Processing for Visual Artists

Processing
for Visual Artists

How to Create Expressive Images
and Interactive Art

Andrew Glassner

CRC Press
Taylor & Francis Group
Boca Raton London New York

CRC Press is an imprint of the
Taylor & Francis Group, an **informa** business

AN A K PETERS BOOK

Editorial, Sales, and Customer Service Office

CRC Press
Taylor & Francis Group
6000 Broken Sound Parkway NW, Suite 300
Boca Raton, FL 33487-2742

First issued in hardback 2018

ISBN 13: 978-1-138-46085-0 (hbk)
ISBN 13: 978-1-56881-716-3 (pbk)

Visit the Taylor & Francis Web site at
http://www.taylorandfrancis.com

and the CRC Press Web site at
http://www.crcpress.com

Library of Congress Cataloging-in-Publication Data

Glassner, Andrew S.
   Processing for visual artists : how to create expressive images and interactive art / Andrew Glassner.
      p. cm.
   Includes index.
   ISBN 978-1-56881-716-3 (alk. paper)
   1. Digital video. 2. Digital graphics. 3. Computer animation. 4. Image processing–Digital techniques. 5. Computer art. I. Title.

T385.G5853 2010 006.6'96--dc22

2010014927

Set in Times, Officina Sans, and Courier using TeX
Cover design: Darren Wotherspoon

In general, textbooks seem to confine the material solely to problem and solution, or to technical analysis. . . . Since [in this book] we are dealing not with organic material like nuts and bolts, but with human qualities like hope and ambition, faith or discouragement, we must throw out the textbook formulas. . . . I cannot participate in all your personal problems, but I can certainly remember my own, and assume that yours will not be greatly different. Therefore this book anticipates the solution of these problems even before you meet them. . . . It is my job here to give you the working materials with which to make your own effort successful.

–Andrew Loomis, *Drawing the Head and Hands*, Viking Press, 1956

If the student is tenacious enough, barriers and problems will dissolve; forms hitherto not seen or conceived will move freely and easily within the infinite spatial realm of the picture plane.

–Burne Hogarth, *Dynamic Figure Drawing*, Watson-Guptill, 1970

Web Materials

Complete programs for every project and every Processing-generated image in this book may be downloaded, for free, from http://www.akpeters.com/processing.

One of the wonderful things about Processing is that people are constantly coming up with new ideas and applications. The starting point for information on Processing is the official website at http://processing.org.

You can also find updates to this book, locate more Processing resources, and connect with other creative people by visiting http://coyote-wind.com/Processing.htm.

Legal Disclaimer

Contents

Preface

Hi!

I know we haven't met, but we already know a few things about each other. I know that you're a creative, intelligent person. I bet that you're visually inventive and you like to make pictures. You may have even created some animations or interactive programs, or you'd like to try your hand at making some.

And you know a few things about me: I like making pictures and animations with Processing, I like to write, and I like to teach.

That's a great start for both of us. This may be the beginning of a beautiful friendship.

Using a computer to create visuals can be a lot of fun. Of course, the process and results are nothing like what we get from painting, sculpting, playing the piano, or going for a hike, and it doesn't replace any of those activities. It's a whole new thing. You can create pictures with so much rich detail, they would have taken you days to create by hand. You can create the simplest kinds of images, but give them mesmerizing, subtle motion that you can't stop watching. Your animations can run all by themselves, or they can respond to your viewer's mouse movement, keyboard taps, or other gestures through custom input devices. You can create games, and you can create art. Your works can be still or moving, simple or complex. Your color palette can be warm or cool, or it can even change over time. You're basically creating your own little interactive world where the only rules are the ones that you invent.

Computer graphics really is a new creative medium. And computer hardware and software has now reached the point where you can create your own computer graphics, on your own system, using software you download for free. How great is that?

If any of that sounds interesting to you, then you're the person I wrote this book for.

I've assumed in this book that you don't have any programming background. And although a big part of this book involves helping you learn to program, this really isn't a programming book. I'm not teaching programming here in the abstract. Instead, it's just a means to an end: making gorgeous, expressive visual imagery.

A great analogy to programming is riding a ten-speed bicycle. There's so much to think about just to get going: which hand brake controls which wheel, which lever controls which set of gears, which gear you're in right now and which one you want to be in, and that doesn't even include whether your helmet's strapped on right or whether you remembered to roll up your pants legs. Then there are the rules of the road, navigating around cars, making sure you don't hit a pedestrian or get blindsided by a car coming out of a driveway or someone opening their car door without warning. There are bike lanes to navigate, signs to read, traffic lights to obey, potholes to avoid, and so on.

When you first started riding a bike in city traffic, you might have been overwhelmed by all the things you had to think about. From just working the bike to riding in a safe and legal way, managing this encyclopedia of information probably required your sustained, concentrated effort. Over time, I'm sure some of the little things (like which brake lever is which) became second nature, and you were able to direct your attention to larger issues, like safely making left-hand turns in traffic.

Then, even that became natural, and as time went on, things just got more and more fluid. Before long, you probably became comfortable riding your bike, and it's turned into a perfectly natural thing to do. Whether you're on a bike trail or in traffic, you feel comfortable and at home on your bike. You can even look around and talk to friends while you're riding, since your body "knows" how to keep you balanced and pedaling.

So it is in programming a project in Processing. It might seem like an overwhelming flood of detail at first. You might feel like it's all too much and that managing all these logical details isn't the way your brain works anyway. Don't fall for it. If you can ride a bike on city streets, you can write a terrific program. It can be weird and strange and unusual and overwhelming at first, no question. But stick with it for a while and you'll find that what originally seemed hard and mysterious is really pretty straightforward. There's no special "programmer's mind," any more than there's a special "dinner-cooking mind" or "bike-riding mind." It's all stuff you can do pretty naturally once you get it under your belt.

Two wonderful things about Processing are that it's free and is available for both Macs and PCs. Did I mention that it's free? If I haven't, I probably should. Processing is free. Perfectly legally. Just download and enjoy!

And frankly, working with Processing is a lot of fun. The whole thing has been designed so that you can create interesting results very quickly. The streamlined nature of the language just scoops you up and delivers you, like an express train, to the land of image making.

So why this book? There are already a few excellent books on Processing, and tons of books that cover programming in general. My experience is that the best learning happens when both teacher and student are on the same wavelength. There's no one "right" or "best" way to learn Processing or read a book or write a book. The core information on Processing that I present in this book is the same as what you'll find in other books—after all, the language is what it is. But this book is for people who like an informal, project-oriented style. If you just want a reference manual, that's also available (in fact, it's online at the Processing website, and it too is free).

When you first get started with Processing, you may find that programming requires you to focus nearly exclusively on the logical, analytical part of your brain. That's natural, and that's part of getting up to speed. There's no debating the point that computer programs have to be nearly perfect in order for them to do what you want them to, and that requires a Mr. Spock kind of approach: logical, reasoned, and focused on working step by step. That's the most unusual aspect of programming compared to other arts, but it's not the most important thing.

Every art form has its idiosyncrasies. If you're a photographer, odds are that you work with math every day to figure out which lenses to use and how long to expose each shot. If you're creating makeup prosthetics for a movie, you know a lot about the chemistry of molding compounds and the practical techniques for making molds. These are the logical, rational sides of those fields. Almost every field has at least a few of these kinds of elements. Computer graphics happens to have lots of them.

And like these other fields, once you're comfortable with the mechanical technique you can start to work intuitively. It may sound crazy if you're not yet a programmer, but once you have the tools under your belt, you really can work by the seat of your pants when building up images and animations. Maybe something in an animation just doesn't *feel* right; a picture of a helium balloon isn't floating the way you'd like, for example. In the back of your head, you try out some possible recipes for how to get it to move the right way. Maybe the balloon should move more slowly? Maybe it should bob up and down a little, as though there was a breeze? If so, how would you create that bobbing motion? Should it be rhythmic or random? You ask the questions that interest you, and you answer them in a way that pleases you.

At this point, you're able to express yourself using images and motion. You can say to yourself, in effect, "Here is the way that I think this balloon should be moving," and then you can write the steps in Processing that bring that about. And almost always, you'll then tune it up by adjusting some of the numbers, making the balloon bob up and down more quickly, for example, or maybe rise higher and drop lower. There are no rules; the balloon will do anything you want it to. The hard part isn't the programming because you'll get good at that more quickly than you might expect. The hard part is figuring out how the balloon should move. That's art. That's self-expression. And that's what this book is all about: getting you to where you can be thinking about the art.

My favorite times with Processing are when I'm balancing analytic and creative skills. My intuitive brain is thinking, "I don't know, maybe a smidgen more of ... whatever, I don't know what to call it, but something sort of like *this*," and my analytical brain is simultaneously figuring out how to write code to capture that vague, fleeting feeling and turn it into pictures and motion. When those two engines are purring together at the same time, it's a great feeling. My goal in this book is to help you find that feeling for yourself.

To that end, I have written this book in a style that's informal and conversational. The technical material isn't presented as it often is in technical books, in a tightly structured sequence where each topic is explored in depth before moving on to the next. Instead, I'll mostly move through a series of projects, from little things to bigger ones, and I'll introduce the technical material that we need as we go. When we do hit a new topic, I only go into it to the depth we need. Later on, we might need to delve deeper and get into more detail, so we'll do that. By the time we're done, we'll have explored every nook and cranny offered by Processing.

The approach is one of shared discovery. As I work on projects, you'll see each step along the way: where I make both simple and big mistakes and fix them, where I change my mind about things, and how the programs evolve. These aren't contrived examples; these are exactly the programs that I wrote, as I wrote them. I saved each version of each program along the way, even if it had bugs and errors, so you can see not just the final results (which we do reach!) but all the steps that got us there.

I did this that way because I think attitude and approach are absolutely key to successful programming. I've written many thousands of programs in my life, and I've worked with hundreds of other programmers, some of whom are enormously productive and skilled. And every great programmer I know, when exploring a new project for the first time, expects to make lots of errors. From simple typos to major conceptual stumbles, everyone does it. We often only come to understand a program as we work on it. So I want you to feel as comfortable with your errors as I feel with mine: ho hum, another error, I'll just fix that and move on.

In this way, you'll see how an experienced programmer works. I'm pretty productive and good at what I do, so I'm willing to hold up my process as a good place for you to start (and my process is a lot like that of many other programmers, so you'll be in good company). Of course, once you feel comfortable, I'm sure you'll find your own style, and that's a wonderful thing. Until then, you can see how I do it, and I hope that will give you a good start.

There are few things that are as rewarding as the chance to publicly thank my friends and colleagues who helped me with this book. They read my drafts and offered many comments that greatly improved the text, the figures, and the programs. For sharing their significant time, expertise, and help, I thank Steven Drucker, Leanna Gingras, Eric Haines, Evan Haines, and Jeff Hultquist. Thank you also to Richard Brauer, Ben Hemmendinger, Jack Kern, and Philippe Lhoste for reviewing the manuscript, catching bugs, and suggesting many useful improvements. Thank you to Ben Fry, Adam Finkelstein, and Julie Steele for encouragement during the early days. Big thanks go to everyone at AK Peters, who have been (as always) a pleasure to work with: Camber Agrelius, Sarah Cutler, Susannah Sieper, and of course Alice and Klaus Peters. And thank you to Neale Simpkin and the staff at Tully's Coffee in Seattle's Wallingford neighborhood for offering such a nice environment (and delicious coffee), where I wrote and edited much of this book.

I hope you find that this book gives you the tools to create new visuals that float your boat and make your friends smile. Have fun, and make great stuff!

Chapter 1
Overview

Hi again!

You're about to start an exciting journey. I've taken this ride before, so I'll be your guide, but what you respond to and get stimulated by is all up to you.

Our ride into making visuals with Processing will be more of a river kayak trip than a theme-park ride. In other words, you'll have to paddle. And I won't kid you, paddling is work. It can feel like hard work, particularly in the beginning when everything seems new and unfamiliar. But you'll be surprised how quickly the paddle comes to fit naturally and comfortably in your hand. You'll come to look forward to the fast sections of water because they give you a chance to stretch out and use your skills, paddling around the rocks and up and down the rapids. You might even show off a little to your friends. It's still work, but it's work that feels great! So hang on past the initial unfamiliar stages and you'll get the swing of it.

In the next chapter, we'll download Processing and enter our first program. But if you haven't done much programming before, jumping into the deep end can be a little disorienting. Sure, you can click the right buttons and type in the right characters, but what does it all *mean*? This chapter will give you a bird's-eye view of the process. With this overview in mind, the mechanics in the next chapter will make sense to you, and you'll already be on your way to creating your own original work.

In this book, I'll focus on creating visuals using the Processing language. I talked about this a little in the Preface, but basically, Processing is a modern system that has been designed from the ground up specifically for making great visuals. It's about as straightforward as something like this can be. And it runs on both Macs and PCs. And it's free!

One of the great things about working with Processing is that once you're comfortable with the language, it's usually not hard to pick up any of the other popular languages in common use. That's because today's popular languages, including Processing, all pretty much share the same central concepts. The differences tend to be in the nuts and bolts of how they do things. There are definitely meaningful, important differences between computer languages, but relatively speaking, they're more alike than they are different.

1

So if you join a group of people who are working in, say, Java, you'll be able to get up to speed and contribute far more quickly than if you were starting from scratch. Or if you find some code posted to the web in a language like Ruby or C++ or Python, you'll usually be able to read it without too much trouble and understand what's generally going on. Processing's specialty is definitely graphics, but it's a modern, general-purpose language that you can use for just about anything, and it's a great foundation for launching into other languages and systems that might appeal to you.

1.1   What Is Processing?

When I refer to Processing in this book, I'm actually referring to four different things, all of which share that name.

First, there's the Processing program itself. This is the thing you download from the web and install on your computer (we'll see how to do that in the next chapter). It's just a file that sits on your hard drive.

Second, there's the *Processing language*. The language defines the rules for the text that you type to create your program. Your program is like sheet music. Sheet music doesn't make any noise by itself (unless you crumple the page), but by following the rules of music notation, you can create a specific sequence of musical notes to be played on a musical instrument. When a performer interprets the marks on the page, music results. Similarly, when the computer interprets your program's text, a running program results.

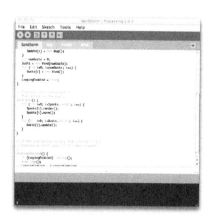

Figure 1.1. The Processing environment.

Third, there's the *Processing development environment*. That's a multipart window that pops up on your screen when you run the Processing file you downloaded. A typical window is shown in Figure 1.1. You can see a piece of a program in the text editor window in the middle of the screen (I'll go over this window in detail in Chapter 2). This Processing window is your home base for writing, fixing, and running Processing programs. Everything you need to develop your programs is right there.

Finally, there's the *Processing run-time environment*. That's the whole complex collection of libraries and other software that have been written for you to call upon when you write your own programs, and it provides all the extra machinery that is necessary for your programs to run. This run-time environment is like the engine in your car; you rarely interact with it directly, but it's always there, providing the unseen power for everything you do.

In Processing, each program you write is called a *sketch*; this is just a friendlier term for "program." A sketch is saved on your hard drive as a file with the extension .pde (an acronym for Processing development environment). Despite the odd extension, this is just a plain text file, so you can open it, read it, and even freely edit it with any text editor (though Processing only pays attention to what appears in its own windows).

When you save a sketch, Processing creates a folder for you with the name of the sketch and then puts the sketch inside the folder. If your sketch gets large, you might want to break it up into several smaller files for your own convenience. In that case, they're all saved in the same folder, and if you open any of the files, Processing opens them all up, with one tab for each file. Figure 1.1 shows a sketch with four files, and thus four tabs.

By long-standing convention, programs are also called *code* or *source code* by programmers, as in, "I finally got that code to run" or "Check out my awesomely fast source code!" Sadly, the word *code* in this context has nothing to do with elegant spies seducing one another on warm balconies overlooking the Mediterranean. The terms *program*, *sketch*, *source*, *source code*, and *code* all refer to the same thing: the text you type into the text editor. I'll use all of these terms interchangeably.

1.2   Experiment Freely!

Programs are imperfect beasts. There's almost no program in the world that does anything interesting that is flawless. The imperfection may only be that it's slightly slower or slightly bigger than it needs to be. Or there might be a very subtle error that only shows up one time in a billion. Of course, programmers work hard to make their programs as correct as possible. But since every program is essentially a brand-new creation that nobody has ever seen before, it's almost inevitable that something, somewhere will be off a little bit. We call any imperfection in a program a *bug*, and it's the rare program that has no bugs. Every time your favorite software company releases an update for your operating system or your programs, it's either because they're adding new features or fixing old bugs (or both). The best programmers in the world write buggy code, and more of the best programmers in the world find and fix those bugs. Nobody wants bugs, but they're a part of life.

Whether or not a given bug is a problem in your program is entirely dependent on context. If you've written a program that is used by air-traffic controllers, and you discover a bug that causes planes to unpredictably disappear from a controller's screen, I'd consider that a pretty serious bug, and one that I'd like fixed right now, this very second, please. If you've written an art piece that displays text on the screen, but when the text is longer than you expected, it shoots past the end of the screen and disappears, you might consider that a serious bug that you need to fix. On the other hand, you might view that behavior as a happy accident; maybe on viewing it, you decide that this quirk actually adds to the meaning of your work. Or you might see it as a problem you want to fix, but since the doors of the gallery are going to open in two hours, you decide you can live with it.

Bugs in programs used by surgeons, astronauts, and bank tellers had better be as free of bugs as possible; programmers call this kind of code *bulletproof*, though in reality no code is bulletproof. But they test it long and hard before they let it out the door. On the other hand, programs that you write for yourself only have to work as quickly and accurately as you want them to.

I've written plenty of programs that I know have bugs in them. But I also know that nobody but me will use one of these little informal programs, and I know that I'll never use them in a way that will trigger the bug, so I don't spend the time and energy to track down and fix the problems (though I'll usually write myself a comment in the program so I don't forget the problems are there). If I'm sharing the program, I might leave a bug in but warn the people I'm sharing the program with, perhaps by including a statement like "never set the volume to 11!" Lots of people share their mostly working code with these kinds of warnings so that other people can build on their work without having to start from zero. After all, if someone is just knocking around some ideas to see how they look, they might not mind a problem here and there, as long as it doesn't come as a bad surprise. More commonly, people work hard to find and fix every bug before they share their code with the world, even if it's just an informal post on a public forum.

Of course, in this book I've tried to make my programs as free of bugs as possible. You'll see the programs as they grow, and you'll see me squash as many bugs as I can find. I hope I've caught them all.

There are a few different kinds of bugs. The first is the *syntax error* or *compile-time error*. These bugs are easy to catch because Processing will explicitly tell you about each one (in fact, they're so common and easy to fix that some programmers don't even consider them "bugs," saving that term for problems that are harder to diagnose and repair). Usually syntax errors are nothing more than typos: you forgot a required semicolon, for example. Computers are obsessive about this kind of precision. Spelling matters: if you don't spell your words perfectly, the computer won't understand you. Case matters: if you use a capital letter where a lower-case letter was expected, or vice versa, the computer won't understand you. You can't have a single one of these syntax errors in your program, or it won't even get to the point where it can run.

This would make people crazy in the real world. Imagine that you wrote a 400-page essay on some complicated subject that took you forever to write, say, the structure of the eyes of some obscure species of shrimp found in tropical reefs. Suppose that when you're finally done and you submit it to your publishers, they send it back within two seconds, telling you that on page 371 you spelled one instance of "the" as "teh," and therefore your entire book was rejected. That publisher wouldn't last very long. But that's exactly how Processing (and all other programming languages) behave. Ninety-nine percent right is not good enough. Not even 99.9 percent. But happily, the computer will instantly spot every syntax error and it will usually even point you right to it along with a helpful error message. Processing even highlights the problematic line in bright yellow. By and large, syntax errors are quick and easy to fix.

When your program is actually running, it can have a different kind of problem. Maybe your program tries to access more memory than you've installed in your computer, or the program tries to talk to an external device that hasn't been connected to that computer. There are called *run-time errors* because they happen while your program is *running*. Many of these will be handled for you by Processing. The others you'll need to catch for yourself. If you don't, your program could behave in an unexpected way, or it might even *crash*.

That's a harsh word, but all it means is that your program stops running. It's as though you'd exited (or quit) the program in a normal way, except that a crash is usually an unexpected (and undesired) surprise. Typically when a program crashes, you'll get an error message from Processing, or a dialog box will pop up on your screen alerting you that your program has crashed.

This is a huge step forward. Not too many years ago, when a program crashed, it took the whole computer down with it. Suddenly the thing wouldn't respond; it was just an inert box. You'd have to physically turn it off and turn it back on again. But that wasn't even the worst case. Sometimes, if the problem was particularly bad, the computer wouldn't just become unresponsive, but it would actually get its memory so scrambled that the entire operating system and all the programs would've had to be reloaded, just as if it was being turned on for the very first time at the factory before any programs were put onto it at all.

When I was first learning to program on a Digital PDP-8/E computer, some of my crashes resulted in exactly this kind of total meltdown. All the software was gone; the hardware was intact but that was all.

I'd turn it off and then back on. The front of the computer had a long row of colored plastic toggle switches. We kept a plastic laminated card near the machine that had rows and rows of numbers on it. Reading from the card, I'd manually flip the switches to form a particular pattern, then push another button to save those settings. Then I'd flip the switches again, push the button, flip, push, flip, push, over and over. This process was actually putting a tiny little program into the computer's memory that enabled it to communicate with the Teletype machine next to it, which we used as our terminal. The program was very short, but entering it by hand still took five or ten minutes, and it had to be done perfectly.

Once that little program was in place, it was time to put the operating system back into the machine. Happily, I didn't have to use the front-panel switches to enter the many thousands of commands for that! The Teletype had a paper-tape reader on the side. You'd feed it a long strip of yellow paper tape, about an inch wide. The tape was punched with holes, and as the tape was automatically fed through the reader, the Teletype sensed where the holes were and sent them to the computer. It was something like a player-piano reader, only instead of making piano keys play, it put 1's and 0's into the computer's memory.

The operating system was kept in the supply cabinet (under lock and key). It was a stack of fan-folded yellow paper tape about eight inches long by six inches tall. I'd feed the first inch into the paper tape reader on the Teletype, make sure the little feeding mechanism was engaged, push a button, and go away for 45 minutes. If all went perfectly, when I came back, there would be a huge mess of paper tape on the floor, but the computer would be back up and ready for use. I would always try very hard to fix the bug in my program before running it again, but there were days when I crashed the computer over and over again. The computer was a shared resource, and though we all crashed it, nobody was ever happy when their turn was delayed as the tape chug-chug-chugged through the reader, agonizingly slowly.

Today, thanks to huge advances in operating-system software, a crash is a lot less disastrous. Once in a great while a crash will take down the operating system, forcing you to reboot, but with rare exceptions, the days of a buggy program destroying the operating system are long gone. In fact, most of the time, a program crash won't affect the operating system at all. If your program crashes, it simply stops, you usually get an error message, and life goes on as before.

But here's the important thing: nothing you do can hurt the computer. I'm mentioning this because exploding computers are a staple of movie and television science fiction, but this is one case where art is definitely not imitating life. Even in the old days I described above, it just took some time and patience to put things right. Today it's much easier. But programming of the sort we're doing here is essentially risk free.

You can't damage the computer.

I have made every error, every mistake, every stupid bug and oversight and dumb move it's possible to make in programming. On hundreds of computers. And not once has a bug resulted in a shower of sparks or caused smoke to billow from the box. I've never made a disembodied voice repeat, "Does not compute, does not compute," faster and faster until the machine blew up. No matter how exciting that is in the movies, real computers don't fail like that, and modern computers just can't get broken by the sort of programs we'll be writing with Processing. Don't fear a crash. It's annoying but harmless. For our purposes, the computer is essentially indestructible.

Write your programs and run them freely. Experiment like mad. Play fearlessly! Try wild stuff that might produce crazy and unpredictable results. There's no risk. The worst that can happen is that, very rarely, you'll have to reboot the computer. So don't worry about the hardware: you can't damage the computer.

If you're working at home, it's a drag to see your program crash, but as I said, it happens to us all. So you *debug* your program, using the techniques we'll see throughout this book. You find the cause of the crash, you fix the program by typing in new lines of text to replace the ones that were making trouble, and you run your program again. If it crashes again, you fix it again. Once you get your programming sea legs, your programs will crash a lot less frequently, and you'll be able to find and fix the problems faster and faster.

Of course, if your program is running at an art gallery, party, dance club, courtroom, or some other public space, a crash would be embarrassing (at the least). So you'll want to test your program pretty thoroughly at home before taking it out into public. Everyone loves a puppy even if it's not yet housebroken, but nobody loves a buggy program, no matter how cute it is.

One way to get your code to work right is to try lots of little side experiments. Suppose you're a chef developing a new salad recipe, and you want to include spiced, candied walnuts. But not just any spice will do; you need to find just the right taste. You'd probably cook up a bunch of walnuts and taste them, adjust your recipe, and try again, over and over. You probably wouldn't create the whole salad every time, particularly during this early stage. You'd focus just on the walnuts in isolation. When they seemed close to right, then perhaps you'd mix them into the whole salad to see how they'd taste in context. Then you could continue to adjust them until they fit in the mix just right.

So too with programming. When you're having trouble figuring out how to do a particular thing, you'll often write a new little program. I think of this as writing a program "off to the side." It lets you focus on just one issue, without all the other stuff in your program complicating matters. When you solve the problem, you can then copy and paste your solution into your big program and tweak it as needed to make it fit smoothly with everything else your program does.

Although it's rare, sometimes your program can cause Processing to lock up and become unresponsive, or the Processing environment itself can crash and essentially stop running. If you hadn't saved your work before you ran your program, and Processing freezes or crashes, then it will be too late to save it.

Some development environments save your changes each time you run your program, but the most recent version of Processing as of now (Version 1.1) doesn't do that. Until Processing saves your changes for you automatically, I recommend you get in the habit of saving your changes every time you run your program. Saving your work frequently is a good idea no matter what program you're running on your computer, from a word processor to an image editor, and Processing is no different. Over time, my fingers have become trained to press the shortcuts for Save and then Run every time I make a change. If for any reason things do go horribly wrong and Processing crashes, then I can restart Processing and pick right up where I left off.

1.3 Planning

So far I've been describing programming as a kind of seat-of-the-pants process, and that's the kind of work you'll probably do most of the time when you're developing visual pieces using Processing. These projects tend to be small and self-contained, and are the sort of thing you do all by yourself or with a small group of collaborators. These kinds of projects develop and change as you work, as you discover new approaches, throw out old ideas and create new ones, and adjust and changes things as you proceed. If this sounds to you like the process of painting with acrylics, or writing a song, or developing a character for a movie, that's no coincidence. Change and discovery are parts of all creative processes.

This is not, however, the way big commercial software gets made. There is an entire professional discipline called *software engineering* that has produced a wealth of techniques and tools for building big programming projects. This is hard stuff, and for some projects (like a new national air-traffic control system), it is almost unbelievably complex. Everything has to be thought out and planned ahead of time, every possible bug has to be anticipated (as much as possible), every possible kind of user input and user error and computer failure has to be considered, every tiny thing has to be thought through and checked and double-checked. It's like planning the world's tallest skyscraper.

Operating systems share this kind of huge complexity. So the next time your computer's operating system freezes up or misbehaves, rather than feel fury at the incompetent boobs who wrote that software (which I admit is a natural reaction), think of the millions (literally, millions!) of lines of code that they had to write and the billions (again, literally billions) of things it's done correctly for you over the last day or two (many of these things are happening behind the scenes, but every time your computer talks to the web, or reads the disk, or moves the cursor when the mouse moves, it's happening because of some piece of code somewhere, written by a real human being). There just isn't any way to make something like that bug free. So people work incredibly hard to try to design the system up front, before the first line of code is typed, so that the bugs are minimized.

In some ways, it's like working out the chord progression for a song before starting on the melody, or making color studies and sketches before starting an oil painting. You hope that by planning your project well beforehand, you'll have a better chance of pulling it off successfully.

And you can indeed plan out your sketches in Processing. If you start writing some big projects, a little planning can help. When we get to Chapter 24, I'll invite you to develop a couple of projects that will reward a bit of planning and strategizing. But you usually don't have to go too far in the process, and you often don't have to plan at all. One of the pleasures of the Processing language is that because it's been so streamlined for graphics, you can really make it up as you go along and get a fine result. If when you're done you want to rewrite the whole thing so that it's faster or better organized, that's fine, but you don't have to do that.

1.4 Commenting

Although we all try to write programs that are easy to read and make sense of, sometimes it helps to have a little note to explain (or remind you) what's going on and why. So all computer languages, including Processing, make it easy to include text in your program that you know the computer will ignore. It's there just for the human beings who read the code. This kind of free-form text is called a *comment*. Often a comment will be just a single line, describing what its related code is meant to accomplish. You can also write whole paragraphs or more, and people often do.

It's a generally agreed truth in programming that comments are good, and generally speaking, more comments are better. You can go overboard, of course, but that's very rare. The much more common case is code with no comments at all. If the names of the objects in a program are short or cryptic, trying to figure out what a program is doing can become a serious challenge. If you have to read someone else's code and there are no comments to guide you, you'll probably wish they had provided some. If you're reading your own code months after you wrote it and there are no comments to guide you, you'll have some choice words for your past self.

The main reason why people don't comment is, of course, laziness. The computer doesn't care if you have comments (because it ignores them), so there's no material advantage while programming to write a comment. And writing a comment will slow you down. And if you later change your code, you'll have to remember to go back and change your comments. And comments can make your program look longer. And besides, surely your code is so beautiful and crystal clear that it's self-explanatory. All true, and all rationalizations. Comments are good. More comments are better.

Yet you'll find that in this book there are very few comments in the code. After what I just said? Yes, I'm granting myself an exemption. The real reason is because the entire book can be seen as comments on the code! Most of the prose here discusses the strategies and techniques of the programs that we'll be discussing, so in a real sense, the book itself is a giant set of comments. Also, I build up each program slowly, often just a few lines at a time, with discussion, so if you're reading along, you'll be familiar with each line. Even so, I'd have included more comments except that they really do make a listing longer, and in a book, that's not good. Reading a program in a book is hard; if the comments make the program span multiple pages, that makes it all the more difficult. So my commenting will typically be sparse. Even so, I encourage you to do as I say and not as I've done. In fact, I usually comment my code pretty well, and I deliberately held back in these programs to keep them short and small on the page.

1.5   Entering Programs

Because most of the programs in this book are of a manageable size, and we'll be building them up in pieces, I strongly urge you to type them in yourself.

But you'll see that every time I make a change (or a little batch of changes) to a program, I've included a pointer to a saved version of the program on the website. So you could just download every program and run it and never type a thing yourself. I strongly encourage you not to do that!

The online listings are there to help you follow the changes we make as a program grows. I tried a lot of different ways to help guide you to see just where new code goes into existing programs, but everything from line numbers to graphic diagrams has significant drawbacks that can be more confusing than helpful. So I decided that I'd describe where the new code goes in words, and I'd give you the entire, complete new listing after every change. If you don't see where a new line or two is supposed to go, you can compare the "before" and "after" listings to see where the changes occurred.

Each of these listings is the complete text of the program up to that point. So you can copy the contents of these text files, paste them into your sketch window, and run them. If you get out of sync with the discussion, this will help you get caught right back up again.

I've also included the complete source code that generated every Processing-made figure in this book. Even the buggy ones. You should be able to regenerate every Processing image in the book with these listings.

But as much as possible, type the code yourself. In terms of muscle memory, programming has a lot in common with playing the piano. When I want to play a particular chord in a way I often play it, my fingers are able to just plunk right down on the keyboard in the right place, seemingly all by themselves. That chord is a single "chunk" in my mind. If I'm reading a song from sheet music and the chord symbol says "E-flat major seventh," my left hand goes *thunk* and there it is, positioned over the keys, fingers poised and ready to play. One step, no thinking, freeing me up to think about how to play the melody, or sing the lyrics, or otherwise perform the song. I'm not swamped by the task of translating "E-flat major seventh" into a collection of notes, and then working out which fingers should press which keys. This only comes about one way: having done it over and over and over again.

And so it is with programming. When your head calls for some structure, say "Let's count from 0 to 38 by 2," your fingers can essentially go into action almost by themselves, typing the letters and symbols and semicolons and parentheses and everything else that's required. Bang. Practically all by themselves. This is a great thing because it frees your mind up to stick with the larger concepts you're juggling to make your project.

And as with the piano, this facility comes about in one way only: doing it over and over and over again. In the beginning it takes time and focus. You have to remember each character. You have to think about each statement and where each semicolon goes. Does this need to be a round parenthesis or a square bracket? Do I put a comma here, or there? And so on. And after doing it a bunch of times, you'll find that the answers come more easily, and faster. And then one day when you need to write that kind of code again, it'll just pour right out of your fingers by itself, and you'll be watching with half an eye for little typos while your brain is thinking about the big ideas.

This facility with typing your programs is hard to over-emphasize. It's what lets you move from spectator to participant, and enables you to build rich and interesting programs you can run and share.

So type everything in. The more you do it, the better you'll be at programming. When you can toss around the little ideas freely, the big ideas become easier to find and hold.

1.6   Programming as Expression

This book is not organized like most books that discuss programming. I touched on this in the Preface and a little bit above as well. There are lots of books on programming that are available to you right now. There are books on programming in general and books specifically targeted at every language that's out there. Some of the popular languages have a dozen or more books. And many of those books are excellent. I've learned many programming languages from that type of book.

But those books have always had one thing missing for me and that's the *process* of programming. The *attitude*. That's often the hardest thing to learn. Each programming language and each development environment rewards a particular attitude.

If you've worked in other art media, you're probably familiar with this. In watercolors or sumi ink, for example, you often plan your strokes carefully and then you commit. Once you've made a stroke, it's done, and that's it. You *can* erase it, of course, but part of the mental discipline of the form is to plan and commit. If you want to excel at those media, you're going to find the road is easiest to travel if you adopt that attitude. When carving stone, this kind of working style is even more important.

In contrast, when finger painting, your best work might be done when you're in a completely impulsive mood, acting spontaneously and carefree, choosing your colors and shapes and everything without a thought, just go go go on pure intuition. If you haven't finger painted recently, give it a try; it's just as much fun as it was when you were a kid! Great finger paintings come from this kind of unplanned play.

Every medium can be approached in an infinite number of ways, of course. But many media reward attitudes that are in harmony with the tools and techniques of that medium. By adopting one of those attitudes, you'll find yourself in tune with the materials, and you'll be working with them, not against them. If you're building sandcastles on the beach, don't try to fight the tide. Don't treat marble like clay and try to bend it. Don't push ropes. Address each medium the way it responds to best.

Programming is the same way. Each language, each system, has a slightly different attitude. Some of the specialized programming languages, such as those written for mathematicians or biologists, really shine when you come to them with a mathematician's or biologist's state of mind.

So where do you find that attitude? Where do you find the work style, the habits? Where do you learn how to start a project, how to build it up, when to go forward, when to go back? How do you know when you're on the right track, or running down a dead-end street? How do you take a big idea and turn it into manageable pieces that you can build up one step at a time? These questions, and many others, are the essence of programming. The mechanics of semicolons and syntax you'll pick up in no time; that's just typing. Writing a program is mostly about thinking through the ideas, inventing approaches, and making them work. How do you do that? What's the right attitude?

Every successful programmer will give you a different answer. But you have to start somewhere.

You can, of course, start at zero and come up with a style all by yourself. Lots of very successful people have done that.

But a perfectly valid alternative is the model of the apprentice: you work under a master and learn attitude and technique by watching and emulating. Over time, you can experiment with those work habits, varying them and trying alternatives, developing your own style. If you've chosen a good model to emulate, then you get a huge head start on the process.

After decades of writing untold thousands of programs, I think I've found a good style and a good attitude. I'm productive and I write code that I can read, debug, and maintain. Other people have used my programs for their own work. I've come up with a process that works very well for me.

So this book is my version of inviting you into an apprenticeship program. My model is that we're sitting side by side, and you're watching over my shoulder as I program. I'm going to share with you my programs each step of the way. When I write code with bugs, you'll see the code, you'll see the bugs, and you'll see the error messages. When I have to find those bugs and fix them, you'll see each step along the way. When the results don't look quite right to me, you'll see me adjust them.

In short, you'll see my process. And I hope that will help you adopt that process for your own projects. And then, over time, I'm sure you'll start to customize it, adding to it, and removing from it, and changing it, until it fits you like a comfortable shirt.

In short, programming can initially look hard and challenging and weird. But it's not. It's really about inventing and creating and dreaming. The rest is typing. If you type in the programs as we go, your fingers will get used to the typing. If you stick with the discussions, you'll pick up a style and an attitude that will see you through many projects. And before you know it, you'll be a master programmer yourself, with your own process and your own style, and you'll be watching your fingers type the code all by themselves while you're dreaming of shapes and color and motion.

In other words, you'll no longer be thinking about the brush, or the keyboard, or the pen, or the code. You'll be thinking about the ideas and how to communicate them.

You'll be making art.

You're going to love this.

Let's dig in.

Chapter 2
Setting Up
and Getting Started

The first step in getting started with Processing is to download and install it. That's easy, because Processing is free, and it runs beautifully on both Macs and PCs that use Windows or Linux. You can download and install it without any worries about viruses or other undesired surprises. Point your web browser to

```
http://www.processing.org/
```

Choose "Download" (if you're on a Windows-based PC, I suggest you choose the link labeled "Windows" and ignore the one labeled "Windows (Without Java)").

You may be offered your choice of versions. Most of the examples in this book were produced with Version 1.1. Generally, you should pick the most recent version available. If your version is newer than the one I used, everything in this book should still run perfectly well. You may even find that some of the bugs I encountered (and I point out in the text) have been fixed.

Once you've downloaded the package, install it by following the usual routine for installing programs on your system. The result is a program called Processing installed on your hard drive. Start it up!

When you run Processing, it will pop up a window for you. This is where you do all your communicating with Processing, so let's go over the pieces briefly so you'll know your way around. This window will soon feel like a second home to you.

Processing's window will look something like Figure 2.1.

At the top is the *menu bar*, which has the traditional sorts of menu items like *File*, *Edit*, and so on. You may be used to seeing these at the top of the screen (on Macs, for instance), but in Processing they're all there in the Processing window. Below the menu bar is the *toolbar*, which has just a half-dozen buttons. The round buttons let you run your program and stop it. The square buttons are shortcuts for opening and saving your files.

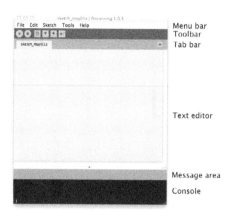

Figure 2.1. A Processing window.

Beneath the toolbar is a strip of *tabs* called a *tab bar*. There's one tab for each file in your project; just click on a tab to activate it. When you're starting a new project, there's just one tab with an automatically-generated default name. That name is usually derived from the current date; in the figure, you can see I took that screenshot on May 1. At the far right, there's a button marked by an arrow in a box, which will open a new menu for tab-related operations.

Below the tab bar is the *text editor*, which is where you'll enter and edit your Processing programs. Below the text editor is the *message area*, where Processing will display any short, important messages, like error statements. Finally, at the bottom of the window is the *console*. This area of the screen does double duty. When you're getting your program to run, this is where the computer will print detailed information about any problems it discovers. When your program is running, if you tell Processing to print out information for you, it shows up here.

You can resize the window by dragging the bottom-right corner. Under the text editor and above the message area there's a little dot. If you drag that up and down you can change how much of the message area and console get displayed. In the bottom-right of the text editor are two tiny arrows. Clicking the downward-pointing arrow gets rid of the message area and console, so the text editor fills the window. Clicking the upward-pointing arrow restores the bottom two areas. Until you're a pro, I strongly suggest leaving the message area and console visible.

2.1 Hello, World!

Let's get Processing to do a little something right away so we know all is well.

Click in the text editor, and type the following exactly as it appears here:

```
println("Hello World!");
```

(Full program in settingup/sketches/HelloWorld/HelloWorld.pde)

It should look like Figure 2.2. Like most text editors, this window contains a *cursor* that indicates where your characters will go when you start to type. You can put the cursor anywhere you want in the text you've written using the mouse; just left-click where you want to start typing, and the cursor will go there. In most word processors, the cursor is indicated with a visual symbol like a blinking box. In Processing, your cursor is a vertical blinking bar. Because this bar can be a little hard to spot sometimes, Processing helps you by highlighting in light gray the entire horizontal row of text around the cursor. The line number where the cursor is located is displayed in the bottom-left corner of the window, just under the console.

In the line I just asked you to type, the first word `println`, is in lower case (in Processing, upper- and lowercase letters are considered different letters, so case matters). Note that the letter after the *t* is an *l* (as in lightbulb),

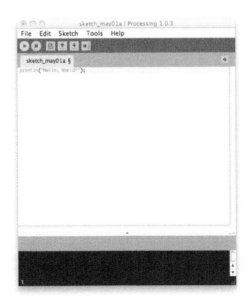

Figure 2.2. A sketch to print "Hello, World!"

and not an *i* (as in incandescent). You must enter the word `println` in just this way, with no spaces, and entirely lower case; if you type it in any other way you'll get an error.

The name may make a bit more sense once you know that `println` is shorthand for "print line."

You might wonder, then, why it isn't just `printline`. After all, what was really saved by leaving off that last *i* and *e*? Not much, that's for sure. But programmers do this kind of thing all the time, leaving off vowels and extra letters to save a little bit of typing. I do it too, and you'll see me do it lots of times in the examples yet to come. For example, to keep track of the number of points in a drawing, I might name my counter `NumPoints`. Why not `NumberPoints`, or better yet, `NumberOfPoints`? There's no single reason for this. The more you have to type, the more you can make a typo, so short names have a little advantage there. They're also faster to type and can be easier to read. I don't know, those might all just be rationalizations for being lazy. The bottom line is that this is the nearly universal style shared by programmers the world over. Some people use fully written-out and descriptive names, and you're welcome to join their elite ranks, but most people abbreviate this way throughout their code.

For example, in later chapters you'll see me build colors out of three values, one each for red, green, and blue. And when I make objects to hold those values, I often call the three objects some variant of `red`, `grn`, and `blu`. On the one hand, that makes them look good to my eye when they're on separate lines: they all have three letters

Figure 2.3. Running "Hello, World!"

and when they appear one under the other it reinforces the idea, at a glance, that they're basically a connected group. On the other hand, it's kind of silly. But as I said, this is a very common practice, so I'm not going to try to hide it from you. The designers of Processing were clearly part of this tradition, using many of these kinds of abbreviations in the language definition itself.

So the "print line" command is written `println`, and after a while, that'll seem perfectly natural to you, too.

OK, with that half apology, half explanation out of the way, let's let Processing loose.

Give it a shot! Click the *Run* button; it's the left-most button in the tool bar, shown by a circle with a right-pointing triangle. Alternatively, you can run your program by clicking on the *Sketch* entry in the menu bar, and choosing *Run*. Or you can use your keyboard to type in the shortcut for *Run* (it will be listed next to the command on the menu). Figure 2.3 shows what happened on my system.

When you clicked the *Run* button, Processing probably did two things: it created a little square window filled with gray somewhere on the screen, and it printed "Hello World!" in the console at the bottom of the Processing window. If so, congratulations! You have a running copy of Processing, ready for playing and messing around with. If something went wrong, make sure you typed in that line exactly as I gave it. If you're sure it's right (remember the parentheses, the quotes, and the semicolon at the end) but Processing is still not giving you this result, you can download the file *HelloWorld.pde* from the website. You can either open that from within Processing, or copy and paste it into your own text window. If that doesn't work either, try talking to a knowledgeable friend in order to determine what may have gone wrong, and how to put things right again. Finally, if things are still not working, try looking on the Processing website and user forums for help.

When you pressed the *Run* button, Processing ran through a two-step procedure. The first was to take the text in the text editor and translate it into another language, which made it more convenient for the computer. The second step was then to run that translated program. So your program first gets turned into something else, and then that something else takes over to create your pictures and animation.

If anything goes wrong during either of these steps, Processing will let you know by giving you an error message.

During the first step, Processing reads what you typed and translates it into another language called *Java*. Sometimes we also say that the program is *compiled* into Java.

The relationship between Processing and Java is something like that between a general contractor and subcontractors. If you're remodeling your kitchen, you probably spend most of your time talking to the general contractor. In some jobs you'll never talk to the subcontractors at all. But they're the ones actually doing the work. The general contractor might do some designing and will choose the subcontractors and guide them, but the contractor is rarely pounding nails or gluing cabinets together. In that sense, most of what seems to be happening when you run a Processing program is actually being done by the Java system, running Java code. But in practice, you rarely see the Java underpinnings.

So in this book I'll discuss everything as though Processing was the whole enchilada, even though we know that Java and your computer's operating system are major contributors to everything that goes on.

2.2 Debugging

During the first step of translation, Processing might find that it can't complete the job. Maybe you typed something incorrectly or forgot a letter or a character. As I mentioned before, the *syntax* (or text) of the program at this point has to be perfect or the compilation into Java won't complete, which means you won't have a program to run.

To see this, let's deliberately break the program by introducing a bug. We'll put in a typographic error that will prevent the translation step from running to completion. Click in the text window and delete the closing parenthesis so the line looks like this:

```
println("Hello World!";
```

Press the *Run* button.

Figure 2.4. Error messages galore!

Trouble! Errors! You might be seeing tons of red text in the console window, as in Figure 2.4 (I made the console bigger and wider here so we could see more of those lovely red messages).

Relax, everything is just fine. No need to be worried at all. We have some errors. They happen all the time. Every program you write will have errors. You'll slip up and miss a letter or a parenthesis. You'll spell `println` with an `i` and an `e`. There are a million possible syntax errors, but they're usually innocuous typos. The error reports come in a million flavors, and despite the scary red text, you should expect and welcome them. They're your friends. These error messages are there to help you make your code work as well as it can, and they exist to guide you to places where things are not as expected.

There are two big things to keep in mind when your program produces errors. First: it's no big deal. The most experienced programmer in the world expects to get some errors when they first try to run their code. You dig in and fix them; that's just part of the process.

The second thing is to remember that you can't break the computer. As I mentioned earlier, you can't make it explode in a shower of sparks like the bridge on *Star Trek* when it gets hit with a photon torpedo. You can't scramble your disk, erase your bank statements, or trigger a flood of outgoing spam email. Processing is a safe environment. Despite all that red type, everything is fine.

In fact, everything is better than fine. Processing, in the act of compiling your program into Java, has found something that doesn't look right. Rather than just plow on and finish making the Java program and then running it, only to have it crash or fail in some confusing and inexplicable way, Processing has held up its hand early to let you know something went astray.

Look at the message area (the little horizontal bar just under the text editor). That's where Processing tries to give you a succinct summary of the problem. It probably says something like

```
Syntax error, maybe a missing right parenthesis?
```

Well, that's awfully nice of it. Yup, that's just what's wrong (as we know).

Given such a clear report in the message area, why is there all that crazy red text in the console below it?

The console messages in red are the output of the internal processes that Processing is running for you behind the scenes to turn your program into a working Java program. Feel free to skim that text if you're curious, but unless you were born with the Java-language gene, it'll probably mean little to you. And that's just fine; that stuff is there primarily for experts. When I get an error from Processing, I always first look at the one-line summary in the message area just under the text editor. Usually that does a pretty good job of describing the problem and getting me close to where it happened. If I don't quite follow the problem, I might skim the console messages, but they're usually not helpful. So I keep the console window shrunk down to usually just one or two lines; if anything appears there that I might want to glance at, I enlarge it, scan what's there, and shrink it back down again.

In general, the message area is the first place to look for help on fixing your bugs. Keep in mind that the report in the message area should be taken with a grain of salt: Processing is doing its best to identify what went wrong, but it can sometimes mis-diagnose the problem or get confused about where the error occurred. It usually does a pretty good job on both counts, but as you get more comfortable with Processing, you'll occasionally find yourself doing a little freelance detective work to identify what actually went wrong and where, using Processing's error message as a starting clue.

Notice up in the text editor that Processing has highlighted the problematic line in yellow. That's another nice touch. To get our program to run properly, just go back to that window, click just before the semicolon, and pop the right parenthesis back in there. If you run your repaired program, it should perform as before, printing "Hello, World!" in the console area.

The kind of problem we've just been looking at, resulting from the missing right parenthesis, is called a syntax error because it's a problem with the syntax, or the written text. It's also called a compile-time error, because it gets caught at the time when Processing is compiling, or translating, our program into Java. These kinds of errors are usually easy to fix because they're just the result of typing mistakes rather than something conceptually wrong with the program. They're usually pretty easy to fix.

The other kind of problem is called a run-time error, and we'll be seeing plenty of those as well later on.

2.3 Working With Processing

You can save your source code using the options in the *File* menu, and of course you can retrieve it later. But it's just text, and if you prefer a different editor than the one in Processing's text editor window, you can tell Processing to use that instead (turn on the option *Use external editor* in Processing's *Preferences* menu). Alternatively, you can just cut and paste from a window running your favorite editor.

As I mentioned in Chapter 1, Processing does not automatically save your changes for you when you run your program. If something goes wrong while you're working (maybe your operating system freezes up or someone trips on your computer's power cord) and if you haven't saved your program recently, you might lose all the work you've done since the last save. You can save by choosing the *File* entry on the menu bar and then *Save* or just by entering the shortcut from your keyboard. I find it a good habit to always save my program every time I run it. Every time I make a change and then want to run the new program, I use the keyboard to enter the shortcuts for *Save* and then *Run*. That way the file on my hard drive is always up to date.

You may have noticed that Processing has been quietly changing the colors of some of the words you type into the text editor. This is called *color coding*, and it's another instance of Processing trying to be helpful. I love this feature. It's purely cosmetic, and it doesn't change your code or how it runs in any way, but it helps you see at a glance the different kinds of things you're typing. I predict you'll come to like it as well.

As we'll see, there are a few different kinds of things in a Processing source program. Generally, there's words (made up of letters and numbers) and punctuation (like parentheses and semicolons). To do its job, Processing has predefined a bunch of words to have specific meanings. We saw one of them in the program above: `println`. These are called *reserved words* or *keywords*. Generally speaking, you can't use reserved words for your own objects. For example, in every Processing program, the word `setup` should be used in only one particular predefined way, and you can't change that. If you want to call something of your own by that name, you have to pick something else, like `mySetup`. Some reserved words are actually common words in English, like `for`, `else`, `if`, and `while`. You'll see them as we go along, and a full list appears in Appendix A. To help you spot the reserved words in your program, Processing highlights them in a special color (on my system, they appear in orange).

Processing comes with tons of documentation, all available on the website. There are tutorials on some of the basics, lots and lots of examples of different features, examples of how to do some cool or unusual things, and descriptions of language features. If you have a question, the odds are good that you can answer it from the documents. If not, try searching the web—there are lots of Processing-related discussions out there.

There are also a few other books on Processing, listed on the website. For more information you can visit this book's website at http://coyote-wind.com/Processing.htm.

Searching for help with Processing on the web in general can be frustrating because you'll naturally want to put the word "Processing" in your search, but that's such a common English word that it will match a bazillion webpages that have nothing to do with the Processing language or environment. So I've found it's best to thoroughly scour Processing's own website for information first, and I only move on to more general web searches if I must.

Let's also talk about *reuse* of code. There's absolutely nothing wrong in finding something that already exists and runs and then adapting it to your own needs. In fact, it's encouraged. It's one of the best ways to learn, and it's a great way to build on other people's efforts. There are dozens of example programs on the Processing website and hundreds or thousands more in various personal galleries all over the web. If one of them comes close to what you want to do, or just shows you a way to do one step of what you want to do, then by all means copy and adapt it. Of course, you might want to include a comment in your code to the effect that you're using some programming originally written by someone else, and you could include that programmer's name, or a link to their website, or some other reasonable acknowledgement. But if the code isn't protected by copyright or patent (and most of the code that people have posted on the web is not—otherwise, why post it?), you're not obligated to do that. It's just a nice thing to do. And if you post your code on the web one day, other people may return the favor. The widespread sharing of code is one of the really nice things about the Processing community.

The first time you save yourself an hour, or a day, by using someone else's code, you'll be a fan of code sharing for life. And the first time you see your code in someone else's project, or you get a thank you email, you'll have that great feeling of giving back and being part of a friendly, international community.

Of course, reuse is also a great idea for your own code. If you wrote something a year ago that could be useful today, copy it and adapt it. Reuse is great. In fact, much of the philosophy of object-oriented programming, which we'll talk about in Chapter 14, is based on the idea that the more you can reuse existing pieces of programming, the better off everyone is. After all, if I've designed something, written it, debugged it, and documented it, and it does what you need to do, why should you repeat my effort? Building on other people's experiences and efforts is one of the pillars upon which we built civilization; let it work for you.

Chapter 3
Basic Ideas: Variables

Before we get into programming, I'd like to give you a little piece of Processing to fool around with. Here's a program you can type into the text window and run. As I said earlier, I encourage you to get used to typing these things. Don't worry for now what any of it means. Just type it in. Remember that upper and lower case are different, spelling counts, and include all the punctuation, including the semicolons at the end of most of the lines. The easiest way to indent lines is to use the Tab key, but you can use spaces if you prefer (these indentations are just to make the code easier to read, so you can use any number of tabs or spaces that look good to you). When you're done, press the *Run* button (or use the *Run* menu item or keyboard shortcut). You should see something like Figure 3.1. When it's stopped drawing, either close the window or press the *Stop* button.

```
void setup() {
  size(1000, 400);
  background(255);
  smooth();
}

void draw() {
  translate(frameCount*2, 200);
  rotate(radians(frameCount*3));
  float sclSize = sin(radians(frameCount * 3.5));
  scale(map(sclSize, -1, 1, .5, 1));
  drawFigure();
}

void drawFigure() {
  noFill();
  stroke(0, 0, 0, 128);
  rect(-60, -40, 120, 80);
}
```

(See output in Figure 3.1. Full program in variables/sketches/spinner1/spinner1.pde)

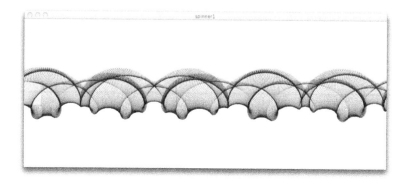

Figure 3.1. A spinning rectangle. (variables/sketches/spinner1/spinner1.pde)

The point here is just to have some fun. Monkey around with the numbers. Just follow your intuition. You can't hurt anything—the worst that can happen is that nothing gets drawn, or you get an error message. If that happens, you can just undo your changes and try something else. Within a few chapters, everything here will be entirely familiar to you, even if it's a meaningless jumble now. Just treat this as a little toy you can fool around with.

Now let's look at how a program like this comes about.

3.1 Naming Things

In the process of writing your program, you're going to create lots of objects, and every one of them will get a name. Processing shares a bunch of weird typographic rules and conventions with virtually every other programming language on the planet, and those rules and conventions apply to every name you invent for every object in your program. If you accidentally break the rules, you can get some very confusing errors when you try to run your program. So let's get the naming rules clear first, before we dig into writing a program.

The first rule is perhaps the strangest-seeming one: when you create something and give it a name, that name can't contain spaces. If your object's name only needs a single word to describe it, then you have no problem: just call it "kettle" or "fruit" and you're set. But you can't name it "my favorite kettle" or "box of blueberries", because those contain spaces, and spaces are always used to separate pieces of text in your code. Spaces are just not allowed in names. But sometimes you really want to name something with a multiword description, like "number of copies." What to do?

There are two popular answers. The first is to separate words with an underscore character. So you could call your object `number_of_copies` and all is well. Don't use a minus sign, though: that means subtraction, and can't be used as part of object names. So never try to use a name like `number-of-copies` because your program either won't compile or else it won't run properly; always use the underscore instead.

The alternative is to run all of the words together, but use capitals to indicate the start of a new word, as in `numberOfCopies`. This style is sometimes called *camel case* because those tall capitals in the middle of a bunch of shorter, lower-case letters might remind you of a camel's humps.

Some people love vanilla and hate chocolate; some adore the accordion and others loathe it. Feelings can also run high when people discuss underscore versus camel case, with people arguing passionately for the pros and cons of each technique. In practice they're both common, and when you look at other people's code, you'll see them both frequently. I suggest you ignore the debate and use whatever feels best to you.

There is also an important rule regarding how names begin. You may not start a name with anything except a letter. A common mistake is to try to use a name like `3musketeers`, but that's not a legal name in Processing. Stick to only letters at the start of your object names. You can use any mix of upper- and lower-case letters, numbers, and underscores in the rest of the name. So you can name your object for your favorite movie by calling it `threeMusketeers` or `three_musketeers` or even `musketeers3`, just as long as you always start with a letter. Remember that case matters, so `milkBottlesize`, `MilkBottlesize`, and `milkBottleSize` are all separate names and are considered to refer to entirely separate objects. Sometimes you'll see a name like `tEaKeTtLe`, which has a mix of upper and lower case that is technically legal, but way too cute unless it's the name of a pet bunny.

For now, I suggest you start every object's name with a lower-case letter (I'll discuss the reason for this in Chapter 4 when I talk about local and global variables).

By the way, one result of the rule that disallows spaces within object names is that generally anywhere you *are* allowed to have a space, you can have as many as you want. So in any Processing program (including those in this book) where you see one space, there could be three or even 100 spaces and the computer wouldn't even notice the difference. Newlines (the character that comes from pressing the Return or Enter key on your keyboard) and tabs (from pressing the Tab key) count as spaces, too. Together, spaces, tabs, and newlines are called *white space*, and generally speaking, you can use as much white space as you like in your Processing programs to make them look good to you.

Coming up with good, short names for your objects is something of an art. Some people focus on this and come up with great, compact, descriptive names for their objects. Most people just pick something reasonable. A few people are lazy and name everything with single letters, like `a` and `b`. Don't do this! Everyone who looks at your code will be driven crazy, including yourself a year after you wrote it, when you come back to add something and you can't figure out what the heck any of those objects are for or what they're supposed to represent. Even a generic name like `counter` tells you something about why the object exists and how it's used.

Of course, every rule has exceptions. For example, when we want to create objects to hold the *x* and *y* coordinates of a point on the screen, variables named `x` and `y` are perfectly appropriate. And we'll see many examples of using a single letter (like i) for objects that control how chunks of code get repeated. But the general rule still applies: pick names that are descriptive and you'll be glad you did.

Finally, there are a few variable names that aren't illegal but that you should really avoid. Don't create any objects named simply I (that's a capital *I*, as in Istanbul) or O (that's a capital *O*, as in Ottawa); they look too much like the numbers 1 and 0. And definitely don't combine just these, like OIO1I. If you want to drive everyone who looks at your code insane (including yourself), pick variable names that are random mixtures of I, O, 0, and 1. You will be long remembered by anyone who has to look at a line like this:

```
OOII00IO = IOOIO1I + OOOOI1I;
```

This is legal, but deranged.

The lower-case letter o is also best avoided, again because of possible confusion with the digit 0. But oddly enough, the lower-case letter i probably the single most popular variable name in all of programming (we'll see why in Chapter 12).

As I mentioned in Chapter 2, the Processing language and its core utilities are defined using about 300 words (and a few dozen symbols). These words are called *reserved words* or *keywords*, and you shouldn't (and often can't) use them in your own programs. These words appear in Processing's text editor in a special color, and if you try to use them in your own way, you'll usually get a syntax error message. Appendix A provides a list of all keywords, with short descriptions. Some keywords are common English words (like for) and some are words that would be incredibly useful if they weren't reserved (like red). As we go through the book, we will eventually see and discuss every one of these keywords.

3.2 Types

Suppose you've just moved across the country, but the movers lost all your stuff. But they apologized and gave you a lot of money to replace it all, so now you're busy buying new versions of what you've lost. And that includes shoes. You're going to need several pairs of shoes, including sneakers for your tennis game next week, hiking boots for climbing mountain trails, and formal shoes for a friend's upcoming wedding. So one day, you're at the store and you purchase a new pair of shoes.

You get on the phone with your butler (did I mention the insurance company paid for a butler? They did), and you tell him, "Charles, I've just bought a new pair of shoes." Since he's good at his job, Charles says, "I'll prepare a special box in which to store them upon your return home. What size are these shoes?"

That's a reasonable question. After all, a pair of slippers would only need a small box, though thigh-high river waders would need something large. So you tell him they're formal dress shoes and need only a medium box.

"Excellent," Charles says, "and what shall I write on the box so that I can retrieve this particular pair of shoes when they're needed?"

Again, even though Charles needs to loosen up a little bit, this is a reasonable question. Since you might end up with a whole lot of boxes of shoes, writing a descriptive label on each box will help you find the one you want quickly. So you tell him to label the box "Black formal shoes," and the conversation's done.

We've just seen the basics of a fundamental idea in programming called *variables*. Variables are like shoeboxes: they're named containers for things. Some variables contain a number (like 3 or −6.2), some contain a string of characters (like "Appalachian Spring"), some contain a color, and so on. You give every variable in your program a unique name so that you can refer to it unambiguously. You can put stuff into the box (which we call *assigning* a value to the variable), and you can look inside the box to get its contents (which we call *retrieving* the value from the variable).

To create a variable, you follow exactly the same recipe as we just did in the phone call. First, you tell the computer the *type* of the variable; this lets the computer know if it's going to hold a number, a color, a string, and so on. Then you give it a name, using the naming rules I discussed above. From then on, you can use that variable to store information and then retrieve it later.

These storage containers are called variables because their value can change over time. If a variable is a number type, you might put the number 6 into the box early in your program and then replace that with the number 18 later. You don't have to change the value if you don't want to, but even if you never choose to change it, you could, so we still call it a variable. Variables are the most general way to store objects in a program, and every program contains lots of variables of different types.

The process of identifying the variable's type and name is called *declaring* the variable.

Declaring the type of each variable has a few advantages. The most important one for you is that it helps you catch errors. If you know that a variable is supposed to hold text (like someone's name) and you try to put a number into that variable, then you probably have made a mistake, like trying to put a sewing machine into a box sized for a paperback book. Generally speaking, if you try to put something of one type into a variable that has been declared with an incompatible type, the computer will flag that as an error. So using types helps both you and the computer make sure you've always got the right kind of information in your variables. It's not a foolproof way of making sure your program is accurate, but over the years, people have discovered that this mechanism is incredibly helpful for finding errors, which is why it's part of most languages.

For some variables, like a number variable holding the current temperature, you'll probably change the value quite often. Other variables, like those holding the mass of the sun or the year you were born, will probably never change at all. In some languages, an object that never changes is called a *constant,* and you can in fact tell the computer which objects are variables (meaning they can change) and which are constants (meaning that they cannot change). In Processing, everything's a variable, so if you want to keep a certain number constant, just don't change it. (Technically, you can force a variable to be a constant if you precede it with the keyword `final` but that's rarely used in practice. Typically, if you want something to be a constant, you just don't change it.)

Let's look at three of Processing's built-in types very quickly. I'll show you how to use them, and then we'll return to consider how to choose among them for different jobs.

The first basic type is the *integer*, written `int` (with a lower-case i). This holds a number with no fractional part, but it can be positive, negative, or zero. Some legal values for an `int` are $-3, 572$, and 0, but not 8.4.

The second basic type is the *floating-point number*, written `float` (with a lower-case f). This is the catch-all type for numbers that can (but don't have to) have a fractional part. A `float` can hold integers, too, since they're just floating-point numbers with a 0 after the decimal point. Legal `float` values include $-3.6, 572.1308$, and 0.0.

A third basic type is for holding text, and it's written `String` (note the upper-case S). A `String` can hold any sequence of characters that you can type, including white space like tabs, spaces, and newlines.

To declare a variable, you need to tell the computer only two things: the type of the variable and its name. You put those two pieces of information on a line by themselves and end it with a semicolon.

Here are a few legal variable declarations:

```
int frogs;
float appleSize;
String my_name;
```

Note that these lines aren't a complete program. I'll typically call a few isolated lines like this a *snippet* or *fragment*. Sometimes when I show isolated lines of code in this way, I'll be giving you new versions of lines in a program we've already entered, and sometimes they'll be new lines to add to that program. And sometimes they'll just be little examples of things that you might use in a program, as they are here. If you type in this particular fragment and hit the *Run* button Processing will actually proceed without errors, since these three lines could be technically considered a program (though a completely useless one). More often, little fragments like this won't run all by themselves; they're only meant as examples of a specific point.

In this fragment, I'm declaring an integer to tell me how many frogs are in my backyard pond, a floating-point number to tell me the weight of the apple I'm going to have for lunch, and a string of characters to hold my name.

The lines above are perfectly legal, and you'll find things like them in almost every Processing program. But, of course, a variable has not just a type but also a value, or it wouldn't be of much use. You assign a value to a variable using an *assignment statement*. That has four parts: the name of the variable, an equals sign (=) (in this use, called the *assignment operator*), the value to be assigned, and a semicolon. Here are some legal assignments, using the types declared just above:

```
frogs = 3;
appleSize = 7.1;
my_name = "Captain Stroganoff";
```

Here are some illegal assignment statements, using the variables (and their types) we just made. If you try to make these assignments (following the declarations above), Processing will report them as errors:

```
frogs = "Prince Bob";   // Illegal: assigning a String to an int
frogs = 3.5;            // Illegal: assigning a float to an int
my_name = 5;            // Illegal: assigning an int to a String
```

You'll see that I've put comments on each line; a *comment* in Processing starts with two slashes (//) and continues to the end of the line. Processing ignores everything between those two slashes and the end of line, so you can put anything you want in there: text descriptions, reminders to yourself, very short poems, or even snippets of code you want to keep around but not actually use yet. Here I've used my comments to make, well, comments.

Because it's so common to want to give variables a starting value, you can combine the declaration and assignment statements:

```
int frogs = 3;
float appleSize = -43.9;
String my_name = "Captain Stroganoff";
```

Here I've assigned a negative number to `appleSize`. This doesn't make much sense if we're literally thinking of apples, but the computer doesn't know that. As far as Processing is concerned, `appleSize` refers to a variable of type `float`, and −43.9 is a floating-point number, so this assignment is perfectly legal. Whether it's sensible or not is up to our interpretation.

After you've declared a variable (and perhaps assigned it a starting value), any subsequent assignments must leave off the type declaration. You can only declare the type once. Writing the following two lines one after the other in a real program would be an error:

```
int frogs = 3;
int frogs = 7;  // Illegal: we've already declared frogs
```

And since you can't declare something twice, you certainly can't change its type:

```
int frogs = 3;
float frogs = 7;  // Illegal: we've already declared frogs
```

In other words, you declare a variable's type once, and it has that type as long as it exists.

Here's a legal assignment statement worth noting:

```
float weight_of_apple = 5;
```

So I've put an integer value (that is, a whole number with no decimal part) into a variable of type `float`. And that's perfectly reasonable; the number 5 could be written 5.0, so the fractional part is simply 0.

So if a `float` can hold an integer, why have `int` variables at all? There are two main reasons: error detection and precision.

Error detection is kind of like defensive programming. Suppose you know that some particular variable should never have a fractional part; that is, it will never need a floating-point type to hold it. For example, a variable might contain the number of chairs in your apartment. And you've decided that there are no such things as "fractional" chairs, like chairs that are broken or too fragile to be used; instead, a thing is either a chair or it is not. There can only be whole numbers of chairs. So you declare your variable this way:

```
int numberOfChairs;
```

Suppose that later in your program you do this:

```
numberOfChairs = 5.7;
```

The computer will report an error during the compilation step, before the code even starts to run. When you look at this line, you'll realize the problem. You might decide it was just a typo, and 5.7 should have been 5, so you use your editor to delete the .7. Or you might decide that this is really what you meant, and that fractional chairs make sense to you after all, and so you go back and change the declaration to make `numberOfChairs` a `float` rather than an `int`.

Again, people have found over the years that distinguishing integer-only variables from floating-point variables has helped them find and fix a whole lot of unintentional mistakes, so the distinction has remained in most languages.

You might be tempted to take the easy way out and make everything a `float`. There are a few reasons not to do this. One is that you're defeating the error-catching ability of the computer, which is, after all, a good thing designed to help you write bug-free programs. The second reason not to make everything a `float` is precision, or more precisely, the lack of it.

It's a sad fact but true: when the computer stores a floating-point number, it often gets it wrong. Ever-so-slightly wrong, but wrong. The problem is due to *finite* or *limited precision*. Suppose that you have a garden that's going to be shared by three gardeners, and each one gets an equal share of the available area. The field covers one acre, so everyone gets one-third of an acre. So you write this program:

```
float total_acres = 1.0;
float number_of_people = 3.0;
float acres_per_person = total_acres/number_of_people;
```

(If you guessed that the last line calculates the value of `total_acres` divided by `number_of_people`, you'd be right!) If you print out the value that is now stored in `acres_per_person`, it will look something like this: `0.333333`. Depending on your computer and installation and other details, you might see more or fewer digits, but the thing to note is that mathematically, the digit 3 should repeat *forever*. If you write down 1/3 then you've written down a perfectly exact and perfectly correct value for "one-third." But when the computer actually calculates that number, it has to store the result, and it can't store the infinite train of repeating 3's. It has to stop somewhere. So it stores lots of digits, but no more. Whatever value that does get stored is going to be close to 1/3, but not exact.

Happily, in this case "close" can be very close indeed. Close enough to get to the moon and back, for instance. Of course, whether it's close enough for your purposes will depend on what you're doing, but for everyday image-making purposes, the value that can be stored in a floating-point number is usually good enough (though it will almost never be exact, and in a moment we'll see a way to make it better).

So 0.33333 is only an approximation of 1/3, and if we start to use it in calculations our results will start to drift from the mathematical ideal. For example, suppose that the computer can only store two digits' worth of the number, so `acres_per_person` has the value 0.33. If we multiply that by three, we get 0.99. But if the value was stored perfectly, it would be 3/3, or 1.0. The real value is a little bit bigger than the one we calculated. (In this case, the difference is $1.0 - 0.99 = 0.01$. If we use more digits we can make the error smaller, but it won't ever get to zero).

As we continue to calculate, the errors will accumulate. Again, these errors are usually so small that we don't have to worry about them in everyday graphics, but they're still there.

By contrast, an `int` value is precise and has no error. A value of 3 is exactly 3. And -78 is exactly -78. Multiply or add two integers and the result is an integer. Add one to an integer and the result is exactly one more than you had before, no more and no less. This is really useful, particularly when counting things and when using a variable to control how many times we repeat something. If I want to draw five green squares, then I want exactly five of them and not 5.001 (I don't even know what 0.001 of a green square ought to look like). So for lots of bookkeeping and counting tasks, the `int` data type is the perfect choice. It's efficient, and if we ever try to store a floating-point value in there, we know it was probably a mistake.

You can't store *any* integer into an `int` variable; the computer does have limits on the largest and smallest values it can store. In Processing, an `int` can hold a value from about -2 billion up to 2 billion (precisely, the range is $-2,147,483,648$ to $2,147,483,647$). If you ever need more than that (which seems unlikely), you can use the `long` data type, which stores integers from about -9 quintillion to 9 quintillion. Wow. But none of the built-in Processing routines accept `long` values, so you'll only be able to use them for your own internal bookkeeping. And a `long` is slower to process than an `int` is. Because of these drawbacks, you rarely see people using `long` variables in practice (I haven't used a single one in this book).

So integers are exact, but floating-point numbers are only approximate. But when you do need floating-point numbers, then by all means use the `float` data type. I don't want to give you the wrong impression. For the kinds of programs we usually write with Processing, `float` variables are more than accurate enough. You can create `float` variables and do what you want with them and never give a moment's thought to precision, and you'll probably never have a problem.

But if there does comes a time when a `float` just isn't accurate enough, there's another data type out there called `double`. This is short for *double precision*, and it's just that: a much more precise floating-point number. You define and use a `double` just like you would use a `float`:

```
double temperature;
temperature = 83.71;
```

So why not use a `double` all the time and forget about `float`? Speed. It takes the computer longer to compute with a `double` than it does with a `float`. The difference isn't huge if you're just adding two numbers, but if you start adding numbers together thousands of times per image (which is entirely reasonable), then the time difference can start to add up to something you can really see. If you're making moving images, the time you save by using variables of type `float` rather than `double` can make the difference between a smoothly flowing animation and something that stutters and jumps. If you don't need the extra precision of a `double`, there's no need to use it.

Which raises the question of how you will know when you need to switch to a `double`? Happily, you can work with Processing for a long time and never need that extra precision. I won't use a `double` for any program in this book. Someday, if you write a program that depends on a lot of math (unlike the ones we'll do here), you may find that your graphics aren't lining up perfectly with each other or that your objects are drifting around on the screen. That's when you can try switching to `double` types and see if it helps. Until then, I suggest avoiding them, though you will see them in other people's code from time to time.

Another downside of `double` is that, like `long`, none of the built-in Processing routines accept numbers in `double` format. If you want to hand a `double` to Processing, you have to turn it into a `float` first by preceding it with the word `float` between parentheses:

```
double doubleNumber = 999999999;
float floatNumber = (float)doubleNumber;
```

Of course, just as you can't put two gallons of milk in a one gallon container, you can't put a giant `double`-sized number into a smaller `float`-sized variable. Processing will do its best to save a floating-point value that's as close as possible to your double-precision value, but if your `double` is too big to fit into a `float`, then Processing will just save the biggest floating-point value it can.

So the general rule I'll use for numbers in this book is to use an `int` when I'm counting, and a `float` for just about everything else. I suggest you do the same in your own projects.

Generally speaking, you can assign variables to those of other types as long as the new object can hold the type it's getting. So a `double` can take on the value held in any other kind of number variable: another `double`, or a `float`, or an `int`. A `float` can't directly take the value of a `double` because it isn't capable of that precision, but it can take on any other `float` or `int`. And finally, an `int` can only take on the value of another `int`.

There are built-in functions that will do their best to convert any type of number to any other type. Each function has the name of the type you want the number to become. So `int(3.78)` will turn the floating-point value 3.78 into an integer.

To do this conversion, `int()` simply throws away the fractional part, leaving you with just 3. Converting a float to an integer is probably the most common example of this kind of *type conversion* (also called *casting*), but you can coerce variables into a `float` if you want to, using `float()`. Normally you don't need to do that explicitly because such assignments are perfectly legal. If you put an `int` into a `float`, that's no problem. It's only when you're risking losing information (like turning the floating-point value 3.78 into the integer 3) that you have to explicitly use one of these conversion functions. Figure 22.9 summarizes all of the type conversion functions in one place.

If you try to assign a floating-point number to an integer variable without running it through `int()` first, Processing will try to protect you from accidentally losing information by flagging it as an error.

The types we've just looked at can only hold numbers. You'll frequently want to store pieces of text in your programs, and the `String` data type exists for just that job.

We'll talk more about `String` types in Chapter 20. where we'll see that they're basically for holding and manipulating text, like someone's name, or the title of a book. We'll see that you can also convert strings to numbers, and vice-versa.

There are only a couple of basic types left to cover (there are a few other special-purpose types that we won't get into here, but of course they're described in detail in the documentation). The `color` type is used to hold (surprise!) a color, and we'll discuss that type in some detail in Chapter 4.

The other useful type is called a `boolean` (pronounced bool'-ee-in), named for the mathematician George Boole. A `boolean` is a special kind of data type because it can only hold two values: `true` and `false`. These two values aren't numbers, and they're not strings; they're just keywords with a special meaning to Processing as the values that a `boolean` variable can take on.

You'll frequently see people using an `int` to do a job better filled by a `boolean`. For example, suppose someone wrote a program to display current weather conditions, and in the program, there's a variable called `it_is_raining`. If it's dry right now that variable has the value 0, otherwise, it's 1. Here's a declaration of the variable with the value 1, to mean "true."

```
int it_is_raining = 1;
```

So why not use a `boolean`? History. Many early programming languages didn't have a `boolean` data type, and people got into the habit of using integers. By universal convention, a value of 0 in an integer means false. Usually a 1 means true, but often anything other than a 0 can mean true as well. Because many people learn to program by reading other people's code (which is a great way to learn), this tradition persists. It's not so bad, but I think if you're trying to represent something that really does seem to have a true/false nature, it's better to use a `boolean`. After all, they were designed for exactly that purpose, and it's a little easier to understand than an integer's value. Here's the same variable but initialized as a `boolean`:

```
boolean it_is_raining = true;
```

To me, this is clearer. Later on, we'll see that we can test a `boolean` to see if it is `true` or `false` and take different actions depending on the result.

3.3   Using = for Assignment

I said earlier that variables can have new values put into them at any time. Just assign them a new value and it's done!

Suppose that it's raining when our program begins. So the `boolean` variable `it_is_raining` might be declared this way:

```
boolean it_is_raining = true;
```

Later on, it stops raining. We'd simply say this:

```
it_is_raining = false;
```

That's all there is to it. The new value gets written into the variable, and the old value is discarded. It's true: variables vary!

A variable's new value can come from all kinds of operations. A very common operation is to count some number of things in your program. Each time you find another one of those things, you add one to the value of some variable. If your variable was named `counter`, you'd write it like this:

```
counter = counter+1;
```

The computer takes the current value of `counter`, adds one to it, and saves that into `counter`, overwriting the value that was there before.

If you're a mathematician, this probably looks like insanity. Clearly, if we read this line of Processing like an equation, it can't possibly be true. There's no value of `counter` that could ever equal its own value plus one. But of course, as we've seen, the equals sign in Processing is not a test of equality but an instruction to assign a value to a variable. We call the equals sign in this context an assignment operator.

In this statement, the right-hand side of the equals sign is evaluated first: take the value of `counter` and add 1 to it. When that's done, the result is put into `counter` (over-writing what it used to have).

Often we pronounce the equals sign as "gets," "takes," or "becomes," so we might read the above line out loud as "counter gets counter plus one". Some people pronounce the equals sign as "equals," but I think that's potentially confusing.

This use of the equals sign is weird. It sure isn't mathematically correct, but this is how almost every language writes assignment statements. Not everyone is happy about that. In some languages, the equals sign is replaced by something else. One choice is a makeshift arrow, `<-`, so that the line above would be written

```
counter <- counter+1;   //This does not work in Processing
```

Though it's not perfect, in a lot of ways I think that this is better. But the equals sign has a lot of history behind it, and it seems to refuse to go away. This use of the equals sign for assignment comes to us from the very first programming languages, and it's just too well embedded now to be easily dethroned.

3.4 Semicolons and Errors

We've seen semicolons at the ends of many lines of Processing code above. Going forward, we'll use semicolons about a million times in every program. Let's see what that's all about.

Almost every sentence in English ends with a period (or occasionally, different punctuation, like a question mark or exclamation point). Even if it's obvious when a sentence is over, that period is still required. There, that sentence just now ended with a period. And so does this one.

In Processing, every *statement* ends with a semicolon. So far, we've seen three kinds of statements: variable declarations, assignment statements, and combined declaration-assignment statements. And just like every English sentence ends with a period, every one of these Processing statements ends with a semicolon. Every single one. And that's the rule: every statement ends with a semicolon. The only tricky thing about this rule is knowing what a statement is!

Until you get the hang of it, you might find yourself including semicolons where they're not required, or leaving one out where one should have gone. Not to worry. I'll identify various statements as we go along, and you'll pick up where the semicolons belong and where they don't. After a while, it'll be second nature to you. Until then, the computer will help you along by reporting a syntax error when a necessary semicolon is missing.

The general principle is that every time you complete an action, you end with a semicolon. If you want to take more than one action at a time, then you wrap the multiple statements in *curly braces*: { and }. The curly braces themselves don't end with a semicolon because they're not actually a statement, they're just a grouping device. The curly braces generally tell Processing "treat all of the statements inside these braces like one chunk of statements."

For example, if you were instructing the computer to bake cookies you might have a step involving adding butter. That would end with a semicolon (don't worry about the parentheses for now):

```
add_butter();
```

If you wanted to add a bunch of things at once, you might wrap them in curly braces:

```
{
    add_chocolate_chips();
    add_walnuts();
    add_mint();
}
```

We'll see later that this lets us package up that group and refer to it conveniently with a single name, like my_winter_cookie_recipe().

Curly braces are used for a few other grouping tasks as well, probably because there are only three kinds of paired grouping symbols on the keyboard. Processing is pretty consistent about using the square brackets [and], though it's a little more flexible with the curly braces { and }, and the round parentheses (and) are drafted into a variety of uses. The angle brackets < and > are used only for math and not for grouping things. Don't worry about keeping all these character pairs straight because there are really just a few patterns and you'll pick those up without even noticing it. But in the beginning, keep an eye out for whether you should be using curly braces or parentheses, and try to get a feel for when a "statement" is over and you need to provide a semicolon.

If you mess up and include an extra semicolon here and there, or leave out a required one, the computer will catch it and tell you.

Which raises an interesting question: if the computer "knows" when you've made a mistake, why doesn't it just fix it for you? For example, when it sees that a semicolon is required, but it's not there, why doesn't it just put one there for you and carry on?

This sounds like a reasonable thing to do, and people have tried it. And over time, they've abandoned it. The problem is that although most of the time it's perfectly reasonable for the computer to fix your simple errors for you, every now and then that can backfire when the computer guesses wrong. And those backfires can be maddening to track down and fix. So maddening that you turn off the auto-fixing entirely.

This is the same reason that spell-checkers and grammar-checkers these days suggest corrections to you rather than automatically fix them. When you wrote "The frog ate the man," maybe that's what really happened, and you don't want the computer to assume otherwise. Or maybe "Hen3ry" really is your character's name (the "3" is silent). The bottom line is that the computer is good at finding things that seem wrong, but because it can't read your mind, it's far less skilled at making them right.

So people have largely given up on having the computer rewrite your program for you. When there's an error and the computer catches it, it tells you that there's a problem, and it tries to identify the problem as clearly and usefully as possible, but then it leaves it up to you to do something about it. And although it can be annoying to spend time fixing a bunch of minor typos, you'll be spared the horrible process of tracking down and fixing computer-generated "repairs."

3.5   Comments and Printing

We're going to start writing code in the next chapter, so I want to make you aware of a couple of really important tools: the comment and the print statement.

As we've seen, when you first hit the *Run* button, Processing first translates your text into the Java language. If something goes wrong during this translation stage, you'll get error messages in the console and a shorter (and usually more helpful) error message in the message area. The line on which Processing got hung up will also be highlighted in yellow in the text editor.

Figure 3.2 shows an example.

Don't worry about the program or the messages here; I just want to illustrate the general way they show up. These kinds of errors are usually typos, like misspelling a word or forgetting a semicolon. Because they are caught as a result of an error in syntax, or the text of the program, these kinds of problems are often referred to in general as syntax errors. Everyone gets lots of them when they first try to run a new piece of code; it's a rare day for me when a new program of more than a half-dozen lines doesn't have at least one syntax error in there somewhere.

If you have enough information to diagnose and fix the problem, then just make your corrections in the text editor and hit *Run* again. Processing will start over again, translating your program with a clean slate. If you repaired this problem, then Processing will keep going. It it hits another problem later on, it will again stop, with the new offending line in yellow and a message about the error.

If the problem isn't obvious to you and you're having trouble isolating it, you can start to *comment out* lines. As we saw earlier, by placing two slashes at the start of a line (/ /), you're telling Processing to ignore everything to the end of that line. It shows up in the text editor, but Processing doesn't try to read it or translate it. You can put any text you want after those characters: a note, a smiley face, anything, and it will be ignored.

The good thing is that this means your error, if there is one, will be ignored as well. Figure 3.2 shows a program with an error. If I was having trouble finding the problem, I could just comment out the highlighted line. The commented version is shown in

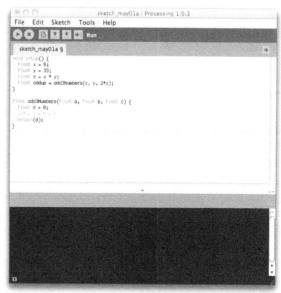

Figure 3.2. A syntax error.   Figure 3.3. Commenting out a line.

Figure 3.3; notice that the commented-out text is automatically shown in light gray. If I run this, there are no problems.

This lets me remove the line from Processing's attention. If the program gets successfully translated (and starts to run), then I'll know that this line is my problem, and I have to dig in a little deeper to fix it.

Sometimes you want to comment out a lot of lines. You can certainly put two slashes at the start of every line, but that can become a hassle. To comment out a whole bunch of code, use the *multiline comment* characters. Write /* to start a multiline comment, and */ to end it. Anything between those marks is a comment.

Warning: Don't put one multiline comment inside another! The first */ ends all comments. You'll be able to see this in the text editor because comments are in gray. After your first */ your code will be colorful again.

Commenting is a great way to isolate the errors that crop up during the translation stage, which are collectively called *syntax errors* or *compile-time errors*.

The other kind of error is the one that occurs when your program is actually running, and that's called a *run-time error*. There is no one best way to handle run-time errors; they're the tricky ones that will occupy most of your debugging attention.

A time-honored way to debug run-time problems is with the *print statement*. In Processing, there are two forms of print statements: `print()` and `println()`. They are identical, except that `println()` adds a newline character to the end of what's printed out (which is like pressing the Return key to start a new line of text).

Figure 3.4. Printing to the console.

Much of the time, you'll use these statements to print out the values of variables. I find that it's very useful to name the variable in the print statement, so if I have a few print statements in my program in different places, I know what I'm looking at:

```
println("a has the value " + a);
```

You can see that `println` lets you print both text and variables. When it sees text between quotation marks, it just prints that directly. A variable is printed with its value. To mix both kinds of things on one line, you use the plus sign (+) as glue. Note that I've included a space in my string, so the value of the variable doesn't come immediately after the last letter. Here's a two-variable example:

```
float x = 3.0;
float y = 8.7;
println("x = " + x+"   y = " + y);
```

Note that I put spaces around the equals sign because I find that makes the output easier to read. Both of the above print statements send their messages to Processing's console. On my system, errors in the console show up in red type, but the messages I generate with print statements show up in white. If I run the program above, I get the results shown in Figure 3.4.

Of course, you can use comments to help you fix run-time errors as well by effectively eliminating chunks of your program (if a line is commented out, it isn't translated, and if it isn't translated, it isn't run). Here, I'll break the print statement above into two lines:

```
float x = 3.0;
float y = 8.7;
println("x = " + x);
println("y = " + y);
```

The output of this program is:

```
x = 3.0
y = 8.7
```

Now I'll comment out the first print statement:

```
float x = 3.0;
float y = 8.7;
//println("x = " + x);
println("y = " + y);
```

The output of this new program is:

```
y = 8.7
```

If my program had been misbehaving and commenting out the line made it work correctly, that would be strong evidence that there was something wrong with that line.

3.5.1 Another Spinner

If you liked playing with the program at the start of this chapter, here's a variation on it that produces a different kind of image. Instead of moving a rectangle around, I'll move an ellipse. Again, kick around the numbers for yourself and have fun with them.

```
void setup() {
  size(600, 600);
  background(255);
  smooth();
  translate(300, 300);
  for (float i=0; i<360; i += 0.5) {
    pushMatrix();
      rotate(radians(i));
      translate(0, 200);
      rotate(radians(i*3));
      scale(map(sin(radians(i*6)), -1, 1, .5, 1),
        map(sin(radians(i*3)), -1, 1, .5, 1));
      drawEllipse();
    popMatrix();
```

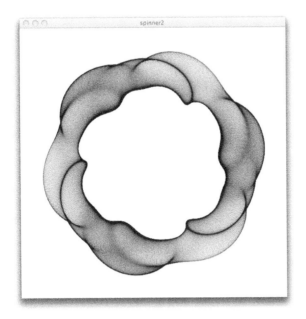

Figure 3.5. A spinning ellipse. (variables/sketches/spinner2/spinner2.pde)

```
  }
}
void drawEllipse() {
  noFill();
  stroke(0, 0, 0, 128);
  ellipse(0, 0, 120, 80);
}
```

(See output in Figure 3.5. Full program in variables/sketches/spinner2/spinner2.pde)

Chapter 4
Functions and Tests

Before we get started, here's another toy project for you to fool around with. As before, you can fiddle with the numbers freely to see what kinds of pictures you can make. This one uses random numbers, so each time you run it you'll get a different picture. Figure 4.1 shows a couple of images from this program. I just kept running it over and over and saved three that I liked.

```
float NoiseScale = 0.005;
float NoiseOffsetX, NoiseOffsetY;

void setup() {
   size(800, 600, P2D);
   background(255);
   smooth();
   noFill();
   stroke(0, 0, 0, 32);
   for (int i=0; i<300; i++) {
      NoiseOffsetX += 5;
      NoiseOffsetY += 7.1;
      drawOneStream();
   }
}

void drawOneStream() {
   float px = 0;
   float py = height/2.0;
   float vx = 1;
   float vy = 0;
   int pcnt = 0;
   while ((px>=0) && (px<width) && (py<height) && (py>=0)) {
      point(px, py);
      float xNoise = noise((pcnt+NoiseOffsetX) * NoiseScale);
      float yNoise = noise((pcnt+NoiseOffsetY) * NoiseScale);
      vx = ((2*vx) + 1 + map(xNoise, 0, 1, -1, 1))/4.0;
```

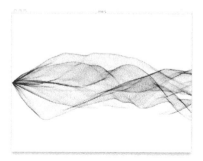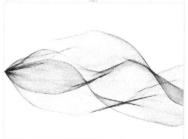

Figure 4.1. A program to draw fabric flowing like a river. (functions/sketches/river1/river1.pde)

```
vy = ((3*vy) + map(yNoise, 0, 1, -1, 1))/4.0;
px += vx;
py += vy;
pcnt++;
    }
}
```

(See output in Figure 4.1. Full program in functions/sketches/river1/river1.pde)

Processing lets you package up collections of actions into chunks that you can invoke all at once. The program above does just that.

Why is this useful? Cooking gives us a perfect analogy here. If you want to tell someone how to make a pasta dinner, but they've never done it before, you might have to walk them through every little step:

1. Fill a pot with water.

2. Put the pot on the stove.

3. Turn on the stove.

4. Wait for the water to boil.

5. Open the package of pasta.

6. Pour the pasta into the water.

7. Many more steps!

If you were careful, they could follow your instructions precisely and prepare a fine meal with pasta, tomato sauce, fresh vegetables, and so on. Now you could package up all those steps and then refer to them as just a single instruction:

1. Cook pasta.

Then you could have other prepackaged collections of steps for choosing a wine, preparing a salad, and so on.

Packaging up multiple steps into a single operation is an efficient way to refer to all of those steps at once. Of course, once you create this packaged version, you have to put it where someone else can find it.

There are lots of words in popular use for describing this kind of packaged-up collection of steps. You'll often see it called a *function*, a *procedure*, a *subroutine*, or simply a *routine*. Although some computer languages distinguish these words, in Processing they all mean the same thing, so I'll use them interchangeably in this book.

You'll also see a function sometimes referred to as a *method*, but in this book I'll use that word only for functions that are part of your own custom objects, as will be discussed in Chapter 14.

Returning to our pasta example, there are lots of different pasta shapes but preparing each of them follows roughly the same process. Rather than have one recipe for macaroni, one for spaghetti, one for wagon wheels, and so on, you might have just one recipe where you can specify the kind of pasta that should be used.

When a function takes one or more values that control or specify what it does, each of those values is called a *parameter*, or (borrowing a term from mathematics) *argument*. Generally speaking, these words both mean the same thing: a value that gets given to a function, that it can then use to do its work.

So the `cook-pasta` function could take an argument that tells it what kind of pasta to include in the description. I'll write this by naming the function and putting the argument in parentheses:

1. `cook-pasta (wagon-wheels)`

2. `cook-pasta (ziti)`

Then the instructions inside `cook-pasta` could conceivably use this information to customize their process. For example, the function might have you boil the wagon wheels for a minute longer than the ziti.

Routines and functions are incredibly useful; almost every program you ever write will have multiple functions in it. So let's dig into them.

4.1 Writing Functions

Let's say that you're writing a program in which you need to constantly add up three different numbers. These might be the last three screen positions of an object, or three shades of red, or any other three things that can be described by a number. Of course, it's easy enough to add three numbers, but let's pretend that it's a mind-bendingly difficult task (maybe instead of just adding the numbers together, we do all kinds of complicated calculations on them instead). Then we'd want to write it once and get it perfect, then save it in a function so we wouldn't have to repeat it over and over.

We start out by declaring a function. This has some elements in common with declaring a variable, but some differences, too. In general, you give the name of the function, its type, the values it takes as inputs (that is, its parameters or arguments), and then the statements you want it to execute.

First off, every function has to have a name. The name must obey the rules we saw earlier for names (it must start with a letter, it must contain no spaces, and it can use only letters, numbers, and underscores). Let's call this one `add3Numbers`. The declaration so far is just the name of the function:

```
add3Numbers
```

Now I'll define the arguments that it takes as inputs. These are just variables like any other, so each argument has an associated name and type.

The list of arguments is naturally enough called an *argument list*. Here's how to type it correctly. The argument list always appears between a pair of parentheses that come after the function name. If there's more than one argument, they're each separated by commas.

These parentheses are *always* required. If you don't have any arguments to go in them, then you just type the parentheses with nothing between them (though you can put in some spaces if you want). This is your way of telling Processing, "This function has no arguments." You might think that an easier way to do this would be to leave the parentheses out altogether, and that's a reasonable idea, but that's not how Processing does it.

So let's start with our empty argument list:

```
add3Numbers()
```

Lots of functions don't take any arguments, and we'll see plenty of them as we go on. But in this example we do have arguments, so let's put them in:

```
add3Numbers(number1, number2, number3)
```

Remember that every variable has a name and a type. The same thing holds for the arguments in a function; Processing has to know the type of each argument. Let's suppose that these are all floating-point numbers, so I'll explicitly give them that type:

```
add3Numbers(float number1, float number2, float number3)
```

We're getting closer.

From here on in the book, anytime I refer to a function, I'll indicate that by using a pair of parentheses after the function name. So if I'm talking about a variable named `numberOfApples`, I'll write it just that way. But let's suppose that this was the name of a function. Then I'll write `numberOfApples()` so that we can tell right away that it's a function. If it takes arguments, I won't list them because it would take up a lot of room and not add much meaning. So when I talk about this function in the text, I'll refer to it as `add3Numbers()`, even though we know it takes three floating-point numbers as inputs.

Remember that the purpose of this function is to add up the numbers we give it. That means it returns a value when it's done, but what's the type of that value?

In this case, it's going to be a floating-point number (because otherwise this would be a pretty lousy function). In Processing, there's a neat conceptual shorthand that lets us conveniently describe the type of a variable that is returned by a function: the function itself is given a type.

In other words, we know that `add3Numbers()` is the name of a function, and when we're done with it, somehow it's going to return a floating-point number as its result. The way we say that `add3Numbers()` returns a `float` is to say that the function `add3Numbers()` itself has a type, and that type is `float`. This is really just a shorthand to save on typing, but it's a good one that makes sense.

To see why, let's look at a line of code that might *invoke*, or *call*, this function:

```
float mySum = add3Numbers(1.0, 2.2, -14.1);
```

When Processing sees `add3Numbers()`, it calls the function with the numbers listed above as arguments (or inputs or parameters). Then when `add3Numbers()` is done, it gives back a `float`, and that gets put into `mySum`. So the value going into `mySum` is a floating-point number. It does make sense to say that the function `add3Numbers()` itself really does have the type `float` because that's the type of the object that results from calling it.

So in the definition of a function, we provide its type just like we would the type of a variable, by simply providing the type before the name:

```
float add3Numbers(float number1, float number2, float number3)
```

Finally, the code that implements this function (called the *body*) follows the definition, between a pair of curly braces:

```
float add3Numbers(float number1, float number2, float number3)
{ }
```

We're so close to having a real function, I can taste it. But if we tried to compile a program with these two lines in it, Processing would highlight the declaration line in yellow and give us an error message in the message area:

```
This method must return a result of type float
```

That's a great error message! Processing knows that `add3Numbers()` must return a `float` (because that's how we declared it), but right now, the function doesn't return anything. In fact, it doesn't do anything at all because there are no statements between the curly braces. There must be at least one statement in order to return a value.

Naturally enough, that's called a *return statement*. It consists of the word `return` followed by the value to be returned and a semicolon (I like to put parentheses around the returned value because I think that makes it easier to read the code, but you don't have to if you don't want to):

```
float add3Numbers(float number1, float number2, float number3)
{
    return (number1+number2+number3);
}
```

Note the semicolon at the end: a *return statement* is a statement like any other, and so must end with a semicolon.

We now have written a complete function in Processing!

The *return statement* is very flexible. You can return all sorts of things from functions: variables of type `int` and `float`, of course, but also variables containing objects of your own design (we'll see these in Chapter 14). Be careful to make sure that the type of the object you're returning is the same type as the function itself, or you'll get an error like the one above.

When the computer executes your `return` statement, that's the end of your function; the computer leaves the function and returns to the calling program that invoked it in the first place.

To use our function, we can write a little test program to call it and then print out the result.

4.2   setup() and draw()

To write a little test program in Processing, put your code inside a function named `setup()` of type `void`; this function takes no arguments (I'll talk about `void` in just a moment).

```
void setup() {
    // testing stuff goes here
}
```

The `setup()` function is special in Processing and effectively tells the system "start here" when it runs your program. It has to have the name `setup()` with a type of `void` and take no arguments. You put your test code between the curly braces that define the `setup()` procedure.

This is the first of two functions you see in almost every Processing program. The other, which we'll see in a moment, is `draw()`.

When you run a program, the first thing Processing does is look for a function named `setup()`. If it can find that, it runs the code that's defined in that function. If there's no `setup()` (like in some of our earlier examples), Processing will just run the commands you've given it in the text window. But except for the very smallest little programs, you're always going to have a `setup()`, and that's always where Processing begins.

Of course, Processing is all about graphics, so your program will probably want to draw stuff. And since Processing is also all about animation, that stuff will probably move over time. Your computer is already redrawing the entire screen for you many times a second. The exact number of times varies from one computer to the next, depending on its speed and the particular choices you've used for your monitor or display. The number is typically around 60 refreshes per second. So if you're looking at your computer monitor right now, odds are pretty good that it's actually being redrawn for you, over and over, 60 times or more every second. Because it's happening so quickly and the electronics are well designed, you don't see any negative effects of this redrawing (if it ran too slowly, you'd see the image *flicker*, like an old-time movie).

Each time the screen is redrawn we say the computer has drawn a new *frame*. So you're probably getting something like 60 frames per second from your computer. For each frame, Processing looks for a function you've written called `draw()`, also with type `void`. If you haven't got such a function, then Processing just doesn't do anything. But if there is a `draw()` procedure, then Processing will call it at the start of every frame. As the name suggests, typically your `draw()` function will draw to the graphics window. Frequently, one of the first things we do when writing a new project is to tell `draw()` to start out by erasing the whole window. This covers the window completely with some background color, so that everything that follows is drawn on top of that. When `draw()` is done with all its work, your computer takes the picture that it created and *bam* it puts it up on the screen in the graphics window. Then 1/60 of a second later it happens again. And again. And again, over and over, as long as your program runs.

So to recap, Processing executes `setup()` once at the start, and then `draw()` for every single new frame as long as your program runs.

Which raises an interesting question: when and how does your program ever stop? There are two ways to stop: when your program itself decides to quit or the user decides to stop it. If you want to stop a sketch that Processing has started up, you can just click the exit button in the window (this varies from one platform to another, but it's the little button that's usually in the top left or top right of the window that makes the window go away).

Sometimes that doesn't work because your program has hit a strange error. If you can't stop a program (that is, dismiss the window) by clicking the graphics window's dismiss button, press the *Stop* button on Processing's menu bar (that's the second round button over, with a square in it).

You might want your program to run for a limited time and then stop itself. For example, it might be part of a museum display. When a museum visitor pushes a button, your program runs, shows them some animation, and stops. You don't want your visitor to have to close the window or press a button to end the program, but instead, you want your program itself to stop when it's done.

You can do that with the function exit(). If you call exit(), that hits the brakes immediately: your program stops right there and the window goes away, just as if the user had pressed the *Stop* button. Most of the programs in this book, though, will be *free running*, so they will just go and go and go until we stop them manually.

So let's get our new setup() function into our example. Where should the definition of add3Numbers() go? Not inside of setup()! Each function in your program is a citizen of the world. No function appears within any other function. If you have three functions, they get listed one after the other. In fact, they can come in any order, and they can even be spread out among multiple source files if that helps you organize your program. Part of the translation step that Processing goes through when you press the *Run* button is to locate each procedure and remember where it is. I'll keep everything in one file for quite a while, since it's the the easiest way to write short programs like this.

So I'll first create setup(), and then put my short test program inside of that procedure. Then after the closing curly brace of setup(), I'll provide the definition of add3Numbers().

Here's our program:

```
void setup() {
    float v1 = 3.0;
    float v2 = 8.7;
    float v3 = -3.0;
    float sum = add3Numbers(v1, v2, v3);
    println("The final sum is "+sum);
}

float add3Numbers(float number1, float number2, float number3)
{
    return (number1+number2+number3);
}
```

(Full program in functions/sketches/addup1/addup1.pde)

If you hit the *Run* button (in the upper-left of the window, at the left-hand side of the toolbar, it's the circular button with a little triangle in it), you'll get this result in the message area:

```
The final sum is 8.7
```

It's a running Processing program! And though it looks simple, don't be fooled. This program is doing a ton of cool stuff. We're creating variables, invoking a function, passing those variables as arguments, using them in a function to compute a result, passing that result back to the calling procedure, storing it in a variable, and printing it out. That's very cool.

Many functions return nothing. For example, you might call a function to draw a square on the screen. Once it's done the job, the function returns, but it doesn't send back any information. How do you tell Processing "this function doesn't return anything"? One approach would be to simply leave off a type on the function. But that's a little risky because the computer wouldn't be able to help you distinguish between when you meant to return nothing and when you did mean to return a value but simply forgot to declare its type. So instead, you explicitly say "this function returns nothing" by saying that it returns the type `void`.

The type `void` is unusual because it's not really a type the way `int` and `float` are types. Its only use in Processing is to give a type to a function that doesn't return anything. In other words, declaring a function with the return type of `void` means "this function does not return anything."

4.3 Curly Braces

Before I march on, I'll make a comment about style. As much as people like to argue over politics and text editors, they can get *really* worked up over the placement of curly braces.

The happy truth is that the computer doesn't care where you put your curly braces, so you can format your code in any way that pleases you. But there are people who feel strongly that one style or another makes it easier to share, change, and debug their programs. Here are the three most popular styles, in no particular order. I've seen them all in practice, and each one works as well as the others. One thing almost everyone does have in common is that they indent the statements inside the block by one tab. It's nice to see everyone agreeing on *something*.

I'm going to compute the sum on one line and return it on another, so that we have at least two lines in each function's body.

1. The opening brace is on its own line and not indented. The closing brace is not indented.

   ```
   float add2Numbers(float number1, float number2)
   {
       float sum = number1 + number2;
       return (sum);
   }
   ```

2. The opening brace is on the same line as the definition. The closing brace is indented.

   ```
   float add2Numbers(float number1, float number2) {
       float sum = number1 + number2;
       return (sum);
       }
   ```

3. The opening brace is on the same line as the definition. The closing brace is not indented.

```
float add2Numbers(float number1, float number2) {
    float sum = number1 + number2;
    return (sum);
}
```

I'm sure you can see why so much blood has been spilled over these choices. It's hard to imagine anything that could be more important.

If each of these styles looks pretty much the same and equally useful to you, then select the one you like most and try to stick with it. If you feel strongly that one of these is vastly superior to the others, you now have a ready-made source for endless hours of entertaining arguments.

I think one reason people get so worked up about this is that when you format your own code the same way for a long time, that consistency does indeed make the code easy to read at a glance. That's a very good thing. Unfortunately, it can make other styles of formatting seem weird, and thus, harder to read. By the same token, people who are used to a style other than yours will think your code looks weird (but of course they're wrong).

I like the last style in the list, where the opening brace is on the same line as the function declaration and the closing brace is indented one tab stop less than the body. There are several places where curly braces are used in pairs like this, and I use this same convention for all those uses.

By the way, once in a while, you can pack a whole function onto one line (if it's short enough):

```
float add2(float n1, float n2) { return (n1+n2); }
```

With occasional exceptions, I find that this usually isn't worth it. Writing your code in a consistent style really does make it easier to write, debug, and change later. The computer doesn't care about your formatting; the one-line version runs no faster than a three-line version. So I usually opt for consistency over a little bit of compactness. On the other hand, sometimes writing something really small on one line is a nice way of visually emphasizing that the function really is doing a tiny little job.

Sometimes very small functions whose principal jobs are just to save you some typing are called *convenience functions* (or *convenience routines*). This isn't a formal term; it's just a way we sometimes describe a little helper function, rather than something that does significant work.

4.4   Integer Division

In add3Numbers() above I added up three numbers using the plus sign, and I hope that seemed reasonable to you. You can add, subtract, multiply, and divide using the standard symbols `+`, `-`, `*`, and `/`. You can use parentheses to control what gets done first:

```
int result1 = 2 * (3 + 3);   // this has the value 2*6 = 12
int result2 = (2 * 3) + 3;   // this has the value 6+3 = 9
```

There are some rules about what happens first if you don't provide parentheses: all the multiplications and divisions in your expression happen before any of the additions and subtractions (we say that multiplication has a higher *precedence* than addition). So if you just wrote `3+2*3`, Processing would multiply first, resulting in a value of 9.

Even though I know the precedence rules, I almost always include the parentheses anyway. That way I don't have to think about precedence, and the intended calculation is instantly clear to me and anyone else who looks at it. The extra parentheses don't slow down the computer even the slightest bit or change how the program runs. Their only cost is two characters in my source file. For the increased clarity, I think that's usually worth it.

There's an odd but very important quirk to keep in mind when you divide numbers: if you divide two integers, the result is always an integer. I don't like this rule very much, and it messes me up all the time, but that's how things are.

For example, if you write `3/2`, the value of that expression is `1`, not `1.5`. That's because both values are integers. Even if you store the result in a `float`, that variable will still have the value of `1.0`, because the variables involved in the expression are all integers. In essence, Processing computes the floating-point result of your division statement and then immediately throws away the fractional value. So an expression like `20*(3/2)` has the value `20`, not `30`.

If you want your division operations to include fractional parts in the result, you need to make sure that at least one of the values involved is a `float`. You can do this with numbers simply by putting a decimal point and a 0 after them. So `3/2.0` or `3.0/2` both evaluate to `1.5`. If your expression involves variables that are all integers, you can multiply one of them by `1.0` to make it a `float`, like this:

```
(weight*1.0)/age
```

Note that if this "promotion" to a `float` is within parentheses, then the promotion ends at those parentheses.

Suppose I have the expression `(1/2)*(1.0*3/2)`. I've made sure that the expression on the right is evaluated as floating-point by multiplying it by 1.0. That makes the rightmost value 1.5. But I'm multiplying that by `(1/2)`, and since that's not inside the parentheses of the other expression, that division has a value of 0. The result of this expression is 0.

Instead, I could write `(1.0/2)*(1.0*3/2)`. Now both values end up as floating-point numbers, and so the final result is `0.75`.

There are two little techniques that can save you a character here and there when you want to make a number into a floating-point value. First, you don't have to include both the decimal point and a 0 after a number to make it floating-point. Just the decimal itself will do. So `3/2.` and `3./2` both return 1.5. Alternatively, you can put the letter `f` after a number to make it floating-point. So `3.0/2` will result in 1.5, as will `3f/2`. My style is usually to include the decimal point and a 0 (that is, I write `3.0` when I want to turn 3 into a floating-point value), but `3.` and `3f` work just as well.

So I could also write our expressions above as `(1./2)*(1.*3/2)` or even `(1f/2)*(3f/2)`.

All of these extra decimal points and letters strike me as a bit messy. But you have to use one of these types of expressions if you want to retain fractional parts in division operations that would otherwise return integers.

This issue applies only to division, because it's the only operator that can create a floating-point value from two integers. You don't have to think about this issue for addition, subtraction, or multiplication.

The thing that triggers Processing to throw away the fraction is the type of the numbers involved, not their values. So as long as one of the variables in an expression is a `float`, then the fractional part is retained.

This takes some getting used to. It can seem strange, but don't feel shy about including a multiplication by 1.0 somewhere in your expression when you're dividing integers. I do it all the time.

4.5   Combined Operators

Processing offers you some very useful notational shorthands that are shared by many modern languages. They make it easy to change the values of variables before or after they get used in an expression. For example, it's very common to want to add or subtract one from a variable, such as when you're counting things:

```
counter = counter + 1;
numItems = numItems - 1;
```

I think I've written lines like this about a billion times (I might be underestimating). To save you typing time, you can use the shorthands `++` and `--`:

```
counter++;
numItems--;
```

These do exactly the same thing as the lines just above; they're just a shorthand way of writing them. Think of `counter++` as a three-step operation:

1. Retrieve the value of `counter`.

2. Add one to that value.

3. Save the result back into `counter`.

This shorthand has another trick up its sleeve, though. Notice that the ++ and --
appear *after* the variable. This means that if the variable appears in an expression, the
add-one or subtract-one operation also happens *after* the variable is used.

To see this in action, consider four games and what happens when a player joins or
quits. The number of people in each game is given by the variable numPlayers.

Suppose you're playing a game where you have some number of tokens or markers
that move around a board. Each player needs a token. Sometime during the game,
another player shows up. So you need to increment the count of the number of players
and the number of tokens so that they stay the same. You can do that in one line:

```
numTokens = ++numPlayers;
```

So the computer retrieves the value of numPlayers, and because the ++ operator appears before the variable, it is first incremented by one and then assigned to
numTokens.

Suppose that later someone leaves. We want to decrease the number of players and
assign that new smaller value to the number of tokens. We could write this:

```
numTokens = --numPlayers;
```

Following the same pattern as last time, the computer gets the numPlayers value,
reduces it by one, and then assigns the result to numTokens.

Now suppose you're playing musical chairs, where there is always one less chair
than players. So if numPlayers is 8, numChairs will be 7. Now someone joins the
game. The number of players has to go up by one, and we need to make sure we have
one less chair than the new number of players. This would be a wrong way to do it:

```
numChairs = ++numPlayers;  // not correct for musical chairs
```

If numPlayers started out as 8, then this would first take numPlayers, add one
to it to make it 9, and then assign the result to numChairs. Both variables would have
the value 9, which isn't what we want.

What we want is to get the current value of numPlayers and assign *that* to
numChairs, and only then increment the number of players. We could write

```
numChairs = numPlayers++;  // correct for musical chairs
```

This statement takes the current number of players, assigns that to the number of
chairs, and *then* adds one to numPlayers. The result is that numPlayers has the
value 9, and numChairs has the value 8 (the previous value of numPlayers). When
the ++ operator comes *after* the variable, it tells the computer to use the value and *then*
increment it.

Finally, suppose we're playing a game that's the opposite of musical chairs, where
there's always one extra, empty chair (it's not a great game, I admit), and one of our
players leaves. We could write

```
numChairs = numPlayers--;
```

So if before this line was executed `numPlayers` was 8, then the computer will take that value, assign it to `numChairs`, and then decrement `numPlayers` to make it 7. That's just what we want: one more chair than there are players.

You'll see this shorthand all over the place; it's incredibly useful. And though I used a lot of words above, you'll soon see something like `baseballs++` and know without even thinking about it that the computer will retrieve the value of `baseballs`, use it in the context of the expression, and then increment it by one when it's done.

If `++` and `--` come after the variable, we call that a *postincrement* and *postdecrement* operation, meaning that the increment or decrement come after the rest of the statement. If they come ahead of the variable, it's called *preincrement* and *predecrement*.

To stay safe, don't use a variable more than once in an expression if you're using one of these operators. For example, don't do the following, where I'm using `grapes` twice, but one occurrence has a postincrement applied to it:

```
int cost_of_fruit_bowl = (2 * grapes++) * (3 + grapes);
                                            // don't do this!
```

And never, ever apply more than one of these to the same variable in a single expression:

```
int cost_of_fruit_bowl = (2 * grapes++) * (3 + --grapes);
                                            // don't do this!
```

As King Lear said, "That way madness lies."

Use an extra line or two to do the calculation one step at a time. It's worth it.

You can, of course, freely mix these operators in an expression as long as they apply to different variables:

```
int cost_of_fruit_bowl = (2 * plums++) * (3 + --oranges);
```

By the way, people pronounce these things in different ways when they read them out loud. I usually just say "plus plus" and "minus minus," which sounds a little funny but communicates just fine.

This shorthand comes in a second, equally important flavor: `+=` that handles the case where you want to add two numbers and store the result back into one of them. For example, if a mouse eats some cheese, his weight goes up by the cheese's weight:

```
mouseWeight = mouseWeight + cheeseWeight;
```

Again, this kind of thing happens all the time in programming. If you were just adding one to `mouseWeight`, you could write:

```
mouseWeight++
```

(or `++mouseWeight`). But here, we want to add something other than one, and the construct `+=` is used to handle this. You can simply write

```
mouseWeight += cheeseWeight;
```

In other words, we have a 4-step process:

1. Retrieve the value of `mouseWeight`.

2. Retrieve the value of `cheeseWeight`.

3. Add the values together.

4. Save the result back into `mouseWeight`.

This shorthand creates the same result as in the previous example, but it's just a little more concise. It has the benefit that you're not typing `mouseWeight` twice. That's nice from a labor-saving standpoint, but even better from a programming point of view. Suppose that the mouse in question is playing hide-and-seek with the household cat. The mouse might find a hiding place and wait, leading you to have a variable in your program called `mouseWait` that tells you how many seconds the mouse waits before moving. If you were working with someone else and you told them what to do on the phone, they might write this code:

```
mouseWeight = mouseWait + cheeseWeight;
```

This could cause very strange results, and you'd have to track down and fix this error. Of course, I picked homonyms here for fun, but when you repeat a variable name a few times on a line, you're asking for trouble if you get one wrong. Eliminating one of those instances is a good thing. In general, the less your code repeats itself (in any way), the better.

There are four of these types of operators, one for each of the four basic functions: `+=` to add and assign, `-=` to subtract and assign, `/=` to divide and assign, and `*=` to multiply and assign. The `+=` form (including `-=`, `*=`, and `/=`) is a terrific tool, and you should get in the habit of using it whenever possible. Consider an expression like this:

```
numberOfApples += 5;
```

Just a glance tells you that you now have five more apples than before. Consider the following:

```
numberOfApples *= 2;
```

You can instantly see that you're doubling the number of apples.

These forms also have the advantage of reducing bugs by helping you not to repeat yourself. Suppose you're creating a neighborhood scene. There are a bunch of cone-shaped objects in your world: ice cream cones, traffic cones, simple teepees, and so on, in addition to a generic "cone" that you use for a child's toy. Each kind of cone has its own variables that define its color, weight, height, and so on. Suppose that near some intersection, you want to make the traffic cones twice as tall as usual. You might write

```
traffic_cone_height = cone_height * 2;
```

Later on, looking at your pictures, something doesn't look right. You eventually decide it's the cones, and after a period of hunting through your code you find the line above. What you wanted to do was double `traffic_cone_height`, but when you typed the code, you accidentally named the generic cone height stored in `cone_height`. What you meant to write was

```
traffic_cone_height = traffic_cone_height * 2;
```

You couldn't have slipped this way if you'd written it with the `*=` shorthand:

```
traffic_cone_height *= 2;
```

So by getting rid of one of the repetitions of the variable name, we also got rid of a possible source of problems.

This is a general theme that we're going to see over and over: minimize repetition.

That's so important, I'll say it again: minimize repetition.

If you can type `traffic_cone_height` just once on a line rather than twice, that's one less thing that can go wrong.

The `*=` shorthand works for all four of the basic operations (+, -, *, and /). For example, consider

```
total_apples = total_apples - order_size;
```

This works, but it's cleaner to write

```
total_apples -= order_size;
```

For another example, consider

```
total_bill = total_bill * (1+taxPercentage);
```

This also works, but it's shorter and clearer to write

```
total_bill *= (1+taxPercentage);
```

It's not a big difference, but it can help you avoid making errors, and it's easier to take in the meaning of the line at a glance.

4.6 Starting a Program

In Processing, as in many other languages, there are a bunch of things you do at the start of almost every program. Particularly while learning Processing, it's usually a good idea to simply type (or copy and paste) these lines into every new program right off the bat, before you even start to create your own program. This kind of recurring language is called *boilerplate* (the term is historical but was adopted by journalists to refer to language that's used over and over again with little to no change; today, lawyers also refer to standard legal language in contracts as boilerplate).

It's reasonable to ask why you have to bother: if these things are so common, shouldn't the system just assume them for you? You have to do them yourself because, eventually, you will want to write a program that doesn't use the boilerplate. If the system always put it in, you might forget it was there. There's not much of it, and it's much clearer to have it in front of you where you can't miss it.

The boilerplate I'll provide here does three things:

1. Puts up a graphics window on the screen.

2. Fills it with a reddish-gray background.

3. Instructs Processing to update the graphics in that window many times a second.

The updating step won't do anything in the boilerplate, but the placeholder will be there for us to modify.

Here's my boilerplate; almost every Processing program I write starts with this skeleton (although I change the specific numbers depending on the size of the graphics window and the color I want to put in it):

```
void setup() {
    size(600, 400);
    background(192, 64, 0);
}

void draw() {
    // drawing goes here
}
```

(Full program in functions/sketches/skeleton1/skeleton1.pde)

This is actually a complete program in Processing. Try it out: type it in and hit the *Run* button. You'll see a window pop up, 600 pixels wide by 400 pixels high, filled with a reddish-gray color. That's all this program does, so once you see it, you can close the window.

If you look at the above code and then take a guess about how this program works (in a general way), you'll probably be right. The first function, setup(), takes no arguments, and because it returns no results, it has type void. It calls two other functions that are built into the Processing language. The first, size(), creates a graphics window of the given width and height. I've chosen to make my boilerplate window a little wider than it is tall because I like how that looks.

Here's something that's important to remember: if you call size(), then it should be the *first line* in setup(). And you will almost always want to call size() because that's what makes the graphics window for you.

Inside of `setup()`, I also call `background()`, which fills the graphics window with a specific color. The three arguments to `background()` define the red, green, and blue components of the color, each on a scale from 0 (meaning dark) to 255 (meaning bright). I'll return to color later on, but for now, if these three numbers don't create a color that tickles your fancy, feel free to change each of them to anything in the range 0 to 255 until you like what you see. You'll find that every graphics object in this book, and every window on which they get drawn, has a color. More times than not, this color is given by three numbers in the range 0 to 255 that appear in a listing, just as the numbers `192, 64, 0` appeared above. Where did these three numbers come from?

I used an online color-picking program and noodled around until I found a color I liked. At the bottom of the window it listed the red, green, and blue values of that color (almost every color-picking program out there will give you these numbers for the colors you pick). I just wrote them down and typed them in.

I used a jazzed-up color picker, but there's a basic one built right into Processing; you can bring it up by selecting *Tools* from the menu bar at the top of the Processing window, and then choosing *Color Selector*.

So my colors aren't the result of any magic—just lots of playing and eyeballing and looking for nice combinations. Except for the leaf project in Chapter 15, where I referenced photographs of autumn colors, I found all of the colors in this book that way.

Returning to our boilerplate, the second function, also of type `void`, is called `draw()`. Right now, our version of `draw()` is empty except for a placeholder comment.

We don't have to tell Processing to call `setup()`, because that's the first thing the system does when it runs the program (after checking for errors). When Processing starts, it looks for a function called `void setup()` and runs it automatically.

The other thing Processing does automatically is to call a function named `void draw()` many times a second. Each time the computer is ready to redraw the picture, which is typically around 60 times per second, Processing will call the function named `draw()` if you've provided one.

If you want to have your own functions named `setup()` and `draw()` you should resist the urge, because those names are special and reserved by Processing for its own use. The same goes for `size()` and `background()`. As I mentioned earlier, Processing has dozens of such reserved words that you can't use for your own purposes. This is a common affair in programming languages, and not such a bad thing. It means that when you look at someone else's code, or even your own, you can quickly identify the function that starts things up by simply looking for `setup()`, and you can find the function that actually draws the picture by looking for `draw()`. It's not uncommon for people to use names like `mySetup()` or `myDraw()` when they really want to use those names for their functions, but with a little thought, you can probably find more descriptive names (like `setupAllFurniture()` or `draw_my_spinning_wheel _of_fate()`).

Both `setup()` and `draw()` must be declared as shown: they take no arguments and have a type of `void`. Of course, this boilerplate doesn't really do anything interesting yet, but it takes care of basic housekeeping: a window of a certain size is made, it's colored in with a background color, and then the `draw()` function gets called once for every frame, over and over (even though it does nothing), until you manually stop the program.

This is the boilerplate for a graphics program. If you're not doing any graphics, you can leave out `draw()`, and if you're not writing any functions of your own, you can even leave out `setup()`. For example, our earlier program that printed out "Hello World!" was just a one-line print statement. I'll continue to use those kinds of bare-bones examples when I want to do something simple, like just printing out a value or two. But since Processing is all about graphics, you'll probably want to use this boilerplate (or something like it) when you start your own projects.

4.7   Animation and Global Variables

The boilerplate above creates the "bones" of a working program, so sometimes I call it a "skeleton" project. It compiles and runs, but it doesn't do too much.

So let's make something happen! Right now the only thing we can see is the color of the background in the graphics window, so let's animate that.

To do this, I'll take the three color numbers out of the call to `background()` and replace them with three variables that I'll define at the top of the file:

```
int redval = 192;
int grnval = 64;
int bluval = 0;

void setup() {
    size(600, 400);
    background(redval, grnval, bluval);
}

void draw() {
    // drawing goes here
}
```

This program does exactly what the last one did, but you can see something new here: three variables that are declared outside of the two procedures. The three variables hold the color's red, green, and blue values. As you can see from the listing above, it's kind of visually nice to see these three variables lined up neatly one under the other; I find that the visual appearance helps reinforce the idea that these three variables are closely related in a kind of "clump." So I used three letters for each of the color names by dropping all the letter *e*'s out of green and blue.

If I'd written the words out in full, it might have looked like this:

```
int redval = 192;
int greenval = 64;
int blueval = 0;
```

I could still get them to line up a bit by making use of the fact that Processing lets us use any number of spaces anywhere that a single space would do:

```
int redval    = 192;
int greenval = 64;
int blueval   = 0;
```

I like the first way best, but these all do the same thing: it's just a question of taste.

By the way, another common spelling trick is to write lo and hi for *low* and *high*. Since each of these has two letters, they stack up nicely. For example, if you wanted to have a range for a variable called v, you might save the low and high ends of the range in variables named something like this:

```
float vlo = 2.0;
float vhi = 8.5;
```

You might be wondering why I didn't just call the color variables red, green, and blue? You guessed it: those are reserved words in Processing (we'll see what they're used for later in this chapter). So I tacked on the redundant val to the end of each name to avoid that conflict.

Returning to the main discussion, I declared these three variables outside the body of any of the functions. Why did I do that? Suppose that I declared the three variables inside of setup() —that is, between the curly braces that mark the beginning and end of that function:

```
void setup() {
    size(600, 400);
    int redval = 192;
    int grnval = 64;
    int bluval = 0;
    background(redval,
        grnval, bluval);
}
```

Figure 4.2. A changing background.

(See output in Figure 4.2. Full program in functions/sketches/animation1/animation1.pde)

That's perfectly fine and it will work flawlessly. But in Processing, as in most other modern languages, variables that are declared inside of a function are only available inside that function. If we want draw() to be able to use these variables, it can't do it. They are "inside" of setup() and not available to lines of Processing code outside of setup(). Lines inside of setup() that come after the declarations can use these variables freely, but to any line outside of that function, they don't exist at all. Trying to refer to them in any way, even just to read their values, will be an error, because outside of setup(), they have no existence.

By analogy, any variable declared inside a function is like a book that exists inside your house. That book is available to anyone in your house, but nobody outside your house can read the book; in fact, they don't even know it exists. If we try to use these variables from within draw(), we'll get an error.

Let's try it. Run this program:

```
void setup() {
    size(600, 400);
    int redval = 192;
    int grnval = 64;
    int bluval = 0;
    background(redval, grnval, bluval);
}

void draw() {
    background(redval, grnval, bluval);
}
```

(Full program in functions/sketches/animation2/animation2.pde)

When you press *Run*, the single line of draw() will be highlighted in yellow, and in the message area, you'll get this short report:

```
Cannot find anything named "redval"
```

That's telling us that when we're inside of draw(), there's nothing it can find with the name redval. And that's exactly right because that variable can only be referred to by lines of code inside the curly braces of setup(), after the variable was declared.

To make variables available to all functions, we declare them outside of all functions. Since they don't belong to any function, they're public property, and they can be accessed from anywhere.

Remember the phrase "Think globally, act locally"? Those are two common terms used to identify these two kinds of variables. The ones defined outside of all functions are called *global variables*, or simply *globals*. Those that are defined inside a particular function are called *local variables*, or *locals*.

You can tell what the type of a variable is by looking at its declaration, but you can only tell whether a variable is local or global by finding that declaration and then looking around to see if it's inside a function or not. Suppose you're looking at someone else's code and you want to know if a variable is local or global; it could be a hassle to go searching around to figure out which it is.

There are many different conventions that people use to distinguish between local and global variables. My convention in this book will be to start global variables with a capital letter and start local variables with a lower-case letter.

So the local-variable version of `setup()` looks like this:

```
void setup() {
   size(600, 400);
   int redval = 192;
   int grnval = 64;
   int bluval = 0;
   background(redval, grnval, bluval);
}
```

All the local variables start with a lowercase letter. The global-variable version looks like this:

```
int Redval = 192;
int Grnval = 64;
int Bluval = 0;

void setup() {
   size(600, 400);
   background(Redval, Grnval, Bluval);
}
```

(Full program in functions/sketches/animation3/animation3.pde)

Now we're getting somewhere. The next step will be to change `draw()`. Each time the function is called, it'll redraw the window with the current background color:

```
void draw() {
   background(Redval, Grnval, Bluval);
}
```

Now we can see why these are globals: I want to use them in more than one function. To make things interesting, I'll change the value of `Redval` on each call:

```
void draw() {
   Redval = Redval + 1;
   background(Redval, Grnval, Bluval);
}
```

I could have used our shorthand to increment `Redval`, say by writing `Redval++` or `++Redval`, but I'll do it this way for now.

Try this out! Type in the whole program as it stands now (because we're going to make the red value grow brighter over time, I'm going to start it here at 12, so it has some room to grow):

```
int Redval = 12;
int Grnval = 64;
int Bluval = 0;

void setup() {
    size(600, 400);
    background(Redval, Grnval, Bluval);
}

void draw() {
    Redval = Redval + 1;
    background(Redval, Grnval, Bluval);
}
```

(See output in Figure 4.3. Full program in functions/sketches/animation4/animation4.pde)

To run this, press the *Run* button. You'll see the window appear and gradually become redder. Congratulations! Your Processing code is animating!

This program works just fine, but you'll notice that the screen gets redder and redder and then stops changing. That's because the value of Redval reaches 255 after a while, and that means "maximum red" (I'll talk more about colors later, and we'll see why this strange number is the maximum value, but for now, please just roll with it: colors range from 0 to 255). If we hand background() a color value greater than 255, it silently assumes you meant 255.

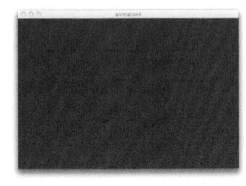

Figure 4.3. The background color animation (frame from animation).
(function/sketches/animation4/animation4.pde)

4.8   If Statements

I'd like the colors in our window to keep changing as time goes on. There are lots of ways to do this. One way is to include another statement in draw(), which will say, "If the value of Redval is larger than 255, then set the value to 0." If we do this, then the next time draw() gets called, Redval will be 0, and then 1, and then 2, and so on, until it reaches 256 again, when it goes back to 0, and the cycle goes on until we stop the program.

Processing (like most languages) gives us a way to do this: the *if statement*. An *if statement* is really just like the expression I wrote above. Conceptually, the *if statement* has a *test* and an *action*: if the test is true, then the action is taken. Let's take a first stab at it by just writing down the English version I gave above:

```
If the value of Redval is larger than 255,
    then set its value to 0
```

Now let's turn this into a bit of Processing. The first thing is to replace the capital *I* in "If" with a lower-case letter:

```
if the value of Redval is larger than 255,
    then set its value to 0
```

Not much of a change, but an important one. Now we'll fix up the test part. In a Processing *if statement*, the test is placed within a pair of parentheses that comes after the word if:

```
if (the value of Redval is larger than 255),
    then set its value to 0
```

Now we'll replace the English text within the parentheses with a little mathematical expression that means the same thing:

```
if (Redval > 255), then set its value to 0
```

Notice here that the greater-than sign, >, is used in its usual way, unlike the equals sign. We're not asserting that Redval really *is* greater than 255, because this is merely the test in the *if statement*. If Redval is indeed greater than 255, we say that the result of the test is true, otherwise it is false. If the test is true, Processing executes the last part of the *if statement*, which tells it what action to take. If the test is false, the action statement is ignored; Processing simply skips right over it. The action statement here is an assignment statement, which we're used to from before:

```
if (Redval > 255), then Redval=0
```

The word "then" is good English, but it's not part of Processing. It's not even a keyword. In an *if statement*, the word "then" is just assumed. If you do include it, Processing will complain. So let's remove it:

```
if (Redval > 255), Redval=0
```

We have two things left to do to make this a real Processing statement. First, we get rid of the comma, which (like "then") is appropriate in English but not for Processing:

```
if (Redval > 255) Redval=0
```

Finally, we add a semicolon to the end to indicate the end of the *if statement*:

```
if (Redval > 255) Redval=0;
```

That's it! Here's the new program:

```
int Redval = 192;
int Grnval = 64;
int Bluval = 0;

void setup() {
    size(600, 400);
    background(Redval, Grnval, Bluval);
}

void draw() {
    Redval = Redval+1;
    if (Redval > 255) Redval=0;
    background(Redval, Grnval, Bluval);
}
```

(See output in Figure 4.4. Full program in functions/sketches/animation5/animation5.pde)

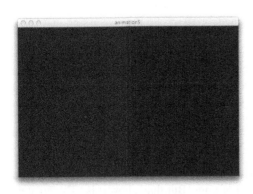

Figure 4.4. The improved background changer (frame from animation).
(function/sketches/animation5/animation5.pde)

Give it a try. You'll find that the red part of the color gets brighter and brighter, and then suddenly goes to zero, then starts to climb again—over and over until you stop the program.

Try messing around with this program. Add a few more lines to get all the colors changing. See what happens when they change by different amounts on each frame. You might even try having one color component get smaller over time, rather than larger (hint: you'll need to change the *if statement* to make sure it stays in the range 0 to 255).

The *if statement* I used above shows another stylistic choice. Remember that I'm happy to let Redval grow until it reaches 256, at which time I want to reset it to 0. I might have written this instead:

```
if (Redval == 256) Redval=0;
```

What the heck is ==? That, unfortunately, is how you test for equality. The equals sign, of course, would be the most sensible choice here, but that's already used to mean assignment, as we've seen. If we forget that and use just a single equals sign in the test, things will become really weird:

```
if (Redval = 256) Redval=0;  // this is wrong
```

This says that the test in the *if statement* is actually an assignment statement (remember, think of the equals sign like an arrow). That's no test! The "test" now reads "Set the value of Redval to 256." So is that true? Is it false? It's neither; it just doesn't make any sense to ask. If you write this, Processing will tell you that you've made an error, flagging the line in yellow and giving you the message

```
cannot convert from int to boolean
```

That's because it's expecting the value of the test to be true or false, the values that can be taken by a boolean. The result of an assignment statement is the value that's being assigned. That's actually very convenient because it lets us *chain* together assignment statements like this:

```
float weight1;
float weight2;
weight1 = weight2 = 103.5;
```

Reading from the right, first we assign the value 103.5 to the variable weight2. The result of that is the value that was assigned, or 103.5. So then we assign that value to weight1. Very nice.

So the value we get by using the single equals sign in our test (Redval = 256) is 256, which is a number and neither true nor false. Hence, Processing reports an error. Since a single equals sign is already used for assigning values to variables, Processing uses two equals signs to test for equality (a choice shared by most modern languages). So to test if Redval is equal to 256 and set it to 0 if it is, we can write this:

```
if (Redval == 256) Redval=0;
```

Using two equals signs to test for equality is a kludge, no doubt about it. Duct tape and string. We're filling a hole with a piece of gum. But that's how it is. The greater-than and less-than signs work as usual, but if you want to test for equality, you use two equals signs. Don't worry, it'll soon become second nature, and in the meantime, Processing will warn you if you get it wrong.

So why didn't I write the test as (Redval==256) to begin with? I could have. But I program defensively. What I was thinking here was, "I want to make sure that Redval never gets larger than 255. If it does, I want it to go back to 0." Now in a simple program like this, I know exactly what's happening to Redval, and I know that once it's 255, it will next be 256, and then 257, and so on. But what if the program was more complicated? Suppose `Redval` is computed by some complex process in another part of the program, and for all I know, it could jump by two or even ten in a single step?

There's also a more subtle possibility. Remember that I said that floating-point numbers are often ever-so-slightly wrong? Here I'm using an `int` for `Redval`. But suppose I used a `float`. I might rewrite the incrementing statement like this

```
Redval = Redval + 1.0;
```

After `Redval`'s been used for a while, and computed with, and maybe is the result of some other computation, it might be 255.0001 before the assignment statement and then 256.0001 after. If that's the case, then the test for equality will fail because 256 is not the same as 256.0001. As far as my intentions for this little program are concerned, they should be pretty much the same thing, but the computer doesn't know that. So `Redval` won't get set to 0, and the next time it'll be 257.0001, and then 258.0001, and so on, and the color on the screen will stop changing.

So my habit is to program defensively. I want `Redval` to be reset to 0 whenever it gets beyond 255. By using the greater-than test, it will be true any time `Redval` is more than 255, whether it's by exactly one or seven or some tiny fraction.

Programming is often about making these little trade-offs as you go. If you program for the more general case when you're first writing your code, it gives you a little more flexibility later on, if and when you make changes. That's something you'll probably grow into over time, as you get more familiar with programming and develop your own style. For now, it's worth trying to understand why other people write code the way they do; then you can adopt the practices that you like and consciously set aside the ones that don't appeal to your sense of style.

Let's add one more twist to our animation. Right now, the red component gets brighter until it hits 255 and then it starts again at 0, and the other colors do nothing. Let's say that when the red component gets to 255, the green component should increase by ten. Here's a first stab at a solution:

```
if (Redval > 255) Redval=0;
if (Redval > 255) Grnval = Grnval + 10;
```

This isn't going to work right. The problem is that the first test resets `Redval` to 0 when it exceeds 255, so by the time we reach the second test, `Redval` will never be larger than 255. We could reverse the order:

```
if (Redval > 255) Grnval = Grnval + 10;
if (Redval > 255) Redval=0;
```

That's better. But as I've said before, there's a strategy I urge you to always keep in mind: never repeat yourself. If you find yourself ever writing the same code twice, or even nearly the same code, you should ask yourself if there's a better way. The most important problem with repeating is that it makes your programs more susceptible to bugs. If you mean to repeat something exactly and you make a small error, you might spend a lot of time trying to track it down. But a bigger problem arises when you later come back to your code and make a change. If for any reason you only adjust one of the repeated sections and not the other, the program can start to behave very strangely, and again, you can spend a long time trying to figure out why some parts seem to work the new way and some work the old way.

We can remove the repetition with one *if statement* that does both of these assignment statements one after the other. To replace any statement with a list of statements, all you have to do is enclose them in curly braces.

Throughout the book I'll often replace a single statement with a list of statements by placing them between curly braces. This use of the curly braces is in addition to their use in defining a function.

Note that the statements between the curly braces all end in semicolons, as usual, but there's no semicolon after the closing curly brace. That's because the closing curly brace as used here is just a grouping tool, and not a statement itself.

So here's how we can combine the two lines above into one statement:

```
if (Redval > 255) {
    Grnval = Grnval + 10;
    Redval = 0;
}
```

Here, I've again used the indenting style with curly braces that I prefer, but you can format the code any way you like. I grant you that this doesn't look like a big efficiency step, since I've traded two lines of program for four. But the braces don't slow down the program at all. And this actually is a better program because we're not repeating the *if statement*, so it's cleaner. By not repeating the *if statement* twice, the program is, in fact, slightly faster! And we can easily add more statements to this list (often called a *compound statement* or *block statement*, or sometimes simply a *block*).

Of course, now that the green value is moving up as well, it will eventually pass 255 itself, and we'll want to reset it to 0 (or do something else interesting). If you're feeling adventurous, try writing code that will catch when the green value goes over 255 and use that to bump up the blue value in a similar way.

By the way, in addition to testing for greater-than (>), less-than (<), and equal-to (==), there's also greater-than-or-equal-to (>=), less-than-or-equal-to (<=), and not-equal-to (!=).

For example, if you want to see if myValue is not equal to 3, you might write

```
if (myValue != 3) {
    // myValue is something other than 3
}
```

Sometimes it's conceptually easier to write a test in a way that tests whether something's false, rather than true. Suppose you have a function out there somewhere called isReady(). It goes off and checks for a piece of hardware connected to your computer and returns a boolean. The result is true if the device is connected and ready to communicate with. You'd like to test this and print a message if it's not ready yet. You could write this:

```
if (isReady() == false) {
    println("Quickly, plug in the flux capacitor!");
}
```

Another way to write the very same test is to see if it isn't true:

```
if (isReady() != true) { ... }
```

It turns out that you can use the exclamation point, !, to *negate* any boolean. So if you put a ! in front of something that's true, you get back false, and vice versa. So we could also write the test this way:

```
if (!(isReady() == true)) { ... }
```

The real beauty comes from noticing that isReady() returns a boolean already, so there's no need for the additional testing. We can write the test this easily:

```
if (!isReady()) { ... }
```

In other words, if isReady() returns false, then the ! makes it true, the test succeeds, and we print the message. We often read the ! out loud as "not," so !isReady() is pronounced "not is-ready." Another common pronunciation of the ! is "bang," so !isReady() is also pronounced "bang is-ready."

If statements have another trick up their sleeve: an optional extra clause called else. After the action statement (or block), you can include the word else and then follow it with another statement (or block). The code associated with the else is executed if the first code is not; in other words, if the test is true, the first block is executed, otherwise (or else) the second one is:

```
boolean ready_for_time_travel = isReady();
if (ready_for_time_travel) {
    println("We're ready, hang on to your hat!");
} else {
    println("We're not ready.  I need the flux capacitor!");
}
```

Here the blocks are only one statement long, so technically, I didn't need the curly braces. But they don't hurt or slow down the code at all. I almost always use the curly braces anyway when I use else with if; that makes it easy to later add lines to either clause. We can get the same result the other way by using the not-equals test:

```
boolean ready_for_time_travel = isReady();
if (!ready_for_time_travel) {
    println("We're not ready.  I need the flux capacitor!");
} else {
    println("We're ready, hang on to your hat!");
}
```

These two snippets produce the same result, but the thinking behind them is different. Sometimes it makes more conceptual sense to think of taking action when something has a given property (for example, if it is a leap year), and sometimes it seems better to act when it doesn't have a given property (for example, if it is *not* a leap year).

If statements can also be used to build tests with multiple testing criteria. Let's suppose you want to do some particular action if you have ten apples on hand and a customer orders five. You could find out if both were true by *nesting* one *if statement* inside another:

```
if (apples_on_hand == 10) {
    if (customer_order == 5) {
        // we have 10 apples, and customer asked for 5
    }
}
```

There's an easier way to do this. Suppose that we had some piece of glue that let us represent the idea of *and*, so we could build a single test that said "ten apples are on-hand *and* the customer ordered five." There is such a piece of glue, and it's written && (this is another odd bit of syntax, but it's common among most modern computer languages). We could write the test this way:

```
if ((apples_on_hand == 10) && (customer_order == 5)) {
    // we have 10 apples, and customer asked for 5
}
```

When read aloud, some people say just "and" for &&, but I find that can be confused with a single ampersand. Some people say "logical and," which is clear and is in fact the formal name for this thing. I usually pronounce it as "and and."

So the code in the curly braces (currently just a comment) only gets executed if *both* of these conditions are true. You can see that my style is to put parentheses around each test. You don't have to do that. I do it because I find that code is easier to read that way.

This is a useful way to write tests of the *and* variety, but as we saw above, it's not strictly necessary because we could just put one *if statement* inside another to get the same result. But suppose we wanted to make an *or* type of test. That is, we want to execute some code if we have ten apples on-hand *or* the customer asks for five. We might write something like this:

```
if (apples_on_hand == 10) {
    // do a thing
}
if (customer_order == 5) {
    // do the same thing
}
```

This has some problems. First, we're repeating code in two places, and that's usually a bad idea. But worse, if both of these conditions are true, we'd end up repeating the code twice. At the very best, that's a waste of time, and at worst, it could cause our code to malfunction. We could write a whole bunch of code to work around this problem, or we could just write | | (that's two vertical bars, one right after the other) to glue the tests together into a compound *or* statement:

```
if ((apples_on_hand == 10) || (customer_order == 5)) {
    // do the thing
}
```

In this case, the code between the braces (now just a comment) will get executed if either (or both) of these clauses are true.

As with the logical and &&, when read aloud some people say just "or" for | |, but I find that can be confused with a single vertical bar, which is also used for a kind of "or" function. Some people say "logical or," but I usually pronounce | | as "or or." It can sound like a seal barking, I know, but it works for me.

You can have as many clauses as you want in a test, and you can make sure they get grouped correctly using parentheses. Here's an example:

```
if (((month==3) || (month==5)) && ((day==1) || (day==15)) {
    // do something
}
```

Now the action (in this fragment, just a comment) will be executed *if* the month is March *or* May, *and* the date is the 1st *or* 15th. In other words, four days out of the year will satisfy this test: March 1, March 15, May 1, and May 15.

Finally, you can negate the result of any test with ! (that's just a single exclamation point). In the last example, we wanted to execute code on the four days I identified. But suppose we want to execute the code if it's March or May, and the date is *not* the 1st or 15th? Here's one way to get there:

```
if (((month==3) || (month==5)) && !((day==1) || (day==15)) {
    // do something
}
```

All I did was put a ! before the second chunk. So now the test succeeds if it's March or May, *and* the day is *not* either the 1st *or* the 15th.

These kinds of compound tests can usually be written in lots of different ways, all of which are logically equivalent. Here's another test that achieves the same result:

```
if (((month==3) || (month==5)) && (day != 1) && (day != 15)) {
    // do something
}
```

This is probably about as complicated as you want one of these tests to get. If you have too many of these tests, it can get very hard to read and understand the code, even if you wrote it! Simpler is usually better, even in programming.

To that end, you might want to build your test in pieces. It takes a little more text and might run imperceptibly slower, but it's easier to read at a glance:

```
boolean marchOrMay = (month == 3) || (month == 5);
boolean neither1or15 = (day != 1) && (day != 15);
if (marchOrMay && neither1or15) {
   // do something
}
```

Breaking things up into pieces like this is usually a much better approach than writing a big complicated *if statement*. You could, of course, explain a complex *if statement* with a comment or two, but writing it out clearly makes it easier to write, understand, and debug.

4.9   Conditional

There are a couple of variants on the *if statement* that can be handy.

The first is called the *conditional*, and it's really nothing more than a text shorthand. Instead of writing

```
if (test) statement1; else statement2;
```

you write

```
test ? statement1 : statement2;
```

This saves you a few characters. The place you see this the most often is in assignment statements:

```
float carSize = ( passengers > 3 ) ? sedan_size : sports_car_size;
```

You don't have to include the parentheses around the test in this kind of conditional statement, but I almost always do anyway. I think they make the test a little easier to read and easier to see, at a glance, that it is indeed a test.

4.10   Switch

Another testing tool is the `switch` statement. This helps you write a complicated *if statement* in a clean way. For example, suppose you've written a game where someone is shooting an arrow at a target. When the arrow hits, you want to draw a glowing ball based on the score value of the location where they hit. Each zone has its own color of ball with a different size; the higher your score, the bigger and brighter the ball. Here's one way to do that sort of thing (rather than implement the whole game, I'll just focus here on drawing the glowing ball).

The function `drawBall()` contains three Processing functions that we haven't discussed yet: `color()` defines a color, `fill()` tells Processing to use that color when drawing, and `ellipse()` draws an ellipse (or circle). We'll discuss `color()` next in Chapter 5, and we'll cover the other two procedures in Chapter 6.

```
void setup() {
   size(600, 400);
   background(87, 66, 8);
   noStroke();
   int score = 40;    // the score of this arrow

   // draw the ball for the current value of score
   if (score == 40) {
      drawBall(160, 212, 20, 20);
   } else if (score == 30) {
      drawBall(80, 231, 48, 3);
   } else if (score == 20) {
      drawBall(40, 255, 93, 8);
   } else if (score == 10) {
      drawBall(20, 255, 140, 5);
   } else {
      drawBall(180, 32, 32, 32);
   }
}

void drawBall(int radius, int redval, int grnval, int bluval) {
   fill(color(redval, grnval, bluval));
   ellipse(300, 200, 2*radius, 2*radius);
}
```
(See output in Figure 4.5. Full program in functions/sketches/target01/target01.pde)

That certainly works, but it's kind of ugly and can be hard to read. The switch statement is a different way to write the same thing. You state the word switch, followed by a pair of parentheses and a pair of curly braces. You put a variable between the parentheses, and this guides Processing to choose one option among many that you provide between the curly braces.

Each of these potential choices begins with the word case, followed by a space and then a value. If the variable that came after switch has the value given in that case clause, the code following case is executed until Processing reaches a break

Figure 4.5. The bull's-eye target.
(function/sketches/target01/target01.pde)

statement. When Processing hits the word break, it jumps immediately to the closing curly brace and continues on from there. On the other hand, if the variable doesn't have the value given after that appearance of case, Processing looks for another case statement and repeats the test. It keeps this up until one of the case statements matches.

If none of them match, then it executes the code after a final clause labeled default (if there is one).

Here's the *if statement* above written in switch form:

```
switch (score) {
   case 40:
      drawBall(160, 212, 20, 20);
      break;
   case 30:
      drawBall(80, 231, 48, 3);
      break;
   case 20:
      drawBall(40, 255, 93, 8);
      break;
   case 10:
      drawBall(20, 255, 140, 5);
      break;
   default:
      drawBall(180, 32, 32, 32);
      break;
}
```

(See output in Figure 4.6. Full program in functions/sketches/target02/target02.pde)

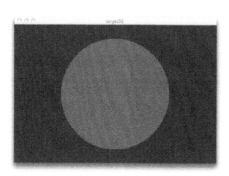

Figure 4.6. Target with the switch statement.
(function/sketches/target02/target02.pde)

This does the same thing, and it's a lot cleaner to read. It's a little longer, granted, but I think it's worth the tradeoff. Each of the case clauses starts a short block of code (in this example, only one line long) that gets executed if the switch variable matches its value. For example, if score has the value 30, then we execute the line

```
drawBall(80, 231, 48, 3);
```

Since the next line reads break, the program jumps to the closing curly brace and proceeds.

Notice the last test, labeled default. This allows you to specify some actions to be taken if none of the earlier conditions are met. It's kind of the equivalent of else in an *if statement*. The default clause isn't mandatory, but I recommend you always use it. Even if you've covered all the possibilities you expect, you can use the default clause to catch any errors. I often use my default clause to contain something like this:

```
switch (score) {
   case 1:
      . . .
      break;
   case 2:
      . . .
      break;
   default:
      println("Error! I don't know how to handle score = "+score);
      break;
}
```

You might think this looks a little odd. Given what we've seen before, you might expect the lines after each case statement to be in a block—that is, within curly braces. When you hit the closing curly brace, you're done with the block and you exit the switch. Why isn't it done that way, instead of using these break statements?

There are two reasons for this. The first is that this form lets you list multiple case statements one after the other, creating an *or*-type test. Let's suppose that you added a 25-point zone to your target, but if the player strikes that, you still want to draw the 20-point ball. Then you could write this clause:

```
case 20:
case 25:
   drawBall(40, 255, 93, 8);
   break;
```

In this fragment, if score had the value 20, the first case statement would match, so Processing would start looking for code to execute. It would skip the next case statement, since there's nothing there to do, and continue on to the call to drawBall(). If score had the value 25, the second case would match, and the same call to drawBall() would be executed.

In other words, the same ball would be drawn for either score. Stacking case statements like this is a way of building a kind of *or* test.

The other advantage of this form is that if you leave out a break statement, Processing ignores the next case statement and keeps on executing each line of code. This continues until Processing hits a break or exits the switch by reaching the closing curly brace.

This lets you pile up choices. For example, let's say that rather than providing just one glow per score, each score gets all the lower-scoring glows as well, for a crazy colorful reward. Here's one way to get that result:

```
switch (score) {
   case 40:
      drawBall(160, 212, 20, 20);
   case 30:
```

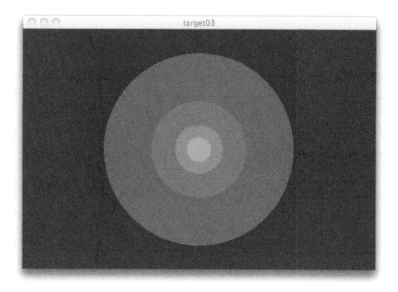

Figure 4.7. The switch statement without breaks. (functions/sketches/target03/target03.pde)

```
    drawBall(80, 231, 48, 3);
case 20:
    drawBall(40, 255, 93, 8);
case 10:
    drawBall(20, 255, 140, 5);
    break;
default:
    drawBall(180, 32, 32, 32);
    break;
}
```

(See output in Figure 4.7. Full program in functions/sketches/target03/target03.pde)

When score is 10, you just get the smallest ball. When score is 20, you get both the score-10 ball *and* the score-20 ball. And so on, all the way up to the big, red score-40 ball.

Be careful with the switch statement, though, because if you forget the break statement where you meant it to appear, you'll get strange results that can sometimes be a challenge to debug. In the example above, I have a break after the case for when score is 10. Try taking this break out. Then every score results in a big dark-gray ball! That's because I'm drawing that ball for the default case, and without a break statement, that case gets executed last, so the circle it draws covers up all the previous ones.

By the way, you don't really need a `break` statement at the end of the last clause in a `switch` statement, because there's nothing after it. It doesn't hurt in any way, but it doesn't help, either; it's kind of a nothing. But I include it anyway because it's good to be in the habit of always including a `break` statement at the end of every case in a `switch`.

Not only is a `switch` statement often easier to make sense of when reading your code, but compared to some big chain of `if` statements, it often runs faster, because the computer can jump directly to the right clause without testing everything along the way.

4.11   Speed and Control

One of the wonderful things about Processing is that it can run on almost any computer. It can even run inside a web browser! But that power brings with it a problem: making things run at the right speed.

Every computer has one or more processor chips inside, and they're responsible for everything that's going on: spinning the fans to keep the insides cool, drawing the screen, responding to the mouse, checking your email, updating the clock in the corner of your screen, playing the music you're listening to on your headphones, and oh yeah, running your program. Who knows how much time it has left to devote to your program? Even if we stripped away every one of these other tasks, the speeds of individual computers varies greatly.

This is relevant to us because we want our animations to run at the speed we want. For example, movies are typically shot and shown at 24 frames per second. Imagine instead if every movie camera shot film at its own random speed, and every movie theater in the world showed its movies at its own, also arbitrary, speed. It would be terrible: some movies would be slightly too fast, others slightly too slow, and some would be so insanely fast or slow that they'd be unwatchable.

But that's the situation we have now with computing. You design your gorgeous animation so it runs perfectly on your computer, which runs at its own speed (like the film camera), and now other people view it on their computers, which run at own their speeds (like the film projectors). Is there any way to be sure that people see on their machine something like what you designed on yours?

This problem is huge and not limited to animation. Color, for instance, is a giant problem, as you know if you've ever ordered clothing online and were surprised by the color of the actual product when it arrived. A lot of people have worked very hard on the color problem, but we're not quite there yet.

Solving the animation problem is also tough, because it's so hard to figure out how much time a computer has to draw each frame for you. So there are two essential questions: how many frames per second can a particular computer draw, and how much time can it spend on each frame, given the other things it has to do?

You can tell Processing that you'd like it to aim for a certain *frame rate*, or number of frames per second. If you call `frameRate()` with an integer value, Processing will aim for that number of frames per second. The default is 60 frames per second.

If your computer can't do all the work you're asking of it and still draw your frames at this speed, you'll get a slower *update rate*. You can ask Processing how many frames per second you're actually getting (as opposed to the number you asked for) by checking the variable `frameRate`. Note that this has the same name as the function, but is lacking the parentheses. Processing keeps this variable up-to-date as time goes by (because sometimes your computer might be busier than others, or your graphics might take longer to draw sometimes, which could slow down your frame rate). The value in `frameRate` is only an estimate, but it's usually pretty close.

A related idea to the frame rate is the *frame count*. This is just a number that tells you how many times your `draw()` function has completed. So when you start, it's zero. After the first frame is completed and shown, it's one, and so on. You can find out the current frame count from the variable `frameCount`. It's surprisingly handy for all kinds of things that you want to change from frame to frame. I'll use `frameCount` often in this book.

If you don't include a `draw()` function, then of course it never gets called. But there are times, particularly when debugging your programs, when you only want to call `draw()` once. As we've seen, if you have a `draw()` function defined, then normally Processing will start producing your graphics as soon as the program begins.

But sometimes you might not want your program to start drawing immediately. For example, your animation might be part of a museum kiosk. You've designed it so the program normally sits there silently until one of the museum's visitors pushes a button. Then it starts and runs through a full performance of the animation, and then stops again.

As we saw before, you can call `exit()` to quit the program, but then it would be hard for the user to start it again. What you want is a way to tell Processing, "Start calling `draw()` now," and later, "Stop calling `draw()`." When it's calling `draw()`, your animation is updating at the current frame rate. When it's not calling `draw()`, nothing's getting drawn.

If you want Processing to stop calling `draw()`, you call the function `noLoop()`.

As we'll discuss in Chapter 7, you can still respond to user events like keyboard presses and mouse clicks even when you're not animating. So if your visitor pushes a button on the display, that might correspond to hitting (say) the space key on a keyboard. If your program used that as the trigger to start calling `draw()` again, it can respond to this key press by calling `loop()`.

The names of these two functions comes from a mental picture of Processing running around and around in a loop, like a car going around a race track. Each time it passes the starting point, it calls `draw()`. If you don't want Processing to call `draw()`, then you tell it to stop running around that loop with `noLoop()`. And to turn it back on, you just tell it to start running around the loop again with `loop()`.

If you want `draw()` to run just once, you can call `redraw()`.

Using `frameRate()` can help us regulate the speed of our program, but just asking for a huge frame rate doesn't guarantee we're going to get it. If we want our program to run at a certain speed, and the computer we're running it on just can't deliver that much horsepower, then we won't get the performance we want. To make sure our programs run as fast as possible, we have to write them so that they are as efficient as possible.

Efficiency is a broad and deep topic. It's usually not as important in Processing as in other languages, but it can be an issue, so I'll mention efficiency considerations from time to time as we work through our projects. Generally you'll want to keep it in the back of your mind while working, but don't let it be your main focus. The goal of any program is to make it work. Making it fast is secondary.

But from time to time, I'll talk about some operation or process as *expensive*. This usually means either that it's slow or that it consumes a lot of the computer's memory (which often makes it slow). Sometimes you just have to do expensive things. If you're showing a flying bird and you really need to show each feather moving individually, you're going to have to draw each feather, and that's that. But you can still try to draw each one as quickly as possible.

Some expensive things can be made cheap—by reorganizing them or by *cheating*.

When we talk about cheating in programming, we almost never mean some nefarious, morally objectionable process. We mean faking it: finding a cheap way to do something that looks expensive. Suppose I'm showing a parade at the zoo, and there are dozens of animals walking across the screen. Lions, tigers, elephants, etc., and every one of them is a complicated object with tons of moving pieces and fur and muscles and textures. Drawing those animals is going to take a lot of time.

Then I notice that the flamingos are far away the entire time. And even then, from where I stand, they are almost always obscured. In fact, I really only see a little flash of bright pink every now and then between the legs of the other animals.

I might get rid of the 30 individual flamingos altogether and replace them all with a single big pink rectangle that I draw behind all the other animals. The result, from the viewer's point of view, is identical. But I've saved myself an enormous amount of work.

I might then go on to notice that I only see the near side of each animal. There's no reason to draw the far away parts that I can't see. So I'll cut my animals in half and only draw the near part. As long as everything is positioned and moves in just the right way that the cheat isn't given away, I've managed to draw my graphics faster than before, but they'll look just as good.

That's the essence of "cheating" in this context: you find a way to reduce your workload, typically in a way that is specialized to exactly the situation at hand.

So in the projects we'll see throughout the book, I'll keep an eye open for places where something that is obviously expensive can be replaced with something that's cheaper and not much more complicated. I'll rarely sweat the tiny details because all of our programs will be relatively bite-sized. But the issue of efficiency can be important when we start to do a lot of work for every frame, so I'll come back to efficiency in Chapter 18.

Chapter 5
Color

In this chapter, I'll talk about colors. But before we get into it, here's another program for you to play around with. This program creates images that move over time, so the real fun comes from watching it run.

```
float StartAngle = 0;
float AngleBump = 0;
color Color1 = color(180, 95, 10);
color Color2 = color(0, 80, 110);

void setup() {
   size(400, 400);
   smooth();
}

void draw() {
   background(Color2);
   noStroke();
   float radius = 400;
   int circleCount = 0;
   float angle = StartAngle;
   while (radius > 0) {
      fill(Color1);
      ellipse(200, 200, radius, radius);
      fill(Color2);
      arc(200, 200, radius, radius, angle, angle+PI);
      radius -= 30;
      angle += AngleBump;
   }
   StartAngle += .01;
   AngleBump += .005;
}
```

(See output in Figure 5.1. Full program in color/sketches/wheels01/wheels01.pde)

Figure 5.1. Spinning wheels (frame from animation). (color/sketches/wheels01/wheels01.pde)

Figures 5.1–5.3 show three screenshots of this running program, taken at different moments as it ran.

Colors are everywhere in a Processing sketch. Everything you draw has a color, and sketches often cook up new colors and even random colors as they run.

We've already seen the two key elements that usually go into a color description: colors are usually constructed with three numbers (one each for red, green, and blue), and each number is in the range 0 to 255. Let's look more closely at this.

The three-number, red-green-blue (or RGB) format is a very common one in computer graphics. It started before computer graphics even existed. When engineers were inventing color television, they had to find a way to display the broadest possible range of colors on a screen. They were guided by an important feature of our biology: human eyes contain three types of cells that respond to color. One type responds largely to reddish colors, another to greenish, and the last to blueish. They reasoned that they could probably make people see any color they wanted if they were able to stimulate these

Figure 5.2. Spinning wheels a bit later.

Figure 5.3. Spinning wheels even later.

three types of cells the right way. So they coated the inside of the display screen with chemicals called *phosphors* that glowed when hit with a beam of electrons. Happily, you can go digging in the Earth and find rocks that contain phosphors that glow with different colors. So they found some red-, green-, and blue-glowing phosphors, and it all worked out very well: you can create a huge variety of colors just by mixing different amounts of red, green, and blue light.

Figure 5.4 shows the *RGB Color Cube*. In one corner, where all three values are 0, you find black. In the opposite diagonal, where all three values are 255, you find white. At the ends of the red, green, and blue edges you'll find the strongest versions of each of

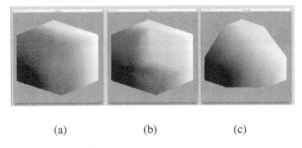

(a)   (b)   (c)

Figure 5.4. The RGB Color Cube. (a) The RGB Cube. (b) A box taken out of the near corner. (c) The cube sliced along the diagonal, revealing the middle.

those colors. The other corners hold mixed pairs of these strongest colors: red + green = yellow, red + blue = magenta, green + blue = cyan. In part (a) of the figure I've shown the entire color cube. The green axis is hidden from us, so in part (b) I've removed a chunk from the near corner, revealing the cube's insides. In part (c) I've sliced the cube in half along a plane through the center of the cube, perpendicular to the line from the black corner to the white corner.

If you're familiar with mixing pigments, you probably think something is wrong here, because the primary colors for pigments are red, yellow, and blue. It turns out that when you're mixing light, you use three different primary colors than when you're mixing pigments like paints or polymer clay. The reasons for this are fascinating, but it would take us too far afield to go into it here. If your curiosity is aroused, there is a ton of information on this all over the web. You can search on the term *subtractive mixing* for discussions of pigment mixing (for example, using the primaries cyan, magenta, and yellow) and *additive mixing* for discussions of light mixing (with the primaries red, green, and blue).

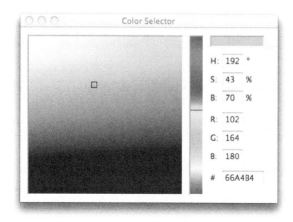

Figure 5.5. Processing's Color Selector.

If you'd like to see how red, green, and blue light is mixed to make colors on the computer, go to the Processing window and from the *Tools* menu choose *Color Selector*. There you'll be able to select colors interactively and watch the live feedback as the tool shows you how much of each primary hue is in each color. Figure 5.5 shows the Color Selector in action.

Processing's built-in color selector is useful in a pinch, but it's a pretty bare-bones affair. There are lots of much more powerful programs out there for picking colors and even for picking sets of colors that need to work together. You can find them embedded in other packages (like the Color Selector in Processing), as well as in stand-alone commercial packages, and even free web apps. In that last category, I like Kuler (http://kuler.adobe.com/).

So red, green, and blue are the primaries for mixing light, but why represent their strengths with numbers from 0 to 255? The answer comes from the early days of computer graphics.

When computer graphics was just getting started, color TV monitors were the best way to show computer-generated pictures, particularly those that moved. So naturally, people stored their pictures in the three-color format, so they could directly drive the

TV electronics. Thus, every dot in the picture corresponded to one or more dots on the screen, and it was described with three numbers, one each for the red, green, and blue brightness of that dot.

A value of 0 seems perfectly reasonable to mean a given color component should be "fully off," but how about "fully on"? You want some range of values between off and on, and generally speaking, more is better. If we had only, say, ten values, you would see all kinds of artifacts in the images. One of the most obvious is called *posterization*, which looks like a poster printed with only a few colors: you get big flat regions of color, with very visible boundaries between regions of different colors. To get smooth color transitions, you need lots of intermediate colors. So how many?

You might have a USB thumb drive in your pocket. It might hold something like four or eight gigabytes of memory. That's four or eight *billion* bytes. A byte is eight bits, and a bit is a single 0 or 1. It's hard to believe now, but not too long ago, every byte was precious. For example, the entire computer system onboard the Apollo spacecraft that went to the moon had only 60 kilobytes of memory. That's 60,000 bytes. For everything: regulating the systems, planning the descent to the moon, running life support, firing the jets, getting into the right position for reentry, getting to the moon, getting home again, everything. Sixty thousand bytes. Every single byte was precious, and programmers had strict limits on how many bytes they could use. The entire Apollo spacecraft computer system wouldn't have been big enough to hold even a single typical song in mp3 format. Not one. Amazing.

This was the situation in the early days of computer graphics. So when people needed to represent color values, they tried economizing on storage by using a single byte per color. A byte can hold numbers from 0 (which is all 0's) up to 255 (which is all 1's). That's it—there aren't any more beads on the abacus: a byte can hold a number from 0 to 255, end of story. So colors were represented with three bytes, one each for red, green, and blue. If we count the numbers from 0 to 255, there are 256 values total (remember to include the 0!).

The choice of a byte for each color was driven largely by the need to save memory, but it turned out to be a pretty good choice. By and large, pictures created with 256 levels per color looked good and were mostly free of artifacts, so that way to describe colors became very popular. That's not the end of the story, of course. There are other ways to describe colors than in combinations of red, green, and blue (and even then, to be careful, you have to specify just exactly what you mean by "red, green, and blue"). And 256 levels per component isn't enough for applications like feature films or high-end photography; people working in those fields use more levels per color.

But the one-byte-per-component model, with 256 levels for each of red, green, and blue, has become a standard in much of computer graphics. It's like having four wheels on a car: maybe three or five would be better, but four is the norm. The move to have more levels per color component has picked up steam in recent years, with previously professional-grade rendering and photo-editing software coming down in price, but the eight-bit approach is still popular, and that's what Processing uses. For the kinds of things we do with Processing, 256 levels per component is usually just fine.

To create a color in Processing, you declare an object to be of type `color` (with a lower-case c):

```
color myColor;
```

To actually fill that in with a color value, you call the built-in function `color()` and hand it three numbers, one each for red, green, and blue. Here's a list of some common colors:

```
color pure_red = color(255, 0,   0);
color pure_grn = color(0,   255, 0);
color pure_blu = color(0,   0,   255);
color yellow   = color(255, 255, 0);
color cyan     = color(0,   255, 255);
color magenta  = color(255, 0,   255);
color white    = color(255, 255, 255);
color black    = color(0,   0,   0);
```

Happily, `color()` can take either three `int` or three `float` variables as arguments (so you could use, say, 153.6 as one of the color values).

Um, wait a second. What was that I just said, that the function `color()` can take either three `int` or three `float` arguments? That doesn't seem to fit the rules we've seen so far, but it sounds useful. Can we write our own procedures that do that?

We sure can. Let's see how.

5.1   Function Overloading

Suppose that we write two versions of a procedure but give them both the same name. They'll differ only in the argument list. The first time, the argument list will have one parameter. The second time, the argument list will have two parameters. Processing considers those two different procedures. When you call one of them, it automatically goes to the version of the function that matches the number and types of arguments you're calling it with.

For example, let's suppose that we want to find the size of some things lying around the house. Some things have only length (like a yardstick), some have area (like a sheet of paper), and some have volume (like a microwave oven). I'll write three versions of a function I'll name `findSize()` that will return to us a floating-point number with the proper measurement. In `setup()`, I'll call each of these:

```
void setup() {
    float length = findSize(3);
    println("length = "+length);
    float area = findSize(4, 6);
    println("area = "+area);
```

```
    float volume = findSize(2, 3, 5);
    println("volume = "+volume);
}

float findSize(float length) {
                    // 1D size - just returns the input length
    return (length);
}

float findSize(float width, float height) {
                    // 2D size - return area
    return (width*height);
}

float findSize(float width, float height, float depth) {
                    // 3D size - return volume
    return (width*height*depth);
}
```

(Full program in color/sketches/overload1/overload1.pde)

The output of this program appears in the console window:

```
len = 3.0
area = 24.0
volume = 30.0
```

There's nothing wrong in defining a version you never call, but don't try to call a version you haven't created. That's like calling any other function that doesn't exist. If I try to call

```
float f = findSize(1, 2, 3, 4);
```

I'll get an error.

Writing multiple versions of a procedure is a useful technique, but it can be a dangerous one. If the different versions of your functions do very different things, you can accidentally find yourself calling the wrong one.

To see how easy it is to get mixed up, let's rewrite findSize() in two versions. They both return a float, but one of them takes a float as input, the other an int:

```
void setup() {
    float len = findSize(3);
    println("len 3 = "+len);
    float flen = findSize(3.0);
    println("len 3.0 = "+flen);

}
```

```
float findSize(float len) {  // return the input
   return (len);
}

float findSize(int len) {  // return the input * 5
   return (len*5);
}
```

(Full program in color/sketches/overload2/overload2.pde)

Here's the output:

```
len 3 = 15.0
len 3.0 = 3.0
```

The technique of using multiple versions of a function that are selected based on their definitions goes by a few names, the most common of which is probably *overloading*. Processing uses overloading all over the place internally; that's why color() can take any mixture of int and float values as inputs. But this technique can make debugging tricky, since in complex situations, it can be hard to be sure which function is being called.

In this example, if we pass findSize() a float we get back the number we sent it, but if we pass it an int, we get back that value multiplied by five. Suppose that while developing this program you originally use both versions of findSize(), but over time, you remove the int-based calls one at a time until none happen to remain. Then you put the project aside.

A month later, you have a great idea for improving your project. You pop it open and find yourself working on a section that passes a float to findSize(), and you want to add a few more calls to that function as part of your new code. But you've forgotten that there are multiple versions of findSize() out there (perhaps the function is in a different source file, so it's not even on your screen at all). So you add some new lines of code, including some new calls to findSize()...and you know where this is going. One or more of your new calls passes an int rather than a float. Your code compiles perfectly cleanly (because, of course, there *is* an int-based version of findSize() out there to be called), but your new program goes haywire. You scratch your head and you read the code over and over, but it looks perfect. In order for you to find this bug, you're going to have to rediscover those multiple versions of findSize() that are sitting out there, innocently helpful, but also crazy dangerous.

Overloading can be a great time-saving trick and a handy convenience, but with great power comes great responsibility. Definitely use overloading when appropriate, but be very, very careful.

A good rule of thumb for overloading in Processing is to restrict your overloads to different versions of the input parameters that all do identical operations. For example, one version of `color()` takes three `int` variables, and the other takes three `float` variables, but they both create a color from those numbers. That's pretty safe.

If you want to do different things based on the number of arguments or their types, I strongly recommend that you write several different procedures, each with its own unique name. It's only a tiny amount of additional work, but it can save you from some very frustrating debugging sessions.

5.2   De ning Colors

When used with care, overloading can be very useful. For example, `color()` has yet another overloaded version that's frequently handy. If you give `color()` just one number, it uses it for all three values, creating a shade of gray:

```
color black       = color(0);
color dark_gray   = color(64);
color mid_gray    = color(128);
color light_gray  = color(192);
color white       = color(255);
```

Note that the word `color` is used in these examples in two different but related ways: to declare the type of object (on the left of the equals sign) and to invoke a built-in function to create one of those objects (on the right).

You'll get used to talking about colors in this fashion very quickly. If you set all three values to the same number, you get grays from black to white. So here are the same colors as above, only more explicitly described:

```
color black       = color(0,   0,   0);
color dark_gray   = color(64,  64,  64);
color mid_gray    = color(128, 128, 128);
color light_gray  = color(192, 192, 192);
color white       = color(255, 255, 255);
```

Once you've made a color this way, you can hand it off to Processing to use when drawing things. For example, instead of giving `background()` the three red, green, and blue values directly, as we have been, you can just hand it a color variable instead. Here's a rewrite of our background-changing program:

```
int Redval = 192;
int Grnval = 64;
int Bluval = 0;
color MyColor;

void setup() {
   size(600, 400);
```

```
   MyColor = color(Redval, Grnval, Bluval);
   background(MyColor);
}

void draw() {
   Redval = Redval+1;
   if (Redval > 255) Redval=0;
   MyColor = color(Redval, Grnval, Bluval);
   background(MyColor);
}
```

(Full program in color/sketches/color1/color1.pde)

Of course, this isn't much of a savings in this example, but later on, the ability to save colors this way will be very convenient.

If you want to disassemble a color variable, Processing offers you three built-in functions, quite sensibly called `red()`, `green()`, and `blue()`. They each take a `color` as input, but they each return a `float`, even though the value is always an integer. Remember that to convert a `float` to an `int`, hand it to the built-in function `int()`:

```
color MyColor  = color(Redval, Grnval, Bluval);
   // create a color
float newRed   = red(MyColor);      // get the red component
float newGrn   = green(MyColor);    // get the green component
float newBlu   = blue(MyColor);     // get the blue component
newRed = newRed * 2;                // make the red double-bright
color NewColor = color(newRed, newGrn, newBlu);
   // save the new color
```

For this little example I didn't check the value of newRed, but in general, you should always make sure your color values are in the range 0 to 255. Processing won't complain if they're not, but you probably won't see the results you were hoping for.

You'll see this quite a lot in some Processing programs: people compute a color in one function and then they take it apart in another function, change it, and save it again. There's a trade-off here: the packing/unpacking business takes some time, but it's very convenient to have the color packaged up in a single variable rather than having to deal with the three red, green, and blue components all the time. If program speed is a significant concern, you might want to keep them separate, otherwise, it's probably conceptually easier to keep them together as a `color` and pull it apart when needed.

5.3   HSB Colors

The red-green-blue color specification is used throughout computer graphics, but it's notoriously difficult to get a good intuitive feeling for how to find particular colors with

RGB. If you look at Figure 5.4, it might not be obvious how to maneuver through this cube to find a particular color. If you want to take a shot at mixing up some colors using RGB, go to the Processing window and under the *Tools* menu choose *Color Selector*. You can mix RGB values there using the color design tool. But if you have a particular color in mind, say a dark brown or a light lime green, it can be frustrating to try to find the right RGB values to get there.

Computer graphics researchers and vision scientists have invented a variety of more useful ways to describe colors. Processing offers you one of the more popular variations, called the *hue-saturation-brightness* (or simply HSB) model. A similar (but different) way of describing colors that's available in some other graphics programs is called the *hue-saturation-lightness*, or HSL, model; be sure that you don't accidentally use HSL values in your Processing program or things won't look right! The Color Selector also shows you the HSB values for your colors, as in Figure 5.6.

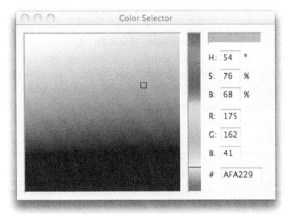

Figure 5.6. Processing's Color Selector. Note the HSB values in addition to RGB.

Colors described with HSB use three values that normally run from 0 to 255, just like RGB values, but of course the numbers mean different things.

The idea behind HSB is that all the colors are arranged in a cylinder, as in Figure 5.7. Black is at the middle of the bottom face, and white is directly above it. Between them,

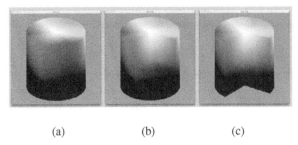

(a)   (b)   (c)

Figure 5.7. The HSB Color Cylinder. (a) The full cylinder. (b) Removing a wedge from the top half of the cylinder. (c) Removing a wedge from top to bottom.

along the axis of the cylinder, are the different values of gray. We say that *brightness* has a value of 0 at the bottom of the cylinder, and 255 at the top.

In part (a) of Figure 5.7 I've shown the whole cylinder. Notice that all the colors at the bottom, where brightness is 0, are black. In part (b) I've removed a chunk from the upper half, revealing the insides. And in part (c) I've extended that removal so you can see what's going on all the way up the cylinder. The black-to-white axis lies in the middle of the cylinder, and colors get more saturated as we move to the edges.

You can move away from the central core grays with the other two values. Suppose you want to create a red-like color. Then you choose a value for *hue* that directs you towards red (in Processing, that's 0). Increasing values of hue run around the cylinder clockwise in this figure, from the reds into the yellows, the greens, and the blues. The distance you move out from the core towards the edge of the cylinder is given by *saturation*, which is 0 at the core and 255 out at the edge.

This is a much easier way to design a color, particularly when using an interactive tool. If you want a light lime green, for instance, you'd pick a hue value toward green, a pretty large value of brightness (since you want a light color) and then you'd push outwards with saturation to move from grays to greens.

By the way, you might be wondering why the RGB color space is a cube and the HSB space is a cylinder. Why not the other way around? Or maybe they should both be cones, or spheres? These shapes are partly by convention, but they also make sense. The three RGB axes are independent and equal, so it makes sense that they should all have the same function in the space: three straight lines forming the edges of a cube does that nicely. In HSB, we have the idea that hue "wraps around" the spectrum, as you can see from Figure 5.7. So saturation and brightness are both straight lines, but it makes sense to give hue a geometric shape that matches its cyclic nature. A circle does that job, so hue gets mapped onto a circle and the result is a cylinder.

If you're intrigued, try recreating these figures with RGB on the cylinder and HSB on a cube and see if that looks any more convenient to you. Or try some other 3D shapes that occur to you and see if they better match your intuition for organizing colors.

When you create a color with `color()`, Processing normally assumes the three values you're handing it are in RGB, each in the range 0 to 255. You can tell it you'd rather it interpreted your colors in HSB values by using the built-in function `colorMode()`. In its basic form, you call this function with just one argument: either RGB or HSB (remember to use all capitals). Here's two ways to create the same blue color:

```
colorMode(RGB);                          // default mode
color c1 = color(102, 164, 180);        // set RGB values
colorMode(HSB);                          // now use HSB
color c2 = color(136, 110, 180);        // set HSB values
```

Internally, both `c1` and `c2` represent the exact same color; Processing doesn't even remember which mode you used to make the color.

Just as you can extract the RGB values of a color with `red()`, `green()`, and `blue()`, you won't be surprised to learn you can get the HSB values with `hue()`, `saturation()`, and `brightness()`. Since Processing doesn't care how you created the color, you can get the RGB or HSB values of any color at any time, no matter how it was originally defined.

We'll see that Processing has a variety of similar mode commands. They all tell the system how to interpret numbers that are given to a function, just as `colorMode()` tells `color()` whether you're giving it RGB or HSB values. My general advice will be to avoid mode commands, but they're a necessary evil when creating colors: if you want to specify a color as HSB there's just no other reasonable way to go about it. My suggestion is that you stick with the default color mode RGB as much as possible. If you really want to use HSB, then use `colorMode()` to go into HSB, create your colors, and then immediately use `colorMode()` to go back to RGB. That way, you'll know that your program is always in the RGB mode, unless you're explicitly setting colors and just a few lines below a call to `colorMode()`. That's what I'll do from now on.

The HSB color space is a great place to work if you want to adjust your colors in your program. To make a color darker, for instance, you would just reduce its brightness. Here's one way to do that:

```
// assume we have a color myColor
float myBrightness = brightness(myColor);
myBrightness = myBrightness - 10;
colorMode(HSB);
myColor = color(hue(myColor), saturation(myColor), myBrightness);
colorMode(RGB);
```

One very interesting quality of hue is that it is defined around a circle. That is, if you increase hue from 0 to 255, you'll start from red and come back to red. So let's write a version of our color-changing program that just rolls the hue value around and around the circle.

```
int Hueval = 0;
int Satval = 110;
int Brival = 110;
color MyColor;

void setup() {
    size(600, 400);
    colorMode(HSB);
    MyColor = color(Hueval, Satval, Brival);
    colorMode(RGB);
    background(MyColor);
}

void draw() {
```

```
        Hueval = Hueval+1;
        colorMode(HSB);
        MyColor = color(Hueval, Satval, Brival);
        colorMode(RGB);
        background(MyColor);
}
```

(Full program in color/sketches/hsb1/hsb1.pde)

Very nice. But if you let it run, you'll find it stops when it gets back to red. That's because `Hueval` grows beyond 255, so Processing simply interprets it as 255 since it knows that's its maximum value. This isn't a general feature of all languages or even all functions in Processing; it's just a special feature of `color()` that values less than 0 or greater than 255 are "clamped" to 0 and 255 respectively (you can change these maximum and minimum values with additional parameters to `colorMode()`, but there's rarely any need to). In one of our background animations in Chapter 4 I stopped `Redval` from getting out of control this way:

```
Redval = Redval+1;
if (Redval > 255) Redval=0;
```

It turns out that there's a built-in shortcut to handle just this kind of situation. It's called the *modulo operator*, and it's written with a percent sign (`%`). Like the plus sign, it takes two numbers, one on the left and one on the right. Let's call those `L` and `R`. In words, it does this:

As long as `L >= R`, subtract `R` from `L`

Here, `>=` means "greater than or equal to."

So suppose we write `10 % 3` (when said out loud, this is pronounced "ten modulo three"). Since $10 >= 3$, we subtract 3 from 10 getting 7, and since $7 >= 3$, we subtract 3 again getting 4, and since $4 >= 3$ we subtract 3 yet again and get 1. That's now smaller than 3 so we stop, and that's the result of `10 % 3`: the number 1. Let's try the number 9: since $9 >= 3$, we subtract 3, getting 6, and since $6 >= 3$, we subtract 3 again, getting 3, and (this is the interesting part) since $3 >= 3$ (remember the equals sign), we subtract 3 again, getting 0, and since 0 is less than 3, we stop. So the result of `9 % 3` is 0.

This is also called the *remainder* of dividing one number by another. For example, 16/3 is 5 with a remainder of 1 (that is, 3 fits into 16 a total of 5 times, with 1 left over), so `16 % 3` is 1.

Using `L` and `R` again, `L%R` is what's left when you remove `R` from `L` as many times as you can before `L` becomes smaller than `R`. The modulo operator is the perfect way to make numbers "loop around"; that is, when they get too large for a given range, they pop back to the beginning of the range. Suppose `Hueval` has the value 250. Then `Hueval % 256` is simply 250. When `Hueval` makes it to 254, then `Hueval%256` is just 254, and when `Hueval` is 255, then `Hueval%256` is 255. But when `Hueval` hits 256, then `256 % 256` is 0: we've popped back to the start.

Now we have two choices. We can assign 0 back into `Hueval` and start it over again from there. Or we can just let `Hueval` increase forever, getting bigger and bigger, but using the result of the modulo operator when we make the color. For example, the next time around, `Hueval` will be 257, so `Hueval % 256` is 1. The next time it'll be 2, and so on. Even when `Hueval` reaches 2560000, the modulo operator will still wrap it around to 0 (internally, the operator uses a much more efficient process to compute this result; it doesn't actually do all those subtractions, so feel free to use it with giant numbers). The first approach could be written this way:

```
Hueval = Hueval+1;
MyColor = color(Hueval % 256, Satval, Brival);
```

Here I'm using the modulo operator when I make the color. The second approach could be written this way:

```
Hueval = (Hueval+1) % 256;
MyColor = color(Hueval, Satval, Brival);
```

They both produce the same results, but I think the second version is much better. It keeps the value of `Hueval` in a reasonable range, so if we examine it (say while debugging), we don't have to figure out the modulo step in our heads.

Here's a full listing of the new program, using the second approach:

```
int Hueval = 0;
int Satval = 110;
int Brival = 110;
color MyColor;

void setup() {
    size(600, 400);
    colorMode(HSB);
    MyColor = color(Hueval, Satval, Brival);
    colorMode(RGB);
    background(MyColor);
}

void draw() {
    Hueval = (Hueval+1) % 256;
    colorMode(HSB);
    MyColor = color(Hueval, Satval, Brival);
    colorMode(RGB);
    background(MyColor);
}
```

(Full program in color/sketches/hsb2/hsb2.pde)

If you use Processing's built-in color tool (under *Tools* and then *Color Selector*) you'll find that the H, S, and B fields are labeled with, respectively, a degree marker, and two percent signs. Traditionally, the hue is written as an angle from 0 to 360 degrees, and saturation and brightness are written as percentages from 0 to 100. Unfortunately, even in HSB mode Processing expects the three numbers you give it to be in the range 0 to 255. That means you can't just copy the HSB numbers into your Processing code, the way you can with the RGB numbers.

Instead, you have to convert each one. Multiply the hue by 255.0/360.0 and saturation and brightness by 255.0/100.0 (of course, you can precompute these numbers to save a little bit of computation time). If you want to copy the numbers from the Color Selector and paste them right into your code (let's call them simply H, S, and B), then plug them into this template:

```
MyColor = color(H * 0.71, S * 25.5, B * 25.5);
```

Although you have to multiply the numbers as above to use them, at least Processing's built-in Color Selector gives you the values in HSB. Many other color tools use alternative color definitions, which can be a challenge to convert into HSB. If you want to convert RGB values to HSB, here's a little program that does the job. Enter the RGB values at the top, and the HSB values will be printed to Processing's console window.

```
void setup() {

    // replace these values with your RGB color
    float r = 102;
    float g = 164;
    float b = 180;

    colorMode(RGB);
    color clr = color(r, g, b);
    float hue = hue(clr);
    float sat = saturation(clr);
    float bri = brightness(clr);

    println("RGB ("+r+", "+g+", "+b+") = HSB ("+hue+", "+sat+",
        "+bri+")");
}
```

(Full program in color/sketches/hsb3/hsb3.pde)

When I run this with the values given above, I get these results:

```
RGB (102.0, 164.0, 180.0) = HSB (136.21794, 110.5, 180.0)
```

Having all those digits of precision is nice, but it makes for a lot of typing (and possible typos) if you're using these kinds of results to manually enter colors. Except for the most precise kinds of color applications, when you're describing colors by hand, you can probably ignore everything to the right of the decimal point; I would call this color simply (136, 110, 180) in HSB.

Note that if you like to use short variable names like r, g, and b, you need to be careful when changing color models, because you might be tempted to use b for "brightness," and you run the risk of all kinds of confusing bugs if you lose track of whether b refers to "blue" or "brightness." I speak from experience here. Don't suffer as I have. Heed these words of wisdom, Grasshopper, and name your variables well.

In Chapter 7 I'll talk about the idea of *linear interpolation*, or *lerp*. It's basically a means for finding a new value between two others. For example, if you had endpoints 10 and 20, then a lerp halfway between them would be the value 15. A lerp a quarter of the way would be 12.5.

Processing provides a built-in means for doing the same thing with colors. This lets you compute colors in between two other colors, which can be handy for tasks like blending and making smooth gradients. The function lerpColor() takes two colors and a number between zero and one, and it produces a color at the specified point along the range between the two inputs.

Note that the color space in use at the moment makes a very big difference in how colors get interpolated by lerpColor(). Here's a little test program to show the difference:

```
void setup() {
    color c0 = color(199, 172, 115 );
    color c1 = color( 46, 106, 148 );
    size(800, 450);
    noStroke();
    int numSteps = 700;
    for (int i=0; i<numSteps; i++) {
        float a = i/(numSteps-1.0);

        // RGB upper
        colorMode(RGB);
        fill(lerpColor(c0, c1, a));
        rect(50+i, 50, 1, 150);

        // HSB lower
        colorMode(HSB);
        fill(lerpColor(c0, c1, a));
        rect(50+i, 250, 1, 150);
        colorMode(RGB);
    }
}
```

(See output in Figure 5.8. Full program in color/sketches/lerpColors/lerpColors.pde)

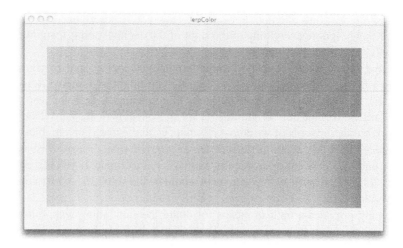

Figure 5.8. Blending the same colors. Using the RGB color space (above), and the HSB color space (below). (color/sketches/lerpColors/lerpColors.pde)

The upper row in Figure 5.8 shows the result of blending in RGB space. In essence we draw a straight line in the RGB cube between the two points, and then pull out colors along that line.

The lower row shows the result of blending the exact same colors, only in the HSB space. The model here is that we're making a kind of spiral in the HSB cylinder, curving around in hue while moving in or out in saturation and up or down in brightness. The yellows and greens in the lower row are a result of all those hues we pass through on our way from the beige to the blue.

These are very different results! Neither one is "right" or "wrong"; which one works for you best depends on how you want your work to look.

When you blend two bright colors in RGB, it's not uncommon for the intermediate colors to become gray or muddied, since the closer you get to the center of the cube, the more gray your colors become. When you blend two bright colors in HSB, they'll typically stay bright throughout since the brightness is blended separately from the hue and saturation, but you can often see unexpected colors appearing between your end-points. While you're getting used to working with colors on the computer, it's often useful to see the results you get from blending in both color spaces and then choosing the one that looks best to you. Just remember that if you do switch the color mode to HSB, switch it back to RGB when you're done!

Chapter 6
Graphics Primitives

Let's move on from changing the background color and actually draw some pictures!

Before we dig in, I'll give you another little program for messing around with.

This chapter's little program draws a 3D wave that pulses and flows outward, forever and ever. If you want to play with the shape and speed of the wave, the place to start is three lines from the end, where the variable z is set. Try adjusting those numbers and see what effect it has on the wave. You can even try out entirely new types of waves by cooking up your own expressions for z.

```
import processing.opengl.*;

void setup() {
  size(600, 400, OPENGL);
}

// a pulsing sinc made of a single quadstrip spiral

void draw() {
  background(108, 131, 166);
  lights();
  translate(width/2, 3*height/8);
  rotateX(radians(55));
  scale(height/2, height/2);

  fill(225, 215, 170);

  float ringWidth = .04;
  int ringSteps = 8;
  int maxi = 240;
  beginShape(QUAD_STRIP);
  for (int i=-ringSteps; i<maxi; i++) {
    float r0 = ringWidth * (i*1.0/ringSteps);
    float r1 = r0 + ringWidth;
```

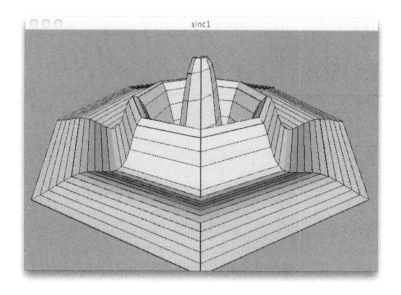

Figure 6.1. A flowing, pulsing wave (frame from animation). (graphics/sketches/sinc1/sinc1.pde)

```
    if (r0 < 0) r0 = 0;
    float theta = i * (TWO_PI / ringSteps);
    makeVertex(r0, theta);
    makeVertex(r1, theta);
  }
  endShape(CLOSE);
}

void makeVertex(float r, float theta) {
    float x = r*cos(theta);
    float y = r*sin(theta);
    float z = 100 * exp(-3*r*r) * cos((r * 2 * TWO_PI)
                    - (frameCount/50.0));
    vertex(x, y, z);
}
```

(See output in Figure 6.1. Full program in graphics/sketches/sinc1/sinc1.pde)

Now let's see about making pictures!

6.1 Naming Points

The most important thing to fix in your mind before we start to draw is that the world is a *checkerboard*. Well, the graphics world of Processing is, anyway. Everything we do is with respect to this checkerboard. When we create a graphics window, as in the calls we've been making so far to `setup()`, we're creating a checkerboard the size of the window. So in the examples we've seen, the world has been a grid

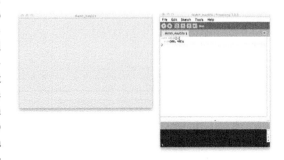

Figure 6.2. A graphics window.

that is 600 units wide by 400 units high, as shown in Figure 6.2.

Almost always, each of these "units" will be a single *pixel* or dot, on your screen. So if your computer monitor has a resolution of, say, 800 dots wide by 600 dots high, then a window that is 800 by 600 will fill the screen (actually, it'll be a little bit bigger than the screen, because your operating system probably includes some borders around the window). Filling in all those dots takes time; in general, the smaller your window, the faster your program will run. But many computers are so fast these days that you can use a huge window on the screen and draw a ton of graphics and everything will still be smooth and responsive.

The reason for thinking of the window as a checkerboard is because that's how you tell Processing where to put things. If you want to draw a circle, you identify the circle's center by naming a point on the checkerboard and you specify the circle's radius in terms of a number of checkerboard squares. To draw a rectangle, you identify the upper-left corner as a point on the checkerboard, and then you give the width and a height. You get the idea by now: every point in the window is identified by its location on that checkerboard.

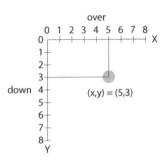

Figure 6.3. Naming points in the graphics window.

Points are always described in terms of how far they are from the left side of the window and how far down they are from the top, as in Figure 6.3. The locations of points are always given in that order: over, then down.

We often call these directions the *x-axis* and *y-axis*, respectively. We call the point (0,0) the *origin*, and of course, it is in the upper-left corner. A point 100 units to the right of that is (100,0), and a point 50 units down from the origin would be (0, 50). If we plotted those three points, the remaining point of a rectangle would be at (100,50). We could say that the point's *x*-coordinate is 100, and its *y*-coordinate is 50.

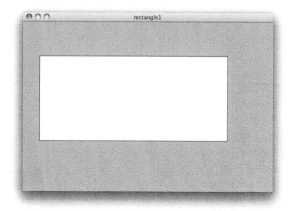

Figure 6.4. Drawing a rectangle. (graphics/sketches/rectangle1/rectangle1.pde)

6.2   Basic Shapes

Now that we know about the underlying (but invisible) checkerboard, let's actually draw a rectangle. Here's my starting skeleton, ready for us to start filling up with graphics:

```
void setup() {
   size(600, 400);
   background(163, 143, 109);
}

void draw() {
   // drawing goes here
}
```

Let's make a rectangle. It takes just one line of code, in the form of a call to the system-defined rect() function (here again we see how programmers like to use short names for everything, but in this case, *rect* seems to me a fair shorthand for *rectangle*):

```
void draw() {
   rect(50, 100, 400, 200);
}
```

(See output in Figure 6.4. Full program in graphics/sketches/rectangle1/rectangle1.pde)

The rect() function takes four arguments: the *x*-coordinate of the rectangle's upper-left corner, the *y*-coordinate of the upper-left corner, the rectangle's width, and its height. So this tells Processing to draw a rectangle that has its upper-left corner at (50, 100) (that is, 50 units to the right of the upper-left corner of the window, and 100 units below the top), and give it a width of 400 units and a height of 200.

Figure 6.5 shows where these points lie on the graph paper of our graphics window. If you try it out, you'll see it works! The system draws a white rectangle with a black border right where we told it to.

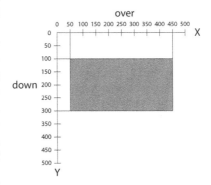

Depending on how you like to work and how your program is organized, specifying a rectangle this way might not be the most convenient approach. Processing lets you tell it to interpret the values in rect() in any of four ways. You always give rect() four numbers separated by commas, but if you change the mode, you're telling Processing to interpret those four numbers in a different way.

To tell it which mode (or style) you intend to use, you first call rectMode() before you make your rectangles. The rectMode() function takes four possible arguments: CORNER,

Figure 6.5. A rectangle in the graphics window.

CORNERS, CENTER, or RADIUS (remember to use all upper-case.) Let's look at each one. They're illustrated in Figure 6.6.

CORNER. This is the default. The four values identify the upper-left x, upper-left y, width, and height.

CORNERS. In this mode, the first two values identify the *x* and *y* of any corner of the rectangle, and the next two values identify the diagonally opposite corner. Which pair of opposite corners you want to use is up to you; in the figure, I used the upper-left and lower-right corners.

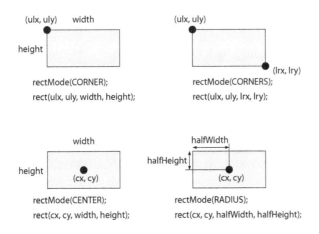

Figure 6.6. Rectangle modes.

CENTER. The first two values identify the center of the rectangle, and the next two identify its width and height.

RADIUS. The first two values identify the center of the rectangle, and the next two identify its half-width and half-height

In general, I advise against using rectMode(). The main reason is that there's no way to tell, just by looking at your code, what mode you're in for any given line of your program; you'd have to backtrack and try to find the most recently called mode command, which can become time-consuming and difficult in complicated programs.

Suppose your program is big enough that it fills up several screens full of text. Maybe it's even spread out over multiple files. In the process of drawing your graphics, you draw lots of rectangles in lots of different routines. Now suppose that you want to add another rectangle somewhere in the middle of the process. So you add a new procedure and compute the points, but what mode are you in? There's no way to tell. Either you spend your time searching the files, trying to figure out what mode is in effect, or you throw up your hands and set the mode explicitly, thereby perhaps breaking another routine later down the line that expected to be in the mode that you just changed. Neither of these options is appealing.

A million times worse is when you're debugging your program (or even someone else's). You identify some particular piece of code as a possible source of the bug, and there you see a call to rect() with four numbers. What do they mean? Are they a center and width and height? Or a corner and half-width and half-height? Or what? At this point, you have to become a detective, and spend your time and energy trying to unravel the code, finding out which procedure is calling which other procedure when, and going through who knows how much source code, just to figure out what mode is in effect when that rect() call is being made. To me, that's a real waste of energy.

Generally, I find the maintenance cost (in terms of time and attention) demanded by these modes far outweighs the convenience they offer. You may recall during the discussion of colorMode() in Chapter 4 that I said using that routine was a necessary evil when you needed to create HSB colors (because there was no other practical way), but I recommended switching back to RGB immediately. You could do the same thing with rectangle modes, switching in and out of the default, but given the hassle of keeping track of the right kinds of variables and what they mean and the difficulty of tracking down the problem when you forget to switch the mode back, I don't think it's worth it.

These modes are all similar enough that you can live with the default forever, and even if another mode is more convenient, you can still use the default with just a little bit of time and code. That's what I'll do throughout this book, and it will never take more than a smidgen of effort. You'll see other people use rectMode() from time to time, as well as some of the other mode commands we have yet to cover, but I suggest that in your own code, you avoid rectMode() and the other mode functions altogether.

Returning to Figure 6.4, looking at that image opens up a lot of questions. Why is the rectangle filled in with white? For that matter, why is it filled in with anything? Why does it have a border? Why is the border black? Why is the border so thin?

All of those questions have the same answer, and it's based on Processing's idea of something called the *graphics state*. This is like a big list of global variables that you can change, and together they tell Processing the answers to all of these questions. Generally, when Processing draws something, it can do all kinds of things in the drawing process, and which things it does, and how, are controlled by the variables in the graphics state.

Our call to `rect()` above was like calling someone up and telling them, "Paint my house." If you don't give them any other information, they'll make their own decisions about what color to use, how many coats to apply, whether or not to paint the trim around your windows, and, if so, what color the trim should be, and so on. If you have specific ideas in mind for those choices, you have to tell them beforehand.

If you don't tell them your own preferences, the painters will use their *default value* for each option. That way they can still do something reasonable, even if you don't explicitly tell them what you want. If you do provide your own choices, we say that those choices *override* or replace their corresponding values (a default value is often simply called a *default*).

So it is in Processing. Each time you draw something, it gets drawn as specified by the graphics state, even if you've never set a single value in it. Processing starts the graphics state out with default values. As we've seen, these values include the following: draw shapes with a white interior, draw a black border around them, make the border one pixel thick, and draw everything so that it's opaque. We'll change each of these choices (and some others) below, but for now, let's stick with these defaults and explore the other shapes we can draw.

Think of these built-in shapes as building blocks. Just as a child can build a cool tower out of simple wooden blocks, you can make complicated and rich images using the right combinations of basic shapes. Some of these shapes are pretty simple (like the rectangle), but some are complex, and when you put them all together in creative ways, you can make some cool imagery.

There's no special way to draw a square. If you want a square, draw a rectangle with equal width and height. So a square is just a standard rectangle, drawn with the same length for both width and height.

```
void draw() {
    rect(40, 80, 200, 200);
}
```

Figure 6.7. Drawing a square.
(graphics/sketches/square/square1.pde)

(See output in Figure 6.7. Full program in graphics/sketches/square1/square1.pde)

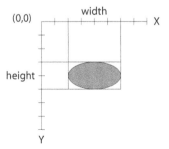

You can draw an ellipse inside of a rectangle by calling `ellipse()`. The default format is a little bit different than the format for a rectangle: the first two numbers give the center point of the ellipse in *x*- and *y*-coordinates, and then the next two numbers, like the rectangle, give the overall width and height, as shown in Figure 6.8.

Figure 6.8. An ellipse sits inside its defining rectangle.

Here's how to draw an ellipse:

```
void draw() {
    ellipse(250, 200, 400, 250);
}
```

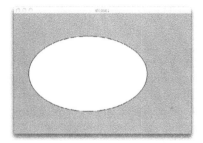

Figure 6.9. An ellipse. (graphics/sketches/ellipse1/ellipse1.pde)

(See output in Figure 6.9. Full program in graphics/sketches/ellipse1/ellipse1.pde)

Like rectangles, you can use `ellipseMode()` to set how you want the four numbers in the `ellipse()` call to be interpreted. You have the same options and they produce the same results: They're illustrated in Figure 6.10.

Note that the default rectangle mode is CORNER (the upper-left point, followed by width and height), while the default ellipse mode is CENTER (the center point, followed by width and height).

As with `rectMode()`, I recommend that you never call `ellipseMode()`. Stick with the default mode for both shapes (even though the defaults are different), and you'll never have to spend your time trying to unravel your code to figure out which mode is being used for any particular shape.

There's also no special way to draw a circle. If you want a circle, just draw an ellipse inside a square (that is, a rectangle with equal width and height), as shown in Figure 6.11.

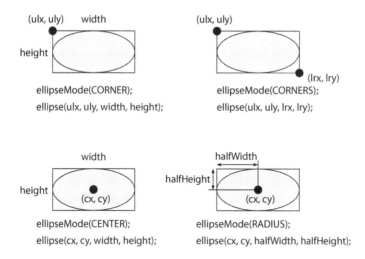

Figure 6.10. Ellipse modes.

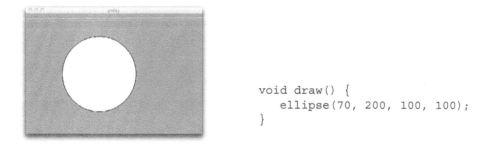

```
void draw() {
    ellipse(70, 200, 100, 100);
}
```

Figure 6.11. Drawing a circle.
(graphics/sketches/circle1/circle1.pde)

(See output in Figure 6.11. Full program in graphics/sketches/circle1/circle1.pde)

Note that if you want to draw a circle with a given radius, say 50, you have to specify the width and height values as twice that radius (in this case, 100) because they're the *total* width and height of the figure. In other words, they specify the circle's *diameter*, not its radius. You'll often see circles created like this:

```
ellipse(xcenter, ycenter, radius*2, radius*2);
```

Of course, you could switch to RADIUS mode instead and then you wouldn't have to multiply the values, but as I've said, I recommend against that.

Sometimes you want to draw just a part of a ellipse. Processing lets you do this by calling arc(). Like an ellipse, the first four values give the *x* and *y* of the center of the ellipse, followed by the width and height. But rather than drawing the whole thing, two more numbers tell `arc()` how much of the ellipse to draw. These two numbers are the starting and ending *angle* of the ellipse. You may recall that a circle has 360 *degrees* going around. Seen from the center of the ellipse, 0 degrees corresponds to three o'clock and then the angles increase clockwise: 90 degrees is at six o'clock, 180 degrees is at nine o'clock, and so on. So if you just want a quarter-circle that extends from, say, three o'clock to six o'clock, you'd give the starting and ending angles of 0 and 90 degrees.

Well, that's what you would do if Processing used degrees. But Processing expects its angles to be expressed in *radians*. There are lots of nice tutorials on the web on the relationship between degrees and radians; there's even one on the Processing website itself. If you don't care about that, all you need to know is that Processing provides a built-in routine to convert degrees to radians. Quite sensibly, this routine is called `radians()`. You give it your angle in degrees, and it returns that angle in radians. As you might expect, you can get the number of degrees from an angle in radians with `degrees()`. Both accept a `float` as input and return a `float`.

By the way, you'll sometimes find people performing this operation manually in their code. I think this is mostly from force of habit, since the cost of making the call to `radians()` or `degrees()` is normally so small it's negligible. But you'll see it in other people's code. To convert from degrees to radians, the formula is:

```
radians = degrees * PI / 180;
```

The system-wide variable `PI` corresponds to the Greek letter π used in geometry and has a value of about 3.14159. This is a built-in constant in Processing. There are also a few convenient slices of `PI`: `HALF_PI` $(\pi/2)$, `QUARTER_PI` $(\pi/4)$, and `TWO_PI` $(2*\pi)$. Note that these names use underscores and not dashes. If you wrote `HALF-PI`, Processing would try to subtract the value of `PI` from the variable `HALF`. If you haven't defined a variable named `HALF`, Processing would report this as a compile-time error. To convert from radians to degrees you can write

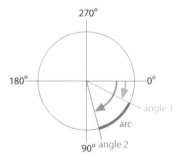

Figure 6.12. Describing an arc by degrees.

```
degrees = radians * 180 / PI;
```

In general, I suggest using the built-in routines to convert from degrees to radians (and back); the routines are fast and easy to use, and using them gives you one less place to make a typing error that you'd later have to track down and fix. Figure 6.12 shows how your two angles define the start and end of an arc.

In most of this book, I'll create my angles in degrees and use `radians()` to convert them as needed. But when this extra work could really slow us down, I'll sometimes save a little time by working things out directly in radians. For example, the little toy project at the start of Chapter 5 computes the angles given to arc() directly in radians because I wanted to keep that code as short as possible.

Let's draw an arc centered at (300, 180) and part of a circle of radius 125 (or diameter 250). The arc will run from three o'clock (0 degrees) to six o'clock (90 degrees): Here's the Processing code to draw that arc:

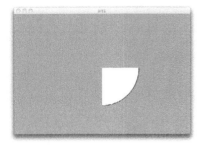

```
void draw() {
    arc(300, 180, 250, 250,
        radians(0),
        radians(90));
}
```

Figure 6.13. A circular arc.
(graphics/sketches/arc1/arc1.pde)

(See output in Figure 6.13. Full program in graphics/sketches/arc1/arc1.pde)

Note that there's a black line along the circular part of the arc, but there are no lines along the straight boundaries of the white region. We'll get into the details behind that in a bit. For now, think of the arc as being the part that's drawn in black; that is, it's just the piece of the circle's rim. The white area "inside" the arc is associated with it, but it's not part of the arc itself (and as we'll see, we don't have to draw this filled-in area; drawing this "fill" region is just one of the defaults).

Of course, you can draw an arc as part of an ellipse (rather than a circle) if you want:

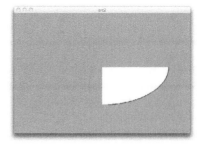

```
void draw() {
    arc(300, 180, 450, 250,
        radians(0), radians(90));
}
```

Figure 6.14. An elliptical arc for a quarter of an ellipse.
(graphics/sketches/arc2/arc2.pde)

(See output in Figure 6.14. Full program in graphics/sketches/arc2/arc2.pde)

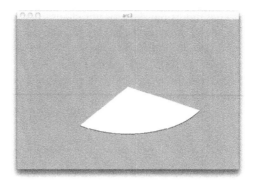

Figure 6.15. An elliptical arc. (graphics/sketches/arc3/arc3.pde)

It turns out that radians(0) is 0, but I often write it out anyway so I can easily change the angle later if I want.

You can draw arcs that start and end at any angles you like:

```
void draw() {
    arc(300, 180, 450, 250, radians(30), radians(125));
}
```

(See output in Figure 6.15. Full program in graphics/sketches/arc3/arc3.pde)

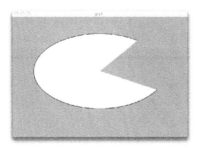

Arcs can wrap around as much of the circle as you need:

```
void draw() {
    arc(300, 180, 450, 250,
        radians(30),
        radians(305));
}
```

Figure 6.16. An elliptical arc that is nearly a full ellipse.
(graphics/sketches/arc4/arc4.pde)

(See output in Figure 6.16. Full program in graphics/sketches/arc4/arc4.pde)

You can easily draw a *triangle* if you want. Just list the *x* and *y* points sequentially; that is, the *x* location of the first point, then the *y* location of the first point, then the *x* location of the second point, then the *y* location of the second point, then the *x* location

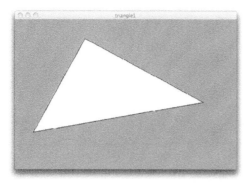

Figure 6.17. A triangle. (graphics/sketches/triangle1/triangle1.pde)

of the third point, and of course the *y* location of the third point, and pass the whole shebang off to `triangle()`:

```
void draw() {
    triangle(50, 300, 510, 220, 190, 50);
}
```

(See output in Figure 6.17. Full program in graphics/sketches/triangle1/triangle1.pde)

You can draw any four-sided figure by calling `quad()` (this is short for *quadrilateral*, which is the formal name for a figure made of four straight sides). This takes the same arguments as `triangle()`, except of course for one more pair of *x* and *y* values at the end for the fourth point:

```
void draw() {
    quad(40, 60, 550, 250,
         400, 350, 150, 300);
}
```

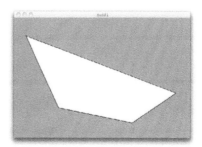

Figure 6.18. A quad.
(graphics/sketches/quad1/quad1.pde)

(See output in Figure 6.18. Full program in graphics/sketches/quad1/quad1.pde)

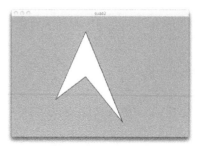

Figure 6.19. An arrow-shaped quad. (graphics/sketches/quad2/quad2.pde)

A 4-sided quad can make an arrow-like shape:

```
void draw() {
   quad(250, 50, 150, 275, 250, 200, 375, 350);
}
```

(See output in Figure 6.19. Full program in graphics/sketches/quad2/quad2.pde)

A quad can even cross over itself, creating a "bow-tie" quad. Note that Processing fills this in as though it was two triangles:

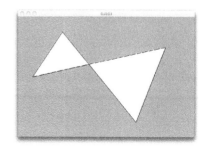

```
void draw() {
   quad(150, 50, 50, 200,
        500, 100, 400, 350);
}
```

Figure 6.20. A bow-tie quad. (graphics/sketches/quad3/quad3.pde)

(See output in Figure 6.20. Full program in graphics/sketches/quad3/quad3.pde)

You can use quad() to draw rectangles and squares, if you like, but rect() will save you a little bit of typing.

You can draw a *line* by simply giving the *x* and *y* values of the starting and ending points to line(). Here's how to draw a pair of lines:

```
void draw() {
   strokeWeight(1);
```

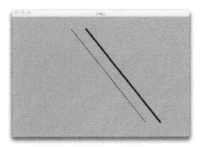

Figure 6.21. A pair of lines. (graphics/sketches/line1/line1.pde)

```
    line(200, 40, 450, 350);
    strokeWeight(4);
    line(250, 40, 500, 350);
}
```

(See output in Figure 6.21. Full program in graphics/sketches/line1/line1.pde)

You can see I've snuck in a few calls to the system routine `strokeWeight()`, which tells Processing how thick the lines should be. For the first line (on the left), I used the default value of one pixel wide. The line on the right was drawn after I'd set the weight to four pixels wide.

And finally, you can draw a single *point* with `point()`:

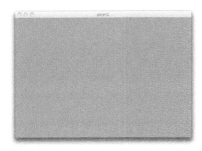

```
void draw() {
    point(300, 200);
}
```

Figure 6.22. A single point.
(graphics/sketches/point1/point1.pde)

(See output in Figure 6.22. Full program in graphics/sketches/point1/point1.pde)

This point is right in the middle of the screen. Don't worry if you can't see it; it's only one pixel large. If you want to make a point larger, use `strokeWeight()`, just like for a line.

You might think that `point()` is kind of useless, but in fact, it's an essential part of lots of beautiful Processing projects. It's great for things like dust clouds, sprays of

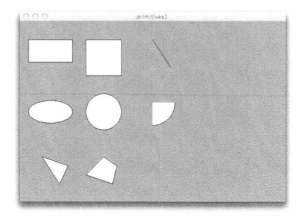

Figure 6.23. Nine primitives. (graphics/sketches/primitives1/primitives1.pde)

water, and other effects where many little points combine to form a complicated and organic texture. Like the humble ant, the tiny `point()` isn't much to look at all by itself, but it can accomplish great deeds when joined by hundreds or thousands of others.

You might not need `point()` right now, but don't forget about it! Later in the book, we'll see some projects that rely on `point()` (for example, see Figure 15.42 and Figure 15.43).

Here are all the basic shapes (or *primitive shapes*) we've seen so far, drawn together:

```
void draw() {
  rect(20, 40, 100, 50);
  rect(150, 40, 80, 80);
  ellipse(70, 200, 100, 50);
  ellipse(190, 200, 80, 80);
  arc(300, 180, 100, 100, radians(0), radians(90));
  triangle(50, 300, 110, 320, 90, 360);
  quad(190, 300, 220, 320, 210, 360, 150, 340);
  line(300, 40, 340, 100);
  point(300, 320);
}
```

(See output in Figure 6.23. Full program in graphics/sketches/primitives1/primitives1.pde)

6.3   Graphics State

So far I've been using the default graphics state for all of these pictures, so they all look pretty much the same. It's time for that to end!

Let's cover a few basic ideas from the graphics state that will give you control over how all of these objects appear.

Processing distinguishes the drawing of the *outline* of a shape from the *interior* of the shape. For example, the outline of a rectangle is four lines, but the interior is a rectangular area. Processing calls the outline the *stroke* and the interior the *fill*. You can specify a color to use for the stroke, and a different color for the fill. You can even turn off either, or both (though if you turn off both, nothing will get drawn). The stroke and fill values apply to everything we've seen so far, except for lines and points. Lines and points use the stroke settings, but they don't pay attention to fill (since they have nothing to fill in). Points have no size, but they use the stroke color to determine the color of the point.

Let's look at fill colors first. You identify the color you want to use to paint the inside of your shapes by handing your color to the routine `fill()`. The idea is simply that the shape is "filled in" with the color. Your new color is saved in the graphics state, overwriting whatever fill color was there before. From then on, until you specify a new fill color, that color gets used for every object.

When you call `fill()`, you can pass it three color components. Unless you changed the color mode, these will be the red, green, and blue components of your color, each in the range 0 to 255:

```
fill(0, 130, 185);   // fill shapes with a turquoise color
```

Even more simply, if you just want a gray color, you can give `fill()` just a single value. It will assume you want to use that value for all three components:

```
fill(192);  // fill shapes with (192, 192, 192)
```

Alternatively, you can create a `color` variable and then just hand that variable to `fill()`:

```
color turquoise = color(0, 130, 185);
fill(turquoise);
```

In this little program, I'll set the fill color and then draw a few rectangles (since I'm going to use this same basic image to demonstrate strokes, I'll use `strokeWeight()` to make the outlines nice and thick and visible):

```
void setup() {
    size(600, 400);
    background(106, 158, 155);
    strokeWeight(10);
}

void draw() {
    fill(198, 209, 173);
```

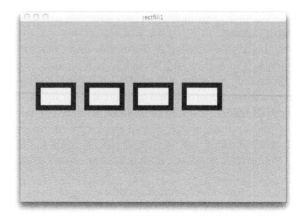

Figure 6.24. Changing the fill color. (graphics/sketches/rectFill1/rectFill1.pde)

```
    rect(40, 140, 80, 50);
    rect(150, 140, 80, 50);
    rect(260, 140, 80, 50);
    rect(370, 140, 80, 50);
}
```

(See output in Figure 6.24. Full program in graphics/sketches/rectFill1/rectFill1.pde)

I've set the background color (using the background() call in setup()) and then, in draw(), I called fill() to change the default fill color. You can see that all the rectangles got filled with the new color, instead of the default color of white that was used in our earlier figures.

Now I'll change the fill color before each rectangle:

```
void draw() {
    fill(122, 99, 12);
    rect(40, 140, 80, 50);

    fill(194, 176, 100);
    rect(150, 140, 80, 50);

    fill(240, 231, 166);
    rect(260, 140, 80, 50);

    fill(198, 209, 173);
    rect(370, 140, 80, 50);
}
```

(See output in Figure 6.25. Full program in graphics/sketches/rectFill2/rectFill2.pde)

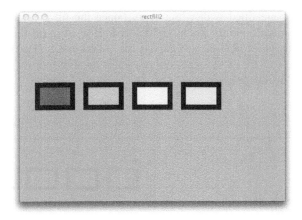

Figure 6.25. Changing the fill color for each rectangle.
(graphics/sketches/rectFill2/rectFill2.pde)

You can see that each rectangle gets filled with the color that's specified immediately before its drawn. So I change the current fill value, draw a rectangle, change the current fill, draw another rectangle, and so on.

The stroke is still black on all of them, so let's change that. To set a new stroke color, just pass that color to stroke(). Here, I'll just replace my calls to fill() with calls to stroke() (like fill(), stroke() can take one or three color values or take a color variable):

```
void draw() {
    stroke(122, 99, 12);
    rect(40, 140, 80, 50);

    stroke(194, 176, 100);
    rect(150, 140, 80, 50);

    stroke(240, 231, 166);
    rect(260, 140, 80, 50);

    stroke(198, 209, 173);
    rect(370, 140, 80, 50);
}
```

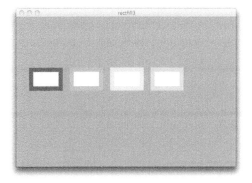

Figure 6.26. Changing the stroke color.
(graphics/sketches/rectfill3/rectfill3.pde)

(See output in Figure 6.26. Full program in graphics/sketches/rectfill3/rectfill3.pde)

Now the boxes are filled with white again (since the fill color is once again its default), but the lines around the boxes are colored. If we turn off the fill completely, we will see see only the strokes around the outside. To do that, call `noFill()`. From then on, until you call `fill()` again (with a color as an argument) everything you draw will have its insides left alone:

```
void draw() {
   noFill();
   rect(40, 140, 80, 50);
   rect(150, 140, 80, 50);
   rect(260, 140, 80, 50);
   rect(370, 140, 80, 50);
}
```

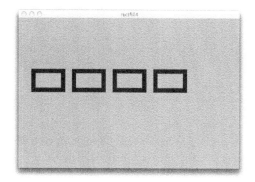

Figure 6.27. Rectangles with no fill.
(graphics/sketches/rectfill4/rectfill4.pde)

(See output in Figure 6.27. Full program in graphics/sketches/rectfill4/rectfill4.pde)

As you might guess, we can go the other way around: instead of calling `noFill()`, I'll call `noStroke()`. That will suppress the stroke (which would otherwise be drawn in the default black):

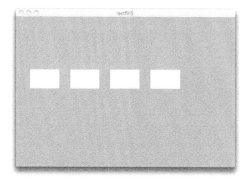

```
void draw() {
   noStroke();
   rect(40, 140, 80, 50);
   rect(150, 140, 80, 50);
   rect(260, 140, 80, 50);
   rect(370, 140, 80, 50);
}
```

Figure 6.28. Rectangles with no stroke.
(graphics/sketches/rectfill5/rectfill5.pde)

(See output in Figure 6.28. Full program in graphics/sketches/rectfill5/rectfill5.pde)

As we've seen, you can tell Processing how thick the stroke should be using the routine `strokeWeight()`, which lets you specify the thickness of the line in window units (normally, one unit is one pixel, but we'll see in Chapter 9 that you can change that).

In addition to using `strokeWeight()` to determine how thick a line is (the default is 1), you can also control the look of the ends of your lines with `strokeCap()`. This gives you a variety of ways to draw your line ends. The default setting is `strokeCap(ROUND)`, which puts a little circle at the end of each line. Here's an example where two lines meet in a V shape; in the lower pair I've drawn them in different colors to make each line more obvious:

```
void setup() {
   size(600, 400);
   background(224);
   strokeCap(ROUND);
   stroke(0);
   strokeWeight(30);
   line(100, 100, 300, 200);
   line(300, 200, 500, 100);

   stroke(196, 32, 83);  // red
   line(100, 200, 300, 300);
   stroke(28, 115, 45);  // green
   line(300, 300, 500, 200);
}
```

(See output in Figure 6.29. Full program in graphics/sketches/roundCaps1/roundCaps1.pde)

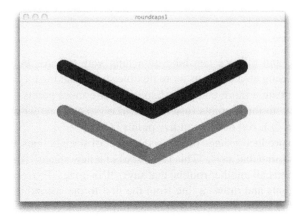

Figure 6.29. Rounded end caps. (graphics/sketches/roundcaps1/roundcaps1.pde)

Figure 6.30. ROUND, SQUARE, and PROJECT line ends and joins.

Rounded ends are nice because they cause the two line segments to join up smoothly. By calling strokeCap(SQUARE) or strokeCap(PROJECT), you can square-off the ends of your lines, which may give you the look you're after in some situations.

When you draw a bunch of lines using a beginShape()/endShape() pair (as we'll see in just a moment), you can exert similar control over the joints using the strokeJoin() function. Figure 6.30 shows how these look.

As I mentioned, all of these stroke and fill adjustments work on all the primitives we've seen so far: rectangle ellipses, arcs, triangles, and quads. Lines and points ignore the fill settings, taking their color from the current stroke.

With control over stroke and fill colors, this is a pretty good collection of geometric shapes, or primitives, that you can use to start building up more complicated graphics.

6.4   Irregular Shapes

Triangles, quads, and ellipses can take us a long way towards building interesting shapes, but Processing also offers us more flexible shape-making tools as well.

One way to create a more complex shape is to use more points. We've seen how to make a shape with three points (use triangle()) and one with four points (use rect() or quad()). But how about five points? Or 13?

If you want to produce a shape out of any number of straight lines, the mechanism is to call a special routine that says, "This is the start of a new shape." Then you provide a bunch of points, and call another routine that says, "I'm done." Processing then bundles up all of those points and draws a line from the first to the second to the third and so on. It even fills the shape when it's done (assuming you haven't disabled filling with noFill(), of course).

The opening and closing routines to this process are called beginShape() and endShape(). In between, you call vertex() once for each point.

Let's build a simple seven-point leaf object using these calls. In Figure 6.31 I've drawn a leaf with points named a through g. In the code, I'll refer to their x and y values as ax and ay, then bx and by, and so on.

In setup(), I'll create the window and set the background color. I'll call strokeWeight() with an argument of three, so that the line around the leaf is 3 pixels thick and a little easier to see. I'll also call strokeJoin(ROUND). As we saw a moment ago, this helps the lines join up nicely.

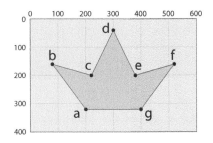

Figure 6.31. A simple leaf of seven points.

I'll also call smooth(), which we haven't seen before. In general, Processing tries to draw your graphics quickly, so that it can finish drawing in the time available between frames. But if you're willing to let it take a little more time, it can improve a few of the details in your images so that they look a little nicer. Taken together, these image-improving techniques are called *anti-aliasing*. Often the results of anti-aliasing are subtle, but taken together, they usually help your lines look a little smoother (hence the name of the function call), and some of the edges of your shapes that might otherwise have looked a little ragged come out nice and clean. Because it's not necessary to use smooth() to illustrate most of the ideas we'll be talking about, I won't bother to call smooth() much in this book. That's not because I don't like how it looks, but rather just because I want to save a single line of code on every example, and make the examples in this book just that little bit easier to read.

But you can always put a call to smooth() into any sketch (most frequently, right after calling size()), and though the resulting images will take a little longer to get drawn, they'll usually look at least a little better, and sometimes they'll look a lot better.

We'll talk about *renderers* near the end of this chapter; they're the software libraries that actually create the graphics you see on the screen. Processing lets you choose among several different renderers, each with their own strengths and weaknesses. Some renderers ignore smooth() because they don't support anti-aliasing, other renderers ignore it because they do anti-aliasing all the time and can't turn it off. The default renderer, which we've been using so far, does pay attention to this call.

If you want to disable anti-aliasing, call noSmooth(). Just as with turning anti-aliasing on, this command will turn anti-aliasing off if your renderer supports that.

Next I'll call drawLeaf(). That routine will simply call beginShape(), name all seven points using vertex(), and wrap up by calling endShape(). The routine vertex() takes two values (or three, as we'll see in Chapter 21), and simply adds that point to the growing list that began when you called beginShape().

To create the x and y values for each of these points I simply drew my leaf on a piece of graph paper, and then read off the x and y values for each point. I moved them around a couple of times before I decided that these positions looked good to me.

```
float ax = 200;   float ay = 320;
float bx =  80;   float by = 160;
float cx = 220;   float cy = 200;
float dx = 300;   float dy =  40;
float ex = 380;   float ey = 200;
float fx = 520;   float fy = 160;
float gx = 400;   float gy = 320;

void setup() {
    size(600, 400);
    background(222, 217, 177);
    fill(131, 209, 119);
    strokeWeight(3);
    strokeJoin(ROUND);
    smooth();
    drawLeaf();
}

void drawLeaf() {
    beginShape();
    vertex(ax, ay);
    vertex(bx, by);
    vertex(cx, cy);
    vertex(dx, dy);
    vertex(ex, ey);
    vertex(fx, fy);
    vertex(gx, gy);
    endShape();
}
```

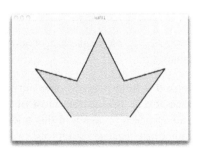

Figure 6.32. A simple leaf with beginShape() and endShape(). (graphics/sketches/leaf01/leaf01.pde)

(See output in Figure 6.32. Full program in graphics/sketches/leaf01/leaf01.pde)

That's a lot of code! But if we take it in chunks, it's not so bad. The first chunk just defines the *x* and *y* values for each point. The second chunk is setup(), and it does a few housekeeping chores in sequence: it creates the window, clears it to the background color, sets some values in the graphics state, and then calls drawLeaf(). Finally, drawLeaf() does nothing but call beginShape(), name each point in sequence, hand it to Processing using vertex(), and then wrap up with a call to endShape().

Notice that this leaf doesn't *close*. That is, the black stroke doesn't run all the way around. That's because the last point (point g) isn't the same as the first, so there's no line from point g to point a. The green fill does close the gap, because it has to draw some kind of filled-in region. But Processing is just making a guess here and finishing the fill by joining the last point to the first one. That's a good guess, but it's not always right.

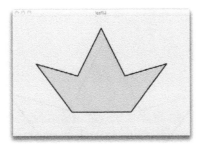

Figure 6.33. Closing the leaf by repeating the first point. (graphics/sketches/leaf02/leaf02.pde)

If we want to close off the figure, we have two choices. The first is to explicitly repeat the first point (a) again at the end of the vertex() list. That will create another line in the figure from g to a:

```
void drawLeaf() {
   beginShape();
   vertex(ax, ay);
   vertex(bx, by);
   vertex(cx, cy);
   vertex(dx, dy);
   vertex(ex, ey);
   vertex(fx, fy);
   vertex(gx, gy);
   vertex(ax, ay);
   endShape();
}
```

(See output in Figure 6.33. Full program in graphics/sketches/leaf02/leaf02.pde)

An easier way to achieve the same result is to tell endShape() to explicitly close the shape itself. You do this by giving it the argument CLOSE (as always, case matters):

```
void drawLeaf() {
   beginShape();
   vertex(ax, ay);
   vertex(bx, by);
   vertex(cx, cy);
   vertex(dx, dy);
   vertex(ex, ey);
   vertex(fx, fy);
   vertex(gx, gy);
   endShape(CLOSE);
}
```

(See output in Figure 6.34. Full program in graphics/sketches/leaf03new/leaf03new.pde)

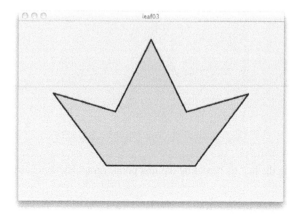

Figure 6.34. Closing the leaf with endShape(CLOSE).
(graphics/sketches/leaf03new/leaf03new.pde)

That gets us to the same result, but we don't have to repeat the first point. This form is especially useful when we're computing the points rather than just using existing variables, as we're doing here. If you had to repeat the first point to close the shape, you'd either have to save it, or compute it again. With endShape(CLOSE), you let Processing remember (and repeat) the first point for you.

In my example above, I called beginShape() with no arguments. That tells it to interpret each vertex as another point in a list, one after the other, that should be joined up into a single big shape. And that was just what we wanted.

But beginShape() can interpret the points in a bunch of different ways, or modes. You tell it which mode you want with an optional argument. We've seen the default (no argument) version already. Let's run through three of the options (each one of these is ended with a call to endShape() that can take either no arguments, or CLOSE).

No Argument. The points are joined up with lines to create a shape. The current fill and stroke settings are used to draw the shape (including noFill() and noStroke(), if you want to suppress either of those qualities).

POINTS. The points are drawn as single points. The value of strokeWeight() tells Processing how big the points should be (the default is one pixel), and the color of the stroke sets the color of the points.

```
beginShape(POINTS);
```

(See output in Figure 6.35. Full program in graphics/sketches/leaf04new/leaf04new.pde)

Figure 6.35. beginShape(POINTS). (graphics/sketches/leaf04new/leaf04new.pde)

LINES. Your input is interpreted as a sequence of independent lines, each made of two points. So a line is drawn between the first and second points, then another line between the third and fourth points, and so on, taking the points in pairs. No filling is done, even if you've specified a fill color. The value of strokeWeight() tells Processing how thick the lines should be (the default is one pixel). This style is useful for drawing a sequence of lines with just one function call.

```
beginShape(LINES);
```

(See output in Figure 6.36. Full program in graphics/sketches/leaf05new/leaf05new.pde)

We'll see in Chapter 21 that we can give beginShape() other arguments that let us build up complicated shapes more efficiently. Those modes are primarily of value when we're making 3D images; in 2D, the no argument form of beginShape() is most common, with the POINTS and LINES forms of occasional value. In Chapter 16, we'll see that we can give additional optional arguments to vertex() that will allow us to attach a photograph (or other image) to a shape as we draw it.

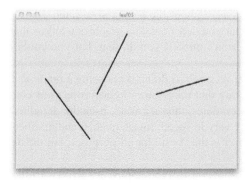

Figure 6.36. beginShape(LINES). (graphics/sketches/leaf05new/leaf05new.pde)

6.5   Graphics Windows

So far, I've been pretty casual about how I've started up the graphics window. I just called `size()` inside of `setup()` and I figured all the work was done. That was a pretty fair assumption, but let's look a little deeper.

The function `size()` actually does two things. The first and most obvious step is that it sets the size of the graphics window on your screen. From then on, the system variables `width` and `height` contain the size of that window, so it's easy for us to later get the size of the window in another part of the program.

Both `width` and `height` are truly variables, by the way, and you can assign new values to them. This will trick Processing into thinking that the window is larger (or smaller) than it actually is, but it won't cause the window to change. Modifying Processing's internal representation of the window size this way is a risky thing to do, because once you've changed one of these variables, unless you squirreled its previous value away yourself, you'll never be able to recover the size of your window. So I recommend that you never do that and treat these as *read-only* variables, that is, variables that you never change. A better way to make your pictures bigger or smaller is to use the transformation commands that we'll see in Chapter 9.

Both `width` and `height` are integers, so if you want to divide them by something, remember that dividing one integer by another throws away any fractional part. So if I want to find the middle of the screen, I compute the points as `width/2.0` and `height/2.0`, where the floating-point `2.0` guarantees me a floating-point value as a result (as we've seen, writing `2.` or `2f` would have been just as good as `2.0`).

Along with these variables that tell you the size of the graphics window, you can find out the size of the screen itself (that is, your graphics monitor) by looking at two *properties* of the global variable `screen`. A property is like a variable that belongs to an object. You get at a property by naming the object, then giving a period and the name of the property. In this case, the object is `screen` and the properties are `width` and `height`, so `screen.width` and `screen.height` tell you the dimensions of your display.

Normally, you only care about the screen size when you're first setting up your graphics window, so that you don't create a graphics window that's larger than can be displayed (the system won't mind if you do that, but you could end up drawing stuff that nobody will see).

The other thing that `size()` is doing is choosing a *renderer* for you. The renderer is the underlying software that takes care of converting your commands into pictures. If you don't specify a renderer, then `size()` uses the default. But not all renderers are created equal. They vary in speed, image quality, and number of features. Unfortunately, no single renderer is the "best" for all purposes, but the default is a pretty good choice in general.

We'll see in the discussion of typography in Chapter 20 that some renderers are capable of producing beautiful typography in some situations, but lousy typography in others. And it's a sad fact, but true, that some renderers have bugs in them. The challenge of getting complex software to work across many different types of hardware, software, and operating systems is a formidable one, and not every renderer has completely conquered every problem. In fact, some renderers specifically ignore some function calls that they either cannot handle or are known to mishandle. These things all change with time, as new versions of Processing are released.

To specify a particular renderer, you name it as a third option in `size()`. So if you want, for example, the P2D renderer for a window that's 600 by 400 pixels, you'd say `size(600, 400, P2D)`.

Here's a short summary of the five standard renderers. If you want to use one of the nondefault renderers, I suggest consulting the latest release notes so that you can review the known limitations and bugs for that version of the renderer.

JAVA2D. The default renderer. It's usually not the fastest one, but it has the most features and usually produces good results. Almost all of the examples in this book were produced with the JAVA2D renderer, since they don't specify a different choice with a third argument in `size()`.

P2D. The "Processing 2D" renderer. On many systems, it will run faster than the default, but the images might not look quite as nice.

P3D. The "Processing 3D" renderer. If you get into working with 3D objects and you want your pictures to look the same on every computer, this is the one to pick. It does all of its work in software, so it cuts a lot of corners in the interest of speed (which can create artifacts in your images that you may find objectionable, but at least those same artifacts will appear on everyone's screen).

OPENGL. This is a high-quality 3D renderer based on the OpenGL (pronounced "Open-G-L") standard. It's a great all-around renderer and can make use of 3D hardware if it's installed on the machine. To use this renderer, you have to include this line at the top of your sketch:

```
import processing.opengl.*;
```

The drawback is that not every computer supports every option in the OpenGL standard, and different hardware and software can produce different results. So your images and animations might look different on different computers. The developers and programmers behind OpenGL work hard to minimize these differences, but it's difficult to iron them all out.

PDF. This renderer saves your drawings directly to a PDF format file. To use this renderer, you have to include this line at the top of your sketch:

```
import processing.pdf.*;
```

To view a PDF file, you'll need software that can read and display PDF images; happily, there are many such programs available for free for all platforms. One big advantage of a PDF file is that it's *resolution independent*, meaning that you can blow it up to a large size and things will still look great. We'll see more on this in Chapter 17.

Although you'll probably never need to adjust any of these renderers, you can set some of their internal parameters using the `hint()` routine. The information passed into `hint()` varies for each renderer and can change with each release, so check the documentation for your version of Processing if you need to tweak the renderer settings this way.

Chapter 7
Human Input

Here's another little toy program to fool around with while we're building up our Processing skills. As always, feel free to play around with the numbers. This one's particularly fun to watch while it runs.

```
void setup() {
  size(600, 400);
  smooth();
  noStroke();
}

void draw() {
  background(255);
  pushMatrix();
  translate(width/2, height/2);
  fill(0, 0, 0);
  drawStar();
  popMatrix();

  pushMatrix();
  translate(width/2, height/2);  // mouse input will go here
  rotate(TWO_PI * frameCount/800);
  translate(0, 70);
  fill(0, 0, 0);
  drawStar();
  popMatrix();
}

void drawStar() {
  int numSpokes = 100;
  for (int i=0; i<numSpokes; i++) {
    float t0 = map(i, 0, numSpokes-1, 0, TWO_PI);
    float t1 = t0 + (TWO_PI/(2*numSpokes));
```

Figure 7.1. An animated Moire effect
(frame from animation). (human/sketches/moire1/moire1.pde)

```
    arc(0, 0, 1000, 1000, t0, t1);
  }
}
```

(See output in Figure 7.1. Full program in human/sketches/moire1/moire1.pde)

To control this with your mouse, change the line with the comment to this:

```
translate(mouseX, mouseY);
```

(See output in Figure 7.2. Full program in human/sketches/moire2/moire2.pde)

A big part of the fun of Processing is that your programs can be interactive, respond-ing to your actions as they run. There are two principal devices that you can use to talk to the computer: the keyboard and the mouse.

This isn't the whole list, of course. People are cooking up new kinds of input meth-ods all the time. For instance, some VJs use Processing as part of their rig during dances and events, creating images based on the music that's being played. But let's stick with the keyboard and mouse for now.

I'll start with the mouse.

Design first: what actions should we take based on the mouse position? I'm going to pick up with the program we wrote in Chapter 4 that changes the color in the background of the graphics window. To keep things simple, the horizontal position of the mouse will

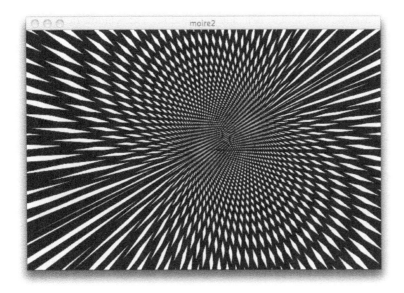

Figure 7.2. Controlling the Moire effect with your mouse (frame from animation). (human/sketches/moire2/moire2.pde)

control the red component of the background color, so moving to the right will make the red component bigger. And the vertical position of the mouse will control the green component, so moving the mouse down will make the green component brighter. Poor blue is left out of this for the moment.

Because dealing with the mouse is so useful in Processing, it's designed to be easy. The system creates and maintains two variables for you, named mouseX and mouseY (as elsewhere in Processing, the capitalization is important, even in camel-case variables like these). The values of these variables tell you where the mouse is *in Processing's graphics window*.

This is important: on most systems, when you move your mouse outside of the graphics window that Processing creates for you in response to your call to size(), Processing loses the ability to respond to the mouse; your computer presumes you mean to be pointing at something else on your screen, and it doesn't even bother to tell Processing you're out there. Processing will continue calling draw() at the current frame rate (typically 60 times a second), but the variables mouseX and mouseY won't change no matter what you do with the mouse. In fact, they will simply hold the last values they had from when your mouse was in the window. Processing only knows what your operating system tells it, and the operating system won't tell Processing anything if your mouse isn't inside the graphics window. This makes sense. Why should Processing change an animation on one part of the screen when you're clicking around inside a web browser somewhere else?

So let's assume your mouse is inside the window. The window defines an x, y grid. The origin of the grid—that is, point (0,0)—is at the upper-left. The coordinates run like you read a page in a book: left to right, top to bottom. So increasing values of x go to the right, and increasing values of y go down.

If (0,0) is at the upper left, what's the value of the point in the lower right? It doesn't have a formal name, but it's easy to determine: it's what we told Processing it should be! In my standard skeleton version of `setup()`, I call `size(600, 400)`. That means that the window should be 600 pixels wide and 400 pixels high. The mouse coordinates are in pixels, so the right edge is 600 pixels from the left, and the bottom edge is 400 pixels from the top. So as we move the mouse around in the window, Processing is constantly updating the values of the variables `mouseX` and `mouseY`. If we use those variables in our program, we will automatically be using their most recent values.

Here's another thing that might seem weird on first reading but will very soon become second nature to you: *computers start counting at zero*. If you have five apples, humans number them 1, 2, 3, 4, 5, but the computer numbers them 0, 1, 2, 3, 4. That's weird. But it's such a perfect way to do things when you're programming that almost every language on the planet does it that way. Once you start programming larger programs, particularly those using loops (as we'll discuss in Chapter 8), you'll come to love this approach too. But if you haven't seen this before, it might seem strange. And here's that strangeness in action: what's the value of the mouse's x-coordinate when the mouse is at the far right of the window?

We've told Processing that the window is 600 units across; think of it as a giant grid with 600 boxes laid out in a row. The computer starts labeling with 0. So the first box is 0, so when the mouse is in that box, the value of `mouseX` will be 0. The box to its right is 1, so when the mouse is in that box, `mouseX` has the value 1. And so on. What's the number of the rightmost box?

It's 599. If we started counting at one, we'd have boxes numbered 1, 2, ... 598, 599, 600. That's 600 boxes. But because we're starting at zero, we end one number sooner: 0, 1, ... 597, 598, 599. If you resist this way of thinking and try to stick with the counting numbers (1, 2, 3...), then it's going to hurt your brain, because you're always going to be one off every time you count things. So I suggest keeping the ideas separate. When you're counting things as a human, start at one. When you're counting things in your program, you start at zero. Forgetting this leads you to get results that are off by one. Such problems are (reasonably) called *off-by-one errors*. They tend to show up as odd things that happen at the fringes of your code, when something happens one time too many or one time too few.

For example, you might write a program that's supposed to draw 12 eggs in basket. But when you run the program, you find that it draws 11 or 13. That's probably an off-by-one error. Don't sweat these things too much now. If you find your program is off by one, keep these ideas in mind, make sure you start counting at zero, and you'll be able to set things right. Gradually, it'll become second nature. Better yet, you'll like it this way. This rule of starting from zero isn't something that's been forced on us by cruel Martians; it's a deliberate design decision that's been adopted by the creators of almost every computer language ever written. And people keep defining languages that way because it works so well for programs. Starting with zero turns out to be such a convenient way to do all kinds of programming tasks that it's worth the initial strangeness.

Now we can finally see why color values end at 255 and not 256. With one byte (eight bits), you can store 256 different values. Since the computer starts with 0 as one of those values, the last one is 255.

So because our window is 600 units wide, the variable mouseX will take on the values from 0 to 599. Similarly, the variable mouseY will have the values 0 to 399.

How do we convert these into a color component? Let's look at the x value first. We've seen that that's going to range from 0 to 599 as the mouse moves from the left to the right of the window. What we'd like is to compute a value for the red component of the color such that it's 0 at the left (when mouseX is 0) and 255 at the right (when mouseX is 599).

This is a standard problem in computer graphics, and it comes up all the time. So Processing offers us some helpful tools to carry off just this kind of job. Let's take a look.

7.1   Interpolation

Surprise! You just walked into your home and a group of friends jumped out, waving their arms and smiling. They've thrown you a surprise birthday party!

After cake and ice cream, one of your friends asks you, "On a scale of 1 to 10, how surprised were you?" You might look inwardly for a second and try to get a feeling for how surprised you were. Then you compare this to your own personal range of "surprise" and decide you were quite surprised, and so on a scale of 1 to 10, that might be a 9.

Your friend could have asked you to describe your level of surprise on lots of different scales. Maybe by holding out your hands (palm to palm would be no surprise, arms stretched out wide would be huge surprise), or maybe on a scale of height (how high did you jump), and so on. In each case you need to determine your amount of surprise, find out where it is on your internal scale, and then translate that into the scale the person is looking for.

We need to do this numerically all the time when programming. We have a number that we know is within some range, and we want to find its corresponding location in another range.

We also do this all the time in real life. For example, suppose someone tells you the temperature outside in degrees Celsius. In that scale, water freezes at 0 degrees and boils at 100 degrees. But you want the temperature in Fahrenheit, where water freezes at 32 degrees and boils at 212 degrees. Somehow you have to convert the temperature from the range 0 to 100 to the range 32 to 212. Happily, Processing gives us a great little built-in routine to do exactly that.

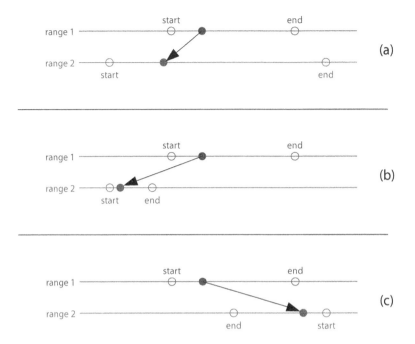

Figure 7.3. The map() function. (a) The two ranges overlap. (b) The second range does not overlap with the first. (c) The second range overlaps with the first, but runs from right to left.

The routine map() takes five arguments. First comes the number you want to translate. Then come the start and end values of the input range and then the start and end values of the output range. Figure 7.3 shows the idea graphically. Typically, your starting value will lie somewhere between the low and high values of the input range, but it doesn't have to.

In the figure, the red range is the first range and the blue is the second. We give map() the two ranges and the location of the solid red dot in the first range, and it will return the value of the solid blue dot in the second range.

In each of the examples in the figure, the solid red dot is 25 percent of the way from the start to the end of the red range, so map() will position the blue dot at 25 percent of the way from the start to the end of the blue range.

Notice that the ranges don't have to be the same size. They don't have to overlap. In fact, they don't have to be related in any way. As far as map() is concerned, it just gets five numbers; it's up to us to interpret them. In part (c) I've reversed the blue range, so the starting value is larger than the ending value; map() doesn't mind a bit, and, as before, finds the location that's 25 percent of the way from start to end.

To convert a temperature degreesCelsius to another variable named degreesFahrenheit, we could use map() like this:

```
degreesFahrenheit = map(degreesCelsius, 0, 100, 32, 212);
```

That's all there is to it!

It takes the input value (degreesCelsius), finds out where that's located in the range from 0 to 100, and returns its corresponding position in the range from 32 to 212.

One of the nice features of map() is that it doesn't just rescale the value we're interested in (as we might when converting from, say, pounds to kilograms). Instead, it finds where that value is in one range and tells us where it would be in a second, entirely unrelated range.

Let's look at using map() with a variety of different inputs:

```
void setup() {
    float r1 = 10.0;
    float r2 = 20.0;
    float s1 = 30.0;
    float s2 = 40.0;
    float a = 12.0;
    showmap(a, r1, r2, s1, s2);
    showmap(a, r2, r1, s1, s2);
    showmap(a, r1, r2, s2, s1);
    showmap(a, r2, r1, s2, s1);
}

void showmap(float a, float rlo, float rhi, float slo, float shi)
{
    println("map "+a+" from ("+rlo+", "+rhi+") to ("+slo+", "+shi+") = "+
        map(a,rlo,rhi,slo,shi));
}
```

(Full program in human/sketches/map1/map1.pde)

It produces this output:

```
map 12.0 from (10.0, 20.0) to (30.0, 40.0) = 32.0
map 12.0 from (20.0, 10.0) to (30.0, 40.0) = 38.0
map 12.0 from (10.0, 20.0) to (40.0, 30.0) = 38.0
map 12.0 from (20.0, 10.0) to (40.0, 30.0) = 32.0
```

Does this make sense? Sure does.

I've illustrated the four cases in Figure 7.4.

The first line is no surprise. We're giving map() the first range from 10 to 20 (in that order) and the second range from 30 to 40 (in that order). The arrows in part (a) of the figure match that: they both start with the smaller value in the range and point to the larger one. Since 12 is 20 percent of the way from 10 to 20, we get back the value 32, which is 20 percent of the way from 30 to 40.

The second line mixes things up a little, because now the first range runs in the opposite direction, from 20 to 10, as shown in part (b). Now the input value, 12, is 80

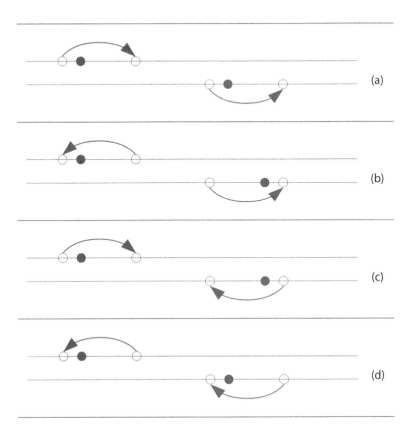

Figure 7.4. Illustrating different calls to map(). Each arrow starts at the first value in the range and ends at the second. (a) Both ranges run left to right. (b) The red range runs right to left. (c) The blue range runs right to left. (d) Both ranges run right to left.

percent of the way from the start (20) to the end (10). So we get back an output value that's 80 percent of the way from the output range's start to its end, or 38.

The third line flips things the other way, as shown in part (c). The input range is again from 10 to 20, so the input value is 20 percent along. But I've reverse the output range, so it now runs from 40 to 30. And 20 percent of the way from 40 to 30 is just 38.

Finally, part (d) of the figure shows when both ranges run from large to small. Again, the value 12 is now 80 percent of the way through the range, and thus we get a value that's 80 percent of the way through the output range, which is 32.

So map() is remarkably egalitarian: it doesn't care about the directions of the two ranges, whether they overlap or not, or even whether the input value is within the starting range or not. Many people (including me) often refer to the start and end values of these ranges as the "low" and "high" values, since that's how they're most frequently used, but that can be misleading. As we've seen, the first value can be larger than the second. But because the majority of the time people use map() by giving the ranges in ascending order, so the language has stuck. Just don't forget that map() can handle either range going in either direction, and the input need not even be in the first range.

We will use map() frequently in this book, and I encourage you to use it freely in your own code.

Not every language offers a map() function, and rather than write their own, many programmers directly type in the expressions needed to convert one range to another, essentially creating their own specialized one-time-use version of map(). I'll show you such a use here so you can see not only how much nicer it is to use map() but so you can recognize this other technique when you see it.

For example, suppose you're creating an animation to show the progress of your favorite cycling team in a multiday race. Today's race starts at mile 17 and runs to mile 34. Your graphics will show the position of the team on a map on the screen. Luckily, today's route is perfectly straight, so the 17-mile stretch corresponds to a straight line on your screen. On the map, this line starts at $x = 25$ and is 25 pixels long. So we need to convert a variable mileage from 17 to 34 to a variable xLocation from 25 to 50.

Here are two lines to calculate that value. They compute identical results, but the second one implements the map() operation explicitly:

```
// compute the location using map()
float xLocation1 = map(mileage, 17.0, 34.0, 25.0, 50.0);

// compute the location explicitly
float xLocation2 = 25.0+(((mileage-17.0)/(34.0-17.0))*(50.0-25.0));
```

The second version is a mess! Obviously, we could simplify some of those expressions (for example, we could write 25.0 instead of 50.0-25.0), but lines like this one are, sadly, not uncommon.

When you use map(), your code is clear and easy to write and maintain. I think it's a great little utility.

A related idea is *interpolation*. An interpolation technique is a method for smoothly changing one value into another. You usually use this when you have the starting and ending values for some range, and you want to get a value between them.

For example, suppose your animation has a balloon floating across the screen. You know where the balloon starts, and you know where it ends 60 frames later. For each in-between frame, you need to somehow calculate an in-between value. In other words, you need to interpolate the starting and ending values.

There are endless ways to do this. But more times than not, the very simplest method is just fine. This method is called *linear interpolation*. Here, *linear* means "straight line." The idea is that you draw a straight line from your starting value to your ending value, and you can find any in-between value by finding its position on that line. Figure 7.5 shows the idea graphically.

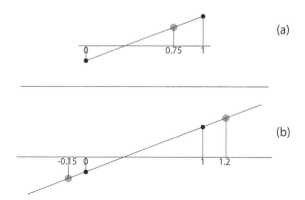

Figure 7.5. Linear interpolation. (a) Interpolating a value between 0 and 1. (b) Interpolating a value at −0.15, which is outside the (0,1) range.

To perform a linear interpolation in Processing, you use the built-in function `lerp()` (that's a common contraction of the full name "linear interpolation"). You give three values to `lerp()`: the starting and ending points of your variable and a control value. The control typically has the values 0 to 1. When the control is 0, you get back the low end of the range. When the control is 1, you get back the high end. When the control is in between, you get back the corresponding in-between value. So if the control is, say, 0.25, then you get back a number that's one-quarter of the way from the low end to the high end of the range.

Figure 7.5 (a) shows a pair of values corresponding to 0 and 1, and I've marked in red the value that would result if we asked `lerp()` for the value corresponding to a control of 0.75, or three-quarters of the way from 0 to 1. You can see that the values in between the two extremes are figured out by imagining a straight line from the value at 0 to the value at 1, hence, *linear* blending, or interpolation.

If you give `lerp()` a control value outside the range 0 to 1, it will give you back the value corresponding to a position on the line passing through the input points. Usually that will give you a number that's less than the low end (if the control is less than 0) or more than the high end (if the control is more than 1). Figure 7.5 (b) shows a couple of queries from the same pair of numbers I used in part (a), except I'm using one control value less than 0 and another greater than 1.

You'll often see the control variable named `t`; that's just a long-standing convention. It's also often called `alpha` (from the mathematical equation that describes how `lerp()` works), but `alpha` is a reserved word in Processing, so sometimes people just call it something like `myAlpha` or the deliberate misspelling `alfa`, or they just use the letter a instead. Of course, you can name the control variable anything you like; these are just common names.

Figure 7.6 shows a little animated example of `lerp()` in action. You can run the sketch yourself; it's in the same directory as the other sketches in this chapter and is

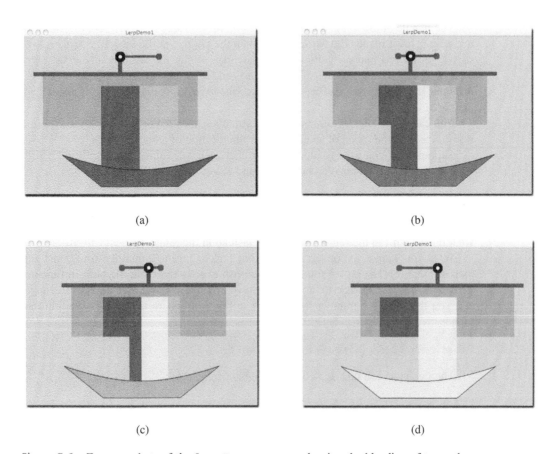

Figure 7.6. Four snapshots of the `lerpDemo` program, showing the blending of two colors using `lerp()`. The handle changes the lerp value from 0 to 1, changing the amount of red and yellow that flows into the bowl below. (a) The control variable is at 0, giving us a red result. (b) The control variable is at 1/3, so we get an orange color that is 2/3 red and 1/3 yellow. (c) The control variable is at 2/3, so we get an orange color that is 1/3 red and 2/3 yellow. (d) The control variable is at 1, giving us a yellow result. (human/sketches/lerpDemo/lerpDemo.pde)

called `lerpDemo` (I won't discuss the internals of the sketch here because we haven't yet covered everything that goes into it, but feel free to read it and mess around with it if you like.)

In Figure 7.6 there's a pair of colored boxes in the upper part of the screen: one red and one yellow. Mixing red and yellow light gives us orange. Superimposed over the color sources is a gray window that can be moved left and right with the little black-and-white handle at the top. Any part of each color that isn't covered flows downward, into the bowl, where the colors mix.

The handle at the top is a graphical version of the value of control that we give to lerp() as it blends the two colors. When the knob is at the far left, control=0, so we get all red and no yellow, as in part (a). When the knob is at the far right, control=1, so we get all yellow and no red, as in part (d). In between, we get different shades of orange. Parts (b) and (c) show values for control of about 1/3 and 2/3.

You can use lerp() to blend anything that's controlled by numbers: the size of a flower's leaves, the speed of an airplane, or the location of a hockey puck.

Suppose that you want to blend (or lerp) between two values, say out1 and out2. If your control variable var is between 0 and 1, you could write

```
float newValue = lerp(out1, out2, var);
```

As var goes from 0 to 1, the value of newValue will go from out1 to out2. But what if var isn't in the range 0 to 1 but is instead in the range, say, in1 to in2?

What you want is to convert a value from in1 to in2 to a number from 0 to 1 and then use that for lerp(). You can accomplish exactly that with the built-in function norm(). Just give norm() a value, followed by the low and high ends of its range, and you'll get back a number from 0 to 1 telling you where that value is within that range:

```
float var0to1 = norm(var, in1, in2);
```

Then you can use that as a control variable to lerp():

```
float var0to1 = norm(var, in1, in2);
float newValue = lerp(out1, out2, var0to1);
```

And of course you could roll these together:

```
float newValue = lerp(out1, out2, norm(var, in1, in2));
```

If something's tickling at the back of your brain, you've jumped a step ahead of me. This combination of lerp() and norm() is the same thing as map()! In fact, map() is just a one-stop shopping convenience that computes the very same result:

```
float newValue1 = lerp(out1, out2, norm(var, in1, in2));
float newValue2 = map(var, in1, in2, out1, out2);
```

In this fragment, both newValue1 and newValue2 have identical results.

Careful! Important! In both map() and norm() the control value comes *first* in the argument list. In lerp() it comes *last*. That trips me up all the time. If your interpolations come out wacky, then make sure you're putting the control value in the right place for each of these routines.

Let's use map() to solve our mouse-positioning issue. The numbers that come to us via mouseX are from 0 to 599. We want to turn those into numbers from 0 to 255.

So we want to tell map() to take mouseX, find where it is from 0 to 599, and give us a number at the same relative position in the range 0 to 255. We just need to give it those five numbers:

```
float mouseX0to255 = map(mouseX, 0, 599, 0, 255);
```

Without map() we'd have had to write some little equations. But this one-liner does all the work for us.

Note that Processing might be updating the value of mouseX dozens or even hundreds of times a second. Every time the mouse twitches, the values are updated. Most of those values are lost to the sands of time. What matters is that when this line is executed, the most recent value of mouseX is used, and that tells us where the mouse is right now.

If you're feeling adventurous, come up with a similar statement to calculate the value of the green component. Remember that the window is 400 units high.

Here's my solution, integrated into our color-changing program:

```
float Redval = 192;  // background red
float Grnval = 64;   // background green
float Bluval = 0;    // background blue
color MyColor;

void setup() {
   size(600, 400);
   MyColor = color(Redval, Grnval, Bluval);
   background(MyColor);
}

void draw() {
   Redval = map(mouseX, 0, 599, 0, 255); // convert 0-599 to 0-255
   Grnval = map(mouseY, 0, 399, 0, 255); // convert 0-399 to 0-255
   background(MyColor);
   MyColor = color(Redval, Grnval, Bluval);
}
```

(Full program in human/sketches/mouse1/mouse1.pde)

I set my globals to be of type float because that's what comes out of map(). Since color() is happy to take float values for input, it's just simplest to make everything a floating-point number, even though I know that mouseX and mouseY are always integers.

Try fooling around with this. As the mouse moves right, the background gets more red. As it moves down, it gets more green. Moving into the lower right gives you a blend of red and green (which makes yellow).

7.2 Mouse Buttons

The mouse has buttons, so let's use them! Processing maintains another variable called mousePressed. This is a boolean, so it has only two possible values: true or false.

Let's add some code to make the background go white as long as a mouse button is pressed (I'm only going to show draw() here, since the rest of the program will be unchanged):

```
void draw() {
   Redval = map(mouseX, 0, 599, 0, 255);
   Grnval = map(mouseY, 0, 399, 0, 255);
   MyColor = color(Redval, Grnval, Bluval);
   if (mousePressed == true) {
      background(255, 255, 255);
   } else {
      background(MyColor);
   }
}
```

(Full program in human/sketches/mouse2/mouse2.pde)

Try it out!

Let's bring blue back into the game. Remember that I'm using global variables for the red, green, and blue values, so they're always around each time we enter draw(). So let's say that if the mouse button is pressed, the horizontal position of the mouse sets the blue value. If the mouse isn't pressed, the horizontal position of the mouse sets the red and green values as before:

```
void draw() {
   if (mousePressed == true) {
      Bluval = map(mouseX, 0, 599, 0, 255);
   } else {
      Redval = map(mouseX, 0, 599, 0, 255);
      Grnval = map(mouseY, 0, 399, 0, 255);
   }
   MyColor = color(Redval, Grnval, Bluval);
   background(MyColor);
}
```

(Full program in human/sketches/mouse3/mouse3.pde)

Now when the mouse button is pushed, the horizonal position of the mouse sets the amount of blue, and otherwise, it sets the amount of red. This is kind of fun to play with. If you click the button near the left side of the screen, then red and green will be very dark, and moving the mouse to the right with the button down will get you a brighter blue background. If you click near the right side of the screen, then red and green will have large values, and moving to the left will reduce the amount of blue, changing the color from white to yellow.

By the way, note that my test reads

```
if (mousePressed == true)
```

Something's funny about that. The variable `mousePressed` is a `boolean`, so it has the value `true` or `false`. The result of the test is either `true` or `false`. So the test is redundant. We could just test the value of `mousePressed` all by itself:

```
if (mousePressed)
```

That's neater and cleaner. But you'll still see people testing `boolean` variables this way. I'll admit I sometimes use the redundant test for `true` myself, just to emphasize the fact that the variable I'm testing is a `boolean`, but it's definitely redundant. You'll also see tests like this:

```
if (mousePressed == false)
```

You could write this more simply using the `!` operator, which, you'll recall, turns `true` into `false`, and vice-versa:

```
if (!mousePressed)
```

Again, both of these tests achieve the same results. I find that explicitly testing for `false` sometimes makes it clearer to see what's happening at a glance, but it's really just a question of personal style.

Testing the value of `mousePressed` every time we go through `draw()` certainly works, but Processing offers us a different way to get to the same result, and this alternative is usually a better way to go. There's a philosophy in Processing that you should keep your `draw()` routine as short and simple as possible. After all, `draw()` gets called for every frame, and it's where your program will probably spend the majority of its time. The faster `draw()` can run, the more responsive your program will be. And the smaller and more compact the source code for `draw()` is, the more likely you can keep it narrowly focused.

Our version of `draw()` here is pretty darned short, but we can make it even shorter by taking out the whole testing clause. In fact, we'll be able to return from `draw()` almost as soon as it's been called.

To set the stage for this revision, note that the colors only change when the mouse actually moves. So if the mouse hasn't moved, the colors haven't changed, and we can return from `draw()` immediately. It would be nice if, instead of testing the conditions of the mouse and then executing code, we could have Processing automatically call routines for us when a mouse button goes down or the mouse moves.

Processing offers us just this ability. The trick is that it has predefined names for the routines it will call in certain situations. If you have written a routine with that name,

Processing will call it for you automatically at the right time (we've already seen this; for example, if we have implemented a draw() routine, Processing will call it at the start of every frame).

If you don't provide one of these special routines (that is, you don't declare the routine in your program and give it some code to execute), Processing just proceeds in the normal way. But if one of these routines exists, Processing will call it at the right time.

It's like a filter on your email that alerts you when you have a message from your best friend. Each time email arrives, the filter checks who sent it. If the sender isn't on your alert list, nothing happens. But if email from your friend comes in, you hear a music clip.

There are five key routines that get called in response to mouse events. Let's look at them.

We'll start with mouseMoved(). If you provide a routine by this name (with no arguments and with return type void), then Processing will call it automatically each time the mouse moves and none of its buttons are down. The routine takes no arguments and returns nothing. Here's how we can use it to make draw() simpler:

```
void draw() {
    background(MyColor);
}

void mouseMoved() {
    if (mousePressed) {
        Bluval = map(mouseX, 0, 599, 0, 255);
    }
    Redval = map(mouseX, 0, 599, 0, 255);
    Grnval = map(mouseY, 0, 399, 0, 255);
    MyColor = color(Redval, Grnval, Bluval);
}
```

(Full program in human/sketches/mouse4/mouse4.pde)

From the point of view of draw(), this is an improvement. Now when the mouse is moved, Processing invokes our routine to handle it and update the background color. The rest of the time, draw() isn't burdened with recomputing things that haven't changed. It's a longer program but a more efficient one, both faster and more responsive.

Except that it's wrong. It's buggy. This almost does what we want, but not quite. The blue value doesn't update when the button is down. What went wrong?

Remember that I said that mouseMoved() is only called if no mouse buttons are down. So the program works fine for red and green, but the blue value never updates because the test never succeeds: if mousePressed is true (that is, a button is pressed), then mouseMoved() wouldn't get called in the first place. Happily, the solution isn't far away: there's another routine called mouseDragged() that you can define. This is kind of the mouse-down partner of mouseMoved() and is called every time the mouse moves *and* a mouse button is held down:

```
void draw() {
    background(MyColor);
}

void mouseMoved() {
    // update red and green
    Redval = map(mouseX, 0, 599, 0, 255);
    Grnval = map(mouseY, 0, 399, 0, 255);
    MyColor = color(Redval, Grnval, Bluval);
}

void mouseDragged() {
    // update blue
    Bluval = map(mouseX, 0, 599, 0, 255);
    MyColor = color(Redval, Grnval, Bluval);
}
```

(Full program in human/sketches/mouse5/mouse5.pde)

This is almost right. It's so close I can taste it. But it's still not right. The problem is that mouseDragged() only gets called when the mouse is down and moved. But how about if we just click? Right now, if you simply click the mouse, nothing happens. That's because mouseDragged() is only called if a button is down and the mouse is moved, so if you press down a button and let go again without moving, none of our new functions gets called. I'd like the program to work the way it did in the first version above, where simply clicking the mouse caused the blue value to be updated.

As you might guess, one more routine comes to the rescue. If you define the routine mouseClicked(), it gets called when a mouse button is pushed down and then immediately let up, with no motion of the mouse in between. Adding that in gives us the ability to respond to only a click, rather than a click followed by a drag:

```
void draw() {
    background(MyColor);
}

void mouseMoved() {
    Redval = map(mouseX, 0, 599, 0, 255);
    Grnval = map(mouseY, 0, 399, 0, 255);
    MyColor = color(Redval, Grnval, Bluval);
}

void mouseDragged() {
    Bluval = map(mouseX, 0, 599, 0, 255);
    MyColor = color(Redval, Grnval, Bluval);
```

```
}

void mouseClicked() {
    Bluval = map(mouseX, 0, 599, 0, 255);
    MyColor = color(Redval, Grnval, Bluval);
}
```

(Full program in human/sketches/mouse6/mouse6.pde)

That does the job. But remember what I said before about never repeating yourself? I see two functions with identical code: mouseDragged() and mouseClicked(). My repeat-detector is going off, warning me to get rid of this redundancy now, while I'm thinking about it, rather than two weeks from now when I change one line but forget to fix the other and have to spend an hour trying to figure out why the program's acting funny. So let's fix it now. I'll make a new routine that does these two steps, and each of these mouse-handling routines will call it. Here's the result:

```
void draw() {
    background(MyColor);
}

void mouseMoved() {
    Redval = map(mouseX, 0, 599, 0, 255);
    Grnval = map(mouseY, 0, 399, 0, 255);
    MyColor = color(Redval, Grnval, Bluval);
}

void mouseDragged() {
    updateBlueValue();
}

void mouseClicked() {
    updateBlueValue();
}

void updateBlueValue() {
    Bluval = map(mouseX, 0, 599, 0, 255);
    MyColor = color(Redval, Grnval, Bluval);
}
```

(Full program in human/sketches/mouse7/mouse7.pde)

That does the job. If you move the mouse with the buttons up, the red and green values get updated. If you click a button, or hold a button down and drag, the blue value gets updated. There are a couple of other mouse functions that round out the collection: mousePressed() gets called when a button goes down, and mouseReleased() gets called when a button comes back up.

Suppose you've implemented all five of these functions. As you move your mouse in the graphics window with no buttons down, mouseMoved() will get called over and over each time you move. If you push down a button, then mousePressed() is called. If you let go right away, without moving, then mouseReleased() is called, followed by mouseClicked(). On the other hand, if you move around with the button down, then mouseDragged() is called for each new position of the mouse until you let the button back up, and mouseReleased() is called.

For any of these functions to make sense, you need a graphics window in your sketch (so your mouse can be inside of it). You also need to have draw() implemented, even if you never do anything with it. One of the things that the draw() function does for you is to keep Processing "awake" after your setup() function. If you don't need to actually draw anything, you can simply use an empty draw(),

```
void draw() {  }
```

You won't see this terribly often, but in some sketches, all the work is done by the mouse procedures (and the keyboard procedures we'll see in the next section), and then a blank draw() is all you need.

You've now seen just about everything you'll need to know about the mouse, and you've seen how the pieces go together. As you start to play with the mouse, you'll find that these different routines are a convenient and flexible way to organize your thinking and your program.

Sometimes it's useful to know how much the mouse has moved recently. A common technique in many systems is to save the values of the mouse coordinates when you're done responding to them. Then the next time your routine gets called, you can look at the saved versions to see how far you've moved since the last time. Processing saves you the effort by providing the built-in variables pmouseX and pmouseY, which, respectively, hold the previous values of mouseX and mouseY the last time draw() was called (think of the starting p as meaning "previous").

These variables work in different (and subtle) ways, depending on whether you're using them inside or outside of mouse routines like mouseMoved().

When you're inside of draw(), pmouseX and pmouseY hold the value of the mouse the last time you entered draw(). So Processing ignores any mouse motion in-between frames when it comes to these variables and draw(). As far as draw() is concerned, the values of pmouseX and pmouseY identify where the mouse was the last time the system called draw().

But inside a mouse routine, they hold the value at the time *that* routine was called. If the mouse moves a lot, these routines can be called more often than draw(). For example, in the following little program I'll set the frame rate to one frame per second. You can probably move your mouse across dozens of pixels in a second. Since mouseMoved() is called each time the mouse changes position, it can potentially be called dozens of times between frames. And each time you enter mouseMoved(), the variables pmouseX and pmouseY tell you where the mouse was the last time you entered mouseMoved().

```
void setup() {
  size(600, 400);
  frameRate(1);
}

void draw() {
  println("======================");
  println("draw!  mouse = "+mouseX+" "+mouseY);
  println("      pmouse = "+pmouseX+" "+pmouseY);
}

void mouseMoved() {
  println("moved!  mouse = "+mouseX+" "+mouseY);
  println("       pmouse = "+pmouseX+" "+pmouseY);
}
```

(Full program in human/sketches/mouseUpdates1/mouseUpdates1.pde)

Try running this code and moving your mouse around. You'll see that the previous values reported by draw() are different than the previous values reported by mouseMoved().

The bottom line is that the variables pmouseX and pmouseY mean different things, and can take on different values, depending on where they appear. This can easily become confusing, particularly when you're debugging.

Generally, I think it's best to think of the variables pmouseX and pmouseY as actually two different sets of variables: one set for draw() (which gets updated once per frame) and one set for everywhere else (which gets updated for every mouse procedure that's called). If you only refer to these variables in one place or the other, you'll never have a conflict; if you mix and match, proceed with care and check your program as you build it up in stages.

One other thing you might want to use that I haven't covered yet is the variable mouseButton, which tells you which of the three buttons has been pressed. Let's put that into updateBlueValue() such that if the user presses the left button, the program does what it did before, but if it's any other button then the blue value goes to zero no matter where the mouse is. The value of mouseButton is set by Processing to LEFT, CENTER, or RIGHT (as always, case is important):

```
void updateBlueValue() {
  if (mouseButton == LEFT) {
    Bluval = map(mouseX, 0, 599, 0, 255);
  } else {
    Bluval = 0;
  }
  MyColor = color(Redval, Grnval, Bluval);
}
```

(Full program in human/sketches/mouse8/mouse8.pde)

You're now a Mouse Master. It might take a little getting used to, but if you have the rough ideas in mind, with a little experimentation and experience, you'll find that handling the mouse usually doesn't take much time or code.

7.3 The Keyboard

Just as we can read the mouse, we can also read the keyboard. Think of the keyboard as just another input device that you can use to control your program. You might draw a spinning ball and increase or decrease its speed with the + and - keys. Or, taking a cue from classic computer games, you could move around an onscreen character with the *A*, *S*, *D* and *F* keys.

If you implement a function named keyPressed(), it will be called each time a key is pressed. To find out which key is down, test the system variable key:

```
void setup() {
}

void draw() {
}

void keyPressed() {
    if ((key == 'a') || (key == 'A')) {
        println("You pressed the A key!");
    }
}
```

(Full program in human/sketches/keyboard1/keyboard1.pde)

You can test the value of key for any character, as above. You can test for any lower- or upper-case letter on the keyboard just by naming it between single quotes. You can also test for a half-dozen nonprinting characters by using their special codes: BACKSPACE, TAB, ENTER, RETURN, ESC, and DELETE (as always, case matters).

Like the mouse routines, keyPressed() is only called if your code has a draw() function defined. If you don't need to draw anything, you can use the empty one-line version I offered earlier.

The Shift, Alt, and Control keys count as keys, too, and you can test for them directly with the codes ALT, CONTROL, and SHIFT.

But often these keys are combined with others. For example, the user might press *Control-A* which the computer treats as a single character. Our test above for 'a' or 'A' would not match *Control-A* (though it does match *Shift-A* because we're explicitly testing for that as the character 'A').

There's an international standard for how these kinds of *extended characters* should be handled. The standard is known by its acronym, ASCII (pronounced ask'-ee). Virtually every keyboard with the letters A through Z on it is an ASCII keyboard, meaning that when you type a particular letter, with or without modifier keys, the keyboard sends the corresponding ASCII value for that key (or modified key) to the computer. You can learn a lot more about ASCII in many books and on the web.

For example, the ASCII value for a capital letter *A* is 65, the ASCII for a lower-case *a* is 97, and the ASCII for *Control-A* is simply 1. You can print out the value of the key system variable as an integer if you want:

```
println("The value of the key you pressed is "+int(key));
```

If you print out the value of key with various *modifier keys* held down, you'll find that the Control key supersedes the Shift key. That is, if Control is pressed, the status of the Shift key is ignored. So although we usually write *Control-A*, technically it should probably be written *Control-a*.

If you really need to dig into the subtleties of Control and Alt and other modifier keys, you can find out the precise details of what keys are down on the keyboard through the variable keyCode and the routine keyTyped().

Let's print out each letter that's typed by both key and keyCode:

```
void setup() {
}

void draw() {
}

void keyPressed() {
  println("key="+key+" keyCode="+keyCode);
}
```

(Full program in human/sketches/keyboard2/keyboard2.pde)

If I type in *Hello* (one letter at a time, of course), I get this output:

```
key=H keyCode=72
key=e keyCode=69
key=l keyCode=76
key=l keyCode=76
key=o keyCode=79
```

If at any time in your program you want to know if a key is pressed (maybe you don't want to use the functions above), the system-wide boolean variable keyPressed will have the value true if a key is down, and otherwise it will be false. You would probably then check key to see which key is down.

If you want to know when a key is released, provide the function keyReleased(), and Processing will call that function when the user lets the key come back up.

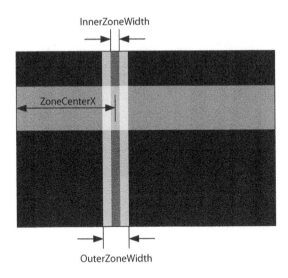

Figure 7.7. Laying out the simple game.

7.4   A Simple Game

I've got an idea for a great game! OK, not really a *great* game, but still a game.

In this game, a tall green bar moves across the screen, left to right and back again, forever. The bar isn't very wide. If you can click your mouse in the bar as it goes by, you get 20 points. But that's really hard, so there's a wider yellow zone around the narrow green one. If you can click in that yellow bar, you get 5 points. If you miss both bars entirely, you lose 5 points.

To write this game, I'll take my standard skeleton and add a few global variables. The score is an integer value, so I'll declare a global `int` by the name of `Score` and initialize it to 0. For the other values, I'll use a bunch of `float` types since none of them require whole-number accuracy. The vertical bar's center at any given time will be stored in `ZoneCenterX`. The green (bull's eye) zone around it will have width `InnerZoneWidth`, and the yellow, low-scoring zone that surrounds that will have width `OuterZoneWidth`. At the start of each frame, the bar will move by a number of pixels given by `ZoneSpeed`.

Figure 7.7 shows the three variables that control the location and size of the moving bar.

When the game starts, the bar is located at the left side (so `ZoneCenterX` has a value of 0), and the bar is moving to the right. So I want to add a positive value, given by the speed of the bar `ZoneSpeed` to `ZoneCenterX` every frame.

Here's the code to cover what we've got so far. I toyed with the values for these global variables until the bar seemed about the right size and moved at a reasonable speed on my computer. You may want to adjust them for your system.

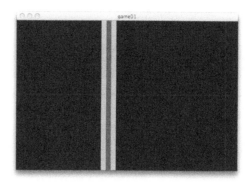

Figure 7.8. Starting a very simple game (frame from animation).
(human/sketches/game01/game01.pde)

```
int Score = 0;

float ZoneCenterX, ZoneSpeed, OuterZoneWidth, InnerZoneWidth;

void setup() {
  size(600, 400);

  ZoneCenterX = 0;
  ZoneSpeed = 1.5;       // pixels per frame
  InnerZoneWidth = width/50.0;
  OuterZoneWidth = width/15.0;
}

void draw() {
  ZoneCenterX += ZoneSpeed;
  background(115, 40, 22);
  noStroke();
  fill(186, 186, 115);
  rect(ZoneCenterX-OuterZoneWidth/2, 0, OuterZoneWidth, height);
  fill(46, 118, 56);
  rect(ZoneCenterX-InnerZoneWidth/2, 0, InnerZoneWidth, height);
}
```

(See output in Figure 7.8. Full program in human/sketches/game01/game01.pde)

That's a start, except that the bar goes to the right and then disappears! We need to turn it around and get it to move back to the left.

There are lots of ways to keep track of which way the bar is moving and how to flip it around. You might keep a boolean that tells you if the bar is moving to the right (if it had the name barIsMovingRight, then it would be false if the bar's moving left) and use an *if statement* to either add or subtract the speed from the zone's position on each frame.

Instead, let's use a numerical approach. I'll make a global integer with the name `ZoneDirection`. Before I add the speed to the zone's center, I'll multiply it by this value. When the game starts, `ZoneDirection` will be $+1$. When the bar passes the right side of the screen, I'll change it to -1. When the bar hits the left side, the direction goes back to $+1$, and so on.

When I multiply the speed by the value of `ZoneDirection`, I end up with a negative number when the bar should be moving left and a positive number when it should be moving right. Which is just right, since adding a positive value to the zone's center will move it right, and adding a negative value will move it left.

So I'll add the declaration for this variable outside of all routines, so it's a global:

```
int ZoneDirection;
```

I'll initialize it in `setup()`:

```
ZoneDirection = 1;
```

Now I can use it in `draw()`:

```
ZoneCenterX += ZoneDirection * ZoneSpeed;
if ((ZoneCenterX < 0) || (ZoneCenterX >= width)) {
    ZoneSpeed *= -1;
}
```

(See output in Figure 7.9. Full program in human/sketches/game02/game02.pde)

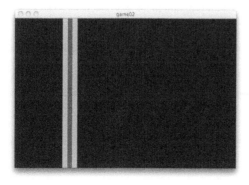

Figure 7.9. Getting the bar to bounce (frame from animation).
(human/sketches/game02/game02.pde)

Figure 7.10. Playing a very simple game (frame from animation).
(human/sketches/game03/game03.pde)

That does it—the bar bounces back and forth, changing direction when it reaches the sides.

Let's now turn this amazing animation into an equally amazing game. I'll implement mousePressed(). Now, each time a mouse button goes down, I can check its position relative to the moving center. If the mouse click is within the smallest zone, we award big points. If it's in the larger zone, we award fewer points. And, of course, a click anywhere else will have a few points removed.

I'll just find the distance of the mouse click from the bar (and make sure it's positive). Then I'll compare it to the distances and award points.

I'll print the results to the console. Bull's-eye hits get a congratulatory message printed out, total misses get a condolence card, and hits in the yellow zone get no message. Every click causes a new printout of the score.

(See output in Figure 7.10. Full program in human/sketches/game03/game03.pde)

```
void mousePressed() {
  float distance = ZoneCenterX - mouseX;
  if (distance < 0) distance = -distance;
              // better: distance = abs(distance);
  if (distance < InnerZoneWidth/2.0) {
    Score += 20;
    println("BULLS EYE! ");
  } else if (distance < OuterZoneWidth/2.0) {
    Score += 5;
  } else {
    println("oops ");
    Score -= 5;
  }
  println(Score);
}
```

Figure 7.11. The console output for our simple game.

You can see a little comment I added to the second line of `mousePressed()`. The *if statement* I have there now works perfectly well. But the statement in the comment does the same thing, and it's shorter, easier to read, and cleaner:

```
distance = abs(distance);
```

We'll see in Chapter 18 that `abs()` is the built-in *absolute value* function. It takes a single number as input, and if the number is positive, it simply returns the number. If the number is negative, it basically drops the minus sign. So `abs(7)` is 7, and `abs(-7)` is also 7. I'm mentioning it here because it's such a perfect tool for this job.

Figure 7.11 shows my Processing window after I played the game for a few moments. In the console you can see my score: a couple of bull's eyes, a couple of okay hits, and one miss. Good thing there's no organized international competition for this game that I need to practice for. At least, not yet.

Chapter 8
Loops and Transparency

This chapter's opening program is a little longer than those of previous chapters, but it makes a more complicated sort of image. Each time you run this program, you'll get a different result because it uses random numbers as part of the process.

There's also a variable at the top that you can change. In this listing, the variable `DrawTiles` is set to `false`. That gives you an image like Figure 8.1. If you set this to `true`, you'll get an image like Figure 8.2.

In this program I'm using a lot of language tools that we haven't seen yet, and much of this notation may look really strange to you. I've still tried to keep it pretty clear so that if you do come back later, it will be easy to follow. We'll cover everything here in the following chapters, of course, and before long, you'll be able to look at this program and very easily see what it's doing and how.

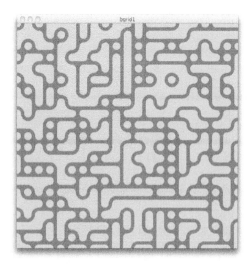

Figure 8.1. A kind of traffic-pattern abstract image. (loops/sketches/Bgrid1f/Bgrid1f.pde)

Because this program's a little longer and more complicated, making random changes might cause you to get weird results more easily than in some of the earlier examples. But even if it crashes, there's no harm done. Just undo your change, or reload the whole file, and try something else!

```
Cell [][] Board;
int Bwid = 20;
int Bhgt = 20;
boolean DrawTiles = false;
        // set to false if you don't want background tiles

void setup() {
   size(600, 600);
   smooth();
   background(230, 212, 167);
   Board = new Cell[Bhgt][Bwid];
   for (int y=0; y<Bhgt; y++) {
      for (int x=0; x<Bwid; x++) {
         Board[y][x] = new Cell();
      }
   }
     buildGrid();
   drawGrid();
}

void buildGrid() {
   for (int y=0; y<Bhgt; y++) {
      for (int x=0; x<Bwid; x++) {
         placeCell(x, y);
      }
   }
}

void placeCell(int x, int y) {
   int numExits = 0;
   while (numExits < 2) {
      Board[y][x].t = Board[y][x].r = Board[y][x].b
         = Board[y][x].l = -1;
      if (x > 0) {
         Board[y][x].l = Board[y][x-1].r;
      }
      if (y > 0) {
         Board[y][x].t = Board[y-1][x].b;
      }
      if (Board[y][x].t < 0) Board[y][x].t
         = random(100) > 50 ? 1 : 0;
      if (Board[y][x].r < 0) Board[y][x].r
```

```
                = random(100) > 50 ? 1 : 0;
            if (Board[y][x].b < 0) Board[y][x].b
                = random(100) > 50 ? 1 : 0;
            if (Board[y][x].l < 0) Board[y][x].l
                = random(100) > 50 ? 1 : 0;
            numExits = Board[y][x].t + Board[y][x].r
                + Board[y][x].b + Board[y][x].l;
        }
    }
}

void drawGrid() {
    float cwid =  width*1.0/Bwid;
    float chgt = height*1.0/Bhgt;


    for (int y=0; y<Bhgt; y++) {
        for (int x=0; x<Bwid; x++) {
            float lx =  x * cwid;
            float hx = lx + cwid;
            float ly =  y * chgt;
            float hy = ly + chgt;
            float mx = (lx+hx)/2;
            float my = (ly+hy)/2;

            noStroke();
            fill(130, 68, 54);

            if (DrawTiles) {
                if (Board[y][x].t == 1) triangle(lx, ly, mx, my, hx, ly);
                if (Board[y][x].r == 1) triangle(hx, ly, mx, my, hx, hy);
                if (Board[y][x].b == 1) triangle(hx, hy, mx, my, lx, hy);
                if (Board[y][x].l == 1) triangle(lx, hy, mx, my, lx, ly);
            }

            noFill();
            stroke(88, 138, 119);
            strokeWeight(9);
            if ((Board[y][x].t == 1) && (Board[y][x].r == 1)) {
                arc(hx, ly, cwid, chgt, HALF_PI, PI);
            }
            if ((Board[y][x].r == 1) && (Board[y][x].b == 1)) {
                arc(hx, hy, cwid, chgt, PI, 3*HALF_PI);
            }
            if ((Board[y][x].b == 1) && (Board[y][x].l == 1)) {
                arc(lx, hy, cwid, chgt, 3*HALF_PI, TWO_PI);
            }
```

Figure 8.2. Setting `DrawTiles` to `true`.

```
        if ((Board[y][x].l == 1) && (Board[y][x].t == 1)) {
            arc(lx, ly, cwid, chgt, 0, HALF_PI);
        }
        if ((Board[y][x].t == 1) && (Board[y][x].b == 1)) {
            line(mx, ly, mx, hy);
        }
        if ((Board[y][x].l == 1) && (Board[y][x].r == 1)) {
            line(lx, my, hx, my);
        }
      }
    }
}

class Cell {
    int t, r, b, l;
    Cell() {
        t = r = b = l = -1;
    }
}
```

(See output in Figure 8.1. Full program in loops/sketches/Bgrid1f/Bgrid1f.pde)

Now let's dig into this chapter's material, starting with transparency.

Transparency is a great visual effect. Transparency lets you draw objects that don't completely obscure what's already on the screen.

Processing lets you specify transparency by including it with your choice of color.

To illustrate transparency, I'll draw a blue box and then a row of yellow circles that overlap it. The basic geometry is in Figure 8.3. I'll make the graphics window a little shorter than before, only 250 pixels high (to save some room). Inside the window I'll draw a blue box, but I'll leave a 25-pixel wide border around the top and sides, with a little bit more below. Inside the box I'll draw a row of five circles. Since the box is 550 pixels wide, 550/5 = 110, so if each circle had a radius of 55, they would all just barely touch. I'd like some space, so I'll back off the radius to 40. The first circle starts at 80 units from the blue box's left side, then the next circle is at 80 + 110 = 290 units, and each following circle is 110 units to the right again.

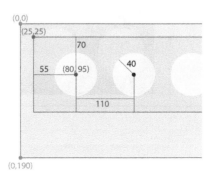

Figure 8.3. The geometry of a row of circles.

If you're thinking that all of these numbers are starting to look like a lot of messy work, I completely agree. A lot of this chapter will be all about how we can do away with manually figuring this out. But even though I found them by hand, there's nothing magical about any of these numbers; I just wanted something that looked pleasing to my eye, and these choices for the box size, circle radius, and spacing looked good to me.

Here's the code:

```
void setup() {
   size(600, 250);
   background(200);
}

void draw() {
   background(200);
   fill(47, 64, 84);
   rect(25, 25, 550, 140);

   fill(249, 246, 155);
   ellipse (80, 95, 80, 80);
   ellipse(190, 95, 80, 80);
   ellipse(300, 95, 80, 80);
   ellipse(410, 95, 80, 80);
   ellipse(520, 95, 80, 80);
}
```

(See output in Figure 8.4. Full program in loops/sketches/row1/row1.pde)

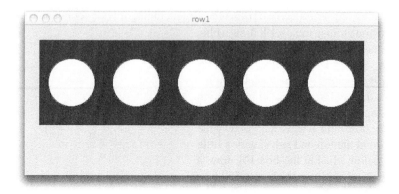

Figure 8.4. A row of circles. (loops/sketches/row1/row1.pde)

Before we go further, the code in draw() is making some of my repeat detectors go off. Those last five lines are almost the same—only the first value is changing. I know that this program is going to get more complicated as we get into the example, and it's going to become more and more of a hassle to change each of those lines the same way every time. And I'll probably mess up a few times, too, and then have to diagnose and fix my mistakes.

What to do?

8.1 Loops

This is a good time to introduce the idea of a *loop*. In a loop we specify a set of instructions that we want to run over and over. Processing itself offers a nice example of a loop: it calls draw(), waits a little bit, then calls draw() again, waits a little bit, and so on.

We have to be careful about what we ask for, or we can end up repeating ourselves forever. A loop is good, but like all good things, it must come to an end sometime. So when we set up a loop, we also have to set up some way to make it stop.

Processing, like most modern computer languages, offers a few different ways for you to create a loop. Let's detour into loop country for moment, and then we'll come back to transparency. That way the code we'll use for the transparency examples will be shorter, cleaner, and easier to understand.

The simplest loop is probably the while loop. To make one of these, you write the word while and then a test within a pair of parentheses (like the test used by an *if statement*). Then you supply a bunch of statements in curly braces (like the block of statements that follows an if test). When Processing first hits the word while, it evaluates the test. If the result is true, then all the statements in the block are executed, also just like an *if statement*. When Processing reaches the end of the block (that is, the closing curly brace), it jumps back up to the `while` and repeats. As long as the test is `true`, the statements will repeat.

The shorthand way to think of a *while loop* is this: "While the test is true, do the statements in the block."

To avoid repeating forever, you'll want to make sure that your test eventually becomes `false`. If it doesn't, your program is said to have gone into an *infinite loop*.

If your program does get stuck in an infinite loop, don't worry about it; it happens to everyone. You'll know it's happening if your program suddenly becomes unresponsive, or something starts happening wildly out of control. Generally, an infinite loop makes itself known in some obvious way. Then you stop the program and try to track down the cause. Again, don't sweat it—the most experienced programmers in the world still accidentally write infinite loops now and then. It's a really easy mistake to make, but happily, it's also usually easy to fix.

Sometimes a program that's in an infinite loop won't respond when you hit the close box in the graphics window. If that happens, try pressing the *Stop* button in the Processing window (that's the round button with a square in it).

Here's a loop to draw our five circles (for now, I won't bother with the other stuff in `draw()`, but I'll just focus on the loop stuff). The circles are all the same except for their *x* center locations, which are 80, 180, 280, 380, and 480; in other words, the *x* location starts at 80 and goes up by 110 each time. To get started, I'll put down the basic structure of the loop:

```
int ellipseNumber = 0;
while (ellipseNumber < 5) {
    // make an ellipse
    ellipseNumber++;
}
// more code
```

So what's happening here? First, I declared a variable called `ellipseNumber` that I'm going to use to count how many times I go through the loop. The first time we hit the word `while`, the variable `ellipseNumber` has the value 0. We carry out the test: is 0 less than 5? Yes! Since the test is `true`, we start executing the block. First, we do something related to the ellipse (here I have just a comment), and then I add 1 to `ellipseNumber`. It now has the value 1. We hit the end of the block and go back to the `while` statement. We test again: is 1 less than 5? Yes again. So we repeat. Over and over. Finally we come back to the top and `ellipseNumber` has the value 5. We ask if 5 is less than 5? Nope. So the test is `false`, and that's the end of the loop. We jump down to just after the closing curly brace and continue with the program (here the comment `more code`).

So we executed the loop once for each value of `ellipseNumber` from 0 to 4. That's five times.

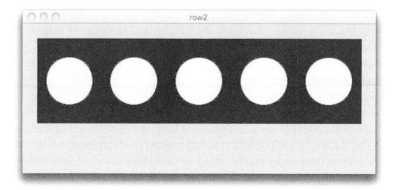

Figure 8.5. A row of circles, version 2. (loops/sketches/row2/row2.pde)

This is a very common form of the *while loop*. Generally speaking, when you see a test in a *while loop* of the form counter < N for some number N, you'll probably start when counter has the value 0, and increment it by one each time through the loop. So you'll something repeat N times, where counter (or whatever your variable is named) takes on the values 0 to N-1.

Now that the structure of the *while loop* is in place, let's populate it with the steps to draw the ellipses. We need a variable that will tell us the current *x* value of this ellipse. I'll call it xValue, initialize it to 80, and add 110 to it each time through the loop:

```
int xValue = 80;
int ellipseNumber = 0;
while (ellipseNumber < 5) {
   ellipse(xValue, 95, 80, 80);
   ellipseNumber = ellipseNumber + 1;
   xValue = xValue + 110;
}
```

(See output in Figure 8.5. Full program in loops/sketches/row2/row2.pde)

As Figure 8.5 shows, this works fine. The new results look just like the old, and we've done away with the repetitions and a lot of that by-hand calculating we saw earlier.

There is nothing wrong with this piece of code. It is 100 percent good Processing, and you can hang it on the wall. But experienced programmers would tighten this up a little bit to make it more concise. Since a lot of the code you're likely to see from other people will have gone through that kind of refinement, let's do it on this little loop.

First, we can shorten the last two lines of the loop using the ++ and += shorthands, so we have

```
int xValue = 80;
int ellipseNumber = 0;
while (ellipseNumber < 5) {
   ellipse(xValue, 95, 80, 80);
   ellipseNumber++;
   xValue += 110;
}
```

We can do even better. Notice that the variable ellipseNumber is never used for anything but counting the number of times we go through the loop. So there's no reason not to increment it right away in the test itself, and then we can get rid of the line that adds one to it:

```
int xValue = 80;
int ellipseNumber = 0;
while (ellipseNumber++ < 5) {
   ellipse(xValue, 95, 80, 80);
   xValue += 110;
}
```

Remember that this means that Processing will test the value of ellipseNumber, and then after it's determined whether it's less than 5 or not, it'll add one to the value.

Now I'm going to be sneaky and tighten this up one more notch. Notice what's happening to xValue? It's starting at 80 and going up by 110 each time we go through the loop. So it's 80, 190, 300, and so on. What if I write this loop this way?

```
int ellipseNumber = 0;
while (ellipseNumber++ < 5) {
   int xValue = 80+((ellipseNumber-1)*110);
   ellipse(xValue, 95, 80, 80);
}
```

What's the value of xValue the first time through? The first time through the loop, ellipseNumber has the value 1 (because it was incremented right after the test). So then the assignment statement is 80+((1-1)*110). But 1-1 is 0, so this is 80+(0*110) or simply 80. The second time through the loop, ellipseNumber has the value 2, so the expression becomes 80+((2-1)*110) or 80+(1*110) or 190. The next time it's 300, and so on. So I've used this little piece of math to calculate the position of the ellipse.

While I'm on a roll, I'll get rid of the `xValue` variable and put that value right into the ellipse call itself:

```
int ellipseNumber = 0;
while (ellipseNumber++ < 5) {
    ellipse(80+((ellipseNumber-1)*110), 95, 80, 80);
}
```

When you look at other people's code, you'll often see expressions like this where there's some seemingly crazy bunch of math jammed into an argument for a routine. Usually it came about the way I showed you here: it was a straightforward bit of code that got squeezed and squeezed. So don't let it throw you. If you see that first argument to `ellipse()` above and it looks like a mess to you (and it sure looks like a mess to me), just grab a piece of scratch paper if you like and unwind it one step at a time to discover the pattern.

One thing I find useful for figuring out these kinds of cryptic expressions is to plug in the values for the variable and see what comes out. So here I'd evaluate (by hand) that expression when `ellipseNumber` is 1 (and I'd get 80), then when it's 2 (and I'd get 190), and so on. Often that will give me a hint as to what the pattern is supposed to be. Then I can look at the expression again and gradually I'll be able to explain it myself. It's kind of reverse engineering the code. Of course, a comment or two from the programmer can make this process a lot more pleasant. And maybe it would be even better not to jam all this in there in the first place and calculate that value over the course of a line or two. But people do write their code this way, and in time, you might as well. You can always make sense of it if you take it one step at a time, essentially undoing the steps that the programmer followed to make this dense little nugget.

All of the examples we just looked at produce the same image as in Figure 8.5; they just get there by different means.

Until you're used to writing tight little clusters of code (like the first argument in the last `ellipse()` call above), be nice to yourself and put every step on its own line. I often still do it that way when I'm writing code, and I've written tens or even hundreds of thousands of loops. Tight code is nice, but code that runs correctly is way, way more important. If it's clearer to you to use lots of lines of code, by all means, use lots of lines of code. Spreading out a calculation over many lines of source code might slow down your program by a miniscule, imperceptible fraction of a second, but it could save you minutes or hours of writing and debugging.

Clarity is good. Except for rare cases where every microsecond matters, a long but easily understood program will be better than a shorter but denser one.

There's a useful variant of the *while loop* called the *do loop*. The *while loop* starts with `while` and a test, followed by a body, and it repeats the body as long as the test is `true`. But sometimes you want to put the test at the end.

For example, you might be writing a little reaction-time training program. You put up a random circle somewhere on the screen and then measure the time it takes your user to click the mouse inside the circle, repeating the process until they get a response in less than some amount of time. In this case, the test would be something like testing a variable `reaction_time` against a threshold time `threshold_time`.

Here's one way to do this:

```
while (reaction_time > threshold_time) {
   reaction_time = run_test();
}
```

The problem here is that before we've run the test the first time, we don't have a value for `reaction_time` yet. Sure, we could give it some huge initial value to force the test to succeed the first time through, or we could manually run the test once before the loop, but the *do loop* (sometimes called a *do-while loop*) offers a better solution.

To create a *do loop*, you give the keyword `do` followed by a body (either one statement or a block of statements between curly braces), and then the keyword `while` followed by the test in parentheses, all wrapped up with a semicolon at the end. It's like writing a *while loop* in reverse order, but you need the extra word `do` in there.

Here's our example from above in *do loop* form:

```
do {
   reaction_time = run_test();
} while (reaction_time > threshold_time);
```

This will first execute `run_test()` to get a value for `reaction_time` and then test that against our threshold. If it's too big, we repeat the block again, over and over as long as the test is `true`.

Anything you can do with a *while loop* you can also do with a *do loop*, and vice versa. They're very similar. Which one you'll choose for any given situation depends on the exact nature of what you're doing and how you like to think about it: are you testing and then doing something (the *while loop*), or are you doing something and then testing (the *do loop*)? Use the form that feels right to you for each situation.

Like most modern languages, Processing offers you yet another way to write loops: the `for` loop. It's really the same sort of thing as the *while loop* (and *do loop*), you just arrange the pieces differently. And, of course, the keyword that distinguishes it is `for`, rather than `while` or `do`.

Remember where we started with the *while loop*:

```
int ellipseNumber = 0;
while (ellipseNumber < 5) {
   // loop body
   ellipseNumber++;
}
```

The *for loop* just packages these elements up into a different form, which usually lets you put them all on one line. Here's the *for loop* version of this *while loop*:

```
for (int ellipseNumber = 0; ellipseNumber < 5; ellipseNumber++) {
   // make an ellipse
}
```

Notice that all I did was rearrange the pieces and insert some semicolons. The *for loop* does the same job as the *while loop*. You just write the pieces down a little differently, and because you can pack them all onto one line, it looks more compact.

The structure of the *for loop* begins with the word `for`, and then a bunch of stuff in parentheses, and then the body of the loop in curly braces. The body of the loop is just like the body of the *while loop*: a series of statements that gets executed over and over again.

Inside the *for loop*'s parentheses are three separate statements, separated by semi-colons. A semicolon ends the first and second statements. It seems to me that there really should be a semicolon after the third statement, too, just for consistency, but there isn't. In fact, if you put one in, Processing reports it as a syntax error. So there are three statements, but just two semicolons.

In a `for` loop, you first provide the starting statement, which gets executed only once when the *for loop* begins. In this example, we declare the variable `ellipseNumber` and set it to 0 (so we're really doing two things here—declaring a variable and initializing it—but that counts as just one statement).

It's common to decleare a variable in a *for loop* like this, but it's just as common to use an existing variable, too.

The second statement in the structure of the *for loop* is the test, and this is just like the one in the *while loop*.

When Processing first starts the *for loop*, it executes the initialization step and then it runs the test. If the test is `true`, then the statements in the block are executed. At the end of the body, when we hit the closing curly brace, the third statement is executed. Then we jump back up to the top, execute the test again, and repeat.

So the *for loop* version of our first version of the ellipse builder might look like this:

```
int xValue = 80;
for (int ellipseNumber = 0; ellipseNumber < 5; ellipseNumber++) {
   ellipse(xValue, 95, 80, 80);
   xValue += 110;
}
```

If we squeeze things together the same way I did for the *while loop*, we can replace all the `xValue` stuff with a calculation:

```
for (int ellipseNumber = 0; ellipseNumber < 5; ellipseNumber++) {
   ellipse(80+(ellipseNumber*110), 95, 80, 80);
}
```

(See output in Figure 8.6. Full program in loops/sketches/row3/row3.pde)

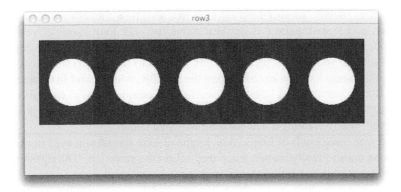

Figure 8.6. A row of circles, version 3. (loops/sketches/row3/row3.pde)

That's the complete *for loop* that does the very same job. Note that I used simply `ellipseNumber` in the calculation, rather than `(ellipseNumber-1)` because in a *for loop*, the third statement (in this case, `ellipseNumber++`) is applied at the end of the loop. So the first time through, `ellipseNumber` has the value 0, then 1, then 2, and so on.

So suppose you want something that runs through 12 values; maybe you're simulating printing the name of a soft drink on 12 cans. You'd write something like

```
for (int canNumber=0; canNumber<12; canNumber++) {
}
```

The first time through, `canNumber` would be 0. Then 1, then 2, and finally the last time through that `canNumber` would be 11. Remember that at the end of the pass where `canNumber` is 11, at the bottom of the loop it gets incremented again (by the third statement in the *for loop*) so it's 12, and then the test fails and we exit the loop. So the general rule is that if you want a loop to cycle through N times, you start the counter (also sometimes called the *index*) at 0, test for <N, and bump by 1 each time:

```
for (int index=0; index<N; index++) {
}
```

And that will give you N cycles through the loop, where `index` will take on the values 0 to N-1.

One of the lovely things about the *for loop* is that you can declare the loop variable right there in the loop statement. In this example, you can see that the first statement is

```
int ellipseNumber = 0;
```

This is inside the parentheses of the `for` loop. That's very convenient. That variable is only defined for the body of the loop (that is, until the loop's closing curly brace). So if you want to include another loop later on that also runs through ellipses, and you decide that ellipseNumber is the best name for your loop variable, you'll want to remember that ellipseNumber doesn't have any meaning after the end of the previous loop. So you can just repeat the int at the start of the loop statement again.

This might seem like you're redeclaring the variable, which I said in Chapter 3 isn't allowed. But the variable ellipseNumber in this example doesn't exist outside of the loop's curly braces. So you're not redeclaring ellipseNumber: as far as Processing is concerned, you're creating a new variable with that name.

We've seen three kinds of loops. Which type of loop should you use? In one sense, the question doesn't really matter, since they all do the same job. The differences are more in how you think about what they're doing.

Though there's no firm answer that tells you which loop to prefer for any given task, in my experience, people use the *for loop* more frequently than the *while loop* or *do loop*. I think that's because it's more compact, and it's easier to see all the relevant pieces at a glance. But every now and then you have a programming job where a *while loop* or *do loop* just makes perfect sense: you really are repeating something *while* something else is true, so one of those loop types feels like the natural way to express the idea. You'll see them all in practice, but the *for loop* form tends to dominate.

Before we leave the land of loops, there are two useful keywords you should know about. These apply in exactly the same way to a *for loop*, a *while loop*, and a *do loop*.

Suppose that the body of your loop (that is, the code between the curly braces) does a whole lot of stuff—it's a big, long, complex calculation that takes a lot of time. And at some point you're able to determine that it's not worth continuing (for example, maybe you're computing the appearance of some object that has gone temporarily offscreen). What you want to do is quit the loop now, at that instant, as though you were back up at the top and the test had failed. In other words, you want to exit the loop and jump down, picking up again at the code that comes after the closing curly brace.

You need only one word to do that: break. It's not a function, so it doesn't have parentheses. Think of it like a command. It tells Processing, "That's it, I quit this loop." Here's an example of break in our circle-drawing program from earlier:

```
void draw() {
    background(200);
    fill(47, 64, 84);
    rect(25, 25, 550, 140);

    fill(249, 246, 155);
    for (int xval=80; xval<550; xval+=110) {
        if (xval == 300) break;
        ellipse(xval, 95, 80, 80);
    }
    // after loop
}
```

(See output in Figure 8.7. Full program in loops/sketches/break1/break1.pde)

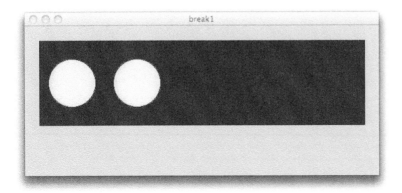

Figure 8.7. Using break in a *for loop*. (loops/sketches/break1/break1.pde)

As before, I'm drawing a line of circles, where each circle is one unit to the right of the one before. The first time through, xval is 80, so the if test fails (since 80 is not equal to 300), and we draw a circle at (80, 95). Then we go though again, and once again the if test fails, since xval is only 190, so we get a circle at (190, 95). The third time through the test evaluates to true because now xval is 300. So the statement following the if is executed, and that's the break. That causes us to jump to the end of the loop body, here marked by the comment after loop. There's no more code to execute there, so we're done, and that's the end of the draw() routine. The result is a picture with only two circles near the left side of the screen.

In this case, I tested the variable xval, which was part of the *for loop*'s definition. But you can call break at any time, for any reason. If you do, Processing just declares, "That's it, the loop ends right now," and it jumps to the first line of code after the loop's body (that is, after its closing curly brace).

A similar and equally useful tool is continue. Like break, it has no parentheses. Also like break, it stops the loop body from executing. But while break stops the loop completely and jumps to the end of the loop, continue just jumps back down to the bottom, where it executes the third statement in the loop's construction. It then continues normally, jumping back up to the top and executing the test. In other words, continue says, "This time through, the loop's body is done right now. Go down to the bottom, execute the third statement of the loop, and then try the test again, as usual."

Let's repeat the program above, but I'll make just one change. I will substitute continue for break:

```
void draw() {
   for (int xval=80; xval<550; xval+=110) {
      if (xval == 300) continue;
      ellipse(xval, 95, 80, 80);
```

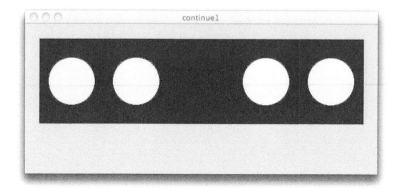

Figure 8.8. Using continue in a *for loop*. (loops/sketches/continue1/continue1.pde)

```
    }
    // after loop
}
```

(See output in Figure 8.8. Full program in loops/sketches/continue1/continue1.pde)

In this case, there's a gap after the second circle, but then the pattern continues. As before, the test succeeded on the third time through. But the continue statement, rather than exiting the loop, just stopped executing the loop body and applied the *for loop* test again, continuing on as before.

The break and continue statements are not used in every loop. Some programmers love them, but I tend to use one or the other of these in perhaps ten percent of my loops, if that many. But every now and then one of these tools is exactly the thing you need.

8.2   Transparency

Now that we have loops under our belt, we can mess around with bunches of circles without writing nearly identical lines of code over and over.

Here's a version of our starting picture, created with a *for loop*:

```
void draw() {
    background(200);
    fill(80, 10, 255);
    rect(20, 100, 520, 160);
    fill(255, 255, 0);
    for (int eCount = 0; eCount<11; eCount++) {
        int xValue = 60 + (eCount * 48);
```

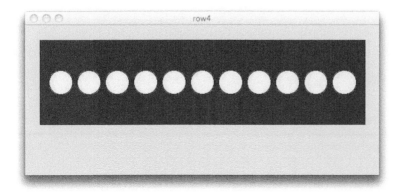

Figure 8.9. Another row of circles. (loops/sketches/row4/row4.pde)

```
    ellipse(xValue, 95, 40, 40);
  }
}
```

(See output in Figure 8.9. Full program in loops/sketches/row4/row4.pde)

Since we have a loop now and I don't have to type in each circle by hand, I've made them a little smaller so we can fit in more of them, and it took almost no effort. Another big win for loops! There are now ten circles in a row across the blue box.

What I'd like to do is to make the left-most circle entirely transparent, the right-most one opaque, and assign the ones in-between with in between transparencies.

It may seem a little strange, but in Processing, the amount of transparency with which objects are drawn is bound up with the color rather than with the object. It's as though our can of yellow paint becomes a can of partly transparent yellow paint.

Everywhere in Processing where you can provide a color, you can also provide a fourth number after the red, green, and blue values to define the transparency of that color. Historically, that value is called *alpha*, for the Greek letter α. (For once, this term doesn't come to us from another field. In the seminal computer graphics research paper where the mathematics of transparency were first presented, the author used the Greek letter α to stand for the transparency value, and the name stuck.) Like the other color values, transparency is defined in the range 0 to 255.

It might be better to think of this as *opacity*, because the higher the number, the more opaque the paint becomes. Let's draw the circles from above with different opacities, starting with 0 and ending at 255. I'll do this by simply adding a fourth number to the call to fill(). Remember that fill() wants a color. If it gets only three values, it assumes that you meant an opaque color and it sets the alpha value to 255. But if you give it a fourth value, that becomes the alpha it uses.

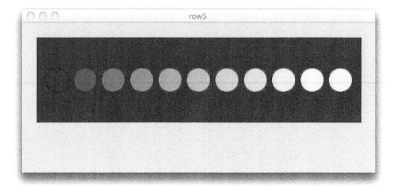

Figure 8.10. Circles with transparency. (loops/sketches/row5/row5.pde)

In this version of the loop, I've moved the `fill()` call inside the loop, so it's just prior to the `ellipse()` call. And I'm calculating alpha so it has a value of 0 for the first circle, and 255 for the last one. Since loop counter `eCount` will run from 0 to 9, I'll use `map()` to get a value of `myAlpha` by transforming it from the range 0 to 9 to the range 0 to 255:

```
void draw() {
   background(200);
   fill(80, 10, 255);
   rect(20, 100, 520, 160);
   for (int eCount = 0; eCount<10; eCount++) {
      float xValue = 60 + (eCount * 50);
      float myAlpha = map(eCount, 0, 9, 0, 255);
      fill(255, 255, 0, myAlpha);
      ellipse(xValue, 180, 40, 40);
   }
}
```

(See output in Figure 8.10. Full program in loops/sketches/row5/row5.pde)

Pretty cool! You can stack up one transparent thing on top of another on top of another as many times as you want. With lots of layers, things can start to look really interesting.

Note that I called my variable `myAlpha`, because `alpha()` is a reserved word (it's the function you call to get back the amount of opacity in a variable of type `color`, just as we use `red()` to get back the red component).

Adding a fourth value works anywhere you can specify a color. So instead of these explicit calls to `fill()`, we could define our colors using a call to `color()` and then handing `fill()` that value. Here's an example that illustrates the idea. I've moved the circles down a bit so they straddle the darker box and the background.

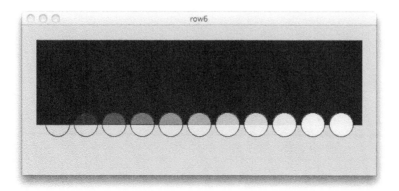

Figure 8.11. Transparent circles, using alpha with color. (loops/sketches/row6/row6.pde)

```
void draw() {
   background(200);
   fill(80, 10, 255);
   rect(20, 100, 520, 160);
   for (int eCount = 0; eCount<10; eCount++) {
      float xValue = 60 + (eCount * 50);
      float myAlpha = map(eCount, 0, 9, 0, 255);
      color myColor = color(255, 255, 0, myAlpha);
      fill(myColor);
      ellipse(xValue, 165, 40, 40);
   }
}
```

(See output in Figure 8.11. Full program in loops/sketches/row6/row6.pde)

Chapter 9
Transformations

Starting with this chapter, I won't be giving you little programs at the beginning of each chapter any more. You now have enough power in your hands to start creating your own interesting projects, and the examples we'll be seeing within the chapters will be getting a little more complicated and interesting on their own as well.

We've made a lot of still images so far, but animation is a big part of making a cool interactive project, so let's get things moving. How about a spinning red box? Nothing to it. Getting started is easy enough—just grab the skeleton and draw a box:

```
void setup() {
    size(600, 400);
}

void draw() {
    background(210, 177, 68);
    fill(139, 49, 30);
    rect(150, 100, 250, 150);
}
```

See output in Figure 9.1. Full program in transforms/sketches/box1/box1.pde.

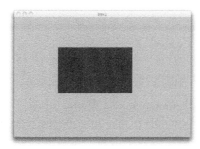

Figure 9.1. A simple box. (transforms/sketches/box1/box1.pde)

Figure 9.2. The box rotated by
20 degrees.
(transforms/sketches/box2/box2.pde)

OK, now we have to get it to rotate. That's no problem at all. Processing comes with a bunch of built-in commands to *transform* graphics. These *transformation* commands let us *move*, *scale*, and *rotate* shapes. Again borrowing a term from mathematics, movement is called *translation*, so we might say "I'm going to translate that circle," or, "The triangle is translated three units to the right."

The call to rotate() will spin an object around by an angle you provide that's expressed in (you guessed it) radians. Remember that to convert degrees to radians, we pass our angle through the built-in function radians().

So let's rotate the box by something small, say 20 degrees. The way to do this is to call rotate() before we draw the object:

```
void draw() {
    background(210, 177, 68);
    fill(139, 49, 30);
    rotate(radians(20));
    rect(150, 100, 250, 150);
}
```

(See output in Figure 9.2. Full program in transforms/sketches/box2/box2.pde)

Um, something doesn't seem right. The box rotated, but it seems to have moved as well. Let's draw a dark yellow box before calling rotate() and the red box after. I'll make the red one semitransparent so we can see all the details.

```
void draw() {
    background(210, 177, 68);
    fill(149, 93, 13, 128);
    rect(150, 100, 250, 150);
    fill(139, 49, 30, 128);
    rotate(radians(20));
    rect(150, 100, 250, 150);
}
```

(See output in Figure 9.3. Full program in transforms/sketches/box3/box3.pde)

Oh yeah, the red box is definitely moving. Why is that?

Remember that all these numbers that describe the rectangles are expressed with respect to the coordinates of the window. The origin, or point (0, 0), is in the upper left. So the point (200, 150) that defines the upper-left corner of the box is 200 units to the right, and 150 down, from the upper-left.

When you give the `rotate()` command, Processing has to know what point you're rotating around. In fact, the answer is fixed. You can't change it. You always rotate around the point (0,0), called the origin. That's the rule.

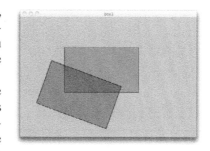

We can prove this by drawing a big circle centered at (0,0), with a radius that just touches the upper-left corner of the yellow box. If we really are rotating around the point (0,0), then the upper-left corner of the red box will also land on that circle. It's as though we placed a stick on top of the picture, with one end of the stick at the upper-left corner of the image and the other end at the upper-left corner of the box. Then we spin

Figure 9.3. The box before and after rotation.
(transforms/sketches/box3/box3.pde)

the stick around the upper-left corner of the window. The box rotates with the stick, but it also gets moved.

The radius of the circle we've been discussing can be found by using a rule discovered by Pythagoras (if you remember it from school, you can type it in and calculate the circle's radius yourself with it). I use the much more convenient built-in function `dist()`. This takes the *x*- and *y*-coordinates of two 2D points, and tells you how far apart they are (we'll see a complete list of handy functions like this one in Chapter 18). The arguments come in the order *x* and then *y* for the first point, then *x* and then *y* for the second.

So we can find the distance from the origin to the point (150, 100) by writing

```
float radiusUL = dist(0, 0, 150, 100);
```

By the way, we could make this a little shorter by using `mag()`. This is a specialized version of `dist()` that assumes the first point is the origin. We could get the same result as above with

```
float radiusUL = mag(150, 100);
```

This is nice, but for now I'll stick with `dist()` so we don't forget what's going on.

So let's use that calculation to draw the circle (I'll put it under everything else by drawing it first, and I'll temporarily increase the thickness of the stroke with a call to `strokeWeight()` to make it easier to see):

```
void draw() {
    background(210, 177, 68);
    stroke(0);
    noFill();
    strokeWeight(2);
    float radiusUL = dist(0, 0, 150, 100);
    ellipse(0, 0, radiusUL*2, radiusUL*2);
```

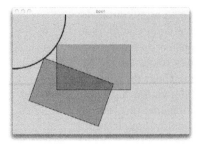

Figure 9.4. Adding a circle from the upper-left to (150, 100).
(transforms/sketches/box4/box4.pde)

```
    strokeWeight(1);

    fill(149, 93, 13, 128);
    rect(150, 100, 250, 150);
    fill(139, 49, 30, 128);
    rotate(radians(20));
    rect(150, 100, 250, 150);
}
```

(See output in Figure 9.4. Full program in transforms/sketches/box4/box4.pde)

Note that I had to use radiusUL*2 in the call to ellipse() because, in the default mode, that routine wants the *diameter* of the circle (which is two times the radius).

So this confirms what I was saying: the box is getting rotated around the origin. For fun, let's draw circles out to the other corners as well:

```
void draw() {
    background(192, 192, 192);
    stroke(255, 0, 0);
    noFill();

    drawCircleTo(200, 150);
    drawCircleTo(200, 250);
    drawCircleTo(400, 250);
    drawCircleTo(400, 150);

    fill(255, 255, 0, 128);
    stroke(0, 0, 0);
    rect(200, 150, 200, 100); // the yellow box

    rotate(radians(10));        // rotate
```

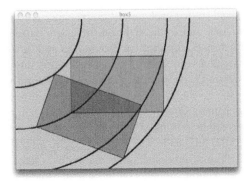

Figure 9.5. Circles to the original box's corners. (transforms/sketches/box5/box5.pde)

```
    fill(64, 64, 255, 128);
    rect(200, 150, 200, 100); // the red box
}

void drawCircleTo(float x, float y) {
    float r = dist(0, 0, x, y);
    ellipse(0, 0, 2*r, 2*r);
}
```

(See output in Figure 9.5. Full program in transforms/sketches/box5/box5.pde)

To keep things neat, I added the little routine at the end. It draws a circle around the origin, out to the point that you pass it.

You know this can't be the end of the road. Who would write a graphics system where you could only rotate around the upper-left corner of the window? We want our box to spin in place, around its own center, not the center of the window.

The way forward involves understanding just what it is that `rotate()` actually does. Then we'll see how the other transformation routines do similar jobs, and all the pieces will fall into place. By the way, sometimes people refer to a transformation simply as a *transform*.

9.1 Understanding Transformations

Here's the key point: `rotate()` does not rotate the objects that you draw. Instead, it rotates the *world*.

Think of it this way: when Processing first creates your window, it hauls out a giant piece of transparent graph paper. It's much, much bigger than the window. But the origin of the graph paper—the point (0,0)—is placed in the upper-left corner of the window. The paper is sized so that each unit of graph paper is equal to one pixel on the screen. So if you move one unit to the right on the graph paper, you move one pixel to the right on the screen, and similarly for moving up and down. The paper can be thought of as living just under your screen, so you're looking through the screen at it.

This is called Processing's *coordinate system*. Every time you name a point in Processing, it's with respect to this system. Because up until now we've always used Processing's default coordinate system, and because that system perfectly matches the window's pixels, we were able to think of them as the same thing.

So a point at (250, 100) tells us to first find the origin, no matter where it happens to be. Then we move 250 units along the x-axis, no matter what direction it happens to be pointing in or how big a "unit" appears on the screen. And then we move 100 units along the y-axis, again no matter what direction y is pointing or how big a "unit" in y would appear. But because the origin and the axes are all set up in a standard way when we start Processing, until now (250, 100) has always meant a pixel at (250, 100) relative to the window's upper-left corner. Now we'll see what happens when we change the coordinate system from this standard form.

To completely define a coordinate system, we need just a few pieces of information. First is the screen location of the coordinate system's point (0,0), which as we've seen is also called the origin. No matter where that point is located, that's the point that objects rotate around. The coordinate system also has two axes, x and y. As I said, they are initially scaled and placed to precisely match the pixels on your screen. Moving one unit to the right in Processing's coordinate system moves you one pixel to the right on the screen.

When you call `rotate(radians(10))`, you're telling Processing to rotate the graph paper, and of course, that means to rotate it around its origin. So your screen stays in place (of course), but the graph paper you're looking at rotates around its origin. Now when you tell Processing to go to (200, 100) it does what it always does and moves 200 units along x and 100 along y, but it does that in its own coordinate system. And that system has just been spun around by ten degrees.

Seen another way, suppose you go out to the park with a friend, and you spot a push carousel (also called a merry-go-round). This is a round wooden platform with metal bars running around the outside, and it spins around its central axis. The idea is that kids stand on the ground just on the edge of the carousel, grab a bar, and push. Faster and faster, they run around and around, accelerating the carousel until it's going at some crazy speed. Then they jump on and whiz around in circles until they throw up.

Suppose a friend is sitting in the middle of the carousel, and you paint a clock face around him on the surface of the carousel, so he's looking at twelve o'clock. Three o'clock is near his right hand, six o'clock is behind him, and nine o'clock is near his left hand. You climb up on a ladder and look straight down at your friend, so that you're both in the same orientation. That is, twelve o'clock is in front of you, three o'clock is to your right, and so on. But your ladder is fixed to the ground and it doesn't rotate with the carousel.

Suppose you ask your friend to take off one of his shoes and put it on the carousel at twelve o'clock. If he agrees, he must like you a lot. But if he does, then you'd both say that the shoe is at twelve o'clock. You ask him to retrieve his shoe.

Now someone rotates the carousel 90 degrees clockwise. Your ladder stays fixed. Your twelve o'clock is just where it's always been. Now you ask your friend to put his shoe back down at twelve o'clock again. And he does. Quite naturally, he puts it right in front of himself, just where he did before, right where it says twelve o'clock on the carousel.

But to you, he's put the shoe down at three o'clock. His coordinate system has rotated with respect to yours. Your coordinate system is like that of the screen: it's fixed and always stays put. The carousel's coordinate system is like that of Processing: it can rotate, and if it does, everything that comes after will get drawn in that rotated system.

This analogy isn't perfect because when the carousel moves, it brings along everything on it as well. But because Processing draws objects as you request them, anything you draw before you rotate the system stays in place. Only the new objects appear in the new system.

So returning to our example of the two boxes, when we start out, we're in the original coordinate system: x to the right, and y down. We draw the yellow box. Then we rotate the coordinate system by ten degrees, which is like rotating the carousel. Now x points to the right and a little bit down, and y points down and a little bit to the left. Drawing a box in *this* coordinate system still results in a box that has its upper-left corner at (150, 100) in Processing's coordinate system, but because that system has been rotated with respect to your screen, the red box appears rotated and moved on the screen as well.

To show the idea, here I've taken out the circle-related stuff and replaced the calls to `rect()` with calls to `drawBox()`. That's a little routine I wrote to draw the box and then draw a little grid over it. You can see that when `drawBox()` thinks it's drawing perfectly vertical and horizontal lines, it's actually drawing them in the current coordinate system. If that system is rotated, so are the lines.

```
void draw() {
    background(210, 177, 68);
    stroke(0);

    fill(149, 93, 13, 128);
    drawBox(150, 100, 250, 150);
    fill(139, 49, 30, 128);
    rotate(radians(20));
    drawBox(150, 100, 250, 150);
}

void drawBox(float left, float top, float wid, float hgt) {
    rect(left, top, wid, hgt);
    // draw perfectly vertical lines
```

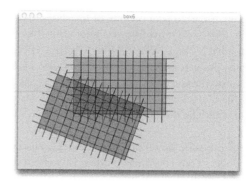

Figure 9.6. Each box has its own coordinate system. (transforms/sketches/box6/box6.pde)

```
for (int x=0; x<wid; x+=20) {
  line(left+x, top-20, left+x, top+hgt+20);
}
// draw perfectly horizontal lines
for (int y=0; y<hgt; y+=20) {
  line(left-20, top+y, left+wid+20, top+y);
}
}
```

(See output in Figure 9.6. Full program in transforms/sketches/box6/box6.pde)

9.2   Accumulating Transformations

Now you can probably guess the trick to getting the coordinate system to rotate around somewhere other than the upper-left corner: we just move the coordinate system to the place we want it! Then we rotate. This is called *accumulating* our transformations.

We want to put the origin in the middle of our boxes. Each box has its center at (275, 175). Before we call rotate(), we'll call translate() to move the origin to that spot (remember that "translate" is just another word for "move"):

```
void draw() {
  background(192, 192, 192);
  stroke(255, 0, 0);
  noFill();

  drawCircleTo(200, 150);
  drawCircleTo(200, 250);
  drawCircleTo(400, 250);
  drawCircleTo(400, 150);
```

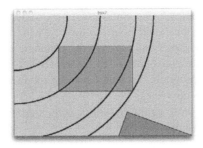

Figure 9.7. Adding a call to `translate()` before `rotate()`.
(transforms/sketches/box7/box7.pde)

```
    fill(255, 255, 0, 128);
    stroke(0, 0, 0);
    rect(200, 150, 200, 100); // the yellow box

    translate(300, 200);
    rotate(radians(10));       // rotate

    fill(64, 64, 255, 128);
    rect(200, 150, 200, 100); // the red box
}
```

(See output in Figure 9.7. Full program in transforms/sketches/box7/box7.pde)

Blech. That didn't work as advertised at all. That's because we didn't think it all the way through. Remember that translation moves the *origin* of the system. That means that when we draw the red box with its upper left at (150, 100) it's going to be at (150, 100) units away from the origin, which is now at the center!

The way to clean this all up is to change how we think of the box. Let's imagine it's centered on the origin (for the moment, we don't care where the origin is). So the box's upper-left corner is at $(-125, -75)$. It still has the same width and height, of course.

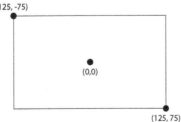

Figure 9.8. The centered box.

Figure 9.8 shows the idea. Instead of thinking of our box as something that's located at a particular place on the screen, we think of it as a kind of abstract box. It's a rectangle that's centered around the origin. When we want it to appear on the screen, we move the origin to the place where the box's center should be and then we draw the box.

As I mentioned in Chapter 6, we could use `rectMode()` to tell Processing that our box will be defined by the center point, followed by the width and height (or even half-width and half-height), but I like to leave the rectangle and ellipse modes at their defaults, so I don't have to constantly keep track of what they happen to be at any particular location in my program. So let's leave the mode alone and just change the values we give to `rect()` ourselves.

If we draw a box with these values, it will be centered on the origin (wherever that happens to be at the time we draw the box):

```
rect(-125, -75, 250, 150); // the red box
```

Now the box will be drawn centered at the origin and not some point far from it.

To recap, rotation always happens around the origin. But we can put the origin anywhere we want to on the screen and then rotations will seem to happen from there.

Let's put the pieces together now. I'll move the coordinate system before I draw anything. Then the yellow and red boxes will both be drawn centered at the origin, but the red box will come after the rotation. I'll also put the circles back in. The circles will also be drawn at the new origin, of course. They don't know that the origin has moved; a circle just draws itself around the origin, regardless of what transformations we've carried out beforehand.

```
void draw() {
   background(210, 177, 68);
   stroke(0);
   noFill();

   // move the origin to the center of the screen
   translate(300, 200);

   strokeWeight(2);
   drawCircleTo( 125,   75);
   drawCircleTo( 125,   75);
   drawCircleTo(-125,  -75);
   drawCircleTo(-125,  -75);
   strokeWeight(1);

   fill(149, 93, 13, 128);
   rect(-125, -75, 250, 150);
   fill(139, 49, 30, 128);

   rotate(radians(20));

   rect(-125, -75, 250, 150);
}
```

(See output in Figure 9.9. Full program in transforms/sketches/box8/box8.pde)

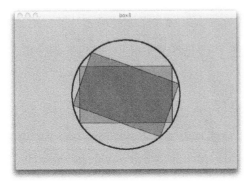

Figure 9.9. The correctly rotated box! (transforms/sketches/box8/box8.pde)

Finally, success! So we *move* the origin, then *rotate* the coordinate system, and then *draw* the box centered at the origin.

All the circles overlap because all four corners of the rectangle are the same distance away from the center.

9.3   Order Matters

A really, really important thing to keep in mind is *you have to execute all your transformations in the correct order*. This is because *all* your transforms accumulate. Each one does its job based on the coordinate system it receives as a result of the preceding transformations. If you translate the coordinate system from its default position, it's moved. If you then rotate, it's the moved system that gets rotated, and then you have a

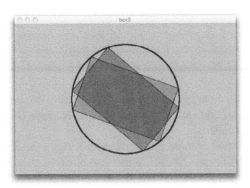

Figure 9.10. Rotating the whole thing after translating. (transforms/sketches/box9/box9.pde)

system that's been moved and *then* rotated. If you do more operations, they continue to accumulate.

For fun, let's rotate the whole system by another 20 degrees right after the first translation:

```
translate(300, 200);
rotate(radians(20));
```

(See output in Figure 9.10. Full program in transforms/sketches/box9/box9.pde)

Right, just what we'd expect: the whole world got rotated by 20 degrees. Now let's put these in the opposite order:

```
rotate(radians(20));
translate(300, 200);
```

(See output in Figure 9.11. Full program in transforms/sketches/box10/box10.pde)

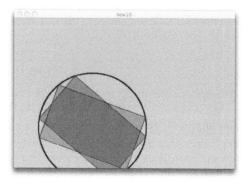

Figure 9.11. Rotating the whole thing before translating.
(transforms/sketches/box10/box10.pde)

Different! First we rotated the world and then we translated. So the translation didn't go 300 units to the right on the screen and 200 down on the screen but instead went 300 units right and 200 units down in Processing's coordinate system, which had just been rotated.

The order in which you apply transformations is really important. If things start to appear in screwy places, odds are you've gotten one or more of your transformations out of the order you intended.

We've seen two of the big three transformations. The remaining one is scale(). This is unlike the others because it takes either one or two arguments.

With just one argument, scale() uniformly enlarges everything. As always, the transformation happens with respect to the origin. Let's go back to our previous example (from Figure 9.9) and put in a scale() just after the translate():

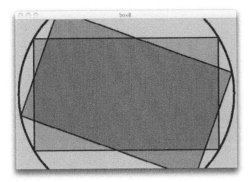

Figure 9.12. Adding a uniform scale operation. (transforms/sketches/scale1/scale1.pde)

```
scale(2.0);
```

(See output in Figure 9.12. Full program in transforms/sketches/scale1/scale1.pde)

Bam, everything gets bigger by a factor of two. Even line thicknesses! Of course, we can use a smaller number to shrink everything instead:

```
scale(0.5);
```

(See output in Figure 9.13. Full program in transforms/sketches/scale2/scale2.pde)

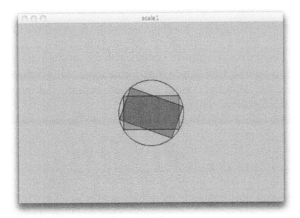

Figure 9.13. Scaling by 0.5. (transforms/sketches/scale2/scale2.pde)

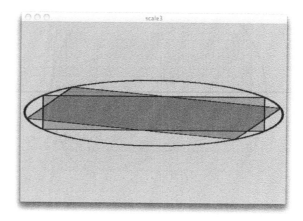

Figure 9.14. Nonuniform scaling. (transforms/sketches/scale3/scale3.pde)

If we give scale() two arguments, then it will use the first to scale things in *x* and the second in *y*. Let's make things twice as big in *x* and half as big in *y*:

```
scale(2, 0.5);
```

(See output in Figure 9.14. Full program in transforms/sketches/scale3/scale3.pde)

This is sometimes called *nonuniform scaling* or *differential scaling*. Scaling by the same size in all directions is called *uniform scaling*.

We've now seen all three of the basic transformations. To recap, translate() lets us move the coordinate system in *x* and *y*, rotate() spins the system around the origin, and scale() grows or shrinks the system (uniformly or separately in *x* and *y*). Each time you change the coordinate system with one of these transformations, that becomes the starting point for all future transformations. All graphics you draw after these operations are drawn in the current coordinate system, and they show up on the screen where the coordinate system is.

9.4 Nested Transformations

The fact that transforms accumulate is incredibly useful in all kinds of situations. We sometimes say that accumulated transformations are *nested* inside one another. Here's a simple example, but a cool one.

The sun sits in the center of the solar system, static and immobile. The Earth orbits the sun. The moon orbits the Earth. Let's do that!

```
float SunDiam = 80;

float EarthDiam = 30;
float EarthOrbitRadius = 130;
float EarthAngle = 0;

float MoonDiam = 10;
float MoonOrbitRadius = 50;
float MoonAngle = 0;

void setup() {
   size(600, 400);
}

void draw() {
   background(0, 0, 0);     // inky blackness of space
   translate(300, 200);     // move origin to center of screen
   noStroke();

   fill(255, 200, 64);                  // yellow-orange
   ellipse(0, 0, SunDiam, SunDiam);   // the mighty Sun

   // rotate around the sun
   rotate(EarthAngle);

   // move out to Earth orbit
   translate(EarthOrbitRadius, 0);

   fill(64, 64, 255);                       // blue-ish
   ellipse(0, 0, EarthDiam, EarthDiam);   // the noble Earth

   // rotate around the Earth
   rotate(MoonAngle);

   // move out to Moon orbit
   translate(MoonOrbitRadius, 0);

   fill(192, 192, 180);                   // gray-ish
   ellipse(0, 0, MoonDiam, MoonDiam);   // the friendly Moon

   EarthAngle += 0.01;
   MoonAngle += 0.01;
}
```

(See output in Figure 9.15. Full program in transforms/sketches/orbits1/orbits1.pde)

Pretty sweet. Imagine if you had to figure out an equation to describe the path of the moon! This is way easier and makes lots of sense.

By the way, all of the numbers in this example, from the sizes of the objects to their colors to how much the angles change, were all chosen pretty much from thin air. I guessed at them and then played with them a few times until everything fit on the screen and looked nice to my eye. This depends a lot on my computer's screen size and running speed. Feel free to change anything that doesn't feel right to you.

If you'd like to see more clearly how things are happening, you can change the circular Earth to a box:

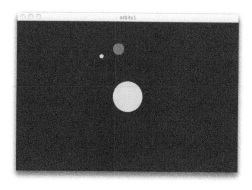

Figure 9.15. A single frame of animation from the solar system.
(transforms/sketches/orbits1/orbits1.pde)

```
rect(-EarthDiam/2, -EarthDiam/2, EarthDiam, EarthDiam);
                                // the noble Earth
```

(See output in Figure 9.16. Full program in transforms/sketches/orbits2/orbits2.pde)

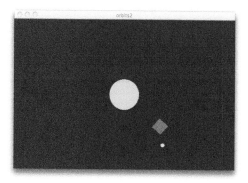

Figure 9.16. The Earth as a box. (transforms/sketches/orbits2/orbits2.pde)

We can make the moon a box as well:

```
rect(-MoonDiam/2, -MoonDiam/2, MoonDiam, MoonDiam);
                                // the friendly Moon
```

(See output in Figure 9.17. Full program in transforms/sketches/orbits3/orbits3.pde)

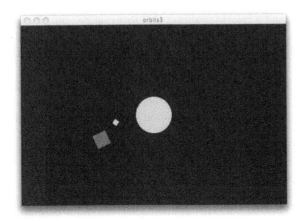

Figure 9.17. The moon as a box as well. (transforms/sketches/orbits3/orbits3.pde)

As we've seen, transforms accumulate. But there are two exceptions to this rule.

The first is that each time you enter `draw()`, all transformations are reset. In essence, each time `draw()` begins, it puts down a fresh sheet of graph paper in the default starting position, orientation, and size. Any transformations you carried out during a previous execution of `draw()` are forgotten and lost.

The second exception lets you bring this about yourself, so you can tell Processing you want to forget all the transformations that are in place right now and return to the default coordinate system. Why would you want this?

Suppose you've just made the little solar system above, but now you want to add another planet and another moon. But by the time you've drawn the moon, you've got several transformations stacked on top of each other. One way to draw a new moon is to toss out all the transformations, so you can start fresh for a new planet.

Processing lets you reset all the transformations at once if you want to, basically going back to a clean slate, like at the start of each call of `draw()`. The name of the routine that does this is a little strange, though. The name comes from the fact that, internally, Processing stores transformations using a mathematical structure called a *matrix*. This is nothing more than a bunch of numbers, typically arranged in a rectangular grid.

You absolutely do not need to know or care about what a matrix is, or what's in this matrix. Or what's in any matrix, anywhere. But the transformation is represented internally in that format, so you'll often see references to things like the *transformation matrix*. Because the matrix is directly responsible for the transformations that get applied to your objects, we often use "transformation matrix" as a synonym for "transformation."

So to reset the transformations, you reset the matrix. Happily, this has a reasonable name:

```
resetMatrix();
```

No arguments, and it returns nothing. Call that routine, and all of your transformations so far go away, and the coordinate system goes back to its default state. Of course, anything you've drawn so far remains where it appeared, but from now on, you have a clean slate, and you can start accumulating new transformations if you want.

That's a pretty drastic step. Wouldn't it be nice if you could undo one or more transformations, like you can undo in a graphics or word processing program? Then you could make some transformations, undo one or two, make some new ones, and so on.

Or, alternatively, what if you could save the current transformation somehow, make changes on top of that, and then later restore the version you saved?

Processing supports just that kind of save and recall feature for transformations. The matrix that describes the transformation in effect at any moment is called the *current matrix*. That's the one that's actually applied when you draw something.

But off to the side, there's a place where you can temporarily save and recall matrices. It's called the matrix *stack*.

A stack is a computer term for a general concept that shows up in Processing in a couple of places. A computer's stack is like a real stack of books. You can put things onto the top of the stack, and you can also remove the top thing off the stack (assuming there's anything in the stack, of course). When you add to the stack, the metaphor is that you're placing it on the top, and the extra weight pushes everything else down. So adding something to the top of the stack is called *pushing* that object onto the stack. When you take the top item off of the stack, it's called *popping* that object off the stack.

So you might say "I pushed the book *Jitterbug Perfume* on top of the stack," or, "I popped the stack and got the book *Jitterbug Perfume* back."

Processing maintains a stack of the matrices that define the transformations you've made to the coordinate system. When you enter draw(), the stack is empty; that is, there's nothing in it. The current transformation is the default one that Processing sets up for you.

As you go on, any time you have a transformation you'd like to keep for later, you can push it onto the top of the stack with the routine pushMatrix(), which you call like this:

```
pushMatrix();
```

The routine pushMatrix() takes no arguments and returns nothing. It just makes a copy of whatever the current transformation is at the time you call it and pushes that copy onto the top of the stack of matrices. You can now continue making whatever changes you want to the current matrix, knowing that there's a saved copy of the older one sitting on the stack for you. Any time you want to retrieve the matrix you most recently pushed, you can pop it with popMatrix():

```
popMatrix();
```

As a result, whatever you pushed most recently gets taken off the stack and becomes the current matrix (whatever transformation was represented by the current matrix just before you did the pop is discarded). The stack now has one less item in it.

Remember that you can only pop the stack if there's something on it already.

Let's write a little program that just draws a box:

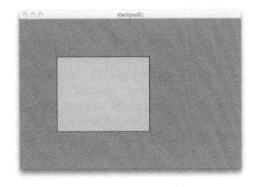

Figure 9.18. Drawing a single box.
(transforms/sketches/stackpop01/stackpop01.pde)

```
void setup() {
    size(600, 400);
}

void draw() {
    background(128);
    fill(128, 202, 83);
    rect(100, 100, 250, 200);
}
```

(See output in Figure 9.18. Full program in transforms/sketches/stackpop01/stackpop01.pde)

Now let's pop the stack. I'll just put in a call to popMatrix() after we set the background color:

```
void draw() {
    background(128);
    popMatrix();
    fill(128, 202, 83);
    rect(100, 100, 250, 200);
}
```

(Full program in transforms/sketches/stackpop02/stackpop02.pde)

When we run this, the program crashes, the console fills up with red error messages, the message area turns red, and it gives me the message

```
missing a popMatrix() to go with that pushMatrix()
```

That error message gets it backwards (it implies we have a pushMatrix() without a matching popMatrix()), but it's got the general idea right. When using a stack, every pop has to have a preceding push.

If you try this, you may find that Processing does make a graphics window for you but then gets hung up with this error, and you can't dismiss the graphics window by clicking on its close button. When that happens, click the *Stop* button on Processing's tool bar.

Stacks are very convenient because of the push and pop mechanism. This lets you push lots of things onto the stack freely and then pop them back off, always retrieving the items back in the opposite order in which you saved them. Of course, this convenience comes at a price: you can't retrieve an item from somewhere deep in the stack without first popping (and possibly losing) all the values above it. But using a stack for saving transformations has proven itself to be the most useful way to organize your transformations for graphics programming, and almost every graphics language around has some means for you to push and pop transformation matrices on a stack.

To use push and pop for transformations, the general plan is that you build your picture, accumulating transformations as you go, until you reach a branching point. Then you push the matrix (that is, you save a copy). You continue on, accumulating new transformations and drawing things. Then you pop the matrix, and it restores the transformation in effect at the time you pushed.

Here's an example. I'll extend our solar system to give the Earth a second moon, named Nem (for Nemesis, the moon's evil sibling). I'll push the transformation just before I make the transformations for the first moon. I'll rotate and translate out to the moon and draw it, then pop the matrix, which brings me back to the coordinate system of the Earth. Then I'll make the transforms for Nem, as though I'd never made the moon transforms at all. For variety, I'll use rectangles this time for the planets and moons.

```
float SunDiam = 80;

float EarthDiam = 30;
float EarthOrbitRadius = 130;
float EarthAngle = 0;

float MoonDiam = 10;
float MoonOrbitRadius = 50;
float MoonAngle = 0;

float NemDiam = 20;
float NemOrbitRadius = 40;
float NemAngle = 0;

void setup() {
   size(600, 400);
}

void draw() {
   background(0, 0, 0);      // inky blackness of space
   translate(300, 200);      // move origin to center of screen

   noStroke();
```

```
fill(255, 200, 64);              // yellow-orange
ellipse(0, 0, SunDiam, SunDiam); // the mighty Sun

// rotate around the sun
rotate(EarthAngle);

// move out to Earth orbit
translate(EarthOrbitRadius, 0);

fill(64, 64, 255);                                    // blue-ish
rect(-EarthDiam/2, -EarthDiam/2, EarthDiam, EarthDiam); // the noble Earth

// push this transform so we can return to it later
pushMatrix();

// rotate around the Earth
rotate(MoonAngle);

// move out to Moon orbit
translate(MoonOrbitRadius, 0);

fill(192, 192, 180);                                  // gray-ish
rect(-MoonDiam/2, -MoonDiam/2, MoonDiam, MoonDiam); // the friendly Moon

// pop the stack, recovering the old transformation
popMatrix();

// rotate around the Earth
rotate(NemAngle);

// move out to Nem orbit
translate(NemOrbitRadius, 0);

fill(220, 75, 75);                                    // red-ish
rect(-NemDiam/2, -NemDiam/2, NemDiam, NemDiam); // the evil Nem

EarthAngle += 0.01;
MoonAngle += 0.01;
NemAngle += 0.015;
}
```

(See output in Figure 9.19. Full program in transforms/sketches/orbits4/orbits4.pde)

So now the slightly larger Nem rotates around the Earth, a little faster and a little closer than does the moon. By pushing the matrix and then popping it, I was able to use the very same process to draw Nem that I used to draw the moon.

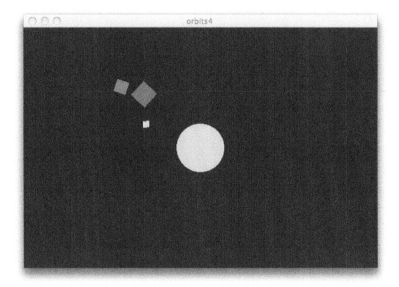

Figure 9.19. A second moon around the Earth. (transforms/sketches/orbits4/orbits4.pde)

Notice that the rectangular Earth always presents one of its sides directly to the sun, and both the moon and Nem also present flat sides to the Earth. That's because they're each being drawn in their own, transformed coordinate system in which the y-axis points in the direction I moved to reach that object's orbit.

By the way, if you're curious to see what the current transformation matrix looks like at any time, you can print it out to the console with command `printMatrix()`. If you're into the mathematics of these things, you can give Processing the 16 (yes, 16) numbers that make up your own matrix and have it combine that with the current matrix with the command `applyMatrix()`. This is very specialized stuff; if you're keen to learn more, you'll want to read up on a field of mathematics called *linear algebra*. The name might be off-putting, but much of that field is visual and geometric, and the ideas are beautiful.

Extend this little program to create a rich solar system of your own design. Use loops to create lots of orbiting bodies, and use `pushMatrix()` and `popMatrix()` to keep things straight. You might even put up some satellites around the moons, which would give you yet a third level of transformation. Maybe you could include a comet or two. If you're really feeling the vibe, try using the built-in `random()` function to create a different, random solar system every time you run the program (we'll cover `random()` later on in Chapter 11, but you can read about it in the documentation now if you want a head start).

If you're of a scientific and mathematical bend of mind, look up Kepler's laws of planetary motion and modify your simulated solar system so that it obeys those laws.

Chapter 10
Recursion

Because transforms accumulate, they let us easily create complicated motions that would otherwise be almost impossible to produce.

Let's write a new project, in some ways like the solar system but a little different. It's inspired by the Spirograph toy, which has been the source of endless different computer graphics projects. A picture of a Spirograph set and its use is shown in Figure 10.1.

The basic version of the toy contains two types of plastic gears. One is a big ring, like a letter O, with gear teeth lining both the inside and outside of the ring. The other type of gear is a smaller circular disk with teeth around the outside. Inside this disk are a bunch of holes.

To make a drawing, you lay down a piece of cardboard, then put a piece of paper on top of that, and then put the ring on top of the paper. You push a couple of little pins through the ring and into the board beneath, fixing everything into position. Then you put the little disk into the inside of the circular ring, put your pen into one of the holes, and then use your pen to push the gear around the ring. Your pen leaves a trail behind as the gear rotates inside the big ring, creating a beautiful, curvy pattern. If you switch out the

Figure 10.1. The *Spirograph* set of plastic gears. In use, the ring gear is pinned to a sheet of cardboard and a circular gear is pushed around and around with a colored pen.

gears every now and then for bigger or smaller ones, and change the color of your pen, you can layer one drawing on another and create really gorgeous results. Figure 10.2 shows a few drawings I made with my Spirograph set.

Mathematicians have studied these kinds of curves quite a lot; if you're curious about them, you can find more information on the web using the terms *hypotrochoid* and *epitrochoid* or *hypocycloid* and *epicycloid*. I know those terms seem strange, but if history had gone a slightly different way they might have been everyday words. Back in 1875, a ride opened up in Atlantic City, New Jersey. It consisted of four wheels about 15 or 20 feet tall, standing vertically, like they were forming the four sides of a box. Mounted along the spokes of each wheel were eight chairs capable of holding two people each. An axle went through the center of each wheel, and all the axles met in the center of the box at a single vertical column. The whole assembly rotated around this center shaft. As a motor spun that shaft, the four wheels turned as they rotated around it, so the people sitting in the seats were lifted up and down as the wheel turned around its own axis, and the wheel rolled on the ground as it spun about the central axis. This ride was patented as the "Rotary-Swing," but when it was built it was called the Epicycloidal Diversion. It was such a popular ride that the basic idea reappeared a few years later in 1893 at the World Columbian Exposition in Chicago. The four spinning, rotating wheels of the Epicycloidal Diversion were replaced by a single spinning wheel of much larger size. That ride was built by George Ferris and was called the Ferris Wheel. The name stuck, people forgot about its predecessor, and "epicycloid" never became a household word.

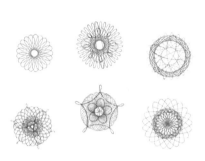

Figure 10.2. Some *Spirograph* patterns.

10.1 Recursive Teacups

Let's take Spirograph one step further and make a moving, kinetic animation. Let's start out with a square window in which we'll draw a big circle. Then inside the circle I'll draw a smaller circle that spins around the inside of the larger one. Inside of that, a smaller circle will spin. Inside of that, yet another circle. And so on.

Coincidentally, this sounds like another amusement park ride known as the spinning teacups. It consists of a giant circular platform under control of the ride operator. Mounted on the platform are a bunch of smaller, circular platforms. On each one of these platforms, three or four bowl-shaped "teacups" are mounted; these have seats (and safety belts!) inside them. When the operator starts the ride, the big platform starts to rotate. Each of the little platforms on it, already going around in a big circle, rotates around its own center. And then each teacup itself spins around its own center! Spinning on spinning on spinning.

Our version will just be pictures on a screen, and I hope it will make us all a bit less dizzy.

So as usual, we'll start with a skeleton:

```
void setup() {
    screen(500, 500);
}

void draw() {
    background(192);
    // drawing stuff here
}
```

Not too exciting, but now we get to strategize. Each circle is going to contain multiple smaller circles. And they will contain multiple smaller circles, and so on. And I don't know yet how far down that should go.

A natural way to think about this would be for draw() to essentially call a routine with the instruction, "Draw a circle that contains several smaller circles." Then that routine, to draw each of those circles, would do the same thing: "Draw a circle that contains several smaller circles." And so on and so on. In other words, the circles-drawing routine would want to call itself to draw its own elements.

This is a natural kind of thing that pops up in programming on a regular basis. It's called *recursion*. The essence of recursion is that a routine calls itself, usually with slightly different arguments each time.

That's not enough, though. Recursion has its own flavor of the infinite loop, which you may recall happens when a loop, like a *while loop*, gets stuck and repeats itself forever without end.

Here's a flawed example of recursion that demonstrates that problem:

```
// a flawed example of recursion
void setup() {
    doRecursion();
}

void doRecursion() {
    int x = 5;
    doRecursion();
}
```

You can probably guess that nothing good would come of this program. But as I've said, you can't break the computer, so give it whirl.

If your machine is like mine, it froze up for a moment and then you got a bunch of red-on-black error messages in the console. My message area reported

```
StackOverflowError: This sketch is attempting too much recursion.
```

Yup, that broke pretty quickly. We call this *runaway recursion*.

Why is this a problem? Each time doRecursion() calls itself, it has to create a new copy of the variable x (after all, each time the computer starts the routine, x is a new local variable to that version of the routine). And then doRecursion() calls itself again, which means allocating another x, and so on, endlessly, until the computer runs out of memory. Processing is smart enough to know that it isn't simply an out-of-memory problem, but in fact, it's the result of this routine calling itself too many times.

The stack in this error message refers to an internal stack used by Processing. We saw in Chapter 9 that Processing lets you use a stack to manage your drawing transformations. Stacks are so useful that Processing uses them for its own purposes as well when compiling and running your program, and here, one of those stacks has grown too big as a result of this runaway recursion.

Even if we didn't create the variable x, Processing still has to save a bunch of information each time you call a routine (like where you were when you called it and other internal information for its own bookkeeping). This eats up memory. When your recursion goes crazy, like this one did, you eventually run out of memory.

Why doesn't this happen in other programs? Well, suppose you have a routine called drawCircle(), and you write a loop that calls this routine 10,000 times. Each time you call drawCircle(), the computer uses some memory to keep track of where you were when you called the routine, and it uses some more memory for the routine's local variables and other internal needs. When drawCircle() finishes and returns, all of that memory gets freed up. After all, there's no need to keep it around anymore, since we're back from the routine. So calling drawCircle() once requires a chunk of memory, but calling it 10,000 times requires nothing more: each time, the computer grabs some memory, uses it, and returns it. The key here is that drawCircle() finished, or returned. That's how Processing knew it could reclaim the memory it used.

You can call the same routine over and over again, without any problem, as long as it finishes up naturally each time (that is, it ends and returns, either by reaching the last statement in the function or by encountering a return() statement). In fact, we've been doing this all along! In every program we've run that has a draw() function, Processing calls that function 60 times a second. After an hour, that's almost a quarter of a million function calls. But these programs can run for hours, or days, or even months without running out of memory.

The problem in our recursion example above is that the doRecursion() routine never finished up! Not once. All that function does is call itself, allocating more memory every time, never freeing it, in a never-ending process until the computer can't store even one more call. Then, crash.

This runaway recursion happens now and then to everyone.

That's why every recursive program must have something called a *stopping condition*, also called a *termination condition*. This is a test that tells the routine, in essence, don't recur any more. Stop here. Don't call yourself.

One simple way to achieve this is to keep track of the *recursion level*, also called the *recursion depth* . That's an integer that tells us how many times a routine has called itself. Here's an example of a version of our program with such a test:

```
// a better example of recursion
void setup() {
   doRecursion(1);
}

void doRecursion(int depth) {
   int x = 1;
   if (depth < 5) {
      println("depth="+depth);
      doRecursion(depth+1);
   }
}
```

You can see that I'm printing out the depth. If we run this program, the results are

```
depth=1
depth=2
depth=3
depth=4
```

After that, the program is done. Whew. We've avoided runaway recursion. Recursion is a great tool, but you've got to remember to have a good, working stopping criterion built into the code, or you risk having it run away from you. When I write recursive routines, the stopping criterion is usually the first thing I write, and the first thing I test. Only once I'm sure it's working correctly do I move on to the body of the routine.

So let's flesh out our circles-in-circles project with a recursive routine that has a stopping condition:

```
int MaxDepth = 4;

void setup() {
   screen(500, 500);
}

void draw() {
   background(119, 112, 127);
   drawCircles(1);
}

void drawCircles(int depth) {
   if (depth > MaxDepth) return;
```

```
    // draw the big circle
    // for each internal circle, call drawCircles(depth+1);
}
```

I've created a global variable called MaxDepth to control the maximum depth that the recursion can go to. Manually tracking the depth is not the most elegant way to control recursion, but it works fine and it's a common practice. Something nicer would be to end the recursion based on what drawCircles() is actually doing. For example, if the circles are less than one pixel large, that would be a good time to stop. But a hard limit on the recursion depth is a perfectly good solution here.

I'd like drawCircles() to have an easy time of things, so let's say it always intends to draw a circle of radius 1 (or diameter 2), centered at the origin. So I'll add a translate() call to put the origin of the coordinate system at the center of the window and then I'll add a scale() call so a circle of radius 1 is a little bit smaller than the screen (if I scaled by 250, then a circle of radius 1 would be drawn as circle of radius 250, and it would just touch the edges of my 500-by-500 window. So I'll scale by 240, which gives me a little 10-pixel cushion around the outside). Then I'll add the circle-drawing command to drawCircles(). I'll set the circle's color to dark red. Since I don't want any outlines now, I'll call noStroke() once in setup():

```
int MaxDepth = 4;

void setup() {
    size(500, 500);
    noStroke();
}

void draw() {
    background(119, 112, 127);
    translate(250, 250);
    scale(240.0);
    drawCircles(1);
}

void drawCircles(int depth) {
    if (depth > MaxDepth) return;
    fill(89, 9, 21);
    ellipse(0, 0, 2, 2);
}
```

(See output in Figure 10.3. Full program in recursion/sketches/spinners1/spinners1.pde)

This is fine, but there's no evidence of recursion yet. So let's put in something simple. After we draw the circle, we'll scale the coordinate system down and then call drawCircles() again. That will draw a smaller circle inside of this one:

Figure 10.3. Starting the recursion project. (recursion/sketches/spinners1/spinners1.pde)

```
void drawCircles(int depth) {
   if (depth > MaxDepth) return;
   fill(89, 9, 21);
   ellipse(0, 0, 2, 2);
   scale(0.75);
   drawCircles(depth+1);
}
```

(See output in Figure 10.4. Full program in recursion/sketches/spinners2/spinners2.pde)

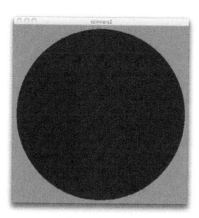

Figure 10.4. Adding recursion (I think). (recursion/sketches/spinners2/spinners2.pde)

Well, maybe that worked. It's hard to tell, since we're just drawing dark red circles on top of dark red circles. Let's turn the stroke back on to see the outlines. I'll call

Figure 10.5. First results from recursion. (recursion/sketches/spinners3/spinners3.pde)

stroke() and set the color to black:

```
void drawCircles(int depth) {
   if (depth > MaxDepth) return;
   stroke(color(0,0,0));
   fill(255, 255, 0);
   ellipse(0, 0, 2, 2);
   scale(0.75);
   drawCircles(depth+1);
}
```

(See output in Figure 10.5. Full program in recursion/sketches/spinners3/spinners3.pde)

What the huh?

If you mess around with this for a while, drawing different circles at different levels of recursion, you'll discover that the stroke thickness is scaling along with everything else. So the black line around the biggest circle, which was originally just one pixel thick, is now 240 pixels thick! So that thick black stroke pretty much fills the screen, and the ones that follow (though they get thinner, thanks to the decreasing scale factor) are still way too thick.

I've never found a good way to handle this. What I want is to have the current transformation in place but have my strokes and lines get drawn only one pixel thick.

This is an explicit option in some 2D drawing programs, which offer you a check box that says something like "Scale line weights with transformations," and you can turn it off if you don't want that to happen. In Processing, we've seen that `strokeWeight()` lets you set line thickness, but the value you give it is transformed along with everything else. So scaling up an object means scaling up the line weight, too.

A natural thought then is to scale the stroke weight by the same amount, only in reverse. So if I scale a circle up by 250, I could set the stroke's weight to 1/250.

But if you've scaled by different amounts in x and y, then no single scaling value will work to give you a uniform-looking stroke. Differential scaling could work, but now we're starting to get complicated. Things get out of control if you rotate, then scale, then rotate, and so on, so there's no one simple scaling factor that's going to make lines one pixel thick in all directions. And even worse, the online Processing manual says that the `strokeWeight()` function has a bug in most platforms for the current release and doesn't work correctly anyway. This is so frustrating that my response is to just forget about strokes altogether in any program that does scaling, except for the most limited and simple cases. If I absolutely need what strokes can do, I end up writing some kind of custom code just to draw them.

So let's do away with the stroke. I'll take out the call to `stroke()`, and so the call to `noStroke()` that's currently in `setup()` will stay in force. Instead, I'll change the color of each circle. I've got some colors that I like, so I'll choose the fill color based on the recursion depth.

I'll use a bunch of *if statements* to control the colors. A nice benefit of this approach is that I can roll the recursion-stopping test right into the same big *if statement*.

```
void drawCircles(int depth) {
        if (depth == 1) fill(color(89, 9, 21));
   else if (depth == 2) fill(color(148, 14, 35));
   else if (depth == 3) fill(color(181, 86, 70));
   else if (depth == 4) fill(color(199, 172, 115));
   else return;

   ellipse(0, 0, 2, 2);
   scale(0.75);
   drawCircles(depth+1);
}
```

(See output in Figure 10.6. Full program in recursion/sketches/spinners4/spinners4.pde)

There, that's kind of nice.

These *if statements* are notable for two reasons. First, there are no curly braces after each test: that's because there's only one statement in each body. Remember that the function of the curly braces in an *if statement* (or a loop) is to create a block, or a chunk of statements, where Processing was expecting only one. If we have only one statement, as we do here, we can just plunk it right down without curly braces. If you want to include the curly braces when you have only one statement, that's fine; there are

Figure 10.6. Finally, some nice recursion results. (recursion/sketches/spinners4/spinners4.pde)

no negative side effects to that except that your source code is a few characters longer.
Your program runs exactly the same either way. I often use the curly braces even for a
block with only a single statement, but I decided not to here because I wanted to show
visually how these tests are related.

And that brings us to the second notable feature: I've formatted the lines a little
strangely. I wanted the `if` keywords to all line up. In fact, I wanted the lines to stack
up as much as possible to show that they're nearly identical repeats of each other. That
way, if I make a typo in one of them, I can catch it more easily. Of course, I would
rather do away with these repetitions altogether, and in Chapter 13, I'll show how to do
that using arrays. For now, though, I'll live with the repetition.

We saw in Chapter 4 that we can use *switch statements* in this kind of situation.
Here's the `switch` form for this code:

```
switch (depth) {
   case 1:  fill(color(89, 9, 21));      break;
   case 2:  fill(color(148, 14, 35));    break;
   case 3:  fill(color(181, 86, 70));    break;
   case 4:  fill(color(199, 172, 115));  break;
   default: return;
}
```

(Full program in recursion/sketches/spinners4a/spinners4a.pde)

This does the same job, but it looks a little better to my eye. It's also a tiny bit more efficient than all those `if` statements. That efficiency isn't a big deal in this program, but it doesn't hurt.

One thing bears noting when you use `switch` this way, though. Notice that the last line (the `default` case) doesn't have a `break` statement, even though I said back in Chapter 4 that I usually like to include one in the default clause anyway. Suppose we do include one, like this:

```
default: return; break;
```

If you try this, Processing will flag it in yellow and report this error:

```
Unreachable code
```

This makes sense. After all, when Processing hits the `return` statement, that means its done, and this function is wrapped up. Anything that comes after `return` in that clause (even something as benign as a `break` statement) can't ever get executed. So Processing considers that to be code that it can never actually get to, or code that is "unreachable." All you have to do is remove the `break` statement (which really wasn't necessary in the first place) and all is well.

Returning to our image, notice that the circles are not getting uniformly smaller; that is, they're not shrinking by, say, 20 pixels in radius each time. Instead, the radius is going down by 75 percent, so each circle has a radius three-quarters the size of the one that surrounds it.

Now we're cooking. The recursion is working, and we're nesting transformations on each call. Now all we have to do is write the code to put the circles where we want them.

To get things working, let's draw just one circle. I'll translate in *y* by 0.6 (so now the origin of the coordinate system is 0.4 units from the edge of the circle) and I'll scale by 0.4. That way, the next time we draw a circle with radius 1, it will just touch the bottom edge of this first circle:

```
void drawCircles(int depth) {
   if (depth > MaxDepth) return;

   float rval = 255;
   float gval = 255 * depth / MaxDepth-1;
   float bval = 150 * depth / MaxDepth-1;
   fill(color(rval, gval, bval));
   ellipse(0, 0, 2, 2);

   translate(0, .6);
   scale(0.4);
   drawCircles(depth+1);
}
```

(See output in Figure 10.7. Full program in recursion/sketches/spinners5/spinners5.pde)

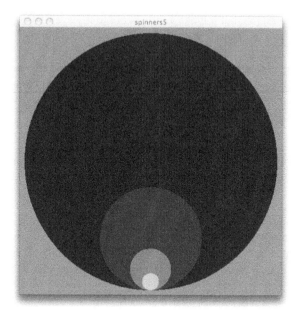

Figure 10.7. Recursion with translation. (recursion/sketches/spinners5/spinners5.pde)

OK, now let's get this moving! I'll call `rotate()` before I call `translate()`, which will cause the new circles to appear rotated around the center of their parent circle. I'll create a global variable called `Theta` (the Greek letter theta, θ, is often used in graphics to refer to an angle). It'll start at 0, and then for every new frame, when `draw()` is called, I'll increment it by one degree. Here's the overall picture:

```
int MaxDepth = 4;
float Theta = 0;

void setup() {
   size(500, 500);
}

void draw() {
   background(192);
   translate(250, 250);
   scale(240.0);
   drawCircles(1);
   Theta += radians(1);
}

void drawCircles(int depth) {
```

```
if (depth > MaxDepth) return;

float rval = 255;
float gval = 255 * depth / MaxDepth;
float bval = 150 * depth / MaxDepth;
fill(color(rval, gval, bval));
ellipse(0, 0, 2, 2);

rotate(Theta);
translate(0, .6);
scale(0.4);
drawCircles(depth+1);
}
```

(See output in Figure 10.8. Full program in recursion/sketches/spinners6/spinners6.pde)

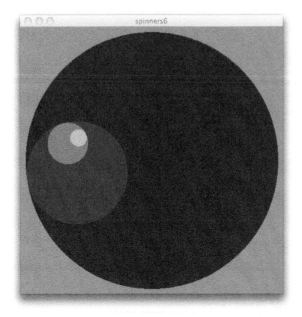

Figure 10.8. Spinners with recursion (frame from animation).
(recursion/sketches/spinners6/spinners6.pde)

If you run this, you'll see the circles spinning around inside of each other. If it's spinning too fast on your system, reduce the number added to Theta in draw(). If it's going too slow for your taste, increase that number.

This animation is nice, but it's not what I originally had in mind. I wanted three circles inside of each larger circle. That's easily done; I'll just put a loop inside of drawCircles(). The first time through, I'll rotate by Theta degrees. The second time, I'll rotate by Theta+120 degrees, which will place the new circle one-third of the way around the bigger circle (remember, there are 360 degrees in a circle). Then the third time, I'll rotate by Theta+240. To make sure that the transforms don't interfere with each other, I'll put each one into its own little pushMatrix()/popMatrix() block. I'll indent the statements between those calls, even though there's no curly braces, because I think of them as a paired set enclosing some statements.

Here's the entire program:

```
int MaxDepth = 4;
float Theta = 0;

void setup() {
   size(500, 500);
   noStroke();
}

void draw() {
   background(119, 112, 127);
   translate(250, 250);
   scale(240.0);
   drawCircles(1);
   Theta += radians(1);
}

void drawCircles(int depth) {
   switch (depth) {
      case 1:  fill(color(89, 9, 21));      break;
      case 2:  fill(color(148, 14, 35));    break;
      case 3:  fill(color(181, 86, 70));    break;
      case 4:  fill(color(199, 172, 115));  break;
      default: return;
   }
   ellipse(0, 0, 2, 2);

   for (int i=0; i<3; i++) {
      pushMatrix();
         rotate(Theta + radians(i*120));
         translate(0, 0.6);
         scale(0.4);
         drawCircles(depth+1);
      popMatrix();
   }
}
```

(See output in Figure 10.9. Full program in recursion/sketches/spinners7/spinners7.pde)

Very cool. This was what I wanted!

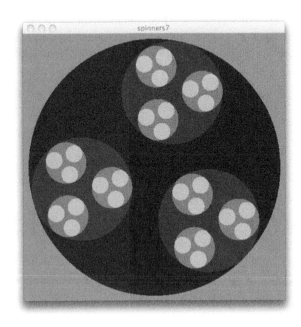

Figure 10.9. Multiple spinning spinners (frame from animation). (recusion/sketches/spinners7/spinners7.pde)

This code is pretty darned short considering what it does. The key, of course, is the beauty of recursion. By calling itself, drawCircles() is able to stay nice and focused. The first half of the procedure just computes a color and draws one circle. The second half runs a loop that builds a transformation and then calls itself three times, creating three new circles inside the big one; each of those will have three smaller circles, and so on.

Recursion is one of those great techniques that you want to have in your bag of tricks. It's not used nearly as often as some of the other programming techniques we've seen, and you can probably program for a long time and never need it. But when you do have a project in which each step is assembled from smaller steps of the same form, recursion has no equal: it is the perfect tool for that kind of job, and with it, you will write shorter, cleaner, more efficient, and more elegant code.

And it's a surprising amount of fun to use. Every time I solve a problem with a recursive technique, I feel like I've just cut a Gordian knot: a problem that appeared very complex was solved with a simple stroke.

10.2 Extending the Teacups

You can take this program in lots of directions. You can, of course, just mess around with the essentially arbitrary numbers I chose. Use more or fewer levels of recursion, change the colors to your liking, change the sizes of the circles or where they're located, or change how fast they move.

You can also build on this as a starting point for your own art. For example, find a way to let the colors change slowly over time. Maybe the sizes or positions of the circles can change over time, or the rotation speed of each set of circles could be based on its depth of recursion so the smaller ones go faster (or slower) than the larger ones. Maybe you could have lots more than three circles, or maybe you'd prefer boxes or some other, more complex shapes, rather than circles. You could add some more graphics; I like the simplicity of these solid-colored circles, but maybe you'd like something richer or more subtle. My circles are in perfect formation; you might like adding some random values to their positions, colors, or motions to add some variation to this perfectly-ordered ballet of moving shapes.

10.3   Drawing Boxes within Boxes

Let's nail down recursion with another project.

I'll write a routine that takes a box on the screen and cuts it in half along its largest dimension (so a wide box would get cut into two boxes side by side, and a tall box would be cut into two boxes stacked on top of each other).

I'll start with a basic `setup()` that makes the graphics window. Then it'll hand off the dimensions of the window, along with a medium-gray color, to another routine that will take care of drawing things; I'll call that `handleBox()`.

```
void setup() {
   size(600, 400);
   noStroke();
   handleBox(0, 0, 600, 400, 128);
}

void handleBox(float ulx, float uly, float wid, float hgt,
               int gray) {
   fill(gray);
   rect(ulx, uly, wid, hgt);
}
```

(See output in Figure 10.10. Full program in recursion/sketches/recurbox01/recurbox01.pde)

Figure 10.10. Start of a new recursion project. (recursion/sketches/recurbox01/recurbox01.pde)

It's not much of a picture, but it's a start. Right now handleBox() just takes a box and a gray value, sets the fill color to that gray, and draws the box.

So now let's do the slicing I talked about earlier. Inside of handleBox() I'll cut the input box in two and then call handleBox() to draw each new box.

Before I type even a single character, I want to stop and think about how to stop the recursion from running away forever. In other words, what are my stopping conditions?

I think it should be based on the size of the box. If either edge of the input box is smaller than some minimum size, then we just return. Because we no longer call handleBox(), there's no more recursion. So let's get that test in there first. I'll create a variable to hold the minimum side length (just so it's easy to find and change later) and then test the box's sides against it:

```
int minSide = 20;
if ((wid < minSide) || (hgt < minSide)) {
    return;
}
```

If you like to squeeze things down, you might notice that I could have written this on one line, like some of the *if statements* we saw in earlier examples:

```
if ((wid < minSide) || (hgt < minSide)) return;
```

Either way works, and lots of people use the one-line version all the time.

So, now that we know how to stop the recursion, what happens if the box is big enough to continue? First I'll test to see if the width is larger than the height. If so, I'll slice the box horizontally, otherwise, I'll cut it vertically. I'll want to remember to use the input parameters wid and hgt and not the global variables width and height, which contain the size of the graphics window!

I'll also change the color of the box when I call handleBox() again, so one box is a little darker than the input box, and the other is a little lighter:

```
void setup() {
    size(600, 400);
    noStroke();
    handleBox(0, 0, 600, 400, 128);
}

void handleBox(float ulx, float uly, float wid, float hgt, int gray) {
    fill(gray);
    rect(ulx, uly, wid, hgt);
    int minSide = 20;
    if ((wid < minSide) || (hgt < minSide)) {
        return;
    }
    if (wid > hgt) {
        float wid2 = wid/2.0;
```

```
      handleBox(ulx, uly, wid2, hgt, gray-10);
      handleBox(ulx+wid2, uly, wid2, hgt, gray+10);
   } else {
      float hgt2 = hgt/2.0;
      handleBox(ulx, uly, wid, hgt2, gray-10);
      handleBox(ulx, uly+hgt2, wid, hgt2, gray+10);
   }
}
```

(See output in Figure 10.11. Full program in recursion/sketches/recurbox02/recurbox02.pde)

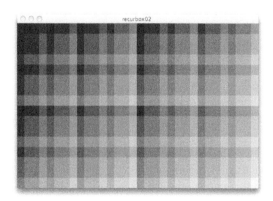

Figure 10.11. Recursive box making.
(recursion/sketches/recurbox02/recurbox02.pde)

That's pretty cool—and easy! Using recursion made this project a snap: all handleBox() has to do is take a box, draw it, and if it's big enough, cut it in two and call handleBox() on each new box.

You can see that each call to handleBox() does a little bit of work to compute the proper upper-left corner, width, and height of each box.

We can jazz this up without too much extra effort, so let's add a few more graphical tweaks. First, let's not cut each box right in the middle but instead cut at a random point somewhere near the middle. To find this random value, I'll call the built-in function random(). I'll talk more about random() in Chapter 11, but the basic idea is that you give it two numbers, the smaller one first, and random() gives you back an unpredictable number that's somewhere between them.

Each time you call random(), you get a different result somewhere between the low and high arguments. Let's use this to cut the boxes. Here's that piece of code using the random value:

```
if (wid > hgt) {
   float leftWid = wid * random(0.25, 0.75);
                  // width of the left box
   handleBox(ulx, uly, leftWid, hgt, gray-10);
   handleBox(ulx+leftWid, uly, wid-leftWid, hgt, gray+10);
} else {
   float topHgt = hgt * random(0.25, 0.75);
               // height of the top box
   handleBox(ulx, uly, wid, topHgt, gray-10);
```

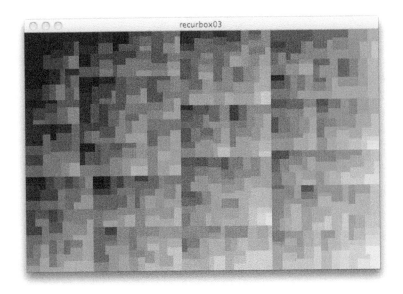

Figure 10.12. Improving recursive boxes. (recursion/sketches/recurbox03/recurbox03.pde)

```
        handleBox(ulx, uly+topHgt, wid, hgt-topHgt, gray+10);
    }
```

(See output in Figure 10.12. Full program in recursion/sketches/recurbox03/recurbox03.pde)

Now we're getting somewhere!

Each cut happens at a position that's not halfway across the width or height of the box but somewhere between 25 and 75 percent of the way.

Let's add some color to this field of gray. Instead of passing around a single int for the color, I'll pass around an actual color variable. To change it as we work our way through the recursion, I'll call a new function called wiggleColor(). This will take an input color and a range of numbers to be added to each component. I'll pick a random number in that range for each of the three color components, add them in, and return the resulting color.

```
color wiggleColor(color clr, float lo, float hi) {
    color newclr = color(red(clr)+random(lo, hi),
                         green(clr)+random(lo, hi),
                         blue(clr)+random(lo, hi));
    return (newclr);
}
```

Now I'll just change the original call to handleBox() so we give it a color rather than a gray value:

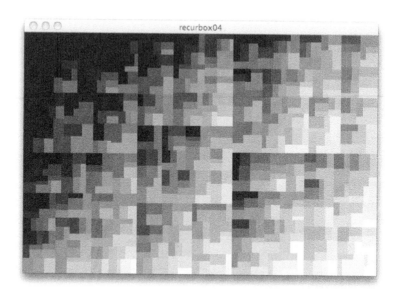

Figure 10.13. Colored recursive boxes. (recursion/sketches/recurbox04/recurbox04.pde)

```
handleBox(0, 0, 600, 400, color(128, 128, 128));
```

I'll need to update the definition of `handleBox()` so that it takes a `color` as input:

```
void handleBox(float ulx, float uly, float wid, float hgt,
                color clr) {
```

That's it except for the four recursion calls to `handleBox()`. The first two are just like they were, only they pass a "wiggled" color rather than a changed gray value:

```
handleBox(ulx, uly, leftWid, hgt, wiggleColor(clr, -20, -10));
handleBox(ulx+leftWid, uly, wid-leftWid, hgt,
          wiggleColor(clr, 10, 20));
```

The other two lines get the same treatment, and we're ready to roll:

```
handleBox(ulx, uly, wid, topHgt, wiggleColor(clr, -20, -10));
handleBox(ulx, uly+topHgt, wid, hgt-topHgt,
          wiggleColor(clr, 10, 20));
```

(See output in Figure 10.13. Full program in recursion/sketches/recurbox04/recurbox04.pde)

I like it!

But I feel like I'm missing a sense of history here. After all, each box is part of a whole chain of boxes, sort of like a family tree. It would be nice to see that.

So let's shrink each box a little after drawing it but before cutting it in half. That way each new box will appear "inside" the one that was cut to make it.

I'll create a variable called inset that will give me a percentage by which to shrink the box. I'll move the upper-left corner right and down by this amount and adjust the width and height as needed. I'll do this just before I cut the box:

```
float inset = 0.025;
ulx += wid*inset;
uly += hgt*inset;
wid *= 1 - (2*inset);
hgt *= 1 - (2*inset);
```

(See output in Figure 10.14. Full program in recursion/sketches/recurbox05/recurbox05.pde)

Figure 10.14. Colored recursive boxes with history.
(recursion/sketches/recurbox05/recurbox05.pde)

Ah, that's got the look I wanted to see.
I added a couple of lines of this form:

```
hgt *= 1 - (2*inset);
```

Note that this tells Processing to first compute the right-hand side (that is, find the value of 1-(2*inset)) and then multiply hgt by that result.

Imagine trying to write a program that would create a picture like this but without using recursion. You *could* do it, of course. But I think it would be difficult and take a lot of code. Here we have a program that's only 33 lines long (and that's including a couple of blank lines), and it does the whole job.

You won't use recursion on every project you make, and you might even find yourself not using it much at all. But when you're doing something that *does* fit the recursive approach to programming, no other technique comes close.

Chapter 11
Randomness and Arrays

With just a few exceptions, the programs we've written so far have produced the same results every time we've run them. That certainly makes sense, since the whole point was to write programs that drew what we intended!

But in the real world, events are rarely perfectly repeatable. If you pluck a note on your guitar today, and you pluck it again tomorrow, the two notes will not be identical. The differences might be subtle, but they'll be there. Even if you were able to pick the note with exactly the same amount of force and speed, variations in temperature and humidity and the clothes you're wearing and where in the room you're sitting and a million other variables would combine to cause the music from the guitar to be ever so slightly different every time you play it.

So the real world *varies* when we repeat things.

We can sometimes harness this variation for our own creative purposes. You might pour paint on a canvas and then set it outside in the rain for a half hour, letting nature erode away the paint and push it around. You might put a stone in a rock tumbler and let it bounce around for a few hours. Or you might buy a grab bag of yarn of different colors and commit yourself to knitting a sweater from the bag's contents.

In each of these cases, you're incorporating *randomness* into your work. Randomness is often a wonderful tool for creating interesting projects. It lets you inject some unpredictable complexity into your work.

Processing has a couple of types of built-in randomness that you can take advantage of in your projects. With careful control, you can create images and animations that follow a general plan that you cook up but also have just enough variation in them so that they come out differently each time. So rather than creating just one image, for example, you can make an endless family of related images. Of course, you may want to pick and choose from that family to select the ones you like the best, or you may embrace the unpredictable nature of the results and appreciate the unique qualities of each variation.

The examples of random values I gave above are quite different. Raindrops create a spatial pattern, while fragments of yarn provide random colors. The outside temperature on any given day is a single number that varies over time, while the changing shape of a tumbled rock involves complicated 3D randomness. How can we describe all of these?

Processing takes a simple, practical approach and offers you two sources of random numbers. In this chapter we'll look at them in turn, with a detour in the middle to talk about how we can save lists of numbers.

11.1   Random Numbers

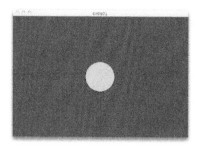

Figure 11.1. A circle in the center of the window.
(random/sketches/circ01/circle01.pde)

Generally speaking, there are two kinds of programs: *deterministic* and *random*. A deterministic program is called that because its output is completely determined by the program and its input values. Every time you run the program with those inputs, you get back the same result. Most of the programs we've built so far have been deterministic.

Everything else is random, even if there's only one tiny little bit of randomness in the program. It means that what comes out is not completely predictable from the program itself and the inputs.

Let's say that we want to draw a circle in the middle of the screen. Here's a little program to do just that:

```
void setup() {
  size(600, 400);
  background(150, 90, 65);
  fill(250, 200, 90);
  ellipse(width/2, height/2, 100, 100);
}
```

(See output in Figure 11.1. Full program in random/sketches/circle01/circle01.pde)

That's a completely deterministic program: every time we run it, we'll get precisely the same output.

But what if we want to fill up the window with a whole bunch of circles? Each circle requires three numbers: the center *x* and *y* coordinates and a radius. In this example, I typed those values in, but if we wanted, say, 20 or 30 circles, then typing them all in one by one would become tedious very fast. If we didn't really care about the precise location and size of each circle but just wanted a general pattern made up of lots of circles, then creating the pattern by hand would be a drag.

Of course, this is where random numbers come to save the day! Processing offers a function called `random()` to provide us with random numbers. It takes two floating-point arguments that give it a range of values from which to produce the results. It gives back a single floating-point number from within the range.

For example, if we call `random(0,1)` then the result is an unpredictable value that is somewhere between 0 and 1. There are two important things to remember when using `random()`.

First, the value that comes back is equal to or greater than the low end of the range but is always less than the upper end. So if we call `random(0,1)`, we will usually get back numbers that are somewhere between 0 and 1. We might, conceivably, get back the value of 0. But we will never get 1. The value that comes back could be as small as the start of the range, and anything up to (but not including) the end of the range.

Let's print out a bunch of random numbers:

```
void setup() {
  println("Random number 1: "+random(0, 1));
  println("Random number 2: "+random(0, 1));
  println("Random number 3: "+random(0, 1));
}
```

(Full program in random/sketches/random01/random01.pde)

Every time you run this, you'll get back three different random numbers between 0 and 1 (which very occasionally could include 0). Here's the result of a run I just made:

```
Random number 1: 0.6363256
Random number 2: 0.81206316
Random number 3: 0.25354677
```

Here's another run:

```
Random number 1: 0.51650345
Random number 2: 0.74579674
Random number 3: 0.19302225
```

Every time we run this program, we'll get back three different numbers.

We say that the numbers that come out of the `random()` function are *uniform*, or *uniformly distributed*.

This means you're as likely to get any number as any other. In other words, every number in the range has an equal chance of coming out.

The second thing to keep in mind is that when you provide the range, the smaller value must come first. Try replacing the ranges (0, 1) in the program above with (1, 0) You'll find that the result is always 1. It would be nice if `random()` was smart enough to use the whole range no matter what, but it isn't.

This can be confusing if you're choosing random numbers from a range that includes negative values. For example, if you want random values between −10 and −5, you need to call random(-10, -5) because −10 is smaller than −5. If you call random(-5, -10), the result will always be −5.

So now we can use random() to make a pattern of circles. Just call random() once to get the circle's center *x* value, again for the circle's center *y* value, and again for the radius. For the *x* value I'll use a range between 0 and width (that is, the width of the window). Likewise, for the *y* value, I'll use a range between 0 and height. For the radius, I'll just guess and say that I want values between 10 and 40; if the results don't look good, I can adjust that range.

```
void setup() {
  size(600, 400);
  background(150, 90, 65);
  fill(250, 200, 90);

  int numCircles = 30;
  for (int count=0; count<numCircles; count++) {
    float xCenter = random(0, width);
    float yCenter = random(0, height);
    float radius = random(10, 40);
    ellipse(xCenter, yCenter, radius*2, radius*2);
  }
}
```

(See output in Figure 11.2. Full program in random/sketches/circle02/circle02.pde)

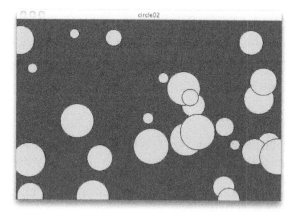

Figure 11.2. A random pattern of circles. (random/sketches/circle02/circle02.pde)

Every time we run this program, we'll get a different pattern of circles.

Notice that some of the circles are falling off the edges of the window. That makes sense because the centers are being computed with the full range of the window. For

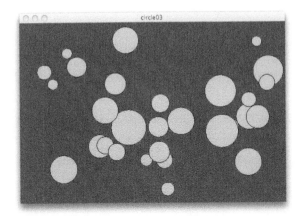

Figure 11.3. A random pattern of onscreen circles. (random/sketches/circle03/circle03.pde)

example, the window is width units wide, and we're calling random(0, width). Because of how random() is defined, this gives us values that could be as low as 0, or as high as something very close to width, but never quite reaching it. If we want the circles to stay onscreen, we want to make sure the centers are at least as far away from the edge as the circle's radius.

If we wanted the circles to all be onscreen, we can do that easily. I'll compute the radius first and then use that value to control the range of the center. In the x direction, for example, the new range will start at radius and run up to width minus the value of radius. Here's the new loop (everything else is unchanged):

```
for (int count=0; count<numCircles; count++) {
  float radius = random(10, 40);
  float xCenter = random(radius, width-radius);
  float yCenter = random(radius, height-radius);
  ellipse(xCenter, yCenter, radius*2, radius*2);
}
```

(See output in Figure 11.3. Full program in random/sketches/circle03/circle03.pde)

Just to be crazy, let's change the color of each circle. We'll pick a random value from 0 to 256 for each color component (remember, by using an upper value of 256 we'll get numbers up to 255.999... but never 256). Here's the new loop:

```
for (int count=0; count<numCircles; count++) {
    float redval = random(0, 256);
    float grnval = random(0, 256);
    float bluval = random(0, 256);
    fill(redval, grnval, bluval);
```

```
    float radius = random(10, 40);
    float xCenter = random(radius, width-radius);
    float yCenter = random(radius, height-radius);
    ellipse(xCenter, yCenter, radius*2, radius*2);
}
```

(See output in Figure 11.4. Full program in random/sketches/circle04/circle04.pde)

Figure 11.4. A random pattern of randomly colored onscreen circles.
(random/sketches/circle04/circle04.pde)

That's pretty ugly!

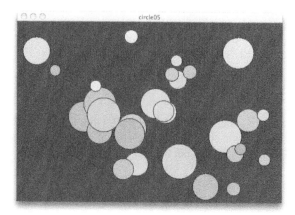

Figure 11.5. Nudging the circle around. (random/sketches/circle05/circle05.pde)

For any finished work, you'll probably end up tuning your random numbers more carefully. For example, maybe we could use the fill color (250, 200, 90) from the earlier examples and just nudge that around a little bit:

```
float redval = 250 + random(-30, 30);
float grnval = 200 + random(-30, 30);
float bluval =  90 + random(-30, 30);
fill(redval, grnval, bluval);
```

(See output in Figure 11.5. Full program in random/sketches/circle05/circle05.pde)

That's not perfect, but it is a lot more harmonious to my eye.

11.1.1 Random Choices

We often use `random()` to create numbers to assign to variables, as we did above. This is a great way to add some variety to your images and animations.

Another popular use of `random()` is to choose among a variety of operations in your code. Suppose that you've created an animation where there are a lot of objects bouncing around. Every now and then, two of them will hit each other. You've decided that half the time you'd like them to just bounce off each other, and the rest of the time they should annihilate each other in a burst of light.

You might write something like this:

```
if (random(0, 1) < 0.5) {
   bounceObjects();
} else {
   blowUpObjects();
}
```

This will work just perfectly.

In some older languages, the random number routines only returned integer values, so people would pick a random number from a huge range and test against a value in the middle:

```
if (random(0, 1000) < 500) {
```

This is just fine, and if you look at other people's code, you'll often see this kind of test. I do it myself sometimes. There's no drawback to using this range rather than (0, 1); it's just a question of style.

If you don't want the odds to be exactly 50/50, of course, they don't have to be. Maybe you want the flash of light to happen rarely, say one-tenth of the time. Sticking with the range (0, 1000), you could write

```
if (random(0, 1000) < 900) {
   bounceObjects();
```

```
} else {
   blowUpObjects();
}
```

That would do it. Or you could use `random()` to choose among multiple options. Suppose when the objects hit they could bounce off each other or blow up or create a third object or pass through each other, and each of these was equally likely.

Then each time two objects hit, you could have one of these four things happen with equal probability with something like this:

```
int randomVal = random(0, 1000);
if (randomVal < 250) {
   bounceObjects();
} else if (randomVal < 500) {
   blowUpObjects();
} else if (randomVal < 750) {
   createThirdObject();
} else {
   passThrough();
}
```

These four choices are happening with equal odds, but by changing the numbers you're testing against, you can make each one more or less likely.

11.1.2 Random Seeds

Debugging graphics can be hard because sometimes your objects land on top of one another, and it's difficult to make out what's being drawn. When that happens, using entirely random colors, as we did in Figure 11.4, is a great technique. This will cause most of the shapes to stand out clearly from one another, so you can see each one.

Debugging programs that use random numbers has its own challenges because sometimes when you run the program, you might get values that cause your bug to appear, but the next time you run it, the random numbers are such that your program runs perfectly. What you'd like is some way to say to Processing, "Every time I run this program, I want you to give me the same random numbers in the same order." That way you can run the program over and over, and you'll always get the same results, even though you're calling `random()`.

Happily, you can do exactly this. The function `randomSeed()` takes a single number as input. This call adjusts Processing's random-number generator so that each subsequent call to `random()` will be the same as in the last run of your program. The value you give to `randomSeed()` controls the sequence of numbers that come out of `random()`, but not in any way that you can easily predict. I usually just pick something simple like 5 and leave it at that. If the numbers that come out of `random()` don't trigger my bug, then I'll change the value to 6, and run the program again. And I'll keep adding 1 to this value until the bug appears. From then on, I can run the program over and over and the bug will always appear.

Once I've fixed my problem, I'll remove (or comment out) the call to `randomSeed()` so that each time I run the program, I'll get new results.

If you use this technique, make sure to call `randomSeed()` *before* you make any calls to `random()`. I usually call `randomSeed()` near the very start of `setup()`.

In the examples we've seen so far in this chapter, I haven't used a `draw()` routine. Why not?

Suppose I put the drawing code into `draw()`. Then for every frame, we'd get new random numbers and a new pattern and the image would jump around. Let's try it! I'll just put all of our drawing stuff into `draw()`:

```
void setup() {
  size(600, 400);
}

void draw() {
  background(150, 90, 65);
  fill(250, 200, 90);

  int numCircles = 30;

  for (int count=0; count<numCircles; count++) {
    float redval = 250 + random(-30, 30);
    float grnval = 200 + random(-30, 30);
    float bluval =  90 + random(-30, 30);
    fill(redval, grnval, bluval);

    float radius = random(10, 40);
    float xCenter = random(radius, width-radius);
    float yCenter = random(radius, height-radius);
    ellipse(xCenter, yCenter, radius*2, radius*2);
  }
}
```

(See output in Figure 11.6. Full program in random/sketches/circle06/circle06.pde)

This is crazy; the circles just jump around madly. That's what happens when we draw them with new, random positions and sizes on every frame.

What we want is to create these random numbers but *save* them, so we can draw the same circles on every frame, even though they originally came from `random()`. We could, of course, create a huge number of variables and store each circle's center and radius in them, but there's a much better way.

Processing gives us a built-in mechanism for storing lists of numbers. It's perfect for this task, and for endless others, so let's take a look at it.

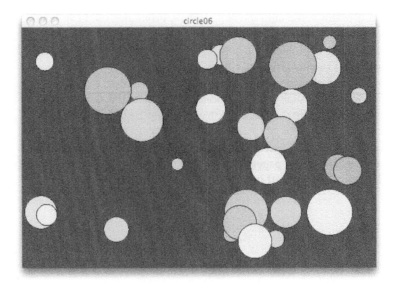

Figure 11.6. Drawing new circles each frame (frame from animation).
(random/sketches/circle06/circle06.pde)

11.2   Arrays

Our goal is to store a list of numbers in a way that we can easily get at them and reuse them.

In programming, a list is often called an *array*. Let's see how to create and use an array in Processing.

Suppose I want to create a piece of art that starts with eight circles side by side, each a different size. For now, let's forget about random numbers and suppose that I'm making a deterministic image. I know roughly the radius of each circle in my piece, but I also know that once I see the picture I'll want to adjust each radius, draw it again, adjust them again, and so on, until the image looks just right. So I want to begin with my initial list of sizes, see how they look, and then tweak them. From left to right, my starting radii are

```
30, 50, 90, 20, 44, 76, 22, 30
```

I'll also say that I want 20 units of space between each circle (I hope my curator likes minimalism!). Here's a really lousy way to start off this work of art.

```
void setup() {
    size(600, 400);
    background(2, 59, 71);
```

Figure 11.7. A simple work of art. (random/sketches/array1/array1.pde)

```
    fill(155, 226, 242);
    noStroke();
}

void draw() {
    ellipse(50, 100, 30, 30);
    ellipse(110, 100, 50, 50);
    ellipse(200, 100, 90, 90);
    ellipse(275, 100, 20, 20);
    ellipse(327, 100, 44, 44);
    ellipse(407, 100, 76, 76);
    ellipse(475, 100, 22, 22);
    ellipse(521, 100, 30, 30);
}
```

(See output in Figure 11.7. Full program in random/sketches/array1/array1.pde)

This isn't good at all. I had to calculate the x position of each circle by hand, and then type it in. I made mistakes and had to fix them. If I want to change the diameter of the second circle, say, I'm going to have to manually figure out all the new positions of all the circles after it and type them all in, and I'll make more mistakes that I'll have to fix, and eventually I'm going to get tired of the whole thing and give up on my dream of creating and showing the masterpiece in my mind. That's not good.

The way out of this is to create an array. I'll build an array, or list, of these eight diameters and then write a loop that generates the circles from the array. The loop can take care of all the calculations.

In Processing, you can make an array out of almost anything: objects of type `int`, `float`, `color`, or even your own objects (we'll see those in Chapter 14). For now, we just need `int` types, so let's stick with those. Here's how to declare an array to hold a list of `int` objects:

```
int [] diameters;
```

The way to think of this is that the type of the variable `diameters` is `int []`. That is, the `int` and the square brackets `[]` should be thought of as one composite thing, so the type is `int []`. The pair of brackets means "array". So `int []` means "array of `int` variables" or "list of `int` variables." The square brackets are used exclusively in Processing for declaring arrays and accessing their contents.

So far, we don't have anything inside of `diameters` because we've only told the computer that it's going to ultimately be a list of `int`s. You can think of `diameters` at this moment as a kind of potential list but one that doesn't exist yet. The computer can't actually use this variable as a list yet; if you try, you'll get an error. Before we can use this, we have to tell Processing that we want it to actually take `diameters` from its status as a potential list and turn it into an actual list. But how big a list should it be? How does that list actually get created?

Of course, we answer both of these questions ourselves. After you've declared the array, as in the line above, you can *create* (or *allocate*) it. When you create the array you tell Processing exactly how big you want it to be by giving it the keyword `new` followed by the length of the array in square brackets. In this case we want 8 entries, so we'd write this:

```
diameters = new int[8];
```

That tells the computer, "The value of `diameters` is an array of 8 `int`s." At this point, the computer builds the array for us, and we're ready to start using it. The key elements here are the word `new` and the type identifier `int`. If you were making an array of, say, `float`s, you'd declare it this way:

```
float [] float_array;
float_array = new float[10];
```

You may wonder why we have to declare and then allocate an array, but not something like an `int` or a `float`. The reason is that Processing already knows how much memory it needs to store a built-in type, but until you tell it the size of your array, it doesn't know how much memory it will need to store it. Because an array can be of any size, you have to explicitly tell Processing how big an array you want it to make.

Returning to our `diameters` array, the statement above may seem redundant to you. After all, the system knows that `diameters` is a list of `int` variables—that's how we declared it. Why did we have to say int again when we told it how big the list should be?

It is redundant, but it's kind of a safety check. You can't put a list of floats into something you declared to be a list of ints, for example. The need to explicitly identify what you're putting in there is meant to help you catch those times when you accidentally try to put the wrong type of list into your variable.

Of course, we can combine these two steps:

```
int [] diameters = new int[8];
```

With this one statement we've declared the variable diameters to be of type int [] (that is, a list of ints), and we've told the computer that the list has 8 entries and that it should actually go ahead and set things up internally so we can use the list.

Each of the 8 entries in the array diameters is also called an *element* of the array. So diameters contains 8 elements, each of which is an int. To refer to the first element, we write

```
diameters[0]
```

Remember that in the computer, we start counting at zero, so the eight elements of diameters are called diameters[0], diameters[1], and so on, with the last one at diameters[7].

We can use diameters[0] like any other integer—we can put stuff into it:

```
diameters[0] = 30;
```

And we can use diameters[0] as a variable like any other:

```
int triple_diameter = diameters[0] * 3;
```

The number inside the brackets is called the *array index*, or sometimes (borrowing again from mathematics) the *subscript*. People usually pronounce diameters[0] out loud as "diameters sub zero," where "sub" is short for subscript, or array index.

What happens if you refer to a value that's outside the array? Suppose you write

```
int subscript = -1;
int new_value = diameters[subscript];
```

If you try this, you'll find that it compiles cleanly (that is, there's nothing wrong with the code itself), but when you run it you get an error:

```
ArrayOutOfBoundsException: -1
```

Something about that error makes sense, since we are asking for entry −1 of the array. But what's the problem? Unlike when we draw a circle off the edge of the screen, Processing can't simply ignore this request. You're specifically trying to read a value out of the array `diameters` from an index that is less than 0, which puts it before the beginning of the array. That entry simply doesn't exist, and it would be terrible for Processing to try to guess what that value should be (it would often be wrong, and it could be a nightmare to debug that problem). So the program quits with an error (also called an *exception*) telling you that the index you're asking for is outside the range, or *bounds*, of this array. Hence, `ArrayOutOfBoundsException`.

The same problem will happen if you try to read from too large an index:

```
int subscript = 10;
int new_value = diameters[subscript];
```

Again, crash! Here's the error message:

```
ArrayOutOfBoundsException: 10
```

Array indexing errors happen to everyone, all the time. They're not good, of course, but if you catch them early, you can often fix them without too much work. When you get one, don't worry about it. Sooner or later you will write code with an indexing error because you are human.

This kind of error is variously called an *out-of-bounds error*, a *range error*, or a *subscripting error*. All of these terms mean that you're trying to read or write to an array using an index (or subscript) that is beyond the bounds of the array.

Finally, trying to read from an array element before anything has been put into it is also going to result in an error. This isn't unique to arrays; the same problem appears even with garden-variety `int`s. Here I'll try to use an `int` before it's been given a value:

```
int i1 = 3;
int i2;
int i3 = i1 + i2;
```

This is an error because `i2` has never been assigned to. Processing tells me

```
The local variable i2 may not have been initialized
```

Yup, that's right. We never assigned anything to `i2`.

Returning to my list of circles, I can fill up the `diameters` array manually, one at a time, like this:

```
diameters[0] = 30;
diameters[1] = 50;
diameters[2] = 90;
diameters[3] = 20;
diameters[4] = 44;
diameters[5] = 76;
diameters[6] = 22;
diameters[7] = 30;
```

That works perfectly well. But you know there's got to be a better way. The better way is to assign these values to the list when you declare it. The syntax for that is to place the values between curly braces, separated by commas. So here's our better declaration-and-assignment statement:

```
int [] diameters = { 30, 50, 90, 20, 44, 76, 22, 30 };
```

Unlike our previous use of curly braces, this time we're not using them to create a block of statements. This use of curly braces is a different, specialized use just for initializing arrays. But they're part of the combined declaration and assignment statement they belong to, so the statement ends with a semicolon just like any other variable declaration and assignment. Compare this to our earlier declaration:

```
int [] diameters = new int[8];
```

The version with braces does away with the need for new, and it doesn't require you to repeat that int type twice. But best of all, it automatically counts up the number of entries and makes an array of that size. I often put a space after the int and before the brackets, but it's entirely optional.

The curly-brace form of array assignment can only be used when you're declaring the array. Unfortunately, you can't use that nice shorthand to fill up an array somewhere inside your code after it's been declared.

Let's now draw our masterpiece. I'll create a little loop that runs through all the diameters and draws a circle for each one. Just to make sure that I have things working correctly, I'll keep the code very simple for now and just draw all the circles on top of each other. I'll turn strokes back on so I can see some evidence of the different circles:

```
void draw() {
    int [] diameters = { 30, 50, 90, 20, 44, 76, 22, 30 };
    stroke(0);
    for (int i=0; i<8; i++) {
        ellipse(100, 100, diameters[i], diameters[i]);
    }
}
```

(See output in Figure 11.8. Full program in random/sketches/array2/array2.pde)

Perfect. Well, perfect if my goals are modest. In this case, I just wanted to make sure that I was drawing a batch of circles, and it looks like I am. The open question is whether I'm drawing all eight of them. I think I should be, given that the loop is pretty simple, but I'll find out for sure later when I space them out.

One thing I might do for efficiency's sake is to move the definition of the variable diameters outside of draw() and turn it into a global variable. That way it doesn't have to get built from scratch every time we enter draw(). Because draw() gets called for every frame, we want draw() to be as small and fast as possible. Creating

Figure 11.8. Drawing the circles with an array. (random/sketches/array2/array2.pde)

this tiny array doesn't take a huge amount of time, but keeping draw() as small as possible is a good habit to get into. Following my convention, when I make this variable a global I'll make sure to change its name to start with a capital letter.

```
int [] Diameters = { 30, 50, 90, 20, 44, 76, 22, 30 };

void draw() {
   stroke(0);
   for (int i=0; i<8; i++) {
      ellipse(100, 100, Diameters[i], Diameters[i]);
   }
}
```

(See output in Figure 11.9. Full program in random/sketches/array3/array3.pde)

Figure 11.9. Using a global array. (random/sketches/array3/array3.pde)

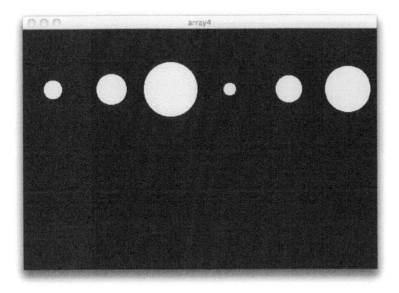

Figure 11.10. Spacing out the circles. (random/sketches/array4/array4.pde)

Beautiful—the same result, but a little bit cleaner and even a tiny smidgen faster. Now let's get the circles spaced out horizontally. I'll make a variable called xpos to represent the *x* value of the center of the circle we're about to draw. The variable xpos begins at 50, since that's where I want the first circle to be centered. Again, to build up the code, I'll bump xpos by some arbitrary number—say 100—on each iteration. That'll confirm that I have all the pieces in there correctly. That will also let me get rid of that call to stroke() I put in a moment ago:

```
void draw() {
    int xpos = 50;
    for (int i=0; i<8; i++) {
        ellipse(xpos, 100, Diameters[i], Diameters[i]);
        xpos += 100;
    }
}
```

(See output in Figure 11.10. Full program in random/sketches/array4/array4.pde)

This is a good result. They're falling off the right side of the screen, but that's no surprise—I just guessed at their spacing, and I clearly overestimated. No worries.

We're not ready for the museum, but we're getting closer. Let's stop the circles from disappearing off the right of the window. How do I compute the amount xpos should be increased each time around the loop? To get from the center of each circle to its right

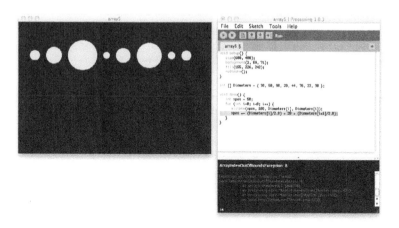

Figure 11.11. Improving the spacing, but not correctly.
(random/sketches/arraybug1/arraybug1.pde)

edge, I have to move to the right by its radius. That's `Diameters[i]/2` units—that's what the radius is, after all: the distance from the center to the outer edge of the circle. Then I want to move 20 more units to the right to create the space. Then I want to move to the right by the radius of the next circle; that will land me in the center of the next circle. That sounds about right. So we can write

```
xpos += (Diameters[i]/2.0) + 20 + (Diameters[i+1]/2.0);
```

(See output in Figure 11.11. Full program in random/sketches/arraybug1/arraybug1.pde)

Note that I divided `Diameters[i]` and `Diameters[i+1]` by 2.0, not simply 2. Since the `Diameters` array holds `int` variables, if I divided by 2, I'd be dividing an `int` by an `int`. While that's legal, it loses some precision (as I discussed in Chapter 4, dividing one integer by another gives us an integer result, so 7/2 gives us 3, not 3.5). By including the floating-point 2.0 in there, I got Processing to "promote" the calculation to a floating-point division with a floating-point result.

If you run this, something unfortunate happens. The picture gets drawn but then there are a lot of errors. If you look at the console area on your screen, you'll see a bunch of red type. You can see it in my window in Figure 11.11. And the message area has turned dark red as well, indicating an error. In the message area you'll see a message like this:

```
ArrayIndexOutOfBoundsException: 8
```

Uh-oh. That's like the error we saw before. We've asked for `Diameters[8]`, but the only legal values are 0 through 7. How did we end up asking for index 8?

Figure 11.12. Fixing the bug. (random/sketches/array5/array5.pde)

It's an off-by-one error. When I drew the last circle, I tried to move xpos in anticipation of the next one, so I tried to refer to Diameters[8]. But there is no next circle and no value out there for me to get.

There are a lot of ways to fix this problem. One way is to realize that we don't need to update xpos after the last circle. So we can put that line inside an *if statement*, executing it only if there is another circle yet to come. Here's the complete program:

```
void draw() {
    int xpos = 50;
    for (int i=0; i<8; i++) {
        ellipse(xpos, 100, Diameters[i], Diameters[i]);
        if (i < 7) {
            xpos += (Diameters[i]/2.0) + 20 + (Diameters[i+1]/2.0);
        }
    }
}
```

(See output in Figure 11.12. Full program in random/sketches/array5/array5.pde)

That's what I was after. I don't know if people are going to be lining up for me to sign this great work of art, but I do know that I've written a clean piece of Processing.

I said earlier that I would probably want to adjust the sizes of the circles once I saw the image. With this program, that's easy: just change the numbers in the array and run the program again. You can take over the art making from here; just tweak the values in the array to your heart's content, and when you run the program again, you'll get a row of perfectly spaced circles with your chosen sizes.

In the examples above, I knew how long my array was, so I just used that number explicitly (when I wrote `i<8` as my test in the loop). But suppose you pass an array as an argument to a routine. How can it know how long the array is?

One solution is to always maintain another variable, probably an `int`, that has the length of the array in it. That works, but it's kind of a pain. A better solution is offered by Processing: the array itself can report on its length. The length is a property of the array.

Recall from Chapter 6 that we can get an object's property by writing the object's name, followed by a period, and then name the property. The length of an array is stored in a property that is quite sensibly named `length`, so the length of the array `Diameters` is found with `Diameters.length` (note that there are no square brackets here because we're not asking for an element of the array; the property belongs to the array as a whole).

We could use this to make our loop work for any length of the array:

```
for (int i=0; i<Diameters.length; i++) {
   ellipse(xpos, 100, Diameters[i], Diameters[i]);
   if (i < Diameters.length-1) {
      xpos += (Diameters[i]/2.0) + 20 + (Diameters[i+1]/2.0);
   }
}
```

If the array has 8 elements (as in this example), then the length reported by this property will be 8. So a loop for that array would run through the values 0 to 7.

11.3 Manipulating Arrays

Arrays are perfect for storing lists of items. But like any list, you'll frequently find yourself wanting to change an array's contents. You might want to add an entry to the end, get rid of an entry, change the value of an entry, and so on. Processing offers a variety of built-in routines to help you manipulate lists and their contents.

As you manipulate your lists, perhaps making them larger and smaller, Processing will keep track of their lengths and keep each one's `length` property up to date automatically.

Some of the routines we'll see below return a new array that holds the result of their actions. For example, `append()` takes an array and a new element as inputs. It puts the new element at the end of the array, and returns a new array with the result. You'll almost always want to save that array (otherwise, why call the function?), and typically, you'll even save it right back into the input array, so the result is that you've put the new element at the end of that array.

To demonstrate these little array manipulators, I'm going to write a skeleton test program. This is a common way to explore a new function, or test out a new idea in isolation while working on a larger program. It lets you focus your thinking just on the one thing you want to explore. In this case, I'll create three arrays and initialize them, and include a function that prints out an array. Then I'll create a little procedure that gets called to do some array process (this will be where we'll put our experiments).

Here's the skeleton:

```
int [] A = { 1, 2, 3, 4, 5, 6};
int [] B = { 10, 20, 30, 40, 50};
int [] C = { };

void setup() {
  println("Before:");
  print("A: "); printArray(A);
  print("B: "); printArray(B);
  print("C: "); printArray(C);
  doArrayThing();
  println("After:");
  print("A: "); printArray(A);
  print("B: "); printArray(B);
  print("C: "); printArray(C);;
}

void printArray(int[] v) {
  for (int i=0; i<v.length; i++) {
    print(v[i]+" ");
  }
  print("\n");
}

void doArrayThing() {
}
```

When we run this as is (that is, the routine doArrayThing() does nothing), we get this output:

```
Before:
A: 1 2 3 4 5 6
B: 10 20 30 40 50
C:
After:
A: 1 2 3 4 5 6
B: 10 20 30 40 50
C:
```

The arrays have what we'd expect (including C, which has length 0 and no entries), and nothing happens between the two printouts. From here on, I'll leave off all the skeleton except for the routine doArrayThing() at the end. I'll also leave out all of the array printouts except for the final version of C, because they won't change from one run to the next.

I'm using arrays of numbers here because they're such a compact way to show what each of the following routines does. I encourage you not to think of arrays as just numbers in some abstract sense, but instead think of the numbers as descriptions of some graphic element in your own pictures or animations. Maybe these numbers represent the heights of people in a cheering crowd, the speeds of cars going around a track, the sizes of the petals on a flower, or the amount of rain waiting to fall from a cloud.

A big advantage of storing lists of numbers is arrays is that we can make use of a wide variety of powerful built-in operations for manipulating those lists. Let's use these A, B, and C arrays to see what we can do with Processing's built-in functions.

11.3.1   append(), expand(), shorten()

Let's begin with adding and removing elements.

You can add a new element to the end of an array with append().

```
void doArrayThing() {
   C = append(A, 98);
}
```

This results in the printout

```
C: 1 2 3 4 5 6 98
```

Note that A hasn't been changed; instead, a copy was made, 98 was stuck on the end of the copy, and then that copy was assigned to C.

If you want to put a whole bunch of objects on the end at once, you can call append() over and over, but a quicker way is to use expand(). If you just give it the name of the array, it will double the array's size. If you give it a second argument, the array will be made that many elements longer. Remember to assign values into the new elements that expand() makes for you.

You can eliminate the final element in an array with shorten():

```
void doArrayThing() {
   C = shorten(A);
}
```

This results in the printout

```
C: 1 2 3 4 5
```

If you want to shorten an array by a whole lot of elements, it would probably be quicker to use subset(), described below.

11.3.2 arrayCopy()

You can make a copy of an entire array, or just some piece of it, using `arrayCopy()`. This function has three overloaded versions. With just two arguments, the first array (called the *source array*) is copied to the second (called the *dest array*, for "destination").

There are two special things to note about `arrayCopy()`. First, unlike the other functions we've seen, `arrayCopy()` does not create any new arrays; both of the arrays you give it must already exist (that is, not simply declared but allocated either with curly-brace notation or a `new` command). Second, both arrays must be large enough to contain all the indices you're going to read from and write to. For example, if you try to copy all of array A in our example to array C, you'd get an error because C has length 0.

To put a copy of array A into array C, we first make sure that C is long enough by creating a new array of `int` variables and assigning that to C. Now we can copy each element of A into C, confident that there are enough slots to hold the values:

```
void doArrayThing() {
    C = new int[A.length];
    arrayCopy(A, C);
}
```

This results in the printout

```
C: 1 2 3 4 5 6
```

If you give `arrayCopy()` a third argument, that tells it how many elements to copy:

```
void doArrayThing() {
    C = new int[A.length];
    arrayCopy(A, C, 3);
}
```

This results in the printout

```
C: 1 2 3 0 0 0
```

The array C was padded with 0's because the `new int[]` call initialized the entries of the new C array with 0.

Finally, a more advanced form of `arrayCopy()` takes five arguments. Unlike the other forms, the first two arguments are not the two arrays, so be careful!

In the five-argument form, the first two arguments are the source array and the location in the source array from which copying should begin. The next two arguments are the dest array and the starting location in that array where values should be stored. As always, the first element is at index 0, the second is 1, and so on. The final argument states how many elements should be copied.

So for example, if you told `arrayCopy()` to start copying from position 3 in A and start storing at position 7 in C and to copy two elements, it would copy `A[3]` to `C[7]` and `A[4]` to `C[8]`. Make sure both arrays are big enough so that the indices you're going to access all exist, or you'll get an `OutOfBounds` error.

Here's an example of the five-argument form of `arrayCopy()`:

```
void doArrayThing() {
  C = new int [10];
  for (int i=0; i<10; i++) C[i] = 101+i;
  arrayCopy(A, 2, C, 3, 4);
}
```

After creating the array C, I initialized it with the values 101 to 110. Then I overwrote four entries. This results in the printout

```
C: 101 102 103 3 4 5 6 108 109 110
```

Note that we started copying from `A[2]` (which had the value 3), and started copying into `C[3]` (which had the value 104). We copied 4 elements total.

The `arrayCopy()` routine is optimized to be very fast, so if you need to copy over big pieces of arrays, you should use this function rather than write your own code.

It's a good rule in general to use system functions whenever you can because they almost always will be faster than equivalent versions you can write for yourself. Sometimes the savings are modest, sometimes they're significant (as with `arrayCopy()`), but even if you get nothing but increased clarity and simplicity in your code, it's usually worth it.

11.3.3   concat() and splice()

You can glue two arrays together, one after the other, with `concat()` (this is short for *concatenate*, which means to unite two objects, one after the other).

```
void doArrayThing() {
  C = concat(A, B);
}
```

This results in the printout

```
C: 1 2 3 4 5 6 10 20 30 40 50
```

If you'd rather paste the second array somewhere inside the first one, rather than at the end, you can use `splice()`. The first argument to `splice()` is the array you want to put things into. The second is either an element you want to insert or another array (in which case, the whole second array will be inserted). The third argument is the position in the first array where the new object (or array) should be placed.

```
void doArrayThing() {
  C = splice(A, B, 3);
}
```

   This results in the printout

```
C: 1 2 3 10 20 30 40 50 4 5 6
```

11.3.4   reverse() and sort()

You can reverse the order of an array, so that the first element becomes the last, the second becomes second-to-last, and so on, by calling `reverse()`:

```
void doArrayThing() {
  C = reverse(A);
}
```

   This results in the printout

```
C: 6 5 4 3 2 1
```

   If you want to sort the array, there's a function for that, too. You'll never, ever guess that it's named `sort()`.   If your entries are numbers, they get put into ascending order; if they're `Strings`, they're put into alphabetical order (`sort` ignores case). In this example, I'll make `C` by putting `A` after `B`; the `sort()` function will put all the resulting values into ascending order.

```
void doArrayThing() {
  C = concat(B, A);
  C = sort(C);
}
```

   This results in the printout

```
C: 1 2 3 4 5 6 10 20 30 40 50
```

11.3.5   subset()

If you'd like to make a new array out of some piece of your first array, say by taking just the third through eighth entries, use `subset()`. It takes three arguments: the name of the array, the starting point where the extraction should begin, and how many elements you want:

```
void doArrayThing() {
  C = subset(A, 2, 3);
}
```

   This results in the printout

```
C: 3 4 5
```

11.4   Deleting an Array Entry

One thing you can't conveniently do with an array is to delete an element from some-where inside. That's kind of a drag. However, you can accomplish the same end with two calls to subset () and one to concat (). The first call to subset () gives you everything up to the element you want to delete, and the second gives you everything after. Then concat () pastes them together.

It's easy to put these together into a single little utility function. The function deleteElement (), which takes an array of ints as input, along with an index, and it returns a new array of ints that matches the input array, except the selected item has been removed.

```
void setup() {
   int [] a = { 0, 1, 2, 3, 4, 5, 6, 7, 8 };
   print("a before deleting: ");
   printArray(a);
   int [] b = deleteElement(a, 4);
   print("a after deleting:  ");
   printArray(a);
   print("b:                 ");
   printArray(b);
}

void printArray(int [] array) {
   for (int i=0; i<array.length; i++) {
      print(array[i]+" ");
   }
   print("\n");
}

int [] deleteElement(int [] array, int num) {
   int [] s1 = subset(array, 0, num-1);                    // get 1st part
   int [] s2 = subset(array, num, array.length-num);       // get 2nd part
   int [] result = concat(s1, s2);                         // combine parts
   return(result);
}
```

(Full program in random/sketches/deleteElement01/deleteElement01.pde)

I added some spaces to the print statements so the array entries would line up nicely. Here's the output:

```
a before deleting:  0 1 2 3 4 5 6 7 8
a  after deleting:  0 1 2 3 4 5 6 7 8
b:                  0 1 2 4 5 6 7 8
```

As you can see, the fourth element (with value 3) was removed from the array a.

Processing is perfectly happy to pass arrays around as arguments to routines or as results from them. The one tricky thing is that they care about what type they are. So if you want to be able to delete an element from an array of `int`s as well as an array of `float`s, you'll need two distinct routines. In other words, you can overload your routines by giving multiple versions, one for each type of array, and Processing will choose the appropriate one when you call it.

Here's another version of the program above. I've got two versions each of the functions `printArray()` and `deleteElement()`, one for arrays of `int` variables and one for arrays of `float` variables.

```
void setup() {
    int [] ia = { 0, 1, 2, 3, 4, 5, 6, 7, 8 };
    print("ia before deleting: ");
    printArray(ia);
    int [] ib = deleteElement(ia, 4);
    print("ia after deleting:   ");
    printArray(ia);
    print("ib:                  ");
    printArray(ib);


    float [] fa = { 0.1, 0.2, 0.3, 0.4, 0.5, 0.6, 0.7, 0.8 };
    print("fa before deleting: ");
    printArray(fa);
    float [] fb = deleteElement(fa, 4);
    print("fa after deleting:   ");
    printArray(fa);
    print("fb:                  ");
    printArray(fb);
}

void printArray(int [] array) {
    for (int i=0; i<array.length; i++) {
        print(array[i]+" ");
    }
    print("\n");
}

void printArray(float [] array) {
    for (int i=0; i<array.length; i++) {
        print(array[i]+" ");
    }
    print("\n");
}

int [] deleteElement(int [] array, int num) {
    int [] s1 = subset(array, 0, num-1);                // get 1st part
```

```
    int [] s2 = subset(array, num, array.length-num);
                                              // get 2nd part
    int [] result = concat(s1, s2);           // combine parts
    return(result);
}

float [] deleteElement(float [] array, int num) {
    float [] s1 = subset(array, 0, num-1);
                                              // get 1st part
    float [] s2 = subset(array, num, array.length-num);
                                              // get 2nd part
    float [] result = concat(s1, s2);         // combine parts
    return(result);
}
```

(Full program in random/sketches/deleteElement02/deleteElement02.pde)

There's a lot not to like about this program! The biggest problem, of course, is that it's basically the same program as before but repeated twice. The entire body of `printArray()` is identical in both versions; the only difference between them is that one says `int` in the function declaration and the other says `float`. And `deleteElement()` is almost the same way, except that the change from `int` to `float` happens five times. Otherwise, these routines are identical. And the code in `setup()` for testing this all out is basically the same thing twice in a row as well.

That's really too bad. But there's a significant upside to writing these overloaded routines, which is that once they've been written, we can just call `deleteElement()` on our arrays, and we never have to worry if the array contains elements of type `int` or `float`. Of course, if the array contains some other type of object, neither of these routines will get called, but at least we've covered our bases for two of the more popular data types.

This new code prints out the following:

```
ia before deleting: 0 1 2 3 4 5 6 7 8
ia after deleting:  0 1 2 3 4 5 6 7 8
ib:                 0 1 2 4 5 6 7 8
fa before deleting: 0.1 0.2 0.3 0.4 0.5 0.6 0.7 0.8
fa after deleting:  0.1 0.2 0.3 0.4 0.5 0.6 0.7 0.8
fb:                 0.1 0.2 0.3 0.5 0.6 0.7 0.8
```

Writing our own function to delete an array element is admittedly a bit of a messy solution. If you need to do a lot of complicated array manipulation, it might be worth taking a jump into the world of the `ArrayList`.

This is actually an object of its own kind, like a `color` or `String`, only it holds an array. The `ArrayList` isn't technically part of Processing. It comes from Java (the language that Processing gets translated into), but Processing still gives you access to it.

Because it's part of Java, using an `ArrayList` requires working with a whole bunch of other object types that we will never use in this book. Generally speaking, you can get a long way with just regular arrays if you're willing to do a little bookkeeping on your own. Since `ArrayList` is not really a part of Processing, I won't go deeper into the topic here. If you really need to do fancy array work, you can find information online on `ArrayList`. I suggest you find some code that uses the `ArrayList` to do something close to what you need and adapt it; that will get you to your goal a lot faster than trying to come up to speed on all the Java stuff that you'd otherwise have to learn first.

There's another advanced, and completely different, technique for working with arrays that is available to you. It's variously called an *associative array*, *hash table*, or *hash array*. Processing supports this idea through a data type called `HashMap`. The idea behind using a `HashMap` is that rather than referencing an array by its index number, you reference it with a string that identifies the entry. Associative arrays are powerful, but we don't need them here so I'm not going into them, but again, you can find some great starting points online.

11.4.1 Array Names

When you name your array, there's an important question you have to answer: is the name singular or plural?

This is a small and subtle choice, but it can have an influence on how you think about your array.

For example, if you've been told to watch a group of children at a park, but you haven't met them individually, you might think of them collectively as a group: the children. You might even address them that way ("Children, don't go near that bear!").

If you know each of them individually, though, you would probably address each one by name ("Sally, don't put any more ice cream in your hair."). So we can think of them as a group of individuals or as individuals who are part of the group. Like I said, it's subtle, but sometimes it's helpful to make the right choice.

For another example, suppose I have an array of 88 `float`s describing a piano keyboard. Each entry tells me how far down its corresponding key has been pressed, where 0 means not pressed at all, and 1 means fully down. I can give that a plural name:

```
float [] pianoKeys;
```

Then each time I refer to a key, say number 63, I'd write `pianoKeys[63]`. Conceptually, this tells me it's the collective that's most important, and I'm momentarily addressing one element of it.

Alternatively, I can give the array a singular name:

```
float [] pianoKey;
```

Then the 63rd entry is `pianoKey[63]`, and to me, it means that this is an individual thing, a particular key, that happens to belong to a larger group.

Whether the name for your array should be singular or plural is a question of attitude and what you want your code to say to someone who reads it. Are you dealing with primarily a group of things or primarily some things that happen to belong to a group?

So if I was writing a program to show where children were spending their time at the park, and I was using actual data from real children, I would probably call my array `Child` because `Child[14]` is a very particular, specific person in my data and in my mind. But if I was writing a program to simulate how a bunch of computer-simulated children moved around a park, I would probably call the array `Children` because I'm really focused conceptually on what they're all doing as a group, and element `Children[14]` is to me just another one of the group.

Of course, the running program will perform exactly the same way no matter what names you choose for your variables. And probably most of the time this singular versus plural distinction doesn't matter. But it's worth being aware of for those times when the difference can help you think about your code in the most natural way.

11.4.2   Some Array Projects

There are a few projects you might like to try on your own to get some personal experience with how arrays work. Try adapting the circle-drawing program from before (the one that drew a bunch of differently sized circles in a row) so that you can also adjust the space between each pair of circles using another array.

If you really want to stretch, extend that program so that you can adjust the circle sizes interactively: if you click the mouse inside a circle and then drag, the size of the circle gets larger if you move away from the center or smaller if you move closer, and all the other circles adjust their locations, of course, to accommodate the change. When you let go of the mouse, everything stays the way it was when you let go.

Warning: this last project is a substantial challenge. But you already have all the tools you need to pull it off, and the work is well worth the reward.

11.5   Noise

Let's get back to random numbers.

The `random()` function is useful in many situations, but the numbers that come out of `random()` are completely unpredictable. If you call `random(-1, 1)`, you'll get back a number from −1 to up to (but not including) 1. If you call it again, you'll get back an entirely different number from that range. The values will jump around in that range with nothing else in common.

There's a whole different kind of randomness available in Processing called *noise*. That's a general term, but here noise refers to something very specific.

Noise is your go-to source of randomness when you want a smoothly changing sequence of random numbers. Suppose you want to make a simple ball that bounces around the screen, but the radius of the ball changes over time so it's a little more interesting. To get started, let's write a little bouncing ball. In Chapter 14, I'll build up this bouncing-ball technique step by step. For now, I'll just put together something that moves the ball in a straight line until it hits a wall and then reverses its direction.

```
float Cx, Cy;          // ball center
float Vx, Vy;          // ball velocity
float Radius;          // ball radius

void setup() {
   size(600, 400);
   Cx = 300;
   Cy = 200;
   Radius = 30;
   Vx = 2;
   Vy = 3;
}

void draw() {
   // update the ball
   Cx += Vx;
   Cy += Vy;
   if ((Cx-Radius < 0) || (Cx+Radius >= width)) {
      Vx = -Vx;
      Cx += 2 * Vx;
   }
   if ((Cy-Radius < 0) || (Cy+Radius >= height)) {
      Vy = -Vy;
      Cy += 2 * Vy;
   }

   // draw the ball
   background(128, 103, 103);
   noStroke();
   fill(224, 199, 37);
   ellipse(Cx, Cy, Radius*2, Radius*2);
}
```

(See output in Figure 11.13. Full program in random/sketches/noise01/noise01.pde)

Let's change the radius on each frame using `random()`. I'll use `constrain()` to keep the radius in the range (10, 50). This is another little helper function that we'll see in detail in Chapter 18. It takes two floating-point numbers that form a range and a third floating-point number. If that third value is in the range, that's the value of the function. Otherwise, we get back the nearest end of the range. So in this case, it means the result of `constrain(Radius, 10, 50)` will be that Radius is never smaller than 10 or greater than 50.

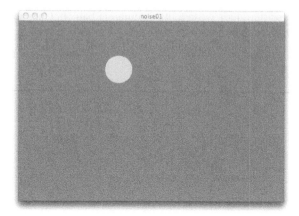

Figure 11.13. A bouncing ball (frame from animation). (random/sketches/noise01/noise01.pde)

Let's put these lines at the top of `draw()`:

```
Radius += random(-2.0, 2.0);
Radius = constrain(Radius, 10, 50);
```

So that we can see what's happening even in a still image, I'll turn on the black stroke around the ball and comment out the line to clear the background:

```
//background(128, 103, 103);
//noStroke();
stroke(0);
fill(224, 199, 37);
ellipse(Cx, Cy, Radius*2, Radius*2);
```

(See output in Figure 11.14. Full program in random/sketches/noise02/noise02.pde)

Wow. That's one twitchy ball. The radius is jumping up and down with no continuity at all. You can really see this if you run the program and uncomment the line to draw the background in `draw()`. The ball's size jumps up and down in a harsh and choppy way.

That might be a nice effect sometime but for now I'd like the ball's size to change smoothly, just as the motion of the ball itself is nice and smooth.

The way to pull this off is to use the function called `noise()`. Like `random()`, it gives you back random numbers. Unlike `random()`, it doesn't take a range: it always returns values from 0 to 1. Instead of a range, `noise()` takes a location. In its most basic form, you give `noise()` a location along the *x*-axis (that is, any floating-point value), and it gives you back a single number between 0 and 1. If you give it that same location again, it'll give you back the same number. So that value "lives" at that

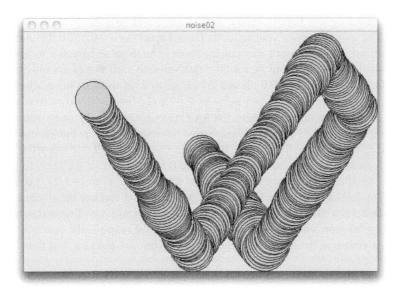

Figure 11.14. The twitchy ball's trail (frame from animation).
(random/sketches/noise02/noise02.pde)

position, and you'll always get that value at that location until you restart your program
(and Processing builds a whole new noise pattern for you).

Suppose you gave `noise()` the position 0.5, and so of course you got back a
number from 0 to 1. Now you give `noise()` a position just a little different than you
did before, say 0.51. You'll get back a value that's just a little different than the last one
(maybe this result will be a little more than the one before, maybe a little less). If you
move your position a little bit again, say to 0.52, the value from `noise()` will be a
little different from the result you got for 0.51. In other words, if you give `noise()`
locations that change smoothly and slowly, you'll get back random numbers that change
smoothly and slowly.

This is great, but I've glossed over something critical: how close do your inputs
have to be for `noise()` to give you back numbers that also seem "close" together?
The answer is tied up with the mathematics of the algorithm that creates the noise.
You don't have to know that math or go anywhere near it. A little trial and error will
guide you to good values for your project (and frankly, even if you do know the math,
you usually need to do the trial and error anyway). The rule of thumb offered by the
Processing documentation is that if you ask for values that are about 0.01 apart, the
results will probably put you in the ballpark for tuning. So your first call to `noise()`
might be with a value of 0, then 0.01, then 0.02, then 0.03, and so on.

If the numbers you're getting back are changing too quickly for your use, put your
requests closer together (so you might try using half of 0.01, or 0.005 as your increment,

thereby generating numbers 0, 0.005, 0.01, 0.015, and so on). If the results aren't changing fast enough, space your requests farther apart (say, 0.02 or 0.03 units apart). This is the trial and error part I was talking about. The usual approach is to assign this scaling value to a variable and then adjust that variable until things are moving at the rate you like. I've found that 0.02 is usually closer to what matches my aesthetics than 0.01 is, so I usually start scaling my noise by 0.02 and adjust up or down from there.

Let's demonstrate this. I'll adjust the `Radius` variable not by using `random()`, but by using `noise()`. I'll hand it the current frame number (from the system variable `frameCount`), scaled by the variable `noiseScale`, which I'll start out at 0.02. Since `noise()` gives me back a number in the range 0 to 1 and I want `Radius` to get both bigger and smaller, I'll use `lerp()` to convert the range $(0, 1)$ to $(-1, 1)$. I could have used `map()` instead, but since the input range is $(0, 1)$, I can use the three-argument function `lerp()` rather than the five-argument function `map()`. This makes my code just that tiny bit more concise and clear. Note that unlike `map()`, the controlling value in `lerp()` comes at the end of the argument list. Here are the new first three lines of `draw()`:

```
void draw() {
   float noiseScale = 0.02;
   Radius += lerp(-1, 1, noise(frameCount*noiseScale));
   Radius = constrain(Radius, 10, 50);
```

(See output in Figure 11.15. Full program in random/sketches/noise03/noise03.pde)

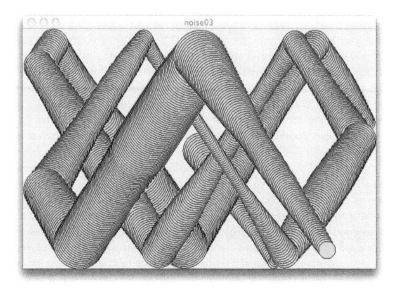

Figure 11.15. Smoothly changing radius (frame from animation).
(random/sketches/noise03/noise03.pde)

As before, to make a more meaningful still image for the printed page, I commented out the calls to `background()` and `noStroke()` and put in a call to `stroke()`; if you're running this on your computer, remove the extra call and uncomment the other two lines to watch the ball.

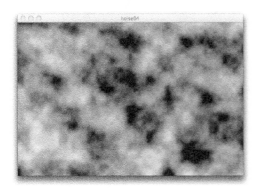

Figure 11.16. Some 2D noise.

That looks pretty swell to me. The twitchy behavior is gone, and the ball changes size randomly but smoothly. That's because the random values coming out of successive calls to `noise()` are also smooth (that is, they don't change by too much from one call to the next). If you want the ball to change in size more quickly, make `noiseScale` bigger. To slow it down, make `noiseScale` smaller. This is the trial and error process I referred to before. There's no substitute for tuning up these numbers to make objects look and behave the way you want them to.

The `noise()` function has another trick up its sleeve: it can take two arguments. These correspond to a point in a 2D plane. In this case, the `noise()` function moves slowly in both directions.

Maybe the easiest way to see this is to draw the values from `noise()` right into the pixels of a window, where each pixel directly shows the noise function's value at that (x, y) location (appropriately scaled by `noiseScale`, of course). Let's use the `point()` primitive to set the color of each pixel (that's a slow way to do this, but it gets the job done—we'll see a faster way to do this sort of thing in Chapter 16). Remember that `point()` uses the current stroke color from the graphics state when it draws a point:

```
void setup() {
    size(600, 400);
    float noiseScale = 0.02;
    for (int y=0; y<height; y++) {
        for (int x=0; x<width; x++) {
            float noiseVal = noise(x*noiseScale,y*noiseScale);
            noiseVal *= 255;  // scale up from [0, 1] to [0, 255]
            stroke(noiseVal);
            point(x, y);
        }
    }
}
```

(See output in Figure 11.16. Full program in random/sketches/noise04/noise04.pde)

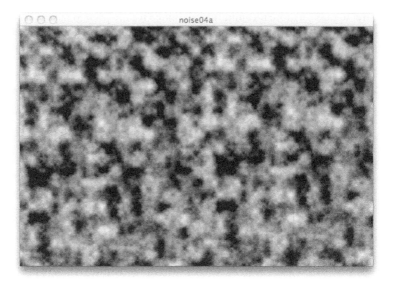

Figure 11.17. Noise with a larger scale factor. (random/sketches/noise04a/noise04a.pde)

If you want noise that changes more quickly, you only need to increase the size of the scaling factor, so that you ask for values of noise that are spaced farther apart.

```
float noiseScale = 0.05
```

(See output in Figure 11.17. Full program in random/sketches/noise04a/noise04a.pde)

It might seem a bit counter-intuitive that using larger values causes the noise to get more closely spaced and bumpier. The reason that this happens is because by taking larger steps at each pixel, we're moving a larger distance across the underlying noise function. The hills and valleys don't get closer together, but because we move farther on each step, we see a larger change in the value of function than if we took a smaller step.

If you want noise that changes more slowly than in Figure 11.16, then change the scaling factor in the other direction, making it smaller, so that you ask for values of noise that are spaced closer together. Now the function changes only a little bit on each step, making the resulting field look smoother.

```
float noiseScale = 0.005
```

(See output in Figure 11.18. Full program in random/sketches/noise04b/noise04b.pde)

If we use different scale factors in x and y, we can stretch the noise out asymmetrically. In this example, I'll change the scale in x across the image. Note that the noise still looks good, even though the size of the features is changing.

Figure 11.18. Noise with a smaller scale factor. (random/sketches/noise04b/noise04b.pde)

```
float xScale = map(x, 0, width, .02, .05);
float yScale = .01;
float noiseVal = noise(x*xScale,y*yScale);
```

(See output in Figure 11.19. Full program in random/sketches/noise04c/noise04c.pde)

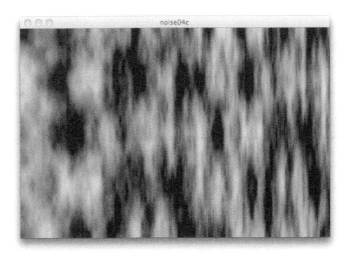

Figure 11.19. Noise with a changing horizontal scale. (random/sketches/noise04c/noise04c.pde)

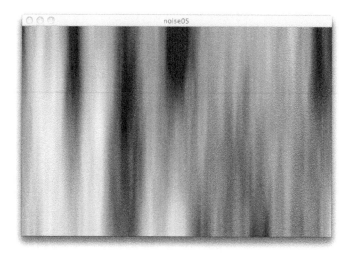

Figure 11.20. Noise stretched out vertically. (random/sketches/noise05/noise05.pde)

Here I'll keep the scale on *x* as it was before, but I'll change the scale on *y* to make it one-tenth that of *x*, so the noise will change vertically one-tenth as quickly as it changes horizontally:

```
float noiseVal = noise(x*noiseScale,y*noiseScale*.1);
```

(See output in Figure 11.20. Full program in random/sketches/noise05/noise05.pde)

What a great texture for a hanging curtain! Let's enhance that feeling a little bit by using `noiseVal` to blend between a dark red and a dark orange color (we could use `lerpColor()` here, but I'll use three calls to `lerp()` instead):

```
float noiseVal = noise(x*noiseScale,y*noiseScale*.1);
float redVal = lerp(114, 194, noiseVal);
float grnVal = lerp( 32, 106, noiseVal);
float bluVal = lerp( 12,  14, noiseVal);
stroke(redVal, grnVal, bluVal);
point(x,y);
```

(See output in Figure 11.21. Full program in random/sketches/noise06/noise06.pde)

It doesn't have quite the feel I'd like; it looks a little bit more like wood grain to me than a curtain. I think there should be more dark areas, to suggest shadows. So I want `noiseVal` to still run from 0 to 1, but I want the numbers that come out to get massaged a little bit, so that numbers near 0 get a bit smaller, but they eventually

Figure 11.21. 2D noise stretched vertically. (random/sketches/noise06/noise06.pde)

reach 1. You can make this happen in a million ways. I've gone down this road before, so I know that a quick and easy way to do this is just to multiply noiseVal by itself. This makes all the numbers from 0 to 1 smaller, but they finally do make it to 1 (because after all, $1 * 1$ is still 1).

Let's do this just after the calculation of noiseVal:

```
noiseVal *= noiseVal;
```

(See output in Figure 11.22. Full program in random/sketches/noise07/noise07.pde)

Figure 11.22. 2D noise pushed a little into darkness. (random/sketches/noise07/noise07.pde)

If you're keen to take a leap into the unknown, try replacing the line above with this one:

```
noiseVal = pow(noiseVal, 1.8);
```

We'll discuss pow() in Chapter 18. This function raises the first argument to the power of the second. If that means nothing to you now, don't worry about it—you can still type in that line and play around with the 1.8 value until the pattern looks good to you.

Back to our bouncing ball: we can use this 2D version of noise to control the ball's radius. Instead of calling the 1D version of noise() with a scaled frameCount, we could call the 2D version with scaled values of the ball's center, given by Cx and Cy. That way every time the ball passes over a particular point, it will always have the same radius, but the radius associated with every point on the screen will be slightly different than the radius of the points next to it.

You probably won't be stunned to learn that there's a 3D version of noise as well, which takes three numbers and lets you get values of a 3D pattern. But 3D is where the story ends. If you need more dimensions, you can use different chunks of the same noise function, as I'll discuss below.

The patterns made by noise() change each time you run your program, but they all tend to have a similar "feel." You can tweak the noise algorithm to generate a slightly different feel (or if you just want to play with it and see what else it can do). The details are in the documentation for noiseDetail(). The controls there are pretty tightly based on the mathematics, but even if you don't dig into the math, you can play with the values and see if you like what happens.

There's also a function called noiseSeed(). Like randomSeed(), you can call this function with a number and then, rather than getting a noise pattern that's different each time you run your program, it'll always be the same. You might even design your program to use random() to pick one of a bunch of seeds that you like and then pass that to noiseSeed(). That way your users will always get one of the noise patterns you've handpicked, but they won't know which one they'll get on any given run of the program. That's pretty rare, though; usually noiseSeed() is used only to help you get consistent patterns when you're trying to debug a program.

There are times when you want to have multiple noise functions around at once. For example, suppose you want to control the color of our bouncing ball. You'd use one 2D noise for the red component, another for green, and a third one for blue. Unfortunately, Processing doesn't let you maintain multiple noise functions. There's just one for the whole system, and that's it.

To get around this, you might think of using noiseSeed() to generate different but repeatable patterns for each call to noise(). You'd probably use three different, arbitrary numbers for the seeds that you'd pick off the top of your head; generally, there's no way to predict what kind of pattern you'll get from any particular seed value. So to draw a color pattern over the face of the window, you might do something like this (but *don't* do something like this!):

```
// warning: VERY SLOW CODE ahead!
int redSeed = 55;
int grnSeed = 103;
int bluSeed = 222;
for (int y=0; y<height; y++) {
   for (int x=0; x<width; x++) {
      noiseSeed(redSeed);
      redValue = noise(x*noiseScale, y*noiseScale);

      noiseSeed(grnSeed);
      grnValue = noise(x*noiseScale, y*noiseScale);

      noiseSeed(bluSeed);
      bluValue = noise(x*noiseScale, y*noiseScale);

      stroke(redValue, grnValue, bluValue);
      point(x, y);
   }
}
```

You'll find that this is a one-way ticket to Sleepsville. Your computer will compile the program, start running it, and then you should go off and get a cup of coffee, watch a movie, or take that week-long vacation you were planning. Each time you call noiseSeed(), Processing has to do a lot of work for you. Doing this once at the start of the program takes the blink of an eye, but doing it three times for every pixel adds up very fast.

Happily, you don't have to do this. The pattern created by noise() is infinite, and extends forever in all dimensions. Better yet, it doesn't repeat. Best yet, the values produced by noise() are computed on demand, so you can freely ask for values from any location in the infinite sea of noise.

So you can use one noise pattern over and over, just by selecting different chunks of it. This example will show a noise pattern in color on the screen much more quickly by using three different regions from the infinite plane of noise to supply the three different color values:

```
void setup() {
   size(600, 400);

   float rx = 0;
   float ry = 0;
   float gx = 1000;
   float gy = 1000;
   float bx = 5000;
   float by = 8000;

   float noiseScale = 0.02;
```

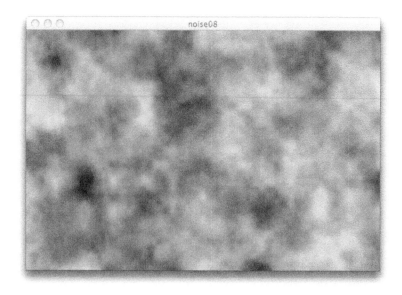

Figure 11.23. Multiple noise patterns. (random/sketches/noise08/noise08.pde)

```
for (int y=0; y<height; y++) {
    for (int x=0; x<width; x++) {
        float redVal = noise((x+rx)*noiseScale, (y+ry)*noiseScale);
        float grnVal = noise((x+gx)*noiseScale, (y+gy)*noiseScale);
        float bluVal = noise((x+bx)*noiseScale, (y+by)*noiseScale);

        stroke(255*redVal, 255*grnVal, 255*bluVal);
        point(x, y);
    }
}
}
```

(See output in Figure 11.23. Full program in random/sketches/noise08/noise08.pde)

In this example, to make use of three different noise patterns, I just arbitrarily selected three different rectangles out of the one giant noise pattern. The pattern for red starts at (0,0), the pattern for green starts at (1000, 1000), and the pattern for blue starts at (5000, 8000). I picked those numbers out of thin air. I knew the window was 600 by 400, so I picked upper-left corners to create rectangles that wouldn't overlap.

Not that overlap is necessarily a bad thing. Let's shift the green pattern just a little bit down and to the right of the red and shift the blue to the right of the red:

```
float rx = 0;
float ry = 0;
float gx = 10;
```

Figure 11.24. Offsetting noise patterns. (random/sketches/noise09/noise09.pde)

```
float gy = 10;
float bx = 10;
float by = 20;
```

(See output in Figure 11.24. Full program in random/sketches/noise09/noise09.pde)

That's kind of an interesting pattern, too.

Let's go back to the ball and use this cool kind of noise to push the ball around. Just after using noise to change the radius, I'll use it to change the velocity of the ball.

```
float Cx, Cy;
float Vx, Vy;
float Radius;

void setup() {
    size(600, 400);
    Cx = 300;
    Cy = 200;
    Radius = 30;
    Vx = 2;
    Vy = 3;
}

void draw() {
```

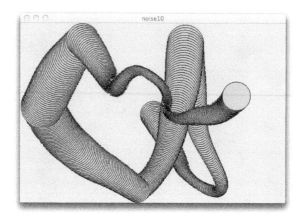

Figure 11.25. A wandering ball (frame from animation).
(random/sketches/noise10/noise10.pde)

```
float noiseScale = 0.02;
Radius += lerp(-1, 1, noise(frameCount*noiseScale));
Radius = constrain(Radius, 10, 50);

Vx += lerp(-0.25, 0.25, noise(noiseScale*Cx, noiseScale*Cy));
Vy += lerp(-0.25, 0.25, noise(noiseScale*Cy, noiseScale*Cx));

Cx += Vx;
Cy += Vy;
if ((Cx-Radius < 0) || (Cx+Radius >= width)) {
    Vx = -Vx;
    Cx += 2 * Vx;
}
if ((Cy-Radius < 0) || (Cy+Radius >= height)) {
    Vy = -Vy;
    Cy += 2 * Vy;
}

//background(128, 103, 103);
//noStroke();
stroke(0);
fill(224, 199, 37);
ellipse(Cx, Cy, Radius*2, Radius*2);
}
```

(See output in Figure 11.25. Full program in random/sketches/noise10/noise10.pde)

I repeated the trick at the end of not clearing the window, so you can see the trail of the ball. If you restore the calls to background() and noStroke() and remove the call to stroke(), you'll see the ball wandering all over the screen in a way that I found really interesting and appealing.

I used scaled values of Cx and Cy to find the strength of the noise pushing the ball left and right. Since I didn't want to use the same indices for the vertical values, I just exchanged them, and it looks great.

Chapter 12
Catmull-Rom Curves

There's another group of 2D shapes we haven't covered yet: free-form curves. We've seen ellipses (and arcs), but what if you want a flowing kind of curve that isn't part of a circle or ellipse?

Processing offers us two flavors of curves. We'll look at one type of curve in this chapter and the other type in Chapter 13.

We'll see that each type of curve starts with a group of four points and draws a piece of curve based on those points. Since I know these four points are going to be important, I'll make a new version of our skeleton program. In this adapted skeleton, I'll store the *x*- and *y*-coordinates of each point in their own variables, and I'll put code into draw() to draw a little circle around each point.

Here's the general plan:

```
void setup() {
    size(600, 400);
    background(242, 240, 174);
    noFill();
}

void draw() {
    stroke(0);
    int x0 = 100;  int y0 = 100;
    int x1 = 300;  int y1 = 100;
    int x2 = 300;  int y2 = 300;
    int x3 = 100;  int y3 = 300;
    ellipse(x0, y0, 15, 15);
    ellipse(x1, y1, 15, 15);
    ellipse(x2, y2, 15, 15);
    ellipse(x3, y3, 15, 15);
    // and now do some curve drawing
}
```

(See output in Figure 12.1. Full program in cmcurves/sketches/cmcurves1/cmcurves1.pde)

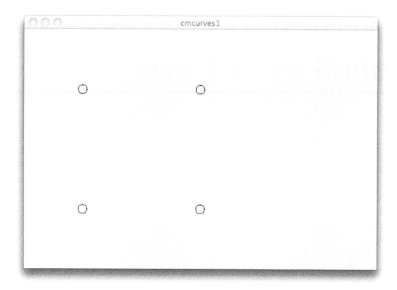

Figure 12.1. Curves skeleton showing curve points.
(cmcurves/sketches/cmcurves1/cmcurves1.pde)

You probably know what's coming next: we've hardly begun, but already my repeat sensors are pinging. The four lines of assignments are causing a yellow alert, but the four lines of nearly identical calls to ellipse() turn on the red lights. What if I decide I want to change the size of the circles? Then I'd have to change the value 15 in eight places. In this example that's probably not going to be overwhelming, but if we had 16 or 50 points, the repeated definitions and calls to ellipse() would get completely out of hand. I want to nip this in the bud, so I'm going to use arrays instead of explicit variables for each x and y value.

Now we're ready to get into curve drawing.

12.1   Knots and Control Points

Before we dig into the details, I want to give you a little heads-up. Curves are fun! Curves are really cool. You can do some really subtle and beautiful things with curves. Not only can you draw them but you can use them to move things around: you can define a curve and then use that as the path of an object that moves on the screen.

But curves are weird beasts. Rectangles and circles and lines are familiar objects to most of us. But curves are based on mathematics that is pretty unfamiliar to most people. Happily, Processing has put all of that math under the covers where it belongs, so you never see any of it. But curves are still weird. The biggest reason is that there's no good universal answer for how to describe or control a loose, free-flowing curve.

Figure 12.2. Two cusps in an otherwise smooth curve.

So in computer graphics we take a practical approach. To create a curve, we give the computer a collection of points, and we let it draw a curve based on those points (it usually goes through some of them and is influenced, or shaped, by others). If the curve doesn't go where you want, you move the points.

That's a pretty good answer, but even that isn't enough to get rid of the weirdness. The problem is that there are lots of different curves that we can draw that will all go through the same points. Which one is the best one? Which is the right one? The answer to those questions is that the "right" curve is the one that helps you express your creative ideas.

Good luck finding a ready-made computer program that does that!

So here's how we do it. Rather than provide tools to make a big complicated curve, Processing gives you the tools to make simpler, more easily controlled little curves. Then you can make a rich, flowing curve by combining these smaller pieces.

To make this big composite curve look good, it needs to have two qualities: *continuity* and *smoothness*. Continuity simply means that it's one long curve without any gaps. That's easy to achieve: make sure that the first point of each little curve is in the same place as the last point of the previous curve. But smoothness is harder because it needs to be controllable. You don't always want a curve to be smooth. Sometimes you want it to be continuous but form a corner. Or you want a cusp, like the pointed tip of a circus big top. Figure 12.2 shows a couple of these sharp changes in direction.

So what you really need is something that will be smooth where you want it to be smooth and pointy where you want it to be pointy.

How can we express that? I suppose there could be some very complicated functions you could call, where you give all kinds of numerical information on how the curve should bend and how pointy or smooth it should be and so on, but that would be complicated and worlds away from the friendly, natural style of Processing.

So Processing keeps it simple and lets you directly assemble the big curve you want out of many little pieces. That's good, but it means that when you want your little curves to look like one big smooth curve, it's your job to make sure you build and assemble them to achieve that.

To get started, I'll talk about how to draw one little curve. Once we have that under our belts, I'll talk about how you can build your curves so that when you draw one after the other, they'll look like one big, smooth curve.

I mentioned earlier that Processing gives you two types of curves (the ones we'll cover in this chapter and those in the next). One thing they both have in common is that each individual curve section is defined by four points: the curve passes through only two of these points, but its shape is influenced by the other two. In computer graphics, the points that the curve actually passes through are usually called *knots*, and the points that steer the curve indirectly are usually called *control points*.

In everyday use, it's not unusual for people to treat these terms as synonyms, referring to all the points involved in a curve definition as simply "knots" or "control points."

So to describe one piece of a curve, we need to store eight numbers (the x and y values for four points). What's the best way to do this?

There are a few ways to go. One way is to store all eight numbers one after the other in an array of eight floats. Another is to have two arrays, each of four floats, one array for the x values and one for the y. There's yet another way, which we'll see later in Chapter 15, that involves an object called a PVector, but let's stick with these arrays for now.

Let's follow the second course and make two arrays, one each for x and y. I'll initialize them with starting values and then use a loop to draw a circle at each one.

```
float [] Xp = { 100, 300, 300, 100 };
float [] Yp = { 100, 100, 300, 300 };

void draw() {
    for (int i=0; i<4; i++) {
        ellipse(Xp[i], Yp[i], 15, 15);
    }
    // draw curves here
}
```

(See output in Figure 12.3. Full program in cmcurves/sketches/cmcurves2/cmcurves2.pde)

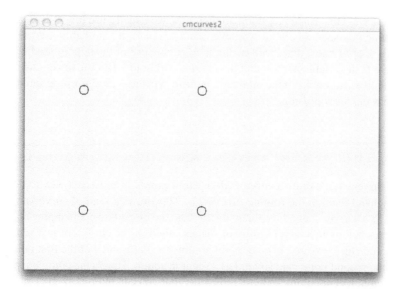

Figure 12.3. The new curve skeleton. (cmcurves/sketches/cmcurves2/cmcurves2.pde)

This produces the same results as before, but the code is a million times easier to maintain and less likely to fall prey to typos. I've used the variable i for the loop counter. I could have used a more descriptive name for this variable, for example, point_counter or circleNumber. But in these short little loops, most programmers prefer to use a short little "throwaway" name for the loop variable. This is not only easier to type but it reinforces the idea that the loop variable in this case isn't very important to us. In most of our previous programs, the loop variable meant something, like the position of a circle on the screen. In this loop, the variable i really means nothing more a count of how many times we've gone through the loop.

I mentioned in Chapter 3 that i is probably the most frequently used variable in all of programming. That's because it's used so frequently in these little loops; when you have a quick loop to toss together and the variable that controls the number of times you've gone around doesn't need a complex name, often that variable gets called i. Why is that? Historical inertia.

In the early days of programming, the language FORTRAN was king. In many early versions of FORTRAN, such as FORTRAN77, variables were written entirely in upper case and didn't have to be declared with explicit types. Instead, the rule was that any variable that wasn't declared explicitly but started with the letters I through N, was an integer (as in INteger), and all others were floating-point. The first variable starting with I is of course just I itself, so that variable became instantly popular, with J a close second, and then K. So when you needed an integer for some momentary use but didn't feel like actually coming up with a real name, the first, shortest name was just the letter *I*. This usage has stuck, though now we usually use lower-case i, j, and k. Any time you see a one-letter variable like i, j, or k, it's probably used to control some little loop. I know that I said earlier to avoid the use of the upper-case letter *I* and upper-case *O* in variable names, and that advice still holds. But the lower-case letter i is sufficiently different from the number 1 in most typefaces used for programming that there's less risk of confusion.

12.2   Catmull-Rom Curves

Back to curves! Let's draw a curve with our four points. The easiest way to do that is to simply hand them to the routine curve(). This draws a kind of curve known as a *Catmull-Rom curve*, named for the two men who developed its mathematics. Catmull-Rom curves belong to a larger family of shapes called *spline curves*, or just *splines*.

The procedure curve() takes eight arguments: the *x* and *y* of the first point, the *x* and *y* of the second point, and so on. Let's see it in action. Here's the complete program so far (though I'm not doing so here, remember that you can put smooth() at the start of any sketch to make things look a little nicer, if you're willing to let it take a little longer to draw):

```
void setup() {
   size(600, 400);
   background(242, 240, 174);
   noFill();
}

float [] Xp = { 100, 300, 300, 100 };
float [] Yp = { 100, 100, 300, 300 };

void draw() {
   for (int i=0; i<4; i++) {
      ellipse(Xp[i], Yp[i], 15, 15);
   }
   curve(Xp[0], Yp[0], Xp[1], Yp[1], Xp[2], Yp[2], Xp[3], Yp[3]);
}
```

(See output in Figure 12.4. Full program in cmcurves/sketches/cmcurves3/cmcurves3.pde)

What the heck kind of a curve is that?

The interesting thing here is that although all four points are part of the process, the curve is only drawn between the two middle points. So in this form, the first and last points are the control points (or control vertices) because they influence (or control) the curve that gets drawn, but the curve doesn't actually pass through them. The middle two points are the knots because the curve actually does pass through them.

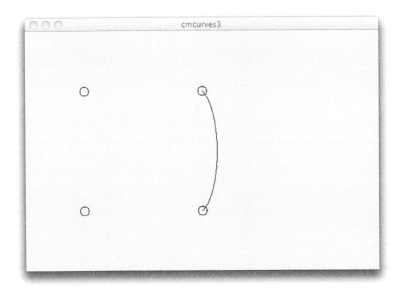

Figure 12.4. A curve between two points. (cmcurves/sketches/cmcurves3/cmcurves3.pde)

Let's explore this a little. The four points I've created here make up a square, starting in the upper left, then moving to the upper right, the lower right, and the lower left. Those points correspond to the indices 0, 1, 2, 3 in the array; I've labeled the points in Figure 12.5. The curve we're drawing now takes them in that order, so point 0 is a control point, then points 1 and 2 are the knots, and point 3 is the other control point.

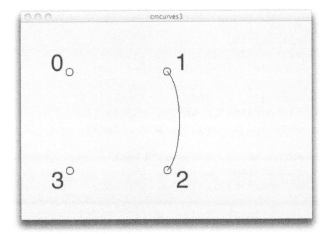

Figure 12.5. Labels for the curve points.

To try to make things a little clearer, I'm going to change the graphics a little. I'll draw the first control point in red and draw a line from it to point 1. I'll draw the last control point in blue and draw a line from that to point 2:

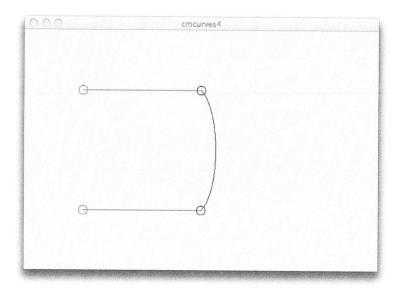

Figure 12.6. A Catmull-Rom curve with supporting graphics.
(cmcurves/sketches/cmcurves4/cmcurves4.pde)

```
void draw() {
    stroke(255, 0, 0);    // red
    ellipse(Xp[0], Yp[0], 15, 15);
    line(Xp[0], Yp[0], Xp[1], Yp[1]);

    stroke(0, 0, 255);    // blue
    ellipse(Xp[3], Yp[3], 15, 15);
    line(Xp[3], Yp[3], Xp[2], Yp[2]);

    stroke(0, 0, 0);    // black
    ellipse(Xp[1], Yp[1], 15, 15);
    ellipse(Xp[2], Yp[2], 15, 15);

    curve(Xp[0], Yp[0], Xp[1], Yp[1], Xp[2], Yp[2], Xp[3], Yp[3]);
}
```

(See output in Figure 12.6. Full program in cmcurves/sketches/cmcurves4/cmcurves4.pde)

I'm kind of sad to lose our lovely little loop and replace it with all this explicit drawing code, but it will help us see what's going on. To keep draw() nice and tidy, though, I'm going to push this extra stuff into its own little routine. Then I can call it once from draw(), and I don't have to look at and think about it every time I want to change draw():

```
void setup() {
   size(600, 400);
   background(242, 240, 174);
   noFill();
}

void drawCurve(boolean drawCircles, boolean drawLines,
int p0, int p1, int p2, int p3) {

   // control point 1
   stroke(255,   0,  0);   // red
   if (drawCircles == true) {
      ellipse(Xp[p0], Yp[p0], 15, 15);
   }
   if (drawLines == true) {
      line(Xp[p0], Yp[p0], Xp[p1], Yp[p1]);
   }

   // control point 2
   stroke(0, 0, 255);   // blue
   if (drawCircles == true) {
      ellipse(Xp[p3], Yp[p3], 15, 15);
   }
   if (drawLines == true) {
      line(Xp[p3], Yp[p3], Xp[p2], Yp[p2]);
   }

   // the knots
   stroke(0, 0, 0);   // black
   if (drawCircles == true) {
      ellipse(Xp[p1], Yp[p1], 15, 15);
      ellipse(Xp[p2], Yp[p2], 15, 15);
   }

   curve(Xp[p0], Yp[p0], Xp[p1], Yp[p1], Xp[p2], Yp[p2], Xp[p3], Yp[p3]);
}

float [] Xp = { 100, 300, 300, 100 };
float [] Yp = { 100, 100, 300, 300 };

void draw() {
   drawCurve(true, true, 0, 1, 2, 3);
}
```

(See output in Figure 12.7. Full program in cmcurves/sketches/cmcurves5/cmcurves5.pde)

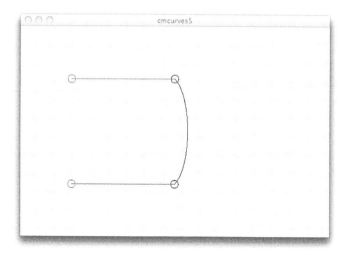

Figure 12.7. A Catmull-Rom curve with extra information.
(cmcurves/sketches/cmcurves5/cmcurves5.pde)

Admittedly, the program is longer now. But it's a step forward in terms of clarity and convenience because we can essentially ignore drawCurve() from here on in and focus our attention on the much simpler draw().

Let's look at drawCurve() briefly before we ignore it, though. The purpose of this routine is threefold: draw circles around the curve's four points (using blue and red for the first and last), draw lines between the first and last pairs of points (again, in blue and red), and then draw the curve in black. The first argument tells it whether or not to draw the circles around the curve's four points. The second argument tells it whether or not to draw the lines. The function drawCurve() knows that all the points come from the Xp and Yp arrays, so it just needs to know which index to use for which point, and that's what the last four arguments tell it.

Now we can run some experiments pretty easily.

Let's see what would happen if instead of handing the points to curve() going clockwise starting in the upper left, we started in the the upper right. Then point 1 (in the upper right) would be the first control point, points 2 and 3 in the lower right and lower left, respectively, would be the knots, and point 0 in the upper left would be the new last control point. Figure 12.8 shows the idea.

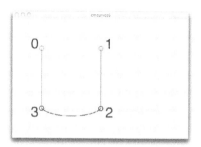

Figure 12.8. The curve points taken in the order (1, 2, 3, 0).

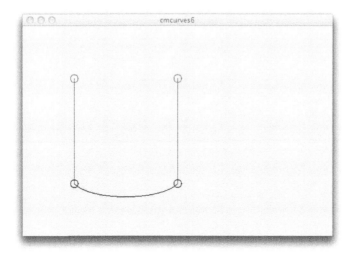

Figure 12.9. Another Catmull-Rom curve. (cmcurves/sketches/cmcurves6/cmcurves6.pde)

So let's hand the values to curve in that order and see what happens:

```
void draw() {
    drawCurve(true, true, 1, 2, 3, 0);
}
```

(See output in Figure 12.9. Full program in cmcurves/sketches/cmcurves6/cmcurves6.pde)

This isn't too shocking—we're simply drawing the bottom part of a square of control points, rather than the right side. But what if we draw them both?

```
void draw() {
    drawCurve(true,  false, 0, 1, 2, 3);
    drawCurve(false, false, 1, 2, 3, 0);
}
```

(See output in Figure 12.10. Full program in cmcurves/sketches/cmcurves7/cmcurves7.pde)

Since I only want to see the circles around the points, I turned that option on in the first call to `drawCurve()` and turned the other options off from then on.

Look at the bottom-right corner. The two curves not only join up but they do it smoothly. I certainly am not going to go into the mathematics here, but this smoothness is no accident! In fact, that's the whole reason for having the two extra control points.

I am *definitely* coming back to this issue of smoothness. But first, let's draw the curves based on the other two sides of the square:

```
void draw() {
    drawCurve(true,  false, 0, 1, 2, 3);
```

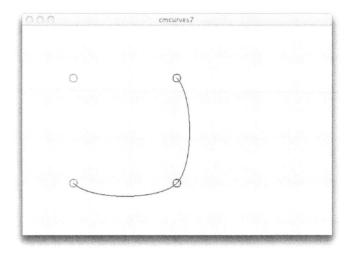

Figure 12.10. Two curves. (cmcurves/sketches/cmcurves7/cmcurves7.pde)

```
    drawCurve(false, false, 1, 2, 3, 0);
    drawCurve(false, false, 2, 3, 0, 1);
    drawCurve(false, false, 3, 0, 1, 2);
}
```

(See output in Figure 12.11. Full program in cmcurves/sketches/cmcurves8/cmcurves8.pde)

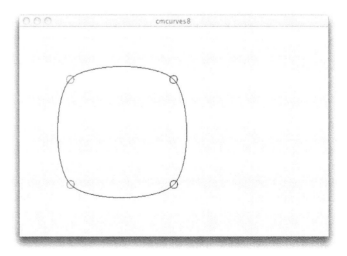

Figure 12.11. Four curves. (cmcurves/sketches/cmcurves8/cmcurves8.pde)

This is called a *closed curve* because it forms a closed loop. And notice that the last part smoothly joins up with the first part as well.

All that wonderful smoothness is no coincidence, and it's not because of good luck. It's a result of the mathematics and how we draw the curves. There's a rule for smoothness with these curves, and as long as we obey the rule, the curves will be smooth, smooth, smooth. If we disobey the rule, the curve won't be smooth and may contain pinches and points and other non-smooth features.

Here's the general rule for smoothness when using `curve()`: if you have two curves and you want them to join up smoothly, then make sure that the *first three* points of the second curve are the same as the *last three* points of the previous one. In our example above, the first curve uses points 0, 1, 2, and 3, and the second curve uses point 1, 2, 3, and 4. Since the first curve ends with points 1 to 3, and the second curve starts with the same points, they join up smoothly. And that's why the curve closes smoothly as well—the last curve ends with points 0, 1, 2, which are the first three points of the first curve.

Overlap means smoothness!

Here's a little visual representation of the four curves we've drawn. Each curve is on its own line, with points given in the order left-to-right:

```
curve 0:   0 1 2 3
curve 1:     1 2 3 0
curve 2:       2 3 0 1
curve 3:         3 0 1 2
```

Again, we see that the first three points of each curve are the same as the last three points of the one that preceded it.

Note that the curve in Figure 12.11 is not a circle. In fact, you cannot make a perfect circle with Catmull-Rom curves, though of course you can get close by using lots of tiny curves.

12.3   Assembling Curves

Let's write a new program to experiment with how to assemble little curves into a bigger one. It will create a bunch of random points, and then hand them to `curve()` four at a time, making sure that each successive pair overlaps as we just discussed. We'll also make sure it closes up smoothly.

The first step is to decide how many points to use; I'm going to say six points. Now we need to create our arrays of points filled with random screen locations.

To keep our random points all on the screen, I'll ask `random()` to create *x* values from 100 to 500, and *y* values from 100 to 300. Here's the skeleton:

```
int NumPoints = 6;
float [] Xp;
float [] Yp;

void setup() {
    size(600, 400);
    background(194, 216, 242);
    noFill();
    Xp = new float[NumPoints];
    Yp = new float[NumPoints];
    for (int i=0; i<NumPoints; i++) {
        Xp[i] = random(100, 500);
        Yp[i] = random(100, 300);
    }
}

void draw() {
    // draw curves
}
```

Now that we've created our arrays, let's do a quick check and make sure that we're making points correctly:

```
void draw() {
    for (int i=0; i<NumPoints; i++) {
        ellipse(Xp[i], Yp[i], 10, 10);
    }
}
```

(See output in Figure 12.12. Full program in cmcurves/sketches/bigcurve1/bigcurve1.pde)

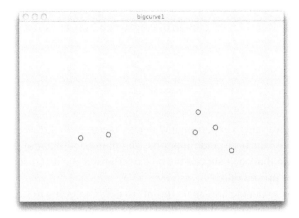

Figure 12.12. Starting a new curve project. (cmcurves/sketches/bigcurve1/bigcurve1.pde)

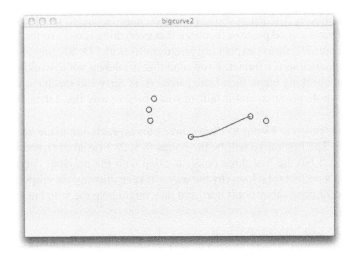

Figure 12.13. Drawing just one curve. (cmcurves/sketches/bigcurve2/bigcurve2.pde)

Perfect. Each time we run the program, we get six different scattered points, so your results will almost surely be different from mine. If you don't like a particular run and you want to run it again with a new batch of random values, on most systems, you don't have to close the sketch first. Just press the *Play* button again (or type its shortcut), and your program will restart with a fresh new batch of random numbers.

As one last sanity check, I'm going to manually draw a curve through the first four points (resulting in one curve segment between two points). If something's going screwy, this will let me know:

```
void draw() {
    for (int i=0; i<NumPoints; i++) {
        ellipse(Xp[i], Yp[i], 10, 10);
    }
    curve(Xp[0], Yp[0], Xp[1], Yp[1], Xp[2], Yp[2], Xp[3], Yp[3]);
}
```

(See output in Figure 12.13. Full program in cmcurves/sketches/bigcurve2/bigcurve2.pde)

So far, so good. I like doing these little tests along the way when I'm developing code because they're a quick way to confirm that everything is working correctly. It's really a matter of style, because I prefer simple debugging to complex debugging. Right now, I expect that I should be able to call curve() with the first four points from the array, and it should work and draw a curve and not cause an error. So I do just that and confirm it.

You might think this is a waste of time—after all, what else could have happened? All kinds of things could have gone wrong! I could have filled the arrays with zeros. Or all negative numbers. The list is endless. So I do a quick check: can I draw this little curve? If so, I have a good piece of feedback that everything is okay so far. I expect it to work, but of course, I always expect my programs to work! Debugging is what you do when your expectations are unmet. I've found that if I debug while working, by taking little steps and checking them, then I can catch errors early and much more easily than if I write the whole program and it fails in some bizarre way that I then have to try to figure out.

Back to our project. I want to create three curves, each one made up of four successive points. The first curve will be the points 0, 1, 2, 3 (as above), and the next one will be 1, 2, 3, 4 (so the first three points overlap with the previous curve), and then 2, 3, 4, 5. That's perfect for a loop (by the way, I'll keep drawing the ellipses around the curve vertices for now—they don't hurt, and they might help me with later debugging):

```
void draw() {
    for (int i=0; i<NumPoints; i++) {
        ellipse(Xp[i], Yp[i], 10, 10);
        }
    for (int i=0; i<NumPoints; i++) {
        int p0 = i;
        int p1 = i+1;
        int p2 = i+2;
        int p3 = i+3;
        curve(Xp[p0], Yp[p0], Xp[p1], Yp[p1], Xp[p2], Yp[p2],
            Xp[p3], Yp[p3]);
    }
}
```

(See output in Figure 12.14. Full program in cmcurves/sketches/bigcurve3/bigcurve3.pde)

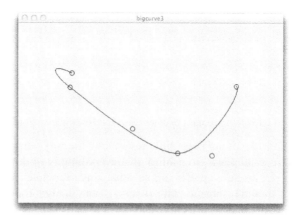

Figure 12.14. Drawing all the curves, but with a bug.
(cmcurves/sketches/bigcurve3/bigcurve3.pde)

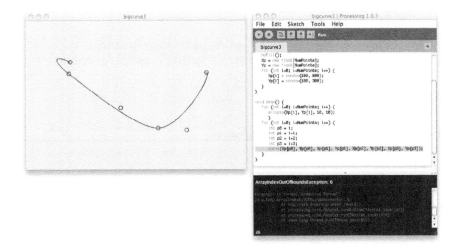

Figure 12.15. A problem with the last program.

So, another baby step. How's it look?

Uh-oh.

The error window has a bunch of messages, as Figure 12.15 shows, and Processing is reporting

```
ArrayIndexOutOfBoundsException: 6
```

Closing the graphics window doesn't work because Processing is hung up. So I'll move it out of the way of the main Processing window and hit the *Stop* button at the top of the Processing window (that's the circular button with a square inside it).

What went wrong? You might already know, but let's take it one step at a time. The error is telling us that we're asking for a value beyond the limits of an array. We're only accessing array elements in two places in this program, once in setup() and once in our new code at the end of draw(). I'm pretty sure the code in setup() is working because it was fine the last time we ran the program, and it hasn't been changed since, so I'm suspecting the new code.

The array indices are called p0, p1, p2, and p3. Let's print them out and see what their values are, and maybe that'll give us a clue about why things went wrong.

```
void draw() {
    for (int i=0; i<NumPoints; i++) {
        ellipse(Xp[i], Yp[i], 10, 10);
    }
    for (int i=0; i<NumPoints; i++) {
        int p0 = i;
        int p1 = i+1;
```

```
            int p2 = i+2;
            int p3 = i+3;
            println("p0="+p0+ " p1="+p1+" p2="+p2+" p3="+p3);
            curve(Xp[p0], Yp[p0], Xp[p1], Yp[p1], Xp[p2], Yp[p2],
                Xp[p3], Yp[p3]);
        }
    }
```

Here's what I get, before the error messages:

```
p0=0 p1=1 p2=2 p3=3
p0=1 p1=2 p2=3 p3=4
p0=2 p1=3 p2=4 p3=5
p0=3 p1=4 p2=5 p3=6
```

So okay, that's fair enough. I'm asking Processing for Xp[p3] and Yp[p3] when p3 is 6, and I know they only have six elements, so the legal range is only 0 to 5.

So this is an error on my part, but why is this happening? I know what I want are four successive points. But these points are going to form a loop, like in our square example above. After point 5, I want to go back to point 0. So when I ask for point 6, I really want to be asking for point 0. When I ask for point 7, I really want point 1.

More generally, any time I ask for a point equal to or greater than NumPoints, I want to subtract NumPoints from it. This is a perfect job for the modulo operator, written %. Recall that for any integer a, the value of a%NumPoints is simply a itself if a is less than NumPoints. Otherwise we keep subtracting NumPoints from a until it *is* less than NumPoints, and whatever is left is the result of the expression. For example, 5%8 is 5, and 10%8 is 2, and 100%8 is 4.

As before, I'll leave in all the debugging stuff so far. I find it's usually better to leave that stuff in until I'm all done with the code. I might want it again later, so why bother typing it all back in? If I don't want to see it on the screen, I'll comment it out. Like most people, I try to delete my debugging statements before I release my code to the world, but sometimes I forget, or miss one or two. When you look at other people's code, you'll sometimes see these kinds of debugging statements still lying around, commented out and forgotten but not deleted.

```
void draw() {
    for (int i=0; i<NumPoints; i++) {
        ellipse(Xp[i], Yp[i], 10, 10);
    }
    for (int i=0; i<NumPoints; i++) {
        int p0 = (i  )%NumPoints;
        int p1 = (i+1)%NumPoints;
        int p2 = (i+2)%NumPoints;
        int p3 = (i+3)%NumPoints;
```

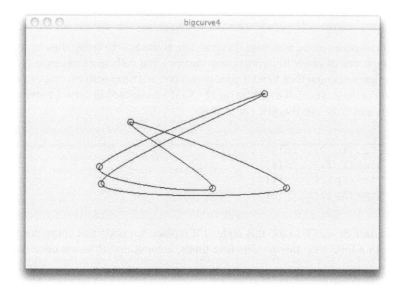

Figure 12.16. A nice smooth curve. (cmcurves/sketches/bigcurve4/bigcurve4.pde)

```
    //println("p0="+p0+ " p1="+p1+" p2="+p2+" p3="+p3);
    curve(Xp[p0], Yp[p0], Xp[p1], Yp[p1], Xp[p2], Yp[p2],
        Xp[p3], Yp[p3]);
    }
}
```

(See output in Figure 12.16. Full program in cmcurves/sketches/bigcurve4/bigcurve4.pde)

You'll see that I rolled the modulo operator right into the calculations for the p variables. I even applied it to p0, though obviously I don't have to. I even put parentheses around the variable i in that expression! Why? Because if I *must* repeat lines of code, I want them to look as much like one another as possible. Then later if I make a change, it will be obvious to me if the other lines need to be changed as well, and it will be equally obvious, at a glance, if I accidentally miss one.

Let's run this new code. That did it! Each time you run the program you'll get a different crazy curve that goes through six random points. The curve is smooth and closes up on itself. You'll notice that the curve in Figure 12.16 has some tight corners. It needs to turn around quickly in places in order to go through all the random points, but it never actually pinches.

I think I'll leave in the little ellipses around each point; it's kind of fun to see how the curve flows from one to the next.

As you might expect, all those lines of code that are near duplicates of each other are bugging me. One way to get rid of them is to use a different technique to specify the points of the curve.

12.4 Curves from Vertices

Processing offers a second way to build up a complicated curve rather than by manually assembling it out of many little four-point curves. You call beginShape() (which takes no arguments) and then hand it your points one at a time with curveVertex(). When you're done, you call endShape(). So if you wanted to draw a curve with the first four points from our list, you could write

```
beginShape();
curveVertex(Xp[0], Yp[0]);
curveVertex(Xp[1], Yp[1]);
curveVertex(Xp[2], Yp[2]);
curveVertex(Xp[3], Yp[3]);
endShape();
```

Let's adapt draw() to use this style. I'll replace our code that computes the four indices with a little loop that repeats four times, computing the points once each time through:

```
void draw() {
    for (int i=0; i<NumPoints; i++) {
        ellipse(Xp[i], Yp[i], 10, 10);
    }
    for (int i=0; i<NumPoints; i++) {
        beginShape();
        for (int j=0; j<4; j++) {
            int p = (i+j)%NumPoints;
            curveVertex(Xp[p], Yp[p]);
            }
        endShape();
    }
}
```

(See output in Figure 12.17. Full program in cmcurves/sketches/bigcurve5/bigcurve5.pde)

This version of creating a curve has two benefits. First, if you compute your vertices on the fly (rather than using precomputed elements from an array, as I'm doing here), then this is a much easier way to program. You just call beginShape() to get started, call your vertex-making routine a bunch of times, and then call endShape() to conclude. If you wanted to use curve(), you'd have to compute and save up four points at a time, which might be less convenient.

The other advantage of this form is that you can name more than four points between beginShape() and endShape(). If you do that, Processing uses the first four points to draw a curve, and then it uses points 1, 2, 3, and 4, then points 2, 3, 4, and 5, and so on. In other words, Processing creates a nice smooth curve for you by automatically drawing the curves using the overlap rule we saw before. Let's change draw() so it draws one curve built from all six points at once:

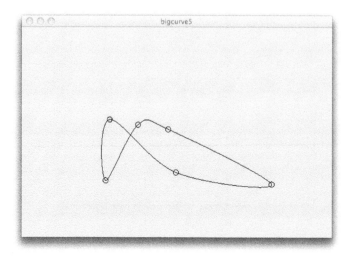

Figure 12.17. A smooth curve named one vertex at a time.
(cmcurves/sketches/bigcurve5/bigcurve5.pde)

```
void draw() {
    for (int i=0; i<NumPoints; i++) {
        ellipse(Xp[i], Yp[i], 10, 10);
    }
    beginShape();
    for (int i=0; i<NumPoints; i++) {
        curveVertex(Xp[i], Yp[i]);
    }
    endShape();
}
```

(See output in Figure 12.18. Full program in cmcurves/sketches/bigcurve6/bigcurve6.pde)

Well, that was a lot easier! But it didn't close up. That's because even in this format, the first and last points are used only as control points, just like when you use `curve()` and hand it four points. If you want the curve to close, you need to repeat the first three points at the end. I'll simply raise the upper limit in the *for loop* from `NumPoints` to `NumPoints+3` and let a little temporary variable and the modulo operator take care of wrapping the value of `i` back around to 0 for me:

```
void draw() {
    for (int i=0; i<NumPoints; i++) {
        ellipse(Xp[i], Yp[i], 10, 10);
    }
    beginShape();
```

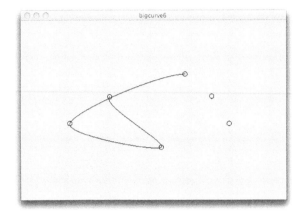

Figure 12.18. A smooth curve that doesn't close. (cmcurves/sketches/bigcurve6/bigcurve6.pde)

```
for (int i=0; i<NumPoints+3; i++) {
    int j = i%NumPoints;
    curveVertex(Xp[j], Yp[j]);
}
endShape();
}
```

(See output in Figure 12.19. Full program in cmcurves/sketches/bigcurve7/bigcurve7.pde)

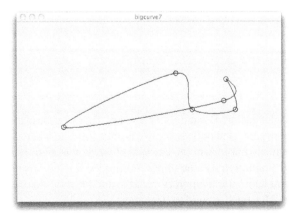

Figure 12.19. Closing the curve. (cmcurves/sketches/bigcurve7/bigcurve7.pde)

12.5   Tightening Curves

There's only one thing left that you can do with Catmull-Rom curves in Processing and that's to tighten them up. If you think of the curve like a piece of string that runs over a board with nails at the control points, then you can imagine what would happen if you pulled the string taut: the nice flowing curves would straighten out. If you pulled the string as tight as it could go, you'd get all straight lines from one point to the next.

The function `curveTightness()` lets you control curves to do just that. If you call it with the value 0, then it's just like not calling it at all: you get Catmull-Rom curves. If you call it with a value of 1, you get straight lines between the points. Values between 0 and 1 give you results between these extremes:

```
void draw() {
    for (int i=0; i<NumPoints; i++) {
        ellipse(Xp[i], Yp[i], 10, 10);
    }
    curveTightness(0.8);
    beginShape();
    for (int i=0; i<NumPoints+3; i++) {
        int j = (i+1)%NumPoints;
        curveVertex(Xp[j], Yp[j]);
    }
    endShape();
}
```

(See output in Figure 12.20. Full program in cmcurves/sketches/bigcurve8/bigcurve8.pde)

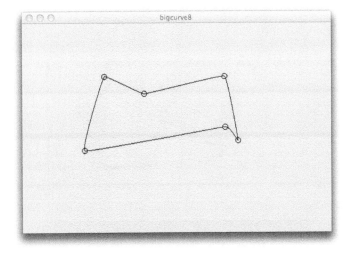

Figure 12.20. Tightening the curve. (cmcurves/sketches/bigcurve8/bigcurve8.pde)

Let's see what this looks like when animated. For fun, I'll bump the number of points up from six to ten. I'll also use the current frame number (from the systemwide variable `frameCount`) to sweep the value given to `curveTightness()` from 0 to 1 and back again. I'll use the built-in math function `sin()` to create a nice pattern. (When you give `sin()` increasing values as arguments, it gives you back a sequence of numbers that smoothly go back and forth from 1 to −1 and back to 1, over and over, forever. To get them to the range (0,1) I'll use our old friend `map()`. I'll talk more about `sin()` in Chapter 18).

```
float [] Xp;
float [] Yp;
int NumPoints = 10;

void setup() {
   size(600, 400);
   noFill();
   Xp = new float[NumPoints];
   Yp = new float[NumPoints];
   for (int i=0; i<NumPoints; i++) {
      Xp[i] = random(100, 500);
      Yp[i] = random(100, 300);
   }
}


   void draw() {
   background(194, 216, 242);
```

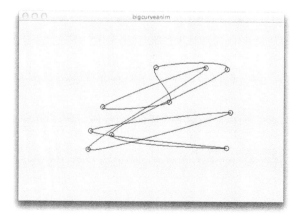

Figure 12.21. Changing tightness (frame from animation).
(cm-curves/sketches/bigcurveanim/bigcurveanim.pde)

```
for (int i=0; i<NumPoints; i++) {
    ellipse(Xp[i], Yp[i], 10, 10);
}
float tightness = map(sin(frameCount * .1), -1, 1, 0, 1);
curveTightness(tightness);
beginShape();
for (int i=0; i<NumPoints+3; i++) {
    int j = (i+1)%NumPoints;
    curveVertex(Xp[j], Yp[j]);
}
endShape();
}
```

(See output in Figure 12.21. Full program in cmcurves/sketches/bigcurveanim/bigcurveanim.pde)

I multiplied `frameCount` by 0.1 because that looked good on my computer. If the animation is too slow for you, make that number bigger; if it's too fast, make it smaller.

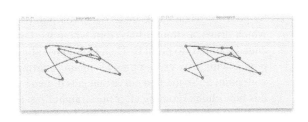

Figure 12.22. A couple of frames from the tightness animation.

A couple of frames at different levels of tightness are in Figure 12.22.

If you're in an experimental mood, try giving `curveTightness()` values that are outside the "official" range of 0 to 1. Just go to the `map()` call above and change the output range from $(0, 1)$ to something nutty, like $(-8, 8)$. You can't break the computer! The worst that can happen is you get an error message. Hint: you won't get an error message.

By the way, you can include straight segments in your big curve if you want. In the midst of your calls to `curveVertex()`, you can instead call `vertex()` with the location of your next point, and Processing will draw a straight line from the most recent point to that location.

In fact, you may recall from Chapter 6 that if you *only* call `vertex()` between `beginShape()` and `endShape()`, you can create an arbitrary drawing of all straight lines (just as though you'd used a curve but set the `curveTightness()` to 1).

If you do call `vertex()` and then you want to continue drawing curves, you'll need to provide at least four additional points using `curveVertex()` to define the next curved segment.

For example, here's a variation on the last program, where I'm going to draw a straight line from point 5 to point 6. To make it easily visible, I'll first draw that line with a thick white stroke and then I'll draw the curve over it.

```
strokeWeight(8);
stroke(255);
line(Xp[5], Yp[5], Xp[6], Yp[6]);
stroke(0);
strokeWeight(1);

beginShape();
for (int i=0; i<7; i++) curveVertex(Xp[i], Yp[i]); // points 0-6
vertex(Xp[6], Yp[6]);                               // point 5
for (int i=5; i<10; i++) curveVertex(Xp[i], Yp[i]);// points 5-9
endShape();
```

(See output in Figure 12.23. Full program in cmcurves/sketches/lineInCurve/lineInCurve.pde).

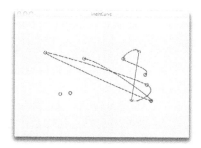

Figure 12.23. Drawing a straight line in the curve. (cmcurves/sketches/lineInCurve/lineInCurve.pde)

To draw the curve, I hand curveVertex() all the points up to, and including, point 6. So the last curve that's drawn uses the four points 3, 4, 5, 6, and thus runs from 4 to 5, influenced by point 6. Then I call vertex() on point 6, which draws a straight line from where we last ended (point 5) to point 6. Then I start providing points with curveVertex() again, starting with point 5. So the first curve that gets drawn by this new chunk (coming after the straight line) is built from the first four points of this loop. Those are points 5, 6, 7, 8, which is a curve from 6 to 7, but the starting direction is influenced by point 5. Thus, we have a curve that smoothly turns into a straight line from point 5 to 6 and then smoothly curves again after.

If you don't want (or need) smoothness going into and coming out of the straight segment, you don't have to overlap the curves and the straight segment so carefully.

That's about all there is to using curve() and curveVertex(). You might be thinking to yourself that this seems like a pretty complete tool: you give it a bunch of points and it draws a smooth, curved line that passes through them all. You can even get it to close up smoothly. And you can pull it tighter if you want, and even insert straight segments. What else could anyone want?

Control. Specifically, control over the shape of the curve. If you hand curve() a bunch of points, you'll get a smooth curve that goes through them. But what if you want that curve to be a little floppier or looser? You can adjust the points, but each time you move a point you're going to also affect multiple segments of the curve since each point is shared by four segments. So you do have some control, but it's not localized to the region you want—moving a point adjusts a big chunk of the the curve. And that still doesn't let you adjust the shape with much precision: maybe you want it to take this corner tightly but that corner loosely. If that's what you want, you're in for a challenge.

Basically, the curves we've seen here are just perfect if you simply want a smooth, graceful curve that passes through a bunch of points. But if you have your own ideas about the shape of that curve, because it's part of your creative expression, you're pretty much out of luck. Catmull-Rom splines are simple, but they lack control. This isn't a limitation of Processing. It's just how the mathematics of these curves work out. We'll see in the next chapter how a different kind of curve can offer us more control.

12.6 Working with Curves

There are three useful routines associated with curves that we haven't discussed yet.

When Processing draws your curve (either using `curve()` directly, or by using a list of `curveVertex()` entries), it actually draws it as a sequence of very short straight lines. By default, Processing draws 20 of these little lines, which usually is more than enough for a smooth-looking curve. But if for some reason (perhaps your curves are enormous on the screen) this isn't enough and you can see those little lines, you can tell it to use more of them. Call `curveDetail()` with the number of lines you want it to use (note: as of Version 1.1, the default renderer ignores this call).

One popular use of curves is to control the motion of an object. A falling snowflake, a galloping horse, and a fish swimming in a bowl can all be controlled by moving them along an invisible curve. But how do you find out the value of the curve? All we've done with curves so far is draw them.

It turns out that you can ask Processing for the x and y value of any point on the curve. The technique is to think of each section of curve (that is, each piece made up of four points) as running from 0 to 1. You give Processing a number in this range, and it gives you back the point. When the control is 0, you get back the first knot, and when the control is 1, you get the second knot.

The interesting thing is that you don't actually hand this routine all four points. Instead, you hand it just the four x values, or just the four y values. It turns out that the underlying mathematics of these curves is completely independent for both coordinates. So to find the x value of a point at a location t from 0 to 1, you'd call `curvePoint()` with the four x values of the curve and t. With the variables we've been using in our code, here's a line that will tell you the x value of any point on the curve. When t is 0, you get the first endpoint of the curve (not the first control point, but the first point of the curve itself), and when t is 1, you get the other endpoint, with values of t in between giving you all the points of the curve.

```
float xValue = curvePoint(Xp[0], Xp[1], Xp[2], Xp[3], t);
```

If you want the y value at point t, you just call `curvePoint()` with the y values:

```
float yValue = curvePoint(Yp[0], Yp[1], Yp[2], Yp[3], t);
```

If you wanted to actually draw your own curve, you could do it by taking lots of little steps and drawing short lines between them. But if you want to move an object along a curve, you need only get the x and y values and position your object there.

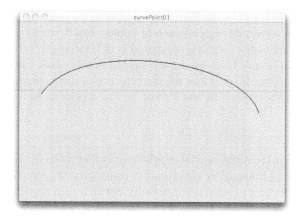

Figure 12.24. A single curve. (cmcurves/sketches/curvePoint01/curvePoint01.pde)

Let's see this in action. I'll make a four-point curve that fills much of the screen:

```
float [] Xp = {  40,  50, 540, 300 };
float [] Yp = { 940, 160, 200, 900 };

void setup() {
  size(600, 400);
  background(237, 180, 198);
  noFill();
  curve(Xp[0], Yp[0], Xp[1], Yp[1], Xp[2], Yp[2], Xp[3], Yp[3]);
}
```

(See output in Figure 12.24. Full program in cmcurves/sketches/curvePoint01/curvePoint01.pde)

Now let's move an object along this curve. I'll pick something so complicated, so rich in detail and subtlety, that you won't be able to look away. I shall draw ... a circle.

```
int numSteps = 8;
for (int i=0; i<numSteps; i++) {
  float t = map(i, 0, numSteps-1, 0, 1);
  float xPos = curvePoint(Xp[0], Xp[1], Xp[2], Xp[3], t);
  float yPos = curvePoint(Yp[0], Yp[1], Yp[2], Yp[3], t);
  fill(255);
  strokeWeight(1);
  stroke(0, 0, 0);
  ellipse(xPos, yPos, 10, 10);
}
```

(See output in Figure 12.25. Full program in cmcurves/sketches/curvePoint02/curvePoint02.pde)

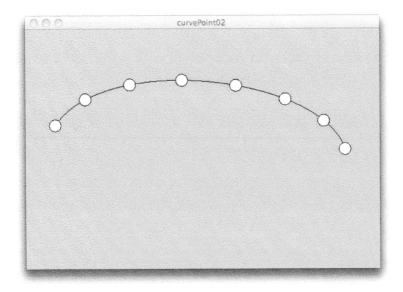

Figure 12.25. Points on a curve. (cmcurves/sketches/curvePoint02/curvePoint02.pde)

Pretty amazing, I know. But the key thing here is that we're able to get points along the curve and do something with them.

Note that although I used equally spaced values of t from 0 to 1, the points that came back were not equally spaced along the curve. That's again due to the underlying mathematics.

12.7 Tangents and Normals

Getting the *x* and *y* of the curve at a value of t is definitely useful, but we can get a little bit more information at each point. We can ask Processing for the *tangent* at every point. The tangent at a specific point on a curve is the straight line that just grazes the curve at that point. If you imagine that an object was moving along the curve like a car on a track, and the track was suddenly cut at some point and the car could then move freely, the tangent is the name of the line corresponding to the direction the car would go off in.

To get the tangent at a point, you call curveTangent(). It takes the same arguments as curvePoint(), and it works the same way in the sense that you call it once with all the *x* points for the tangent's *x* value, and again for the *y*.

Here I'll add a few lines to get the tangent and then I'll draw a little line centered at the curve point that goes in the direction of the tangent.

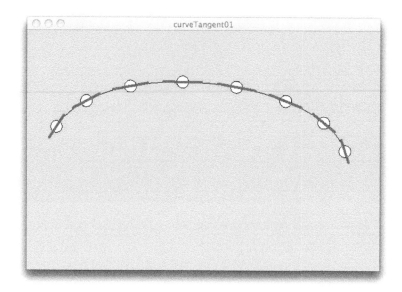

Figure 12.26. Drawing the tangent lines in blue.
(cmcurves/sketches/curveTangent01/curveTangent01.pde)

The mathematics used by Processing to compute the tangent produces lines of different lengths. They go in the proper direction (that is, they are always tangent to the curve), but some are short in length, and others are long. When the curve is changing fast, like in a hairpin turn, the tangent will have small values (so if we draw the line, it would be short). When the curve is mostly flat, the tangent will be large (so the line would be long). Sometimes this is useful, since the tangent thus tells us not only what direction the curve is going in but how fast it's changing.

Let's draw the tangents as we get them back, but I'll draw them symmetrically around the point we're testing. When I first ran the following program the tangents were huge on the screen, so I scaled down the x and y components. A scaling of 1/20 looked good to me. You'll be able to see in the figure how the lengths vary with the sharpness of the curve.

```
float xTan = curveTangent(Xp[0], Xp[1], Xp[2], Xp[3], t)/20;
float yTan = curveTangent(Yp[0], Yp[1], Yp[2], Yp[3], t)/20;
strokeWeight(3);
stroke(40, 62, 209);
line(xPos-xTan, yPos-yTan, xPos+xTan, yPos+yTan);
```

(See output in Figure 12.26. Full program in cmcurves/sketches/curveTangent01/curveTangent01.pde)

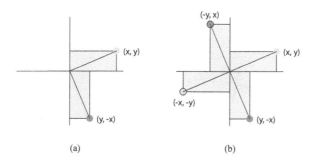

Figure 12.27. Finding the perpendicular. (a) The original line runs from the center to the blue point at (x, y). The perpendicular line runs from the center to the red point at (y, -x). (b) The original line also runs through (-x, -y). Another line perpendicular to the original runs from the origin to the red point at (-y, x).

A related idea to the tangent is the *normal* . The normal to a curve at a given point is perpendicular to the curve at that point. Since the tangent lies right on the curve, the normal is perpendicular to the tangent.

So if we have the tangent, we can find the normal just by rotating the tangent line by 90 degrees. There is a super-easy, super-fast trick for doing just this operation on a line.

Suppose that you have a line from the origin (at $(0,0)$) to some point (x,y). In Figure 12.27a I've marked that point in blue. If you want to find a line that's perpendicular to this one (that is, it's at right angles), you only need to draw a line from $(0,0)$ to $(y,-x)$. This point is marked in red.

This is a great general method for finding a line that's perpendicular to any other line. By the way, as the figure shows in part (b), the line from the origin to (x,y) will also pass through $(-x,-y)$, and the perpendicular line will also pass through $(-y,x)$. That can be useful information when you want to draw the line passing through the point—just join up the two extremes.

This little perpendicular-finding trick is just one of those little useful bits of knowledge you pick up over time, like the fact that the word "separate" has an *a* (not an *e*) in the middle or that you should lift with your legs, not your back.

We can use this trick to draw normals from the tangents:

```
stroke(0);
line(xPos-yTan, yPos+xTan, xPos+yTan, yPos-xTan);
```

(See output in Figure 12.28. Full program in cmcurves/sketches/curveTangent02/curveTangent02.pde)

Notice that the normals vary in length, too. This should be no surprise, since they're just the tangent lines rotated by 90 degrees.

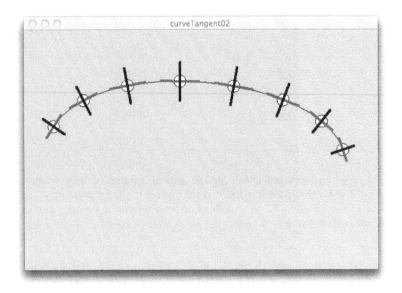

Figure 12.28. Drawing the normal lines in black.
(cmcurves/sketches/curveTangent02/curveTangent02.pde)

By joining up the endpoints of the normals, we can create an *offset curve*. This is a curve that sits roughly on the inside (or outside) of another curve. As you can see from the figure, if we took lots of steps along the curve, found the normals, and joined their endpoints, we could create two new curves inside and outside the main curve. So let's do that! In this program, I'll take the time to scale the lines, so that the normals all have length 20 (that will make sure that the offset curve is always 20 units away from the center line).

The strategy will be to take a bunch of steps along the curve. At each step I'll compute the location of the point on the curve and the tangent. Because I want the tangents to have the same length, I'll call the mag() function. We'll see this in depth in Chapter 18, where we'll find that it tells us the distance between the point (0,0) and a point that you give it. So in our case, mag() will give us the length of the line that comes from the computation of the tangent. If I divide both of the line's components by that value, the line itself will have length 1.

Then I'll multiply each component by 20. The result is a pair of points that are each 20 units away from the center curve. If this isn't the first point along the curve, I'll draw a line between the old values above the curve (called oldx0 and oldy0) and the new point above the curve and between the old values below the curve (called oldx1 and oldy1) and the new point below the curve. Then I'll save the current point values in these "old" variables, and take another step. The result is that I'll draw one curve above (or "outside") the input curve, and another one below (or "inside") it. I'll do all of this explicitly, so the code is a bit long and repeats itself, but it shows you every step.

```
float oldx0 = 0;
float oldy0 = 0;
float oldx1 = 0;
float oldy1 = 0;
float newx0 = 0;
float newy0 = 0;
float newx1 = 0;
float newy1 = 0;
int numSteps = 20;
strokeWeight(2);
for (int i=0; i<numSteps; i++) {
  float t = map(i, 0, numSteps-1, 0, 1);
  float xPos = curvePoint(Xp[0], Xp[1], Xp[2], Xp[3], t);
  float yPos = curvePoint(Yp[0], Yp[1], Yp[2], Yp[3], t);
  float xTan = curveTangent(Xp[0], Xp[1], Xp[2], Xp[3], t);
  float yTan = curveTangent(Yp[0], Yp[1], Yp[2], Yp[3], t);
  float tanlen = mag(xTan, yTan);
  xTan *= 20/tanlen;
  yTan *= 20/tanlen;
  newx0 = xPos-yTan;
  newy0 = yPos+xTan;
  newx1 = xPos+yTan;
  newy1 = yPos-xTan;
  if (i > 0) {
    line(oldx0, oldy0, newx0, newy0);
    line(oldx1, oldy1, newx1, newy1);
  }
  oldx0 = newx0;
  oldy0 = newy0;
  oldx1 = newx1;
  oldy1 = newy1;
}
```

(See output in Figure 12.29. Full program in cmcurves/sketches/curveTangent03/curveTangent03.pde)

Offset curves are great for all kinds of things. If you want to draw a roadway, for instance, you could just maintain the center of the road as a curve, but you could draw two yellow lines down the middle of the road by drawing two curves just slightly offset from the center. Curves farther away could be the curbs or shoulders.

If you're using curves to control motion, then offset curves give you objects with related motion. For instance, you might have a bird flying along a curve. By finding the value of two offset curves at a time slightly in the past, you can find the positions of birds to the left and right, and slightly behind, the leader. That gives you three points of a triangle, and you can fill that in with many more birds if you want a flock of them.

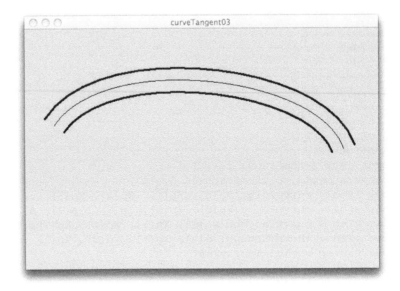

Figure 12.29. Drawing the offset curves.
(cmcurves/sketches/curveTangent03/curveTangent03.pde)

12.8   Finding a Point on a Curve

As we saw in the last section, we can find the *x* and *y* coordinates of any point on a curve by calling `curvePoint()` with a value for t along the curve. And this works just fine for many situations, particularly when you're using a curve to move things around on the screen.

But another great use for curves is in helping you make patterns. The curve does this by transforming one number into another. Consider the following little program that draws a single curve:

```
float [] Xp = {  50,  50, 540, 200 };
float [] Yp = {-650, 150, 110, -290 };

void setup() {
   size(600, 400);
   background(210, 215, 140);
   noFill();
   curve(Xp[0], Yp[0], Xp[1], Yp[1], Xp[2], Yp[2], Xp[3], Yp[3]);
}
```

(See output in Figure 12.30. Full program in cmcurves/sketches/findPoint01/findPoint01.pde)

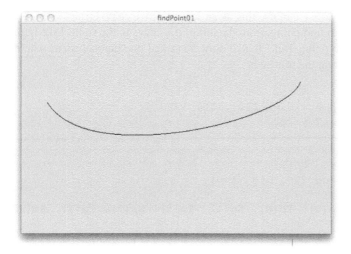

Figure 12.30. A curve with one *y* per *x*. (cmcurves/sketches/findPoint01/findPoint01.pde)

We might use this curve to help us determine how much animation to apply to a crowd at a baseball game. In this example, the height of the curve tells us how excited the people in the crowd are.

At the start of the game (at the left of the curve) their energy is pretty high, since they're looking forward to a good game. But very soon the other guys start scoring runs, and they pull out ahead. The crowd loses some of its enthusiasm. The game goes on for a while longer and then the home team starts to come back. The crowd gets a little more excited with each new run, until finally its team just barely wins the game. The people in the crowd go home feeling a little bit better than when they arrived.

In this scenario, we imagine the horizontal axis as representing time. It starts near the left of the window and runs to the right. At each moment in time, we find the crowd's excitation by finding the value of the curve corresponding to that time (that is, that horizontal location).

We sometimes express this by saying that we can find the crowd's excitement "as a function of" the time. That is, we imagine that there's some function that takes time as an input, and produces the crowd's level of excitement as output. We could even make this a Processing function.

But there's a problem: we don't have a way of finding the value of the curve at any horizontal point. What we do have is the value of the curve at a position t, but that's measured along the curve itself, not along the axis. And that's not the same thing. Often, it's not even close.

To see that, let's add some code to our little example. I'll write a routine that takes a parameter called `percent`, telling us how far along the game we've progressed. When this variable has the value 0, we're at the start of the game, and at 1, we're at the end of the game. So we can use this as an input to curvePoint(), which also uses the values 0 to 1 to find points from the left of the curve to the right. Like before, I'll draw a circle at that point. But I'll also draw a vertical line that shows us where we are as a percentage along the time axis.

```
float [] Xp = {   50,   50, 540, 200 };
float [] Yp = {-650, 150, 110, -290 };
int TimeAxisY = 300;

void setup() {
   size(600, 400);
   background(210, 215, 140);
   noFill();
   curve(Xp[0], Yp[0], Xp[1], Yp[1], Xp[2], Yp[2], Xp[3], Yp[3]);

   line(50, TimeAxisY, 540, TimeAxisY);      // the time axis
   drawMatch(color(194, 54, 17), 0.2);
   drawMatch(color(112, 52, 90), 0.5);
   drawMatch(color(40, 115, 110), 0.8);
}

void drawMatch(color clr, float percent) {
   stroke(clr);
   fill(255);

   float x3 = curvePoint(Xp[0], Xp[1], Xp[2], Xp[3], percent);
   float y3 = curvePoint(Yp[0], Yp[1], Yp[2], Yp[3], percent);
   ellipse(x3, y3, 20, 20);

   float px = lerp(50, 540, percent);
   line(px, 0, px, TimeAxisY);
}
```

(See output in Figure 12.31. Full program in cmcurves/sketches/findPoint02/findPoint02.pde)

In Figure 12.31, I've shown three different values of percent. Consider the first one, when percent=0.2, in red. The red circle shows us the spot that's 20 percent of the way along the curve itself. In other words, if we stretched the curve straight, that point would be 20 percent of the way from the left end to the right end. But of course the curve isn't straight!

Compare this to the red line, which shows our position 20 percent along the way from the left end to the right end of the time axis, drawn under the curve. What we want to find is the height of the curve at this location. In other words, we want the y value of the curve for this value of x.

It's a common mistake when working with curves to forget this and use t as though it was actually an x value. You can see that sometimes they come close, so the bug

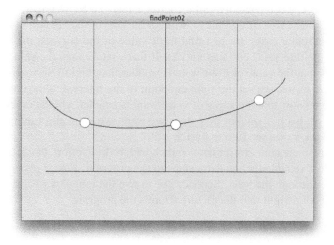

Figure 12.31. Comparing percent along the time axis with percent along the curve. (cmcurves/sketches/findPoint02/findPoint02.pde)

might escape your detection right away, but it's usually not what you really want. What we'd like is a function that lets us give it a percent along the timeline, and it returns the y value of the curve at that percentage. That is, if we give it a percentage of 0.2, it returns the point in Figure 12.31 where the red line intersects the black curve.

Happily, there's a standard technique for this. The idea starts by turning the problem on its head. We ask ourselves, given an x value, what value of t would we need to give to curvePoint() to get that value of x back out?

The trick is to create an *interval*. This is just a pair of values, typically arranged with the smaller one first. The idea is that we start with such a huge interval for the value of t that we're sure the value we want lies somewhere inside the interval (usually we start with the interval $(0,1)$). Then we make the interval smaller and smaller and smaller until the distance between the low and high values is so tiny we decide we're close enough.

In other words, eventually the interval is very small, but we know that there's a value of t in there that, when given to curvePoint() with the x values of the curve's points, will give us back the value of x we started with. If we evaluate curvePoint() at that value of t with the y values of the curve's points, we'll get back the y value of the curve that's directly above the x value we started with. Typically, once we stop dividing, we'll use the value of t in the middle of the final, tiny interval.

Let's do exactly that. I'll take our program from the last example and change it around a little bit. I'll create two new variables, Tlo and Thi, to define my interval. I'll start them out at 0 and 1, respectively, so they enclose the whole curve. After drawing the curve, I'll repeatedly call a routine called `refineInterval()`. Each time we call it, `refineInterval()` will cut the size of the interval in half.

The trick is really easy: we just find the *x* value of the curve at the value of t in the middle of the interval (I call this `tmid`). If that's larger than the value of *x* that we have, we know that the value of t we want is smaller than `tmid`. So we just set `Thi` to `tmid`. In other words, we set the right endpoint of the interval to the current value of `tmid`, since we know that the value of t we want is smaller. On the other hand, if the value of *x* we get back is smaller than the *x* we want, we know the value we're after is larger than `tmid`, so we set `Tlo` to `tmid`.

This trick is so elegant, and it does so much with so little effort, that it can be hard to understand. So I've added a few extra steps to the program. First, I print out the range of t each time through the loop. Second, I've drawn the range of *x* values represented by those values of t right into the picture. Here's the program:

```
float [] Xp = {  50,   50, 540, 200 };
float [] Yp = {-650, 150, 110, -290 };
int TimeAxisY = 300;
float Tlo = 0.0;
float Thi = 1.0;

void setup() {
   size(600, 400);
   background(210, 215, 140);
   noFill();
   curve(Xp[0], Yp[0], Xp[1], Yp[1], Xp[2], Yp[2], Xp[3], Yp[3]);

   line(50, TimeAxisY, 540, TimeAxisY);     // the time axis
   float targetX = 120;
   for (int step=0; step<10; step++) {
      refineInterval(step, targetX);
      println("step "+step+":   Tlo = "+Tlo+"
         Thi = "+Thi+"   (width = "+(Thi-Tlo)+")");
   }

   line(targetX, 0, targetX, TimeAxisY);
   float tmid = (Tlo+Thi)/2.0;
   float px = curvePoint(Xp[0], Xp[1], Xp[2], Xp[3], tmid);
   float py = curvePoint(Yp[0], Yp[1], Yp[2], Yp[3], tmid);
   ellipse(px, py, 20, 20);
}

void refineInterval(int step, float targetX) {
   float xLeft = curvePoint(Xp[0], Xp[1], Xp[2], Xp[3], Tlo);
   float xRight = curvePoint(Xp[0], Xp[1], Xp[2], Xp[3], Thi);
   float barY = TimeAxisY - ((step+1)*10);
   line(xLeft, barY, xRight, barY);
```

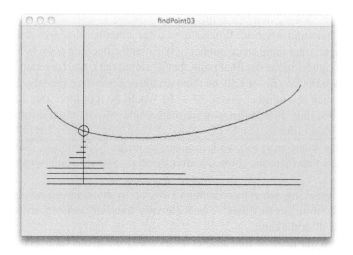

Figure 12.32. Finding the value of *t* for a given *x*.
(cmcurves/sketches/findPoint03/findPoint03.pde)

```
float tmid = (Tlo + Thi)/2.0;
float xval = curvePoint(Xp[0], Xp[1], Xp[2], Xp[3], tmid);
if (targetX < xval) Thi = tmid;
              else Tlo = tmid;
}
```

(See output in Figure 12.32. Full program in cmcurves/sketches/findPoint03/findPoint03.pde)

You can see what happens to the range visually in the figure. We start with the interval $(0, 1)$ and find that the *x* value we want is in the left half. So that becomes our new interval, and we test the midpoint again and again select the left half. Then we select the right half, then the left half again, and so on, until the interval is tiny in width.

Here are the numbers that show the range getting smaller each time:

```
step 0:  Tlo = 0.0   Thi = 0.5   (width = 0.5)
step 1:  Tlo = 0.0   Thi = 0.25   (width = 0.25)
step 2:  Tlo = 0.125   Thi = 0.25   (width = 0.125)
step 3:  Tlo = 0.125   Thi = 0.1875   (width = 0.0625)
step 4:  Tlo = 0.15625   Thi = 0.1875   (width = 0.03125)
step 5:  Tlo = 0.171875   Thi = 0.1875   (width = 0.015625)
step 6:  Tlo = 0.1796875   Thi = 0.1875   (width = 0.0078125)
step 7:  Tlo = 0.1796875   Thi = 0.18359375   (width = 0.00390625)
step 8:  Tlo = 0.1796875   Thi = 0.18164062   (width = 0.001953125)
step 9:  Tlo = 0.18066406   Thi = 0.18164062   (width = 9.765625E-4)
```

That strange-looking number at the end $(9.765625E - 4)$ is a number printed in a format called *scientific notation*. Whenever you see a number that ends with something like E-4, it means that there are a number of 0's after the decimal point before the digits that are given (ignoring the decimal point that's printed out). So, for example, $9.5E - 4$ is the same as 0.00095 ($E - 4$ tells us there are three 0's before the 95). Since there's one less zero than the number given, $8E - 12$ would be a number that has a decimal point, eleven 0's, then an 8. It's a way for the computer to give you information about the number without forcing you to plow through (and count) a long list of 0's.

It works the other way, too, with a plus sign instead of a minus. Something like $9.5E + 4$ means that there are three 0's after the digits, so we could write $9.5E + 4$ as $95,000$.

Generally speaking, when the computer switches to showing you numbers with scientific notation, it means that they've become very small or very big, involving lots of zeros before or after the digits.

Returning to our quest to find a point on a curve for a given value of *x*, you can see that this routine homed in on the right value very fast. In ten steps we found the value of t in an interval that was less than 1/1000 wide. Each step after that would halve the size of the interval yet again.

So how many times do we repeat this process? The easiest answer is to simply pick a width for your interval ahead of time. Whenever the process narrows down the interval to that size (or smaller), it stops. We call that a *threshold*. So let's rewrite the routine to use that strategy. We'll call it just once, with a desired value of *x* and a threshold, and it will return the value of t that lies in the middle of an interval that is no larger than that threshold.

Here's the change to the calling routine and the graphics that come after it:

```
float targetX = 120;
float threshold = 0.0001;
float answerT = findTfromX(threshold, targetX);

line(targetX, 0, targetX, TimeAxisY);
float px = curvePoint(Xp[0], Xp[1], Xp[2], Xp[3], answerT);
float py = curvePoint(Yp[0], Yp[1], Yp[2], Yp[3], answerT);
ellipse(px, py, 20, 20);
```

We don't need the global Tlo and Thi variables any more. Everything happens inside the new function findTfromX(), which returns the identified t when it's done.

```
float findTfromX(float threshold, float targetX) {
  float tlo = 0;
  float thi = 1;
  float xLeft = curvePoint(Xp[0], Xp[1], Xp[2], Xp[3], tlo);
  float xRight = curvePoint(Xp[0], Xp[1], Xp[2], Xp[3], thi);
  int numSteps = 500;
  while (numSteps-- > 0) {
```

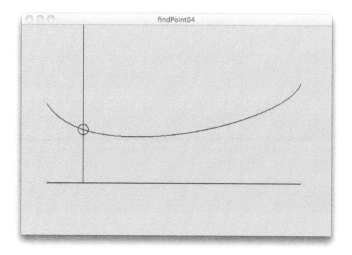

Figure 12.33. Better routine for finding *x*. (cmcurves/sketches/findPoint04/findPoint04.pde)

```
    float tmid = (tlo + thi)/2.0;
    if ((thi - tlo) < threshold) {
        return(tmid);
    }
    float xval = curvePoint(Xp[0], Xp[1], Xp[2], Xp[3], tmid);
    if (targetX < xval) thi = tmid;
                else tlo = tmid;
    }
    return((tlo+thi)/2.0);   // we couldn't find the point
}
```

(See output in Figure 12.33. Full program in cmcurves/sketches/findPoint04/findPoint04.pde)

The only interesting change here is that I added a new variable called numSteps, and I stopped the loop if we ran it that many times. Why did I do that?

It's just defensive programming. If there's something wrong with my code (for example, I missed a bug), then I might end up with an infinite loop and the program would seize up. I'd rather get back a wrong answer. Then I can see my problem and dig into the code and fix it. If the program just suddenly stops running, I really don't have any options except to stop it and then step by step try to find the place it's getting stuck. Since the interval is getting halved each time through the loop, even if you ask for an interval that's narrower than one-millionth of the original $(0, 1)$ interval, it shouldn't go through the loop more than 20 times. If we go through this loop 500 times then something has gone seriously wrong!

I've been assuming all along that we have a curve that obeys a basic rule: every value of *x* has a single value of *y*. But there's no reason that should be the case.

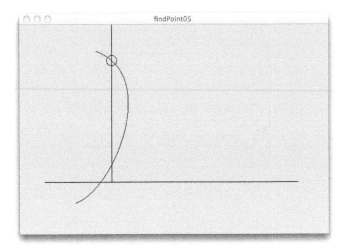

Figure 12.34. A curve with two values of *y* for a given value of *x*.
(cmcurves/sketches/findPoint05/findPoint05.pde)

Let's create a very similar curve, but rotated 90 degrees from the last one, and then run our program on it. I'll adjust the value of *x* that we're looking for by a little bit, too, so it's within the new range.

```
float [] Xp = { -650,   150, 110, -290 };
float [] Yp = { 50, 50, 340, 200 };
```

(See output in Figure 12.34. Full program in cmcurves/sketches/findPoint05/findPoint05.pde)

In this backwards C-shaped curve, there are two values of *y* for this value of *x*. In other words, there are two possible results for t that the routine can return. If we didn't know what was going on inside the function, we wouldn't be able to predict which one we'd get back.

So this technique, while very useful, depends on your making sure that you only call it with the right kind of curves, namely, those that have a single value of *y* for each value of *x*.

Often people will call these *well-behaved* curves. That term is pretty flexible because something that's well behaved with respect to one technique might be a nightmare for another. Often, "well behaved" is something of a synonym for "appropriate," so it strongly depends on what's being discussed.

The technique we just saw is called a *binary search* or *binary subdivision*. The "binary" part comes from the idea that our searching process involves cutting the interval in two pieces each time through.

You can use this technique any time you want to control any variable in your program, whether it's the color of the sky, the motion of a bungee-jumper, or the pulsing glow around a blinking light in the fog. We'll see in Chapter 18 that Processing offers us a wide variety of built-in functions for creating sequences of numbers that we can use to control all the elements in our images and animations. If you find that none of those built-in tools produce just the kind of patterns that you want, using a curve in this way is an alternative.

Chapter 13
Bézier Curves

The second type of curve offered by Processing is the Bézier curve. It's pronounced bez'-yay, and named for the man who developed its mathematics. The functions for creating Bézier curves look a lot like those for Catmull-Rom curves, but they produce quite different results.

13.1 Bézier Curves

Bézier curves are popular in graphic arts because you can easily control their shape (in fact, they were originally developed to help automobile designers create smoothly shaped car parts). Programs like Photoshop and Illustrator use Bézier curves for their curve-drawing tools, so if you're familiar with those programs, you're already an old hand at Bézier curves.

Just for fun, and to see what happens, let's take our curve program from the last chapter (which drew Figure 12.11, showing curves joining up at the four corners of a square), but instead of calling `curve()` for each set of four points, I'll call `bezier()`. Since `bezier()` also takes four points as input, whatever happens, it ought to at least run. Whether the results will be interesting or not, we'll find out! The only changes in this program from the earlier one are a new background color and the one call to `bezier()` in place of `curve()`:

```
void setup() {
   size(600, 400);
   background(242, 207, 194);
   noFill();
}

void drawCurve(boolean drawCircles, boolean drawLines,
               int p0, int p1, int p2, int p3) {

   // control point 1
```

```
    stroke(255,  0, 0);   // red
    if (drawCircles == true) {
        ellipse(Xp[p0], Yp[p0], 15, 15);
    }
    if (drawLines == true) {
        line(Xp[p0], Yp[p0], Xp[p1], Yp[p1]);
    }

    // control point 1
    stroke(0, 0, 255);   // blue
    if (drawCircles == true) {
        ellipse(Xp[p3], Yp[p3], 15, 15);
    }
    if (drawLines == true) {
        line(Xp[p3], Yp[p3], Xp[p2], Yp[p2]);
    }

    // the knots
    stroke(0, 0, 0);   // black
    if (drawCircles == true) {
        ellipse(Xp[p1], Yp[p1], 15, 15);
        ellipse(Xp[p2], Yp[p2], 15, 15);
    }

    bezier(Xp[p0], Yp[p0], Xp[p1], Yp[p1], Xp[p2], Yp[p2],
        Xp[p3], Yp[p3]);
}

float [] Xp = { 100, 300, 300, 100 };
float [] Yp = { 100, 100, 300, 300 };

void draw() {
    drawCurve(true,  false, 0, 1, 2, 3);
    drawCurve(false, false, 1, 2, 3, 0);
    drawCurve(false, false, 2, 3, 0, 1);
    drawCurve(false, false, 3, 0, 1, 2);
}
```

(See output in Figure 13.1. Full program in bcurves/sketches/box01/box01.pde)

It's a nice image, but it's not obvious what's going on.

Let's back up a step and draw just the first curve. The points are taken clockwise from the upper left, since we're starting with the same four points we started with in the last chapter, in the same order.

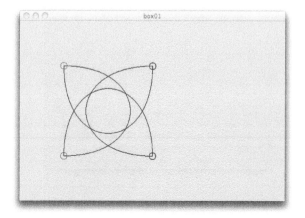

Figure 13.1. Bézier curves on a box. (bcurves/sketches/box01/box01.pde)

```
void draw() {
   drawCurve(true,  true, 0, 1, 2, 3);
   }
```

(See output in Figure 13.2. Full program in bcurves/sketches/box02/box02.pde)

The first thing that hits me when I compare this to what `curve()` gave us (in Figure 12.4) is that the relationship of the control points and knots has reversed. In Catmull-Rom curves, the first and last points are the controls, and the curve is drawn between the middle two points. In a Bézier curve, the curve is drawn from the first point to the last, and the second and third points serve as controls.

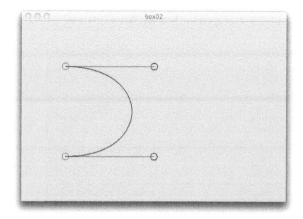

Figure 13.2. One Bézier curve. (bcurves/sketches/box02/box02.pde)

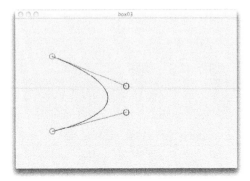

Figure 13.3. Moving a control point. (bcurves/sketches/box03/box03.pde)

But what's the nature of that control? One of the pleasures of using Processing is that exploring is easy. Let's try moving these control points around and see what happens. For the first experiment, I'll move point 1 downward and point 2 upward (but not as much), bringing them closer together:

```
float [] Xp = { 100, 300, 300, 100 };
float [] Yp = { 100, 180, 250, 300 };
```

(See output in Figure 13.3. Full program in bcurves/sketches/box03/box03.pde)

You know what's coming—let's move them apart now:

```
float [] Xp = { 100, 300, 300, 100 };
float [] Yp = { 100,  50, 330, 300 };
```

(See output in Figure 13.4. Full program in bcurves/sketches/box04/box04.pde)

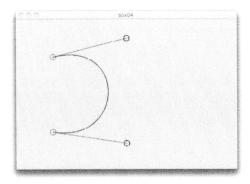

Figure 13.4. Moving a control point to another location. (bcurves/sketches/box04/box04.pde)

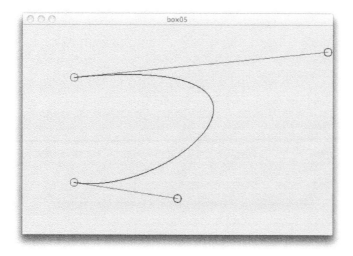

Figure 13.5. Moving a control point far away. (bcurves/sketches/box05/box05.pde)

And finally, let's move point 1 way out to the right:

```
float [] Xp = { 100, 590, 300, 100 };
float [] Yp = { 100,  50, 330, 300 };
```

(See output in Figure 13.5. Full program in bcurves/sketches/box05/box05.pde)

You've probably guessed what these control points do, and if so, you're right. The general scheme of things is that the curve starts at point 0 in the direction of point 1. The farther away point 1 is located, the more the curve tries to go towards it (think of the red line between points 0 and 1 like a magnet: the longer it is, the more pull it exerts on the curve). The same thing happens at the other end: the curve can be thought of as leaving point 3 and heading out towards point 2, again influenced by the length of the blue line to point 2. In between, the curve smoothly blends from one trajectory to the other.

Bézier curves are very flexible. By moving the points around you can can do some wacky things. For example, let's go back to the original square but move point 0 from its position in the upper left to a position right of what was the upper right:

```
float [] Xp = { 500, 300, 300, 100 };
float [] Yp = { 100, 100, 300, 300 };
```

(See output in Figure 13.6. Full program in bcurves/sketches/box06/box06.pde)

Oh, nice. The curve can pinch, too. Let's just reverse the locations of points 1 and 2 on the original square:

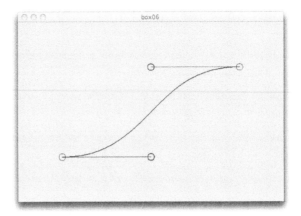

Figure 13.6. Moving a control point to make an S shape. (bcurves/sketches/box06/box06.pde)

```
float [] Xp = { 100, 300, 300, 100 };
float [] Yp = { 100, 300, 100, 300 };
```

(See output in Figure 13.7. Full program in bcurves/sketches/box07/box07.pde)

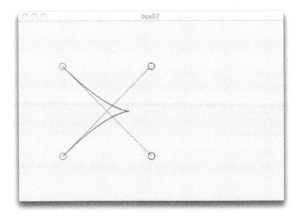

Figure 13.7. Moving a control point to create a cusp. (bcurves/sketches/box07/box07.pde)

So if we *want* a sharp cusp, we can make it.

If we push those points out further, the curve will loop over itself:

```
float [] Xp = { 100, 400, 400, 100 };
float [] Yp = { 100, 400,   0, 300 };
```

(See output in Figure 13.8. Full program in bcurves/sketches/box08/box08.pde)

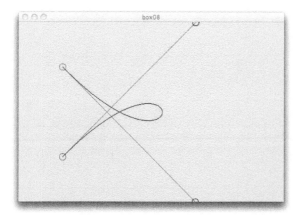

Figure 13.8. Moving a control point to create a loop. (bcurves/sketches/box08/box08.pde)

We've seen that Bézier curves can offer you more flexiblilty than the Catmull-Rom curves we saw in Chapter 12.

But how about smoothness?

You can make adjacent Bézier curves join up smoothly, but the technique is a little different than how you do it with Catmull-Rom curves. The trick this time isn't to overlap the points, but rather, getting points to line up at the proper distances.

Here's the idea for creating one big smooth curve from many smaller Bézier curves. Suppose you have two Bézier curves and you want them to join up smoothly. I'll call the points for the first curve A0, A1, A2, and A3. Similarly, the second curve's points are B0, B1, B2, and B3. Each of these points, of course, has an x and a y value, which I'll write $A0x$ and $A0y$, $A1x$ and $A1y$, and so on.

Think about the last two points of curve A. Point A2 is a control point that influences how the curve is shaped as it approaches point A3. You can draw a line from A2 to A3 (and of course that's exactly the blue line in our program).

Now think about curve B. The curve starts at B0, and it heads off in the direction of B1. I've been drawing the line from B0 to B1 in red.

To draw these two curves, I'll keep using our example program, but I'll double up the length of the arrays. I'll make four points for curve A on the left side of the window and four points for curve B on the right. Here's our example at the starting gate:

```
//                A0    A1    A2    A3    B0    B1    B2    B3
float [] Xp = { 100, 150, 200, 250, 400, 400, 500, 550 };
float [] Yp = { 150, 100, 250, 200, 150, 350, 150, 150 };

void draw() {
   noFill();
   drawCurve(true, true, 0, 1, 2, 3);  // curve A
```

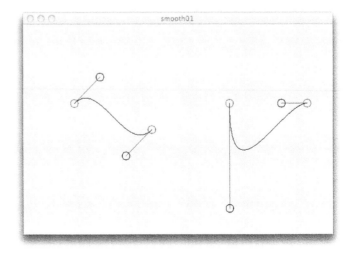

Figure 13.9. Some curves we'd like to join up smoothly.
(bcurves/sketches/smooth01/smooth01.pde)

```
    drawCurve(true, true, 4, 5, 6, 7);  // curve B
}
```

(See output in Figure 13.9. Full program in bcurves/sketches/smooth01/smooth01.pde)

Figure 13.10 shows the same drawing with the names of the points added.

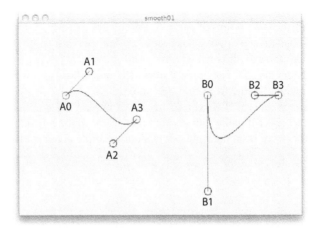

Figure 13.10. Figure 13.9 with labels.

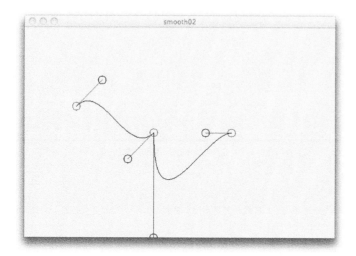

Figure 13.11. Getting two Bézier curves to touch. (bcurves/sketches/smooth02/smooth02.pde)

If we want these to line up smoothly, the first job will be to get them to touch. *A3x* is 250, and *B0x* is 400, so I'll subtract 150 from each of the *x* values in curve B so that it shifts over to the left. I'll also add 50 to each *y* coordinate. Now curve B has the same shape as before, but it's been moved left and down so that B0 has the same values as A3, and the curves touch:

```
//              A0    A1    A2    A3    B0    B1    B2    B3
float [] Xp = { 100,  150,  200,  250,  250,  250,  350,  400 };
float [] Yp = { 150,  100,  250,  200,  200,  400,  200,  200 };
```

(See output in Figure 13.11. Full program in bcurves/sketches/smooth02/smooth02.pde)

Of course, they're not joining up smoothly yet. To get smoothness, we need two things. The first is that points A2, A3, and B1 have to all lie on the same line. Of course, B0 will lie on that line too, since it's at the same coordinates as A3. The second thing is that the distance from A2 to A3 has to be the same length as the distance from B0 to B1. In other words, the change from A2 to A3 has to be the same as the change from B0 to B1.

How you make those things happen is up to you. But if you have curve A in hand, here's the easy way to build B so that it will join up smoothly to A. First, find the change in *x* from A2 to A3 (for instance, here *A2x* is 200 and *A3x* is 250, so the change is 50; that is, point A3 is 50 units to the right of point A2). Now find the change in *y* between the same two points (here *A2y* is 250 and *A3y* is 200, so the change is −50; that is, point A3 is 50 units above point A2).

So to get from A2 to A3, we add 50 in *x* and subtract 50 in *y*.

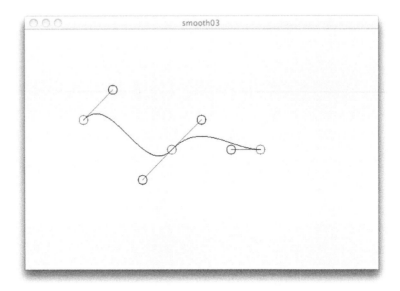

Figure 13.12. Further smoothing of Bézier curves. (bcurves/sketches/smooth03/smooth03.pde)

To get curve B to line up smoothly with curve A, we position point B1 so that it has the same relationship to B0. That is, $B1x$ is found by adding 50 to $B0x$, and $B1y$ is found by subtracting 50 from $B0y$.

We can write all this in Processing, using our names for these points:

```
float dx = A3x - A2x;
float dy = A3y - A2y;
B1x = B0x + dx;
B1y = B0y + dy;
```

You'll commonly see these two steps rolled up into one:

```
B1x = B0x + (A3x - A2x);
B1y = B0y + (A3y - A2y);
```

Let's try that. Using the values we just found, I'll set B1x to 300 and B1y to 150:

```
//                  A0    A1    A2    A3    B0    B1    B2    B3
float [] Xp = { 100, 150, 200, 250, 250, 300, 350, 400 };
float [] Yp = { 150, 100, 250, 200, 200, 150, 200, 200 };
```

(See output in Figure 13.12. Full program in bcurves/sketches/smooth03/smooth03.pde)

It sure looks smooth. Even better, the mathematics guarantees us that it *is* smooth. If you follow this recipe, you will always get a smooth blend between the curves.

Of course, this required changing curve B. But if you think about it, that was inevitable. When we started out, curve A ended by going up and to the right, and curve B started out by going down and to the right. If they were ever to be smooth, one of them was going to have to change.

To recap, two Bézier curves will join up smoothly if the following three conditions are true: the first point of B is at the same place as the last point of A, the first two points of curve B lie on the same line as the last two points of curve A, and the first two points of curve B are the same distance apart as the last two points of curve A.

You can create longer Bézier curves using a technique like we did with Catmull-Rom curves. The general idea is very similar: after calling `beginShape()`, you create a series of curve segments, and then you wrap up with `endShape()`.

But unlike Catmull-Rom curves, where we named one vertex at a time, with Bézier curves we call `bezierVertex()` and name three points each time, creating a complete curve segment. The most recently named point before this call is the first knot, and then our new points become the first and second control points and then the second knot.

Since each call to `bezierVertex()` presumes that the last point of the previous curve is the first point of the new curve, the first curve is in a fix: there's no previous curve to build on! To handle this, the very first call you make after `beginShape()` is to `vertex()`, where you identify the first knot of the first curve. Then you just build on that, calling `bezierVertex()` again and again until you're done, and you call `endShape()`.

So the job of `bezierVertex()` is consistent with `curveVertex()`, but the name might seem a little inconsistent because you're handing it three points. On the other hand, only one of those is actually a knot (the other two are control points), so the two functions have a lot in common. Still, it's strange (and worth remembering) that `curveVertex()` and `bezierVertex()` work in such different ways.

Let's make a version of our multipoint random-curve drawing example from the last chapter, but let's do it for Bézier curves. The basic strategy will have to change to accommodate the different way Bézier curves work. First, we'll need to make more points, since the middle two points of each call to `bezier()` are control points that the curve does not pass through. Second, we'll have to adjust the points before we draw them, so we can enforce the smoothness conditions we just discussed.

So I'll start by making four times as many points. Then I'll make sure that the first point of each curve is the same as the last point of the previous one. Then I'll position the second point of each curve so it's the same distance and direction from the first point as the last two points of the previous curve.

I'll begin just by copying the starting skeleton from last time. In `draw()` I'll draw all the points and make a single call to `bezier()` to make sure I don't have any obvious bugs yet:

```
int NumPoints = 24;
float [] Xp;
```

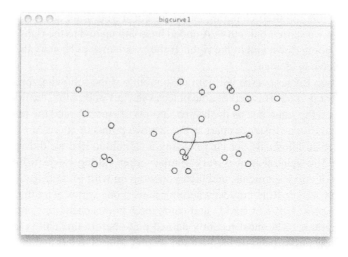

Figure 13.13. Setting up the big Bézier curve. (bcurves/sketches/bbigcurve1/bbigcurve1.pde)

```
float [] Yp;

void setup() {
   size(600, 400);
   background(206, 214, 242);
   noFill();
   Xp = new float[NumPoints];
   Yp = new float[NumPoints];
   for (int i=0; i<NumPoints; i++) {
      Xp[i] = random(100, 500);
      Yp[i] = random(100, 300);
   }
}

void draw() {
   for (int i=0; i<NumPoints; i++) {
      ellipse(Xp[i], Yp[i], 10, 10);
   }
   bezier(Xp[0], Yp[0], Xp[1], Yp[1], Xp[2], Yp[2], Xp[3], Yp[3]);
}
```

(See output in Figure 13.13. Full program in bcurves/sketches/bbigcurve1/bbigcurve1.pde)

Not very inspiring, but it doesn't crash! I think I'll next write the loop to draw all the Bézier curves:

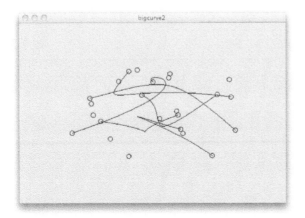

Figure 13.14. Drawing all the Bézier curves. (bcurves/sketches/bbigcurve2/bbigcurve2.pde)

```
void draw() {
   for (int i=0; i<NumPoints; i++) {
      ellipse(Xp[i], Yp[i], 10, 10);
   }
   for (int i=0; i<NumPoints; i+=4) {
      bezier(Xp[i],    Yp[i],    Xp[i+1], Yp[i+1],
             Xp[i+2], Yp[i+2], Xp[i+3], Yp[i+3]);
   }
}
```

(See output in Figure 13.14. Full program in bcurves/sketches/bbigcurve2/bbigcurve2.pde)

Yowch, that's messy code. And it makes an even messier picture. But it works. Note what's happening in the second loop. First of all, I'm incrementing i by four each time; that's because I'm using the points four at a time. Second, I don't have to check for what happens when i gets too big, because it doesn't. We don't have to wrap around because the Bézier curves don't overlap the way the Catmull-Rom curves did. We just grab each chunk of four points and draw a curve through them, and when we've used up each chunk, we're done.

Before moving on, I'm going to adjust the code that draws the points, so it only draws the first point of each curve (that way it leaves out the control points and the fourth point of each curve, which is the same as the first point of the next).

```
for (int i=0; i<NumPoints; i+=4) {
   ellipse(Xp[i], Yp[i], 10, 10);
}
```

(See output in Figure 13.15. Full program in bcurves/sketches/bbigcurve3/bbigcurve3.pde)

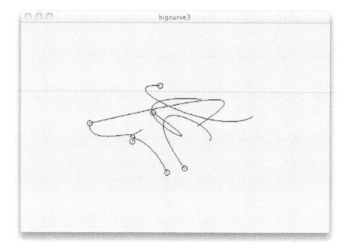

Figure 13.15. Connecting the big Bézier curve. (bcurves/sketches/bbigcurve3/bbigcurve3.pde)

Notice that all I had to do was increment i by 4 each time, rather than by one. That way we draw point 0, then point 4, then point 8, and so on.

Now let's make sure that the first point of each curve is at the same location as the last point of the previous curve. I'll do this the easy way, by simply copying the coordinates over. First, I'll write the skeleton of the loop. I want to get the first point of every curve, which will look like the loop we just wrote:

```
for (int i=0; i<NumPoints; i+=4) {
}
```

Now I'll fill it in:

```
for (int i=0; i<NumPoints; i+=4) {
   Xp[i] = Xp[i-1];
   Yp[i] = Yp[i-1];
}
```

Wait, I know that's going to fail right away. The first time through the loop, i is 0, so Xp[i-1] will be Xp[-1], which is illegal. I want to start resetting points starting with the first point of the second curve. All I have to do is start the loop at 4, rather than 0. Here it is in context:

```
void draw() {
   for (int i=0; i<NumPoints; i+=4) {
      ellipse(Xp[i], Yp[i], 10, 10);
   }
```

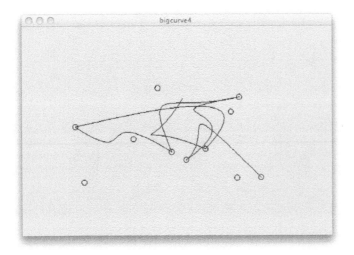

Figure 13.16. Big Bézier curve problems. (bcurves/sketches/bbigcurve4/bbigcurve4.pde)

```
for (int i=4; i<NumPoints; i+=4) {
    Xp[i] = Xp[i-1];
    Yp[i] = Yp[i-1];
}
for (int i=0; i<NumPoints; i+=4) {
    bezier(Xp[i],    Yp[i],    Xp[i+1], Yp[i+1],
           Xp[i+2], Yp[i+2], Xp[i+3], Yp[i+3]);
}
}
```

(See output in Figure 13.16. Full program in bcurves/sketches/bbigcurve4/bbigcurve4.pde)

Take a look at Figure 13.16. Ugh. That's awful. What's going wrong?

The problem is that I'm drawing the points before I've moved them! So let's switch the order. First step: move the points to where they belong. Then I can draw them and then the curves.

```
void draw() {
    for (int i=4; i<NumPoints; i+=4) {
        Xp[i] = Xp[i-1];
        Yp[i] = Yp[i-1];
    }

    for (int i=0; i<NumPoints; i+=4) {
        ellipse(Xp[i], Yp[i], 10, 10);
    }
```

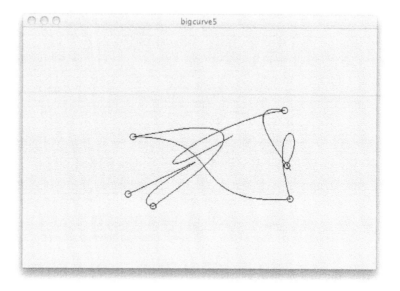

Figure 13.17. The Bézier curve, but not yet closed or smooth.
(bcurves/sketches/bbigcurve5/bbigcurve5.pde)

```
for (int i=0; i<NumPoints; i+=4) {
    bezier(Xp[i],    Yp[i],    Xp[i+1], Yp[i+1],
            Xp[i+2], Yp[i+2], Xp[i+3], Yp[i+3]);
    }
}
```

(See output in Figure 13.17. Full program in bcurves/sketches/bbigcurve5/bbigcurve5.pde)

Closer, but still no cigar. The curve doesn't close. That's because the first point of the first curve didn't get set to the last point of the last curve (remember that I explicitly started the loop at i=4, so the very first point never got moved). So let's move that point manually:

```
void draw() {
    for (int i=4; i<NumPoints; i+=4) {
        Xp[i] = Xp[i-1];
        Yp[i] = Yp[i-1];
    }
    Xp[0] = Xp[NumPoints-1];
    Yp[0] = Yp[NumPoints-1];
    for (int i=0; i<NumPoints; i+=4) {
        ellipse(Xp[i], Yp[i], 10, 10);
    }
```

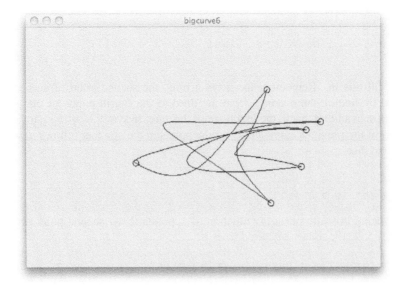

Figure 13.18. A closed Bézier curve. (bcurves/sketches/bbigcurve6/bbigcurve6.pde)

```
for (int i=0; i<NumPoints; i+=4) {
    bezier(Xp[i],   Yp[i],   Xp[i+1], Yp[i+1],
           Xp[i+2], Yp[i+2], Xp[i+3], Yp[i+3]);
}
}
```

(See output in Figure 13.18. Full program in bcurves/sketches/bbigcurve6/bbigcurve6.pde)

This code does the job, but it's setting off another of my code-detector alerts. This time it's the *special-case* sensor. We have a loop that contains two lines of code that moves points, and that's fine. But then when the loop is over we explicitly move point 0 all by itself. So the loop almost handles all the points, except for one special case.

Special cases aren't always a problem that needs attention, but they often indicate something that should at least be considered. When you see special-case code, it means that the general method wasn't really all that general and could probably stand some improvement. For now, I'll let it stay.

Notice that I only moved the first point of each set of four so that it was in the same place as the last point of the previous set. If these curves had some meaning for me, I might have instead moved all four points, but since the points are all random, it wasn't worth the effort.

Now all that's left is to get continuity. Remembering our recipe from above, we can write a second loop. What I want is to get the second point of each curve. So we want point 5, then 9, 13, 17, and so on. Like the last loop, we move forward 4 steps each time, but now we'll begin at 5:

```
for (int i=5; i<NumPoints; i+=4) {
}
```

Let's fill this in. Remember the general rule: the second point of each curve is computed by finding the distance from the third to the fourth points of the previous curve, and then adding that to the first point of this one. In symbols, using p to stand for the points of the previous curve and q for the points in the one that follows it, we want to set q1 so that

```
q1x = q0x + (p3x - p2x)
q1y = q0y + (p3y - p2y)
```

Translating this into our array notation, if i points to the second point of a curve (say, index 5, 9, 13, and so on), we'd have

```
Xp[i] = Xp[i-1] + (Xp[i-2] - Xp[i-3]);
Yp[i] = Yp[i-1] + (Yp[i-2] - Yp[i-3]);
```

Like the last loop, to make the first curve pay attention to the last, I'll remember to manually set the second point of the first curve as a special case after the loop:

```
for (int i=5; i<NumPoints; i+=4) {
   Xp[i] = Xp[i-1] + (Xp[i-2] - Xp[i-3]);
   Yp[i] = Yp[i-1] + (Yp[i-2] - Yp[i-3]);
   }
Xp[1] = Xp[0] + (Xp[NumPoints-1] - Xp[NumPoints-2]);
Yp[1] = Yp[0] + (Yp[NumPoints-1] - Yp[NumPoints-2]);
```

And here it is in the code, so that we move all the first points and then all the second points:

```
void draw() {
   // move first point
   for (int i=4; i<NumPoints; i+=4) {
      Xp[i] = Xp[i-1];
      Yp[i] = Yp[i-1];
   }
   Xp[0] = Xp[NumPoints-1];
   Yp[0] = Yp[NumPoints-1];

   // move second point
   for (int i=5; i<NumPoints; i+=4) {
      Xp[i] = Xp[i-1] + (Xp[i-2] - Xp[i-3]);
      Yp[i] = Yp[i-1] + (Yp[i-2] - Yp[i-3]);
   }
```

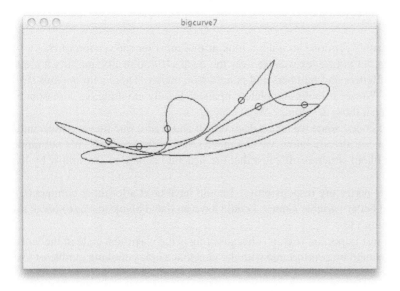

Figure 13.19. The smooth, big Bézier curve. (bcurves/sketches/bbigcurve7/bbigcurve7.pde)

```
    Xp[1] = Xp[0] + (Xp[NumPoints-1] - Xp[NumPoints-2]);
    Yp[1] = Yp[0] + (Yp[NumPoints-1] - Yp[NumPoints-2]);

    for (int i=0; i<NumPoints; i+=4) {
        ellipse(Xp[i], Yp[i], 10, 10);
    }
    for (int i=0; i<NumPoints; i+=4) {
        bezier(Xp[i],   Yp[i],   Xp[i+1], Yp[i+1],
        Xp[i+2], Yp[i+2], Xp[i+3], Yp[i+3]);
    }
}
```

(See output in Figure 13.19. Full program in bcurves/sketches/bbigcurve7/bbigcurve7.pde)

Mmmm. Yummy, delicious smoothness.

By the way, note that by "smoothness" I mean what's happening at the knots. Depending on where the random points fall, the Bézier curves between the knots can form sharp corners or even cusps, as we saw before. But the transition from one curve to the next is nice and smooth.

Since we can control the shape of a Bézier curve directly with the control points, there's no need for a routine corresponding to the Catmull-Rom `curveTightness()` routine.

13.2   Reading Code

If you haven't yet done so, take a look at this most recent version of draw(), all at once. Just let your eyes wander over the code. If you're like me, it's a meaningless jumble of letters and numbers and punctuation marks. There's no obvious structure to any of it. Worse, it looks completely opaque. Hardly anything has a reasonable name (What are all those i's doing? What's an Xp?).

But of course once we take a deep breath and read it one line at a time, and keep in mind what we already know, we can make sense of the madness. It's not random, and it's not without structure. It's just that the structure is hard to see simply by looking at it.

This is partly my responsibility. I could have used a lot more comments. I could have used better variable names. I could have included blank spaces to break things up. So why didn't I?

The most important reason is because this is the way most code in the world looks. I wanted you to be comfortable with the idea that a crazy-looking jumble of text can be understood.

This program would be much easier to unravel if it had comments. Normally, this is where an author would tell you about the importance of comments, and how you have to always comment your code completely and clearly. I very much agree with those ideas. As I discussed in Chapter 1, good comments are golden. Good commenters are beloved by everyone who reads their code. But in actual practice, most people don't comment nearly as much as they should. You'll often find that analyzing someone else's program (or even your own, long after you wrote it) requires doing some detective work. Comments are great, comments are wonderful, but they're not always there.

Of course, figuring out what someone else did is more challenging than remembering what you've done yourself, but the two activities have a lot in common. You read each line, you ask yourself what it's for and what it's doing, and you try to see how it fits into the overall picture. If a line of code isn't clear to you, try to make a guess about the gist of it and move on.

For example, if I was looking at this draw() routine for the first time and I saw a line like

```
Yp[i] = Yp[i-1] + (Yp[i-2] - Yp[i-3]);
```

I'd just say to myself something like, "Okay, whatever this Yp array thing is, one of the elements is being overwritten with a calculation involving the three previous ones. There's some kind of relationship between those three earlier values that tells us what this one should be." And I'd leave it at that. Reading the rest of the code, perhaps a few times, maybe by running it and changing it and trying some experiments, I'd slowly build up a picture of what's going on.

But if I didn't know the mathematics of Bézier curves, I'd probably never, ever figure out what that line is for. I'd be able to tell you what it does, of course—it subtracts these two numbers and adds the result to another one—but it would be pretty amazing if I ever guessed that it had anything to do with continuity.

Happily, when people write programs that depend on math in this kind of obscure way, they usually do include at least some comments. I didn't because I didn't want these code listings to grow and grow in the book. But if I was releasing this code into the wild, I might document it this way:

```
// Draw crazy free-form Bezier curves
// Get a new random curve each time you run the sketch
// Version 1.0 - AG, 15 April 2009
//

int NumPoints = 24;    // The total number of points created
float [] Xp;           // The point X coordinates
float [] Yp;           // The point Y coordinates

// This version of setup() creates the graphics window and
// sets the background color.  It turns off filling so we
// get just the curves, not their interiors.  Then I create
// the two point arrays and fill them up with random numbers.
// From here on, Processing calls draw() automatically for
// every new frame to generate the graphics.
//
void setup() {
   size(600, 400);
   background(206, 214, 242);
   noFill();
   Xp = new float[NumPoints];
   Yp = new float[NumPoints];
   for (int i=0; i<NumPoints; i++) {
      Xp[i] = random(100, 500);
      Yp[i] = random(100, 300);
   }
}

// This version of draw() takes two arrays full of random
// points and turns them into a single closed Bezier curve.
// Input parameters: none
// Output parameters: none
// Global variables used:
//          NumPoints : the number of points in arrays Xp and Yp
//          Xp[]      : float array of point's x coordinates
//          Yp[]      : float array of point's y coordinates
// Side effects: draws the curve on the screen
//
```

```
void draw() {

   // The points need to be turned into a list of 4-element
   // Bezier curves.  First, to get the curves to touch and
   // thus be continuous, we set the first point of each
   // curve to the coordinates of the last point of the
   // preceding curve.  The first curve is handled as a
   // special case after the loop.

   for (int i=4; i<NumPoints; i+=4) {
      Xp[i] = Xp[i-1];
      Yp[i] = Yp[i-1];
   }
   Xp[0] = Xp[NumPoints-1];
   Yp[0] = Yp[NumPoints-1];

   // To create a continuous curve, we need to enforce the
   // mathematical constraint that the change in X between
   // the first two points of each curve is equal to the
   // change in X between the last two points of the previous
   // curve, and the same thing in Y.  The first curve is
   // handled as a special case after the loop.
   for (int i=5; i<NumPoints; i+=4) {
      Xp[i] = Xp[i-1] + (Xp[i-2] - Xp[i-3]);
      Yp[i] = Yp[i-1] + (Yp[i-2] - Yp[i-3]);
   }
   Xp[1] = Xp[0] + (Xp[NumPoints-1] - Xp[NumPoints-2]);
   Yp[1] = Yp[0] + (Yp[NumPoints-1] - Yp[NumPoints-2]);

   // Draw a little circle around the first point of
   // each curve.  The default drawing state makes this
   // a white circle with a black outline, which looks good.
   for (int i=0; i<NumPoints; i+=4) {
      ellipse(Xp[i], Yp[i], 10, 10);
   }

   // Run through the lists of points, taking them 4 at a
   // time.  Hand off each batch of 4 to bezier().  By now,
   // they should all touch and join up smoothly.
   for (int i=0; i<NumPoints; i+=4) {
      bezier(Xp[i],    Yp[i],    Xp[i+1], Yp[i+1],
             Xp[i+2], Yp[i+2], Xp[i+3], Yp[i+3]);
   }
}
```

(See output in Figure 13.20. Full program in bcurves/sketches/bbigcurve8/bbigcurve8.pde)

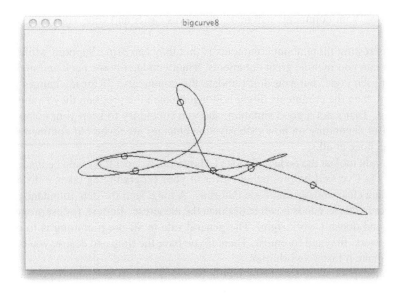

Figure 13.20. The result of the commented code. (bcurves/sketches/bbigcurve8/bbigcurve8.pde)

That might be a bit of overkill, but frankly, that's what I'd love to see when I look at other people's code. But this kind of extensive documentation is rare. I normally comment my code well, but usually, I'm somewhere in between these two extremes, leaving enough information so that someone who's motivated to figure out the program will have a strong head start.

The quantity and quality of the comments you put into your code can also be influenced by the code's intended use and lifetime. If you're just knocking out a little toy program to experiment with an idea, and you plan to abandon it in 15 or 20 minutes comments are probably superfluous. But if you're writing something that will be part of a library that will be used by thousands of people, odds are that at some point you (or someone else) will need to revisit the code. Someone might want to add a new feature a year from now, or something in the underlying operating system might change and require an adjustment in the code, or a new release of Processing may come out that requires you to make a corresponding adjustment in your program. In these situations, comments can make a world of difference. Ten seconds of commenting while programming can save hours of frustration and head-scratching later when trying to figure out what the code does. If your code is destined to be open source, where you'll be sharing it with other people freely, then you should expect that people will want to dig into your code to customize and extend it (that's a big reason for making it open source in the first place). Again, in that situation every useful comment you make is like a gift to everyone who follows. Your comments will make their lives easier and your work more likely to be used.

An interesting thing about comments is that they can *drift*. Suppose while writing your program you include great comments. Then you later come back and make some changes to the code, but you don't update the comments. If those changes become permanent, then the comments might no longer match the program they're supposedly describing. That's not a good situation, and you should try to keep your comments up to date. But depending on how extensive the changes are, even old comments can be better than none at all.

You might look at the code in draw() above and wonder if it could be made shorter or faster. As I've said before, being clever in your programming takes a distant back seat to being clear and writing code that runs. A long, step-by-step, mundane program that runs correctly is hands down better than the cleverest, shortest, fastest program that has bugs and doesn't work right. The general rule in all programming is to get your project to work, first and foremost. Then, if you have the time and desire, you can clean it up and make it faster and shorter.

If you feel passionate about making this program as short as humanly possible, there are a couple of places to start (but be careful of making it so dense that it becomes hard to understand—there's such a thing as being too terse). If you want to give it a go for fun, try combining the first two loops in draw() into just one loop. You can also use the modulo operator (%) to get rid of the special cases after the loops in draw().

13.2.1 Bézier Curve Utilities

You won't be surprised to know that Bézier curves have the same utility routines that I discussed in the last chapter for Catmull-Rom curves.

Specifically, bezierDetail() lets you set the number of short segments that are drawn for each segment of a Bézier curve (the default renderer ignores this call).

If you want to find the position of a point along a Bézier curve, you would call bezierPoint() with either the four *x* values or four *y* values, and a parameter from 0 to 1. Like Catmull-Rom curves, Bézier curves have the mathematical property that their *x* calculation is independent of their *y*. In fact, all I have to do is take the old program and replace curve() and curvePoint() with bezier() and bezierPoint() (although I'll also move the points around a little so the curve looks nice for the example):

```
float [] Xp = {  80,  160, 580, 380 };
float [] Yp = { 300,    0,  80, 300 };

void setup() {
  size(600, 400);
  background(237, 180, 198);
  noFill();
  bezier(Xp[0], Yp[0], Xp[1], Yp[1], Xp[2], Yp[2], Xp[3], Yp[3]);
```

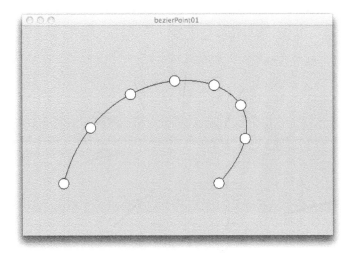

Figure 13.21. Finding points on a Bézier curve.
(bcurves/sketches/bezierPoint01/bezierPoint01.pde)

```
int numSteps = 8;
for (int i=0; i<numSteps; i++) {
  float t = map(i, 0, numSteps-1, 0, 1);
  float xPos = bezierPoint(Xp[0], Xp[1], Xp[2], Xp[3], t);
  float yPos = bezierPoint(Yp[0], Yp[1], Yp[2], Yp[3], t);
  fill(255);
  strokeWeight(1);
  stroke(0, 0, 0);
  ellipse(xPos, yPos, 20, 20);
}
}
```

(See output in Figure 13.21. Full program in bcurves/sketches/bezierPoint01/bezierPoint01.pde)

13.3 Offset Bézier Curves

Just as before, we can find the tangent at any point by calling `bezierTangent()`.
Let's use this to draw the tangents and the normals:

```
float xTan = bezierTangent(Xp[0], Xp[1], Xp[2], Xp[3], t)/20;
float yTan = bezierTangent(Yp[0], Yp[1], Yp[2], Yp[3], t)/20;
strokeWeight(2);
```

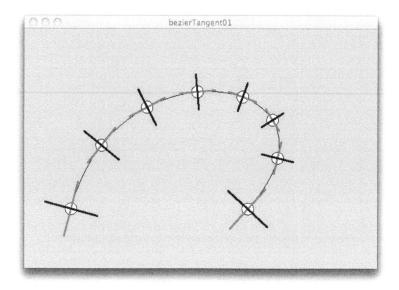

Figure 13.22. The normals and tangents on a Bézier curve.
(bcurves/sketches/bezierTangent01/bezierTangent01.pde)

```
stroke(78, 98, 229);
line(xPos-xTan, yPos-yTan, xPos+xTan, yPos+yTan);

stroke(0);
line(xPos-yTan, yPos+xTan, xPos+yTan, yPos-xTan);
```

(See output in Figure 13.22. Full program in patterns/sketches/bezierTangent01/bezierTangent0
.pde).

And we can join up the normals to make offset curves just as before, too. Again, the
only change to the program in the previous chapter is to change the call to curve() to
bezier():

```
float oldx0 = 0;
float oldy0 = 0;
float oldx1 = 0;
float oldy1 = 0;
int numSteps = 40;
strokeWeight(2);
for (int i=0; i<numSteps; i++) {
  float t = map(i, 0, numSteps-1, 0, 1);
  float xPos = bezierPoint(Xp[0], Xp[1], Xp[2], Xp[3], t);
  float yPos = bezierPoint(Yp[0], Yp[1], Yp[2], Yp[3], t);
```

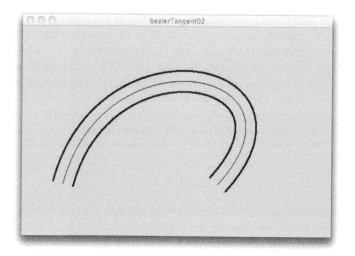

Figure 13.23. Drawing the offsets to a Bézier curve.
(bcurves/sketches/bezierTangent02/bezierTangent02.pde)

```
float xTan = bezierTangent(Xp[0], Xp[1], Xp[2], Xp[3], t);
float yTan = bezierTangent(Yp[0], Yp[1], Yp[2], Yp[3], t);
float tanlen = mag(xTan, yTan);
xTan *= 20/tanlen;
yTan *= 20/tanlen;
if (i > 0) {
  line(oldx0, oldy0, xPos-yTan, yPos+xTan);
  line(oldx1, oldy1, xPos+yTan, yPos-xTan);
}
oldx0 = xPos-yTan;
oldy0 = yPos+xTan;
oldx1 = xPos+yTan;
oldy1 = yPos-xTan;
}
```

(See output in Figure 13.23. Full program in bcurves/sketches/bezierTangent02/bezierTangent02.pde)

13.4   Finding a Point

In Chapter 12 I discussed how to find a y value for a given x in a "well-behaved" Catmull-Rom curve.

The very same technique can be used for Bézier curves as well. We pick a pair of parameter values to create an interval that is sure to include the point we're looking for and then we repeatedly check the point in the middle of the interval, compare it to the input, and replace either the upper or lower limit of the interval with the midpoint. In this way we cut the interval in half each time, quickly zooming in to the point we want.

The technique needs to be carefully applied, because it's only valid for curves that have a single y value for each x. As we've seen, Bézier curves can loop around and make a wide variety of shapes. The binary subdivision algorithm will always find you some value of y for your given x, but making sure that value makes sense for your application relies on your making sure you're using a well-behaved curve.

13.5   Moving Curves Around

If you're feeling adventurous, I have a great project for you to try. Start with the program that draws the big Bézier curve made out of many smaller curves. Change it such that you can click on any little circle around a knot or control point and drag it around, so that the big closed curve on the screen updates and follows your changes. It might be useful to make the circles a little bigger so they're easier to click on. Give the user the choice of drawing Catmull-Rom or Bézier curves through the same set of points.

This project can get pretty involved, depending on how far you want to take it. For example, suppose you grab one of the points, drag it right on top of another point, and let go. And you do that a few times, creating a little stack of points. How can you then pick out the one you want and move it? How can you even determine which one it is you want? Can you invent some way for a person to identify and select the point they want to change and then let them change it, without modifying the other points?

As you play with Bézier curves, you'll probably notice that when the control points are very close to the curve points, the curve can cut a pretty tight corner at that location, but when the control points are far away, the curve swoops into the point gracefully. Consider some way for the user to "tighten" or "loosen" all the points at once (by moving the associated control points closer to, or farther from, the curve point).

You might also want to put something into the `setup()` code where the random points are selected to make sure that no two points are too close to one another to start with. Maybe no point can be closer than some number of units to any other point. How could you make the random points satisfy that condition? (Hint: it may be easier to handle this kind of thing as the points are made, rather than afterwards. Second hint: you don't have to use every number that `random()` gives you; you can use a loop to keep rolling random numbers until you get values that you like.)

Writing a little interactive program can lead to hours of productive exploration and play. As you gain mastery of the tools of programming and Processing, you'll start to think of ever-more interesting and creative ideas, and you'll be able to implement them for your own pleasure, and to share with other people.

Chapter 14
Objects

The history of computer languages has a lot of parallels with the history of cars.

After an initial period of experimentation, people agreed on what generally worked well in automobiles: four wheels, a handheld wheel for steering, a pair of foot pedals to control speed and braking, an internal-combustion engine that runs on gasoline, and so on. There have been lots of cosmetic changes over the years, and lots of really important technical and safety innovations, but these core ideas have been pretty consistent. People have tried tons of alternatives, of course, from flying cars with wings to cars that turn into submarines, but most of these variations didn't move into the mainstream, and the typical idea of a "car" has remained the same. A significant change is in the air, though, with the increasingly popular adoption of electric engines.

Computer languages have had a similar history. The earliest languages were stylistically all over the map. Some languages even invented entirely new alphabets with dozens of custom symbols that required special typewriters just to print out. But most languages eventually stabilized into a world of typed variables, loops, subroutines with arguments, arrays, and so on. Processing is firmly in that tradition. That's one reason why it's a lot faster to learn a second computer language once you've mastered a first; these things are usually a lot more alike than they are different (though there are still lots of unusual languages, of course, and some have very active and vocal supporters).

Like the electric engine, there's recently been a really big change in programming. It's called *object-oriented programming*, often abbreviated OOP. The ideas of OOP don't replace the ideas that I've discussed in previous chapters. Those ideas and techniques are still very much present. Rather, OOP just gives us a different way to organize the pieces, so that conceptually we package up our code in a different way.

This new way has some big advantages, which include making it easier to debug your programs and easier to reuse them. For example, if a year from now you were working on a project where you'd like to draw big floppy curves on the screen you might pull up one of the examples from Chapter 12 or Chapter 13 as a starting point. And then you'd have a lot of work ahead of you. First, you'd have to remember what NumPoints and Xp and Yp were all about, then you'd have to think about the continuity conditions, and ultimately, you'd spend so much time and energy getting back up to speed that you might have been better off just starting from scratch. The appeal of OOP is that you can just grab the "curve stuff" from an earlier program (or from a colleague, or even off the web) and very quickly start to use it with almost no fuss. OOP really does deliver on the promise of making code easy to use and reuse, which is a big reason why it has become so popular.

The ideas behind OOP have spread into almost every new language out there today, including Processing. They've been tried out in endless situations and dozens of languages, and the jury is in: object-oriented programming is definitely a good thing.

Even knowing that, you don't have to use OOP ideas in all your programming. Everything we've done so far has been done without OOP ideas. But they're built into Processing and available for our use, so we'll take a look at what they offer.

Before we dig in, I'll note that the OOP approach isn't perfect for all situations. In particular, simple, little throw-together projects probably don't need OOP. In fact, using OOP for something simple is often counterproductive because it makes your code longer and maybe even a little slower. OOP really shines when you can use it as a conceptual tool to organize big projects, or projects with lots of little pieces.

So how should we get into a discussion of OOP? I could pick some huge complex project, say the design of a new interstate highway system, or a simulation of wildlife on an African savannah, but the size and details of the project would dwarf our discussion of OOP. The other extreme would be to pick a very simple example and work it through with OOP, always with an eye to showing you how the ideas would apply in a bigger, more complicated system. That's kind of unsatisfying too, because it doesn't really show the value of OOP.

So I'm going to try to split the difference. I'll start with a simple OOP skeleton, which is going to look like *way* too much code. Then as the project gets bigger and more interesting, I hope you'll see how the OOP organization helps us manage the growing complexity in a way that keeps everything manageable. And when the project gets large enough, we'll find that OOP actually keeps it from growing as quickly as it would if we weren't using that style.

OOP is a big field, with its own specialized language. This is perfectly reasonable: important new ideas are often well served by new words to describe them. In this chapter (and the rest of the book), I will use the terminology of OOP in a general way, without stressing the shades of precision or mentioning every special case and subtle issue. If you pursue the subject of OOP, you'll find plenty of interesting, detailed subtleties that you can sink your technical teeth into.

14.1 Objects and Methods

Before we get into writing any programs, we need to briefly go over the principles of OOP, so the the starting point will make sense.

The basic idea is simple: the world is made up of *objects* that can be told to take *actions* (also called *methods*). That's it. OOP is mostly about maintaining that attitude and point of view: the world is full of objects that can be told to do things.

For example, if you were the manager of a business office, the objects in your program could be your employees. They're well trained and very capable, so when you need them to do something, you only need to tell them the action you want them to take and provide any materials they need to carry it out. A typical instruction might be: "Frank, here are ten pages. Please make three photocopies of each one."

The object here is Frank. The instruction is to make photocopies. The materials he needs to do his job are the ten pages.

Here's another one: "Sarah, drive this truck to Des Moines."

The object is Sarah, the instruction is to drive to Des Moines, and the material she needs is just the truck.

How about this: "Truck, drive yourself to Des Moines."

OK, we don't have intelligent self-driving trucks yet. But conceptually, that could happen. So the object is the truck, the instruction is to drive to Des Moines, and the materials required are ... well, nothing in this case.

In fact, most of the objects in computer programs are inanimate: they're things like points or rectangles or simulations of elevators or musical instruments. So we might say, "Violin, play this Mozart concerto."

The object we're talking to is the violin, the action is to play, and the material is the music for the concerto.

Closer to home, we might say "Animated steam engine, run faster and emit more puffs of smoke."

Then our animated engine will do what we've asked, and we don't have to worry about the internal variables and procedures that the steam engine uses to produce that visual result.

We can also ask questions of our objects. In that case, they will usually give us back something in return. For example, we could ask, "Cup of coffee, how full are you?"

This would probably return a number representing the amount of coffee in the cup.

As you've probably guessed, the language tools in OOP are designed to help us create objects and send messages to them.

Let's dig into OOP techniques by making a little air hockey table full of moving disks. The graphics window will be our tabletop. The disks will have different colors and sizes, and for now, they'll just move in straight lines and bounce off the walls of the window. What I forgot to mention is that these are really *ghost* disks, the disembodied remains of deceased disks that have remained in our material plane to find emotional closure. Yes, it's a little goofy, but when I first saw this project in my mind's eye, the disks were partly transparent, and they passed through each other without any effect, so they reminded me of ghosts.

Every disk has a current position (x and y), a current speed (x and y), a radius, and a color. That's six pieces of information per disk. So we could represent our collection of disks with six arrays of floats. But that's kind of messy, and it would be really hard to further develop the program. Instead, let's do it the OOP way.

Here's the list of information we need to store for each disk:

1. Current location (*x* and *y*).

2. Current motion (*x* and *y*).

3. Radius.

4. Color.

We're going to create a single structure that will package up all of this information in one place. Such a structure is called a *class*. Think of a class as your own type of object. Speaking conceptually, Processing gives you built-in int and float objects for numbers and color objects for colors. Now we're going to invent our own new kind of object for storing disks.

To create a class, you simply write the word class followed by the name of your class and then a pair of curly braces, which are going to surround all the information about it. Like global variables, class definitions appear outside of all functions. Conventionally, class names are capitalized:

```
class Disk {
}
```

Note that there are no parentheses. This isn't a function, and it's not a variable. Instead, this is a special kind of type declaration. You're telling the system that you're creating a *new type* of object, roughly like an int or a float, only it's of your own design and it's called Disk.

Now let's put in the information that describes a disk. These are just normal variable declarations. You won't be too surprised, I hope, when I tell you these are called *class variables* or *object variables*:

```
class Disk {
   float xPos;    // 1. Current location (X and Y)
   float yPos;
   float xDir;    // 2. Current motion (X and Y)
   float yDir;
   float radius;  // 3. Radius
   color clr;     // 4. Color
}
```

Here, I'm storing the disk's speed in variables called xDir and yDir to tell me how fast it's moving in each direction.

Another note on language. Processing keeps things simpler than some other OOP languages. They might distinguish between class variables and object variables, but

Processing doesn't. I'll use the term *object variables*, or sometimes *instance variables*, to refer to the variables that are part of an object's description. If you read about these variables in other places, you may encounter slightly different terms (such as *class members*).

So now that we've listed all the things that go into a `Disk`, how do we go about telling it to do things?

The first step is to create a `Disk`. So far, all we've done is describe the variables that a disk would have if one existed. We have yet to actually make one.

Happily, that's easy to do. We start with a variable declaration like any other (since I'm going to make this a global variable, I'll stick to my convention and capitalize its name). Because I'm thinking of my disks as ghosts of disks, I'll name my first disk `Ghost`:

```
Disk Ghost;
```

Not too bad. But unlike, say, an `int` or a `float`, this doesn't actually make a `Disk`. That's because a `Disk` is our own type of thing, and Processing doesn't know how to create one for us. All it knows at this point is that there's a variable named `Ghost`, and ultimately, it will contain something of type `Disk`, once it gets created.

To actually put a `Disk` object into the variable `Ghost`, we use a notation that's close to—but different from—what we used to create an array. We still use the keyword `new`, but in a different way, to *initialize*, or create, a `Disk`:

```
Ghost = new Disk();
```

The `new` is familiar, but here we're calling a function whose name is the same as the name of the class. It returns a new *instance* of the class, that is, an actual `Disk` and not just a placeholder.

You can of course combine the declaration and initialization:

```
Disk Ghost = new Disk();
```

You might be wondering if `Disk()` is a function like the others that we've seen. Yes, it is. Okay, then where is it? The answer is that Processing automatically provides you with a default function to create objects of each class. That default is just the name of the class with no arguments. So the default function that creates objects of the class `Disk` is `Disk()`. It takes no arguments, and returns a new `Disk` object. When you call this function it has to be preceded by the keyword `new` or you'll get an error. In a moment, we'll look more closely at how this object creation works, and how we can replace the default `Disk()` with something of our own.

But first, what happens if you just declare an object, but you don't initialize it? That is, you don't call `new Disk()` or its equivalent before you try to read or write one of the object's variables? Processing will report that as an error during the compilation step, warning you that you're using an object before anything has been put into it.

Remember, just declaring an object doesn't actually make the object; it simply tells Processing what type the object will be once it's brought into existence. You must always explicitly create it using new. If not, you're reading and writing to an uncreated object, which is an error.

Processing's detection apparatus for this situation isn't perfect, so every now and then you can compile and run a program where you're using a variable that hasn't been initialized yet. It's also possible to write a complicated (and buggy) program where you end up with a variable that doesn't point to anything. A variable that points to nothing still has to have *something* in it. In Processing, that special something is called null. You almost never use null yourself in Processing, but you'll see it sometimes in error messages when you've encountered a variable that doesn't point to anything; it's the value that Processing prints to tell you "This object doesn't have anything inside it."

This might remind you of void. The distinctions between null and void can become subtle, but roughly, we use void when programming to tell Processing that a routine doesn't return anything, and the system uses null when running to tell you that an object has nothing inside of it,

Returning to our project, we've now declared and initialized (or created) our object. That's everything Processing needs, so it should happily go off and build a disk for you. Here's what we have so far:

```
Disk Ghost = new Disk();

void setup() {
   size(600, 400);
   background(164, 164, 164);
}

void draw() {
   // draw something
}

class Disk {
   float xPos;    // 1. Current location (X and Y)
   float yPos;
   float xDir;    // 2. Current motion (X and Y)
   float yDir;
   float radius;  // 3. Radius
   color clr;     // 4. Color
}
```

(Full program in objects/sketches/disk01/disk01.pde)

If we run this, nothing much happens, but that's okay, because at least it doesn't crash. In fact, it's a little better than that because the very first line is creating a Disk object. In other words, we're making an object of our own custom type! That's pretty cool. So if you wanted a type that combined, say, an int and a color in one place, you could do it. In our example, we've got an object that combines five floats and one color into a single object, and the code compiles and runs.

But let's ask ourselves now, what's in that variable Ghost? It seems reasonable that it would have values for all those object variables, but what values are they?

In most languages, the answer would be simple: *junk*. I don't mean this in some technical way; the values would simply be random, meaningless junk. Lots of 1's and 0's with unpredictable values and no meaning. These variables were never explicitly assigned values, so they would hold values made up of whatever happened to be sitting in that part of memory at the time. Those previous contents might have been anything, so those values would be random junk.

Processing, in its efforts to be helpful, automatically assigns a default value of 0 to all float and int variables that aren't otherwise assigned. It even puts 0's into all three fields of any color variables.

Of course, we would usually prefer to put our own values into these variables. To do so, the first thing we need to add to our class is called a *constructor* routine. It's a special kind of routine in two ways. First, it doesn't declare a return type (not even void). Second, the name of the constructor routine is the name of the class.

Here's a constructor for Disk, with a little bit of the Disk class around it for context:

```
class Disk {
    // object variables go here
    Disk() {            // the constructor
        radius = 10;
    }
}
```

This is a very simple constructor—in fact, it's a lousy one, and I'll improve it in a moment. But let's see what this does.

It takes no arguments. As I said, it doesn't return anything at all (not even void). But it does set the variable radius to 10. This raises two big questions: how is this called, and what specifically does that radius refer to?

The first answer comes from the definition of how classes work. Consider the line

```
Ghost = new Disk();
```

When Processing sees this, it realizes you're trying to assign to the variable Ghost an object of type Disk. So it starts off by going to the Disk class definition. It makes a new chunk of memory big enough to hold that object's variables and then sets them all to default values (like 0), if it can. Now you actually have a Disk. Next, Processing tries to finish the construction process that we initiated with our call to new Disk().

This tells Processing something very specific: look for a routine in the class Disk that has the name Disk(), takes no arguments, and has no return type. That lack of any return type is a special property of constructors. Of course, Processing knows that, so it looks for a function with that definition (that is, a constructor called Disk()).

If it can't find a routine called Disk(), Processing uses the default version which simply gives you back what it's made so far. But if you have provided your own version of Disk() (and you almost always will), then Processing runs it. In this case, it would run the little routine we just wrote.

Inside the routine, we have an assignment statement to radius. We're now working with a very specific object, the particular instance of Disk that Processing just created, and so we set its value of radius to 10. Then we reach the end of the routine and Processing hands you back your new object.

It might seem to you that the constructor should explicitly return a Disk object. If it did, the constructor would probably have a return type of Disk in the definition. And at the end of the function, there would be a return statement that hands the new object back to the place where the constructor was called. That would all make sense, but that's not how constructors work.

Constructors are special procedures and have their own rules. You don't declare a type for the constructor, and you don't provide an explicit return statement. Processing just takes those things for granted; they're part of what makes constructors special.

To summarize, the idea is that when a constructor is called, Processing sets aside enough memory for the object and fills all the values it can with 0's. Then it finds a constructor of the form you requested, runs it, and the object that was initially created (and then modified by the constructor) is returned as the result of the constructor.

Why did I say earlier that the constructor above is lousy? First of all, it only sets one variable. That's not very useful. But even worse, it sets the radius of every disk to 10, which isn't very flexible. So let's fix that by changing the constructor so it takes an argument:

```
Disk (float aradius) {
   radius = aradius;
}
```

Much better. Now we give the constructor the value we want radius to have, and we set the disk's variable to that value. You'll notice that I simply stuck an a in front of the variable name in the argument list. There's no universal convention for this kind of thing, but I like to make it really obvious how the arguments to the constructor correspond to the instance variables. So I often just stick an a (for argument) in front of the arguments and then assign them to their namesakes.

If we run the program with this change, we'll get an error:

```
The constructor Disk() is undefined
```

What? It's right there!

But of course, it isn't. The constructor Disk() is gone; it's no longer in our code. We replaced it, and Disk(float aradius) is what we have now.

When we had no constructors of our own, Processing let us get away with using
Disk(). But as soon as we created any constructors at all, then that default goes away.
In other words, if you have no constructors of your own then the default is available, but
if you have at least one constructor of your own the default is no longer available, and
you must then call one of your own constructors to make your object.

So we'd better change the line where we create the disk to use our new constructor:
the one that takes one floating-point argument.

```
Ghost = new Disk(5);
```

And this runs just fine. Now we're running the new constructor, and it will assign
the value 5 to the radius variable for that object. Here's the whole program. I've
moved the construction of Ghost into setup() and added a println statement:

```
Disk Ghost;

void setup() {
    size(600, 400);
    background(164, 164, 164);
    Ghost = new Disk(5);
    println("Ghost radius = "+Ghost.radius);
}

void draw() {
    // draw something
}

class Disk {
    float xPos;     // 1. Current location (X and Y)
    float yPos;
    float xDir;     // 2. Current motion (X and Y)
    float yDir;
    float radius;   // 3. Radius
    color clr;      // 4. Color

    Disk(float aradius) {
        radius = aradius;
    }
}
```

(Full program in objects/sketches/disk02/disk02.pde)

That println statement is really, really interesting. I know, it doesn't look that
way. But it shows us how to look "inside" the object Ghost and find its instance values.
It's like using [and] to get an element of an array. Using the lowly period (.), we
can "open up" that object Ghost, which is an instance of type Disk, and look at its

instance variables. And we do that by giving the name of the object, followed by a period, followed by the name of the variable, just as we did to get properties like the screen's size or an array's length.

We can access any of Ghost's variables with this *dot notation*, and we'll see it's also how we can tell it to tell Ghost to take actions for us.

Note that the print statement refers to Ghost.radius and not Disk.radius. In fact, if you try to use Disk.radius the program won't even compile; that's just not a legal thing to ask for. There is no object that corresponds to Disk. The Disk class is an empty form: it's a set of blueprints, or a recipe in a cookbook. It tells you how to make something, but it's not the thing. You have to call the constructor with new to make an object and then *that* object will have values you can set, retrieve, and print.

In other words, when you see Disk, think of it as a type like int or float. It's not a variable, and it doesn't have a value. When we want an actual instance of a Disk to put into a variable and then use, we call new Disk(), which automatically calls the constructor. A new object of type Disk is made at that moment and returned to us.

When I run this program, it produces the expected output in the console window:

```
Ghost radius = 5.0
```

Inside of this instance, which I'm calling Ghost, are a bunch of variables. We refer to any variable in any object with the dot notation, following the variable's name with a period and the name of the variable, as in Ghost.radius. If we had a second Disk object, named, say, Spooky, then its radius would be Spooky.radius. Because they're separate objects, Ghost.radius and Spooky.radius are completely different variables, belonging to completely different objects.

I replaced the constructor in the last example, but I could have just added the new one in addition to the old. In other words, you can overload class constructors. When you call a constructor with new, Processing looks through all the constructors for that type and tries to find one whose argument list matches the argument list you're calling with.

So for example, new Disk("SpookyName") would try to find a constructor that was defined with a single argument of type String, while new Disk(3, 5) would try to call a constructor that takes two numbers.

Now we're starting to cook with gas. A big benefit of OOP is that the same class definition can give rise to an unlimited number of instances of that class, each with its own set of instance variables.

Let's make a second instance of class Disk and set its radius to something different:

```
Disk Ghost0;
Disk Ghost1;

void setup() {
  size(600, 400);
```

```
    background(164, 164, 164);
    Ghost0 = new Disk(5);
    Ghost1 = new Disk(37);
    println("Ghost0 radius = "+Ghost0.radius);
    println("Ghost1 radius = "+Ghost1.radius);
}
```

(Full program in objects/sketches/disk03/disk03.pde)

This produces the console output

```
Ghost0 radius = 5.0
Ghost1 radius = 37.0
```

So just as we can have a million different variables of type int in our code, all with different values, so too can we have a million different variables of type Disk, each with their own package of six different values.

Earlier I said that I'd fix my lousy constructor. The time has come! Even with the improvement we recently made, this constructor still assigns only to radius and ignores the other instance variables. If there are instance variables that you really know are always going to be the same for every object that's created (like a counter, perhaps, that always starts at 0), that's fine. But in general, you want your constructor to let you set all the instance variables for an object. And it's good programming practice to always initialize your variables, so you're certain they have the starting values you want them to have.

If you don't initialize your variables in the constructor, you'll have to do so in your code after the object is made and that runs against the ideas behind OOP. In a "pure" OOP program, you'll never look inside an object to see its variables (like I did with this print statement). Instead, you create the object with a set of starting values and then you ask it to do things (which can include printing itself). The object is responsible for itself. In some languages, in fact, the instance variables are not even accessible to the outside world unless you explicitly make them available.

Processing is pretty lax about enforcing these kinds of rules. The philosophy is that if you want to be pure and strict with your OOP programming, you're free to do it that way. If you want to peek and poke inside your objects because that style works for you, then Processing will let you do that, too. Your choice.

But let's walk the talk and load up each Disk with a full set of starting variables:

```
Disk (float axPos, float ayPos, float axDir, float ayDir,
float aradius, color aclr) {
    xPos   = axPos;
    yPos   = ayPos;
    xDir   = axDir;
    yDir   = ayDir;
    radius = aradius;
```

```
    clr    = aclr;
  }
```

And now I'll fix the two calls as well:

```
Ghost0 = new Disk(100, 100,  5,  5, 20, color(255, 0, 0));
Ghost1 = new Disk(400, 200, -3, -7, 30, color(0, 255, 0));
```

Now that we have real Disk objects, we can take out the print statement and let draw() show our objects as real graphics on the screen. Here's the new program:

```
Disk Ghost0;
Disk Ghost1;

void setup() {
   size(600, 400);
   background(132, 144, 163);
   Ghost0 = new Disk(100, 100,  5,  5, 20, color(242, 203, 5));
   Ghost1 = new Disk(400, 200, -3, -7, 30, color(209, 117, 4));
}

void draw() {
   fill(Ghost0.clr);
   ellipse(Ghost0.xPos, Ghost0.yPos, Ghost0.radius*2, Ghost0.radius*2);
   fill(Ghost1.clr);
   ellipse(Ghost1.xPos, Ghost1.yPos, Ghost1.radius*2, Ghost1.radius*2);
}

class Disk {
   float xPos;    // 1. Current location (X and Y)
   float yPos;
   float xDir;    // 2. Current motion (X and Y)
   float yDir;
   float radius;  // 3. Radius
   color clr;     // 4. Color

   Disk (float axPos, float ayPos, float axDir,  float ayDir,
   float aradius, color aclr) {
      xPos   = axPos;
      yPos   = ayPos;
      xDir   = axDir;
      yDir   = ayDir;
      radius = aradius;
      clr    = aclr;
   }
}
```

(See output in Figure 14.1. Full program in objects/sketches/disk04/disk04.pde)

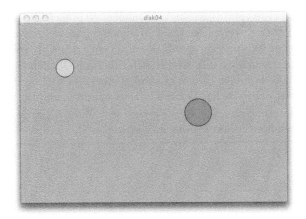

Figure 14.1. Our first disks. (objects/sketches/disk04/disk04.pde)

14.2   Multiple Instances

You can probably guess what I want to do next: I want a whole lot of ghostly disks! It's time for an array. I'll replace our two `Disk` objects with one array to store a group of disks:

```
Disk [] Ghosts;
```

I'm using a plural name here because I don't expect to think of each of these disks as a distinct individual; to my mind, it's the collective that's most important. Remembering our array notation, once I've created the array `Ghosts` (using the array-creating power of `new`), I'll be able to get its length from `Ghosts.length`. We can get at any individual element of this array, say the one at index `ghostNumber`, with `Ghosts[ghostNumber]`.

In `setup()` I'll put in a call to a routine I'll write called `buildGhosts()` to fill up the array with random disks, making sure that each disk starts well inside the window. To do that, I'll create a variable called `border` and generate x and y values that are never less than `border`, and never more than the window's width and height minus `border`, as shown in Figure 14.2. Remember that the global variables `width` and `height` contain the size of the graphics window.

I've also included the two "motion variables" `xDir` and `yDir`, but frankly, I don't know what

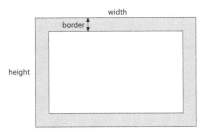

Figure 14.2. The window with an inset border.

they're really going to do yet. I'll just stick the number 10 in each one so they have some value, but I know I'll have to come back and do something better (and more meaningful) later. I'll also try to pick something potentially nice for `radius`. I'll pick these starting values by plucking them out of thin air and then I'll change them once I see what they do so they look good. For now, I'll use random numbers for `color`, but I usually end up picking appealing colors by hand before I finish a project completely.

I'll also put a loop into `draw()` to go through each of the `Ghosts`, set the fill color to its color, and then draw its circle using `ellipse()`.

```
Disk [] Ghosts;

void setup() {
    size(600, 400);
    background(132, 144, 163);
    buildGhosts();
}

// for each of the Ghosts, set the fill color and draw the circle
void draw() {
    for (int i=0; i<Ghosts.length; i++) {
        fill(Ghosts[i].clr);
        ellipse(Ghosts[i].xPos, Ghosts[i].yPos,
                Ghosts[i].radius*2, Ghosts[i].radius*2);
    }
}

// create a bunch of random Disks and put them into Ghosts
void buildGhosts() {
    Ghosts = new Disk[10];
    int border = 50;
    for (int i=0; i<Ghosts.length; i++) {
        float xPos = random(border, width-border);
        float yPos = random(border, height-border);
        float xDir = 10;
        float yDir = 10;
        float radius = random(10, 30);
        color clr = color(random(20, 255),
                          random(20, 255),
                          random(20, 255), 128);
        Ghosts[i] = new Disk(xPos, yPos, xDir, yDir, radius, clr);
    }
}

// The Disk class
class Disk {
    float xPos;    // 1. Current location (X and Y)
```

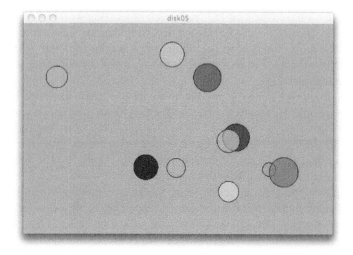

Figure 14.3. A batch of Ghost disks. (objects/sketches/disk05/disk05.pde)

```
float yPos;
float xDir;    // 2. Current motion (X and Y)
float yDir;
float radius; // 3. Radius
color clr;     // 4. Color

Disk (float axPos, float ayPos, float axDir,  float ayDir,
float aradius, color aclr) {
    xPos   = axPos;
    yPos   = ayPos;
    xDir   = axDir;
    yDir   = ayDir;
    radius = aradius;
    clr    = aclr;
    }
}
```

(See output in Figure 14.3. Full program in objects/sketches/disk05/disk05.pde)

I put an alpha value of 128 in the call to color() after the three random values for red, green, and blue. After all, these pucks are ghosts, so they should be partly transparent, right? I figured half-transparent would look nice.

If you think about this, you might wonder about the benefit of calling the constructor. After all, I just computed all those values in buildGhosts(). Why not skip the constructor altogether and load the values directly into the variables for Ghosts[i]?

Because I don't have Ghosts[i] yet! Each object Ghosts[i] is only created when I call new Disk(...) to construct one. But let's say I created Ghosts[i] at the start of the loop. Surely then I could put my variables right into Ghosts[i]'s fields, rather than passing them as arguments to the constructor and letting the constructor make the assignments.

I certainly could, but it's not a good habit to get into. As I mentioned above, you really want to let objects create and initialize themselves in their constructors as much as possible.

Suppose that this object was complex and written by someone else. The person who originally wrote the Disk object might have written it to carry out some important tasks at creation time, based on the values you hand it.

For example, suppose I want an object to look like a glowing, rotating sun on the screen. I find something perfect on the web, wrapped up as a Processing class, and I drop it into my program. I know the object uses a location and a radius to define the glowing shape.

So I might create my sun with the default constructor that takes no arguments and then manually fill in the radius and location variables, thinking I'm saving myself a line or two of code. But suppose that the author of the object knew that it was very taxing for most computers to draw that fuzzy, moving object because it uses tons of graphics primitives. The author might have some code that checks the computer's speed and reduces the complexity of the object it draws based on how fast that computer runs, the location of the sun, and its size. All of this happens in the constructor when the object is first made.

By not letting the object construct itself, I'm cheating myself out of some very useful optimization.

In other situations, a constructor's work might not be merely helpful, but actually essential. So the general rule is that constructors are good, and we should use them! You can adjust an object's variables yourself if you must after the constructor's done its work, but at least give the object every advantage when you're constructing it.

Returning to our ghostly air hockey pucks, this is the longest program we've seen yet in this book. And all it does is draw ten circles on the screen!

You probably remember that I said OOP is at its best in bigger projects, and now you see why. There's a bunch of overhead in this code for creating and maintaining the disks that we could have written directly by manipulating global arrays.

If we were to compare the number of lines it would take to write this program in a "traditional" way to the number of lines it's taken (so far) to write it in an OOP way, we'd find we're coming out a little bit behind. As the program gets more complicated, those numbers will even out. And then once OOP starts to pull out ahead, it will pull out ahead fast. But one step at a time!

So let's see that happen, because it's worth it. I'll show you how we can issue commands to the objects to get them to do things. Once that's in place, we'll have covered all the basics of object-oriented programming. Then I'll push this little framework and make it do more interesting stuff for us.

14.3   Object Methods

Here's the big thing we haven't tackled yet: actions. So far, these disks don't do anything. They're just packages of data. The program we have now only touches the disks twice: once to make them and then later to retrieve their variables so we can draw them.

So let's get the disks to draw themselves. The command will be, "`Ghosts[i]`, draw yourself on the screen."

The object we're talking to is `Ghosts[i]` (that is, an object of type `Disk`), the action is "draw yourself," and in this example, there's no additional material or information required.

To teach the `Disk` class how to take an action (and thus also teach every object of type `Disk`), we simply create a function inside of `Disk` with the name of the action. This is a normal function like any other: it can take arguments, and it can return a result. The one thing that makes it special is that it has access to the rest of the `Disk` object: it can call other `Disk` actions, and it can look at, and even change, the instance variables that belong to a variable of type `Disk` (like `radius`).

Recall that from outside the class, we refer to an object's variables with dot notation, like `Ghost.radius`. But when you're writing code inside an object (that is, between the curly braces that follow the `class` keyword), you don't use the name of the object or the dot because Processing knows that your action is talking about the object itself.

In other words, when you call a function, such as `Ghost.changeRadius()`, the procedure `changeRadius()` inside of `Disk` will be run. The particular instance of this `Disk`, named `Ghost`, is the one you sent the message to, so that's the one whose instance variables are used by the function. So when the code in `changeRadius()` refers to the variable `radius`, it's referring to the value of `radius` inside of the particular instance named `Ghost`. If you call `Spooky.changeRadius()`, then references to `radius` inside `changeRadius()` will refer to the instance variables for `Spooky`.

If you wanted to use the dot notation inside of your class actions, you'd need some way of referring to the particular object that is running that code. That is, your code would need some way to refer to "myself." Processing offers that in a special variable called `this`. Inside of a class action, `this` refers to the object that received the message to run that action. So instead of `radius`, you could write `this.radius`. Normally, this would just be wasted effort, giving you nothing but another chance to make a typo. However, there are some places where `this` comes in handy, and I'll come back to them later.

Returning to our code, let's teach `Disk` how to draw. We might be tempted to actually call this `draw()` because it's a good name for what the function does. This is legal, and you can do it, but remember that `draw()` is the name of the special system function that draws the screen. By declaring a function named `draw()` inside of the class, you're inviting confusion. Maybe not today, maybe not tomorrow, but someday you'll see an implementation of `draw()` in your code (or someone else's), and you'll mistake a class-specific version for the systemwide version, or viceversa. That could lead to all kinds of misunderstandings that you'd later have to clear up. So I suggest avoiding this problem right off the bat, and let Processing completely own its special names. There are plenty of synonyms in the world. I commonly use render() or display() for my class functions that draw graphics.

Of course, if I have two (or more) classes in my program, they can both have functions called render(), that are entirely distinct from one another. If you think that might cause confusion as well, you can pick yet other synonyms for each one. You could also include the class name in the function names, like renderDisk(). I think that's overkill. It's easy enough to know that a function defined inside a class belongs only to that class, and there's no confusion when you see something like Ghost.render(); that clearly means, "Ghost, call the render() function for your class," and not the same-named function for any other class. I try not to duplicate Processing's reserved names, but it makes a lot of sense, for consistency's sake, for every object that can draw itself to implement a function called render().

So now that we want a class function called render(), let's put it inside the class. I'll put it in right after the constructor (by convention, in a class definition, you first give the variables, then the constructors, then the other actions):

```
void render() {
    fill(clr);
    ellipse(xPos, yPos, radius*2, radius*2);
}
```

And now in draw() we'll just call this for each Ghost:

```
void draw() {
    for (int i=0; i<Ghosts.length; i++) {
        Ghosts[i].render();
    }
}
```

(See output in Figure 14.4. Full program in objects/sketches/disk06/disk06.pde)

You can see that just like we use the dot to look "inside" of a Disk object and get at its variables, we also use the dot to get at the actions (or functions or routines) defined inside of Disk. A function that belongs to a class, like render() above, is often called a method.

Remember that this works because each Ghosts[i] has its own package of data, and when you call render(), the variables xPos, yPos, and so on, have the values for that particular Disk and no other.

So now we have a clean object-oriented program. We create some objects using a constructor and then we ask them to do things for us. If we got the code for Disk off the Internet, all we would have to know is the format of the two routines it implements (the constructor and the render() routine), and we could use it.

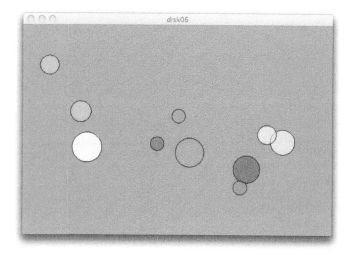

Figure 14.4. A batch of self-drawing disks. (objects/sketches/disk06/disk06.pde)

In fact, it's now possible for us to yank out all the code that implements `Disk`—that is, the entire block in curly braces after `class Disk`—and put new code in there. We could even completely change the variable names, or do away with the variables altogether.

The other parts of our program (the ones that aren't inside of `Disk`) at this point know nothing about what's inside that class. They only know that there are two function calls, the constructor `Disk()` (and its arguments) and the drawing method `render()`. In essence, my main code first says, "`Disk`, make one of yourselves according to this specification," and then later "`Ghosts[i]`, draw yourself." Note that the first instruction is to the class, to create an instance, and the second is to that instance itself. What happens inside of `Disk` to fulfill the drawing request could involve a few variables and loops, or it could harness the power of a global network of nuclear-powered hamsters, and the rest of my program neither knows nor cares.

This is sometimes called *data hiding* or *encapsulation*, and generally, the OOP philosophy is that this kind of separation of responsibilities is a very good thing, and you should try as much as possible to develop and maintain it.

Let's see the value of data hiding in action by changing `Disk` significantly: I'm going to reimagine our `Disk` as a box. To keep things simple the constructor will still take five `float`s followed by one `color`, but as far as `Disk` is concerned, some of these variables will have different meanings. Nothing in our program changes except the code that defines the `Disk` class:

```
class Disk {
    float xPos;
    float yPos;
```

```
float strokeSize;
float angle;
float sideLength;
color clr;

Disk (float axPos, float ayPos, float astrokeSize, float aangle,
float asideLength, color aclr) {
   xPos       = axPos;
   yPos       = ayPos;
   strokeSize = astrokeSize;
   angle      = aangle;
   sideLength = asideLength * 2;
   clr        = aclr;
}

void render() {
   fill(clr);
   strokeWeight(strokeSize/2.0);
   pushMatrix();
     translate(xPos, yPos);
     rotate(radians(angle));
     rect(-sideLength/2.0, -sideLength/2.0, sideLength,
        sideLength);
   popMatrix();
}
}
```

(See output in Figure 14.5. Full program in objects/sketches/diskbox/diskbox.pde)

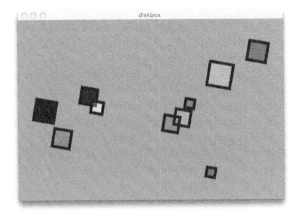

Figure 14.5. Changing the definition of a Disk. (objects/sketches/diskbox/diskbox.pde)

If we wanted `Disk` to draw an elephant, an espresso machine, or a tough-looking guy in a pinstripe suit, we could make that change to `Disk` and our main program wouldn't need to change even a single character (though, admittedly, the name `Disk` might not be such a great fit anymore).

Of course, this example's pretty simple so far, but it lays all the basic groundwork. Let's return to our circular disks, and teach them some new tricks.

14.4   Moving Disks

I want our disks to move. I could reach "into" each object and move it on every frame, but then I'd have to know what's inside of the `Disk` object, which violates my intention to follow the OOP philosophy. So I'm going to pretend I don't know what's inside of `Disk` at all, and instead, I'll issue an action to each disk telling it to move. I'll set it up so that `draw()` moves the disks on every frame by calling a routine `move()` (which doesn't yet exist):

```
void draw() {
   for (int i=0; i<Ghosts.length; i++) {
      Ghosts[i].move();
      Ghosts[i].render();
   }
}
```

I've put `move()` before the `render()` so that I move each disk and then draw it. In this situation, we could have called these methods in the opposite order, but I generally like to put things in position and then draw them.

Now I want to teach the disks to move. Just to get started, I'll do something quick and dirty to make sure the pieces are working right. I'll simply move the center of each disk by a random number based on `xDir` and `yDir`, and if it moves offscreen, I'll just move it back somewhere random on the screen.

```
void move() {
   xPos += random(-xDir, xDir);
   yPos += random(-yDir, yDir);
   if ((xPos < 0) || (xPos > width)) {
      xPos = random(0, width);
   }
   if ((yPos < 0) || (yPos > height)) {
      yPos = random(0, height);
   }
}
```

(See output in Figure 14.6. Full program in objects/sketches/disk07/disk07.pde)

This animation is kind of cool, like squiggly worms.

Figure 14.6. Some moving disks (frame from animation). (objects/sketches/disk07/disk07.pde)

Another image of a different run that I let go for a while longer is in Figure 14.7.

Figure 14.7. Another run of the ghost disks.

Just for fun, let's change the radius over time too:

```
void move() {
   xPos += random(-xDir, xDir);
   yPos += random(-yDir, yDir);
   if ((xPos < 0) || (xPos > width)) {
      xPos = random(0, width);
   }
   if ((yPos < 0) || (yPos > height)) {
      yPos = random(0, height);
   }
   radius += random(-1, 1);
```

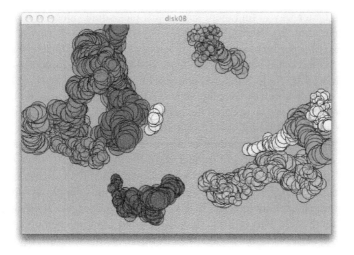

Figure 14.8. Changing position and radius (frame from animation).
(objects/sketches/disk08/disk08.pde)

```
    if (radius < 5)  radius++;
    if (radius > 20) radius--;
}
```

(See output in Figure 14.8. Full program in objects/sketches/disk08/disk08.pde)

Another image of a different run that I let go for a while longer is in Figure 14.9.

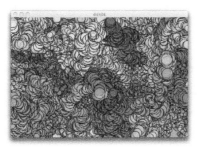

Figure 14.9. Another run of the radius-changing ghost disks.

I had no particular reason for picking 5 and 25 here for the `radius` extremes, I just tried a few numbers, and these felt right. When you're writing programs to draw pictures, you'll find yourself picking these kinds of numbers all the time; how big should something be, how fast should it move, how much should it change over time, and so on. There's no better way to find them than to just pick some values, try them out, and then adjust them until they feel right to you.

If you'd like to experiment a little, try adjusting the color on each new frame as well.

When we started out, I said I wanted these disks to bounce around like they were on an air-hockey table. So let's get that going. The values of xDir and yDir will tell us how much each disk moves on each update. All we need to do is add those into the current position. Once we've updated the center of the disk, we check to make sure it hasn't left the window. If it has, we'll turn it around.

For example, if the new *x* position in xPos is less than 0, it means that xDir is negative (on each update, xPos got smaller, until finally it dropped below 0). So we'll "flip the sign" on xDir (the phrase "flip the sign" means that if a variable has a positive value, we'll make it negative, and vice versa; we can do this simply by multiplying it by −1). So now on each update, the disk will move to the right. If xPos is greater than width, then xDir was positive (the disk moved right on each update) and now we want it to be negative again, so again we'll flip its sign. So if the *x* position is off screen on either side, we can replace xDir with -xDir, and now the puck will reverse its horizontal direction.

We'll do the same thing with yPos and yDir. For now, I'll take out the radius-changing stuff so we can focus just on the disk's motion.

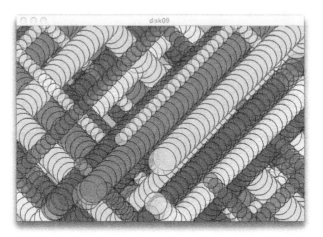

Figure 14.10. Disks bouncing off the wall (frame from animation).
(objects/sketches/disk09/disk09.pde)

```
void move() {
   xPos += xDir;
   if ((xPos < 0) || (xPos > width)) {
      xDir = -xDir;
   }
```

```
    yPos += yDir;
    if ((yPos < 0) || (yPos > height)) {
        yDir = -yDir;
    }
}
```

(See output in Figure 14.10. Full program in objects/sketches/disk09/disk09.pde)

This is another great example of a very object-oriented change. I *completely changed* what move() does, and the rest of the program never heard a peep and didn't change at all.

All of these Disk objects are moving fast, and initially they're all going down and to the right (after all, xDir is initially 10 which is positive, so that moves the disks right, and yDir is also initially 10 which is also positive, so they move down). I'll change the assignment statements in buildGhosts() so xDir and yDir are both random numbers that can be positive or negative:

```
float xDir = random(-8, 8);
float yDir = random(-8, 8);
```

(See output in Figure 14.11. Full program in objects/sketches/disk10/disk10.pde)

They're still moving a little too quickly for me, so I'm going to back those 8's down to 4's. And eventually, I'll want to get rid of those trails. But there's something else that's bugging me.

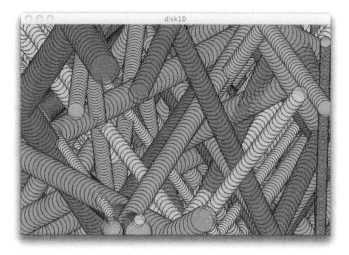

Figure 14.11. Disks bouncing off the wall and moving in different directions (frame from animation). (objects/sketches/disk10/disk10.pde)

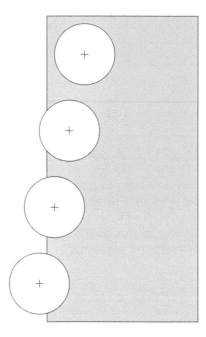

Figure 14.12. At the top, the center of this disk of radius 8 is at $x = 10$. The disk below is centered at $x = 6$, then $x = 2$, then $x = -2$.

Look at where any of the disks "bounces" off a wall. It's actually going deep into the wall before it bounces. It's because I'm checking the location of the center of the disk, and not its edge.

Figure 14.12 shows a disk of radius 8 heading for the left wall. At the top of the figure the center of the disk, xpos, is at $x = 10$, so the left edge edge of the disk is at $10 - 8 = 2$. If the speed xDir is -4, then on the next frame the center moves to xPos=6. The center is still to the right of the wall, but the left edge of the disk is now at $6 - 8 = -2$. The left edge of the disk has now gone past the left edge of the screen. It should have bounced already, but it hasn't because the center is still to the right of the window's edge, so the disk is heading off-screen. And then it's going to happen again, on the next update, xPos=2, so now the left edge is at $2 - 8 = -6$. Finally, on the next update, xPos= -2 and we will turn things around, but it takes two more frames for the left edge to re-appear.

I'd like for the disk to never go off the screen. So I'll change my tests. I'll see if the left edge is less than zero, or the right edge is greater than width; if so, I'll change direction in x. I'll use a similar test to check the top and bottom edges, and if they're respectively less than 0 or greater than height, I'll reverse direction in y.

```
void move() {
    xPos += xDir;
```

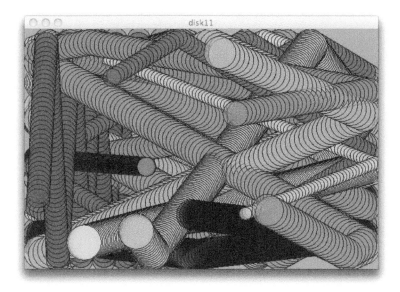

Figure 14.13. Disks not penetrating the walls (frame from animation).
(objects/sketches/disk11/disk11.pde)

```
    if ((xPos-radius < 0) || (xPos+radius >= width)) {
        xDir = -xDir;
    }
    yPos += yDir;
    if ((yPos-radius < 0) || (yPos+radius >= height)) {
        yDir = -yDir;
    }
}
```

(See output in Figure 14.13. Full program in objects/sketches/disk11/disk11.pde)

We're getting much closer, but notice that changing directions isn't quite enough (I'll come back to this issue later). When one of these tests succeeds it means that the disk has already left the screen. What we really want to do is undo that last move, and instead move the disk in the other direction.

Suppose xdir is -4, so the disk is moving left. We just subtracted, say, four from xPos and now xPos is negative. So we want to add four back into xPos (to put it where it was before it went offscreen), and then add four back in again (so it's moving in the direction it should be going). If you think it through, that same logic applies in all four directions: if the disk goes offscreen, we want to flip the direction around and add it back in twice to create the new position.

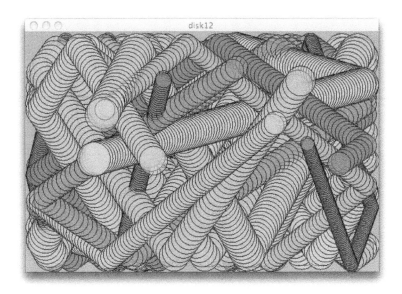

Figure 14.14. Improved wall bouncing (frame from animation).
(objects/sketches/disk12/disk12.pde)

```
void move() {
   xPos += xDir;
   if ((xPos-radius < 0) || (xPos+radius >= width)) {
      xDir = -xDir;
      xPos += 2*xDir;
   }
   yPos += yDir;
   if ((yPos-radius < 0) || (yPos+radius >= height)) {
      yDir = -yDir;
      yPos += 2*yDir;
   }
}
```

(See output in Figure 14.14. Full program in objects/sketches/disk12/disk12.pde)

There we go. Now we can get rid of the trails. They're the result of drawing new circles on top of the old ones each time we enter draw(). If we call background() at the start of draw(), it will clear the previous image. Here's the whole shebang:

```
Disk [] Ghosts;

void setup() {
   size(600, 400);
```

```
      buildGhosts();
}

void draw() {
      background(132, 144, 163);
      for (int i=0; i<Ghosts.length; i++) {
            Ghosts[i].move();
            Ghosts[i].render();
      }
}

void buildGhosts() {
      Ghosts = new Disk[10];
      int border = 50;
      for (int i=0; i<Ghosts.length; i++) {
            float xPos = random(border, width-border);
            float yPos = random(border, height-border);
            float xDir = random(-8, 8);
            float yDir = random(-8, 8);
            float radius = random(10, 30);
            color clr = color(random(20, 255),
                              random(20, 255),
                              random(20, 255), 128);
            Ghosts[i] = new Disk(xPos, yPos, xDir, yDir, radius, clr);
      }
}

class Disk {
      float xPos;    // 1. Current location (X and Y)
      float yPos;
      float xDir;    // 2. Current motion (X and Y)
      float yDir;
      float radius; // 3. Radius
      color clr;     // 4. Color

      Disk (float axPos, float ayPos, float axDir,  float ayDir,
      float aradius, color aclr) {
         xPos    = axPos;
         yPos    = ayPos;
         xDir    = axDir;
         yDir    = ayDir;
         radius = aradius;
         clr     = aclr;
      }

   void render() {
```

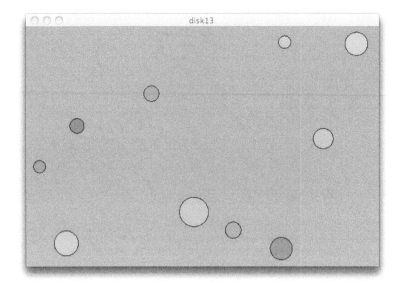

Figure 14.15. The ghostly disks (frame from animation). (objects/sketches/disk13/disk13.pde)

```
    fill(clr);
    ellipse(xPos, yPos, radius*2, radius*2);
  }

  void move() {
    xPos += xDir;
    if ((xPos-radius < 0) || (xPos+radius >= width)) {
      xDir = -xDir;
      xPos += 2*xDir;
    }
    yPos += yDir;
    if ((yPos-radius < 0) || (yPos+radius >= height)) {
      yDir = -yDir;
      yPos += 2*yDir;
    }
  }
}
```

(See output in Figure 14.15. Full program in objects/sketches/disk13/disk13.pde)

I like how this looks: ghostly air-hockey pucks bouncing around, searching for the secret truths that will let them leave this mortal coil and advance to the next level of spiritual air-hockey puck growth.

Depending on your computer, the disks may appear to be jumping or popping as they move. If you're seeing this, or some other image artifact that you think shouldn't be there, you can try a couple of things. As we discussed earlier, you can call smooth() in your setup() routine and see if that cleans things up. If there are still some aspects of the image you don't like, you can tell Processing to change the underlying libraries that it's using to draw graphics. I suggest trying the OpenGL library, as discussed in Chapter 6. To do that, you need to add one line and make one change to the size() routine we're calling in setup(). The new line, which should appear at the very top of your program, is

```
import processing.opengl.*;
```

Type the line in just like that. Then in the size() call, add a third parameter OPENGL (in all caps):

```
size(width, height, OPENGL);
```

That probably will make things look better (they look a whole lot nicer on my computer—the disks look smoother and they move more gracefully). If this doesn't make your graphics look better, or something goes wrong when you try to run the program, try one of the other renderers and see what works best on your system.

14.5 Using this

Sometimes it's useful for object methods to explicitly refer to the object that they're working with.

For example, let's imagine a couple of procedures we could add to Disk. One of them changes the size of the object by scaling radius up or down by some amount, and the other adds a specific value to the red component of its color. We might call these two routines on our Ghost object this way:

```
Ghost.scaleRadius(2.5);   // make Ghost bigger
Ghost.addToRed(10);       // make Ghost redder
```

There's nothing wrong with that at all. But if we were going to do a lot of those sorts of things, it might be nice if each of those routines returned Ghost itself. Then we could chain the calls together.

To see how, let's make a simple skeleton just to look at this idea. I'll create a new class called TestClass (catchy name, eh?). It will be very simple, with just two variables and a constructor. But I'll give it two methods, named print1 and print2, because they'll just print the numbers "1" and "2." This is one of those rare times when functions are so short I'll put the whole thing on a single line:

```
TestClass MyTester;
void setup () {
   MyTester = new TestClass();
   MyTester.print1();
   MyTester.print2();
}

class TestClass {
  TestClass() { }
  void print1() { println("1"); }
  void print2() { println("2"); }
}
```

(Full program in objects/sketches/this1/this1.pde)

This produces the output

```
1
2
```

Let's now assume that our class has a few dozen of these little functions, and we'll be calling them constantly. We might end up with long lists of calls to `print1()` and then `print2()` and so on, but we'd like to save some lines of code.

What if each function returned the object it was working with? Here's a new version of `print1()`:

```
TestClass print1() { println("1"); return(this); }
```

I made two changes. First, I changed the type of the function from `void` to `TestClass`, and then I added the statement `return(this)`. Remember that `this` refers to the object that the method is working with; `this` corresponds to the object that called the method in the first place.

Consider just a single call to `print1()`:

```
MyTester.print1();
```

Now `print1()` returns the object `MyTester`. In the line above, that return value would be ignored (since it's not assigned to anything). But what if we used the return value? We could assign it to another variable, for instance. Or (and here's the payoff), we could use it as the object that invokes another action:

```
MyTester.print1().print2();
```

This kind of notation can be a big space-saver in complex programs, saving you the hassle of creating lots of little temporary variables to hold intermediate results.

If you pull this statement apart, it takes the following steps:

1. Gets the object `MyTester`.

2. Calls `print1()` on that object.

3. Gets the value returned by `print1()`.

4. Calls `print2()` on that object.

Here's the new program, with changed versions of both methods and this new call in `setup()`:

```
TestClass MyTester;
void setup () {
   MyTester = new TestClass();
   MyTester.print1().print2();
}

class TestClass {
  TestClass() { }
  TestClass print1() { println("1"); return(this); }
  TestClass print2() { println("2"); return(this); }
}
```

(Full program in objects/sketches/this2/this2.pde)

The result of this program is exactly the same as before:

```
1
2
```

Whether or not this floats your boat is a matter of taste. There are people who absolutely love this kind of thing and write their objects to return `this` from almost every method. Other people never do it at all.

I find that this technique is useful for small objects that you want to manipulate repeatedly, and that returning `this` is less useful as the objects get larger or more complex. But again, this is a matter of taste and style, and as you look at people's code, you'll see lots of examples of both approaches.

Returning to our first example, if the two imaginary `Disk` routines we considered both returned `this`, then we could make `Ghost` bigger *and* redder using just one line:

```
Ghost.scaleRadius(2.5).addToRed(10);
```

14.6 Controlling Access

When you create an object, the variables and procedures that are inside it are, by default, visible to everything else in your sketch.

For example, suppose we had an instance of the `Disk` object above; let's call it `ghost` (I'm thinking of this as a local variable now, so I'm using a name that starts with a lower-case letter). Then you can use `ghost.xPos` anywhere in your code to access the xPos variable in that object. You can read it and even change it. You can also call any method implemented by Disk by calling it through ghost, as in ghost.render().

We say that the variables and methods in the object are *public*. If you wanted to make this explicit, you could put the keyword public in front of the variable and method definitions, but since that's the default, there's no reason to bother.

But the reason you have the option is because you can also say that you want one or more of your variables and methods to be *private*. When a variable or method is private, then it can only be accessed from within the object itself; outside objects cannot "reach in" as we did with ghost.xPos or ghost.render(). To make something private, you put the keyword private before its definition.

Making variables and methods private to an object is a central part of the object-oriented philosophy. The idea is that the object itself is responsible for what goes on inside it, and nobody else can change things from the outside. In essence, the object is a closed-off fortress, and the only information that can go in or out is through the variables and methods that are explicitly defined to be public. Usually none of the variables are public, and the only way to set or retrieve them is through a method offered by the object for just that purpose.

This is great stuff for big projects, but it's usually overkill for the sorts of smaller sketches we write in Processing. Here, object-oriented ideas are perfect for structuring our code cleanly and keeping things nicely separated, and not really so much for enforcing a strict set of controls. The Processing philosophy is generally that everything is public all the time.

In some programming languages, you define an *interface* when you first create an object. The interface defines all of the variables and methods, but that's all it has: just the definitions. To actually flesh out the methods, you then write an *implementation*. Typically you put the interface and implementation in different files. You can do this in Processing by using the implements keyword to start off an implementation of an interface. But again, this is something we rarely do, because it's overkill. Usually our objects are manageable, and we can put the interface and implementation together in one file without any problem.

Another idea that's common in larger object-oriented systems, but not so much in Processing, is that of *class variables* and *class methods*. These are variables or methods that are shared by all instances of the class.

A typical use of a class variable is to count the number of instances that have been made of a given object. For example, suppose we want to count the number of times we make a Strawberry object. Let's write a class definition that keeps track of the number of berries created. Each berry will also have a weight. We'll make three berries and print out the variables for each one:

```
void setup() {
  Strawberry s1 = new Strawberry(4);
  println("s1 = "+s1.numberOfBerries+"  weight="+s1.weight);
```

```
   Strawberry s2 = new Strawberry(5);
   println("s2 = "+s2.numberOfBerries+"  weight="+s2.weight);
   Strawberry s3 = new Strawberry(6);
   println("s3 = "+s3.numberOfBerries+"  weight="+s3.weight);
}

class Strawberry {
   int numberOfBerries = 0;
   float weight;
   Strawberry(float aweight) {
      numberOfBerries++;
      weight = aweight;
   }
}
```

(Full program in objects/sketches/static01/static01.pde)

Here's the output:

```
s1 = 1   weight=4.0
s2 = 1   weight=5.0
s3 = 1   weight=6.0
```

So that's not right. The first value printed out on each line should go up by one for each berry, indicating its sequential number in the number of berries made so far.

The problem is that each time we create a new object of type Strawberry, we're creating a new set of all the variables that are part of that object. So each new Strawberry object gets its own copy of numberOfBerries, and in the constructor it increments that by one, so it goes from 0 to 1. Every new berry goes through the same process, so every time we look at this variable, for every berry, it has the value 1. Normally, this is exactly what we want; it would be crazy if different objects normally shared the same variables. But every once in a while, as in this situation, we *do* want a single, shared variable.

We can accomplish this by making numberOfBerries a class variable. We do that by putting the keyword static in front of the variable's declaration:

```
static int numberOfBerries = 0;
```

It's a rule in Processing that if a class contains one or more static variables, then we have to put the keyword static in front of the class declaration as well:

```
static class Strawberry {
```

(Full program in objects/sketches/static02/static02.pde)

Then when we run this, we get

```
s1 = 1   weight=4.0
s2 = 2   weight=5.0
s3 = 3   weight=6.0
```

Now that's more like it! The single instance of the variable `numberOfBerries` is now shared by all the objects. It belongs to the class, not the objects of that class. It's kind of like a global variable, shared by all instances of that class. In contrast, the variable `weight` is not shared; each instance of `Strawberry` has its own weight.

14.7 Some Projects

I promised earlier to return to how the disk bounces off the screen and discuss a subtlety I overlooked in my solution. Yes, the disks no longer go off the screen. But something else is a little off. Probably nobody would see it in a million years, and in a fun little piece like this, the only real measure is whether things look right or not. But still, if you're into dotting i's and crossing t's, you'll find that there is a little problem with my algorithm. Can you catch it and devise a repair? (Hint: think about how far the puck moves on each frame. Then think about when the puck gets close to the edge and is about to hit—it shouldn't actually bounce until it hits the wall. Is my code taking that into account?)

Also, a disk could move towards a corner and hit two walls at the same time. Or it could hit one wall very slightly ahead of the other. Does this code handle those situations correctly? If it doesn't, can you make it do so?

A general issue to keep in mind when you go after little issues like these is to be sensitive to costs and benefits. Right now, any work you do in Processing is going to pay off, because you're learning and getting comfortable with the way things work. At this stage, every minute of design and programming is well spent, so if you're inclined to tackle any problems I suggest, or any that you dream up yourself, you should definitely dig in!

But once you're a master, you'll want to choose your battles. Not every detail is worth your time, particularly if it's a subtlety that doesn't affect the viewer's experience of your work, which is of course the ultimate goal. Always measure your effort against its contribution to the experience that you're trying to communicate. If there's a detail that affects that result, by all means, roll up your sleeves and make it rock solid, unquestionably, exactly right. But if some detail is just a little rough edge that will never be appreciated by anyone except yourself (and maybe another master who looks at your code), you might be better off letting it go and turning your attention to weightier matters. Nobody can make those trade-offs but you, of course. There's probably no piece of code in the world that does something complex or interesting that couldn't be improved in some way. But just keep in mind that if you strive for perfection in all things, you might never finish anything!

Another project is to extend this program so that the disks bounce off of one another rather than passing through each other. You can find the relevant math by searching the web for the term "perfect elastic collision," and for more information, read up on "conservation of linear momentum." Or you can treat it as an art project and just make the disks react in some way of your own design; maybe they exchange colors, for example, or go spinning off in random directions.

14.8   Managing Memory

Before we leave our discussion of objects, there's one important issue left to cover: memory.

So far we haven't talked about memory much because we haven't needed to. But OOP changes things because without your even realizing it, your OOP program can use up memory in almost no time at all, making your program crash. To avoid that, you need to have a general understanding of the techniques that Processing uses to manage memory for you, so you can make sure you're not accidentally consuming it all. First, let's see where the problem comes from. Then we'll see how to keep it under control.

In all of our programs up until now, we've casually asked for objects whenever we wanted them, with the expectation that we'll always get them. For example, we'd write

```
Disk myDisk = new Disk();
```

And we'd get back a new Disk, just as we asked for. No worries.

This has worked because we haven't asked for very many objects over the life of any program, and the objects we have asked for have been small. But computer memory is a finite resource; there's only a limited amount of it available on any given computer. If you don't need too much, you'll be fine. But object-oriented programs can casually gobble up all the memory you have in no time at all. When your memory's all used up, you're practically guaranteed to get a crash.

What causes this runaway consumption?

It's not the text of your program. Generally speaking, the size of your program (that is, the text that makes up your source code) makes almost no impact on your memory use. Even if your program is 20 or 50 screens full of text, that's basically nothing to a modern desktop computer. Fleas on an elephant. It's almost too small to bother mentioning.

What matters most are the objects you create when your program runs.

To see how quickly and easily these objects can grow out of control in an object-oriented program, think of a model of an orchard, represented by the class Orchard. Inside an Orchard are instances of class Tree. Making up a Tree are instances of class Limb. Here's one way to write up this little scenario, complete with a call to build an Orchard in setup():

```
class Orchard {
   Tree myTrees[];
   Orchard (int numTrees, int numLimbs) {
      myTrees = new Tree[numTrees];
      for (int i=0; i<numTrees; i++) {
         myTrees[i] = new Tree(numLimbs);
      }
   }
}

class Tree {
   Limb myLimbs[];
   Tree (int numLimbs) {
      myLimbs = new Limb[numLimbs];
      for (int i=0; i<numLimbs; i++) {
         myLimbs[i] = new Limb();
      }
   }
}

class Limb {
   // 1 megabyte of variables here
   Limb() {
   }
}

void setup() {
   Orchard myOrchard = new Orchard(2, 3);
}
```

As the comment suggests, let's pretend that a Limb requires a megabyte per instance (that's about a million bytes). That's not very much memory. In that megabyte we might hold the shape of the limb, how it twists and turns, where the bumps and knobs are located, how the color changes over its length, and so on. We also have to store where the leaves are located, how they're positioned, and all the points that describe the outline of each leaf. A megabyte for all of that information is probably pretty conservative.

In the setup() routine you can see that I have asked Processing to make an Orchard out of two Tree objects, each of which has three Limb objects. Two trees isn't much of an orchard, and those trees are little more than sticks. How much memory does it require?

Since each Limb requires one megabyte of memory (let's write a megabyte as M), this little Orchard requires $2 * (3 * M)$ bytes. That's only six megabytes. Most computers can probably handle that. But that's a really weak orchard: two trees, each with three limbs?

Let's make our orchard just a little more interesting and bump it up to 100 trees. Any tree that's going to bear fruit is going to have at least 1,000 limbs, including the little ones. So now we'll need $100 * (1000 * M)$, or 100,000, megabytes. That's 100 thousand million bytes, or 100 thousand megabytes, or 100 gigabytes. I don't know of anyone who has 100 gigabytes of memory in their home computer. And frankly, this still seems like a pretty thin orchard to me: a tree with only 1,000 limbs (including the little twigs) is a shell of a tree, and I only asked for 100 of them. But even this would not run on almost any home computer today.

By the way, you may be aware of an idea called *virtual memory*. This is a technique where the computer tries to make it look like you have more memory installed by using the hard drive as a kind of giant memory chip. This is much slower than using internal memory, and many of today's portable computers (like cell phones, PDAs, and smartphones) don't even have hard drives. Since we want our Processing sketches to run on those devices, too, I won't get into virtual memory here. We need to find a way to get our programs to work with the actual memory available.

14.8.1 Objects and Pointers

Let's look more closely at how memory is managed. This will help us find ways of avoiding the run away consumption we just saw.

A good way to think about the computer's memory is that it's just a huge list of slots that can hold numbers. The slots are relatively small: they're made up of eight *bits* (a bit is large enough to hold either a 0 or 1 and nothing else). This group of eight bits is called a *byte*. So if your memory can hold ten bytes, we call it a ten-byte memory. If it holds 1,000 bytes, that's one kilobyte, and if it can hold a million bytes, it's one megabyte, and so on.

Each of these slots is numbered. The number of a slot is called its *address*, like the street address of your house. We say that the very first byte has an address of 0, the next has an address of 1, then 2, and so on, for millions and billions of slots.

When you ask Processing for an object, say by calling `new Disk()`, it first looks at the object and figures out how many bytes it will take to store it. Speaking roughly, an integer might take two or four bytes, and a `String` of ten characters might take ten bytes.

Then Processing looks at the memory *pool*. Remember that we're thinking of the memory as a single big list of bytes. Conceptually, Processing has marked each byte as either *available* or *used*. If it's used, then it's hands-off; something in your program has reserved that byte for storing something, and that makes it unavailable for anything else. But of course, if a bunch of bytes are available, Processing can grab them, mark them as used, and then use them to build the new object you're trying to construct.

Later, when Processing determines that the object as no longer needed, it can *release* or *return* that cluster, or *block*, of bytes. All that means is that it marks them as once again available. Now when you ask to make another object, those bytes that you were just using are once again available to build something new.

It's like perfect recycling. The same bytes, and the bits that make them, get used over and over to hold different objects. If you watched a single byte over time, it might be part of an int for a while, then part of a float, and then unused, and then part of another int.

The reason we care about this is that when we assign a new object to a variable, the result isn't quite like when we assign a primitive type to a variable.

Here's what I mean. Suppose we have a few int variables, and we assign the value of one to another:

```
void setup() {
   int a = 3;
   int b = 100;
   b = a;
   println("just assigned b=a.   a = "+a+", b = "+b);
   b = 15;
   println("just assigned to b.  a = "+a+", b = "+b);
}
```

(Full program in objects/sketches/memory01/memory01.pde)

Here's the output:

```
just assigned b=a.   a = 3, b = 3
just assigned to b.  a = 3, b = 15
```

This should be no surprise, but I want to point out something important. Recall our shoeboxes analogy from Chapter 3. There, I said each variable corresponds to a shoebox. We can put values into the box or take values out.

So when we assigned a to b using the = sign by writing b=a, we copied the contents of a into b. They are still distinct boxes, and they hold distinct contents. After the first assignment statement, there is no ongoing relationship between the two variables a and b. They happen to have the same value, but that's all.

We can be sure that's the case because the second assignment statement, b=15, does nothing to the variable a. In this second assignment, we're putting the value 15 into the box marked b; box a simply isn't involved at all. It certainly isn't changed, as the printout shows.

This is not how it works when you make one of your own objects!

Instead, Processing does a little two-step. First, it grabs enough memory to hold your object. Then it puts the address of that block into your variable.

For example, suppose we have this little program:

```
class Apple {     // a tiny Apple class
   Apple() { }
}

void setup() {
```

```
    makeAnApple();
    println("back from setup");
}

void makeAnApple() {
    Apple myApple;              // line A
    myApple = new Apple();      // line B
    println("I made an apple");
}
```

(Full program in objects/sketches/memory02/memory02.pde)

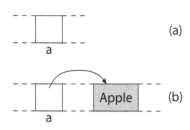

In line A, we declare the variable myApple. As Figure 14.16(a) shows, Processing grabs a little slot of memory that's big enough to hold the address of another piece of memory (that address is just an integer that runs from 0 to the total number of bytes installed in your computer).

Then, in line B, the right-hand side calls new Apple(). As shown in Figure 14.16(b), Processing finds a chunk of memory big enough to hold an Apple object.

Then in the left-hand side of line B, we assign the new object to the variable myApple. This means that Processing puts the address of the new Apple object into the variable myApple. When a variable holds an address, rather than a value, we call the variable holding the address a *pointer*. One of the nice things about Processing is that most of the time you don't need to know or care which variables hold values and which hold pointers to other parts of memory. Processing keeps track of the distinction for you, and any time you ask for a variable's contents, Processing does the right thing, and gives you either the variable's value (in the case of an int or float, for example) or the value of the object that it points to (in the case of an Apple or Disk or any other object you create).

Figure 14.16. (a) Enough memory to hold the pointer a. (b) The pointer a points to the block of memory that contains an Apple object.

So if the computer manages the distinction for us, why should we even bother knowing the difference?

There are two reasons. The first is to understand what happens when we assign one pointer to another, and the other (surprise!) helps us manage memory effectively.

Let's look at these in order.

14.8.2   Pointers and Assignments

Let's merge our two little program from above. I'll assign one variable to another, but instead of using variables of type int, I'll use objects of type Apple.

```
class Apple {      // a tiny Apple class
   float weight;
   Apple(float aweight) {
      weight = aweight;
   }
}

void setup() {
   Apple a = new Apple(3);
   Apple b = new Apple(100);
   b = a;
   println("just assigned b=a.  a.weight = "+a.weight+",
      b.weight = "+b.weight);
   b.weight = 15;
   println("just assigned to b. a.weight = "+a.weight+",
      b.weight = "+b.weight);
}
```

(Full program in objects/sketches/memory03/memory03.pde)

Here's the result of this little program:

```
just assigned b=a.  a.weight = 3.0, b.weight = 3.0
just assigned to b. a.weight = 15.0, b.weight = 15.0
```

OK, that's different.

And maybe surprising. We changed b, and only b, but a changed, too. After we changed the weight of b, the weight of a had the same value. How did that happen? And why?

It's because, just as we saw before, the assignment statement puts the contents of one variable into the other. Back when we had two int objects, initialized with the values 3 and 100, we copied the *contents* of a, which was the number 3, into the contents of b.

But in the newer version, a holds a pointer to the block of memory that describes an apple with weight 3, and b holds a pointer to the block of memory that describes an apple with weight 15, as in Figure 14.17(a). When we copy a to b, we copy what's in a itself, which is that pointer, not the object it points to. Figure 14.17(b) shows

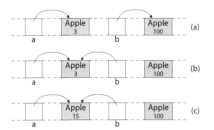

Figure 14.17. (a) The pointer a points to an Apple object with weight 3, and the pointer b points to an Apple object with weight 15. (b) After assigning b=a, both a and b point to the Apple with weight 3. (c) After b.weight changes, the object both a and b point to has the new value.

the result of the assignment b=a. The pointer in b takes on the value of the pointer in a. The poor Apple with weight 100 is abandoned; the memory is still out there, but nothing's pointing to it. And then when we change the weight of the `Apple` pointed to by `b`, the weight of the `Apple` pointed to by `a` changes too, because they're both pointing to the same object.

So in this example, the assignment `b=a` meant that both `b` and `a` point to the same block of memory; in other words, they both point to the same object! So whether we call it `a` or `b` doesn't matter, since they both point to the same place. And if we change anything in that block of memory, say by assigning to `b.weight`, then of course `a.weight` will reflect that change as well. These have become two names for the same thing.

What if you really wanted two different instances of the `Apple` object, but you wanted the new one to have the same values as the old? You could simply create a new object, initialized with the variables of the old one:

```
Apple b = new Apple(a.weight);
```

Now `b` is an entirely new `Apple` that just happens to have a `weight` variable with the same value as that of the `Apple` pointed to by `a`. Changing either one from here on out will not affect the other.

Copying objects by copying their contents is a common thing to do, but if your objects are complicated, with lots of variables, you might find that your constructors become unpleasant, with long argument lists naming every variable. In that case, you might want to create a function that copies one object into a brand-new one. Here's an example of that for our little `Apple`, to which I've now added a variable `size`:

```
class Apple {     // a tiny Apple class
   float weight;
   float size;
   Apple(float aweight, float asize) {
      weight = aweight;
      size = asize;
   }

   Apple() {      // a blank constructor for a default apple
      weight = 1;
      size = 1;
   }

   Apple makeCopy() {
      Apple newApple = new Apple();  // make a default apple
      newApple.weight = weight;
      newApple.size = size;
      return(newApple);
   }
}
```

```
void setup() {
  Apple a = new Apple(4, 5);
  Apple b = a.makeCopy();
  println("a.weight = "+a.weight+"  a.size = "+a.size);
  println("b.weight = "+b.weight+"  b.size = "+b.size);
  b.weight = 5000;
  println("changed the weight of b");
  println("a.weight = "+a.weight+"  a.size = "+a.size);
  println("b.weight = "+b.weight+"  b.size = "+b.size);
}
```

(Full program in objects/sketches/memory04/memory04.pde)

So my intention here is to start with an apple called a, with a weight of 4 and a size of 5. Then I'll make a copy of that apple called b. It will start with the same values, but it will be a different object. I'll print out both a and b.

Then I'll change the weight of b and print them both out again to see what's changed.

Here are the results that this produces:

```
a.weight = 4.0   a.size = 5.0
b.weight = 4.0   b.size = 5.0
changed the weight of b
a.weight = 4.0   a.size = 5.0
b.weight = 5000.0  b.size = 5.0
```

That's just right. The variable b now points to a copy of the apple pointed to by a. Initially b has the same values as a thanks to makeCopy(), but if we change those values, the object pointed to by a is unaffected.

Having multiple pointers that all point to the same object can be an enormously useful tool. For example, you might have a huge list of Apple objects. Sometimes you want to work with that list with the apples sorted by weight, and other times, you'd like to get at them sorted by size.

To be able to refer to either sorted list easily, you could create one array to hold the Apple objects. This array would hold pointers to the memory blocks that describe the apples.

Then you could make two more arrays of type Apple. These, too, are just pointers to those same memory blocks. In one array, the

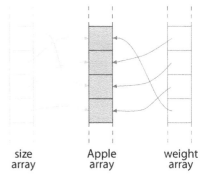

size   Apple   weight
array   array   array

Figure 14.18. The central column represents an array of Apple objects. On the left and right are two different arrays of pointers that point to the Apples. Another array, not shown, also points to the objects in the central column.

pointers will be arranged so that they represent the apples sorted by `weight`, and in the other, they'll be sorted by `size`, as in Figure 14.18 (for clarity, I haven't shown the first array in the figure, but it would just point to the entries in the middle column in order of their creation). Even though you have three lists, they're all just pointers, which take just a few bytes each. You haven't duplicated the objects themselves (in this case, our objects are small, but if they were a few megabytes each, or more, then having three copies of each one would waste a lot of memory).

So by sharing pointers, you can save a ton of memory because you don't have to create and save multiple, identical copies of your objects.

But having multiple pointers to the same object can be risky, since you now have multiple ways to change those objects. If you forget which pointers share an object, and which point to different objects, you can easily get yourself into a crazy jumble of confusing changes, and objects going haywire.

So remember that if you're assigning a primitive type (like an `int` or `float`), then you're assigning the object itself, and you'll end up with two independent variables that happen to have the same value for a while. Changing either object leaves the other unaffected.

If you assign a nonprimitive type (like a `Disk` or `Apple` or any other class that you create), then you're assigning the pointer to that object, and you'll end up with two variables that point to the very same, shared object. Changing either variable changes the other as well.

If you want one object to take on the values of another, or you want a new object with the same values as one you already have around, you must make a new instance of your object first and then put the values you want into it (either with a constructor or by assigning the values yourself).

If you're ever working with an object and you're not sure whether you're copying values or pointers, make a little test program like the one above. Make one of your objects, assign it to a variable, assign that variable to another variable, and then change a value of the object using that second variable. Print out both variables. If changing the second one changed the first, you've got pointers! If changing the second one left the first alone, you've got values.

Keeping this pointer–value business straight can be a real challenge when you're getting started with object-oriented programming. Don't sweat it; it's strange and hardly anyone gets it right away. And even veterans accidentally copy pointers when they want to copy objects, or vice versa. If you suspect something like this is going wrong in your code, use print statements to help you keep track of what's changing and where. I find it very helpful to pick up my pen and draw little diagrams that show me what I intend my code to do. I label the boxes as pointers or values and draw arrows showing me where the pointers are going. Then I can put values into the boxes and watch how they change over time using print statements. If I find the values of objects changing unexpectedly, then I know my code isn't matching my drawing, and I fix one or the other until they're both the same and both doing what I want.

14.8.3   Orphaned Objects

Earlier I talked about how Processing is able to recycle memory when it's no longer needed. That way memory that's used for an object you no longer need can be reused later for something new, rather than being locked up forever.

Processing handles this for primitive types (like int and float) all by itself. For your own objects, you need to keep in mind just one rule: when nothing is pointing to an object, it gets recycled.

If there's even one active variable (I'll define this in a moment) anywhere in your program that is pointing to an object, then that object's memory is considered used. But if nothing points to the object, then it's been cut loose from your program (after all, if nothing points to it, then nothing can read or write it).

It's like holding a bunch of helium balloons, each one tied with a string. Over time, you might tie more strings on each balloon and hang onto them, or you might untie some strings and drop them. As long as you're holding at least one string for each balloon, it's safe in your hands. But as soon as you've let go of all the strings for a given balloon, it flies up and disappears.

Processing recycles memory with a technique that goes by the ungainly name of *garbage collection*, or GC. The idea is that there's a "garbage collector" in the system, looking for objects that nobody points to. If it finds them, it considers them "garbage" and makes their memory available for new objects.

You don't need to do anything to help the garbage collector. You may occasionally see comments or code in other people's programs that refer to "helping" the garbage collector in some way, but that's almost never a good idea and might even work against you. The garbage collector has been developed and optimized to be fast and efficient without your intervention.

As long as you have at least one variable pointing to an object, it's safe from the garbage collector. When no variables point to an object, it gets recycled.

There's an interesting subtlety here regarding local variables. Recall that those are variables that are declared in a routine, which I typically start with a lower-case letter. When we leave a routine, the local variables go away as well. That means that if they were pointing to an object, those pointers go away also. And as we've seen, if nothing else is pointing at a particular object, then it will get recycled.

For example, consider this little program:

```
class Apple {
   Apple() { }
}

void setup() {
   makeApple();
}

void makeApple() {
```

```
   Apple myApple = new Apple();
   // do things with myApple
}
```

I've scaled `Apple` back to a pretty useless class so we can stay focused on the pointers.

In `makeApple()` we declare the variable `myApple`. As a result of the assignment statement, `myApple` will point to an instance of class `Apple`. Because there's at least one variable pointing to it (in this case, exactly one), that instance of `Apple` is protected from the garbage collector and will remain intact and untouched for the duration of the routine.

When `makeApple()` finishes, it returns, and we go back to `setup()`. As part of that process, all of the local variables that belong to `makeApple()` are recycled, and that includes `myApple`. So in effect, the variable `myApple` disappears. That means nothing is pointing to the `Apple` we made. So a little chain reaction happens here: we leave the routine, so the local variables go away, so they no longer point to anything, so the `Apple` object has nothing pointing to it, so the garbage collector will scoop that object up and recycle it.

This is what I meant by *active variable* above. The variable `myApple` is present in your source code all the time (after all, it's right there in the text), but it only gets created when we enter `makeApple()`, and it disappears when we leave it. So in that sense, `myApple` is only active when the procedure `makeApple()` is running.

We've seen that when we leave `makeApple()`, the object we created will get recycled. What if we wanted to keep that object? There are two basic ways to do it: return it from the function or assign it to a global variable. Let's look at these in turn.

We've seen the return technique before. All we have to do is pass back the object in a `return` statement, from a procedure that has the type `Apple`. Processing doesn't recycle the local variables until it's assigned any values that the procedure returns. So to save the `Apple`, we can just return it.

Here I'll change the type of `makeApple()` so that it returns an `Apple`, and I'll include a `return` statement. In `setup()` I'll create a variable to receive that returned value:

```
class Apple {
   Apple() { }
}

void setup() {
   Apple newApple = makeApple();
   // do things with newApple
}

Apple makeApple() {
   Apple myApple = new Apple();
```

```
   // do things with myApple
   return(myApple);
}
```

Since what's getting returned is the value of myApple, which is a pointer to the Apple we made, newApple will also point to that Apple. So even when the local variable myApple disappears, there's still at least one variable pointing to that object we just made, and setup() can continue to use that apple.

Safe!

Of course, in this example, in the very next line after the comment, we finish setup() and the program is over, but we could do other things with newApple after the assignment statement if we wanted.

The other way to save an object is to assign it to a global variable. Because those never get recycled (at least, not until the program exits), anything saved in a global will be safe as well. I've said before that in large programs global variables are generally frowned on because they can be changed in far-apart, different parts of the program (which can be hard to find, and confusing), but in small Processing sketches, globals can often be handy. Here's an example of saving our variable using a global.

I'll unwind our changes back to the version of the program that doesn't return anything, and instead of returning the new Apple, I'll set it to a global variable:

```
class Apple {
   Apple() { }
}

Apple NewApple;   // a global variable

void setup() {
   makeApple();
   // do things with NewApple
}

void makeApple() {
   NewApple = new Apple();
   // do things with NewApple
}
```

In this example, the global variable NewApple points to the newly made object. Since NewApple itself is never recycled, the object it points to is never recycled, either.

Of course, if NewApple is reassigned later to point to some other object, then it no longer will point to the Apple that was made in the routine makeApple(). Unless some other variable was assigned to this value, changing the value of NewApple will leave the object without anything pointing to it, and thus ready for the garbage collector.

We sometimes say that an object that has nothing pointing to it is an *orphan*, or that it has been *orphaned*.

By the way, there may be times when you want to recycle an object by changing the variables that point to it, but you don't have a new object around to point them to. You can always assign the special value null to a pointer; this means, "This pointer doesn't point to anything." The object it previously pointed to gets one step closer to being recycled (because one fewer pointers are directed at it), but now the variable doesn't point to anything. Later, you of course can always set it to the address of a new object.

Here's an example of setting a pointer to null to release the object it points to. I'll use the local-variable version of the program from above and change setup().

```
class Apple {
   Apple() { }
}

void setup() {
   Apple newApple = makeApple();
   // Do something with newApple
   // Now we want to recycle this Apple, so we have room for
   //    other objects we want to make.
   newApple = null;
   // make new objects
}

Apple makeApple() {
   Apple myApple = new Apple();
   // do things with myApple
   return(myApple);
}
```

As soon as we say newApple = null, in this example we've cut loose that object, and its memory will be available for new objects.

This use of null is not used very frequently in practice, but when you really need to free up an object and you don't have something new for your pointers to point to, this technique does the job.

14.8.4   Reusing Objects

We've seen that any object that has nothing pointing to it will be reclaimed by the garbage collector and made available for recycling into new objects.

Abandoning an object is fine, and the garbage collector will do its job for you, but if you need to re-create the object later, then it might be better not to free it up in the first place. That's because each time you create an object, it takes some time for the computer to locate the necessary memory and reserve it for you. And each time an object is orphaned, it takes time for the garbage collector to locate it and then recycle the memory.

If your project calls for regularly creating the same kind of object over and over, you could end up spending a lot of time allocating memory and returning it. It's often faster to reuse the objects you've already got.

Suppose you're creating a museum project that displays a fruit stand. The computer in the museum gets turned on an hour before the doors open, so it's okay if the program takes a while to start up the first time. But while the visitors are around, your program needs to be responsive and fast.

Let's say your program displays a fruit stand containing a half-dozen apples. If someone clicks on one of the apples, that indicates that they'd like to buy it. So that apple disappears from your screen (and maybe you then trigger some piece of hardware that actually gives your visitor an apple!). Now you want to draw a new (and slightly different) apple in the old one's place. You could, of course, just create a new apple. Here's an example of that.

I'll say that we want to show six apples at a time, and we'll keep them in a global array called `DisplayApples`:

```
Apple DisplayApples[6];
```

Ignoring how you might deliver the selected apple, animate its disappearance, and so on, we could just replace the selected apple with a new one like this:

```
int chosenApple = getPickedApple();
                // get index of selected apple
DisplayApples[chosenApple] = new Apple();
                // replace with a new apple
```

That would work, but suppose now that our `Apple` is a complicated 3D object with lots of surface detail and color, and our `Apple` constructor is a crazy mad scientist's dream of how to make an `Apple`. It starts with a seed and simulates its growth, including effects from rainfall to the acidity of the soil, factoring in visits from birds and competition from nearby plants, ultimately producing an apple. It takes ten minutes to run this constructor, but the apples it creates are beautiful.

If we run this constructor first thing when the program starts, that long creation time is no problem because it happens in the morning before the doors open.

But when it's running during the day, this program has a performance problem. Each time someone clicks on an apple, we're calling `new Apple()` in response. So the program will freeze up for ten minutes as we create this new apple. That's not good.

Instead, let's reuse the apple we have. Suppose that the only difference between the apple we were showing before and the one we'll show next is the overall size and color. Let's also assume that those are fast and easy to determine, involving none of the complex calculations we needed to grow the apple from a seed. So if those variables are part of `Apple`, we could write this instead:

```
int chosenApple = getPickedApple();
                    // get index of selected apple
```

```
DisplayApples[chosenApple].size = getNewSize();
                         // new apple's size
DisplayApples[chosenApple].color = getNewColor();
                         // new apple's color
```

Or, if we're feeling really object-oriented ourselves, we can have the object do the work:

```
int chosenApple = getPickedApple();          // get index of selected apple
DisplayApples[chosenApple].setNewSize();     // take on a new size
DisplayApples[chosenApple].setNewColor();    // take on a new color
```

Either way, we now have a replacement `Apple` with a few new values, while all the other (and time-consuming) variables are left untouched. And, the pointer `DisplayApples[chosenApple]` still points to the `Apple` object, so it's never orphaned, and it doesn't get recycled. We just change what's inside of it.

This technique of reuse is popular in situations where you're going to create many of the same kind of object. You just keep around a whole bunch of them all the time, and when you need an object, rather than use `new` to generate a new one, you just grab an existing one and load it up with new values.

That approach requires a little bit of bookkeeping on your part. Typically, each object will have a `boolean` that tells you if it's in use or not. If an object is in use, you try another one, until you find one that isn't being used. You'll need to either know beforehand the maximum number of objects you'll ever want to have around at one time or be willing to take the performance penalty for creating a new one (with `new`) when all of your existing objects are in use and you need another.

You can use this technique to draw our orchard example from earlier in the chapter. You'll need only one `Tree` and one `Limb`, and you can just keep reusing them to build up the entire orchard. It requires a bit more effort on your part (for example, you'd probably want to the draw the farthest-away limb first, and then draw the remaining limbs in order based on their distance from you), but a little programming effort can save you tons of memory, and perhaps even turn a program that can't run at all into one that runs quickly and smoothly.

And with that observation, we've discussed pretty much everything you'll probably ever need to know about memory.

Don't let this memory stuff scare you away from object-oriented programming. I know it seemed like a lot of detail, but I wanted you to see all the different ways to handle the memory problem because you'll see all of these approaches in other people's code. If you don't have a basic idea of what's going on, these kinds of memory-management techniques can seem impossible to figure out. Once you have the general idea, then all you have to do is keep track of the pointers.

OOP is a lot of fun once you get the hang of it, and it's really the best way to write many kinds of programs. Most small projects don't need OOP, but sometimes even a small program can be conceptually perfect for implementation using OOP techniques. And OOP is of course a great choice for big and complicated programs.

This whole memory discussion really boils down to one thing, and it's the only thing you'll probably ever need to know about managing your memory: objects that have at least one variable pointing to them are left alone; objects with nothing pointing to them are recycled by the garbage collector. Just keep in mind how many things are pointing to any given object and you'll be on safe ground.

Once you get a feeling for this pointer business, it will become second nature, and you'll be writing OOP code with confidence and ease.

14.9   Objects and Arrays

In Chapter 11 we saw Processing's routines for manipulating arrays. I illustrated those routines with arrays of ints. As long as you're using one of Processing's built-in primitive types, such as int, float, color, and so on, everything works just as I described.

But there's a subtle difference in how you write your code when you're using arrays of your own objects. The issue appears in the routines that return a new array.

For example, here's a tiny program where I'll define an array of floats and then append another float onto the end:

```
void setup() {
    float [] myArray = { 1, 2, 3, 4 };
    myArray = append(myArray, 5);
}
```

This runs without a hitch, and the result is that the array myArray is now a five-element array that contains the floating-point numbers 1 through 5. Note that to make this work properly, Processing had to notice that in this case append() was taking a list of floats as input, and thus returned a list of floats as output (since we stored the result back into myArray, which has type float []).

That's a lot of work for Processing to do! It's great that it can manage this for us, but it can only do it for its built-in types. If we try this same fragment with our own objects, it will fail. Here's a new version with a super-tiny object named Peach. I'll create an array of Peach objects and then try to add one more to the end:

```
class Peach {
  float weight;
  Peach (float aweight) {
    weight = aweight;
  }
}
```

```
void setup() {
  Peach [] peachList = { new Peach(3), new Peach(4), new Peach(5) };
  peachList = append(peachList, new Peach(6));
}
```

(Full program in objects/sketches/arrayobject01/arrayobject01.pde)

This won't compile. If you try, you'll find that the line with the call to `append()` is highlighted, and the message area will turn red and display this error message:

```
cannot convert from Object to arrayobject01.Peach[]
```

This is a pretty cryptic message! To get a handle on it, we can pull apart the pieces. First, there's a problem with "converting" something. This usually means a type mismatch, like if we're trying to put a `color` into a `float`. Second, the type it's starting with is `Object`. We haven't seen that before, but let's roll with it and keep going. It's trying to convert this to the type `arrayobject01.Peach[]`. That's a mouthful! The first part is the name of the sketch; I saved this as `arrayobject01`. The second part is `Peach[]`, which we know is an array of `Peach` objects. These last two bits are joined with a period. So generalizing from the dot notation we've seen before, this is telling us that the type it's trying to convert to is coming from the program `arrayobject01`, and named `Peach[]`, which tells us it's our array of `Peach` objects.

The only remaining mystery component here is `Object`. It turns out that every object in Processing is derived from a master generic type called `Object`. We almost never see it. It's like saying that every kind of life on Earth is built by using carbon molecules. Carbon has to be there, and its properties are essential to the chemistry that makes life as we know it possible, but we rarely deal with carbon molecules at that level. They're there, but so deep in the system we don't deal with them.

The `Object` type is like that, but every now and then, it rises up and surfaces. That's happening here. It's because Processing knows that `append()` returns *something*, but it doesn't know what that might be in this case. It's just not able to work out the details of the statement and figure out that we're handing `append()` an array of `Peach` objects, and they're in our program, and so that should be what comes back from the function. It sure would be nice if Processing could work that out on its own, but it can't, and it's telling us that.

So the error message says, in effect, "The routine `append()` returns something, but I don't know it's type, so I'll just say it's of type `Object` since that's the primordial type everything else comes from. You're trying to save that into a variable of type `Peach[]`. I don't know how to put an `Object` into a `Peach[]`, so I'm giving up with an error."

To make this work, all we have to do is explicitly tell Processing to take the output of `append()` and consider it a variable of type `Peach[]`. Then it can do the assignment easily, since the types match.

This kind of manual type conversion is called a *cast*. We say "I'm going to cast that to an `int`", or "This has to be cast to an array of `Peach`." To force Processing to change the type of a variable, place the new type, in parentheses, before the variable's name. We want to cast the output of `append()` to the type `Peach[]`, so we put `(Peach[])` in front of it, like so:

```
peachList = (Peach [])append(peachList, new Peach(6));
```

(Full program in objects/sketches/arrayobject02/arrayobject02.pde)

It compiles and runs and does just what we want.

You'll typically use these kinds of casts (or type conversions) when you're working with system functions like `append()` that return different kinds of objects depending on their inputs. Sometimes `append()` will return an array of `float`s, sometimes an array of `Peach` objects. The cast tells Processing to interpret the output as the proper type.

Of course, we can get into trouble if we mess up the cast. For example, if you cast the output of `append()` in this example to, say, `(int [])`, the compiler will complain because it can't put an object of type `int []` into an object of type `Peach[]`.

Chapter 15
Fall Leaves

Little projects are great for demonstrating various features of Processing, but they're not much good for showing how to write a larger program. Of course, the problem with a larger program is that it's, well, larger. Lots of code. Lots of details. And all that code, all those details and trade-offs and stuff—it just gets boring after a while, unless you're the person doing it. It's like the difference between playing a video game and watching someone else play it. If you're a gamer, you know that playing a really great, immersive game is a very pleasurable experience. But I've found that watching someone else play is rarely as much fun.

On the other hand, if we don't do something of some size, then I'd be skipping all the important steps of planning and execution that only come up in larger projects. After all, a large program is not like one of our little examples.

So I'm going to take a middle ground, and together we'll build up a medium-sized project. It's big enough that we'll get into all the relevant issues, but not so big that we'll get endlessly detoured by detail.

The rest of this chapter will be completely devoted to starting from scratch and working our way up to a medium-sized, running project.

In the preceding chapters I've let you watch over my shoulder as I've written each piece of code. When there was a bug, you saw it when I did, and we fixed it. But if I was to do that now for this larger program, it would take forever. On the other hand, I always feel a little cheated when I read a programming book and someone drops a big listing on my head, effectively saying, "Behold! Look at my wonderful program!" That's not much of a learning experience. I'll try to split the difference again. The little stuff that I think we've discussed in detail, or should be straightforward enough to understand by now, I'll just present to you as accomplished fact. But when the going gets interesting, I'll dig into the details, and we'll build things up together.

One central issue that comes with writing a larger program is the question of *structure*. How do you organize a big program? What classes are useful? Should they all go into one file, or across multiple source files? If there should be several files, what goes into which file?

The truth is that very few people know the answers to all these questions when they start a program, particularly creative and arts-based programs. Everyone has their own style, and they figure out these answers as they go, rewriting and reorganizing their code along the way.

Here's how I work.

I usually start out with a vague idea, and I throw together something to see if it works at all. Usually the code is ugly (for example, it'll have lots of global variables or bad organization, and often, the picture (or animation) is not too hot, either. But if it's headed in the right direction, I'll keep at it for a while, trying to refine it a little bit at a time until the images start to look roughly the way I have it in my head.

Almost always, I hit a bunch of problems. This shape doesn't look right, or that color isn't changing the right way, and I don't really know why. Usually it's because I haven't really thought through what it is I want; I'm kind of fumbling my way through the process, writing code to try out this idea and that one, hunting for something that looks good. Often I'll actually manage to match my original idea, but by then I'll have changed what I'm going after! Experimenting with an idea is only partly about finding a way to achieve the original idea. The rest is about discovering alternatives, dreaming up new ideas along the way, and having happy accidents. Lots of times, when I'm trying to do one thing, I'll write code that only does part of the job, or even code with a bug in it, but I'll like what I see even more than what I thought I wanted, or it will give me a new idea to go off in a new direction.

What I'm trying to share here is the idea that writing code for art and visual purposes is a lot like noodling around on a musical instrument or sketching with a pencil. You start with something rough, you change this and change that, you erase whole big chunks and redraw them, and so on. You might start drawing a picture of a dog and end up instead with a picture of two dogs or even a landscape. Your goal is to draw and to express yourself, and to make a picture that does that. How you get there is a very personal experience, and it's rarely a perfectly straight line from inspiration to final result. Rather, you explore all kinds of alternatives along the way, solving problems that crop up, spending time creating stuff that you later throw away, and so on, as the final work slowly comes into focus. Programming can be the same way. When you're familiar with the tools, you get to the point where you're not thinking about the mechanics of semicolons and curly braces, but instead about bigger issues like how images ought to warp or how to make a tree look like it's swaying in the wind.

In this chapter, we're going to create a project inspired by the season of fall.

How should we do that? There are endless possibilities. We could draw impressionistic blobs of color that change from greens to reds and oranges through to browns. We could draw trees that gradually go bare and reveal their limbs.

We need to pick *something*, so I choose this: a picture of a forest floor, with leaves appearing on it over time, overlapping one another and accumulating.

With that as our starting point, let's write the project.

15.1 Basic Skeleton

Here's the basic skeleton for the leaf-drawing program:

```
// Fall leaves project
// version 0.1, Andrew, 16 April 2009
//

// dimensions of the square drawing area
int Window = 400;

void setup() {
   size(Window, Window);
   background(200, 190, 143);
   noFill();
}

void draw() {
   drawOneLeaf();
}

void drawOneLeaf() {
   // draw a random leaf
}
```

(Full program in leaves/sketches/leaf01/leaf01.pde)

Everything here we've seen before. The call to `setup()` creates a square window for us to draw into and sets the background to a light yellow. It also turns off filling of objects. The `draw()` routine is called once per frame, and in turn, it calls `drawOneLeaf()`, which right now does nothing. The code compiles and runs, but all it does is put up a window. That's still a good start!

I saved this as `leaf01`. Processing automatically built a folder for this file, so there's a folder called `leaf01` that contains the file `leaf01.pde`. It's not much, of course, but it's a start.

15.2 PVector Object

As we've seen, when you work with geometry, there are a lot of points floating around. So far, I've been managing each point by storing the *x* and *y* values explicitly (either per point or by using arrays).

It turns out that Processing offers us an easier way, in the form of a built-in object called a `PVector`. Just as a `color` object holds three numbers, one for each color channel, a `PVector` holds two numbers, one each for the *x* and *y* values of a point (we'll see in Chapter 21 that it can hold a 3D point as well).

You create a new PVector as you would any other object, by using new and calling its constructor. Typically when you create a new PVector, you give it two values, one each for the *x*- and *y*-coordinates of that point:

```
PVector myPoint;
myPoint = new PVector(0, 0);
```

Now you can refer to the *x* and *y* values using dot notation:

```
float xValue = myPoint.x;   // get the point's x
float yValue = myPoint.y;   // get the point's y
xValue += 3;                // change xValue, doesn't affect myPoint
myPoint.x += 5;             // change value of x in myPoint
```

The name might be a bit of a mystery. The P at the start is probably for Processing, but why Vector? Shouldn't this be a PPoint?

It turns out that there are two ways to think of the coordinates stored in this object. We can certainly think of them as simply defining a point at (x, y). But sometimes it's useful to think of an arrow that starts at the origin $(0, 0)$ and ends at the point (x, y). In mathematics, an arrow like this is called a *vector*. Most of the time, there's no reason to make much of a fuss over the distinction. After all, the object itself doesn't care; it just has an x and a y, and what you want them to mean is up to you. But we'll see later that there are times when we really do want to think of this as an arrow.

So sometimes this object is best thought of as a point, and sometimes it's best thought of as an arrow (or vector). Neither concept will always be right. Since it can have only one name, the designers gave it the name PVector. So when you see me refer to "a vector," there are times when I could just as well be talking about "a point," or vice versa. On the other hand, some operations only make sense for one thing or the other (for instance, you can get the length of a vector—that's the distance from its base, at the origin, to its tip, at (x, y)—but there's no such thing as the "length" of a point).

The PVector object comes loaded up with a bunch of useful methods. We'll typically use just a few of them, but I'll run through them briefly here so you'll know what options are available to you.

set(). Assign values to the fields of the PVector.

get(). Load up a PVector with the values from another one.

mag(). Returns the length of the vector (distance from origin to point).

add(). Adds two vectors by adding components.

sub(). Subtracts one vector from another.

mult(). Multiplies all components of a vector by a single value.

div(). Divides all components of a vector by a single value.

dist(). Returns the distance between two points.

dot(). Computes the dot product of two vectors.

cross(). Computes the cross product of two vectors.

normalize(). Scales the vector to have length 1.

limit(). Scales a vector to be no longer than the given amount.

angleBetween(). Finds the angle between two vectors.

array(). Returns the vector's components in an array.

The odd ducks in the list above are dot() and cross(). If you get into 2D geometry (and later, 3D geometry) you'll find yourself using these all the time. I won't get into those types of operations in this book, so I won't go into these procedures here. Mostly I'll do basic things with vectors: assign to them, add them, multiply them, that sort of thing. If you're curious about dot() and cross(), you can read up on the large and beautiful branch of mathematics called linear algebra.

One useful idiom is to set a vector to a specific length. For example, suppose you want to move a point A partway towards a point B. One way to go would be to find the difference between them (that is, subtract A from B to create B-A) and then add some or all of that into A:

```
PVector A = new PVector(10, 20);
PVector B = new PVector(40, 80);
PVector change = B.get();     // get value of B
change.sub(A);                // subtract A from B
A.add(change);                // add that back into A
```

Here I made two vectors, or points. In the third line I initialized the vector change with the value in B. Then in the next line I subtracted the value of A from it, which in this case is $(40 - 10, 80 - 20)$ or $(30, 60)$. In the last line, I added that to A, which of course now gives A the same values as B.

But what if I only wanted to move A partway there? What I'd want to do is first scale the vector to something smaller.

Suppose I know that I want to move three units towards B. What's the right scaling factor to apply to change so that the new value of A will be three units from where it started?

The technique to answer this question is so common you'll see it everywhere. You take a little two-step. First, you *normalize* the vector. This simply means you scale it so that it has a length of 1. Then you scale the vector, as before. If we want it to have a length of 3, we just scale it by 3. Figure 15.1 shows the idea.

Because this is such a common process, Processing makes it easy. You start with a built-in action called normalize(). You call this on a vector, and it comes back with length 1.

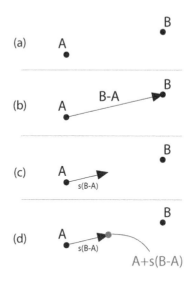

Figure 15.1. Moving from point *A* to point *B*. (a) Points *A* and *B*. (b) The vector from *A* to *B* is $B-A$. (c) Scale the vector by *s* (here, about 0.4). (d) Add that vector to *A* to find the new point.

So to move our point A three units towards B, we first find the difference between them, normalize that difference, scale it by 3, and add that in to A. In this little sketch, I'll do exactly that and then print out the distance from the new value to its original starting point:

```
void setup() {
    PVector A = new PVector(10, 20);
    PVector Acopy = A.get();
    PVector B = new PVector(40, 80);
    PVector changeVector = B.get();
    changeVector.sub(A);
    changeVector.normalize();
    changeVector.mult(3);
    A.add(changeVector);
    println("new A: ("+A.x+", "+A.y+")");
    println("distance from A to original A: "+A.dist(Acopy));
}
```

(Full program in leaves/sketches/pvector01/pvector01.pde)

The result of this is

```
new A: (11.34164, 22.68328)
distance from A to original A: 2.9999993
```

Well, that's pretty darned close to three units away.

Remember the list of PVector actions above when you want to do something with a point or vector. Odds are that you can do what you need with just one or two calls to these built-in actions. Using the built-in routines over doing it yourself is almost always a win, whether you're looking at it from a writing, debugging, or efficiency point of view.

OK, now that we have this new box of tools in our kit, let's get back to the leaf-drawing project!

15.3   Drawing a Leaf

In the starting skeleton, I included this routine:

```
void drawOneLeaf() {
    // something here that draws leaves
}
```

My goal is to put something in there that will take us to the goal of drawing a forest floor. Let's build up the code, one step at a time.

So, what does a forest floor look like? What do leaves look like as they fall? What do they look like when they settle on top of other leaves? What shapes do they have? Do they cast shadows? Do some of them crumple when they hit they ground? Do they have just one color, or are they mottled? Do they have holes in them? How obvious are the veins?

Writing code means asking these questions of yourself, answering them, and finding ways to turn your answers into pictures.

That process of questioning, answering, experimenting, imagining, making tiny changes and making huge changes, and generally just following your instincts is really rewarding. Just because I'm showing you my final results doesn't mean that this is where I started! My first programs were ugly to look at and produced lousy pictures. My approach grew over time. If I were to sit down with the same inspiration and go through the process again, I bet I would end up with a very different program, and probably quite different pictures.

When I write programs, I go through a lot of paper. I keep a box of colored pencils by my desk, and I'm constantly drawing little sketches and trying to figure out how I might program them. I use the colored pencils to indicate the difference between, say, curve control points and knots, or I draw construction lines to show me how to place points versus actual lines I want to draw, and so on. And of course I just doodle a lot, drawing pictures and thinking things through visually. I encourage you to have a generous supply of scratch paper around when you program and a good bunch of writing instruments that you like. Nothing beats pencil and paper for designing, debugging, writing notes, and otherwise making sense of the world and keeping track of your ideas while you're programming.

After lots of playing around, I settled on something very simple. I wouldn't draw the leaves as they fell, nor would I try to do anything with them once they reached the ground. Instead, I'd just draw the leaves on the ground, one on top of the other, and let them accumulate.

So, now we have to decide what general shape the leaves should be, what their margins (or outlines) should look like, what color they should have, how transparent they should be, and so on. As I mentioned before, the general way to figure this out is to write some code that approximates what you want and then play with it until it starts to look good. There's really no good way to guess the answers to a lot of these questions before you begin.

Figure 15.2. A simple leaf.

Because I want to keep things simple, my leaves are not going to be complicated things like maple leaves, but closer to something simple like bay leaves. I'm not going for any specific kind of leaf here, but rather some loose kind of personal impression of what a simple leaf feels like to me. What I do know about these leaves is that they are thin at one end; much, much bigger in the middle; and thin again at the far end. That is it, that is my theory.

So let's get started on something like that. As always, we'll begin with something simple: in this case, a leaf that lies on the horizontal axis. So I'll imagine a horizontal line in the middle of the screen. Half of the leaf lies above that line, the other half below, as in Figure 15.2.

Now what should the edges look like? I'm going to keep it simple and use a Bézier curve. They're easy to control, and they're built into Processing, so it's an easy choice.

Each curve is of course made up of four points. Let's call the endpoints pA and pB; these are the pointy bits at the ends, as in Figure 15.2. So they're shared by both the upper and lower curves. In between, the two upper control points are in the top half of the screen, and the lower control points are in the bottom half. Let's call the upper control points pG1 and pG2 and the lower ones pH1 and pH2 (these are arbitrary names; I just wanted something short and distinct). Figure 15.3 shows the scheme.

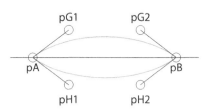

Figure 15.3. Leaf with Bézier curves.

For my own convenience, I'm going to adopt a convention from some other programming languages and name some of my variables for their type. So all of my points will begin with p.

Let's make these points. One thing I've learned is to try to keep the actual dimensions of my graphics window outside of the code as much as I can. For example, suppose I write a beautiful project with a window that's 500 by 500, and someone with a much faster computer wants to display it at 800 by 800, or even bigger. If my code is littered with references to 500 (or 499), I'll have to adjust them all. But much worse, suppose that I've tuned the code so that things move just the way I want—for example, an object moves to the right by 3 pixels every frame, and that's exactly the right speed. So somewhere in my program there's a line like

```
position += 3;
```

And now we want to use a 1000-by-1000 pixel window. Uh-oh. My objects are still moving by three units, only now that makes them move at half the visual speed that I wanted. My spiffy, snappy animation is now happening in a tub of viscous goo. Ugh.

The easy solution to this is to do everything in some other, abstract coordinate system and then determine where the points end up on the screen only when you need to display them.

There are several popular kinds of abstract regions that people like to use.

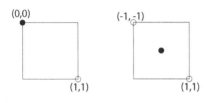

Figure 15.4. Two different coordinate systems. (a) The origin is in the upper left and $(1,1)$ is in the lower right. (b) The origin is in the center, and the corners are all 1 unit away from the origin in each dimension.

As Figure 15.4 shows, one system puts the origin $(0,0)$ in the upper left and places $(1,1)$ in the lower right. The other puts $(-1,-1)$ in the upper left and $(1,1)$ in the lower right. The first one is a little simpler to use, while the second one is symmetrical. They're both just fine, so you can pick the one that appeals to you. Just remember to stick with it!

I'll note that some people prefer to let the y-axis proceed up, rather than down, matching the traditional coordinate system we learned about in geometry class. That idea appeals to me, but I've found that it's easier for me to think of all my coordinate systems using the same directions. Since I can't change Processing's choice that y goes down, I'll use that direction in my coordinate systems as well.

So now everything happens in that little world, using floating-point coordinates. When it's time to actually draw something, we scale the values up to match the screen.

Suppose that we choose the coordinate system that has $(0,0)$ in the upper left and $(1,1)$ in the lower right, and we move an object to the right like this:

```
position += .01;
```

That means it moves 1/100 (or one percent) of the width of the window to the right. It doesn't matter if the window ultimately is 10 pixels wide or 10,000, because one percent is always one percent. So that's the way I'm going to do things here.

For this project, I'm going to use the convention that the screen is a square that runs from $(-1,-1)$ in the upper left to $(1,1)$ in the lower right, as in Figure 15.4(b). I'll turn those into screen coordinates (that is, pixel locations in the window) with another routine before I draw anything based on these points.

Let's get the basics in place first. I'll create the leaf points by hand and draw them, so I know I have this much functioning correctly.

```
void drawOneLeaf() {
    PVector pA = new PVector(-0.5, 0.0);   // left end
    PVector pB = new PVector(-0.5, 0.0);   // right end

    PVector pG1 = new PVector(-.25, -.25);
    PVector pG2 = new PVector( .25, - 25);
    PVector pH1 = new PVector(-.25, - 25);
    PVector pH2 = new PVector( .25, - 25);

    PVector sA = pointToWindow(pA);
    PVector sB = pointToWindow(pB);
    PVector sG1 = pointToWindow(pG1);
    PVector sG2 = pointToWindow(pG2);
    PVector sH1 = pointToWindow(pH1);
    PVector sH2 = pointToWindow(pH2);

    stroke(196, 66, 63);   // red
    bezier(sA.x, sA.y, sG1.x, sG1.y, sG2.x, sG2.y, sB.x, sB.y);
    stroke(64, 135, 36);   // green
    bezier(sA.x, sA.y, sH1.x, sH1.y, sH2.x, sH2.y, sB.x, sB.y);
}

PVector pointToWindow(PVector p) {
    PVector t = p.get();
    t.x = map(t.x, -1, 1, 0, Window-1);
    t.y = map(t.y, -1, 1, 0, Window-1);
    return(t);
}
```

(See output in Figure 15.5. Full program in leaves/sketches/leaf03/leaf03.pde)

The results here are unbelievably awful, so we'll have to figure out the problem. First, let me clear up what the code was *supposed* to do!

The first few lines of drawOneLeaf() create six points and put them on the screen in places I thought they might look nice. Again, I'm thinking the screen runs from $y = -1$ at top to $y = 1$ at the bottom, and similarly, $x = -1$ at the left and $x = 1$ at the right.

The next six lines create copies of those points that have been converted into screen coordinates by the function pointToWindow(). Here, I've extended my naming convention: variables that begin with s are points that are in screen coordinates. Then I draw the top curve in red and the bottom curve in green.

The function pointToWindow() takes one argument: a point that you want to convert. Its job is to return a new PVector that holds the input point in screen coordinates. The question it has to answer is the same for both the x- and y-coordinates: how

Figure 15.5. A first try at drawing a leaf! (leaves/sketches/leaf03/leaf03.pde)

do we turn a number from $(-1, 1)$ to a number from $(0, \text{Window})$? Simple—use our old friend map()!

You can see here what I meant before by the OOP style potentially leading to endless memory consumption. The routine draw() gets called once every frame, and it calls drawOneLeaf(). That routine creates six new PVector objects each time you enter it. Then in the body, it calls pointToWindow() six times, and each of those calls creates a new PVector. If there was no garbage collector, then for every frame this program drew, it would have 12 PVectors less worth of memory to work with, and eventually, after minutes or hours or days, there would be no memory left. Thanks to the garbage collector, though, each time we leave drawOneLeaf(), all the objects within its scope—including the ones made by pointToWindow() but passed back to drawOneLeaf()—will be recycled by the garbage collector.

So what's going wrong? I have tried to do a few things at once here: filling in drawOneLeaf(), creating a bunch of points, moving them all to the screen, and then drawing the curves. I don't know what went wrong, so I'll pick this apart in pieces. The first thing I'm going to check is the pointToWindow() routine; maybe that's not working the way I intended, or maybe my intention was flawed. I'll comment out the code that's in drawOneLeaf() and replace the two Bézier curves with a rectangle and see what happens:

```
void drawOneLeaf() {
    // everything else commented out
    PVector pul = new PVector(-.5, -.25);  // upper left
    PVector pur = new PVector(-.5, -.25);  // upper right
```

Figure 15.6. Using rectangles rather than curves. (leaves/sketches/leaf04/leaf04.pde)

```
PVector plr = new PVector(-.5, -.25);  // lower right
PVector pll = new PVector(-.5, -.25);  // lower left
pul = pointToWindow(pul);
pur = pointToWindow(pur);
plr = pointToWindow(plr);
pll = pointToWindow(pll);
fill(0, 0, 255);
rect(pul.x, pul.y, plr.x-pul.x, plr.y-pul.y);
}
```

(See output in Figure 15.6. Full program in leaves/sketches/leaf04/leaf04.pde)

Yup, something's seriously wrong here. Nothing is getting drawn at all. That's actually a pretty good thing, because this kind of total failure is usually easy to fix. The huge obvious bugs are easy to swat; it's the pesky little ones that take time. So let's print out this rectangle's four points and see where they go wrong. I'll put these lines just before the call to `fill()`:

```
println("pul="+pul.x+", "+pul.y);
println("pur="+pur.x+", "+pur.y);
println("plr="+plr.x+", "+plr.y);
println("pll="+pll.x+", "+pll.y);
```

Here's the printout:

```
pul=100.0, 150.0
pur=100.0, 150.0
plr=100.0, 150.0
pll=100.0, 150.0
```

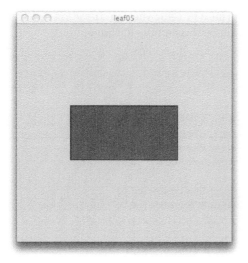

Figure 15.7. Fixing the debugging code. (leaves/sketches/leaf05/leaf05.pde)

```
pul=100.0, 150.0
pur=100.0, 150.0
plr=100.0, 150.0
pll=100.0, 150.0
```

That goes on and on, over and over, every point coming up as (100.0, 150.0). What's up with that?

When I made the four points, I wrote the first line and then copied and pasted it to make the others. I remembered to change the variable names, and I even remembered to change the comments, but I didn't remember to change the points themselves.

There's a bug in the code I wrote to find my bug! Well, that's a shame but it's not too surprising: almost all software has bugs, including debugging software.

This is why I pay attention when my antennae start to quiver when I see repeated lines of nearly-identical code. It's just too easy to forget to keep everything up to date.

So that's easy enough to fix:

```
PVector pul = new PVector(-.5, -.25);  // upper left
PVector pur = new PVector( .5, -.25);  // upper right
PVector plr = new PVector( .5,  .25);  // lower right
PVector pll = new PVector(-.5,  .25);  // lower left
```

(See output in Figure 15.7. Full program in leaves/sketches/leaf05/leaf05.pde)

The picture finally looks right, so that's solved. I know the pointToWindow() routine is working correctly. I'll take out all this new rectangle code and remove the comments. The problem must be somewhere in `drawOneLeaf()` as I originally wrote it. So let's look at it again, more carefully this time:

```
void drawOneLeaf() {
    PVector pA = new PVector(-0.5, 0.0);  // left end
    PVector pB = new PVector(-0.5, 0.0);  // right end

    PVector pG1 = new PVector(-.25, -.25);
    PVector pG2 = new PVector( .25, - 25);
    PVector pH1 = new PVector(-.25, - 25);
    PVector pH2 = new PVector( .25, - 25);

    PVector sA = pointToWindow(pA);
    PVector sB = pointToWindow(pB);
    PVector sG1 = pointToWindow(pG1);
    PVector sG2 = pointToWindow(pG2);
    PVector sH1 = pointToWindow(pH1);
    PVector sH2 = pointToWindow(pH2);

    stroke(196, 66, 63);  // red
    bezier(sA.x, sA.y, sG1.x, sG1.y, sG2.x, sG2.y, sB.x, sB.y);
    stroke(64, 135, 36);  // green)
    bezier(sA.x, sA.y, sH1.x, sH1.y, sH2.x, sH2.y, sB.x, sB.y);
}
```

Sheesh. There's another copy-and-paste error, in the assignment statement for pB. Sigh. We have to lose that minus sign:

```
PVector pB = new PVector( 0.5, 0.0);  // right end
```

OK, that's more promising. The points pA and pB seem okay, but the intermediate points are wrong. Although pG1 looks okay, pG2 is missing the decimal point in front of the *y*-coordinate. And the next three lines are, too. Oh, and while I'm at it, I can see that all the *y* coordinates have minus signs in front of them. Stupid copy-and-paste errors. Let's fix them all.

This is programming, warts and all. This is how it goes. But it's easy enough to fix:

```
PVector pG1 = new PVector(-.25, -.25);
PVector pG2 = new PVector( .25, -.25);
PVector pH1 = new PVector(-.25,  .25);
PVector pH2 = new PVector( .25,  .25);
```

(See output in Figure 15.8. Full program in leaves/sketches/leaf06/leaf06.pde)

All right! Huzzah! Another triumph for the forces of good over evil!

Maybe it's not that big a deal to you, but I'm always happy when I get my code to work properly.

Figure 15.8. Finally, a leaf! (leaves/sketches/leaf06/leaf06.pde)

Now this has got to be the world's most boring leaf. It's symmetrical top and bottom, and symmetrical left and right. Let's mix that up a bit.

The easiest way is just to move the control points around. I'll call `random()` to add some random numbers to the x and y locations of the four points. But how much randomness? I don't know. The whole leaf here is one unit long (it runs from $x = -0.5$ at the left to $x = 0.5$ at the right), and the control points are 0.25 above and below the endpoints, so let's add a random number between 0 and 0.15 to both the x and y values, and see what it does for us.

```
PVector pG1 = new PVector(-(.25+random(0,.15)), -(.25+random(0, .15)));
PVector pG2 = new PVector( (.25+random(0,.15)), -(.25+random(0, .15)));
PVector pH1 = new PVector(-(.25+random(0,.15)),  (.25+random(0, .15)));
PVector pH2 = new PVector( (.25+random(0,.15)),  (.25+random(0, .15)));
```

(See output in Figure 15.9. Full program in leaves/sketches/leaf07/leaf07.pde)

Ugh. Forget the image for a moment, the code is awful. Copy-and-paste madness here. There's going to be some of that, no matter what we do, because these four points are very similar, yet different. But we can avoid repeating all this gunk by packaging it up into its own routine:

```
PVector makeControlPoint(float x, float dxlo, float dxhi,
                         float y, float dylo, float dyhi) {
    float px = x + random(dxlo, dxhi);
    float py = y + random(dylo, dyhi);
    PVector t = new PVector(px, py);
    return(t);
}
```

Figure 15.9. Experimenting with the leaf shape. (leaves/sketches/leaf07/leaf07.pde)

So this takes the starting location of the point (both *x* and *y*), and the range of random values we want to apply to each coordinate, creates an appropriate point, and returns it. (And now we're creating yet more PVector objects. Hooray for garbage collection!)

```
PVector pG1 = makeControlPoint(-0.25, -0.15,  0.15, -0.25, -0.15, 0.0);
PVector pG2 = makeControlPoint( 0.25, -0.15,  0.15, -0.25, -0.15, 0.0);
PVector pH1 = makeControlPoint(-0.25, -0.15,  0.15,  0.25,  0.0, 0.15);
PVector pH2 = makeControlPoint( 0.25, -0.15,  0.15,  0.25,  0.0, 0.15);
```

(See output in Figure 15.10. Full program in leaves/sketches/leaf08/leaf08.pde)

Figure 15.10. Leaf shape experiment with better code. (leaves/sketches/leaf08/leaf08.pde)

That's still much too cut-and-paste like, and each line is even a little longer than it used to be, but now I can see everything cleanly at one glance. I still need to be really careful about my numbers and minus signs, but ultimately, there's no getting around that; the best we can do is make it easy as possible to get it right in the first place and fix any errors that do creep in.

This is kind of like a little spreadsheet now. The first value is the x location of the point, and the next two numbers tell me the range of values that can be added to it. You'll see that I'm letting the x values move left or right up to 0.15 in each direction. Then come the y values, and my idea is that I'll start them out near the y-axis, and only push them away. So positive y value get more positive (I add a random number from $(0,0.15)$) and negative y values get more negative (I add a random number from $(-0.15,0)$).

Remember that the arguments to random() have to be in ascending order. The documentation doesn't explicitly say so, but try this little stand-alone program:

```
for (int i=0; i<10; i++) println(random(10, 1));
```

You'll get back 10.0 every time. If you make sure the numbers ascend (that is, put the smaller one first), you'll get back what you expect (that is, numbers from 1 to 10).

If you're looking closely, you'll see that in the older version of the code I only added numbers in the range $(0,0.15)$ to the x-coordinates. That had the effect of always pushing them to the right, and that was an oversight. Now that I could see all the values in front of me, I made the range symmetrical when I typed them in, not even realizing I was fixing a problem!

Now with these two changes in place, I can tear my eyes away from the code and look at Figure 15.10. It kind of looks like a pair of lips. Maybe I could make them talk? Well, file that away for another time. Right now, I'll stop them from accumulating like that by clearing the window to the background on each new frame:

```
void draw() {
    background(200, 190, 143);
    drawOneLeaf();
}
```

(See output in Figure 15.11. Full program in leaves/sketches/leaf09/leaf09.pde)

This is twitching way too fast! We can tell Processing to slow down by making a call to frameRate(). It wants a number that tells it how many times per second to call draw(). Let's slow it down to one call per second:

```
void setup() {
    size(Window, Window);
    background(200, 190, 143);
    noFill();
    frameRate(1);
}
```

(See output in Figure 15.12. Full program in leaves/sketches/leaf10/leaf10.pde)

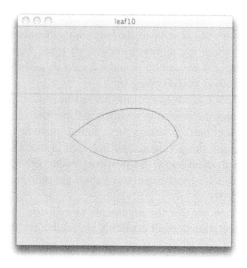

Figure 15.11. Looking at leaf shapes (frame from animation). (leaves/sketches/leaf09/leaf09.pde)

Figure 15.12. Looking at leaf shapes more slowly (frame from animation). (leaves/sketches/leaf10/leaf10.pde)

That's much better. Now we can see our leaf. I don't know about you, but I'm having a hard time seeing where the control points are landing just by looking at these curves. Let's draw a little circle around each point by adding a few lines at the end of `drawOneLeaf()` and show the lines from the endpoints to the control points:

```
stroke(196, 66, 63);  // red
elipse(sG1.x, sG1.y, 15, 15);
elipse(sG2.x, sG2.y, 15, 15);
line(sA.x, sA.y, sG1.x, sG1.y);
line(sB.x, sB.y, sG2.x, sG2.y);
stroke(64, 135, 36);  // green
elipse(sH1.x, sH1.y, 15, 15);
elipse(sH2.x, sH2.y, 15, 15);
line(sA.x, sA.y, sH1.x, sH1.y);
line(sB.x, sB.y, sH2.x, sH2.y);
```

(See output in Figure 15.13. Full program in leaves/sketches/leaf11runbug/leaf11runbug.pde)

This copy-and-paste code makes me uneasy, but I know it's just for temporary visualization while debugging and that I'll delete it soon, so I won't worry about it. Note that I made sure to use the s versions of the points, rather than the originally computed ones, because I wanted screen locations.

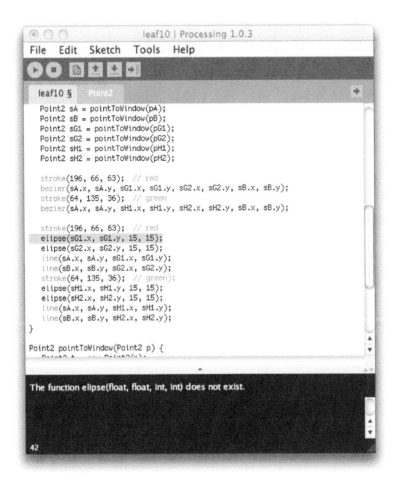

Figure 15.13. Oops—typing error. (leaves/sketches/leaf11runbug/leaf11runbug.pde)

But if I run this, I get an error, with the first call to `elipse()` highlighted:

```
The function elipse(float, float, int, int) does not exist.
```

Oh, I left out one l in "ellipse." If you look at the screen shot, you'll see that the word `elipse` is not in orange, meaning that Processing isn't recognizing it as a keyword. I'll fix that in all four calls. Here's the complete program so far:

```
// Fall leaves project
// version 0.1, Andrew, 16 April 2009
//
```

```
// dimensions of the square drawing area
int Window = 400;

void setup() {
   size(Window, Window);
   background(200, 190, 143);
   noFill();
   frameRate(1);
}

void draw() {
   background(200, 190, 143);
   drawOneLeaf();
}

void drawOneLeaf() {
   PVector pA = new PVector(-0.5, 0.0);  // left end
   PVector pB = new PVector( 0.5, 0.0);  // right end

   PVector pG1 = makeControlPoint(-0.25, -0.15,  0.15, -0.25, -0.15, 0.0);
   PVector pG2 = makeControlPoint( 0.25, -0.15,  0.15, -0.25, -0.15, 0.0);
   PVector pH1 = makeControlPoint(-0.25, -0.15,  0.15,  0.25,  0.0, 0.15);
   PVector pH2 = makeControlPoint( 0.25, -0.15,  0.15,  0.25,  0.0, 0.15);

   PVector sA = pointToWindow(pA);
   PVector sB = pointToWindow(pB);
   PVector sG1 = pointToWindow(pG1);
   PVector sG2 = pointToWindow(pG2);
   PVector sH1 = pointToWindow(pH1);
   PVector sH2 = pointToWindow(pH2);

   stroke(196, 66, 63);  // red
   bezier(sA.x, sA.y, sG1.x, sG1.y, sG2.x, sG2.y, sB.x, sB.y);
   stroke(64, 135, 36);  // green
   bezier(sA.x, sA.y, sH1.x, sH1.y, sH2.x, sH2.y, sB.x, sB.y);

   stroke(196, 66, 63);  // red
   ellipse(sG1.x, sG1.y, 15, 15);
   ellipse(sG2.x, sG2.y, 15, 15);
   line(sA.x, sA.y, sG1.x, sG1.y);
   line(sB.x, sB.y, sG2.x, sG2.y);
   stroke(64, 135, 36);  // green);
   ellipse(sH1.x, sH1.y, 15, 15);
   ellipse(sH2.x, sH2.y, 15, 15);
   line(sA.x, sA.y, sH1.x, sH1.y);
   line(sB.x, sB.y, sH2.x, sH2.y);
}
```

```
PVector pointToWindow(PVector p) {
    PVector t = p.get();
    t.x = map(t.x, -1, 1, 0, Window-1);
    t.y = map(t.y, -1, 1, 0, Window-1);
    return(t);
}

PVector makeControlPoint(float x, float dxlo, float dxhi,
                         float y, float dylo, float dyhi) {
    float px = x + random(dxlo, dxhi);
    float py = y + random(dylo, dyhi);
    PVector t = new PVector(px, py);
    return(t);
}
```

(See output in Figure 15.14. Full program in leaves/sketches/leaf12/leaf12.pde)

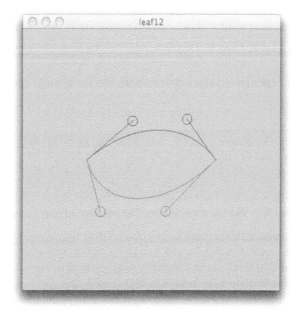

Figure 15.14. Leaf shapes with control points (frame from animation).
(leaves/sketches/leaf12/leaf12.pde)

There's a lot of stuff in drawOneLeaf() right now, but it's mostly for visualization and debugging. It's scaffolding while we build the tower, and I expect to dismantle it (that is, delete the code) before we're done.

Right now I'm tempted to write a `Leaf` class to help me organize this growing sprawl. But for the moment, anyway, I'll resist the impulse. It wouldn't save me much code, and I'm only dealing with one leaf at a time. But in the back of my mind, I'll keep the thought, in case it becomes more attractive later.

There's a lot of code here, and we're not yet accomplishing too much. That's also common while developing. You build up these big flexible structures and objects, anticipating what might be useful later. You keep things general and loose so you can easily manipulate the numbers and steps, making it easy to tune the results. And you accumulate lots of little debugging and visualization steps. I tend to let them stay in until the very end; you never know when you might want to go back and check or draw something again.

The results are pretty good, but not great. The leaves are much too fat for me. I want them to be thinner and more graceful. Maybe the solution is to bring the control points down closer to the middle of the leaf. I'll change the y value from 0.25 to 0.10 and see what happens:

```
PVector pG1 = makeControlPoint(-0.25, -0.15,  0.15, -0.10, -0.15, 0.0);
PVector pG2 = makeControlPoint( 0.25, -0.15,  0.15, -0.10, -0.15, 0.0);
PVector pH1 = makeControlPoint(-0.25, -0.15,  0.15,  0.10,  0.0, 0.15);
PVector pH2 = makeControlPoint( 0.25, -0.15,  0.15,  0.10,  0.0, 0.15);
```

Nope, not quite enough. I played around with this for a while and found that 0.05 looked good to me.

```
PVector pG1 = makeControlPoint(-0.25, -0.15,  0.15, -0.05, -0.15, 0.0);
PVector pG2 = makeControlPoint( 0.25, -0.15,  0.15, -0.05, -0.15, 0.0);
PVector pH1 = makeControlPoint(-0.25, -0.15,  0.15,  0.05,  0.0, 0.15);
PVector pH2 = makeControlPoint( 0.25, -0.15,  0.15,  0.05,  0.0, 0.15);
```

(See output in Figure 15.15. Full program in leaves/sketches/leaf13/leaf13.pde)

The leaves are indeed thinner and more graceful than they were, and the shapes are generally pleasing to me, but they're still lacking a certain something. I invite you to pause for a moment and think about whether you agree with me or not. If you think the leaves could use a little more zing, what would that zing be?

My answer to this is that the leaves need to bend! So far, the middle of each leaf is a straight line.

How to do that? There's no need to move the endpoints pA and pB because that will just rotate the entire leaf (which we'll do by the time we're done anyway). So let's try something with the control points.

When I think about how a leaf grows, it seems to me that it often starts out straight but then curves. How can we curve the leaf? Thinking back to some of our experiments with Bézier curves in Chapter 13, it seems reasonable that if we push some of the control points downward, say, then the curves will be pushed downward as well. Maybe

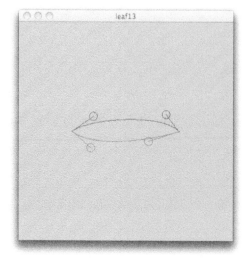

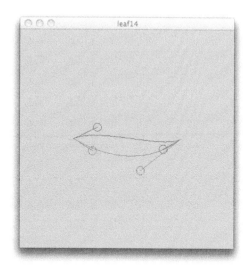

Figure 15.15. Leaf shapes with control points (frame from animation). (leaves/sketches/leaf13/leaf13.pde)

Figure 15.16. Making the leaf bend (frame from animation). (leaves/sketches/leaf14/leaf14.pde)

that'll look good. To try it, I'll manually move the right-most control points down by some amount. I don't know how much that amount should be, so let's try 0.15 and see if it looks encouraging. I'll put in these two lines just after the four calls to `makeControlPoint()`:

```
pG2.y += 0.15;
pH2.y += 0.15;
```

(See output in Figure 15.16. Full program in leaves/sketches/leaf14/leaf14.pde)

Oh, sweet! That's terrific. It's definitely a step in the right direction. I played around with these numbers for a while and decided that 0.35 was as high as I wanted to go. So let's add a random number from 0 to 0.35 to each y value:

```
pG2.y += random(0, 0.35);
pH2.y += random(0, 0.35);
```

(See output in Figure 15.17. Full program in leaves/sketches/leaf15/leaf15.pde)

Uh-oh. Not good. If you let this run for a while, you'll eventually see a leaf where the edges cross one another, as in Figure 15.17. In a moment, I'll invite you to think about this and try to figure out why.

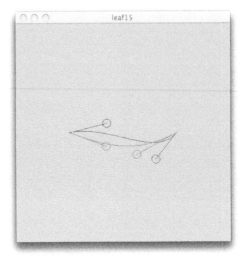

Figure 15.17. Ce n'est pas une feuille [this is not a leaf] (frame from animation). (leaves/sketches/leaf15/leaf15.pde)

A word of warning, though, and that's that my invitation is probably harder than it seems. When you're the one writing the program, you have a much clearer idea of what you're doing than if you're just watching someone else. So as soon as I saw these results I knew what was going wrong, but that's because this is my code that sprang from my mind only a minute ago, and I'm intimately familiar with it. Debugging your own code can be challenging; debugging someone else's code can be like solving a crime. So it's easy for me to tell you to find the error here, but if it's not coming to you, don't sweat it. When it's your own code that's going wrong, it'll be easier to fix (it will often still be a challenge, but it's a lot easier than fixing someone else's program).

So here's the invitation I promised: what's gone wrong in Figure 15.17?

Here's the problem. When the top point, pG2, moves a lot, it pulls the red curve downwards, but if the lower point, pH2, moves only a little, the green curve might not move much at all. The result is that the red curve crosses over the green one in a decidedly non-leaf-like fashion.

In the same spirit as before, when I asked you to figure out why this was going wrong, I'll invite you to pause and dream up a solution.

In general, when you're faced with this kind of a problem (the leaf doesn't look like we want it to), the road forks in front of you. One path is the path of *adjustment*: can you change the algorithm to make it work as you want? The other path is that of *novelty*, or *invention*: can you dream up a new, different algorithm that will get the job done?

Both paths are valid, and you'll take them each many times. Let's look at them one at a time.

The path of adjustment itself has two choices. You need to decide if the code is wrong (that is, there's a typo) or if the strategy needs a change (that is, your way of solving the problem itself has a problem). We saw the typo case earlier, when I realized I'd missed a decimal point in front of some coordinates, causing all my points to go offscreen; that was just a typing mistake. We saw the strategy-changing approach when I realized that the leaf didn't look right, and I decided to make it bend. That meant taking what I had written and making some changes. In that case, it was just adding a few lines to move the control points, but in a big system it can mean big changes, up to and including ripping out whole chunks of code and replacing them with entirely new stuff.

The path of invention is more daunting. When you choose that path, you're saying to yourself that the strategy you've been pursuing so far isn't worth following anymore. No matter what you do, the picture you're trying to make is never going to look right or move correctly, or the problem you're trying to solve is inherently insoluble by this general approach, or it's just become unwieldy or unattractive to you. So you take what you've learned from your experience so far, and you design a brand-new strategy. You might throw away a whole lot of existing code and start over, following a new plan. I haven't had to do that yet in this book, and you won't see much of it in other people's code. That's no surprise; people don't usually discuss their failures. With rare exceptions, painters don't exhibit the paintings that didn't work out, photographers don't show accidentally out-of-focus images, and songwriters don't play for you the songs that drift aimlessly without a point. But we all make failures. Lots of them. Failure is not only an option, it's a requirement of the creative process.

The tricky part, of course, is deciding when you've reached the point of no return and distinguishing a promising failure from a dead end. It can be very difficult emotionally to abandon a plan, because you might have sunk a lot of time and creative energy into something that just isn't working. Maybe it's not even the algorithm that isn't working, maybe it's the whole idea (for example, maybe after deciding I couldn't draw leaves well, I realized that the whole idea of drawing leaves on the forest floor was a lousy one). Nobody can make those decisions but you.

But lots of projects seem to reach a point where they just get stuck in a ditch, and no amount of pushing or pulling will get them out. Whether it's a routine, an algorithm, a project, or even a whole family of projects, it's important to know when to dig in and keep at it and when to let something go and move on.

The saving grace of this, and it's a big one, is that the process that brought you to that point has given you insights that will guide your next steps. By virtue of doing the work, you understand the problems better, you've created new ideas, and you've improved your craft. Successes are great, and they're what we share with the world for all the benefits that come from that sharing, but failures are important, too.

So, back to leaves and the red line crossing over the green one. I don't think I have to abandon the whole project because of this, and I don't think I even have to rethink my whole leaf-drawing approach. I have a theory that describes why this crossover is happening, and I can think of something that I think will fix it. To make sure that the red line can never move farther than the green one, I'll move the green curve at least as far as the red. Then the red line can never dip below the green one. The easiest way to achieve that is to move them both by the same amount:

```
float yMove = random(0, 0.35);
pG2.y += yMove;
pH2.y += yMove;
```

(See output in Figure 15.18. Full program in leaves/sketches/leaf16/leaf16.pde)

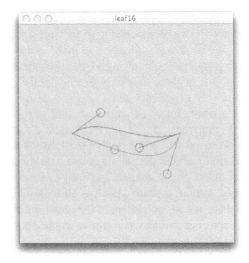

Figure 15.18. Fixing the overlap (frame from animation). (leaves/sketches/leaf16/leaf16.pde)

That does the trick nicely. Just for fun, what if we move the green control point by even more than the red? I'll pull the number 0.2 out of thin air and add an additional random amount from 0 to 0.2 to the green control point. Let's see what it does:

```
float yMove = random(0, 0.35);
pG2.y += yMove;
pH2.y += yMove + random(0, 0.2);
```

To my eye, this doesn't have much effect, except that sometimes the leaf gets fatter. Messing around with this for a while would surely give me a slightly different batch of leaves, but I don't think I'd see much difference. So I'll leave out that extra step. There's no reason to introduce any unnecessary complexity. The simpler the code, the faster it runs, and the easier it is to understand, get right the first time, and debug later if it does have a problem.

So now that I like the leaf shape, let's actually draw the thing. I'll get rid of the code that draws the control points (but I'll save this version of the program in case I want it later). How can I make one shape out of these two Bézier curves?

What if we fill them? I'll just change the call to `stroke()` to a call to `fill()`. I'll also include a call to `noStroke()` just before the curves and one to `noFill()` just after, so the curves don't get lines and the little circles don't get filled in.

```
noStroke();
fill(196, 66, 63);  // red
bezier(sA.x, sA.y, sG1.x, sG1.y, sG2.x, sG2.y, sB.x, sB.y);
fill(64, 135, 36);  // green
bezier(sA.x, sA.y, sH1.x, sH1.y, sH2.x, sH2.y, sB.x, sB.y);
```

(See output in Figure 15.19. Full program in leaves/sketches/leaf17/leaf17.pde)

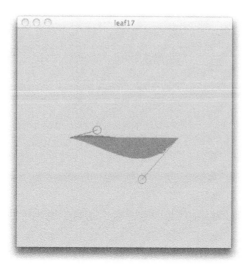

Figure 15.19. Filling the leaf (frame from animation). (leaves/sketches/leaf17/leaf17.pde)

Close, but no cigar. The fill joins up the two endpoints as well as the curve. When the upper curve dips below the bottom of the midline, that graceful bend gets crushed by the horizonal line of the fill from the bottom curve.

The answer is to use the `beginShape()`/`endShape()` approach, so we create one large curve out of the two smaller curves. We'll use `bezierVertex()` to build up the big curve. Remember that we need to start with a single call to `vertex()` to get the process going.

So let's give it a whirl. I'll replace the whole group of leaf-drawing lines (from the `noStroke()` to the `noFill()` we just added, including both of those calls) with this:

```
fill(64, 135, 36);   // green
beginShape();
vertex(sA.x, sA.y);
bezierVertex(sG1.x, sG1.y, sG2.x, sG2.y, sB.x, sB.y);
bezierVertex(sH1.x, sH1.y, sH2.x, sH2.y, sB.x, sB.y);
endShape();
noFill();
```

(See output in Figure 15.20. Full program in leaves/sketches/leaf18/leaf18.pde)

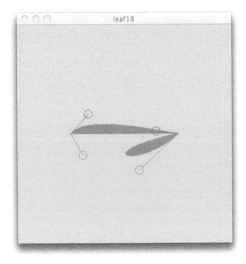

Figure 15.20. Filling the leaf (frame from animation). (leaves/sketches/leaf18/leaf18.pde)

Something has gone horribly wrong! Actually, I kind of like this image (and the others that are produced as this runs), but it's not what I'm after.

The problem is in the second call to bezierVertex(). When I drew the two curves, I drew them both left to right. So to make the first call to bezierVertex(), I just handled the first point manually with vertex(), and then I passed bezierVertex() the remaining three points. Then I made a copy-and-paste error and did to the second line what I did to the first, deleting the first point.

What we're trying to do is make a loop. Going clockwise, the first full curve is (sA, sG1, sG2, sB). The second curve, continuing on from sB and working our way back to sA, is (sB, sH2, sH1, sA). So that's what we need to give to the second bezierVertex() call (though we can leave off the first sB, since that's where the previous curve ended). So let's fix that second call to bezierVertex():

```
fill(64, 135, 36);   // green
beginShape();
```

```
vertex(sA.x, sA.y);
bezierVertex(sG1.x, sG1.y, sG2.x, sG2.y, sB.x, sB.y);
bezierVertex(sH2.x, sH2.y, sH1.x, sH1.y, sA.x, sA.y);
endShape();
```

(See output in Figure 15.21. Full program in leaves/sketches/leaf19/leaf19.pde)

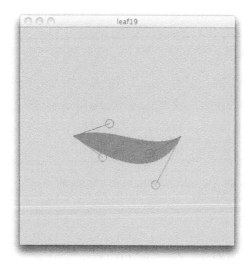

Figure 15.21. Filling the leaf (frame from animation). (leaves/sketches/leaf19/leaf19.pde)

Loverly.

It's hard to tell, but the leaf has a green outline. That's because the last thing we do to the stroke in `drawOneLeaf()` is to set the stroke color to green. When we reenter the routine, the graphics state is just where we left it, so the leaf gets a green stroke. That probably is thickening it up ever so slightly. We can certainly turn that off if we want.

So let's do a couple of things now. I'll turn off the stroke, and I'll pick a random color for each leaf. Right now I'll be entirely carefree about colors, so I'll just roll up three random numbers and make a color out of them.

This code will replace the `fill()` statement:

```
int myRed = int(random(50, 255));
int myGrn = int(random(50, 255));
int myBlu = int(random(50, 255));
fill(color(myRed, myGrn, myBlu));
noStroke();
```

(See output in Figure 15.22. Full program in leaves/sketches/leaf20/leaf20.pde)

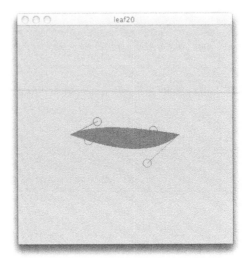

Figure 15.22. Changing the leaf colors (frame from animation).
(leaves/sketches/leaf20/leaf20.pde)

Beautiful. Well, beautiful in function; I'll definitely have to come back to the colors later. Now let's let the leaves pile up. I'll change the fill color to be 50 percent transparent:

```
fill(color(myRed, myGrn, myBlu, 128));
```

And I'll stop calling `background()` on every `draw()`. I'll also remove the code that draws the control points and the lines to them. Now that I think I'm drawing what I want, I'll get rid of the stroke and fill commands in `drawOneLeaf()` and put just a single `noStroke()` into `setup()`. I'll comment out the call to `frameRate()` since I don't want it now but might want it again later. With those changes, here's the complete program now:

```
// Fall leaves project
// version 0.1, Andrew, 16 April 2009
//

// dimensions of the square drawing area
int Window = 400;

void setup() {
    size(Window, Window);
    background(200, 190, 143);
```

```
   noFill();
   frameRate(1);
}

void draw() {
   background(200, 190, 143);
   drawOneLeaf();
}

void drawOneLeaf() {
   PVector pA = new PVector(-0.5, 0.0);  // left end
   PVector pB = new PVector( 0.5, 0.0);  // right end

   PVector pG1 = makeControlPoint(-0.25, -0.15,  0.15, -0.05, -0.15, 0.0);
   PVector pG2 = makeControlPoint( 0.25, -0.15,  0.15, -0.05, -0.15, 0.0);
   PVector pH1 = makeControlPoint(-0.25, -0.15,  0.15,  0.05,  0.0, 0.15);
   PVector pH2 = makeControlPoint( 0.25, -0.15,  0.15,  0.05,  0.0, 0.15);

   float yMove = random(0, 0.35);
   pG2.y += yMove;
   pH2.y += yMove;

   PVector sA = pointToWindow(pA);
   PVector sB = pointToWindow(pB);
   PVector sG1 = pointToWindow(pG1);
   PVector sG2 = pointToWindow(pG2);
   PVector sH1 = pointToWindow(pH1);
   PVector sH2 = pointToWindow(pH2);

   int myRed = int(random(50, 255));
   int myGrn = int(random(50, 255));
   int myBlu = int(random(50, 255));
   fill(color(myRed, myGrn, myBlu));
   noStroke();

   beginShape();
   vertex(sA.x, sA.y);
   bezierVertex(sG1.x, sG1.y, sG2.x, sG2.y, sB.x, sB.y);
   bezierVertex(sH2.x, sH2.y, sH1.x, sH1.y, sA.x, sA.y);
   endShape();
}

PVector pointToWindow(PVector p) {
   PVector t = p.get();
   t.x = map(t.x, -1, 1, 0, Window-1);
   t.y = map(t.y, -1, 1, 0, Window-1);
```

```
      return(t);
}

PVector makeControlPoint(float x, float dxlo, float dxhi,
                         float y, float dylo, float dyhi) {
   float px = x + random(dxlo, dxhi);
   float py = y + random(dylo, dyhi);
   PVector t = new PVector(px, py);
   return(t);
}
```

(See output in Figure 15.23. Full program in leaves/sketches/leaf21/leaf21.pde)

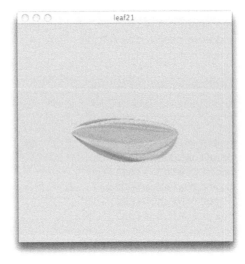

Figure 15.23. Stacking up leaves (frame from animation). (leaves/sketches/leaf21/leaf21.pde)

So far, so good. The colors definitely need attention, but I'll get to that later.

I am ever-so-slightly bothered by the fact that every leaf is the same size, in the same place, and at the same orientation. That doesn't really look like a forest floor as much as a stack. A perfectly vertical stack of identically sized leaves. That's not really the feeling I was going for!

Let's start with size. Right now, the leaf is half the width of the window. How much bigger can it go and still look good?

My first impulse is to use one of Processing's built-in transforms. So just before the call to beginShape(), I'll add

```
scale(2.0);
```

(See output in Figure 15.24. Full program in leaves/sketches/leaf22/leaf22.pde)

Figure 15.24. Making the leaves larger... and wronger (frame from animation).
(leaves/sketches/leaf22/leaf22.pde)

The leaves got bigger as I'd hoped, but they also went offscreen. That makes sense, as the origin of Processing's graphics window (not my little $(-1,-1)$ to $(1,1)$ world) is in the upper-left. By the time we draw the leaf, we're using the s version of the coordinates, which are all in screen coordinates. So if a point of the leaf is at, say, $(400, 300)$, then this scales it up to $(800, 600)$ which is way offscreen. In other words, the world is being scaled around the upper left, not around the middle.

Oh man. This is starting to look complicated. We'll need to move the coordinate system to the middle of the screen, change the coordinates on the leaf so that the origin of the leaf is at (0,0), then apply the scale, and probably we'll want to remember to push the matrix first and then pop it, and ...

Wait a second. We have the coordinates of the leaf with (0,0) in the middle. Those are the coordinates we computed first; they're the ones with the p at the start of the name. If we move the coordinate system to the middle of the screen and then draw those coordinates, we'd get a leaf one pixel large. But if we apply a scale first, we'll get a leaf as large as we want! In fact, if we scale by `Window/2`, we should get the very same results we were just getting before.

Let's try that out. Here's my replacement for the `beginShape()` / `endShape()` block. Remember that all transformations, like `scale()`, have to appear *outside* of the lines enclosed by `beginShape()` and `endShape()`.

```
translate(Window/2, Window/2);
scale(Window/2);
beginShape();
```

```
vertex(pA.x, pA.y);
bezierVertex(pG1.x, pG1.y, pG2.x, pG2.y, pB.x, pB.y);
bezierVertex(pH2.x, pH2.y, pH1.x, pH1.y, pA.x, pA.y);
endShape();
```

(See output in Figure 15.25. Full program in leaves/sketches/leaf23/leaf23.pde)

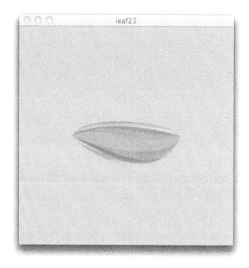

Figure 15.25. Correctly-scaled leaves (frame from animation).
(leaves/sketches/leaf23/leaf23.pde)

The result looks just like the previous version. All I did was add the `translate()` and `scale()` calls and then replace all the s variables (the ones that we computed in screen coordinates) with the original p variables.

This means we can delete all the lines that computed the s versions of the points (since we don't need them anymore), and we can delete the whole `pointToWindow()` function, because we don't need that anymore, either. The new program is a whole bunch shorter than the old one!

I want to take a moment here to stop and enjoy the moment.

This is one of the sweetest things that can happen when writing software. We added a little bit of code, cut a lot more, and the result is a cleaner, clearer, better program. We made the program better by throwing away some of our hard-earned code. That is a really, really good thing.

Making a program better by making it smaller doesn't happen that often, and it's almost always a surprise. But it's always a good surprise. Of course, you can cheat and make a program smaller by smushing together calculations and other things, making each line a dense, little, impenetrable nugget. But that's not at all what we did here. We simply realized that with a little change to our point of view, a lot of work we thought we had to do suddenly went away. We didn't have to compute screen coordinates for all the points, so we didn't need those variables, so we didn't need those lines, and we didn't need that function. Using Processing's built-in transformation routines on the values we already had accomplished the same goal.

Better yet, we know that we can accumulate some more transforms the same way, so we'll be able to move and rotate the leaf pretty easily, too. Very sweet.

I love it when this happens. It's like someone showing up unannounced and giving you a present. The moment when you make a change and realize, "Hey! This means I can cut out a whole lot of code!" is a moment to stop and savor.

By the way, you might be thinking that I'm only feeling so smart now because I was so dumb before. If I'd only used the coordinates this way from the start, I wouldn't have done it the wrong way first.

Yup, that's true.

But I can't see the future, and as I wrote this code, I was making the best choices I could based on what seemed reasonable at the time. Programming is discovery. After exploring the land, we found a beautiful clear pass through the mountains that we otherwise had to climb. If we'd been lucky we'd have found the pass on our first visit to the mountains, but generally, you find the best route only after you've surveyed the area. In other words, we earned this accomplishment!

So here's our shorter, cleaner, better program in its full listing:

```
// Fall leaves project
// version 0.1, Andrew, 16 April 2009
//

// dimensions of the square drawing area
int Window = 400;

void setup() {
   size(Window, Window);
   background(200, 190, 143);
   noStroke();
   //frameRate(1);
}

void draw() {
   //background(200, 190, 143);
   drawOneLeaf();
}

void drawOneLeaf() {
   PVector pA = new PVector(-0.5, 0.0);   // left end
   PVector pB = new PVector( 0.5, 0.0);   // right end
```

```
    PVector pG1 = makeControlPoint(-0.25, -0.15,  0.15, -0.05, -0.15, 0.0);
    PVector pG2 = makeControlPoint( 0.25, -0.15,  0.15, -0.05, -0.15, 0.0);
    PVector pH1 = makeControlPoint(-0.25, -0.15,  0.15,  0.05,  0.0, 0.15);
    PVector pH2 = makeControlPoint( 0.25, -0.15,  0.15,  0.05,  0.0, 0.15);

    float yMove = random(0, 0.35);
    pG2.y += yMove;
    pH2.y += yMove;

    int myRed = int(random(50, 255));
    int myGrn = int(random(50, 255));
    int myBlu = int(random(50, 255));
    fill(color(myRed, myGrn, myBlu, 128));

    translate(Window/2, Window/2);
    scale(Window/2);
    beginShape();
    vertex(pA.x, pA.y);
    bezierVertex(pG1.x, pG1.y, pG2.x, pG2.y, pB.x, pB.y);
    bezierVertex(pH2.x, pH2.y, pH1.x, pH1.y, pA.x, pA.y);
    endShape();
}

PVector makeControlPoint(float x, float dxlo, float dxhi,
                         float y, float dylo, float dyhi) {
    float px = x + random(dxlo, dxhi);
    float py = y + random(dylo, dyhi);
    PVector t = new PVector(px, py);
    return(t);
}
```

(Full program in leaves/sketches/leaf24/leaf24.pde)

I'm very happy with this. Now we can play around with that scale() statement. How big should the leaves get? I first made the leaves 25 percent larger. Since I already have a statement to scale by Window/2, I'll just multiply that value by 1.25:

```
scale(1.25*Window/2);
```

Then I changed this number for a while. I finally decided that to my eye, the original size was just about right; half the screen is about as big as a leaf should get.

Now how about making them smaller? I started with

```
scale(0.25*Window/2);
```

so each leaf was a quarter of the original size. Too small. To my eye, about 0.6 was the right spot. So now I know how big the leaves are: between 60 and 100 percent of the original size. So that means the scale factor should be a random number between 0.6 and 1. Rolling that together with the Window based scaling gives us:

```
float scaleFactor = random(0.6, 1.0);
scale(scaleFactor*Window/2);
```

(See output in Figure 15.26. Full program in leaves/sketches/leaf25/leaf25.pde)

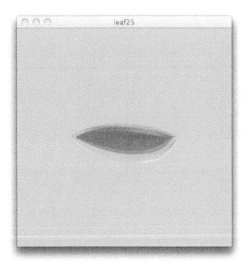

Figure 15.26. Randomly scaled leaves (frame from animation).
(leaves/sketches/leaf25/leaf25.pde)

Trying this out, I like the results. I can always come back and tweak these numbers later if I want the final leaves a little bigger or smaller.

Now let's rotate them. I'd like them to rotate randomly through a full circle. So I'll get a random number of degrees from 0 to 360 and rotate by that (though I'll convert that to radians, of course, when I hand it to `rotate()`):

```
float rotationAngle = random(0, 360);
rotate(radians(rotationAngle));
```

(See output in Figure 15.27. Full program in leaves/sketches/leaf26/leaf26.pde)

This comes right after `scale()`. It could probably go before it, too, but conceptually, I'm thinking of this in the order that we scale the leaf, then rotate it.

Lastly, I need to translate the leaf to a random point on the screen. My first thought is to translate the leaf so the whole thing can land, at the farthest, just barely offscreen. That means a few leaves won't get drawn at all, but it also means that some leaves will just barely show up, maybe poking just an edge or a tip into the picture. I think that'll give the final image a nice feeling, as though it really was just a window of a much larger section of forest floor.

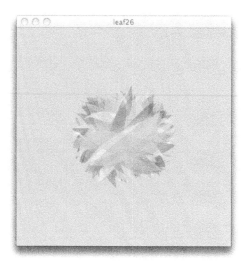

Figure 15.27. Adding rotation (frame from animation). (leaves/sketches/leaf26/leaf26.pde)

Where should the translate() call go? Before the scale(), between the scale() and rotate(), or after the rotate()?

Let's first think about putting it before the scale(). Before the scale() happens, the coordinate system has the default starting size, where one unit means one pixel on the screen. At this point we've already put the origin of the coordinate system in the screen's center. So if we translate to the right by Window/2, that will put us on top of the right side of the window. Let's try that:

```
float xTrans = Window/2.0;
float yTrans = 0.0;
translate(xTrans, yTrans);
```

(See output in Figure 15.28. Full program in leaves/sketches/leaf27/leaf27.pde)

Similarly, moving that much in *y* will put us on the bottom of the window. If we move by -Window/2 in *x*, we'll be at the left side of the window, and -Window/2 in *y* will put us at the top of the window.

The leaf itself is, at the largest, Window/2 units wide by the time it gets drawn. So if I want to move it just barely offscreen to the right, I could push it right by Window units. Then it won't show up at all.

But anything less than that and it might just show a little edge or point (if the leaf is rotated vertically, then it probably still won't show up at all). So let's try moving the leaf somewhere between just off the left side of the window and just off the right side:

```
float xTrans = random(-Window, Window);
```

(See output in Figure 15.29. Full program in leaves/sketches/leaf28/leaf28.pde)

Figure 15.28. First version of translation (frame from animation). (leaves/sketches/leaf27/leaf27.pde)

Figure 15.29. Placing the leaf horizontally (frame from animation). (leaves/sketches/leaf28/leaf28.pde)

That does it. Some of the leaves are surely going offscreen, but most are showing up at least a little bit. Of course, we can do the same thing for *y*. And since the window is square, it's got the same values:

```
float yTrans = random(-Window, Window);
```

(See output in Figure 15.30. Full program in leaves/sketches/leaf29/leaf29.pde)

Figure 15.30. Placing the leaf vertically as well (frame from animation). (leaves/sketches/leaf29/leaf29.pde)

Now we're getting somewhere. Just out of curiosity, what if we put the call `translate()` after the scale, but before the rotation?

Once `scale()` has been called, the coordinate system we're drawing in has been resized; x still points right and y points down, but now moving one unit in x no longer moves us one pixel on the screen. In fact, moving one unit in x now corresponds to `(scaleFactor*Window/2)` units on the screen. So if we want to move `Window` units to the right, we have to do a little algebra. In the following equation, we have to solve for `g` (the letter g has no meaning here; I just wanted something very short that we haven't used yet):

```
g * scaleFactor * Window/2 = Window
```

Some math shows `g = 2/scaleFactor`. If this isn't your cup of tea, don't worry about it: my only reason for looking into how we'd put the `translate()` after the `scale()` is to show how messy it becomes! Anyway, now that we've done the math, let's use it:

```
float scaleFactor = random(0.6, 1.0);
scale(scaleFactor*Window/2);

float g = 2.0/scaleFactor;
float xTrans = random(-g, g);
float yTrans = random(-g, g);
translate(xTrans, yTrans);

float rotationAngle = random(0, 360);
rotate(radians(rotationAngle));
```

(See output in Figure 15.31. Full program in leaves/sketches/leaf30/leaf30.pde)

The results are the same, but this code is not as nice as before. We have this extra `g` variable floating around, which is no bonus. And now it's a little unclear how we'd adjust things if we wanted to move them around later.

Finally, putting the `translate()` after the `rotate()` just means using the same values as above. That's because we already have the origin in the middle of the screen. So `rotate()` will rotate the whole system around the middle of the screen. When we move the leaf in x and y it'll probably go in some crazy directions relative to the screen, but it'll move towards (and off) the window:

```
float scaleFactor = random(0.6, 1.0);
scale(scaleFactor*Window/2);

float rotationAngle = random(0, 360);
rotate(radians(rotationAngle));

float g = 2.0/scaleFactor;
float xTrans = random(-g, g);
```

Figure 15.31. Translating after scaling but before rotating (frame from animation). (leaves/sketches/leaf30/leaf30.pde)

Figure 15.32. Translating after scaling and rotating (frame from animation). (leaves/sketches/leaf31/leaf31.pde)

```
float yTrans = random(-g, g);
translate(xTrans, yTrans);
```

(See output in Figure 15.32. Full program in leaves/sketches/leaf31/leaf31.pde)

When all is said and done, I like the first version best. We avoid the need for thinking about and computing the messy g variable, and it's easier to understand, too.

Now that we have the general program running, let's do some housekeeping. I should probably change the forest floor to some brown dirt color. A little enjoyable time with a color picker led me to (71, 25, 20). I'll also take out the frameRate() call to speed things up , and I'll remove the noFill() from setup() because it's redundant now that we're setting the fill color of each leaf manually. Finally, I'll change scaleFactor so that the leaves can get a little smaller; now that I'm looking at the results, I think they should be able to scale down a little more, let's say 0.5 rather than 0.6.

One little thing has been bugging me for a while. The left part of the leaf is symmetrical, while the right part gets pushed downwards by a random amount. Even after we rotate the leaves, they all have this same clockwise kind of bend.

I don't know if it'll show, but let's bend the leaves up the other way sometimes. Right now, the code to move the right control points looks like this:

```
// move the H control points so that the leaf bends
float yMove = random(0, 0.35);
```

Figure 15.33. Leaves that curve both ways (frame from animation)
(leaves/sketches/leaf32/leaf32.pde)

```
pG2.y += yMove;
pH2.y += yMove;
```

(See output in Figure 15.33. Full program in leaves/sketches/leaf32/leaf32.pde)

If all we want is to move them up or down equally, we can just change the range to include negative numbers as well:

```
float yMove = random(-0.35, 0.35);
```

But for fun, let's say that we want most of the leaves to curl clockwise, say 80 percent of them. Only 20 percent of the adjusted control points will get pushed up rather than down. How can we accomplish that? Here are a bunch of approaches.

First, we could use an *if statement* and a random number:

```
if (random(100) > 80) {
   // move points up
   pG2.y -= yMove;
   pH2.y -= yMove;
} else {
   // move points down
```

```
    pG2.y += yMove;
    pH2.y += yMove;
}
```

Another common trick is to multiply yMove by a variable that is either 1 or −1:

```
float yDir = 1;
if (random(100) > 80) {
    yDir = -1;
}
pG2.y += yMove * yDir;
pH2.y += yMove * yDir;
```

This works, too. This form can be an advantage if figuring out which choice you want is a big or complex process, but you can boil down the result to a single number.

These methods are fine, but we can do it another way, too, and you'll see this technique used all the time. Notice that in one case we're subtracting yMove from the two variables, and in the other case we're adding it in. Let's make this easier and always add in yMove, but we'll make it negative sometimes first:

```
if (random(100) > 80) {
    yMove = -yMove;
}
```

Figure 15.34. Leaves that curve unequally (frame from animation)
(leaves/sketches/leaf33/leaf33.pde)

```
pG2.y += yMove;
pH2.y += yMove;
```

(See output in Figure 15.34. Full program in leaves/sketches/leaf33/leaf33.pde)

That also does the job, and that's how I'll do it.

You have to decide for yourself whether these subtleties are worth your time and effort. I think they are because they make the results look a little more pleasing to my eye.

Let's finally do something about the colors. The easiest way to dig in is to split off the color computation into its own routine. Consider these four lines:

```
int myRed = int(random(50, 255));
int myGrn = int(random(50, 255));
int myBlu = int(random(50, 255));
fill(color(myRed, myGrn, myBlu, 128));
```

I'll replace them with a single call to make a color.

```
color leafColor = makeLeafColor();
fill(leafColor);
```

Then the new routine makeLeafColor() can start out with the old code, and as far as the image appears, we're right back where we started:

```
color makeLeafColor() {
    int myRed = int(random(50, 255));
    int myGrn = int(random(50, 255));
    int myBlu = int(random(50, 255));
    color clr = color(myRed, myGrn, myBlu, 128);
    return(clr);
}
```

(See output in Figure 15.35. Full program in leaves/sketches/leaf34/leaf34.pde)

That's good; it still works. How can we create more leaflike colors?

You might have fun picking things up for yourself at this point. Change the routine makeLeafColor() until the leaves have colors that satisfy your artistic feelings and then make any other changes to the code that you think might create interesting results.

Here's my solution. I searched on the web for pictures of fall leaves, and I found a couple of nice photographs. I then wrote a little program (in Processing, of course, since that's where my head is right now) to look through the pictures and report back to me the 40 most popular colors (I did this by printing out the color values and also drawing a window with a grid of the colors in it). We'll see how to read in an image and examine the colors of its pixels in Chapter 16.

This worked great, but almost all of the colors were slight variations on red. So I changed the algorithm a little to chunk together similar colors in a very rough way,

Figure 15.35. Splitting off the color calculation (frame from animation)
(leaves/sketches/leaf34/leaf34.pde)

and the results were better. Here are the top 40 colors that I picked out by hand from
the results from a couple of photographs (you'll see that the numbers are rounded to
multiples of 16, which is a result of that chunking step):

```
int [] LeafRGB = {
  117,  48,   0,     32,  16,   0,     80,  32,   0,    144,  64,   0,
  128,  48,   0,     80,  16,   0,     48,  32,  16,    144,  80,   0,
   32,  32,   0,    160,  96,   0,    176,  80,   0,     48,  16,   0,
  192, 112,   0,     64,  64,   0,     16,  48,   0,     80,  80,  64,
  224, 160,   0,     48,  64,  32,     32,  80,  32,    176,  48,   0,
  224, 144,  64,     80, 128,  32,    144, 112,  48,    240, 208,   0,
  240, 176,  64,    224, 144,   0,    224, 144,  32,    192, 112,  64,
  208,  16,   0,    240,  80,   0,    224,  48,   0,    240, 224,   0,
  240, 112,  16,    224,  64,   0,     64,  80,  16,    176,  16,   0,
   48,   0,   0,     64,  16,   0,     80, 128,   0,     96,  32,   0
};
```

There's not a lot of blue in there, but that's how fall leaves are.

Figure 15.36. Leaves in fall colors (frame from animation). (leaves/sketches/leaf35/leaf35.pde)

Now that we have a list of RGB values, picking a color is easy. How many colors are in the array? That's just the length of the array divided by three. So we pick a random number in that range, and then use that number to grab the three RGB values that correspond to it, and from them make a color:

```
color makeLeafColor() {
    int w = int(random(LeafRGB.length/3));
    color clr = color(LeafRGB[w*3], LeafRGB[1+(w*3)],
        LeafRGB[2+(w*3)]);
    return clr;
}
```

(See output in Figure 15.36. Full program in leaves/sketches/leaf35/leaf35.pde)

That's more like fall to me. Now let's vary the transparency a little bit. Rather than have every leaf be 50 percent opaque (with an alpha of 128), let's make it anywhere from 25 percent (that is, alpha is 64) to 75 percent (that is, alpha is 192). I'll tack that on to the end of makeLeafColor():

Figure 15.37. Leaves in fall colors (frame from animation). (leaves/sketches/leaf36/leaf36.pde)

```
color makeLeafColor() {
    int w = int(random(LeafRGB.length/3));
    color clr = color(LeafRGB[w*3], LeafRGB[1+(w*3)], LeafRGB[2+(w*3)],
                      random(64, 192));
    return clr;
}
```

(See output in Figure 15.37. Full program in leaves/sketches/leaf36/leaf36.pde)

That's better.

One last thing is that I'll change the background color to a dirty brown. It will eventually get covered up by the leaves, but when the program is just starting it'll look a little nicer.

```
// Fall leaves project
// version 1.0, Andrew, 16 April 2009

// dimensions of the square drawing area
int Window = 400;
```

```
void setup() {
   size(Window, Window);
   background(82, 52, 12);
   noStroke();
   //frameRate(1);
}

void draw() {
   //background(200, 190, 143);
   drawOneLeaf();
}

void drawOneLeaf() {
   PVector pA = new PVector(-0.5, 0.0);  // left end
   PVector pB = new PVector( 0.5, 0.0);  // right end

   PVector pG1 = makeControlPoint(-0.25, -0.15,  0.15, -0.05, -0.15, 0.0);
   PVector pG2 = makeControlPoint( 0.25, -0.15,  0.15, -0.05, -0.15, 0.0);
   PVector pH1 = makeControlPoint(-0.25, -0.15,  0.15,  0.05,  0.0, 0.15);
   PVector pH2 = makeControlPoint( 0.25, -0.15,  0.15,  0.05,  0.0, 0.15);

   // move the H control points so that the leaf bends
   float yMove = random(0, 0.35);
   if (random(100) > 80) {
      yMove = -yMove;
   }
   pG2.y += yMove;
   pH2.y += yMove;

   color leafColor = makeLeafColor();
   fill(leafColor);

   translate(Window/2, Window/2);

   float xTrans = random(-Window, Window);
   float yTrans = random(-Window, Window);
   translate(xTrans, yTrans);

   float scaleFactor = random(0.6, 1.0);
   scale(scaleFactor*Window/2);
   float rotationAngle = random(0, 360);
   rotate(radians(rotationAngle));

   beginShape();
   vertex(pA.x, pA.y);
   bezierVertex(pG1.x, pG1.y, pG2.x, pG2.y, pB.x, pB.y);
   bezierVertex(pH2.x, pH2.y, pH1.x, pH1.y, pA.x, pA.y);
   endShape();
```

Figure 15.38. The final project!

```
PVector makeControlPoint(float x, float dxlo, float dxhi,
                         float y, float dylo, float dyhi) {
  float px = x + random(dxlo, dxhi);
  float py = y + random(dylo, dyhi);
  PVector t = new PVector(px, py);
  return(t);
}

int [] LeafRGB = {
  117,  48,   0,      32,  16,   0,      80,  32,   0,     144,  64,   0,
  128,  48,   0,      80,  16,   0,      48,  32,  16,     144,  80,   0,
   32,  32,   0,     160,  96,   0,     176,  80,   0,      48,  16,   0,
  192, 112,   0,      64,  64,   0,      16,  48,   0,      80,  80,  64,
  224, 160,   0,      48,  64,  32,      32,  80,  32,     176,  48,   0,
  224, 144,  64,      80, 128,  32,     144, 112,  48,     240, 208,   0,
  240, 176,  64,     224, 144,   0,     224, 144,  32,     192, 112,  64,
  208,  16,   0,     240,  80,   0,     224,  48,   0,     240, 224,   0,
  240, 112,  16,     224,  64,   0,      64,  80,  16,     176,  16,   0,
   48,   0,   0,      64,  16,   0,      80, 128,   0,      96,  32,   0
};
```

```
color makeLeafColor() {
    int w = int(random(LeafRGB.length/3));
    color clr = color(LeafRGB[w*3], LeafRGB[1+(w*3)],
                      LeafRGB[2+(w*3)], random(64, 192));
    return clr;
}
```

(See output in Figure 15.38. Full program in leaves/sketches/leaf37/leaf37.pde)

You can remove the ragged edges on the leaves by adding a call to smooth() inside of setup().

We've finished the project! That's always a nice moment.

15.4   More Fun with Leaves

That big list of colors satisfies me because I picked them by hand, and I like them all. But suppose that you want to make a picture with more reds or weaker yellows? If you stuck with a list like this, you'd have to manually pick all those colors, and assembling a list that was just right might take a long time. Is there an algorithmic way to get to the same result? That is, can you replace this array, and the code in makeLeafColor(), with a routine that generates random colors that are like the ones in the table?

How about a routine that lets you somehow communicate an overall theme to the colors (you'll have to invent what a "color theme" means to you, and then how to describe it, and then how to realize it in code)? Are there other ways to create the colors of the leaves that produce images that appeal to you?

Here's one example of algorithmic coloring. I've just shoehorned this into the code rather gracelessly, but it shows you the effect. I'll compute the color of the leaf based on its position: near the middle of the screen leaves are mostly red, towards the edge they're mostly yellow, and they blend along the way. Of course, there's some randomness in there to keep things from looking too neat. This block of code sits just in front of beginShape():

```
float tdist = mag(xTrans, yTrans);     // distance of point to window center
float ddist = mag(Window/2, Window/2); // distance from window center to a
                                       // corner
float td = tdist/ddist;                // how far we are from the center
int rVal = int(random(200, 255));      // random red
int gVal = int(random(-40, 40)) + int(td * 215);  // more green with distance
int bVal = int(random(0, 80));         // random blue
leafColor = color(rVal, gVal, bVal);   // create the color
fill(leafColor);                       // use the color for filling the leaf
```

(See output in Figure 15.39. Full program in leaves/sketches/leaf38/leaf38.pde)

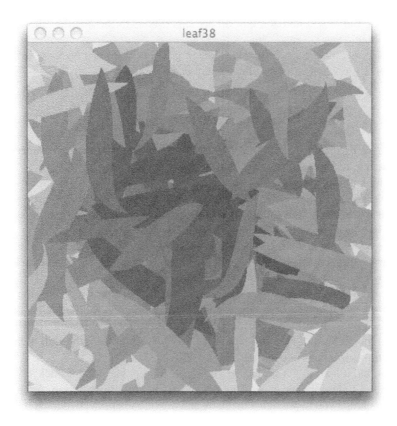

Figure 15.39. Color based on position (frame from animation).
(leaves/sketches/leaf38/leaf38.pde)

Returning to the shapes, do these leaves satisfy your notion of "leaf"? If not, change them in small or large ways until they look like leaves to you.

I mentioned creating a `Leaf` object while building up this project, but I didn't follow up on that idea. So give it a shot and write a version of this project that uses such an object. Here's a hint: you might want to put the forest floor into a class as well, so that `draw()` simply tells the forest floor to update itself. Once you have those classes in place, does it stimulate any new ideas about other things you can add to them to play around with this project?

When you're learning something, messing around is almost always a good idea. When you're thinking of something to share with other people, consider whether maybe less might be more and keep only the elements of the work that really communicate your ideas. If you think the forest floor needs worms, squirrels, birds, shafts of sunlight, and stuff like that, put them in! If after you try them out they really spin your sockets, keep them there. But if you find some or all are superfluous to the mood or the idea, take them back out.

Developing creative works involves lots of going forward and backward. Don't let it bug you. Even when you take things out, that's progress.

15.5 Pointillism Leaves

The leaves in Figure 15.38 look fine, but I'd like them to have a more gossamer quality. I want them to feel just a little different, a little more abstract.

I'm thinking dots. Points. I don't know exactly why; maybe it's the mist from my neighbor's lawn sprinkler, maybe it's another Processing project where I saw someone use points, but something is telling me that these leaves are going to look better if I use points. That's my hunch, anyway, so I'm going to follow through on it.

I'll go about this in a slightly different way than before. Instead of building up the code step-by-step from a skeleton to a final version, I'm going to give you a chance to do it all by yourself.

First, I'll describe the goal in a very general sense. I encourage you to stop reading at that point, and think about how you might write a program to accomplish that idea. You might want to try some little experiments, or you might be able to plan it all in your head. But give it a shot! This will be a great way for you to learn the skill of taking an idea and transforming it into a program.

If you find it hard to get started, or you reach an impasse and get stuck, come back to the book. I'll describe the general approach that I used for my solution. Again, at that point I encourage you to put down the book and dig into the project yourself, taking my approach (or one of your own) and writing the code.

If that doesn't work out, don't get upset, because making that transition from mental picture to running code is hard stuff. So I'll then give you my code, accompanied by a *walkthrough*, where we step through the listing together and I comment on what's going on, and why.

When we're finished, I'll suggest another goal. The approach will be the same as before: I suggest you try it yourself. If you have problems, there's an overview and then a walk-through with code showing you my solution.

One reason I'm doing things this way is that these goals will present you with a pretty tough design challenge. I'm not talking about the programming part. If you've been working through some of the smaller projects I've discussed, or some of your own, you have more than enough Processing knowledge and programming experience to do these. The challenge here is design: coming up with an approach that runs reasonably fast and looks good to your eye.

I went through at least a dozen different solutions myself, trying all kinds of things until I found something I liked.

And that's another reason for this approach: this project is a lot of fun! Each different design solution you come up with will take you in a new direction, and it will inspire a bunch of other solutions. Even bugs and accidents along the way can look really nice, maybe even better than the final result.

So I encourage you to give this a go. If you don't have your Processing sea legs yet, you'll get them pretty quickly. And if you stick with it, I predict you'll start to have a good time. There's no rush.

When I have a problem puttering away in my mind, often I'll be standing in line at the supermarket or walking somewhere and a great new idea will hit me; it's easy and simple and I just *know* this one's gonna work! I'll scribble it down on a piece of paper and implement it when I get home. And once in a while, it really does work! The rest of the time I try it, and even if it has a problem, I learn something new anyway.

So give it a shot. If you have trouble, read the description of my solution. If you still have trouble, read the walkthrough. And ultimately, of course, I'll provide my code.

The project here is really two essentially independent subprojects, so I'm going to present them individually.

15.5.1 Goal 1

Draw the leaves just with dots. The dots are opaque along the (curved) central vein from one tip to the other, and fade out to the edges.

Now go out there and make pictures!

15.5.2 Approach 1

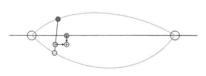

Figure 15.40. Finding the inner dot cloud. First I find the purple and cyan points. Then I pick a random point between them, shown in green. I find a point from left to right, drawn in orange. The point I will draw, shown in yellow, comes from the orange dot's *x* value and the green dot's *y* value.

The code begins with a loop that draws a single random dot; by running through the loop a few thousand times I get a few thousand points.

I start with a pair of points somewhere along the the length of the upper and lower curves. They both come from a value for t somewhere between 0 and 1.

To find the location of the points, I use this value of t for both the upper and lower curves. Then I randomly blend (or lerp) between the two points I just found.

Figure 15.40 shows the idea.

In the figure, suppose I'm at about 20 percent of the way from left to right along the central vein. I find the point on the top curve that's 20 percent along the way; it's colored in purple. Then I find the point 20 percent along the way on the lower curve; that's colored in cyan. Note that these distances are computed by Processing along the length of the curve itself, so the two points generally are not directly above and below each other. Then I find a point randomly between these two. In the figure, that's colored in green. That gives me the *y*-coordinate of the point I'm going to draw.

Rather than compute the x-coordinates of the purple and cyan points and blend them, I just find the point 20 percent of the way from the left to the right; that's marked in orange. That's the x-coordinate of the point.

The point I draw is built from the orange dot's x value and the green dot's y value; that point is marked in yellow.

I also use the y-blending value to determine the opacity. When that value is 0 or 1, it means I'm at the edges of the leaf, so the opacity is 0. When the blending value is 0.5, I'm in the middle of the leaf, so the opacity is 255. In between, the opacity also is in between.

When I looked at the resulting patterns I saw that the tips of the leaves were looking extra dark because they were getting as many points as everywhere else but, all the points were packed into a smaller area (if you think about why this happens, you'll gain a deeper insight into Bézier curves). So I wrote a little correction that nudged t away from the edges and towards the middle.

I encourage you to dig in and write this yourself.

15.5.3   Code Walkthrough 1

The code runs through a loop 5,000 times, each time creating a random dot. That looked nice to me; you might prefer more or fewer dots.

First, I call `random()` to get a value for t from 0 to 1. I found that if I computed the points on the curves using that value of t, the points bunched up at the tips of the leaf. That's because of the mathematics that define these curves. Rather than dig into that math, I decided to try to change t, pushing its values away from the ends of the range and towards the middle (that is, away from 0 and 1 and towards 0.5).

I played around with a bunch of corrections, and eventually came up with something. This is what programmers sometimes call a *hack*. That term has many uses, some positive and some negative, but one common usage refers to something that you cobble together to solve a single, specific problem. A hack is usually something weird and very specialized. It's like using a garden hose to tie a kayak to the roof of your car: it works, but it's probably not a good, general approach you'd want to repeat.

In this case, I played around with different nudges to t until I found something that worked. I decided to nudge t in the positive direction when it was near 0 and in the negative direction when it was near 1, and not at all when it was 0.5. I added a little sine curve, scaled down to a low value, that ran through a half-cycle over the $(0, 1)$ range of t. That did the job (I'll talk about sine curves in Chapter 18). If you're not familiar with the idea of a sine curve or the `sin()` function, that's fine; there are probably thousands of other hacks that would do just as well at solving this little problem.

I compute the x position for the dot just by lerping between the two knot's x positions using t.

To compute the y, I find the y-coordinate of both the upper and lower Bézier curves at that value of t. Then I call `random()` again to get another random number from 0 to 1, and I use that to lerp between the two curve y values. Note that I'm playing kind of fast and loose with the *x* and *y* values here, since I'm not really treating the curve points as (x, y) pairs. But this looks fine, which is the goal.

Then I use map () to convert the *y*-blending value to an opacity. I subtract the blending value from 0.5, and then take the absolute value of the result using abs () (this is the absolute value function which simply turns negative values into positive ones). That gives me something that is .5 at the bottom edge, 0 in the middle, and .5 again at the top. I use map () to turn the range $(0, .5)$ to $(255, 0)$.

Finally, I set the point's color and opacity using stroke and then draw the dot.

15.5.4 My Code 1

This code goes into drawOneLeaf (), right after the call to rotate (). It replaces everything up to the closing brace of the routine.

```
int numPoints = 5000;      // how many dots to draw
for (int d=0; d<numPoints; d++) {

    // create t and nudge it away from the ends
    float t = random(0.0, 1.0);
    t += .07 * sin(TWO_PI*t);

    // X is simple: just lerp the knot's X points
    float px = lerp(pA.x, pB.x, t);

    // find the Y value for the upper and lower curves
    float uy = bezierPoint(pA.y, pG1.y, pG2.y, pB.y, t);
    float ly = bezierPoint(pA.y, pH1.y, pH2.y, pB.y, t);

    // create a blending value a, and find Y
    float a = random(0.0, 1.0);
    float py = lerp(uy, ly, a);

    // find alpha from a
    // the range (0,1) for a should map to 0 to 255 to 0
    float myAlpha = map(abs(.5-a), 0, .5, 255, 0);

    // set the color and draw the point
    stroke(leafColor, myAlpha);
    point(px, py);
}
```

15.5.5 Goal 2

Draw the leaves with an aura of dots outside the curves. It's as though we put down a cardboard cutout of the leaf on a page, lightly spraypainted it, and then removed the cutout. The leaf itself is blank, but there are many dots right at its edge, and they fade out with distance in a cloud. The cloud should look uniform and smooth all around the leaf.

Make it so!

15.5.6   Approach 2

Creating the outer cloud is a harder problem than creating the inner one. I tried a lot of things; here's the solution that I liked best. It's not a great, unified theoretical answer; it's kind of a hodgepodge that works together well.

The overall structure is the same as the inner cloud. Like the inner cloud, I run through a loop, once for each point. I draw many times more points because there's a lot more area to cover in the cloud.

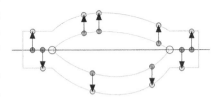

Figure 15.41. Finding the dot cloud.

I call the cloud around the leaf the "aura." The general idea is this: find a point on either the upper or lower curve of the leaf, and push it either up or down, respectively. The farther away it goes, the dimmer it gets.

Figure 15.41 shows the idea.

The ends are trickier because the cloud has to wrap around them as well. So when I use `random()` to create a value of t to use to find these points, I create values not from 0 to 1 but from -b to 1+b for some small value of b.

If t comes out between 0 and 1, I randomly choose either the upper or lower curve and find the point on that curve and then I push it in the appropriate direction by a random amount.

If t is less than 0 or greater than 1, I use a y value equal to that of the nearest knot. And I compute a fading factor based on t that will combine with the overall fading, so that points beyond the left and right edges will get dimmer with their distance from the knot. There's not a lot of theory here; I just figured that the dots should be dimmer with distance and multiplied that into the aura-based fading factor. The result is a cloud with opacities that are like a tent in the middle and like a sagging tent at the ends, but with rare exceptions it looks pretty good to my eye.

The aura is controlled by two parameters. One tells me how far to the left and right it extends (that's the value of b I described above), and another tells me how far out the aura extends (that tells me how far to move the points).

15.5.7   Code Walkthrough 2

The code runs through a loop 30,000 times, once for each dot. That looks pretty good to me, but you could easily change how many dots get drawn.

The code itself is almost a step-by-step implementation of the strategy. I first define values for tbump (to control the width of the cloud at the ends) and aura (to control its thickness).

Then I call random() to find a value for t between -tbump and 1+tbump. As with the inside points, I blend the two knot's x-coordinates to find the x-coordinate for this point. Note that if t is less than 0 or greater than 1, this will give me a point to the left or right of the original leaf segment, which gives me the horizontal extension of the cloud past the ends.

Then I flip a coin to decide if I'm going to draw a dot above the leaf or below it. If above, I find my starting y value from the upper curve and set the variable dir (for direction) to −1; otherwise I choose the lower curve, and set dir to 1.

I then test to see if I'm off the left or right side. If so, I compute a variable tfade that drops from 1 to 0 with distance from the knot.

Then I compute a random value to push the y coordinate and compute the fading value (which will determine alpha) based on how far I pushed it. I needed to somehow combine the sideways fading (from the variable tfade above) with this vertical fading. I tried a few things, but a simple multiplication did the job quickly and looked nice.

Then I run the completed fade value through a half-cycle of the cosine curve, which smooths out the uniform drop in intensity and makes it look a little more cloudlike (cosine is a lot like sine, and I'll discuss it also in Chapter 18). Again, if you're not familiar with cosine or the cos() function, anything that makes numbers that smoothly get smaller with distance would do the trick. Then I push the y value in the direction dir by the distance I computed above, set the color (and alpha), and draw the point.

15.5.8 My Code 2

```
int numPoints = 50000;      // how many dots to draw
for (int d=0; d<numPoints; d++) {

    // tbump tells us how far to the left and right the aura extends
    float tbump = 0.3;

    // aura tells us how far up and down the aura extends
    float aura = 0.5;

    // compute a value of t from (0,1) extended by tbump on both sides
    float t = random(-tbump, 1+tbump);

    // cheap and dirty: find the X position by blending the knots
    float px = lerp(pA.x, pB.x, t);

    // decide if we're moving up from the top or down from the bottom
    float py, dir;
    if (random(1000) > 500) {
        dir = -1;
```

```
      py = bezierPoint(pA.y, pG1.y, pG2.y, pB.y, t);
   } else {
      dir = 1;
      py = bezierPoint(pA.y, pH1.y, pH2.y, pB.y, t);
   }

   // add fading to the left and right and set Y to the
   // knot value
   float tfade = 1.0;
   if (t < 0) {
      tfade = 1-(abs(t)/tbump);
      py = pA.y;
   } else if (t > 1) {
      tfade = 1-((t-1)/tbump);
      py = pB.y;
   }

   // compute a distance to push out into the aura
   float auraD = random(aura);

   // find alpha from the distance
   float aurafade = 1-(auraD/aura);

   // include any fading due to the edges
   aurafade *= tfade;

   // run aurafade through cosine to give it a smoother fade
   aurafade = map(cos(PI * aurafade), 1, -1, 0, 1);

   // compute the Y by pushing the curve point up or down
   py += dir * auraD;

   // set the color and draw the point
   stroke(leafColor, 255*aurafade);
   point(px, py);
}
```

15.5.9 Complete Code

Here's the code that I wrote. It's part of drawOneLeaf(), starts right after the
rotate() statement, and runs to the end of the routine. I changed the declaration
of drawOneLeaf() to tell it whether I want to draw an inside or an outside leaf:

```
void drawOneLeaf(boolean drawInside) {
```

There's also a change in draw() to call this routine. I draw inside leaves seven
times out of ten:

```
void draw() {
   if (random(1000) > 300) drawOneLeaf(true);
                      else drawOneLeaf(false);
}
```

Here's the code:

```
if (drawInside) {
   int numPoints = 5000;        // how many dots to draw
   for (int d=0; d<numPoints; d++) {

      // create t and nudge it away from the ends
      float t = random(0.0, 1.0);
      t += .07 * sin(TWO_PI*t);

      // X is simple: just lerp the knot's X points
      float px = lerp(pA.x, pB.x, t);

      // find the Y value for the upper and lower curves
      float uy = bezierPoint(pA.y, pG1.y, pG2.y, pB.y, t);
      float ly = bezierPoint(pA.y, pH1.y, pH2.y, pB.y, t);

      // create a blending value a, and find Y
      float a = random(0.0, 1.0);
      float py = lerp(uy, ly, a);

      // find alpha from a
      // the range (0,1) for a should map to 0 to 255 to 0
      float myAlpha = map(abs(.5-a), 0, .5, 255, 0);

      // set the color and draw the point
      stroke(leafColor, myAlpha);
      point(px, py);
   }
} else {
   int numPoints = 30000;       // how many dots to draw
   for (int d=0; d<numPoints; d++) {

      // tbump tells us how far to the left and right the aura extends
      float tbump = 0.3;

      // aura tells us how far up and down the aura extends
      float aura = 0.5;

      // compute a value of t from (0,1) extended by tbump on both sides
      float t = random(-tbump, 1+tbump);
```

Figure 15.42. Pointillism leaves.   Figure 15.43. More pointillism leaves.

```
// cheap and dirty: find the X position by blending the knots
float px = lerp(pA.x, pB.x, t);

// decide if we're moving up from the top or down from the bottom
float py, dir;
if (random(1000) > 500) {
   dir = -1;
   py = bezierPoint(pA.y, pG1.y, pG2.y, pB.y, t);
} else {
   dir = 1;
   py = bezierPoint(pA.y, pH1.y, pH2.y, pB.y, t);
}

// add fading to the left and right and set Y to the knot value
float tfade = 1.0;
if (t < 0) {
   tfade = 1-(abs(t)/tbump);
   py = pA.y;
} else if (t > 1) {
   tfade = 1-((t-1)/tbump);
   py = pB.y;
}
```

```
        // compute a distance to push out into the aura
        float auraD = random(aura);

        // find alpha from the distance
        float aurafade = 1-(auraD/aura);

        // include any fading due to the edges
        aurafade *= tfade;

        // run aurafade through cosine to give it a smoother fade
        aurafade = map(cos(PI * aurafade), 1, -1, 0, 1);

        // compute the Y by pushing the curve point up or down
        py += dir * auraD;

        // set the color and draw the point
        stroke(leafColor, 255*aurafade);
        point(px, py);
    }
}
```

(Full program in leaves/sketches/pointLeaves/pointLeaves.pde)

Figure 15.42 and Figure 15.43 show two screenshots from this code.

Chapter 16
Images

So far, all the pictures we've drawn have been of our own making. But the world is full of images that already exist. So Processing offers us a bunch of specialized built-in routines for working with images of all kinds, including photographs.

For computer purposes, a photograph can be thought of as a grid of squares, each filled in with a particular color. This is just like how we've been treating the grid of pixels that we've been using to make our pictures. And in fact you could display a photograph by making thousands of calls to `rect()`. You'd set the color, then draw a rectangle that covers one pixel, then you'd set the next color, draw another tiny rectangle, and so on. You could also use `point()`, which might be a little faster, though either way is going to be incredibly slow.

But this conceptual model is a very good one: a photograph is a grid of colors. The only problem is that we haven't seen any built-in way to represent a grid. So let's take a brief interlude to see how we could do that.

16.1   2D Arrays

An array that can hold 2D information (or 3D, or even more) is conventionally called a *multidimensional array*, referring to the fact that it has more than one (hence *multi*) row (*dimension*). We've already seen array declarations like this:

```
int [] squareSizes = { 3, 4, 5 };
```

This is a *unidimensional array*, meaning an array of one dimension. If you called it that people might look at you funny because when you just say "array," people assume you mean "one-dimensional." It's like calling your car an "automotive car"; it's redundant, but not wrong. But when there are lots of arrays floating around in a program, people will indeed sometimes refer to those with only one dimension as "one-dimensional arrays" or "1D arrays" just to be clear.

How could we make a 2D array, like a checkerboard? Let's actually make this our plan: we want to represent a checkerboard. So it's a grid of integers, which can have any of five values. I'll say the number in each square corresponds to the type of piece on that square this way:

0 empty square

1 red checker

2 red king

3 black checker

4 black king

Our board will be a standard checkerboard: an eight-by-eight grid of squares.

Because people want to build these kinds of grids all the time, Processing makes it easy. Here's the strategy: we'll create an *array of arrays*. That is, we'll create a list, and each entry in the list will be a list itself.

By analogy, suppose you had a lot of shopping to do in a given week: you have to go to the grocery store, the hardware store, the clothing store, and so on. And you have a shopping list for each store. You decide to pace yourself and go to just one store per day. So you might make a list of your shopping lists, so that you could answer questions like "What will I be buying on Wednesday?" or "What do I need from the hardware store?"

In our case, I'll create a list of eight items, where each item is in itself a list of eight checkerboard squares. Thus I'll have an array of arrays. If we think of the first array as containing the eight others, we might say the first array is the *outer* array and the others are *inner*. We might also say the outermost array *encloses* the others.

Following long-standing tradition, I'm going to think of the inner arrays as describing rows of the checkerboard. So the outer list is a list of rows. Let's write a cell in the checkerboard using the letters (r, c); this is the same idea as (x, y) but reminds us that we have distinct rows and columns. To find a given cell at (r, c), we use r as the index for the outermost list (giving us row r), and then we'd use c as the index into that array, giving us the element at column c of that row.

You could of course reverse these conventions and think of the checkerboard as a list of columns rather than a list of rows. There's no formal rule here, and you're completely free to arrange your checkerboard any way you like. But many people arrange their arrays the way I just described, and by sticking to that convention, you'll find that life is a lot easier if you ever collaborate or use someone else's code alongside your own. This convention isn't universal, and the language doesn't enforce it, but this is the most common way to arrange this kind of grid.

Because we're using two values to select a particular square in the checkerboard, we call this array of arrays a *two-dimensional array*, or just a *2D array*.

You can declare a 2D array in one go, all at once:

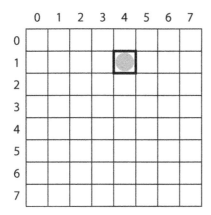

Figure 16.1. `NewCheckerboard[1][4]` is the point $(4,1)$.

```
int [] [] NewCheckerboard;
```

This is just like declaring a 1D array, only there are two sets of square brackets.
You can initialize it using nested sets of curly braces. Here I'll set up a checkerboard's
starting position. Note that I'm using white space to make the setup clear. The outermost
curly braces create the list of lists, and then each inner set of braces (that span one line)
defines a single row of the checkerboard:

```
int [] [] NewCheckerboard = {
    { 3, 0, 3, 0, 3, 0, 3, 0 },
    { 0, 3, 0, 3, 0, 3, 0, 3 },
    { 0, 0, 0, 0, 0, 0, 0, 0 },
    { 0, 0, 0, 0, 0, 0, 0, 0 },
    { 0, 0, 0, 0, 0, 0, 0, 0 },
    { 0, 0, 0, 0, 0, 0, 0, 0 },
    { 0, 0, 0, 0, 0, 0, 0, 0 },
    { 0, 1, 0, 1, 0, 1, 0, 1 },
    { 1, 0, 1, 0, 1, 0, 1, 0 }
};
```

To name an element in a 2D array, you naturally use two sets of brackets. The index
closest to the array's name chooses which list, and the index that follows chooses the
entry in that list. In other words, the first index is the row, the second is the column:

```
NewCheckerboard[1] [4] = 3;  // assign 3 to index (1,4)
```

Figure 16.1 shows this graphically.

The convention here is that we first count down and then over. So the reference
`NewCheckerboard[1][4]` tells us to go down one row, and then over four units.

In other words, first we find NewCheckerboard [1], which is a row of numbers, and then we find the value of entry number 4 in that row.

This is the opposite of the graphical order where we name points as (x, y), corresponding to over and then (in Processing's world) down. This can cause a little confusion when you're getting used to it, but luckily, there's an easy way to keep things straight. The (down, over) convention applies only to these 2D arrays, and they're always visible because of the multiple sets of square brackets.

Just as we wrote loops to access the elements of a regular array, we can write two loops (one nested in the other) to access all the elements of a 2D array. Because we read the indices as "y then x" (that is, reading the numbers in brackets from left to right), we often go through y in the outermost loop, with the x loop inside it:

```
// set all entries in NewCheckerboard to 0
for (int y=0; y<8; y++) {
    for (int x=0; x<8; x++) {
        NewCheckerboard[y][x] = 0;
    }
}
```

When we wanted to know how long a 1D array was, we could ask for its length property using dot notation. We can find the sizes of a 2D array in a similar way. If we ask the array for its length, we'll get back the number of rows it contains. We can then ask each row for its length.

For example, here's a 2D array that holds the scores of nine successive games played by two people. The first row contains the first player's scores, the second row contains the second player's scores.

```
int [][] gameScores = {
    { 3, 5, 7, 3, 9, 3, 2, 9, 5},
    { 1, 3, 2, 6, 4, 9, 2, 0, 1}
};
println("gameScores.length = "+gameScores.length);
println("gameScores[0].length = "+gameScores[0].length);
```

If we run this tiny fragment, we get this output:

```
gameScores.length = 2
gameScores[0].length = 9
```

So the array itself (gameScores) has a length of 2 (it has two rows), but the first row (gameScores [0]) has a length of 9, because there are nine scores for that player.

In the discussion above I've been showing a square checkerboard, but as we've just seen, the x and y dimensions of your array can be completely different. I've also been using int variables, but your array can be of any type, from built-in types like int and color to objects built from your own class definitions.

You can make arrays of any number of dimensions just by piling on more brackets in the declaration.

Multidimensional arrays are useful for all kinds of things that aren't exactly graphical. For example, to collect statistics on the colors used in the leaves project of Chapter 15, I built a 3D array of integers. The thinking went like this: I can imagine a big cube, where the axes are labeled Red, Green, and Blue.

```
int [] [] [] ColorCount;
ColorCount = new int[256][256][256];
```

(When I first tried to run this, Processing complained that I was using too much memory—that's reasonable, since this array alone is more than 16 million integers! I told my operating system to allocate more memory to Processing, and my program ran without problems.)

To start, I initialized every entry in the cube to 0. Then I opened the picture and found the color of the first pixel—that is, I got that pixel's red, green, and blue values. So then in my big array I bumped the corresponding count:

```
ColorCount[thisRed][thisGreen][thisBlue] += 1;
```

This didn't work well because colors have so much variation. I ended up with lots of very tiny variations of red as the most popular colors.

So instead, I made each entry in `ColorCount` cover a 16-by-16-by-16 cube in the original color cube. Happily, that made it a lot smaller:

```
ColorCount = new int[16][16][16];
```

And then I stored colors this way:

```
int red16 = int(thisRed/16);
int grn16 = int(thisRed/16);
int blu16 = int(thisRed/16);
ColorCount[red16][grn16][blu16] += 1;
```

That worked beautifully. So this 3D array didn't really correspond to any 3D object, except abstractly.

If you want to stretch your mind a little, you can think of the parameters to any object as a point in a corresponding "space." For example, the values (x, y) fit nicely onto a page, with axes labeled x and y. We saw above that we can put colors into a cube, with the axes labeled Red, Green, and Blue. Now consider a rectangle that's created with four numbers: the upper-left x and y, and the width and height. Taken together, these four numbers can be thought of as a single point in a 4D space, where the axes are labeled X, Y, Width, and Height. If you're able to actually visualize and "see" a 4D space in your head, you're very unusual; most people (including myself) can only reason about these things by analogy. But that analogy is very powerful, and you can easily imagine spaces with five, six, or any number of dimensions if it helps you organize your project.

For example, you might think of a circle as a point in a 3D space labeled Center-*x*, Center-*y*, and Radius. You could tell whether two circles are "alike" by finding their distance from each other in this space. If you want, you can extend the space to six dimensions by including axes for Red, Green, and Blue; you'll have to write your own function for computing six-dimensional distances, but it turns out that Pythagoras's Theorem (the old one from high school) can be generalized in a snap to any number of dimensions.

For now, though, I'll stick to 2D arrays.

16.2 Displaying Images

We know that photographs are grids of colors, and now we've seen how Processing can easily represent such a grid. Manipulating 2D grids is a great general-purpose tool that comes up in lots of applications. One of the most popular uses of a 2D grid is to save the colors of an image or a photograph. So Processing makes that particularly easy with a built-in object called a PImage.

Sometimes graphics that are based on a grid of colors are called *raster graphics*, because the display grid (that is, the 2D array of colors) was once widely referred to as a *raster* (this term has fallen out of fashion but *raster graphics* remains). Pictures drawn with primitive shapes like circles and rectangles are sometimes called *vector graphics* because many of these shapes are built up out of straight-line segments called vectors (the word vector has lots of other meanings as well).

So the object that holds a grid of colors is a PImage. You can declare one in the usual way:

```
PImage myImage;
```

If this was a user-defined class, then to actually make one of these you'd make a call to new PImage() to run a constructor. But this object's different and uses its own routines that act as alternatives.

To create a blank, empty image, you call createImage():

```
PImage myImage = createImage();
```

It's more interesting to start off with a photograph. You can load up any picture stored in .jpg, .gif, .tif, or .tga formats using loadImage():

```
PImage myImage = loadImage("myPhoto.jpg");
```

The file name follows the usual conventions of naming things on the computer. If you just give the name, as above, Processing expects to find the file with the given name in the same folder where you're saving your Processing source code. If it's located somewhere else on the disk, you'll need to give the computer a longer name that includes the "path" it has to follow through your disk to locate the image. The format of this longer "path" reference varies from system to system, but here are a couple of examples:

```
myImage = loadImage("/Users/Andrew/images/myPhoto.jpg");     // Mac path
myImage = loadImage("C:My Documents/Pictures/myPhoto.jpg");  // PC path
```

Once you've loaded an image, what can you do with it? For the rest of these examples, I'm going to assume you have a jpg-format image called myPhoto.jpg in your directory. Just copy any picture in jpg format on your computer (or from the web) and give it that name. You can of course change the name in the Processing code examples below instead, if you prefer.

The place to start with any image is to show it on the screen. Call image() with the x- and y-coordinates of the upper-left corner of the picture with respect to the window, and it will show up right there:

```
image(myPicture, 0, 0);
```

You can give two more optional arguments to image() to tell it what size the picture should be.

Let's use those arguments to make a little stairstep of photographs (I'll use a picture I took during a recent backpacking trip in New Zealand):

```
void setup() {
   size(600, 400);
   background(110, 120, 126);
   PImage pic = loadImage("myPhoto.jpg");
   for (int i=0; i<5; i++) {
      image(pic, i*100, i*60, 200, 160);
   }
}
```

(See output in Figure 16.2. Full program in images/sketches/stairs1/stairs1.pde)

You can manipulate a picture with transformations just like any other graphics object. I find it's easiest to think of a PImage like a rectangle. Let's redo the above example with transformations instead. Remember that transforms accumulate, so we only have to move one step down and to the right after each picture:

```
void setup() {
   size(600, 400);
   background(110, 120, 126);
   PImage pic = loadImage("myPhoto.jpg");
   for (int i=0; i<5; i++) {
```

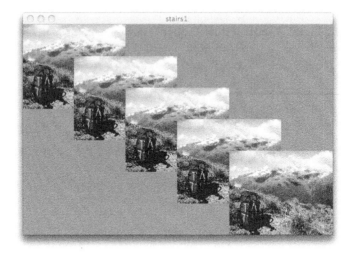

Figure 16.2. Displaying photos. (images/sketches/stairs1/stairs1.pde)

```
        image(pic, 0, 0, 200, 160);
        translate(100, 60);
    }
}
```

(See output in Figure 16.3. Full program in images/sketches/stairs2/stairs2.pde)

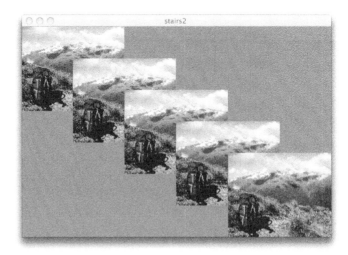

Figure 16.3. Stair steps with transforms. (stairs/sketches/stairs2/stairs2.pde)

Figure 16.4. Spinning the picture. (images/sketches/spin1/spin1.pde)

For fun, we can rotate the picture, too. I'll rotate the first picture by 0 degrees, then −20, then −40, and so on. To keep things simple, I'll just rotate around the upper-left corner:

```
void setup() {
   size(600, 400);
   background(110, 120, 126);
   PImage pic = loadImage("myPhoto.jpg");
   for (int i=0; i<5; i++) {
      pushMatrix();
         rotate(radians(i * -20));
         image(pic, 0, 0, 200, 160);
      popMatrix();
      translate(100, 80);
   }
}
```

(See output in Figure 16.4. Full program in images/sketches/spin1/spin1.pde)

Note that I used pushMatrix() and popMatrix() around the rotation. If I hadn't, then we would have moved along the rotated coordinate system rather than along the x- and y-axes of the screen. Let's try commenting them out:

```
void setup() {
   size(600, 400);
```

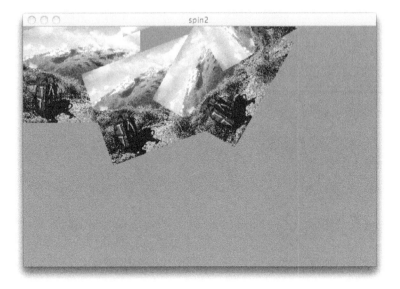

Figure 16.5. Spinning the picture without nesting transforms. (images/sketches/spin2/spin2.pde)

```
background(110, 120, 126);
PImage pic = loadImage("myPhoto.jpg");
for (int i=0; i<5; i++) {
   //pushMatrix();
      rotate(radians(i * -20));
      image(pic, 0, 0, 200, 160);
   //popMatrix();
   translate(100, 80);
}
}
```

(See output in Figure 16.5. Full program in images/sketches/spin2/spin2.pde)

That's not what I was originally going for, but it's kind of interesting in its own way. The pictures are curling up tightly like they're in a seashell. That might be a useful kind of thing to draw one day.

A PImage has three properties that you can use: width, height, and the array pixels. The first two are integers that tell you, naturally enough, the width and height of the picture. The last is a 1D array of colors, one entry for each pixel in the image.

Um, wait. That's a 1D array. And pictures are 2D. What gives? I'll get back to that in a minute.

You can find out the color of any point in the image using the built-in routine get(). To get the color of the pixel at $x = 25$, $y = 30$ (counting from $(0,0)$ in the upper left, of course), you'd write

```
color myColor = myImage.get(25, 30);
```

The arguments to `get()` appear in the usual way, first *x* and then *y*. Actually, `get()` is more powerful. It can read a whole block of pixels at once if you hand it two more arguments for the width and height of a rectangle that starts at the point given by the first value.

As you might guess, you can assign any color you like by using `set()`:

```
myImage.set(25, 30, myColor);
```

Like `rectMode()` and `ellipseMode()`, you can tell Processing to interpret the values you hand to `image()` in several different ways. You can call the function `imageMode()` with one of three values:

CORNER. The default mode. The four numbers following the image are considered the upper-left *x*, the upper-left *y*, the width, and the height.

CORNERS. The first two numbers are any corner of the image, and the next two numbers are the coordinates of the diagonally opposite corner.

CENTER. The first two numbers are the center of the image, followed by the image's full width and height.

As with the other mode-setting commands, I find that changing the image mode can lead to confusion. I suggest you never call `imageMode()` unless you really need to. If you must call `imageMode()`, immediately call it again and put the mode back to the default.

If you try to use `set()` to set the color of a nonexistent pixel (that is, one that's outside of your graphics window), Processing simply ignores the operation. If you try to use `get()` to retrieve a color from a nonexistent pixel, you'll get back the color $(0,0,0)$, which corresponds to black.

Let's have some fun with `get()` and `set()`. I'll load up an image into the graphics window and then each time the system calls `draw()`, I'll run through every pixel in the image and get a random number. If the number is above some threshold, I'll replace that pixel with the color of the pixel above it.

```
void setup() {
    size(600, 400);
    PImage img = loadImage("myPhoto.jpg");
    image(img, 0, 0, 600, 400);
}

void draw() {
    for (int y=1; y<height; y++) {
```

Figure 16.6. Randomly copying a pixel from above. (images/sketches/swap1/swap1.pde)

```
for (int x=0; x<width; x++) {
   if (random(1000) > 950) {
      set(x, y, get(x, y-1));
   }
  }
 }
}
```

(See output in Figure 16.6. Full program in images/sketches/swap1/swap1.pde)

That's a nice kind of vertical dripping effect. Let's change this so that we randomly copy the color of the pixel to the left, right, above, or below (I'll fix the limits of the loops so we don't scan the border pixels; if we did, get() would return black for the offscreen pixels, which wouldn't look nice).

```
if (random(1000) > 950) {
   int j = int(random(1000));
       if (j < 250) set(x, y, get(x, y-1));
   else if (j < 500) set(x, y, get(x, y+1));
   else if (j < 750) set(x, y, get(x-1, y));
   else              set(x, y, get(x+1, y));
}
```

(See output in Figure 16.7. Full program in images/sketches/swap2/swap2.pde)

Figure 16.7. Randomly copying a pixel from any neighbor. (images/sketches/swap2/swap2.pde)

That produces a nice blotchy effect. What if we swap the colors of the two pixels rather than just copying one to the other? I'll write a little utility to trade the color of two pixels and call that for each of our possible cases.

```
void draw() {
    for (int y=1; y<height; y++) {
        for (int x=0; x<width; x++) {
            if (random(1000) > 950) {
                int j = int(random(1000));
                    if (j < 250) swap(x, y, x, y-1);
                else if (j < 500) swap(x, y, x, y+1);
                else if (j < 750) swap(x, y, x-1, y);
                else              swap(x, y, x+1, y);
            }
        }
    }
}

void swap(int x0, int y0, int x1, int y1) {
    color c0 = get(x0, y0);
    color c1 = get(x1, y1);
```

Figure 16.8. Randomly swapping a pixel with any neighbor.
(images/sketches/swap3/swap3.pde)

```
  set(x0, y0, c1);
  set(x1, y1, c0);
}
```

(See output in Figure 16.8. Full program in images/sketches/swap3/swap3.pde)

If you let this run long enough, the pixels eventually migrate far from their start-ing points, and the picture becomes increasingly fuzzy until it's just a big, formless, sparkling sea of colored dots.

I said above that I'd get back to the perhaps surprising fact that `pixels` is a 1D array, and not 2D. The reasons for this are partly historical, and partly for efficiency.

16.3   The Pixel Array

It used to be the case that multidimensional arrays were often a little bit slower to work with than their 1D counterparts. They required just a bit of additional work under the hood, and when we work with images we're often affecting a lot of pixels, so every little bit of performance matters. Modern computer languages are largely free of this problem, but there are still a few lingering issues that can make 1D arrays a little faster and more convenient than 2D versions (or those with even higher dimensions). So

Processing stores the array of pixel colors as a 1D array. This is really just all the rows of the image laid together, one after the other.

For example, suppose our picture was five lines tall by four pixels wide. We could write down the coordinates like this:

```
(0,0)   (0,1)   (0,2)   (0,3)
(1,0)   (1,1)   (1,2)   (1,3)
(2,0)   (2,1)   (2,2)   (2,3)
(3,0)   (3,1)   (3,2)   (3,3)
(4,0)   (4,1)   (4,2)   (4,3)
```

In the 1D array, they're all placed one after the other in a single list. That list comes from the above picture by reading the entries left to right, top to bottom:

```
(0,0)  (0,1)  (0,2)  (0,3)  (1,0)  (1,1)  (1,2)  ...  (4,2)  (4,3)
```

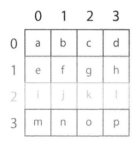

Figure 16.9. The 2D grid in 1D.

We often want to refer to a point with two dimensions (x and y), but we need to find its location in this big 1D array. The method for converting from 2D to 1D is so common that it will eventually become second nature to you. Let's take a look at it now.

Our goal is to find a way to take the x- and y-coordinates of a cell in the 2D array and find the corresponding index (let's call it p, for pixel) in the 1D array `pixels`.

The trick to doing this is in the drawing of Figure 16.9. Essentially, we pull out the rows one by one and lay them one after the other in a single long row.

Let's say that the grid has dimensions w (for width) and h (for height). The first row of the grid has w entries, and those are the first w entries of the array. So when $y = 0$ (that is, we're on the first row), $p = x$ (that is, the 1D array index is just the horizontal position of the pixel). So values from $p = 0$ to $p = w - 1$ correspond to the first row (remember that w entries are numbered 0, 1, ..., $w - 1$).

Next in the array comes row 2, where $y = 1$. So that starts at $p = w$ (that is, one past the last entry from the first row) and runs to $p = w + (w - 1)$.

Next comes row 3, where $y = 2$. So that starts at $p = 2 * w$, and it runs to $p = (2 * w) + (w - 1)$.

You're probably spotting a pattern, and you're right. To find the value of p (that is, the entry in the `pixels` array) from x and y, given a grid that is w across by h high, we write

```
int p = (y * w) + x;
```

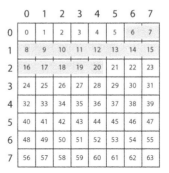

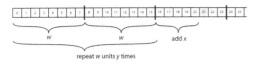

Figure 16.11. The pixels from (6,0) to (4,2) run from index 6 to index 20.

Figure 16.10. Finding $p = 21$ from $x = 5$ and $y = 2$. We add up two row widths and then add the x value to get the index for p.

That's all there is to it! In words, we jump forward by w pixels for each row and then we advance x pixels more. Figure 16.10 shows the idea.

This is why the `pixels` array is so efficient. If we want to run through all the pixels from a given (x, y) up to another (x, y), we only have to compute the two values of p that correspond to those points, and then run a loop between them. Here's what I mean, illustrated in Figure 16.11.

```
// put 0 in all points from (x0, y0) to (x1, y1)
int p0 = (y0 * w) + x0;
int p1 = (y1 * w) + x1;
for (int indexp=p0; indexp<p1; indexp++) {
    pixels[indexp] = 0;
}
```

We can also find x and y from any given value of p.

Let's start by finding y. First, we want to know how many *complete* rows are above the (x, y) we're starting with, as shown in Figure 16.12. That's the integer part of y/w. For example, in our eight-by-eight checkerboard, suppose $y = 27$. Then $27/8 = 3.375$, and the integer part of that is 3. So there are three full rows above this point, and that's the value of y. Subtracting three times the width, or $3 * 8 = 24$, gives us $27 - 24 = 3$, and that's the value of x.

This also works even for the top row. Suppose $p = 3$. Then $p/8 = 0.375$, and the integer part is 0. So $y = 0$, corresponding to the top row. To find the value of x, we only need to find how far we are into the current row. To get that, we find the index at the

Figure 16.12. Finding $x = 3$ and $y = 3$ from $p = 27$.

start of this row and subtract it from p. That index, of course, is just the number of rows above us times the width of each row. So $x = p - (y * w)$.

In code,

```
int y = int(p/w);
int x = p-(w*y);
```

When we do these conversions in practice, we get the width of a `Pimage` named `img` from the property `img.width`.

In fact, this little bit of conversion is one of the things that the routines `get()` and `set()` are doing each time you call them. Here are versions of those routines with the steps made explicit:

```
color myGet(PImage image, int x, int y) {
    int p = (y * image.width) + x;
    return(image.pixels[p]);
}

void mySet(PImage image, int x, int y, color clr) {
    int p = (y * image.width) + x;
    image.pixels[p] = clr;
}
```

There are two very important things to keep in mind, however.

First, `get()` and `set()` are doing something extremely helpful that my little versions above don't do: *bounds checking*. Remember that if you try to access an element of a 1D array that doesn't exist, you'll get an error and your program will crash. Processing's `get()` and `set()` try to help you avoid that by ignoring such requests. Here's a more robust example of `myGet()` that does this kind of bounds checking:

```
color myGet(PImage image, int x, int y) {
   if ((x<0) || (y<0) || (x>=image.width) || (y>=image.height)) {
      return(color(0,0,0));
   }
   int p = (y * image.width) + x;
   return(image.pixels[p]);
}
```

So you can now say something like myGet (myImage, -1000, -30) and get back a black color, and not a program crash. The built-in versions of get() and set() do this kind of bounds checking for you every time you call them, and that takes a little bit of time. When you access pixels directly, you lose this ounce of prevention, but you pick up a bit of speed.

The other important thing is that before you can use the pixels array directly, you have to fill it up! Processing doesn't actually use the pixels array itself. That array is just a convenience for you to get at the pixels in a way that's faster than using get() and set() (for example, you might want to set all the pixels in the image to a background color or make them all twice as bright; you could just run through the array from start to finish and change the colors and avoid all the overhead of calling set() and get() and their bounds checking).

This is an essential point: the pixels array does not contain the pixels of your image until you explicitly copy them in. The array exists, and you can read from it and write to it, but until you tell it to load itself up with the image's pixel colors, it might contain random junk.

Just loading your image with loadImage() does *not* fill the pixels array. If you try to read values from pixels before you explicitly load it up with colors, you'll get back meaningless information. You must manually call a routine that tells Processing, in effect, "Copy the colors from the image to the pixels array." Similarly, any changes you make to pixels have no effect on the image. You need to explicitly call a different routine that says "Copy the colors from the pixels array into the image."

In order to use the pixels array to read colors from a PImage, you have to call loadPixels() to fill it up. Then you have to call updatePixels() to copy your new data back into Processing's internal representation:

```
PImage myImage = loadImage("../myPhoto.jpg");
myImage.loadPixels();
myImage.pixels[35] = color(255, 0, 0);
myImage.updatePixels();
```

If you don't call loadPixels(), then reading values out of pixels will give you junk (or just black). And if you don't call updatePixels(), then your changes will have no effect on the image.

I forgot these rules a few times when learning Processing, and it drove me crazy. I'd write some beautiful complicated algorithm to modify an image in some wonderful way, but every time I drew it, the picture was unchanged! Nothing worked! Finally I realized that I had to call loadPixels() to fill the pixels array with the actual colors from the PImage, and I had to call updatePixels() or Processing would completely ignore my changes.

These rules don't apply to get() and set(). Those built-in functions touch the internal representation directly. Even though the little look-alike versions I gave above use the pixels array, in fact, these routines deal with the PImage directly, and you don't have to load and then update the pixels array when you use get() and set().

In general, you don't want to mix and match your use of get() and set() with use of the pixels array. The problem is that you can get out of sync, and your changes will get lost. For example, suppose you want to work with the pixels array to make some changes to your image. So you call loadPixels() to load it up with values and then you change a few colors in that array. While this is happening, suppose you change a few other colors with set(). Remember that set() affects the image immediately, but the pixels array is, of course, unaffected. Later, when you copy your pixels back to the image using updatePixels(), the values in pixels overwrite all the color in the image, which means they also overwrite the colors you changed with your calls to set(). So I suggest sticking with either the pixels array for all your changes, or get() and set(). If you really need different approaches at different times, try to bunch them up.

The key thing to remember is that when you call updatePixels(), the image becomes whatever is in your pixels array, regardless of anything else you've done to the picture since you called loadPixels(). You can use this as a kind of *undo* mechanism. Save a "snapshot" of the image using loadPixels(). Then let someone modify the image by using get() and set() to change the pixel values. If they ever want to go back to the start, they can press the *undo* button. Then you call updatePixels(), and the image goes back to how it appeared at the time of the snapshot.

To summarize, here are the trade-offs between using get()/set() and the pixels array. The advantages of get()/set() are (a) they always check your pixel coordinates first, so you never need to worry about asking for an invalid pixel; (b) they read from, and write to, Processing's internal representation right away; (c) they use (x, y) in the normal order; and (d) they're perfectly clear, so there's no need to interpret or decode them. The disadvantage of get()/set() is performance. They cost you some time every time you use them.

The pixels array is almost the reverse. It's big advantage is performance: you can write into the pixels you want with no extra overhead. The disadvantages are (a) there's no bounds checking (so if you ask for a negative index, or values past the end of the array, your program will crash), (b) they require you to call loadPixels() before you can do anything and updatePixels() when you're done (and each of these takes time to run), and (c) interpreting the index number as x and y can take some decoding work.

So how do you choose? If you're only changing a few pixels, then get/set() is better. Remember that loadPixels() and updatePixels() take time to run. So if you aren't changing a whole lot of pixels, then avoid the overhead required by these two mandatory calls associated with the pixels array. If you're developing code and it makes sense to talk about your pixels in (x,y) format, it's also probably better to use get()/set() as long as you can, because it'll make your code easier to understand and debug. When you're going to modify tons of pixels on each update, then the array form is probably better because the time you lose to loadPixels()/updatePixels() will be more than made up for. In between, it depends on your own judgment and the nature of the computer you're running on. I generally try to use get()/set() as long as possible, and if I see that my code is running too slow, I bite the bullet and switch to the other form.

By the way, I said that the pixels array would hold nonsense, or junk, before it was loaded up from loadPixels(). On some versions of Processing, you can get away with using that array before loading it up. That is, you can use pixels right away, and it will actually hold the pixels from the image, as though you'd called loadPixels(). But even if skipping the explicit call to loadPixels() works right now, it may not work in future releases. In other words, don't rely on this behavior. The next time Processing is updated, this preloading may stop happening, so using pixels without first calling loadPixels() could leave you working with nothing but random junk. Always call loadPixels() before using the pixels array, and always call updatePixels() to put your changed pixels back into the image.

Let's write a little program that draws every pixel in the window on every frame. First we'll write it using get() and set() and then we'll use pixels. You can run them both on your computer and see how the speeds compare.

The program doesn't have much to it. First, I'll create the window, and then I'll step through every pixel and do something. I know I'll want to do something with a couple of different colors, so I'll pick them now. Here's the skeleton to do that much:

```
int WindowSize = 200;

void setup() {
    size(WindowSize, WindowSize);
}
void draw() {
    background(0);
    color color0 = color(35, 160, 255);
    color color1 = color(255, 116, 0);
    for (int y=0; y<height; y++) {
        for (int x=0; x<width; x++) {
            // do something here with get() and set()
        }
    }
}
```

(See output in Figure 16.13. Full program in images/sketches/pixels01/pixels01.pde)

Figure 16.13. A skeleton for setting image pixels. (images/sketches/pixels01/pixels01.pde)

It's not too interesting, but it puts up a window and it doesn't crash.

Let's now fill in the pixels. I played around with this for a while until I came up with a recipe for a little animation that looked good to me. Rather than rederive the whole thing step-by-step, I'll just describe the approach I ended up with. The idea will be to fill up the image with noise and then slice that noise up into layers. I'll color alternating layers with alternating colors. On each frame, I'll move the boundaries between the layers upward a little bit, so that they seem to be growing over time.

To get started, at each pixel I call `noise()` using scaled values of the x- and y-coordinates. Remember that this gives us back a number between 0 and 1. If I use that to blend between the two colors using `lerpColor()`, we get a nice start. Here's the code that replaces the comment above:

```
float noiseVal = noise(x*.015, y*.015);
color thisColor = lerpColor(color0, color1, noiseVal);
set(x, y, thisColor);
```

(See output in Figure 16.14. Full program in images/sketches/pixels02/pixels02.pde)

That's okay, but not very exciting, and it's not animated. Let's think of this grid of values as giving us the height of a smooth surface. A value of 0 would be the lowest valley, and a value of 1 would be the highest mountain.

I'll break up the range from 0 to 1 into a fixed number of layers and draw each layer in a different color. I'll create a variable `NumLayers` to tell me how many layers to use and compute the height of a single layer as `layerHeight`. Then I'll just divide the height of each pixel by this amount, which tells me how many levels up it is from the lowest valley. Remember that we can tell whether a number `a` is even by finding `a%2`; this result is either 0 or 1 when `a` is even or odd, respectively. I'll set the even-numbered layers to `color0` and the odd-numbered layers to `color1`.

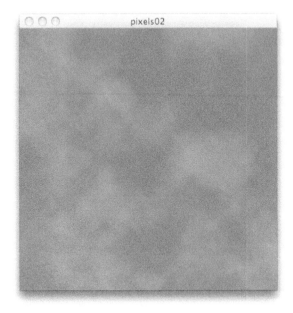

Figure 16.14. Setting the pixels. (images/sketches/pixels02/pixels02.pde)

Here's the new loop that goes into draw():

```
float layerHeight = 1.0/NumLayers;
for (int y=0; y<height; y++) {
    for (int x=0; x<width; x++) {
        float noiseVal = noise(x*.015, y*.015);

        color thisColor = color0;
        int whichColor = int(noiseVal/layerHeight);
        if (((whichColor) % 2) == 0) thisColor = color0;
        else thisColor = color1;

        set(x, y, thisColor);
    }
}
```

(See output in Figure 16.15. Full program in images/sketches/pixels03/pixels03.pde)

Lastly, I want the layers to move. So on each frame, I'll compute a variable I'll call noiseBump that will "bump" the value of the noise up by an amount based on the current frame number (which we get from frameCount). I'll also make a variable called Speed to control the size of the bump, and thus, the speed of the animation.

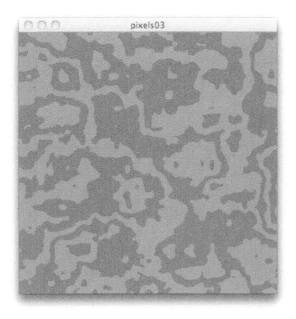

Figure 16.15. Making contours from noise. (images/sketches/pixels03/pixels03.pde)

I'll put the declaration of Speed at the top:

```
int Speed = 20;
```

Here's the new section of the loop, which replaces the four lines set off above. I've moved the declaration of thisColor up, so it's just before the loop:

```
float noiseBump = lerp(0, layerHeight, (frameCount % Speed)/(1.0*Speed));
int whichColor = int((noiseVal+noiseBump)/layerHeight);
if (((whichColor) % 2) == 0) thisColor = color0;
else thisColor = color1;
```

(See output in Figure 16.16. Full program in images/sketches/pixels04/pixels04.pde)

The line for noiseBump is long, but there's not much going on. I find the frame number modulo the value of Speed, which gives me a number from 0 to Speed-1. I divide that by Speed (remembering to multiply it by a floating-point number first, so that I get a floating-point result). That gives me a number from 0 to almost 1. Then I use that as an argument to lerp() to find a value from 0 to layerHeight.

If you run this, you'll find that the contours get bigger and bigger and then something weird happens: everything changes colors. Then the contours get bigger again, until the switch happens again, and this happens over and over. What's going on?

Figure 16.16. Animated contours, but with a problem (frame from animation).
(images/sketches/pixels04/pixels04.pde)

This is a fun little puzzle. You might want to play with it a bit before reading on.

The essence of the problem is that when `noiseBump` reaches 0.1, that means it adds the height of an entire layer to every pixel. That means that pixels that were in layer 0 are now in layer 1, those that were in layer 1 are now in layer 2, and so on. That's a problem because we're coloring the layers using an even/odd scheme. A particular layer should have the same color no matter where it is in the sequence. In other words, if layer 0 starts out as red, then all the pixels in that layer should stay red even as the boundaries of the layer move. So an orange clump, for instance, could start off in layer 0, but then become part of layer 1, and then layer 2, and so on, as it moves "up." But it should stay orange the whole way through.

Since we have just two colors, this is easy to fix. I'll just find out how many times the current frame has passed through `Speed` frames by dividing them. If we've passed through an even number of frames, then we'll start the alternating color sequence with `color0`, otherwise with `color1`.

Here's the final program:

```
int NumLayers = 10;   // smaller values = bigger blobs
int Speed = 20;       // smaller values = faster animation
int WindowSize = 400; // smaller values = smaller window =
                      // smoother animation
```

```
void setup() {
   size(WindowSize, WindowSize);
}

void draw() {
   background(0);
   color color0 = color(35, 160, 255);
   color color1 = color(255, 116, 0);
   color thisColor = color0;
   float layerHeight = 1.0/NumLayers;
   for (int y=0; y<height; y++) {
      for (int x=0; x<width; x++) {
         float noiseVal = noise(x*.015, y*.015);

         float noiseBump = lerp(0, layerHeight, (frameCount % Speed)/(1.0*Speed));
         int whichColor = int((noiseVal+noiseBump)/layerHeight);
         int startingColor = (((frameCount/Speed) % 2) == 0) ? 0 : 1;
         if (((whichColor+startingColor) % 2) == 0) thisColor = color0;
         else thisColor = color1;
```

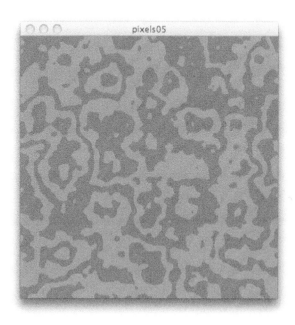

Figure 16.17. Correctly moving, animated contours (frame from animation).
(images/sketches/pixels05/pixels05.pde)

```
        set(x, y, thisColor);
      }
    }
}
```

(See output in Figure 16.17. Full program in images/sketches/pixels05/pixels05.pde)

If you run this, you'll find the contours grow and grow smoothly forever. Of course, they're just running through a loop, but it's still pretty to watch.

On my computer, this program doesn't run smoothly. It's kind of jerky. I printed out the frame rate (by printing the variable frameRate at the end of draw()), and I got about 5.2 frames per second. That's not quite as jerky as early movies, but it's a long way from smooth.

Let's add two lines and change one. I'll put a call to loadPixels() just before the loop and one to updatePixels() at the end. And instead of calling set(), I'll assign the color to pixels:

```
pixels[(y*width)+x] = thisColor;
```

(See output in Figure 16.18. Full program in images/sketches/pixels06/pixels06.pde)

Figure 16.18. Smoothly moving, animated contours (frame from animation). (images/sketches/pixels06/pixels06.pde)

Wow! What an improvement! My computer gives me about 28 frames per second now, just from that one change. Skipping the extra work done by set() brought us nearly a six-fold speedup. That's huge!

But this pleasant increase in speed comes because we're bypassing the bounds checking that set() does for us. Suppose I made a typo and used a multiplication sign rather than a plus sign, like this:

```
pixels[(y*width)*x] = thisColor;    // this is wrong!
```

Right off my program crashes with an ArrayIndexOutOfBoundsException. You can hand essentially any pixel (x,y) to set() and get away with it because it tests them first and ignores anything that's outside the window.

So when you're developing a program, set() is great because it's easy and safe. If you want more speed and you're sure of the *x* and *y* values you're using, you can bracket your changes with loadPixels() and updatePixels() and write to the pixels array instead.

16.4 Image Manipulation

When you read a book and find a passage you want to remember, you'll sometimes use a bright highlighter to mark that section, so that your eye will be drawn to it later. You're not really changing the page of the book, you're just adjusting its color so part of it will stand out.

Processing lets you do that to a region of a picture by *tinting* it. You call the routine tint() with the color that you'd like the picture to take on and then you can show the result using image() and it will be tinted correctly. This is just a display effect that takes place when the picture is displayed; the pixels themselves are not changed.

```
void setup() {
  size(600, 450);
  PImage myPhoto = loadImage("myPhoto.jpg");
  tint(255, 255, 0);
  image(myPhoto, 0, 0);
}
```

(See output in Figure 16.19. Full program in images/sketches/tint1/tint1.pde)

An interesting trick is to use tint() with a color that has some transparency in it. Then the new image will be drawn on top of whatever was on the graphics window before, but the new image will appear to be drawn with a transparent gel. If you want to just get the transparency effect without changing the color, use a tinting color of white. Here's an example where I start with a graphics window that's all black and then I draw a white rectangle to cover the left half of the image. Then I draw my photograph, but I use a white, half-transparent tint. Notice how the new image appears over what was there before, but it's faded out, as though it was on a sheet of tracing paper.

Figure 16.19. Tinting an image. (images/sketches/tint1/tint1.pde)

```
void setup() {
  size(600, 450);
  background(0);
  noStroke();
  fill(255);
  rect(0, 0, width/2, height);
  PImage myPhoto = loadImage("myPhoto.jpg");
  tint(255, 255, 255, 128);
  image(myPhoto, 0, 0);
}
```

(See output in Figure 16.20. Full program in images/sketches/tint2/tint2.pde)

You can turn off tinting by calling noTint().

You can easily shuffle around big rectangles of pixels using copy(). This routine lets you copy pixels from one part of the graphics window to another part or from a file to the graphics window (if you want to copy pixels from the graphics window, you need to use get()).

When you call copy(), you can give it either eight or nine arguments (whew!). In the eight-argument form, you give the starting and ending rectangles for the region you want to copy (you name the rectangles in the order upper-left *x*, upper-left *y*, width, and

Figure 16.20. Tinting over a background. (images/sketches/tint2/tint2.pde)

height). The idea is that you're copying a rectangle from one place in your graphics window to another. In the nine-argument form, you start the list with the name of the `PImage` object you want to copy the pixels from. They still end up in the graphics window.

Notice that you're giving `copy()` two entirely independent rectangles. They can overlap, or they can even be of completely different sizes, and `copy()` will do the right thing, resizing the image as necessary to fit the second rectangle. Here's a little sketch that grabs random rectangles from a source image and copies to them to slightly different rectangles in the graphics window:

```
PImage MyPic;
void setup() {
  size(600, 450);
  MyPic = loadImage("myPhoto.jpg");
  background(0);
}

void draw() {
  float sulx = random(width);
  float suly = random(height);
  float swid = random(width-sulx);
```

Figure 16.21. Copying rectangles in an image. (images/sketches/copy1/copy1.pde)

```
float shgt = random(height-suly);
float dulx = sulx + random(-30, 30);
float duly = suly + random(-30, 30);
float dwid = swid + random(-30, 30);
float dhgt = shgt + random(-30, 30);

copy(MyPic, int(sulx), int(suly), int(swid), int(shgt),
           int(dulx), int(duly), int(dwid), int(dhgt));
}
```

(See output in Figure 16.21. Full program in images/sketches/copy1/copy1.pde)

When copy() draws the new pixels into the image, it simply writes them on top of whatever was previously there. If you're familiar with graphics programs like Photoshop or Painter, you know that many of those systems offer a variety of *blend modes* that let you mix new pixels with the old. Processing lets you use blend modes as well, through the function blend(). To use blend(), you give it the same eight or nine values you gave to copy(), but you include one more at the end: the blend mode, which tells Processing how to merge the images.

Blend modes are very useful, but they're an advanced technique that can take a while to master. Until you get a feel for them, it's often fun and rewarding just to experiment. I won't detail here what each of them does. I suggest exploring with them for a while, and if you're into it, read up on blending modes either in the Processing documentation or any of the many websites or books that go into these modes for programs like Photoshop and Painter (those programs sometimes call these *channel modes*).

As of this writing, the online documentation page for `blend()` incorrectly describes the `BLEND` mode for two images, A and B. The text is correct when it says that this will linearly interpolate the colors involved, but the little expression at the end is wrong; it should be `C = A*factor + B*(1-factor)`, as we'd expect from a function that does linear interpolation (here, you can think of `factor` as the alpha value of a given pixel in the A image).

Figure 16.23 presents a grid that shows each of the 14 different blend modes. I combined my hiking picture from above with Figure 16.22, which is a photo of a really cool rock I found while hiking. The code has so many lines that are nearly identical because `blend()` requires all those arguments, and they're nearly the same every time. The blending mode itself isn't defined as a type (that is, it's not an `int` or a `float`), so we shouldn't try passing it as an argument to a general-purpose routine. Hence, many nearly identical lines.

Figure 16.22. A photograph of a cool rock.

For fun, and because there are only 14 blending modes and the grid has 16 spaces, the last two images in the grid (in the bottom right) show another couple of results from using `tint()`.

```
PImage Hike, Rock;

void setup() {
  size(1350, 1050);
  Hike = loadImage("mountains300.jpg");
  Rock = loadImage("rocks300.jpg");

  background(128);

  for (int y=0; y<4; y++) {
    for (int x=0; x<4; x++) {
      showPictures(x, y);
    }
  }
}

void showPictures(int x, int y) {
  int ulx = x * 350;
```

```
int uly = y * 275;
image(Hike, ulx, uly, 300, 225);
switch ((y*4)+x) {
  case  0: blend(Rock, 0, 0, 300, 225, ulx, uly, 300, 225, BLEND); break;
  case  1: blend(Rock, 0, 0, 300, 225, ulx, uly, 300, 225, ADD); break;
  case  2: blend(Rock, 0, 0, 300, 225, ulx, uly, 300, 225, SUBTRACT); break;
  case  3: blend(Rock, 0, 0, 300, 225, ulx, uly, 300, 225, DARKEST); break;

  case  4: blend(Rock, 0, 0, 300, 225, ulx, uly, 300, 225, LIGHTEST); break;
  case  5: blend(Rock, 0, 0, 300, 225, ulx, uly, 300, 225, DIFFERENCE); break;
  case  6: blend(Rock, 0, 0, 300, 225, ulx, uly, 300, 225, EXCLUSION); break;
  case  7: blend(Rock, 0, 0, 300, 225, ulx, uly, 300, 225, MULTIPLY); break;

  case  8: blend(Rock, 0, 0, 300, 225, ulx, uly, 300, 225, SCREEN); break;
  case  9: blend(Rock, 0, 0, 300, 225, ulx, uly, 300, 225, OVERLAY); break;
  case 10: blend(Rock, 0, 0, 300, 225, ulx, uly, 300, 225, HARD_LIGHT); break;
  case 11: blend(Rock, 0, 0, 300, 225, ulx, uly, 300, 225, SOFT_LIGHT); break;

  case 12: blend(Rock, 0, 0, 300, 225, ulx, uly, 300, 225, DODGE); break;
  case 13: blend(Rock, 0, 0, 300, 225, ulx, uly, 300, 225, BURN); break;
  case 14: tint(255, 255, 0); image(Rock, ulx, uly, 300, 225); noTint(); break;
  case 15: tint(255, 128);    image(Rock, ulx, uly, 300, 225); noTint(); break;
  default: break;
  }
}
```

(See output in Figure 16.23. Full program in images/sketches/blend1/blend1.pde)

A downside to blend() is that it only works on the screen: you can't use this to blend one PImage with another PImage, building up a picture in memory before you display it. If you use blend(), the results go right to the graphics window.

If you want to apply one of these blending modes without displaying the results right away, you can use the function blendColor(). This routine takes two colors and a blending mode (from the list above) and returns a new color resulting from mixing them the way you requested. So you can grab a pixel from one image, another pixel from a second image, combine them with blendColor(), and save the result. This only works on one pair of colors (that is, one pixel) at a time.

Processing also lets you apply eight different types of *filters* to images on the screen. As with blend(), you can't apply these to images in a PImage object in memory, unfortunately: these are strictly operations that are applied to the graphics window. And they are applied to the entire window. These are best thought of as special effects that you can use to give the whole image a particular look. Experiment with these filters a bit before you get too attached to them; some (like blurring by a large amount) can take a while to execute.

To apply a filter to the graphics window, call filter() with the name of the mode. Some of the filters take a single parameter, others do not. If there is a parameter, it's the second argument to filter() after the name of the mode.

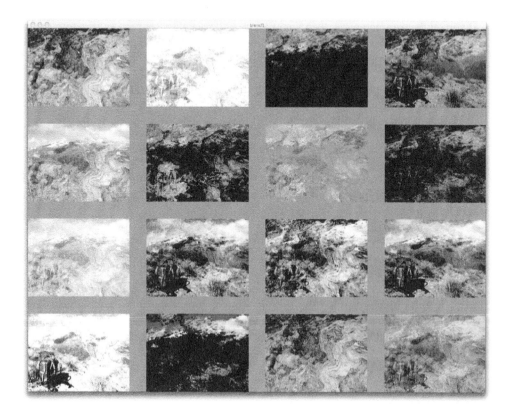

Figure 16.23. Blending modes. The base picture is the mountain image, and the rock image is blended over it. Reading from left to right, top-down, the modes are: BLEND, ADD, SUBTRACT, DARKEST, LIGHTEST, DIFFERENCE, EXCLUSION, MULTIPLY, SCREEN, OVERLAY, HARD_LIGHT, SOFT_LIGHT, DODGE, and BURN. The bottom-right two images show a yellow and white tint. (images/sketches/blend1/blend1.pde)

THRESHOLD. (One optional parameter.) Converts the window to gray, then test each pixel. If it's brighter than the threshold parameter, the pixel becomes white, otherwise it's black. The threshold value runs from 0 (for black) to 1 (for white). The threshold defaults to 0.5.

GRAY. (No parameter.) Converts the window to gray.

INVERT. (No parameter.) Replaces each color component x by $255 - x$.

POSTERIZE. (One parameter.) Each color channel is reduced to just a few colors. The number of colors is given by the parameter, which is between 2 and 255. For example, if you set the parameter to 4, then your picture will have only four red values, four green values, and four blue values. Notice that this can still result in 64 different colors in the image, depending on how the colors overlap.

BLUR. (One optional parameter.) Makes the picture "fuzzier" by blending pixels within a circle around each pixel. The parameter gives the radius of the circle. The default is 1. Higher numbers give blurrier results.

OPAQUE. Sets the alpha channel for the window to be fully opaque.

ERODE. (No parameter.) This operation tries to remove small regions of light-colored pixels. If you apply it multiple times, it will dig deeper and deeper into the regions, removing more pixels.

DILATE. (No parameter.) This is the opposite of ERODE, and it tries to remove pockets of darker-colored pixels. If you apply it multiple times, it too will dig deeper into those pockets.

Because `filter()` modifies the graphics window, it's tricky to show you the results in one big picture. What I've done in the next program is to run each filter on my hiking picture, and then save the results from the screen into memory. When I've done all the filters, then I build a single big image out of the saved images.

```
PImage Hike;
PImage [] Results;

void setup() {
  size(1350, 1050);
  Hike = loadImage("myPhoto.jpg");
  Results = new PImage[16];
  for (int i=0; i<16; i++) Results[i] = createImage(300, 225, RGB);

  for (int i=0; i<16; i++) {
    runFilter(i);
  }

  background(128);

  for (int y=0; y<4; y++) {
    for (int x=0; x<4; x++) {
      copy(Results[(y*4)+x], 0, 0, 300, 225, x*350, y*275, 300, 225);
    }
  }
}

void runFilter(int i) {
  image(Hike, 0, 0, 300, 225);
```

Figure 16.24. Filtering examples. See Figure 16.25 for a key to what's happening in each image.

thresh(0.25)	thresh(0.75)	gray	invert
poster(2)	poster(3)	poster(4)	poster(8)
blur(1)	blur(4)	blur(15)	opaque
erode	erode*3	dilate	dilate*3

Figure 16.25. Filter figure key.

```
switch (i) {
  case  0: filter(THRESHOLD, 0.25); break;
  case  1: filter(THRESHOLD, 0.75); break;
  case  2: filter(GRAY); break;
  case  3: filter(INVERT); break;

  case  4: filter(POSTERIZE, 2); break;
  case  5: filter(POSTERIZE, 3); break;
```

```
      case  6: filter(POSTERIZE, 4); break;
      case  7: filter(POSTERIZE, 8); break;

      case  8: filter(BLUR, 1); break;
      case  9: filter(BLUR, 4); break;
      case 10: filter(BLUR, 15); break;
      case 11: filter(OPAQUE); break;

      case 12: filter(ERODE); break;
      case 13: filter(ERODE); filter(ERODE); filter(ERODE); break;
      case 14: filter(DILATE); break;
      case 15: filter(DILATE); filter(DILATE); filter(DILATE); break;
      default: break;
   }
  Results[i] = get(0, 0, 300, 225);
}
```

(See output in Figure 16.24. Full program in images/sketches/filter1/filter1.pde)

It's often useful to apply a series of filters, for example, to first blur a picture and then posterize it. For fun, I played around with a bunch of different combinations. I found that I liked it when I called ERODE and DILATE filters multiple times, so I packaged up a couple of tiny routines to call them repeatedly.

```
PImage Hike;
PImage [] Results;

void setup() {
   size(1350, 1050);
   Hike = loadImage("myPhoto.jpg");
   Results = new PImage[16];
   for (int i=0; i<16; i++) {
      Results[i] = createImage(300, 225, RGB);
   }

   for (int i=0; i<16; i++) {
     runFilter(i);
   }

   background(128);

   for (int y=0; y<4; y++) {
     for (int x=0; x<4; x++) {
       copy(Results[(y*4)+x], 0, 0, 300, 225, x*350, y*275, 300, 225);
     }
   }
}
```

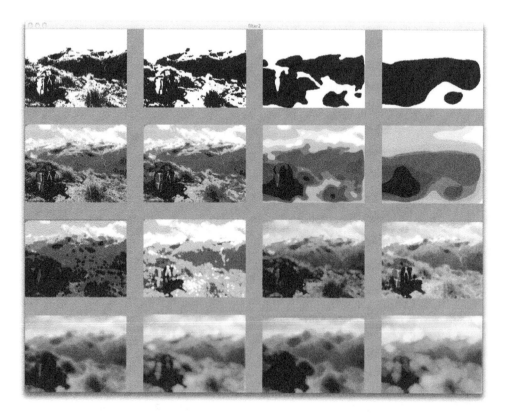

Figure 16.26. Combining filters. See Figure 16.27 for a key to what's happening in each image.

thresh(0.25)	blur(1) + thresh(0.5)	blur(5)+thresh(0.5)	blur(15)+thresh(0.5)
poster(4)	blur(1)+poster(3)	blur(5)+poster(4)	blur(15)+poster(8)
erode*3 + poster(4)	dilate*3 + poster(4)	erode*3 + dilate*3	dilate*3 + erode*3
blur(3) + erode*3	blur(3) + dilate*3	blur(3) + erode*8	blur(3) + dilate*8

Figure 16.27. Combining filters figure key.

```
void runFilter(int i) {
  image(Hike, 0, 0, 300, 225);
  switch (i) {
    case  0: filter(THRESHOLD, 0.5); break;
    case  1: filter(BLUR, 1);  filter(THRESHOLD, 0.5); break;
    case  2: filter(BLUR, 5);  filter(THRESHOLD, 0.5); break;
    case  3: filter(BLUR, 15); filter(THRESHOLD, 0.5); break;
```

```
    case  4: filter(POSTERIZE, 4); break;
    case  5: filter(BLUR, 1);  filter(POSTERIZE, 4); break;
    case  6: filter(BLUR, 5);  filter(POSTERIZE, 4); break;
    case  7: filter(BLUR, 15); filter(POSTERIZE, 4); break;

    case  8: multiErode(3);   filter(POSTERIZE, 4); break;
    case  9: multiDilate(3);  filter(POSTERIZE, 4); break;
    case 10: multiErode(3);   multiDilate(3);   break;
    case 11: multiDilate(3);  multiErode(3);   break;

    case 12: filter(BLUR, 3);  multiErode(3); break;
    case 13: filter(BLUR, 3);  multiDilate(3); break;
    case 14: filter(BLUR, 3);  multiErode(8); break;
    case 15: filter(BLUR, 3);  multiDilate(8); break;
    default: break;
  }
  Results[i] = get(0, 0, 300, 225);
}

void multiDilate(int repeats)
      { for (int i=0; i<repeats; i++) filter(DILATE); }
void multiErode(int repeats)
      { for (int i=0; i<repeats; i++) filter(ERODE); }
```

(See output in Figure 16.26. Full program in images/sketches/filter2/filter2.pde)

16.5 Applying Texture

So far, we've drawn entire images (which are rectangular) or rectangular pieces of images. You can also attach an image to a shape (like a triangle or a quad) and then the image gets drawn with the shape. The idea is that the image is treated like a sheet of flexible rubber, and it's stretched and pulled as needed to fill in the entire shape.

When you use an image to decorate a shape in this way, we call the image a *texture*. When we put a texture onto a shape, we identify a point on the texture and associate it with a point on the shape. This is a potential source of confusion because the texture has its own coordinate system and the shape has another one. So if I talk about a point $(3,5)$, do I mean three units over and five down from the upper left of the texture, or from the upper left of the graphics window?

To keep things straight, conventionally we don't talk about points in the texture using the labels x and y. We still find them by starting in the upper left and going over and then down, but we call the axes u and v (less frequently, people call the texture axes s and t, but I'll stick with u and v). So we say that we associate a particular (u,v) point on a texture with a particular (x, y) vertex on a shape. It's just a change in labels. When you see someone talk about (u, v) coordinates, you know they're talking about points on a texture.

To apply a texture to a shape, you first tell Processing which image to use and then you tell it how to put the image on the shape. Although we've seen a variety of ways to create and define geometric shapes, the only way to apply textures to your own shapes is with the `beginVertex()`-`endVertex()` style.

As usual, you begin a shape by calling `beginVertex()` (with an optional argument, if you want). Then, *before* building any vertices, you call `texture()` with a single argument: the `PImage` that holds your image.

Now you call `vertex()` as before, but in addition to the *x*- and *y*-coordinates, you also include the *u*- and *v*-coordinates, so `vertex()` gets a total of four arguments. When you're done, you call `endShape()` as usual. The texture will then get warped, stretched, or otherwise distorted as necessary so that the points line up as you've specified.

As of Processing 1.1, the default renderer doesn't handle texture at all, and the P2D and P3D renderers produce different results. Let's start with the P3D renderer. In this example, I know my screen is 600 by 400, and my texture is 600 by 450, so I'll use those numbers both to place my vertices and identify texture positions.

```
PImage Hike;

void setup() {
  size(600, 400, P3D);
  Hike = loadImage("myPhoto.jpg");

  background(192);

  // tall thin rectangle
  beginShape();
  texture(Hike);
  vertex(50, 50, 0, 0);
  vertex(150, 50, 599, 0);
  vertex(150, 350, 599, 449);
  vertex(50, 350, 0, 449);
  endShape(CLOSE);

  // short wide rectangle
  beginShape();
  texture(Hike);
  vertex(200, 250, 0, 0);
  vertex(550, 250, 599, 0);
  vertex(550, 350, 599, 449);
  vertex(200, 350, 0, 449);
  endShape(CLOSE);
```

Figure 16.28. Displaying texture. (images/sketches/texture1/texture1.pde)

```
// square
beginShape();
texture(Hike);
vertex(300, 50,    50, 200);
vertex(450, 50,   200, 200);
vertex(450, 200,  200, 400);
vertex(300, 200,   50, 400);
endShape(CLOSE);
}
```

(See output in Figure 16.28. Full program in images/sketches/texture1/texture1.pde)

You can see how the texture has been stretched to fit the shape I'm putting it into. And in the square, I've chosen just a piece of the texture to display by associating only a region of the texture with the square's vertices. The texture is automatically enlarged, shrunk, twisted, pulled, and otherwise transformed to make it fit your shape using the points you provide.

Figure 16.29. Texture with OpenGL. (images/sketches/texture2/texture2.pde)

Compare this result to the image produced by the OPENGL renderer. All I'll do is import the library,

```
import processing.opengl.*;
```

and then specify OPENGL in the size() call:

```
size(600, 400, OPENGL);
```

(See output in Figure 16.29. Full program in images/sketches/texture2/texture2.pde)

You can see that the OPENGL version is a lot smoother and less choppy. To my eye, the OPENGL version looks blurrier, too. The P3D renderer is trying to go as fast as it can, so it's cutting corners on image quality. The OPENGL renderer is a bit slower, but the picture looks less grainy.

I've been showing textures on rectangular shapes so that you can see what's happening easily, but you can attach texture coordinates to any vertex on any shape. Here are some examples of nonrectangular shapes with textures on them.

```
// triangle
beginShape();
texture(Hike);
vertex(100, 240, 0, 400);
vertex( 60,  60, 0, 0);
vertex(240, 100, 600, 400);
endShape(CLOSE);

// fish
beginShape();
texture(Hike);
vertex(160, 320, 0, 300);
vertex(200, 200, 100, 400);
vertex(280, 180, 200, 400);
vertex(300, 100, 400, 400);
vertex(380, 160, 600, 0);
vertex(400, 240, 500, 0);
vertex(320, 220, 400, 0);
vertex(300, 300, 300, 0);
endShape(CLOSE);

// arrowhead
beginShape();
texture(Hike);
vertex(420, 300,   0, 400);
vertex(500,  60, 600, 400);
vertex(580, 360, 600,   0);
vertex(500, 240,   0,   0);
endShape(CLOSE);
```

(See output in Figure 16.30. Full program in images/sketches/texture3/texture3.pde)

In the code above I named the (u, v) coordinates of my textures. You can change the way you refer to texture coordinates using textureMode(). If you give it the argument IMAGE, then you work just as above: the texture values passed to vertex() are interpreted as points in the texture (that is, u and v values that range from (0,0) in the upper left to one less than the texture's width and height in the lower right). If you give textureMode() the argument NORMALIZED, then your texture coordinates are interpreted with (0,0) still in the upper left, but the lower right is (1,1). Using normalized coordinates for your texture can be easier because then you don't have to mess around with getting the texture's width and height from its fields and calculating with them. On the other hand, this is another of those mode changes in Processing that, once applied, is essentially undetectable later. So my advice is to avoid changing the texture mode and leave it at the default of IMAGE. As always, if you must change the mode, I recommend putting it back to the default as soon as possible.

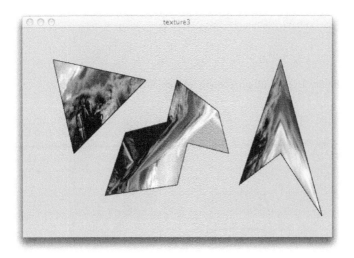

Figure 16.30. Nonrectangular shapes. (images/sketches/texture3/texture3.pde)

16.6   SVG Objects

Somewhere in between images and shapes that you draw out of primitives (like rectangles and circles) are *scalable vector graphics* objects , also called *SVG* objects.

SVG is really nothing more than a file format for collections of shapes and colors. So while a file in, say, jpg or gif formats contains an array of pixel colors, a file in SVG format contains a list of shapes to draw (and their associated drawing information). You can create and save SVG files with a variety of drawing programs, such as Illustrator.

The commands for using an SVG object parallel those for using an image object. You create an SVG object in your Processing sketch by declaring a variable of type PShape to hold it. You read it in with the command loadShape(), which takes the name of an SVG format file. You draw the shape file to the screen using shape(), which takes the PShape variable and the upper-left *x*- and *y*-coordinates of the shape. You can also give it two additional values representing the desired width and height of your drawing.

Like imageMode(), there's a shapeMode() that lets you change how the four numbers you give to shape() should be interpreted. It takes the three arguments CORNER, CORNERS, and CENTER, which have the identical meanings as those given for imageMode() earlier. As always, I strongly recommend leaving the mode at its default value.

Let's load in an SVG picture and display it.

```
void setup() {
  size(350, 500);
  smooth();
```

```
  PShape s = loadShape("lamp.svg");
  shape(s, 50, 50);
}
```

(See output in Figure 16.31. Full program in images/sketches/svg1/svg1.pde)

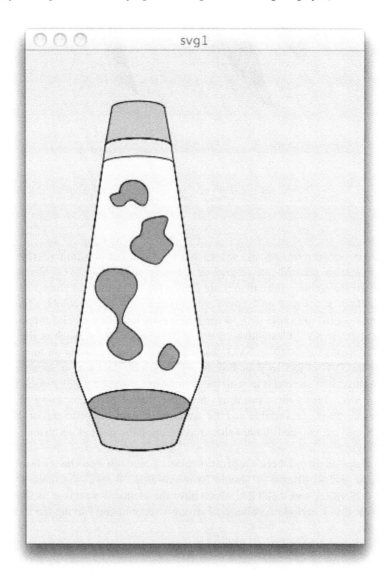

Figure 16.31. Drawing an SVG file. (images/sketches/svg1/svg1.pde)

Figure 16.32. Zooming in on an SVG file. (images/sketches/svg2/svg2.pde)

Figure 16.31 shows an SVG form of Figure 19.1.

One nice quality of an SVG file is that it's *resolution independent*. That means we can zoom in on it and it will still look nice and crisp, unlike a grid of pixels, which would just turn into big fuzzy blocks. Let's zoom in on the last picture and see how nice the curves still look.

```
shape(s, -250, -300, 1000, 1000);
```

(See output in Figure 16.32. Full program in images/sketches/svg2/svg2.pde)

Very nice. If you don't want to use SVG, Processing supports an alternative: as we saw in Chapter 6, we can also use the PDF renderer to produce resolution-independent graphics. We'll return to that topic in Chapter 17.

Chapter 17
Working with Files

The big focus in Processing is what's happening on the screen, but often we need to read in some information that already exists. We might be drawing a program that shows rainfall in the state of Washington, for instance. Then we would need a file with points that define the outline of the state and another file with data on the rainfall.

Processing has a small number of routines available for reading and writing files. Generally speaking, the easiest way to work with files is to treat them as *plain text*. This is the name given to the type of file that you might create with a bare-bones text editor (that is, no color, font changes, or other style information). Processing makes it easy for you to read and write these text files one line at a time. The big advantage of plain-text files is that they're *human-readable*, which simply means that you can open them up and make sense of them.

Processing's own source code files are plain text (the .pde extension helps the computer know that they belong to Processing, but they're still just text files). You can read and write .pde files with any text editor. To get Processing to pay attention to your changes, of course, you'll need to copy the text out of your editor and into Processing's own window (or you can turn on the "Use external editor" check box on Processing's *Preferences* page).

You can also work with *binary files*. These are compressed in a form that's more efficient for the computer. It's faster to read and write binary files, but you can't make sense of them directly with a text editor.

You have tons of binary files on your disk already. All of your pictures are binary, and all of your sound and music files are also binary (though they contain very different types of information, of course). Try opening up a picture or sound file with your text editor. It might not even let you open it, but if it does, unless the program has been specially written to handle those kinds of files, you're likely to end up with a screenful of random junk. The only way to examine an image file is with an image-editing program, and the only way to listen to a sound file is with a music program.

So binary files are efficient, but each kind of binary file requires special software to read and write it. Text files are less efficient, but humans can read and write them and make sense of them.

Generally speaking, when I save my own data out of Processing, I use text. I can look at the results myself and see if they look good, and I can even adjust them if they don't. If performance becomes an issue (that is, my program starts to run too slowly, or I'm going to share it with other people who might have slower computers), I'll consider using binary files.

So let's stick with text files for now.

In this chapter, we'll write a program that lets us digitize and then display a hand-drawn picture. I'll start with a little silhouette guy I drew as part of a bunch of illustrations for last Halloween. An unedited scan from my sketchbook is shown in Figure 17.1.

My overall goal is to write a sketch in Processing that will take this guy, and a bunch of other creatures I drew, and animate them on the screen. I could, of course, just load the drawing as a PImage and show it with image() as we saw in Chapter 16, but I'm thinking that I might like to move some of the pieces around over time. So what I'd like is to turn this picture into a collection of points, so that I can actually draw these shapes using Processing's drawing commands and then later animate them.

There are commercial packages that will do this, and some do a great job. You can digitize your shape as points or even as Bézier curves (which would probably be an excellent choice for this guy). Why not just buy one of these programs? Of course, there's the cost. It might not be worth it to spend whatever these packages charge just to digitize a few shapes once. But even if we found a free (or open-source) package, there's the possible hassle of *file conversion*. Suppose I settle on a particular program to turn my little guy into a collection of points. I push the button and it's done: the program has saved the points in a file. But what's inside that file? How do I get at the points and use them in Processing?

If the program wrote a binary file, I'm probably stuck. I can't just open it and figure out what's there simply by looking. I'll have to dig around the web, maybe read some forums, maybe contact the manufacturer, and if their file formats are confidential, maybe they'll tell me that they won't tell me how to read the data!

Even if the program wrote a text file, it could still be a mess. There might be tons of other information in there, from the date the file was written to color information. The numbers themselves might be in some weird format, with commas in them, or there might be strange codes inserted to tell the program information that it cares about but that I don't.

I've been down this road more times than I can count, and even when it's possible to read a file written by some other program, it's often a long and frustrating task. It can take hours.

So maybe I'm better off writing something quick and dirty in Processing that can do the job. I'll have complete control over everything, and I can even customize the program to work exactly the way I want. It doesn't have to be a great solution that I can sell; it just needs to be good enough to let me digitize my little character and get on with my Halloween plans. It'll probably even be fun to write and then use. So let's go for it.

Here's the general plan. My first program, or sketch, will help me convert the image into a file of points. A second program will read that file of points and draw the object.

Figure 17.1. A little hand-drawn man.

The file of points will be simple as can be, a plain-text file in which each line contains the x and y values of a single point, separated by a tab, like this:

```
...
338.78   -134.74
333.23   -132.73
331.14   -130.12
...
```

I've got a problem right away, though: my little guy has white shapes on top of his black body. In my original design, the white shapes are holes cut out of the black body, so I got in the habit of calling them "holes." For this project, I'll treat them as white shapes, but I'll still call them holes to distinguish them from the "body."

How can I store both the body and the holes? I see two choices. The first is to make everything a little more complicated: somehow I'll tell my digitizing program when I'm digitizing the body and when I'm digitizing a hole and then, in the text file, there will be extra lines that say something like, "The shapes that follow this line are part of a new shape," and then the next line might have the color definition. It might end up like this:

```
...
338.78   -134.74
NEWSHAPE
COLOR 0  0  0
333.23   -132.73
331.14   -130.12
...
```

I wrote my words in all capitals to help them stand out.

This can work just fine, but our simple little program would take a jump in complexity. Reading all these different types of input lines and processing each one correctly is straightforward but takes a lot of lines of code. To keep things simple in this project, I won't take this approach.

Instead, I'll run the program several times, and each time, I'll create a new file of points. Since I have one body and five holes, I'll end up with six text files. It'll be up to me to name them sensibly so I'll know which is which. Then I can just draw the body first, in black, and then draw the white holes on top of it.

I considered writing an automatic program to extract the contours. I might use the mouse to click on a single spot on the edge of the body, for instance, and the program itself would run around the shape, collecting up points, until it returned to the beginning. This is a fun kind of program to figure out and write, but it has some drawbacks. Obviously I want to keep the sharp points in my design (like at his lips, or the corners of his eye). But an automatic program wouldn't know a sharp corner from a smooth edge, so I'd have to program in that intelligence. Now it's a significantly harder and more complex program. Then I want to make sure I don't get too many points (I don't want a figure defined by 20,000 points—it would take forever to read it in and draw), but I don't want too few points, either (or all my graceful curves will turn into chunky straight lines). I don't need many points in smooth areas like the back of his head, but I need lots of them around his fingers. Trying to adjust how many points are needed where would make things even more complex.

So again, I'm going to keep this easy. Who knows where lots of points are needed? Who knows where the sharp corners are located? I do! So I'll drive this train. This will be an interactive program. Processing will put up the picture, and I'll use my mouse to click around the outside of the body or one of the holes, gathering up one point at a time and saving them to a file.

Let's do that.

17.1 Digitizing

As always, I'll start with a skeleton. Because my monitor is wider than it is tall, I'll do all this work with my little guy rotated 90 degrees. I used my favorite image editor to resize the scan to about fill my screen. Here's the skeleton to show me the drawing:

```
PImage Picture;

void setup() {
   size(1600, 630);
   Picture = loadImage("../oddman.png");
   image(Picture, 0, 0);
}
```

(See output in Figure 17.2. Full program in files/sketches/digitize01/digitize01.pde)

Figure 17.2. Showing the scan. (files/sketches/digitize01/digitize01.pde)

I needed to put my drawing oddman.png somewhere that my program could find it, but since I know I'll run through lots of versions of this program while building it up, I didn't want to have to put a new copy of the drawing into every sketch's folder. So I put one copy in the folder above this sketch (that's what the . . / is for) and then all the other sketches to come can point to the same place to find the picture. Since the sketches only read the image oddman.png and never change or overwrite it, they can all share one copy.

So that you can follow along, I've included a copy of this drawing with the sketches for this chapter.

So far, so good. Now let's collect and save mouse clicks.

First, the mouse part. Recalling Chapter 7, I'll just implement mouseClicked(), which gets called when a mouse button is pressed and then released. I know that the mouse location is saved in the variables mouseX and mouseY.

Second, the saving part. This is where our file stuff comes into play.

To write to a file, we create an object called a PrintWriter. This object can be sent lines of text, and it will add them to a text file it knows about. We'll see that this is pretty easy to implement.

It's important to keep in mind that this file writing is not instantaneous. Processing knows that reading and writing files on your hard drive can be slow. If your disk has to spin up first after being idle, for example, your whole animation could freeze up for a few seconds while the disk gets going again. Even when the disk is ready, reading and writing files can take some time. So in an effort to be efficient, PrintWriter will save up, or *buffer*, multiple lines of text. When it has a whole bunch of stuff to write, then it writes everything to the file in one big operation rather than lots of little ones.

Normally this is a great thing and keeps your program running nice and smoothly, even when you work with disk files. You tell Processing to write something, and if it needs to spin up the disk, it stashes your request on the side while the disk gathers speed, and in the meantime, your program keeps running. If you ask it to write a dozen tiny little things, rather than handle each request one by one (and slow you down a little each time), it just waits until there's a whole batch of things ready to be written, and it writes them all at one go.

But sometimes you want the file to really be up to date, right now. In other words, you want to force PrintWriter to write whatever it has to the file, now, regardless of whether that's efficient or not. Thanks to long-standing tradition, this is called *flushing the buffer*. If you want the PrintWriter to write what it has, right now, you call its method, named flush().

Once you've created a PrintWriter, the file it points to is *open*. That is, the operating system considers that this file "belongs" to Processing, and while other programs may be allowed to read it, no other program can write to it. It's good form to *close*, or *release*, a file when you're done with it. If you forget, Processing will close all open files for you when your program exits. But you should get into the habit of manually closing your files yourself so that you don't find yourself one day with a dozen open files floating around your program, and you accidentally write to the wrong ones, clobbering your work. To close a file, you call its method, named close().

Caution! There's a quirk in how Processing handles this operation that you need to keep in mind. If you forget, you can actually lose some of your work. Here's the thing: the close() method doesn't automatically flush the PrintWriter first. That is, when you call close(), if there are things still waiting to get written, they are ignored, the file is closed, and the things you told Processing to write to the file just disappear.

I don't know why it works this way; automatically flushing before closing is definitely a good idea. But that's how it is. If you close your file (either manually or by calling exit()) and you don't flush the file first, anything that was sitting in the buffer is simply lost. Yes, you told the PrintWriter to write your output to the file and that should be the end of it, but if you close the file before it happens to get around to doing the writing for you, it just throws your most recent requests away. In order to make sure that your file is complete when you close it, you must manually flush it first. The rule for writing files correctly is this: *always call* flush() *before you call* close().

Now that we have all the pieces, I'll declare a global variable for our PrintWriter:

```
PrintWriter OutputFile;
```

Like PImage, you don't create a new PrintWriter in the usual way (by calling new followed by a constructor). Instead, it has its own creation routine with its own name: createWriter().

In setup() I'll create OutputFile, with the name of the file where I want the output to go using createWriter():

```
OutputFile = createWriter("DrawingPoints.txt");
```

You'll see I used the .txt extension for my file because that's the generally used extension for plain-text files.

Finally, I'll implement mouseClicked() so that it writes each mouse position to the file. I'll just print them out on the line in order: *x* value, tab, *y* value:

```
void mouseClicked() {
    OutputFile.println(mouseX + "\t" + mouseY);
}
```

You can see that writing to a file is just like writing it using println(), only you call that routine as a method for the file object. Here's the complete program so far:

```
PImage Picture;
PrintWriter OutputFile;

void setup() {
    size(1600, 630);
    Picture = loadImage("../oddman.png");
    image(Picture, 0, 0);
    OutputFile = createWriter("DrawingPoints.txt");
```

```
}

void mouseClicked() {
    OutputFile.println(mouseX + "\t" + mouseY);
}
```

(Full program in files/sketches/digitize02/digitize02.pde)

If you run this and click around a few times and then exit the program, you'll see that there's a new file in your sketch's folder. It's called `DrawingPoints.txt`. But if you look inside, it's probably empty.

Right. Although Processing closed `OutputFile` for us when we exited, we didn't flush it first, so unless your system happened to be pretty aggressive and wrote just a few lines to the file, it got closed before they ever made it.

How do we capture the fact that we're exiting the program? As we know, when Processing starts it always calls `setup()` if it's there, so what does Processing call when it exits?

Sadly, nothing. If we want to run something when Processing quits, we have to quit our own way rather than by using the quit button on the window.

Since we're already using the mouse button, let's use the keyboard. Pressing the letter *Q* (for "quit") will cause the program to flush `OutputFile` and close it and then exit the program. We can do that by implementing `keyPressed()` and checking the value of `key`:

```
void keyPressed() {
    if ((key == 'q') || (key == 'Q')) {
        OutputFile.flush();
        OutputFile.close();
        exit();
    }
}
```

(Full program in files/sketches/digitize03/digitize03.pde)

Hmm, when I run this, nothing happens at all when I press the *Q* key. Let's print out the key value; maybe I'm not testing it correctly.

```
void keyPressed() {
    println("the key is "+key);
    if ((key == 'q') || (key == 'Q')) {
        OutputFile.flush();
        OutputFile.close();
        exit();
    }
}
```

(Full program in files/sketches/digitize04/digitize04.pde)

Another big fat nothing. I can hit keys all day and nothing comes out. Clearly, keyPressed() isn't getting called.

You may recall from Chapter 7 that when you're trying to read from the mouse or keyboard, you'll want to have a draw() routine implemented, even if it does nothing. I haven't written one of those yet. So I'll add an empty draw() (which I'll probably want to have around eventually anyway):

```
void draw() {
}
```

(Full program in files/sketches/digitize05/digitize05.pde)

That does the job. Now the program prints out the key presses, and when I press *Q* it wraps up and exits. Even better, if I click around a few times before hitting *Q*, then those mouse clicks are correctly recorded in the file.

I'll remove the print statement in keyPressed() before moving on, but it was a good contributor and it has my thanks.

What's next? Well, at each step, I'd really like to know where I've clicked so far so I can both be sure that my most recent mouse click got read and see where to click next. Let's draw a little, bright red circle around every mouse press. In setup() I'll add two lines for the style:

```
fill(255, 0, 0);
noStroke();
```

Figure 17.3. Showing mouse clicks with red circles. This is a close-up of the mouth area. (files/sketches/digitize06/digitize06.pde)

And then I just need one line in mouseClicked():

```
void mouseClicked() {
   OutputFile.println(mouseX + "\t" + mouseY);
   ellipse(mouseX, mouseY, 3, 3);
}
```

(See output in Figure 17.3. Full program in files/sketches/digitize06/digitize06.pde)

The ellipse is so small it's coming out as a little square, but that's fine.

I want to capture my outline as accurately as possible, but I'm as human as anyone, and sometimes I slip. You can see in Figure 17.3 a place where I slipped: I started at the corner of his lip and worked my way down and to the left, but I did a pretty bad job on the sixth point. I made this particular mistake on purpose to create the figure, but when I was really using the program to digitize the points, I did start in that place, went in that direction, and eventually I always slipped up somewhere just like this. So then I started over. And messed up again.

That's when I realized I would have to do this a thousand times to get it perfect all the way around the body, and I just wasn't about to do that. I needed some approach that would let me handle problems in some nicer way than starting over again from scratch.

My first thought, of course, was a big fancy system with undo capabilities and stuff like that, but then I remembered that I'm writing a nice little Processing sketch, not a big, monster, do-everything, professional-grade, image-digitizing program. I just needed something to let me get my work done. If someday I need something with tons more features, I can either roll up one of my sleeves and write it or roll up my other sleeve and find an existing package and figure out how to use it and its output. But for now, I just need a way to handle the occasional slip.

Here's my quick-and-dirty answer. When I mess up a dot, I hit the Z key (it's convenient and easy to reach, sitting in the corner of the keyboard). Remember, by the time I see the dot, it's already been written into the file, so I can't undo that. But what I can do is write a new line to the file. So when I hit the Z key, I'll write the line ERROR! to the output file. Then when I'm done, I can open the file with my text editor and search for that word. Each time I find it, I'll delete the word and the point immediately above it. This solution does require a little manual intervention at the end, but that's going to be a lot easier on my time and life than implementing some sophisticated error-fixing system.

So let's just add that little bit to `keyPressed()`:

```
void keyPressed() {
  if (key == 'z') {
    output.println("ERROR!");
    return;
  }
  output.flush(); // Write the remaining data
  output.close(); // Finish the file
  exit(); // Stop the program
}
```

(See output in Figure 17.4. Full program in files/sketches/digitize07/digitize07.pde)

You can see that I messed up the fourth point in Figure 17.4. I remembered to hit the Z key when I did. Here's the resulting `DrawingPoints.txt` output file:

```
446        99
434        103
```

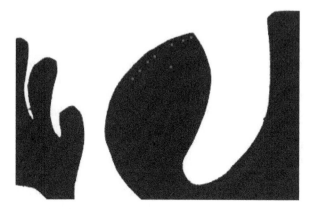

Figure 17.4. The new code. The fourth point is an error.
(files/sketches/digitize07/digitize07.pde)

```
421        108
419        152
ERROR!
399        124
392        132
384        141
377        152
```

In practice, when I screwed up I tried to go back and reclick the point again where I meant it to be; I left that step out of this example so you could see the results more clearly.

There's one big problem remaining, and that's the lousy job I'm doing at capturing the outline of my own drawing. The mouse pointer is pretty big, and even when I get up close to the monitor, it's hard to click on exactly the right spot. These points are ending up in roughly the right place, but it's going to be a pretty rough and craggy outline that I draw from this data. How can I get closer to the smooth forms of my original image?

One choice would be to back off and replace this dot-gathering approach with a curve-drawing approach. I could create a bunch of Bézier curves, enforce smoothness, and it would look like a million bucks. But that would be a whole lot harder than what I'm doing now from a user interface point of view. Well, maybe not excessively harder, but I've picked this road and I'll see where it can take me.

What I'd like is to create some kind of a "magnet" effect. Something that would take the location of my mouse click and find the nearest point on the border of my image. If the picture was made up of smoothly changing grays (or even colors), this might be a very tall order, but I have a crisp black-and-white picture. So I'm encouraged that there must be a way. To give myself more of a fighting chance, I used my image editor and resaved the picture with the contrast cranked up so high that all the black pixels are (0,0,0) and all the white pixels are (255,255,255) (that's actually the version that I've saved with these sketches). There are a few gray pixels still on the boundaries between the regions of constant color.

Let's say that the pixel I click on is the *click pixel*. Then I want to look around at the pixels nearby and see if any of them are on a black–white border. If so, that's probably the pixel I meant to click. So I'll write a routine that takes the click pixel as input (that is, the mouse coordinates) and returns the value of the nearest *border pixel* within some radius.

So we have two questions. The first is what defines a border pixel, and the second is how do you find the nearest one. Let's take these in order.

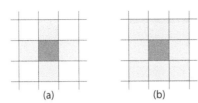

(a)   (b)

Figure 17.5. The two types of neighborhoods around the red pixel. (a) The 4-connected neighbors are shown in blue. (b) The 8-connected neighbors are shown in blue.

I'll say a border pixel is any pixel that has at least one neighbor of a different color. I don't care what color that is; if any of its neighbors are different from itself, it's a border pixel.

So we want a routine that takes a *test pixel* as input and tells us whether or not it's a border pixel. All it needs to do is find the color of the test pixel and check the colors of the neighbors. If any neighbor has a different color, this is a border pixel. If not, it's not on a border.

Which pixels should make up the neighbors? There are two popular choices, called the *4-connected* neighbors and the *8-connected* neighbors. Figure 17.5 shows these. The 4-connected pixels are those to the north, south, east, and west of the pixel we're working with. The 8-connected pixels are those four, plus the four on the diagonals.

Let's go with the 8-connected neighbors. So a simple routine would grab the test pixel's color and test the others, one by one. I'll put all the tests together into one big *if statement* with the logical or operator ||; that way, if any of them are true, the test is true and we return true.

```
boolean onBorder(int tx, int ty) {
    color tcolor = picture.get(tx, ty);
    if ((tcolor != picture.get(tx-1, ty-1)) || // upper left
        (tcolor != picture.get(tx,   ty-1)) || // above
        (tcolor != picture.get(tx+1, ty-1)) || // upper right
        (tcolor != picture.get(tx-1, ty  )) || // left
        (tcolor != picture.get(tx+1, ty  )) || // right
        (tcolor != picture.get(tx-1, ty+1)) || // lower left
        (tcolor != picture.get(tx,   ty+1)) || // below
        (tcolor != picture.get(tx+1, ty+1)))   // lower right
        return(true);
    return(false);
}
```

That does the trick. You know my repeat sensors are going off. I tried to make this a little more tolerable by formatting it clearly. I could tighten this up a bit, say by using one *for loop* nested inside another, and have it run through the little three-by-three square centered on (tx, ty), but then I'd have to explicitly exclude the center square itself, and ultimately, I don't think I'd end up with much improvement in size or clarity. So on balance, I'll leave these lines as they are, though they bug me a little.

I could save a little bit of code by removing the *if statement* altogether. After all, I'm testing to see if something is true, and if it is, I'm returning `true`. If I replace the test with just a phrase for the moment, we could write the above routine like this:

```
if (big-test-here)
    return (true);
return(false);
```

Here's even shorter code that produces the same result:

```
return (big-test-here);
```

After all, if the test is true, then we're returning `true`, otherwise `false`. This second version is definitely tighter and smaller, but I often use the more extended form above. It could be slightly slower to run (by an amount no human could ever detect), but the structure makes it easier to get in there and add other code (like print statements) if I need to someday get in there and debug or extend this routine. It's a question of style and taste; both forms have their merits, and they both do the same job.

So now we have a test that tells us whether a pixel is a border pixel or not. How do we use this to find the nearest border pixel? First we have to decide how far to search. I'm going to arbitrarily say that a distance of about five pixels is far enough. If my click pixel is more than five pixels away from a border pixel, then I probably made a very bad click, and it should ultimately be ignored.

Let's imagine a circle around the click pixel and test every pixel inside it. The first time that we find a border pixel (if we find any), we save it. Then suppose we later find another border pixel. If it's closer to the test pixel, we save that one instead. When we're done looking at all the pixels around the click pixel, if we've saved any pixel at all, it will be the border pixel closest to the click pixel.

So we'll write a routine that takes the mouse position as input and returns the nearest border pixel. I'll return the border pixel's coordinates in the global variables Bx and By (I could use a PVector, but this works just as well).

The routine first initializes Bx and By to the click pixel (the mouse coordinates). That way, if we don't find any border pixels, we'll return the mouse position itself (since there's nothing better to return). Then I'll start the search. Rather than use a circle, let's use a square. So I'll search a square that's 11 pixels on a side (plus and minus 5 around the click pixel).

Before I start, I'll create a `boolean` variable (sometimes called a *flag*) to tell me if I've found any border pixels at all yet. I'll also create a `float` to keep the distance of the nearest one to the click pixel. The first time I find a border pixel, the flag goes to `true`, the globals `Bx` and `By` get set to the border pixel, and I save the distance of the border pixel from the click pixel in `nearestDistance`. Then I keep scanning. If I find another border pixel, and it's closer to the test pixel than the value in `nearestDistance`, then `Bx` and `By` get updated to the new pixel, and `nearestDistance` gets updated too. If I find another pixel of the same distance, I won't bother to update it; for this project, we just want the nearest pixel, or any of the nearest pixels if there are several of them at the same distance.

Here's a little routine called `findBorder()` that returns the nearest border pixel (or one of the nearest) or the mouse point itself if it can't find one. To represent the distance between the points in x and y I'll name my variables `dx` and `dy` (in mathematics, the Greek letter delta (Δ) is often used to represent the distance between two points, so programmers often use the letter d (for delta) when measuring quantites involved in distances). So `dx` is meant to suggest "change in x".

```
void findBorder(int mx, int my) {
    Bx = mx;
    By = my;
    boolean foundBorder = false;
    float nearestDistance = 0;
    for (int dy= -5; dy<6; dy++) {
        for (int dx= -5; dx<6; dx++) {
            if (onBorder(mx+dx, my+dy)) {
                float distance = mag(dx, dy);
                if ((!foundBorder) || (distance < nearestDistance)) {
                    foundBorder = true;
                    nearestDistance = distance;
                    Bx = mx+dx;
                    By = my+dy;
                }
            }
        }
    }
}
```

So the code just sweeps through the square and remembers the nearest border pixel (if there is one). You'll notice that if we find multiple border pixels, I'm setting `foundBorder` to `true` over and over again. That's a little inefficient, but speed is not our priority here. This is not the most efficient way to find the nearest border pixel (you might want to try experimenting with some faster ways), but it's easy to write and more than quick enough to keep up with me as I click my mouse, one point at a time.

We don't want to forget to declare the global variables up top somewhere:

```
float Bx, By;
```

We'll also fix `mouseClicked()` to call `findBorder()` and use the "border" coordinates that come back:

```
void mouseClicked() {
    findBorder(mouseX, mouseY);
    OutputFile.println(Bx + "\t" + By);
    ellipse(Bx, By, 3, 3);
}
```

Here's the complete program, all in one place:

```
PImage Picture;
PrintWriter OutputFile;
float Bx, By;

void setup() {
    size(1600, 630);
    Picture = loadImage("../oddman.png");
    image(Picture, 0, 0);
    OutputFile = createWriter("DrawingPoints.txt");
    fill(255, 0, 0);
    noStroke();
}

void draw() {
}

void mouseClicked() {
    findBorder(mouseX, mouseY);
    OutputFile.println(Bx + "\t" + By);
    ellipse(Bx, By, 3, 3);
}

void keyPressed() {
  if (key == 'z') {
    OutputFile.println("ERROR!");
    return;
  }
  OutputFile.flush();
  OutputFile.close();
  exit();
}

void findBorder(int mx, int my) {
    Bx = mx;
    By = my;
    boolean foundBorder = false;
    float nearestDistance = 0;
    for (int dy= -5; dy<6; dy++) {
        for (int dx= -5; dx<6; dx++) {
```

Figure 17.6. The input process with the magnet code. (files/sketches/digitize09/digitize09.pde)

```
            if (onBorder(mx+dx, my+dy)) {
                float distance = mag(dx, dy);
                if ((!foundBorder) || (distance < nearestDistance)) {
                    foundBorder = true;
                    nearestDistance = distance;
                    Bx = mx+dx;
                    By = my+dy;
                }
            }
        }
    }
}

boolean onBorder(int tx, int ty) {
    color tcolor = Picture.get(tx, ty);
    if ((tcolor != Picture.get(tx-1, ty-1)) || // upper left
        (tcolor != Picture.get(tx,   ty-1)) || // above
        (tcolor != Picture.get(tx+1, ty-1)) || // upper right
        (tcolor != Picture.get(tx-1, ty  )) || // left
        (tcolor != Picture.get(tx+1, ty  )) || // right
        (tcolor != Picture.get(tx-1, ty+1)) || // lower left
        (tcolor != Picture.get(tx,   ty+1)) || // below
        (tcolor != Picture.get(tx+1, ty+1)))   // lower right
        return(true);
    return(false);
}
```

(See output in Figure 17.6. Full program in files/sketches/digitize09/digitize09.pde)

Figure 17.6 shows the result. I started with the body and worked my way around the drawing, clicking near the border. I messed up a few times (near his toes and forehead, for example) by clicking outside the five-pixel radius, but most of the time, my points snapped right to the boundary.

Figure 17.7. A close-up of the magnet results.

One thing I learned was that it was best to always stay on one side of the boundary; that is, always click on black pixels or white ones. Otherwise, there was a tiny bit of jitter in the positions as the pixels snapped to the nearest side of the boundary, which of course is at least one pixel different for the two colors. I found it easiest to always click on the black areas.

Figure 17.7 shows a close-up of the hand, which has the tightest curvy bits. All I did was click near the boundary, and the points snapped right up snugly to the edge.

I repeated this five more times, once for each of the white "holes." I manually renamed the output file after I was done with each run so I knew which file described which piece of the shape.

17.2   Cleanup

So now how do we clean up the errors? Some of them I remembered to hit the Z key for, so I went through the files manually and deleted any line with the word "ERROR" on it, as well as the line above it. But I still had a bunch of bad points.

I decided to write a little program in Processing to help me identify and fix the points. Rather than fix the points interactively with the mouse, I thought it would be faster and easier to simply change the contents of the output file using my text editor. So what I needed was something that would let me quickly find the line number in the file that held each bad point. Then I could go to that line with my text editor and change the values in the file to tweak the point's position. I could even delete that line altogether if I thought the point wasn't needed.

My first thought was to simply draw lines between the points as I'd entered them by running through all the points with a loop. I'll keep the variables ox and oy to refer to the "old" x and y locations (that is, the points from the previous time around the loop) so I can draw a line from the last point to the new one. Then the new points become the old points, and around we go again.

This time around we want to read from the file we just made. This is even easier than writing. The routine loadStrings() takes the name of a file, and returns an array of String variables, one per line. That's it! No need to open the file, flush it, close it, any of that. One call to loadStrings() and you're done.

I'll talk more about the String type in Chapter 20. For now, just think of it as a little snippet of text. If we hand a String to the function int(), that function will turn the text into an actual number of type int. Since each line of our file contains two numbers separated by a tab, we need to split the line up into two pieces, so we can

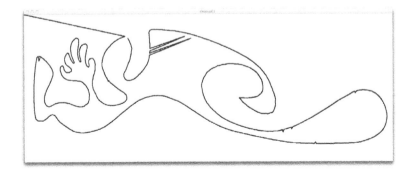

Figure 17.8. The results of digitizing. (files/sketches/cleanup01/cleanup01.pde)

hand each little piece to int(). The function split() will do this for us. It takes a String and a character and chops up the input String into shorter pieces by cutting it anywhere that character appears. In this case, we'll give it a line from our file and the tab character (which is written with the special code '\t'); it will return an array of two elements. I'll discuss all this stuff in more detail in Chapter 20.

Let's put these file-reading and integer-making steps into a new skeleton and join up the points with lines. After I digitized each piece of my input drawing, I renamed the file my program produced. I named the file with the points for the man's body Body-ManPoints.txt, so that's the file I'll read back in.

```
void setup() {
    size(1600,630);
    background(255);
    stroke(0);
    strokeWeight(2);
    String [] lines = loadStrings("../Body-ManPoints.txt");
    int ox, oy, x, y;
    ox = oy = x = y = 0;
    for (int i=0; i<lines.length; i++) {
        String[] words = split(lines[i], '\t');
        if (i>0) {
            x = int(words[0]);
            y = int(words[1]);
            line(ox, oy, x, y);
        }
        ox = x;
        oy = y;
    }
}
```

(See output in Figure 17.8. Full program in files/sketches/cleanup01/cleanup01.pde)

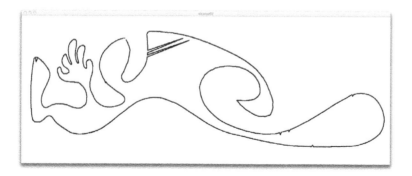

Figure 17.9. Fixing the first point. (files/sketches/cleanup02/cleanup02.pde)

Well, that's not too bad for a start, but I've got something nutty happening at the beginning. It's as though the values of x and y aren't being correctly extracted for the first point.

And they're not! I put those lines inside the loop. Dumb mistake. That's easy to fix. The *for loop*, when repaired, looks like this:

```
for (int i=0; i<lines.length; i++) {
   String[] words = split(lines[i], '\t');
   x = int(words[0]);
   y = int(words[1]);
   if (i>0) {
      line(ox, oy, x, y);
   }
   ox = x;
   oy = y;
}
```

(See output in Figure 17.9. Full program in files/sketches/cleanup02/cleanup02.pde)

That's better, but it's not closing up (see the little gap at the end of his lower lip). So I'll let the loop run for one more step (by changing the < test to <=) and use the modulo operator to make sure the last access will be to index 0 and not one past the actual end:

```
for (int i=0; i<=lines.length; i++) {
   String[] words = split(lines[i%lines.length], '\t');
```

(See output in Figure 17.10. Full program in files/sketches/cleanup03/cleanup03.pde)

That looks right. Now I can start fixing my errors.

Remember, my plan was to find the line number of each problem point in the file, so I could fix it by hand. Since the points are saved in the file one per line, if I can find the number of any point (counting from the first point I entered), that will also be that

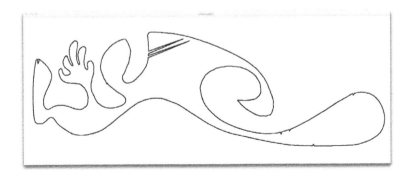

Figure 17.10. Closing the curve. (files/sketches/cleanup03/cleanup03.pde)

point's line number in the file. So how to find the number of each point? I thought of writing the numbers on the screen next to each point, but I realized that would become overwhelming, and the text would sometimes sit right on top of the points themselves. So then I thought I'd break them up into chunks of ten. Each chunk would be drawn in a different, random color. Near the bottom of the loop, we can say

```
if (i%10 == 0) {
    stroke(color(random(50, 200), random(50, 200),
            random(50, 200)));
}
```

(See output in Figure 17.11. Full program in files/sketches/cleanup04/cleanup04.pde)

Figure 17.11. Each chunk of ten points is in a different color.
(files/sketches/cleanup04/cleanup04.pde)

To see the points more clearly, let's also draw the points themselves. I'll make every tenth point larger:

```
if (i>0) {
    line(ox, oy, x, y);
```

Figure 17.12. Showing the points as well. (files/sketches/cleanup05/cleanup05.pde)

```
  float radius = 3;
  if (i%10 == 0) radius = 6;
  ellipse(x, y, radius, radius);
}
```

(See output in Figure 17.12. Full program in files/sketches/cleanup05/cleanup05.pde)

Great, now we have some landmarks. Using them, we can find and fix the little errors.

For example, let's dig into those two big glitches on his upper lip. I know I started at the tip of his lower lip and went counterclockwise, so these glitches are near the end of the file. Counting backwards, using the colors and big dots as reference, these errors are about 45 steps from the end. My text editor tells me that there are 824 lines (one per point), so I'll jump back to line $824 - 45 = 779$, which I think should be near the problem. That line reads:

```
540.0 202.0
```

To see if that's the point I want, I'll push it around. I'll arbitrarily change the 202 to 402 and see what happens. I'll save the file and run the program again; Figure 17.13 is the result.

I'm close, but the point I changed is a little bit past the error. So I put it back to the value it had. Looking at the file, I can see a pretty obvious

Figure 17.13. Looking for the problem points.

jump in the numbers a few lines earlier. Here are five consecutive lines:

```
548.0    136.0
548.0    146.0
700.0    94.0
548.0    156.0
547.0    165.0
```

I deleted the middle line of this set and got Figure 17.14.

Got it! In this way, one by one, I addressed each line that looked bad to me. I hunted for the problem point by changing the numbers of points nearby. When I finally found the line with the point that I didn't like, I sometimes adjusted the values to make them close to the ones nearby, or sometimes

Figure 17.14. Deleting the suspicious line.

I deleted the point entirely. Figure 17.15 shows the result for the body curve.

Figure 17.15. The cleaned-up curve.

I repeated this for each of the six curves (the body and the five holes).

Now let's repackage this drawing routine so I can call it once for each of the point files, allowing me to see everything at once. It just means making lines a global and putting the bottom half of the listing into its own routine. Here's the repackaged version:

```
String [] Lines;

void setup() {
  size(1600,630);
  background(255);
  stroke(0);
  strokeWeight(2);
  Lines = loadStrings("../Body-ManPoints.txt");
  showCurve();
```

```
}

void showCurve() {
  int ox, oy, x, y;
  ox = oy = x = y = 0;
  for (int i=0; i<=Lines.length; i++) {
    String[] words = split(Lines[i%Lines.length], '\t');
    x = int(words[0]);
    y = int(words[1]);
    if (i>0) {
      line(ox, oy, x, y);
      float radius = 3;
      if (i%10 == 0) radius = 6;
      ellipse(x, y, radius, radius);
    }
    if (i%10 == 0) {
      stroke(color(random(50, 200), random(50, 200), random(50, 200)));
    }
    ox = x;
    oy = y;
  }
}
```

(Full program in files/sketches/cleanup06/cleanup06.pde)

Figure 17.16. All the curves at once.

Sometimes reorganizing code in this way is called *refactoring* the code. Generally re-factoring means taking the existing pieces of a program and moving them around a bit so that they're more efficient or more generally useful.

Now I'll just repeat the loadStrings() command for each of the six point files, following each one by a call to showCurve() to see the whole thing, as shown in Figure 17.16
(Full program in files/sketches/cleaup07/cleaup07.pde)

17.3   Final Display

Now that we have the final points, displaying them is pretty easy. It's just a simple variation on the last program. Let's start with a skeleton that runs through the six files and calls something to draw them all:

```
String [] Lines;

void setup() {
    size(1600, 630);
    background(214, 192, 178);
    noStroke();
    smooth();
    color black = color(0, 0, 0);
    color white = color(255, 255, 255);
    Lines = loadStrings("../Body-ManPoints.txt");
    drawShape(black);
    Lines = loadStrings("../BellyHole-ManPoints.txt");
    drawShape(white);
    Lines = loadStrings("../EyeHole-ManPoints.txt");
    drawShape(white);
    Lines = loadStrings("../FootHole-ManPoints.txt");
    drawShape(white);
    Lines = loadStrings("../UpCircleHole-ManPoints.txt");
    drawShape(white);
    Lines = loadStrings("../UpperHole-ManPoints.txt");
    drawShape(white);
}

void drawShape(color clr) {
}
```

(Full program in files/sketches/drawAll01/drawAll01.pde)

In drawShape, I'll call beginShape() and then run through the file, calling vertex() once for each point, and then call endShape().

```
void drawShape(color clr) {
    fill(clr);
    beginShape();
    for (int i=0; i<lines.length; i++) {
        String[] vals = split(Lines[i], '\t');
        int x = int(vals[0]);
        int y = int(vals[1]);
        vertex(x, y);
    }
    endShape();
}
```

(See output in Figure 17.17. Full program in files/sketches/drawAll02/drawAll02.pde)

That does the job, but let's see the guy in his original form. That means reversing the dimensions in the size() statement and flipping the roles of x and y.

Figure 17.17. Drawing the whole figure. (files/sketches/drawAll02/drawAll02.pde)

Figure 17.18. Getting the dimensions right. (files/sketches/drawALL03/drawAll03.pde)

Figure 17.19. The final figure. (files/sketches/drawAll04/drawAll04.pde)

The only hitch is that my screen isn't tall enough for this new size of graphics window! So I'll reduce the dimensions by two and also scale x and y by 1/2 as well:

```
size(315, 800);

int x = int(vals[0])/2;
int y = int(vals[1])/2;
vertex(y, x);
```

(See output in Figure 17.18. Full program in files/sketches/drawAll03/drawAll03.pde)

Oops! He's upside-down. I'll just mirror the whole picture in y:

```
vertex(y, height-x);
```

(See output in Figure 17.19. Full program in files/sketches/drawAll04/drawAll04.pde)

Now we have the complete figure in point form, and we can draw and manipulate it as we like.

Success!

17.4   More File Options

We've covered only one file-related object and a few functions, but they've brought us a long way. There are lots of other file functions available in Processing, many of which have very specialized uses. To my mind, they fall into a few categories.

Dialog boxes. I wrote the names of my files right into my code. That works, but it's hardly flexible. Programmers sometimes call this *hard-coding* the file names into the program, and it's generally considered bad form because it's so inconvenient to maintain. For a little quickie project like this one, hard-coding is no sin. But if you're going to share your programs with other people, generally you shouldn't have any file names written into the code.

A better solution is to use your operating system's built-in file dialog boxes, the ones you see all the time when you want to open or save a file. To display one of these dialogs that allows the user to choose an input file call selectInput(). It will return either a String with the full path to the chosen file or the special value null if the user canceled. If you want to let the user choose an output file, call selectOutput(), which also returns a String to the file, or null if the user canceled. There's also the function selectFolder(), which lets the user select a folder.

Saving strings. We saw the use of loadStrings() to fill up an array of String objects from a file. It should therefore be little surprise that there's a function saveStrings(), which does the opposite job. You give it a file name and an array of Strings, and it writes them to the file, one String per line.

Reading big les. When you use `loadStrings()`, you're reading a whole file into memory. If that file is enormous, you might not have enough memory, and your program could crash. If you're on a computer with a hard drive (unlike a smartphone or handheld device), the computer might try to "fake" more memory for you, but that can cause your program to slow down or even pause. Happily, there's an alternative way to read in a text file that lets you read just one line at a time, when you need it. This will be a little bit slower than `loadStrings()`, but for big files, over the long run your program could run much faster because it's not hogging up all the computer's memory.

To read a file this way, you create a `BufferedReader` object using `createReader()`, which takes the name of a file. From then on, you read a single line by calling the `readLine()` method belonging to the reader object (by the way, note that unlike the ever-present system call `println()`, here we spell out the whole word and write `readLine`—it's just a little inconsistency in the language). The method `readLine()` returns a `String` that contains the next line or `null` if there are no more lines to be read. You don't have to close the file when it's used up.

There's a trick to making this work, though, and it involves an error-catching mechanism we haven't discussed before. Processing catches lots of run-time problems for you (for example, if you try to divide a number by zero in most languages, your program will crash, but Processing sets your number to the special value `Infinity` and keeps going—it still might crash later, of course, but not at that moment). If you want to program very defensively, you can tell the system that you want to handle some of these errors yourself, including perhaps some that Processing doesn't handle for you.

The way to do this is with a mechanism called *try/catch*. The idea is that you take the piece of code that you think might cause a problem, and you put it within a block (that is, a pair of curly braces) after the keyword `try`. Then immediately after that block, you give the keyword `catch` and the name of the error you want to handle and provide another block of code. This second block gets executed if there was a problem in the first block. It's sort of like an *if statement*, where you're saying, "If something in the `try` block generates this particular error, then execute the code in the `catch` block (otherwise, don't)."

To use a `BufferedReader`, you have to wrap up the calls to `readLine()` in a try/catch pair. The catcher is written like a little function: after the word `catch`, there's a pair of parentheses with arguments inside. If an error occurs in a `try` block, the system creates a little object that describes what went wrong and goes looking for a matching `catch` clause that accepts that kind of object. If it finds one, it hands the object to the catcher, which then does whatever it wants.

In the case of `BufferedReader`, the error we want to catch goes by the lovely name `IOException`. I won't go into this; there are tons of possible error types and most of them you'll never come near to using. This particular error type is very general; it just means something went wrong somewhere with input or output. I'll set up my `catch` clause to accept an object of this type. I won't actually do anything about it; I'll just set the input line to `null`, as though we'd reached the end of the file normally. This isn't doing much, but the `try/catch` mechanism must be used for the `BufferedReader` to work correctly.

Here's a little example to print out the contents of a text file. I want to print out the lines one by one, so I'll use `draw()` almost like a loop. Each time the system calls `draw()`, we'll print out the next line from the file (as long as there's still lines to be read):

```
BufferedReader Reader;            // a line-by-line reader
boolean MoreLinesLeft = true;     // are there lines left to read?

void setup() {
    Reader = createReader("file.txt"); // open this file
}

void draw() {
    String line;
    if (MoreLinesLeft) {
        try {                          // try to read a line
            line = Reader.readLine();  // save it in line
        } catch (IOException e) {      // handle IOException errors
            line = null;               // just set line to null
        }
        if (line == null) {            // do we have a valid line?
            MoreLinesLeft = false;     // no, so stop reading
        } else {
            println("next line is "+line); // yes, print it
        }
    }
}
```

(Full program in files/sketches/bufferedRead/bufferedRead.pde)

Saving drawings. One way to save your Processing drawings right off the screen is to use `save()` and `saveFrame()` inside of `draw()`. These functions will save the contents of the graphics window to an image file. A little bit less sophisticated but more impromptu is just to use a screen-capture utility to grab and save your window. There's a third option, but it requires some planning.

The downside of the `save()` and `saveFrame()` routines, and the screen capture, is that you're only getting graphics drawn at the resolution of your graphics window. Suppose you're drawing the floor plan for a building, with tons of little lines. If your graphics window is only ten-by-ten pixels, it's going to be essentially impossible to make out anything. You might have to make the window huge, many thousands of pixels on a side, to be able to read all your detailed graphics clearly.

If you've used vector-based graphics programs, you know that you can save your drawings in a *resolution-independent* format like SVG (which we saw in Chapter 16), or PDF. Rather than saving a grid of colored pixels, vector files save the drawing commands themselves, like, "Draw a line from this point to that one." So you can zoom in all you want, and things will stay crisp and clean, because the computer can always redraw your entire picture from those commands using the current zoom level.

If you want to record Processing's output in a vector format, you can. You need to surround all of your drawing commands with two calls. To start recording, give `beginRecord()` the file name you want to write to. When you're done with your graphics, call `endRecord()`.

If you're going to save your picture in PDF format, you need to include the PDF library in your code. Put this line at the top of your file:

```
import processing.pdf.*;
```

Here's a little program that draws the same picture twice, saving the pixels in png format and then the commands in PDF format.

```
import processing.pdf.*;

void setup() {
  size(600, 400);
  recordPNG();
  recordPDF();
}

void recordPNG() {
  drawPicture();
  save("pixels.png");
}

void recordPDF() {
  beginRecord(PDF, "commands.pdf");
  drawPicture();
  endRecord();
}

void drawPicture() {
  strokeWeight(1);
  background(181, 86, 70);
  fill(212, 201, 143);
  ellipse(200, 200, 100, 150);
  strokeWeight(8);
  fill(214, 192, 178);
  ellipse(400, 200, 50, 180);
}
```

(Full program in files/sketches/recordPDF/recordPDF.pde)

Figure 17.21. Close-up of screen save.

Figure 17.20. Screen save of two ellipses.

You can see the result of the screen save in Figure 17.20. A close-up in Figure 17.21 shows some choppy artifacts.

We can remove some of these by calling `smooth()` inside of `setup()`, but at best, they'll be cleaned up only a little. They'll never have any resolution finer than the pixels they're drawn into. Figure 17.22 and Figure 17.23 show the smoothed versions.

The smoothed versions are better, but if we get too close, those pixels are going to get mighty large and blocky. Figure 17.24 shows a closer view.

By contrast, look at the PDF save in Figure 17.25 and the close-up in in Figure 17.26.

These look great, and they'll continue to look great as we zoom in more and more. Figure 17.27 shows a tight close-up of the PDF versions, and they still look nice and

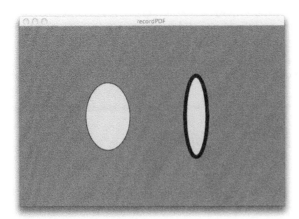

Figure 17.23. Close-up of smooth screen save.

Figure 17.22. Smooth screen save of two ellipses.

Figure 17.24. Closer close-up of smooth screen save.

crisp. We can zoom in as much as we like and we'll never see the blocky artifacts that come from zooming in too closely on the pixels, as in Figure 17.24.

Figure 17.26. Close-up of PDF output.

Figure 17.25. PDF save of two ellipses..

The downside of saving your work this way is that it requires preplanning to wrap up all of your commands. I also found that fonts and onscreen type were a problem, often showing up as just blocks of solid color rather than characters (as I'll discuss in the command `textMode()` in Chapter 20, type can be tricky, and different renderers give different results). You also need a PDF viewer to see these results, unlike a normal image editor.

Figure 17.27. Closer close-up of the PDF output.

Other commands. There are a few other file-related commands that you probably won't need. Just so you're aware of them, there's `saveBytes()` and `loadBytes()`, which let you write and read arrays of `byte` objects in binary form. You can ask your operating system to run an application using `open()`, and you can even pass it some arguments, but there are restrictions on what `open()` can do. If you get into 3D, you can save and read binary files of 3D commands with `beginRaw()` and `endRaw()`. If you're an advanced Java programmer, you can get access to Java's *streams* with `createInput()`, `createOutput()`, and `saveStream()`.

These are deep veins of material, and you can do some powerful things if you "escape" into the world of Java. But if you really want or need the power of the full-fledged Java language on anything more than an occasional basis, then I suggest you consider writing your project entirely in Java rather than a Processing/Java hybrid. Although Processing offers a wealth of conveniences and looks very much like Java, there are both subtle and overt differences, and keeping them straight can become a real challenge.

Finally, you might be aware of the XML file format. It's a standard used for exchanging many kinds of structured information. The files are organized using a set of markers, or *tags*, that tell you what's coming up in each section. XML files can be very complicated, but if you want to dig into them, the `XMLElement` object will give you a head start on reading these files and pulling them apart into useful pieces.

17.5   Extending the Project

I digitized my shapes by collecting a long list of points. Try writing an alternative program that lets you digitize a shape by laying down curves (think about whether you'd prefer to use the Catmull-Rom curves of Chapter 12 or the Bézier curves of Chapter 13). Make sure you can capture both long, graceful curves and tight, little turns. Also make sure you can catch sharp corners.

To find the closest border pixel, I imagined a square around the test pixel and scanned the whole thing. Is there a more efficient way to proceed that will find the nearest border pixel more quickly? I said that if there were multiple border pixels that were all the same distance away from the test pixel, I didn't care which border pixel I chose. Might it make a difference which one gets picked? If it does, can you identify which one is "best" and write some code to choose it?

Chapter 18
Creating Patterns

One of the coolest things that a programming language offers is the ability to create endless types of interesting patterns. Your patterns can repeat over and over, or never repeat until the end of time. They can be pleasantly predictable or continually surprising. They can be slow and comforting or fast and edgy. You can use patterns to control shapes, colors, motion, and everything else in your project.

A staggering variety of great patterns can be created by using some of the building blocks that are already built into Processing. If you've ever used an old-school analog sound synthesizer, you know that it gives you a collection of modules. Some modules produce a kind of sound (for example, a buzz, chime, or whistle). You hook up these sound sources to each other, and then hook the results up to other modules that apply filters that modify their input, maybe making the sound raspier or giving it an echo. Then you add more filters and more effects until the final sound is rich and interesting.

In the same way, you hook up modules in Processing, only instead of making sounds, they make a series of numbers. Most take one or more numbers as input and produce new numbers as output. Then you take those numbers, do more things to them, and eventually you get a pattern of numbers that you use to create graphics that capture the type of behavior or looks that you were after.

Processing's built-in pattern functions are powerful and can be used for all kinds of purposes. You'll find yourself using them in almost every program you write.

After all, most Processing programs are about making patterns with numbers: patterns of shapes, patterns of motion, patterns of color. All the things you see on the screen, all of their attributes, are described by numbers. The shape of a Bézier curve? The eight numbers that make up the control points. The color of a circle? The three numbers that define the red, green, and blue values. The motion of a kite in the wind? The numbers that define its (x, y) location on the screen, and the numbers that specify how those two numbers change with each frame.

The routines we'll see in this chapter (and the old standbys of addition, subtraction, multiplication, and division) are the building blocks that we use to create number patterns.

Although these functions are often described as mathematical operators, don't be spooked if math isn't your thing. You don't need to know what goes on inside these routines to get great results from them. By analogy, people who use hardware sound synthesizers are rarely electrical engineers who understand the electronic circuitry behind the panel. They just know that a certain kind of input can produce a certain kind of output, and they use that knowledge to build up their sounds.

So that's how we're going to look at Processing's pattern-making capabilities in terms of its built-in math functions. Processing uses the names of the underlying equations to name its routines (which makes sense), but feel free to treat those as words from another language and focus just on what the routines do.

Some classical composers learn how to play every instrument in the orchestra, at least a little bit, so that they better understand how to write for it, but most don't go to this extreme. They know what each instrument can do in the hands of a good player, and they leave it up to the performer to master the internal subtleties of the instrument. In the same way, you can use the functions in this chapter with only a basic idea of what they do and how their controls affect the results. You probably won't be surprised to know that I'm one of those people who finds great beauty in the underlying mathematics, so if you're inclined to learn about the underlying theory, I'm totally behind you. So if you're excited by the idea of knowing what's going on inside each one, like the composer who can play everything from the violin to the kettle drum, go for it! But it's strictly optional, and I won't get into any of that stuff here. In this chapter, I'll stick as much as possible to a high level, input–output kind of discussion.

To see how these functions can be joined up to make a particular kind of pattern, let's jump the gun on the various functions that I'll describe below and think about creating an animation of a bouncing ball. The ball will start near the upper left of the graphics window. We'll give it a little push to the right and then let gravity do the work. The ball will fall to the bottom of the window, where it will bounce off the "floor" and then back up. But of course, it doesn't come back up as high as it started. As it rises, it slows down, and then comes back down again, and then it bounces again, comes back up, and so on, each rebound a little less high than before, all the time moving slowly to the right.

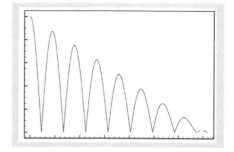

Figure 18.1. The trail left behind by a bouncing ball.

One way to describe this motion is with a picture. Suppose we get a real, physical ball that glows in the dark. We then point a camera at the ball in a dark room, hold the shutter open, and drop the ball to the floor while pushing it a little to the right, as I described above. The result is a time-exposure photograph that shows us the trail left behind by the ball as it bounced while moving right. Our time-exposure photograph might look like Figure 18.1.

We can use this picture to help us create the animation. When the animation starts, let's say we're at zero seconds into the animation. As time goes on, the ball moves to the right and down, then it bounces, and so on. So by tracing the path over time, we can find the (x, y) coordinates of the ball at any given moment.

If we had a function that accepted time as an input argument (say as a floating-point number), then it could produce a point as an output, and that would tell us where to position that ball at that moment. Then creating the animation would be as simple as calling that function each time we enter draw().

Let's actually do that.

```
void setup() {
    size(600, 400);
    noStroke();
}

void draw() {
    background(145, 236, 152);
    fill(6, 119, 120);
    float time = frameCount;
    PVector ballCenter = getBallCenter(time);
    ellipse(ballCenter.x, ballCenter.y, 40, 40);
}

PVector getBallCenter(float time)
{
    PVector center = new PVector(time, 200);
    return(center);
}
```

(See output in Figure 18.2. Full program in patterns/sketches/bounce01/bounce01.pde)

Here, I've set the time from the value of frameCount, which starts at 0 and goes up by one each time Processing calls draw().

This isn't much of a bouncing ball. The disk starts at the left and moves to the right at a fixed speed. Well, we have the horizontal motion working correctly, at least!

Now I'm going to jump ahead because I want to give you the feeling of what we'll be talking about in this chapter. I'm going to rewrite the routine getBallCenter() using some of the pattern-making functions we'll see below. The idea will be to make the ball move in a way that starts to look like the curve of Figure 18.1.

```
PVector getBallCenter(float time)
    float xPosition = time;
    float angle = time/40.0;
    float bounceHeight = max(0, map(time, 0, 600, 1, 0));
    float yPosition = bounceHeight * abs(cos(angle));
    yPosition = map(yPosition, 0, 1, 350, 50);
```

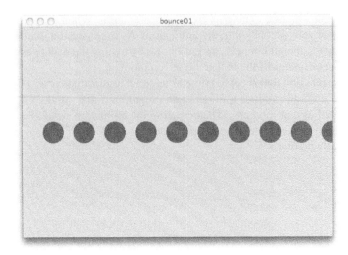

Figure 18.2. The bouncing ball, take one. This images shows multiple images from the animation taken every 60 frames (frame from animation). (patterns/sketches/bounce01/bounce01.pde)

```
PVector center = new PVector(xPosition, yPosition);
return(center);
```

(See output in Figure 18.3. Full program in patterns/sketches/bounce02/bounce02.pde)

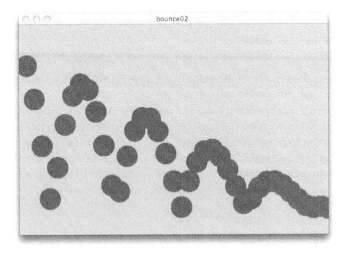

Figure 18.3. The bouncing ball, take two. This images shows multiple images from the animation taken every 15 frames (frame from animation). (patterns/sketches/bounce02/bounce02.pde)

The animation doesn't look real yet, but it has the right general kind of motion, which is good enough for me to demonstrate my point. With a few lines of code, using Processing's built-in functions, we were able to move the ball in a way that matches our intended motion.

You'll notice that there's a bunch of new stuff in `getBallCenter` that we haven't discussed yet. Don't sweat it; we're going to see all of these building blocks soon. They may look unfamiliar to you now, but they're all pretty simple.

You'll also see lots of numbers that I typed in there. There's nothing special about them. They control the speed of the ball, the height of each bounce, how many times it bounces, and so on. The numbers in this listing are the result of trial and error. I picked some numbers out of thin air when I first wrote these lines and then I changed them over and over until the motion of the ball looked about right to me. That's not a bad thing—in fact, it's a good thing! It means that I'm able to use Processing to fine-tune the motion until it looks just the way I want. Without that kind of control we'd never be able to use Processing as an expressive medium.

Of course, if we didn't want to mess about with the numbers this way, we could replace `getBallCenter()` with a realistic physics simulator. It could take the mass of the ball, the strength of gravity, the amount of air resistance at this temperature and humidity, and so on, and it could calculate exactly where the ball would be if it was a real, physical object.

This is entirely possible, and lots of games have this kind of physics simulator built into them. Of course, it means remembering (or looking up) all of those equations, typing them in, debugging them, and so on, but the results are a ball that moves in a physically accurate way.

The downside of this approach, besides the sheer amount of math and programming required, is that you can't do much to tune the resulting motion to make it look the way you'd like. You could adjust some of the values in the simulator, but your options are limited. If you want to produce your animation by matching the real world, you can get accurate-looking results but not a lot of adjustable control. Alternatively, you can forget physics and create your object's motion your own way. Then you can tune it until it looks and feels right to you. You may have to do more work, but you can make the motion look any way you like, even if it's physically impossible.

18.1   Plotting a Function

Many of Processing's pattern-making functions take a single floating-point number as input, and return a single floating-point number as output.

A great way to visualize what these functions do is to make a little *plot* of their values. Along the x-axis I'll show the input value, and along the y-axis I'll plot the value that comes back from the function.

Most of these functions can take as input any floating-point number. That's an enormous range—there's no way we could plot all the possible inputs and outputs on a single page. So we usually take a pragmatic approach and pick some range of values that give us a feeling for the function. If we pick the range well, we can get a good sense for what the function returns for other values.

Let's make a little plotting program. It will call a function over and over to get its value at different inputs, and it will draw a curve on the screen to show the output values. There's only one problem: what kinds of numbers come out of the function? Some functions might return numbers between 0 and 1, others perhaps from -50 million to 100 billion. Somehow we have to adapt what each function gives us to our little screen window.

My solution is pragmatic. I'll run through the whole range of input values first, and find the smallest and largest values returned by the function. Then I'll run through the range of input values again. Each time I get back an output value, I'll find where it lands between the minimum and maximum output values, and I'll use map() to place that on the vertical axis of the plot.

I'll create a couple of global variables that let me define the minimum and maximum values of x that I'll give to the function.

This plotting program isn't really my focus in this chapter because it's just a tool we'll use to see what the functions look like. So rather than slowly build it up piece by piece, I'll show you the final result, mention a couple of issues, and then move on to the pattern-making building blocks.

Here's the code:

```
int WindowSize = 400;
int MinimumX = -1;    // the minimum input value
int MaximumX =  1;    // the maximum input value

void setup() {
   size(WindowSize, WindowSize);
   background(255);

   int border = 20;                       // leave a gap around the plot
   int windowMin = border;                // left and bottom
   int windowMax = WindowSize - border;   // right and top

   // draw a box around the plot
   noFill();
   stroke(0, 0, 0);
   rect(windowMin, windowMin, windowMax-windowMin, windowMax-windowMin);

   // run through the function and find the output range
   float yMin = plotFunction(MinimumX);
   float yMax = yMin;
   for (int screenX=windowMin; screenX<windowMax; screenX++) {
      float xValue = map(screenX, windowMin, windowMax, MinimumX, MaximumX);
      float yValue = plotFunction(xValue);
```

```
        if (yValue < yMin) yMin = yValue;
        if (yValue > yMax) yMax = yValue;
    }

    // now run through the values again, and plot them
    float oldx = 0;
    float oldy = 0;
    for (int screenX=windowMin; screenX<windowMax; screenX++) {
        float xValue = map(screenX, windowMin, windowMax, MinimumX, MaximumX);
        float yValue = plotFunction(xValue);

        float screenY = map(yValue, yMin, yMax, windowMax, windowMin);
        if (screenX > windowMin) {
            line(oldx, oldy, screenX, screenY);
        }
        oldx = screenX;
        oldy = screenY;
    }
}

float plotFunction(float x)
{
    return(x*x);
}
```

(See output in Figure 18.4. Full program in patterns/sketches/functionPlot/functionPlot.pde)

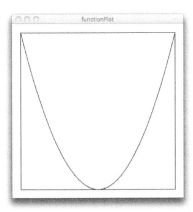

Figure 18.4. Plotting the function $x*x$ from $(-1, 1)$.
(patterns/sketches/functionPlot/functionPlot.pde)

Most of what's going on here should be familiar to you. After `setup()` creates the window and sets the background to white, I find the screen coordinates of the corners of a box that will hold the plot. They're just the window dimensions itself, inset by the value of border.

Then I run a loop that calls our plotting function plotFunction() for all the values I intend to use when I actually draw it. The idea is that a variable screenX will run from the left edge of the plot window to its right edge, one screen pixel at a time. I pass each value of screenX into map(), which turns it into a corresponding value in the range (MinimumX, MaximumX). So at the left side of the plot window, xValue has the value MinimumX, at the right side, it has the value MaximumX, and in between, it has in-between values.

I call the plot function for this xValue to get its output, which I call yValue. Then I test it against yMin: if yValue is smaller than yMin, then yMin gets assigned to yValue. In this way, yMin always holds the minimal number we've gotten back from plotFunction(). I do the same thing for yMax, though of course I test for which one is larger. You'll see later that there's a shorter way to do these tests, but we haven't seen them yet, so I'll leave them this way.

By the way, note that I initially set yMin and yMax to the first value that comes out of plotFunction(). That way, the first time I test them, they already hold reasonable values.

After that, I just repeat the process. I use map() again to transform the values I get back from plotFunction() into the range of screen values in the plotting box (remembering that y goes down). As long as I'm past the first point, I draw a line from the new point to the old point, or the one I computed the previous time through the loop. Then I save the current point into the old point, and repeat.

I know we went through that pretty fast, but I hope you got the general idea. And if you look at the code closely, you'll be able to nail down any details you're interested in.

In the listing (and figure), I plotted a simple function that just returns the value of its input x multiplied by itself:

```
float plotFunction(float x)
{
    return(x*x);
}
```

I plotted this in the range $(-1, 1)$. What happens to this function for other input values? If we look at the picture and the code, we could probably guess that the values just go up and up, becoming ever more positive as the values of x get farther from 0 (which is in the middle of the figure).

Of course, the plot itself doesn't tell us what really happens for inputs that aren't being shown, it's just suggestive. Sometimes when you're plotting a complicated function that you're not familiar with, you'll have to try a bunch of plots over diverse ranges in order to get a feeling for how the function behaves.

18.2   Building Blocks

There are two steps to building up a nice pattern out of Processing's building blocks: picking the blocks you want to use and deciding how to combine them.

These steps are something like planning a flower garden. You need to start with a general familiarity with the basic pieces at your disposal and what variations you can get from them. Then you choose the flowers you'd like in your garden, while thinking about how they would look near one another. You'd probably start by picking some favorites, then adding in a few other varieties, then maybe taking some types of flowers out and putting others in, moving them around and adjusting until you have just the right mix.

Building up patterns out of functions is the same. Like our bouncing ball example, you might start with a rough idea of what you want (it goes down and right, then comes back up but not as high, then down and right again, repeatedly). So you consider the catalog of available functions you'll probably try out different combinations in your head.

One of the fun things about this process is that it's playful. There are usually lots of different ways to build the pattern you're after, each one offering you different methods for controlling and tweaking the results. Experimenting with these patterns, putting them together in new ways and seeing what happens, is rewarding both because it helps you get the results you want and because it's all about playing with and discovering patterns. You probably enjoyed playing with blocks as a child; playing with these pattern-making functions can be just as much fun. You just type a few lines, press *Play*, and watch the results.

Let's look at the catalog of basic building blocks offered by Processing. I'll plot each one to show you the general idea of what the function is about. Rather than include lots of little numbers on the plots themselves, the captions tell you the range I used for the *x* values (generally the input to the function) and the range I got back for the *y* values (generally the output of the function). I'll discuss aspects of each function that I think are special or interesting. Think of this catalog like a listing of birds you might see in your backyard, flowers in your garden, or instruments in an orchestra: many of these functions share some qualities, but each one is different from the others in its own way.

I'll take them in alphabetical order. Generally, I'll show you the function's name, give you a very short description, show a plot of the output for some range, and then discuss it a bit.

abs(x)   (absolute value of *x*). If x>=0, return x, else return -x. See Figure 18.5.

```
abs(3)     // 3
abs(-7)    // 7
```

This function takes a single floating-point number, and if that number is positive, it simply returns it. If the number is negative, it essentially removes the negative sign.

The most frequent use of abs() is to take a pattern with positive and negative values and turn it into a pattern with only positive values. Where the input pattern moves

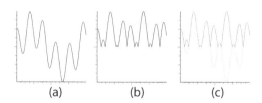

Figure 18.5. The abs() function; (a) A random curve that has output values from $(-1,1)$. (b) The absolute value of that curve. (c) The two curves overlaid.

from positive to negative territory, the output pattern will show a sharp turnaround, as in Figure 18.5. It's as if the line $y = 0$ was a mirror, and the pattern reflects off of it.

But you can use abs to perform this job at any value, not just zero. For example, if you want the "mirror" line at $y = 4$, you can write 4+abs(x-4).

asin(x) (arc-sine of x). The inverse of sine (see sin()). See Figure 18.6.

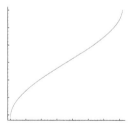

Figure 18.6. The inverse-sine function asin(). $x = (-1,1), y = (-1.5, 1.5)$.

acos(x) (arc-cosine of x). The inverse of cosine (see cos()). See Figure 18.7.

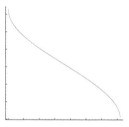

Figure 18.7. The inverse-cosine function acos(). $x = (-1,1), y = (-1.5, 1.5)$.

atan(x) (arc-tangent of *x*). The inverse of tangent (see `tan()`). See Figure 18.8.

Figure 18.8. The inverse-tangent function `atan()`. $x = (-1, 1), y = (-0.8, 0.8)$.

atan2(y, x) (arc-tangent of y/x). The inverse of tangent (see `tan()`). This is the two-argument form of `atan()`. It's often more useful than `atan()`.

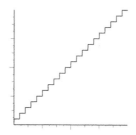

Figure 18.9. The `ceil()` function. $x = (1, 20), y = (1, 20)$.

ceil(x) (ceiling). Round up x to the nearest integer. See Figure 18.9.

```
ceil(4)        //  4
ceil(4.2)      //  5
ceil(-7.3)     // -7
```

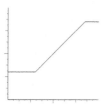

Figure 18.10. The `constrain()` function. The input is from $(0, 1)$ and is constrained to $(0.3, 0.85)$. $x = (0, 1), y = (0, 1)$.

constrain(val, min, max) (constrain to a range). If (x<min), return min, else if (x>max), return max, else return x. See Figure 18.10

```
constrain(-5,   0, 1)    // 0
constrain( 0.2, 0, 1)    // 0.2
constrain( 3.5, 0, 1)    // 1
```

cos(x) (cosine x). Return cos(x) for x in radians (use radians() to convert degrees to radians). See Figure 18.11.

```
cos(0)          //   1
cos(1)          //   0.54030
cos(PI)         //  -1
```

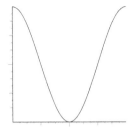

Figure 18.11. The cos() function from 0 to 2π. $x = (0, 2\pi), y = (-1, 1)$.

The cosine curve is a workhorse that appears in many Processing programs, along with its very similar cousin sine (sin()). In fact, sine and cosine only differ by an offset that you can apply to their inputs; for any argument angle, cos(radians(angle)) has the same value as sin(radians(angle-90)).

The input to cosine is an angle. A circle closes back on itself in 360 degrees; the equivalent in radians is 2π, where π is the Greek letter pi, with a value of about 3.14159. Processing provides you the built-in variable PI, as well as HALF_PI, QUARTER_PI, and TWO_PI. Remembering that you can convert any angle in degrees to radians with the function radians(), I'll talk about degrees here.

With an input of 0 degrees, cosine returns a value of 1. That value drops to 0 at 90 degrees. At 180 degrees the value of cosine is -1, and at that point, it turns around and starts back up again, in a mirror image of its left half. At 270 degrees cosine is back up to 0, and at 360 degrees, it's returned to its starting point at 1.

A very useful feature of the cosine curve is that at 0 degrees, 180 degrees, and 360 degrees, the curve flattens out. In other words, it changes direction smoothly and gradually rather than suddenly and abruptly turning around, the way the abs() function sharply flips a curve that dips below 0. This makes the cosine a natural choice for any pattern that needs to start and end gradually rather than abruptly.

Periodic or repetitive movement is a great example of this. When a real object is standing still, it doesn't suddenly start moving at full speed. From a standing start, it picks up a little speed, then a little more, then a little more, and so on. And the process happens in reverse when it comes to a halt: first it has to slow down. Nothing abruptly freezes in place after moving at a high speed.

The smooth nature of the cosine makes it a great choice for this kind of application. Typically you'll use just the first 180 degrees, since that gets you a nice S shape from 1 to −1.

The pendulum on a grandfather clock moves left and right, slowly coming to a stop at the top of each arc before turning around again. That's the kind of motion that cosine provides: move, slow down, gradually stop, reverse direction, pick up speed, slow down, stop, reverse, pick up speed, and so on, over and over, forever.

The cosine curve repeats every 360 degrees, or 2π radians. We say that this is the *period* of this curve.

If you want repeating motion, cosine is great for that, too. Just keep calling it with ever-increasing values. Every time you pass a multiple of 360 degrees, the curve starts over again, giving you a smooth down–up–down sequence over and over forever. Figure 18.12 shows three cycles of the cosine curve.

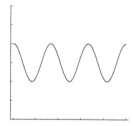

Figure 18.12. Three cycles of the cosine function cos (), plotted from 0 to 6π. For clarity, the y-axis has been enlarged (making the graph smaller vertically). $x = (0, 6\pi), y = (-3, 3)$.

If you want to run cosine in reverse (that is, you have a value from cosine and you want to find the angle that produced it) you can hand it to acos ().

dist(x1, y1, x2, y2) (distance between points). Return the distance from point (x1, y1) to point (x2, y2).

```
dist(10, 20, 37, 48)        // distance from (10, 20) to (37, 48)
dist(10, 20, mouseX, mouseY)   // distance of mouse from (10, 20)
```

exp(x) (exponentiation). Named for *Euler's constant*, a number (written with the single-letter name *e*) with a value of about 2.71828. This function returns *e* raised to the power of *x*. This is useful for many mathematical calculations. The number *e* is named for the mathematician Leonhard Euler (pronounced oy′-ler). See Figure 18.13.

```
exp(0)         // 1            (by definition)
exp(1)         // 2.71828   (Euler's constant)
exp(2)         // 7.38904
```

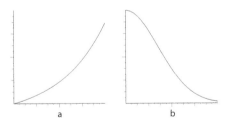

Figure 18.13. The exp() function. (a) The value of exp(x) for $x = (0,2), y = (1,2.718)$. (b) The value of exp(-(x*x)) in the same range; this is the famous "bell curve." $x = (0,2), y = (1,0.018)$.

We'll come back to this function later when we discuss the bell curve.

floor(x) (floor). Round down x to the nearest integer. See Figure 18.14.

```
floor(4)        // 4
floor(4.2)      // 4
floor(-7.3)     // -8
```

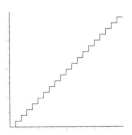

Figure 18.14. The floor() function. $x = (1,20), y = (1,20)$.

lerp(low, high, amount) (linear interpolation).   Return low + ((high-low) * amount). This is useful for blending between two values. When amount=0, this returns low. When amount=1, this returns high. In-between values of amount return in-between outputs. When amount is less than 0 or greater than 1, you'll get values correspondingly below low or above high. **Note:** unlike map() and norm(), the controlling variable amount comes at the *end* of the argument list.

```
lerp(3, 7, 0)        // 3      a=0, return low
lerp(3, 7. .125)     // 3.5
lerp(3, 7. .25)      // 4
lerp(3, 7. .5)       // 5
lerp(3, 7, 1)        // 7      a=1, return high
```

```
lerp(3, 7, -2)      // -5      a<0, return less than low
lerp(3, 7, 2)       // 11      a>1, return more than high
```

$\log(x)$ (natural logarithm). The number y such that exp (y) has the value x. See Figure 18.15.

```
log(1)       // 0.0
log(2)       // 0.69314
log(exp(1)) // 1.0
log(3)       // 1.0986
```

Figure 18.15. The log () function. $x = (1, 4), y = (0, 0.602)$.

$\text{mag}(x, y)$ (magnitude). The distance from the point $(0,0)$ to the point (x, y).

```
mag(0,0)    // 0
mag(1,0)    // 1
mag(1,1)    // 1.41421
```

map(val, low1, high1, low2, high2) (map from one range to another). Find where val sits in the range from (low1, high1). Then use that to find a corresponding value from the range (low2, high2). You could write this as

```
lerp(norm(val, low1, high1), low2, high2)
```

Here are some examples:

```
map( 3, 3, 5, 10, 20)      // 10
map( 4, 3, 5, 10, 20)      // 15
map( 5, 3, 5, 10, 20)      // 20
map(.5, 0, 1,  0, width)   //  width/2
```

$\text{max}(a, b)$ (maximum). Return the larger of a or b. See Figure 18.16.

```
max(-3, -5)      // -3
max(3, 5)        //  5
max(-2, 9)       //  9
```

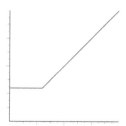

Figure 18.16. The max() function. The plot shows max(x, 0.3) for $x = (0, 1), y = (0, 1)$.

min(a,b) (minimum). Return the smaller of a or b. See Figure 18.17.

```
max(-3, -5)        // -5
max(3, 5)          //  3
max(-2, 9)         // -2
```

Figure 18.17. The min() function. The plot shows min(x, 0.6) for $x = (0, 1), y = (0, 1)$.

norm(val, low, high) (normalize). Tell where val is in the range (low, high). This is the same as map(value, low, high, 0, 1).

```
norm(3, 3, 5)      // 0
norm(4, 3, 5)      // 0.5
norm(5, 3, 5)      // 1
norm(6, 3, 5)      // 1.5
```

pow(a, b) (power). Raise a to the power b. Note that both a and b can be floating-point values. See Figure 18.18.

```
pow(2,3)      //  8
pow(2, 3.5)   // 11.313708
pow(2,4)      // 16
```

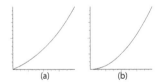

Figure 18.18. The pow(a,b) function. (a) pow(2,x) for $x = (0,1), y = (1,2)$.
(b) pow(x,2) for $x = (0,1), y = (0,1)$.

round(x) (round). Return the integer closest to x. See Figure 18.19.

```
round(8.1)    //   8
round(8.9)    //   9
round(-3.1)   //  -3
round(-3.9)   //  -4
```

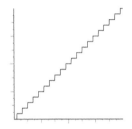

Figure 18.19. The round() function. $x = (1,20), y = (1,20)$.

sin(x) (sine x). Return sin(x) for x in radians (use radians() to convert degrees to radians). See Figure 18.20.

```
sin(0)        //   0
sin(1)        //   0.84147
sin(PI)       //   0
```

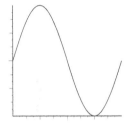

Figure 18.20. The sin() function. $x = (0, 2\pi), y = (-1, 1)$.

The sine function is a close relative of the cosine. Everything in the description of cosine applies just as well to sine. The only difference between them is that the sine starts 90 degrees (or $\pi/2$ radians) earlier.

Like cosine, you can find the angle that corresponds to a given sine using asin().

sq(x) (square). Return x*x. Note that this is not the same as the square root sqrt(). See Figure 18.21.

```
sq(2)          //   4
sq(3)          //   9
sq(3.5)        // 12.25
sq(4)          // 16
```

Figure 18.21. The sq() function. $x = (0,1), y = (0,1)$.

sqrt(x) (square root). Return y such that y*y = x. Note that this is not the same as sq(). See Figure 18.22.

```
sqrt(16)      //  4
sqrt(15)      //  3.87
sqrt(4)       //  2
```

Figure 18.22. The sqrt() function. $x = (0,1), y = (0,1)$.

tan(x) (tangent x). Return tan(x) for x in radians (use `radians()` to convert degrees to radians). See Figure 18.23.

```
tan(0)        //   0
tan(1)        //   1.5574
tan(PI)       //   0
```

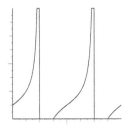

Figure 18.23. The `tan()` function. $x = (0, 2\pi), y = (-\infty, \infty)$.

Tangent is closely related to sine and cosine. In fact, `tan(x) = sin(x)/cos(x)`. It's less frequently used than those other two functions.

To find the angle that produced a given tangent, use `atan()`, but also see the comments for `atan2()` in Section 18.4. The tangent function goes to infinity (which mathematicians write as ∞) each time the cosine function goes to zero, which happens at π, $3\pi/2$, $5\pi/2$, and so on. In the figure, I've zoomed in on the graph so we could see the shape of the curve before it blows up.

18.3 About Pattern-Making Functions

As I've mentioned before, all angles in Processing are described in radians. To convert an angle in degrees into radians, you can call the built-in function `radians()` with your angle in degrees. To convert radians to degrees, call `degrees()` with your angle in radians.

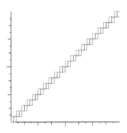

Figure 18.24. The `floor()`, `ceiling()`, and `round()` functions overlaid on the range 1 to 20. The `floor()` function is in green, `ceil()` is in orange, and `round()` is red.

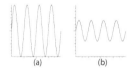

(a)   (b)

Figure 18.25. A sine wave. (a) The vertical scale is $(-1, 1)$. (b) So we can see the shape a bit better, the vertical scale is $(-2, 2)$.

I'm sad to report that there's no arc-cosecant (pronounced ark-koh-see′-kant) function. I've never needed to use this in my life, but I think it has the coolest name in all of trigonometry.

The three rounding functions, `floor()`, `ceil()`, and `round()` are closely related. Figure 18.24 shows how they handle numbers from 0 to 20.

I mentioned above that one of the nicest things about sine (and cosine) is that they repeat over and over, smoothly and forever. Each repetition is called a *cycle*, and it covers 360 degrees. In Figure 18.25(a) I've shown four cycles of the sine wave (to see it a bit more easily, in part (b) I've scaled it down a bit vertically).

I also mentioned that sine and cosine are the same curve, shifted 90 degrees from each other. Figure 18.26 shows the two curves superimposed.

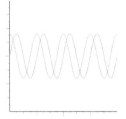

Figure 18.26. The sine is in blue, cosine in orange.

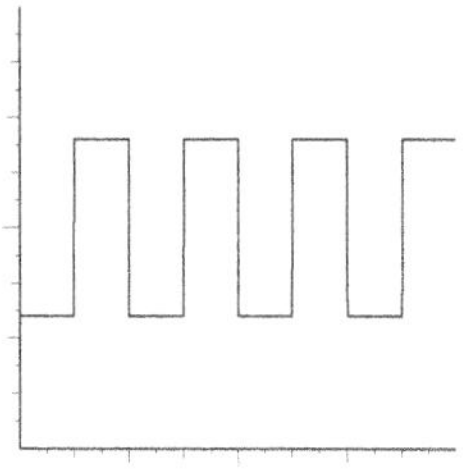

Figure 18.27. Four cycles of a square wave.

There are an infinite number of patterns that you can create from these building blocks. Every one of these patterns can be used to control colors, shapes, motion, or anything else that varies over space or time, or both. For example, Figure 18.27 shows a few cycles of a *square wave*. Useful variants on the square wave involve changing the ratio of the time it's at 1 versus when it's at 0, making it less of a square and more of a pulse.

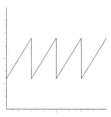

Figure 18.28. Four cycles of a ramp wave.

Figure 18.28 shows a few cycles of a *ramp wave*. This is often useful for animating ratchet-type mechanisms, like the gears inside a clock.

18.4   Finding Angles

The three functions `sin()`, `cos()`, and `tan()` have *inverse* functions. If we have a value that was produced by `sin()`, then we can use the inverse to find what input produced that number. For instance, suppose that somehow we know that a variable named `sinval` corresponds to the sine of an angle. What angle is that? In other words, what input a should we give to `sin()`, so that `sin(a)` produces `sinval`?

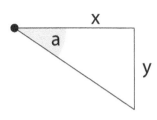

Figure 18.29. The angle *a* in a right triangle with sides *x* and *y*.

That's what the inverse functions are for. You might guess that they're named inverse-sine (and inverse-cosine and inverse-tangent), but mathematicians use the word "arc" here rather than "inverse." So the inverse-sine function is called arc-sin (pronounced ark′-sine), and it's made available in Processing with the function `asin()`. We can use it to solve the problem from the last paragraph: `asin(sinval)` gives us the angle a, so `sin(a)` has the value `sinval`.

We can do the same thing with arc-cosine (using `acos()`) and arc-tangent (using `atan()`). The arc-tangent is used much more frequently than arc-sine or arc-cosine.

The most common use of the arc-tangent is to find one of the two acute angles of a right triangle (that is, one of the angles less than 90 degrees). Figure 18.29 shows the idea: we know the lengths of the sides *x* and *y*, and we'd like to know the angle *a*. We can find that angle (in radians, of course) by calling `atan(y/x)`.

We do this kind of thing all the time in programs when objects are moving around. For example, we might have a car at the far end of our triangle, and we want to find the angle *a* so we can rotate the car so it looks like it's going around a curve, as in Figure 18.30.

But sometimes the car might be directly above or below the origin, so the "triangle" collapses into nothing but a straight line. Figure 18.31 shows the car approaching this position, and then finally reaching it. In this case, the *x* value would be 0. And dividing anything by zero is infinity. In many modern languages, dividing by zero causes a run-time error and your program will crash. In Processing, you'll get back the special value `Infinity`. Your program

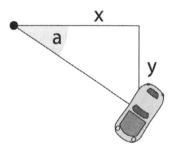

Figure 18.30. Knowing the angle *a*, we can rotate the car correctly.

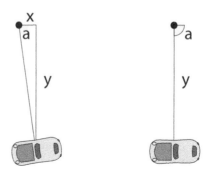

Figure 18.31. When the car is below us, the x component of the triangle is 0. (a) A very small x component. (b) The x component is now 0, which poses a problem if we're using the one-argument `atan()` function.

won't crash, but it'll probably behave in some unexpected way if you start trying to do things with a value of `Infinity`.

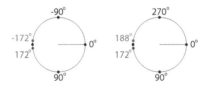

Figure 18.32. The `atan2()` function returns angles from $-\pi$ to π (-180 to 180 degrees), while most of the time we think of the circle with angles from 0 to 360 degrees. (a) Two points at 172 and -172 degrees seem to be numerically far apart, though they're close to one another on the circle. (b) If we label the points as 172 and 188, it's easier to see that they are close to one another.

Because this kind of thing comes up so much when making pictures, almost every language offers a function named `atan2()` that takes the two sides of the triangle as separate arguments (rather than making you divide them first), and it then figures out the angle using a method that doesn't involve actually computing y/x, and thus avoids dividing by zero. In the case of Figure 18.31, if the y value was -5, you could call `atan(-5/0)` but that would give you back an angle of `Infinity`. That's not right! Instead, you could call `atan2(-5, 0)`, and you'd get back the correct value (in this case, about 1.57, which is `PI/2`, or 90 degrees).

Remember when you use `atan2()` that the arguments are named with y first and then x (this is to remind us that the function is going to compute the equivalent of y/x).

Using `atan2()` is straightforward, but it can require you to be very careful depending on your situation. It gives you back angles in the range $(-\pi, \pi)$ (or -180 to 180 degrees). Sometimes this can be confusing if you're trying to compare angles to see if one is near another.

For example, consider Figure 18.32(a). We see two points that are near one another on the left side of the circle. If the angle we rotated around (from 0 at three o'clock) came from `atan2()` (and converted to degrees), then we would find them at 172 and at -172 degrees. Those values look very far apart numerically, though we know the angles are very similar.

In a more conventional circle that is marked from 0 to 360 degrees, shown in part (b) of the figure, the points would be at 172 and 188 degrees, and it would be a bit more obvious (even to a computer) that they're close to one another.

Of course, we can have the very same problem on the 0-to-360 circle, where one angle could be at 359 degrees and another at 1 degree. We know that they're only two degrees apart, but we can't just subtract one from the other to find that out.

The moral of the story is that if you want to compare angles, you'll need to keep in mind what the ranges are (which often depends on where we got the angles from in the first place), and compensate for the fact that angles that seem to be far apart numerically might be very similar geometrically.

18.5 Blending with Cosine

One of the most popular uses of the cosine curve is to create a smooth blend between two values, giving you a smoothed-out alternative to `lerp()`.

For example, suppose you're creating an animation that includes a top-down view of a city. There's a car that's driving from left to right, passing three blocks (and the two intersections between them). Suppose the three different blocks have different speed limits.

What does the car do once it's passed the first block but hasn't yet arrived at the second? Somehow the speed has to decrease.

The easiest way to handle this is to use `lerp()`. Just find the percentage of the way you've made it across the intersection and use that to blend the two speeds. So if your speeds are given by two variables, say `speed1` and `speed2`, the car at any moment is horizontally located at position `x`, and the intersection zone runs horizontally from `zoneLeft` to `zoneRight`, you could handle it this way:

```
a = map(x, zoneLeft, zoneRight, 0, 1);
speed = lerp(speed1, speed1, a);
```

In this little fragment, the value of `a` is 0 at the start of the transition zone and 1 at the end. In between it has values from 0 to 1, and we use those as the control to `lerp()` to tell us the current speed.

Let's write a little program to draw a curve showing the car's speed. I'll include the code for the step we're about to take, where we use the cosine curve to smooth things out.

```
void setup() {
  size(600, 400);
  background(210);
  noFill();
```

```
  stroke(0);
  strokeWeight(2);
  smooth();
  float v1 = 0;
  float v2 = .5;
  float v3 = 1;
  drawSet(v1, v2, v3, false, 50, 50);
  drawSet(v1, v2, v3, true, 50, 250);
}

void drawSet(float v1, float v2, float v3, boolean useCosine,
             int xLeft, int yTop) {
  drawBlend(v1, v1, xLeft,     100, yTop, 100, useCosine);
  drawBlend(v1, v2, xLeft+100, 100, yTop, 100, useCosine);
  drawBlend(v2, v2, xLeft+200, 100, yTop, 100, useCosine);
  drawBlend(v2, v3, xLeft+300, 100, yTop, 100, useCosine);
  drawBlend(v3, v3, xLeft+400, 100, yTop, 100, useCosine);
}

void drawBlend(float v1, float v2, int xLeft, int wid, int yTop, int hgt,
               boolean useCosine) {
  int xRight = xLeft + wid;
  float oldx = xLeft;
  float oldy = yTop + (hgt*v1);
  for (int x=xLeft; x<xRight; x++) {
    float a = map(x, xLeft, xRight-1, 0, 1);
    if (useCosine) a = map(cos(a*radians(180)), 1, -1, 0, 1);
    float y = yTop + (hgt*lerp(v1, v2, a));
    line(oldx, oldy, x, y);
    oldx = x;
    oldy = y;
  }
}
```

(See output in Figure 18.33. Full program in patterns/sketches/blendingWithLines/blendingWithLines.pde)

The top graph in Figure 18.33 shows the car's speed across all three blocks. The speed is constant and then, when the car enters the transition zone, the speed drops down to the slower speed, and it holds that until it enters the second transition zone, when it drops down to the slowest speed.

Mathematically, this does the job, but the human visual system is tuned to pick up these kinds of abrupt changes. Whether it's a change in speed, color, size, or almost anything else, if it changes suddenly, we notice it. In this graph, the start and end of each transition zone has a corner, and even if we couldn't say what it was we noticed we would probably feel that something was attracting our attention at those moments. Worse, we know from a lifetime of experience how things move, from gnats to windsurfers. And nothing changes speed abruptly like this. So our brains respond to it,

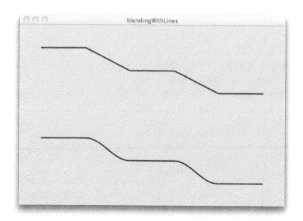

Figure 18.33. The top graph shows the speed of the car using linear blending. The bottom graph uses the cosine curve for blending.
(patterns/sketches/blendingWithLines/blendingWithLines.pde)

and something feels "wrong" about the animation. Most people probably couldn't tell you what it is they're responding to, but something just won't feel right. Of course, you might intend them to feel this way, in which case you'd want to keep this abrupt transition. But let's make the motion feel more natural.

We need only add one more line to our little fragment. I'll run the value of a through the first 180 degrees of cosine.

```
a = map(cos(radians(180*a)), 1, -1, 0, 1);
```

In this new line, I first scaled a up so that it runs from 0 to 180 degrees. Over that range, the cosine curve starts at 1 and ends at −1, so I use map() to transform that range back to 0 to 1.

The result of this single change is shown in the lower graph of Figure 18.33. The corners are gone, and the changes are nice and smooth. Cosine is a popular choice for this kind of transition because it creates these gorgeously smooth changes, and often, that makes images and animations look just a little nicer.

As I mentioned, the tendency of the human visual system to spot corners extends to almost everything we can notice. I'm blending three colors in Figure 18.34, using the same arrangement as in Figure 18.33. That is, there's a region of solid blue, a transition zone, a region of solid orange, a transition zone, and a region of solid green. This is basically the very same program as above, except I'm using colors and stripes rather than floating-point numbers and lines.

```
void setup() {
  size(600, 400);
```

```
  background(128);
  noFill();
  color c1 = color(25, 45, 210);
  color c2 = color(250, 140, 0);
  color c3 = color(65, 120, 80);
  drawSet(c1, c2, c3, false, 50, 50);
  drawSet(c1, c2, c3, true, 50, 250);
}

void drawSet(color c1, color c2, color c3, boolean useCosine,
                int xLeft, int yTop) {
  drawBlend(c1, c1, xLeft,     100, yTop, 100, useCosine);
  drawBlend(c1, c2, xLeft+100, 100, yTop, 100, useCosine);
  drawBlend(c2, c2, xLeft+200, 100, yTop, 100, useCosine);
  drawBlend(c2, c3, xLeft+300, 100, yTop, 100, useCosine);
  drawBlend(c3, c3, xLeft+400, 100, yTop, 100, useCosine);
}

void drawBlend(color c1, color c2, int xLeft, int wid, int yTop,
                 int hgt, boolean useCosine) {
  int xRight = xLeft + wid;
  for (int x=xLeft; x<xRight; x++) {
    float a = map(x, xLeft, xRight-1, 0, 1);
    if (useCosine) a = map(cos(a*radians(180)), 1, -1, 0, 1);
    color stripe = lerpColor(c1, c2, a);
    stroke(stripe);
    line(x, yTop, x, yTop+hgt);
  }
}
```

(See output in Figure 18.34. Full program in patterns/sketches/blendingWithColors/blendingWithColors.pde).

The upper graph uses linear blending (in the default RGB mode). Depending on your eyes and how you're viewing the image (e.g., on a flat-panel LCD, a CRT monitor, or a printed page), you may or may not notice the edges of the transition zones jumping out at you. But it's a sure thing that if you blend regions of colors this way, sooner or later the edges will pop out and grab your attention.

The lower graph uses cosine blending, just as in the previous figure. The transition zones look a bit narrower because some of the zone is occupied by the gradual transitions at the ends. But the transitions look very nice and smooth.

You can also blend the colors in HSB mode, of course. The results will come out differently because HSB blends in the HSB color cylinder, not the RGB cube. I'll just put in a call to change the mode inside of setup(), after we make the colors (so they'll be the same as last time) but before we draw the blends:

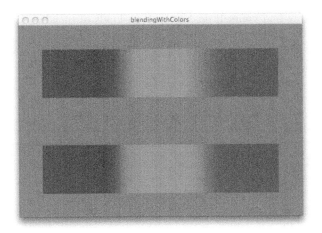

Figure 18.34. The top graph shows three colors using linear blending between solid areas. The bottom graph uses the cosine curve for blending. All blending is done with RGB mode. (patterns/sketches/blendingWithColors/blendingWithColors.pde)

```
colorMode(HSB);
drawSet(c1, c2, c3, false, 50, 50);
drawSet(c1, c2, c3, true, 50, 250);
```

See output in Figure 18.35. Full program in patterns/sketches/blendingWithColorsHSB/ blendingWithColorsHSB.pde).

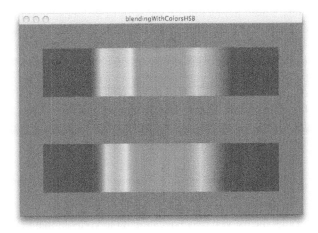

Figure 18.35. Blending linearly and with cosine in HSB mode. (patterns/sketches/blendingWithColorsHSB/blendingWithColorsHSB.pde)

You'll probably find yourself dealing with all kinds of blending situations as you develop your Processing projects. You might blend between different speeds, colors, angles, sizes, or really anything else that describes your images and how things move. Much of the time, a linear blend using lerp() is all you need. But if you're looking for smoothness, remember that cosine is your friend.

Sometimes when I find I'm doing a lot of blending in a project, I'll create two little helper functions that give me cosine-blended versions of lerp() and map(). Naturally enough, I call them coslerp() and cosmap(). These new functions take the same arguments as their namesakes, but they blend smoothly (and take a little more time to do it, of course). Here's the code for these two routines (note that, like their namesakes, coslerp() puts the control parameter at the end of the argument list, while cosmap() puts it at the start):

```
// amt should be in range (0,1)
float coslerp(float value1, float value2, float amt) {
    amt = map(cos(amt*PI), 1, -1, 0, 1);
    return(lerp(value1, value2, amt));
}

// value should be in range (0,1)
float cosmap(float value, float low1, float high1, float low2,
                float high2) {
    value = map(cos(value*PI), 1, -1, 0, 1);
    float amt = norm(value, low1, high1);
    return(lerp(low2, high2, amt));
}
```

In these routines, I used the fact that radians(180) has the value PI (Processing's built-in keyword for the Greek letter π), so I was able to just use that result directly and skip the function call to radians(), saving just a little bit of time.

Note that these routines only behave like lerp() and map() when the control parameter is in the range $(0,1)$. If your control goes outside of that range, the built-in lerp() and map() will assume that your input and output ranges continue as straight lines forever in both directions. These versions don't do that, and may give you some unexpected results. As the comments suggest, coslerp() and cosmap() are really only sensible for control values in the range $(0,1)$.

18.6 Building Patterns

As you looked through the list you may have thought to yourself that I could have made some of the earlier examples in this book shorter if I'd used these functions. That's absolutely true. I've tried to limit my use of these until now, though lerp(), dist(), and map() were too handy to ignore, and I used abs() and a few others from time to time. When you're writing your own code, these functions can all be terrific time-savers, and I encourage you to use them whenever the need arises.

Let's see some examples where these functions are useful for making cool images.

Like its cousin cosine, the sine function `sin()` is fabulous for creating gently changing numbers. You'll often want to control how quickly the numbers change. You can do that by multiplying the argument to `sin()` (that is, the angle) by some number. Multiply the input by two, and the numbers change twice as fast.

Here's an example of a bunch of pulsing circles:

```
float Angle = 0;

void setup() {
   size(600, 400);
   fill(196, 84, 94);
}

void draw() {
   background(135, 125, 112);
   for (int i=0; i<6; i++) {
       float radius = map(sin(Angle), -1, 1, 20, 40);
       ellipse(50+(100*i), 200, 2*radius, 2*radius);
   }
   Angle += .1;
}
```

(See output in Figure 18.36. Full program in patterns/sketches/pulse1/pulse1.pde)

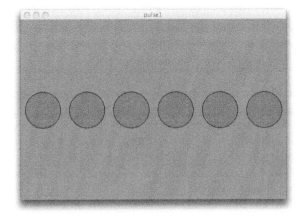

Figure 18.36. Some pulsing circles (frame from animation).
(patterns/sketches/pulse1/pulse1.pde)

We can make this a little more interesting by making them pulse at different speeds. That just means multiplying the value we give to `sin()` by slightly different amounts. A quick-and-dirty choice is to use something based on the loop variable `i`:

```
float sine_angle = Angle * (1+i/5.0);
float radius = map(sin(sine_angle), -1, 1, 20, 40);
```

(See output in Figure 18.37. Full program in patterns/sketches/pulse2/pulse2.pde)

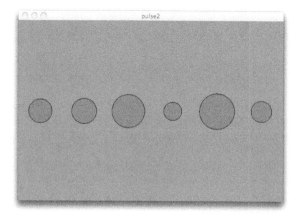

Figure 18.37. Pulsing circles no longer in unison (frame from animation). (patterns/sketches/pulse2/pulse2.pde)

I used the value 5.0 rather than simply 5 because, as I discussed in Chapter 4, an expression like `(1+i/5)` involves only integers, and thus Processing would throw away the floating-point value of the division. By using 5.0 I've got a floating-point value inside the parentheses, so it returns a floating-point result.

Note that when we're using `sin()` this way we don't have to worry too much about the meaning of the angle argument. Just keep in mind that when the angle reaches `2*PI` (which is about 6.2), the output of `sin()` will start to repeat.

As I mentioned earlier, the functions `sin()` and `cos()` are real workhorses. Any time you need something to move back and forth from one value to another, and you want it to happen smoothly, `sin()` and `cos()` are your go-to functions. To avoid repetition I'll just refer to the sine curve in the following discussion, but remember that cosine offers the very same features.

Let's look a little more closely at how to control the sine curve so you can get the results you want.

The basic idea is that `sin()` starts at 0, goes up to 1, then back down to 0, then to -1, then back up to 0 again. It takes 360 degrees to make a full cycle. If you ask it for the value for 361 degrees, it's just like asking for the value at 1 degrees. You could use modulo for this, but you don't have to: the `sin()` function is happy to take values that go up and up and up (or down and down and down).

If you don't want your result to be in the range -1 to 1, just pass it into `map()` with the range you want. If you want your output values to go from a to b, for example, you'd say

```
myValue = map(sin(x), -1, 1, a, b);
```

In this example, x is the angle that's being passed to `sin()`. Your values of a and b can be anything you like, and your output value will smoothly bounce from a to b and back again, over and over, smoothly, forever, as x grows.

A very common use of sine is to control a value that runs through the range $(0, 1)$, rather than the range $(-1, 1)$ that sine produces. We can easily use `map()` to transform the range $(-1, 1)$ to $(0, 1)$, and now the value bounces between 0 and 1:

```
myValue = map(sin(x), -1, 1, 0, 1);
```

By changing x slowly, the value of `sin(x)` will change slowly. Larger changes to x will of course mean more rapid changes in the output. So if you're using `sin()` to control motion, bigger changes to the input from frame to frame will result in faster motion.

A great and common way to control motion is to use the value of `frameCount` as part of the input to `sin()`. The value of `frameCount` just goes up and up over time, so the angle we give to `sin()` goes up and up, and we get that back and forth behavior forever. The trick is to multiply `frameCount` by the right number so you get pleasing motion.

For example, suppose you're drawing a miniature golf course, and on this hole, there's a monkey stomping its foot up and down over the width of the green, so you have to time your shot to get it through. You might control the height of the monkey's foot this way:

```
monkey_foot_height = map(sin(degrees(frameCount)), -1, 1, 6, 0);
```

So in this example, the monkey's foot will move from 6 units to 0 units and back again, up and down, forever (I suppose the units might be inches, or ball heights). But how fast is this happening? Remembering that `sin()` goes through one complete loop over 360 degrees, then the monkey's foot will go through one full up/down/up cycle in 360 frames. At 60 frames per second (which is pretty common) that's six seconds. That's pretty slow! I think that would make the hole much too easy; the foot would barely seem to be moving.

So we can speed it up by multiplying `frameCount`. If we give `sin()` the value `3*frameCount`, it will reach 360 in 120 frames, which is just two seconds. That sounds a lot closer to me.

```
monkey_foot_height = map(sin(3*frameCount), -1, 1, 6, 0);
```

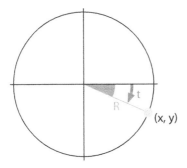

Figure 18.38. A circle of radius R around the origin, and a point (x,y) at an angle t from the x-axis.

Of course, if you wanted the motion to take longer than six seconds you could slow it down by dividing frameCount by some number, or (just as well) multiplying it by something less than one. For example, multiplying by 0.5 is the same as dividing by two.

Finally, the sin() and cos() functions have another trick up their sleeves. We can use them to find points on a circle. Suppose you draw a circle of radius R around the origin, as in Figure 18.38.

In the figure I've also marked a point at t degrees around the circle (starting at the x-axis and going clockwise). Suppose we know the radius R and the angle t, and we want to find the x and y coordinates of the point.

The recipe is easy:

```
x = R * cos(radians(t));
y = R * sin(radians(t));
```

That's all there is to it! When t is 0, then you get back the (x,y) values $(R,0)$ (that is, a point that's R units out along the x-axis). When t is 90, you get back $(0,R)$, and so on, all the way around to 360.

You'll find that this little recipe is useful in a surprising number of situations. One common use is to draw the points of a regular *polygon*, or a figure with a given number of straight, equal sides. For example, suppose you wanted to draw a stop sign. That has eight sides. So you just need to walk around the circle in eight steps, making points as you go:

```
void setup() {
    size(600, 400);
    background(177, 224, 214);

    float centerx = 300;
    float centery = 200;
    float r = 150;

    fill(79, 168, 81);
    beginShape();
    for (int i=0; i<8; i++) {
        float angle = map(i, 0, 8, 0, 360);
        float x = r * cos(radians(angle));
        float y = r * sin(radians(angle));
        x += centerx;
        y += centery;
```

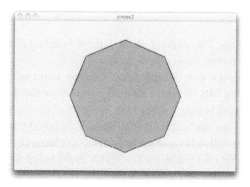

Figure 18.39. A green stop sign made with `sin()` and `cos()`.
(patterns/sketches/sincos2/sincos2.pde)

```
        vertex(x,y);
    }
    endShape(CLOSE);
}
```

(See output in Figure 18.39. Full program in patterns/sketches/sincos2/sincos2.pde)

That's almost right, but it's green, and it's not in the orientation we usually see stop signs mounted in. To fix the orientation, I'll just adjust the angle so we spin the whole thing half of one step on each loop.

```
angle += 360/16;
```

(See output in Figure 18.40. Full program in patterns/sketches/sincos3/sincos3.pde)

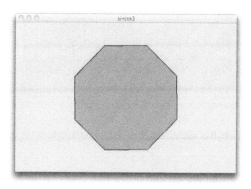

Figure 18.40. A green stop sign in the right orientation. (patterns/sketches/sincos3/sincos3.pde)

18.6.1   A Bouncing Ball

At the start of this chapter, I assembled some of these building blocks to make a simple bouncing ball. Let's see how those pieces went together.

Let's write it so that we give the function a floating-point value `time`, and it gives us back a `PVector` that tells us where the ball is at that moment.

The horizontal motion is easy because the ball is traveling to the right at a constant speed. In fact, since `time` starts at 0 and increases, I assigned `time` to `xPosition`.

How can we get the ball to bounce up and down? Let's start by using a cosine curve. I'll use the plotting program I listed above. The X input range will go from 0 to 1000, which will simulate the value of `time` that would go into `getBallCenter()`.

```
float plotFunction(float x)
{
    float v = cos(x);
    return(v);
}
```

(See output in Figure 18.41. Full program in patterns/sketches/rebounce01/rebounce01.pde)

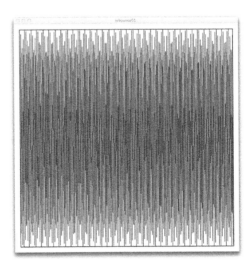

Figure 18.41. Making the ball bounce, step one. (patterns/sketches/rebounce01/rebounce01.pde)

Yikes, that curve is jumping up and down like crazy. If this was the ball, it would be flying up and down the screen. The cosine curve is wiggling much too fast. I'll slow it down by making the angle grow more slowly. Dividing `time` by 40 makes it look much more reasonable:

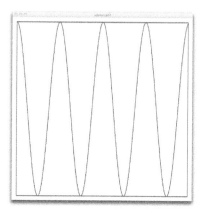

Figure 18.42. Making the ball bounce, step two.
(patterns/sketches/rebounce02/rebounce02.pde)

```
float plotFunction(float x)
    float v = cos(x/40.0);
    return(v);
}
```

(See output in Figure 18.42. Full program in patterns/sketches/rebounce02/rebounce02.pde)

That's better, but it's still too smooth at the bottom. I want the ball to bounce when it hits the ground. By taking the absolute value of the curve with abs (), it will reverse course abruptly at a height of 0.

```
float plotFunction(float x)
    float v = abs(cos(x/40.0));
    return(v);
}
```

(See output in Figure 18.43. Full program in patterns/sketches/rebounce03/rebounce03.pde)

Much better, but the ball is rebounding to its original height on each bounce. Let's compute a variable called bounceHeight that will be 1 when x is 0 and 0 when x is 1,000. That will be a straight line. Here's the value of bounceHeight plotted by itself:

```
float plotFunction(float x)
    float bounceHeight = map(x, 0, 600, 1, 0);
    return(bounceHeight);
}
```

(See output in Figure 18.44. Full program in patterns/sketches/rebounce04/rebounce04.pde)

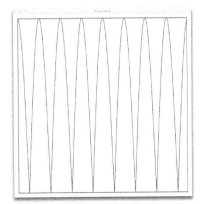

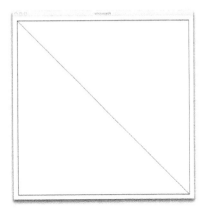

Figure 18.43. Making the ball bounce, step three.
(patterns/sketches/rebounce03/rebounce03.pde)

Figure 18.44. Making the ball bounce, step four.
(patterns/sketches/rebounce04/rebounce04.pde)

If I now multiply the height of the absolute cosine by this straight line, I'll change the height of the curve over time:

```
float plotFunction(float x)
    float v = abs(cos(x/40.0));
    float bounceHeight = map(x, 0, 600, 1, 0);
    float y = v * bounceHeight;
    return(y);
}
```

(See output in Figure 18.45. Full program in patterns/sketches/rebounce05/rebounce05.pde)

Yow! What's going on here?

The problem is that the scaling curve is starting out positive, but then it goes to 0 and then negative. So I really want to change two things here. First, once the height of the ball's bounce is zero, that's the end of it; the ball doesn't start bouncing with a negative height!

So I'll *clamp* the scaling variable bounceHeight to 0 using max(). If one argument to max() is positive and the other one is 0, then the output will be the greater (positive) number. But if that number goes negative, then the output will be 0.

```
float plotFunction(float x)
    float v = abs(cos(x/40.0));
    float bounceHeight = max(0, map(x, 0, 600, 1, 0));
    float y = v * bounceHeight;
    return(y);
}
```

(See output in Figure 18.46. Full program in patterns/sketches/rebounce06/rebounce06.pde)

That's just about right. I'll just slow down the bouncing a little bit so that the curve gets stretched out. Right now, the input x is running from 0 to 1,000. If that stood for frames, at 60 frames per second, 1,000 frames is a little less than 17 seconds. That's a long time for the ball to cross the screen.

So let's cut that in half. Now the input will run from 0 to 500:

```
int MinimumX = 0;    // the minimum input value
int MaximumX = 500;    // the maximum input value
```

(See output in Figure 18.47. Full program in patterns/sketches/rebounce07/rebounce07.pde)

That's the kind of thing I was going for. Obviously we could continue to tune this up to our heart's content to get just the right amount of bouncing at the right speed.

18.7   Pattern Shaping

When we use Processing's built-in `random()` function, we get back random numbers that fall with equal probability throughout the range we ask for. In other words, if we call `random(0,1)` we're equally likely to get back any number from 0 up to (but not including, one). We say that these numbers are *uniform*, or *uniformly distributed*, meaning that every number in the range is as likely as any other. If we ask for `random(100,200)`, the values are still going to come out uniformly between those two new extremes.

That's often perfectly fine. But sometimes we want a different distribution to our random numbers. For example, we might be trying to draw a picture of oranges that grow in our orchard of orange trees. We know that most oranges are about the same size, with only a few being smaller and a few larger. A very few will be very small,

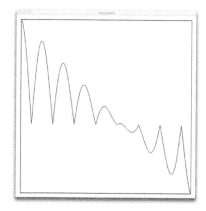

Figure 18.45. Making the ball bounce, step five. (patterns/sketches/rebounce05/rebounce05.pde)

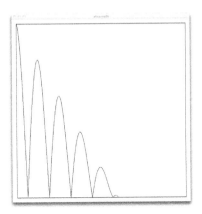

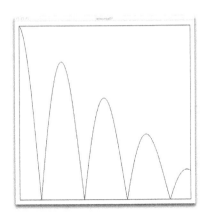

Figure 18.46. Making the ball bounce, step six. (patterns/sketches/rebounce06/rebounce06.pde)

Figure 18.47. Making the ball bounce, step seven. (patterns/sketches/rebounce07/rebounce07.pde)

and a very few will be very large. So when we call `random()` over and over to tell us how large our oranges should be, we'd like it to give us back values that cluster near the middle of the range.

Let's say an average orange has a radius of 2 inches. Then each time we make a random number, we'd like something that's close to 2. Occasionally, we'll get something rather bigger (like 2.5) and occasionally smaller (like 1.5), and very rarely we'll get back something as large as 3 or as small as 1. If we just called `random(1,3)`, then we'd get just as many values near 1 as we'd get near 2 and near 3. So although `random()` might be a good function to call to start our process of finding useful random numbers, we need to do something more to adjust what we get back so that the values have the shape, or distribution, that we want.

There's a general method that will give you any distribution of numbers you like. The idea is that you write a routine that you treat like a black box. You just call the routine and out comes a random number from 0 to 1.

Suppose that I wanted my random numbers to have a particular pattern. For example, I'm creating an animation of people participating in a charity 5K run. About half the people are runners and going pretty fast. And most of the others are walkers and going much slower. Not many people are in between.

What I'd like is to have a random-number generator that I can call over and over, each time getting back the speed of one person. I'd like the numbers to bunch up near the low end and near the high end and rarely be in between. Suppose I call my routine 1,000 times, and I plot the frequency with which each value was produced. If I get back a picture like Figure 18.48, then my custom random-number generator is doing a great job for me.

The way to read Figure 18.48 is to think of the horizontal axis as the range of values that can come out of the generator. In this case, that's a range from 0 to one.

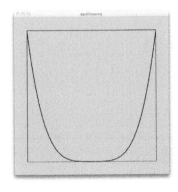

Figure 18.48. We'd like random numbers that come out with this frequency: lots of values near 0, then trailing off, then picking up again with lots of values near 1.

The height of the curve above each of these values tells us how likely it is that the random-number generator will produce that value. So in this figure, we'd get back a lot of numbers at the very lowest and highest ends of the range, none at all in the middle of the range, and a smoothly falling-off density of numbers as we move from the extremes towards the center. This is just the kind of distribution of values that I want for my racers. Many are very slow, there are fewer and fewer that run at increasingly faster speeds until there are no runners at a moderate speed. Then there are a few that are a bit faster, a few more that are faster still, and so on, until there's a lot running at the top speed.

A good way to write this routine is to think about it backwards. Rather than try to produce a particular pattern, take the pattern as an input and generate numbers that match it.

To do this, think of the pattern as a kind of controlling function. For each input value x, there's a corresponding y that tells us how often that value of x should come out.

To produce values of x that follow that pattern might seem like an incredibly hard problem. And it could be, but there's an easy way out.

Think of the pattern as a drawing on a square dartboard. The horizontal x-axis is labeled 0 to 1, and the vertical y-axis is also labeled 0 to 1 (for once, I'm going to assume that y is 0 at the bottom and increases in value as we move upwards). Now you stand some distance away, and you throw darts at the board, one after the other. Let's say that all the darts that fall under the pattern we'll paint green, and the ones above we'll paint red. Looking just at places where the darts hit, after 1,000 darts we'd get something like Figure 18.49.

If we throw darts and return the x locations of the green ones, then they'll create exactly the pattern we're after!

In Figure 18.50 I've thrown 10,000 darts, but I'm only showing the green ones. Note that they match our input pattern very nicely.

This is known, unsurprisingly, as the *dart-throwing algorithm*. It's not the most efficient way to produce random numbers, but it's simple and it can produce any distribution. The pattern doesn't even have to be continuous. As long as you can get a y for every x, you know whether a dart is red or green. The procedure can be written this way (this is just a fragment):

```
do {
    x = random(0, 1);
    y = random(0, 1);
    threshold = patternValue(x);
```

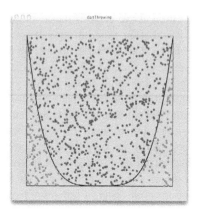

Figure 18.49. Throwing darts at a   Figure 18.50. Throwing 10,000 darts.
square dartboard.

```
} while (y>threshold);
// x is now our random value
```

So we just throw dart after dart. We find the threshold for the dart's value of *x*, and if the dart's *y* value is less than that threshold, we use its *x* value, otherwise we throw another dart.

Depending on your pattern, this can waste some time throwing away lots of red darts. In Figure 18.50, I threw 10,000 darts, but only 1,990 ended up under the curve and getting returned. So I threw away a little more than 80 percent of the points that I computed. If your project is running too slow, a dart-throwing technique might not be a good way to generate your random numbers. But if you don't mind this bit of wasted time, it's a great option because it's so simple and flexible.

Often the height of the pattern is called a threshold, since we're comparing our values of *y* to it and only taking those that pass below (so it acts something like a limbo bar: you only get through if you're low enough).

Processing's built-in function `random()` can be pictured this way, where the pattern is simply a straight horizontal line. So if the range you give it is 0 to 1, every value from 0 to 1 has an equal probability of coming out.

Let's explore the dart-throwing technique a little, but for fun I'll take everything up a notch and use two random number patterns, creating *x* and *y* values for points.

I'll write a little program that will generate lots of points by throwing darts to get an *x*, and more darts to get a *y*. Then I'll plot that point and repeat.

The code is straightforward, so I won't build it up line by line, but here's the general approach. The `setup()` routine makes the window and chooses the patterns I'll use for *x* and *y* (I cooked up seven patterns, and simply numbered them 0 through 6; I'll talk about the specific patterns in a moment).

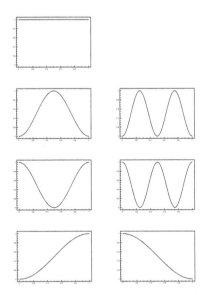

Figure 18.51. Different patterns for random numbers. Except for the top row, these are all just different pieces of the cosine curve. Top row: Pattern 0 is a uniform value of 1, like Processing's built-in system. Second row: Patterns 1 and 2 are one and two humps. Third row: Patterns 3 and 4 are one and two dips. Fourth row: Pattern 5 is an S shape, pattern 6 is a reversed S.

The heart of the program is `getRandom()`. You hand it a choice of pattern, and it gives you back a random number from 0 to 1, shaped to match that pattern.

The function `drawPatterns()` just runs a value of x from 0 to 1, gets back the threshold for the x pattern for each value, and plots it. It does the same thing for y. That way, we can see our choice of pattern laid up right against the window holding the dots.

The dots themselves come from `drawDots()`, which just calls the shaped random-number maker twice, getting an x and then a y. It plots that point and repeats.

The routine `getThreshold()` is responsible for making the patterns. You give it a value from 0 to 1, and a pattern choice, and it tells you the height of the pattern at that value. In other words, it gives you a number from 0 to 1, telling you how likely it is that the given value should come out of the random-number function. A value of 0 means that number should never appear, while 1 means no other number is any more likely. Values in between represent probabilities between these extremes.

I cooked up seven patterns to play around with. They're illustrated in Figure 18.51.

The first (pattern number 0) is just a flat line at 1; that is, every number from 0 to 1 has an equal probability of coming out. That's what we get from `random(0,1)`.

The other six patterns use pieces of the cosine curve, scaled from 0 to 1. Patterns 1 and 2 contain one hump and two humps, respectively (where a "hump" starts at 0, rises to 1, and drops back down again to 0). Patterns 3 and 4 contain one and two dips,

respectively (where a "dip" starts at 1, drops down to 0, and rises back to 1). Pattern 5
creates an S shape that starts at 0 and rises to 1, and pattern 6 creates a reversed S that
starts at 1 and drops to 0.

Here's the program that uses these patterns to generate random values:

```
void setup() {
    size(750, 550);
    smooth();
    background(173, 180, 125);
    int hPattern = 0;
    int vPattern = 0;
    drawPatterns(hPattern, vPattern);
    drawDots(hPattern, vPattern);
}

float getRandom(int patternChoice) {
    float x, y, threshold;
    do {
        x = random(0, 1);
        y = random(0, 1);
        threshold = getThreshold(x, patternChoice);
    } while (y>threshold);
    return(x);
}

void drawPatterns(int hPattern, int vPattern) {
    fill(240, 218, 180);
    stroke(0);
    rect(125, 25, 600, 100);  // horizontal plot area
    rect(25, 125, 100, 400);  // vertical plot area

    fill(240, 275, 180);
    rect(125, 125, 600, 400);  // the main dots area

    noFill();
    stroke(3, 125, 135);
    float oldpx = 0;
    float oldpy = 0;

    // draw the horizontal pattern
    for (int x=0; x<600; x++) {
        float ax = x/599.0;
        float y = getThreshold(ax, hPattern);
        float px = 125+x;
        float py = 125 - (100*y);
        if (x>0) line(oldpx, oldpy, px, py);
        oldpx = px;
```

```
         oldpy = py;
      }

   // draw the vertical pattern
   for (int y=0; y<400; y++) {
      float ay = y/399.0;
      float x = getThreshold(ay, vPattern);
      float px = 125 - (100*x);
      float py = 125+y;
      if (y>0) line(oldpx, oldpy, px, py);
      oldpx = px;
      oldpy = py;
   }
}

void drawDots(int hPattern, int vPattern) {
   noStroke();
   fill(205, 125, 28);
   int numEllipses = 1800;
   for (int i=0; i<numEllipses; i++) {
      float px = 600 * getRandom(hPattern);
      float py = 400 * getRandom(vPattern);
      ellipse(125+px, 125+py, 8, 8);
   }
}

float getThreshold(float x, int patternChoice) {
    float loAngle, hiAngle;
    switch (patternChoice) {
       case 0:  // uniform
          loAngle = hiAngle = 0;
          break;
       case 1:  // one hump
          loAngle = PI;
          hiAngle = 3*PI;
          break;
       case 2:  // two humps
          loAngle = PI;
          hiAngle = 5*PI;
          break;
       case 3:  // one dip
          loAngle = 0;
          hiAngle = 2*PI;
          break;
       case 4:  // two dips
          loAngle = 0;
```

```
            hiAngle = 4*PI;
            break;
        case 5:   // S
            loAngle = PI;
            hiAngle = 2*PI;
            break;
        case 6:   // backwards S
            loAngle = 0;
            hiAngle = PI;
            break;
        default:
            println("I don't know pattern choice "+patternChoice);
            loAngle = hiAngle = 0;
            break;
    }
    float angle = lerp(loAngle, hiAngle, x);
    float threshold = map(cos(angle), -1, 1, 0, 1);
    return(threshold);
}
```

(See output in Figure 18.52. Full program in patterns/sketches/randomPatterns/randomPatterns.pde)

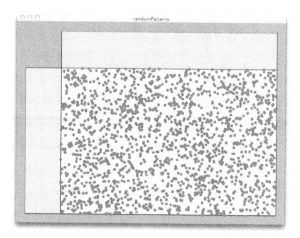

Figure 18.52. Using two random patterns to generate points (x,y). Here the two patterns are the default, uniform distributions. (patterns/sketches/randomPatterns/randomPatterns.pde)

Let's use this code to make some 2D patterns that follow different distributions. In Figure 18.52, you can see the result of using pattern 0 on both axes; this is like just calling random(0,1). The dots are uniformly distributed throughout the yellowish rectangle.

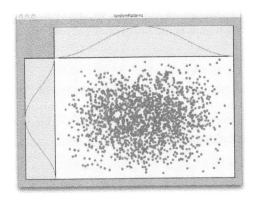

Figure 18.53. Random dots using pattern 1 for both horizontal and vertical locations.

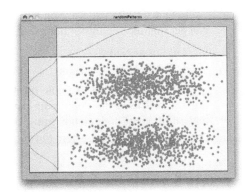

Figure 18.54. Random dots using pattern 1 for horizontal and pattern 2 for vertical locations.

In Figure 18.53, I used the single-hump pattern 1 on both x and y. The dots clump up in the middle of the image.

```
int hPattern = 1;
int vPattern = 1;
```

In Figure 18.54, I used the one-hump pattern 1 for x, but the two-hump pattern 2 for y. We get two clouds of dots, following the double hump in y.

```
int hPattern = 1;
int vPattern = 2;
```

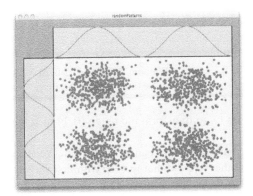

Figure 18.55. Random dots using pattern 2 for both horizontal and vertical locations.

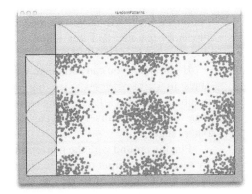

Figure 18.56. Random dots using pattern 4 for both horizontal and vertical locations.

Let's try using pattern 2 on both axes. The result, in Figure 18.55, shows that we can get four nice clouds of dots, following the humps in the distribution curves.

```
int hPattern = 2;
int vPattern = 2;
```

Let's turn this last example on its head and use dips rather than humps. In Figure 18.56, I used the double-dip pattern 4 for both axes. We can think of this as a pattern of about nine clouds (most of them only partly in the rectangle), or a kind of "negative" grid pattern where the dots are not absent.

```
int hPattern = 4;
int vPattern = 4;
```

Finally, in Figure 18.57, I used the S-shaped pattern 5 in the horizontal direction and the reverse-S pattern 6 in the vertical (remember that the vertical pattern is plotted from the top downwards, so the vertical reverse S starts at 1 and drops to 0). The points clump together in the corner of the space.

```
int hPattern = 5;
int vPattern = 6;
```

The big value of this approach is that it lets us conceptually separate getting and using random numbers from the process used to shape their distribution. All our program needs to think about is calling `getRandom()` with the pattern number instead of `random(0,1)`. The random numbers that come back are "shaped" the way we want automatically. If they don't have the right shape (that is, the distribution we want) we can just change the threshold pattern, and our main code doesn't need to be touched.

If you want, you can add range variables to `getRandom()` so that the numbers come back from a range other than $(0,1)$. Alternatively, you can call `lerp()` to transform the range $(0,1)$ to some other range.

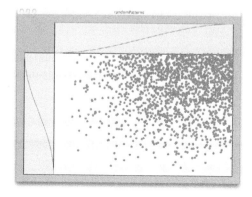

Figure 18.57. Random dots using pattern 5 for horizontal and pattern 6 for vertical locations.

Playing around with the pattern-making building blocks can be a lot of fun. You can try feeding the output of one function to another (we did that in a very limited way by applying the output of `map()` to `max()`). A deep discussion of all of these functions could fill another book (and it would be a wonderful book). But that's not this book, and in the meantime, you can discover all kinds of patterns and pattern-making techniques on your own using Processing's deceptively simple pattern-making functions.

18.8   Circle Packing

Let's make some interesting images by mixing together a few of the pattern-making functions we saw above, then adding in a handful bit of geometry, slowly stirring in some 2D arrays, and finally adding a splash of image-loading.

One class of cool patterns can be built by taking a starting shape and packing many copies of it into another shape. For example, you might start with a circular region and fill it with squares. You'd start with the biggest square you could fit, and then you'd add in the next-biggest square in the remaining space, and so on, until the only gaps left were smaller than a pixel.

Let's do just that, but with circles instead of squares.

The program will take as input a black-and-white picture from the disk. Black regions mean "don't touch", and white means "fill me in with circles."

To get started, let's make a simple `Disk` class to hold a circle. I'll give it the usual object variables: a center, radius, and color. I'll give it a simple constructor and a simple `render()` routine that we can control to draw just the outline of the circle, the interior, or both.

The `setup()` routine will do almost nothing yet.

There won't be any `draw()` routine in this program because it just makes one picture and shows it.

Here's the starting skeleton:

```
class Disk {
    PVector center;
    float radius;
    color clr;

    Disk(PVector acenter, float aradius, color aclr) {
        center = new PVector(acenter.x, acenter.y);
        radius = aradius;
        clr = aclr;
    }

    void render(boolean drawStroke, boolean drawFill) {
        noFill();
        noStroke();
        if (drawFill) fill(clr);
        if (drawStroke) stroke(clr);
        ellipse(center.x, center.y, 2*radius, 2*radius);
    }
}

void setup() {
    size(600, 600);
    background(0);
```

```
    smooth();
}
```

(Full program in patterns/sketches/circlefill01/circlefill01.pde)

It doesn't do anything, of course, but it gets us off the ground.

Now we need a strategy that will help us determine where to put down the circles and how big they should be. There are probably a million ways to do this. Although I've seen pictures of packed circles, I don't know how they were made. It's a fun problem to kick around in your head for a while; if you like this kind of puzzle, I encourage you to think about it for a bit before continuing on.

In my solution, the goal is to create a 2D array, which I'll call `Distance`. The array is the same size as the graphics window, so each array entry matches one pixel. The value of `Distance[y][x]` tells us the distance to the nearest "occupied" pixel. Initially, nothing is occupied except the black pixels in the input image. But as soon as we place a circle, all of its pixels are then occupied, and we have to update the array. So if we draw a circle at `(x,y)` with radius `Distance[y][x]`, it will stay within the boundaries of the input image, and it won't overlap any previous circles.

Once we have this array, making the picture is easy: find the largest value in the `Distance` array and draw a circle of that radius right there. Update the array and repeat. Keep doing this until the largest value in `Distance` is too small (say one pixel or so) and then just draw the image.

So, how should we create `Distance`? The obvious solution is to write two sets of nested loops. The outermost one scans the `Distance` array one pixel at a time. For each pixel, it looks up the corresponding pixel in the input image (which I'll call the "mask"). If the mask pixel is black, then the `Distance` value for that pixel is 0 (that is, we're zero pixels away from a black pixel). Otherwise, we put some huge value into that entry of `Distance`, and we go into the second, inner set of loops. Here we look at every pixel in the mask, and if it's black, we compute how far away it is from the `Distance` entry. Then we update that entry of `Distance` to hold the minimum of what it used to have and this new distance.

In other words, for a given `Distance[y][x]`, we look at every single pixel in the mask and find the distance to the closest such pixel that's black, which is of course our goal.

This works perfectly well. Rather than build up each piece of this program together, as we usually do, I'll just give you a description of each step and then share the code. There's nothing tricky here in the programming, but the full programs are of course available for you to download and experiment with.

To set things up, I'll need to declare the array as a global:

```
float [][] Distance;
```

I'll also have to allocate it inside of `setup()`:

```
Distance = new float[height][width];
```

In setup(), I'll add two new calls: one to buildDistance() and one to showDistance(). The first will do what I just described. The showDistance() routine will be just a quick, little throw-together thing to find the maximum and minimum distances and then set each pixel in the image. It's just to give us a rough idea of what the Distance array looks like.

In buildDistance(), I'll read the input image from a file named mask0.png. I really shouldn't be putting absolute file names into my code, of course, but it'll work for this little project. The mask needs to be the same size as the graphics window, so I'll check for that, and if the sizes don't match, I'll print out a message and quit.

Here's buildDistance(), implemented just as I described above:

```
void buildDistance() {
   PImage maskImage = loadImage("mask0.png");
   if ((maskImage.width != width) || (maskImage.height != height)) {
      println("Please use a mask of width "+width+" and height "+height);
      exit();
   }
   maskImage.loadPixels();
   color clr;

   for (int dy=0; dy<height; dy++) {
      for (int dx=0; dx<width; dx++) {
         clr = maskImage.pixels[(dy*width)+dx];
         if (red(clr) == 0) {
            Distance[dy][dx] = 0;
         } else {
            Distance[dy][dx] = width*height;
            for (int py=0; py<height; py++) {
               for (int px=0; px<width; px++) {
                  clr = maskImage.pixels[(py*width)+px];
                  if (red(clr) == 0) {
                     float d = dist(px, py, dx, dy);
                     Distance[dy][dx] = min(d, Distance[dy][dx]);
                  }
               }
            }
         }
      }
   }
}
```

And here's the little showDistance so we can see what the last routine did for us:

```
void showDistance() {
   float minD = Distance[0][0];
```

```
float maxD = Distance[0][0];
for (int y=0; y<height; y++) {
    for (int x=0; x<width; x++) {
        minD = min(Distance[y][x], minD);
        maxD = max(Distance[y][x], maxD);
    }
}
println("show: minD="+minD+"  maxD="+maxD);
for (int y=0; y<height; y++) {
    for (int x=0; x<width; x++) {
        float mapD = map(Distance[y][x], minD, maxD, 0, 255);
        set(x, y, color(mapD, mapD, 0));
    }
}
}
```

(See output in Figure 18.58. Full program in patterns/sketches/circlefill02/circlefill02.pde)

Figure 18.58. The distances from the edge. (patterns/sketches/circlefill02/circlefill02.pde)

For this run, I used the mask shown in Figure 18.59, which is a white picture with a row or two of black pixels around the outside.

Just to make sure things are working, let's try out a second mask, shown in Figure 18.60. Here I've added a black box in the upper right of the image.

Figure 18.59. The first mask: a white box with a black border.

Figure 18.60. The second mask: a white box with a black border and a black box inside.

We just need to change the name that's wired into the code:

```
PImage maskImage = loadImage("mask0box.png");
```

(See output in Figure 18.61. Full program in patterns/sketches/circlefill03/circlefill03.pde)

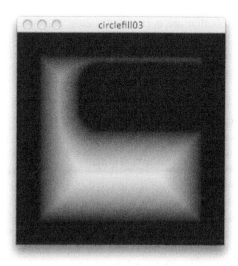

Figure 18.61. The distances from the second mask.
(patterns/sketches/circlefill03/circlefill03.pde)

That looks about right to me. The brighter the yellow, the farther we are from a black pixel. So all seems to be fine.

Well, not exactly fine. If you run this code, you'll see that it's *slow*. I mean *really* slow. With a few exceptions, we fill in each pixel in the image by scanning the *entire* mask and computing a distance for every pixel. These pictures were made at a resolution of 300 by 300, and they took almost a minute. If we scale this up to 600 by 600, that will go up to about four minutes, and that's before we even start creating the circles!

You might want to knock this around in your own mind for a while and see if you can think of a faster way to fill in the Distance array.

Here's what I came up with. I'll make a number of passes through the original mask image, and fill in a few more entries in Distance with each pass. To keep track of this, I'll create a second 2D array called pass, which will be the same size as the mask (and the graphics window).

The idea is that I'll slowly "thicken" the black parts of the mask image. We could also say that I'll erode, or wear away, the white areas. So each entry in the pass array will tell me how many times I've gone through this erosion step until I reached that entry.

Initially, every entry in pass will be −1, except those that are directly over a black pixel in the mask. Those are set to 0 because they required zero steps of erosion to get to black.

Now I'll go through the pass array, over and over, eroding away the white parts until none are left. For every pixel in pass (well, not *every* pixel; I'll come back to this in a moment) I'll check to see if it's been handled already (that is, if it has a value greater than −1). If so, I'll move on. Otherwise, I'll check its 8-connected neighbors (recall these are the pixels that are north, south, east, and west of this pixel, plus the diagonals, as shown in Figure 17.5). If any of those were handled in the last pass, then this pixel should be handled, too. In other words, as we erode the white areas, if any white pixel is next to a pixel that was just eaten away on the last pass, it will get eaten away on this pass.

Because I'm checking the eight neighbors, I don't bother with the pixels on the very outermost border of the image. This way I don't have to bother checking to make sure I don't accidentally ask for a pixel off the image, causing an OutOfBoundsError. I could write code to do that, of course, but it would be a little long and messy and I want to keep this short, so I'm just ignoring those pixels for now.

The beauty of this approach is that the number of steps of erosion it took to reach a pixel is roughly the distance of that pixel from the nearest black pixel, where the eroding started. I say "roughly" because we're only computing distance along horizontal, vertical, and diagonal lines, and even then, the diagonals are counting for one unit of distance (when they should be slightly more).

Here's the new version of buildDistance():

```
void buildDistance() {
  PImage maskImage = loadImage("mask0box.png");
```

```
maskImage.loadPixels();
int[][] pass = new int[height][width];

// anything with a black pixel has distance -1, else 0
for (int y=0; y<height; y++) {
    for (int x=0; x<width; x++) {
        color clr = maskImage.pixels[(y*width)+x];
        pass[y][x] = -1;
        if (red(clr) == 0) pass[y][x] = 0;
    }
}

// dilate black pixels repeatedly, each newly-dilated
// pixel has a distance equal to number of steps of dilation
boolean dilateAgain = true;
int passNumber = 1;
while (dilateAgain) {
    dilateAgain = false;
    for (int y=1; y<height-1; y++) {
        for (int x=1; x<width-1; x++) {
            if (pass[y][x] >= 0) continue;
            if ((pass[y-1][x-1] == passNumber-1) ||
                (pass[y-1][x  ] == passNumber-1) ||
                (pass[y-1][x+1] == passNumber-1) ||
                (pass[y  ][x-1] == passNumber-1) ||
                (pass[y  ][x+1] == passNumber-1) ||
                (pass[y+1][x-1] == passNumber-1) ||
                (pass[y+1][x  ] == passNumber-1) ||
                (pass[y+1][x+1] == passNumber-1)) {
                dilateAgain = true;
                pass[y][x] = passNumber;
            }
        }
    }
    passNumber++;
}

// copy the temporary mask into the Distance array
for (int y=0; y<height; y++) {
    for (int x=0; x<width; x++) {
        Distance[y][x] = pass[y][x];
    }
}
}
```

(See output in Figure 18.62. Full program in patterns/sketches/circlefill04/circlefill04.pde)

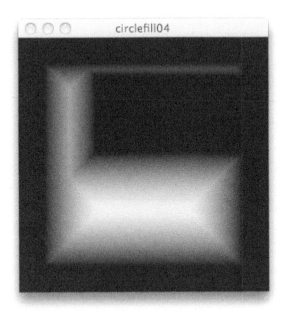

Figure 18.62. The fast version of the distance-finding routine.
(patterns/sketches/circlefill04/circlefill04.pde)

Compare Figure 18.62 and Figure 18.61. The new version is roughly like the accurate one, but not exactly. On the other hand, it runs in about one second!

If this was a scientific simulation, then this approximation might not be acceptable. But since my goal here is to make an interesting image, I think it should work just fine. The downside here is that large distances will be underestimated, so when I ask a pixel for the largest circle I can place there (that is, I check Distance[y][x]), the result will be a little smaller than it could be. But the problem diminishes with size, and the smallest distances will be more accurate. This means I can expect that my biggest circles won't be as large as they could be, but the smallest circles will still hug the boundaries of the white shapes pretty closely.

To me, the speed advantage is worth changing my original idea a little. If later I decide I really want the more accurate version of buildDistance(), I can always put it back in there.

This is really the only conceptually tricky part of the program. The rest is straightforward and gets a bit long, so as I said earlier, rather than build this up together, I'll just walk through the steps of my approach.

The big idea will be to find the largest circle that's available. I'll create a Disk object to hang onto this new circle and add it to a growing array of Disks. Finally, I'll update each entry in Distance to reflect the fact that these pixels are now occupied.

When there are no more gaps left large enough to hold another circle, I run through the `DiskList` array and draw them all into the graphics window.

To get this going, I'll make a new global to hold the list of `Disk`s:

```
Disk [] DiskList;
```

I'll add a line to `setup()` to create this array. Since it starts out with no entries, I'll create an array of length 0:

```
DiskList = new Disk[0];
```

The only other change to `setup()` is to call `buildPicture()` to kick the process into action.

That routine finds the biggest circle that can be placed in the picture. The radius of this circle is called `goalRadius`. Then it enters a loop. The routine tries to place a circle of size `goalRadius` into the picture. If it can't, it decreases `goalRadius` by one and tries again. This continues until `goalRadius` is just one pixel. When that happens, we draw the circles and we're done. Here's `buildPicture()`:

```
void buildPicture() {
    float goalRadius = maxDistance();
    while (goalRadius > 1) {
        if (!fitCircle(goalRadius)) {
            goalRadius--;
        }
    }
    background(0);
    for (int i=0; i<DiskList.length; i++) {
        DiskList[i].render(false, true);
    }
}
```

This routine first calls `maxDistance()` to find the starting radius.

There's not much to this little helper function. It just runs through the `Distance` array and returns the largest value it holds. The function uses `max()` along the way:

```
float maxDistance() {
    float maxd = Distance[0][0];
    for (int y=0; y<height; y++) {
        for (int x=0; x<width; x++) {
            maxd = max(Distance[y][x], maxd);
        }
    }
    return(maxd);
}
```

Returning to buildPicture(), once it has a desired radius, it tries to put a circle of that size into the picture using fitCircle(), so let's look at that routine next.

Here's the code for fitCircle():

```
boolean fitCircle(float radius) {
    float maxRadius = maxDistance();
    if (maxRadius < radius) {
        return(false);
    }
    PVector center = getAnyPixelWithDistance(radius);
    updateDistance(center, radius);
    color clr = color(random(100,255), random(100,255),
                      random(100,255));
    Disk newDisk = new Disk(center, radius, clr);
    DiskList = (Disk[])append(DiskList, newDisk);
    return(true);
}
```

The goal of fitCircle() is to place a new circle of the requested radius into the picture. If it can, it returns true, otherwise it returns false.

It does its work using a series of helper routines. First, it calls maxDistance(), which we just saw. This tells it the largest radius we can draw right now. If that largest radius is smaller than the requested radius, we return false.

If we haven't returned, I call getAnyPixelWithDistance() with the desired radius. This finds any pixel in the image that has a Distance value equal to or larger than the radius we want to draw. This routine returns a PVector that tells us the center of the new circle. We already know the radius, so I then call updateDistance() to adjust the Distance array for the presence of the new circle.

Finally, I create a new Disk object to save this new circle, give it a random color, add that to the growing list of Disks, and return true.

Let's look at each of these little helper routines.

When we're looking to place a circle of a specific radius, we can use any entry from Distance with that value or greater. We want to pick a random entry from those possibilities so that the circles will be equally distributed across the image. If I always scanned the array top to bottom and left to right, for example, and selected the first pixel that was large enough, the big circles would bunch up in the upper left of the image, and the bottom right would have more of the smaller circles. That might actually look kind of cool, but right now I want the circles to be evenly distributed around the image. So I first scan the array and count up the number of pixels that satisfy our minimum radius. I pick a random number in that range and then scan again from the start until I find the pixel with that entry.

```
PVector getAnyPixelWithDistance(float d)
{
    int numPixels = 0;
```

```
for (int y=0; y<height; y++) {
    for (int x=0; x<width; x++) {
        if (Distance[y][x] >= d) {
            numPixels++;
        }
    }
}
int whichPixel = int(random(0, numPixels));
int pixelCount = 0;
PVector result = new PVector();
for (int y=0; y<height; y++) {
    for (int x=0; x<width; x++) {
        if (Distance[y][x] >= d) {
            result.x = x;
            result.y = y;
            if (pixelCount++ == whichPixel) {
                return(result);
            }
        }
    }
}
// we should have returned by now, but safety first
return(result);
}
```

Finally, we need to update the Distance array so that it "knows" this circle has been drawn. It just checks the distance of each pixel to the edge of this new circle (that's the distance to its center minus its radius). If that distance is less than the value currently stored in Distance, the stored value is updated.

```
void updateDistance(PVector center, float radius) {
    for (int y=0; y<height; y++) {
        for (int x=0; x<width; x++) {
            if (CircleNumber[y][x] == CircleCount) {
                Distance[y][x] = -1;
            } else {
                float d = dist(x, y, center.x, center.y);
                Distance[y][x] = min(Distance[y][x], d-radius);
            }
        }
    }
}
```

Here's the whole listing in one place. I've enlarged the window to 600 by 600, so I enlarged the mask image as well.

```
float [][] Distance;
Disk [] DiskList;
```

```
class Disk {
  PVector center;
  float radius;
  color clr;

  Disk(PVector acenter, float aradius, color aclr) {
    center = new PVector(acenter.x, acenter.y);
    radius = aradius;
    clr = aclr;
  }

  void render(boolean drawStroke, boolean drawFill) {
    noFill();
    noStroke();
    if (drawFill) fill(clr);
    if (drawStroke) stroke(clr);
    ellipse(center.x, center.y, 2*radius, 2*radius);
  }
}

void setup() {
  size(600, 600);
  background(0);
  smooth();
  //randomSeed(5);

  DiskList = new Disk[0];
  Distance = new float[height][width];
  buildDistance();

  buildPicture();
}

void buildPicture() {
  float goalRadius = maxDistance();
  while (goalRadius > 1) {
    if (!fitCircle(goalRadius)) {
      goalRadius--;
    }
  }
  background(0);
  for (int i=0; i<DiskList.length; i++) {
    DiskList[i].render(false, true);
  }
}
```

```
void buildDistance() {
   PImage maskImage = loadImage("mask0box.png");
   maskImage.loadPixels();
   int[][] mask = new int[height][width];

   // anything with a black pixel has distance -1, else 0
   for (int y=0; y<height; y++) {
      for (int x=0; x<width; x++) {
         color clr = maskImage.pixels[(y*width)+x];
         mask[y][x] = -1;
         if (red(clr) == 0) mask[y][x] = 0;
      }
   }

   // dilate black pixels repeatedly, each newly-dilated
   // pixel has a distance equal to number of steps of dilation
   boolean dilateAgain = true;
   int passNumber = 1;
    int markCount = 0;
   while (dilateAgain) {
      dilateAgain = false;
      for (int y=1; y<height-1; y++) {
         for (int x=1; x<width-1; x++) {
            if (mask[y][x] > 0) continue;
            if ((mask[y-1][x-1] == passNumber-1) ||
                (mask[y-1][x  ] == passNumber-1) ||
                (mask[y-1][x+1] == passNumber-1) ||
                (mask[y  ][x-1] == passNumber-1) ||
                (mask[y  ][x+1] == passNumber-1) ||
                (mask[y+1][x-1] == passNumber-1) ||
                (mask[y+1][x  ] == passNumber-1) ||
                (mask[y+1][x+1] == passNumber-1)) {
               dilateAgain = true;
               mask[y][x] = passNumber;
            }
         }
      }
      passNumber++;
   }
   // copy the temporary mask into the Distance array
   for (int y=0; y<height; y++) {
      for (int x=0; x<width; x++) {
         Distance[y][x] = mask[y][x];
      }
   }
}
```

```
boolean fitCircle(float radius) {
   float maxRadius = maxDistance();
   if (maxRadius < radius) {
      return(false);
   }
   PVector center = getAnyPixelWithDistance(radius);
   updateDistance(center, radius);
   color clr = color(random(100,255), random(100,255),
                     random(100,255));
   Disk newDisk = new Disk(center, radius, clr);
   DiskList = (Disk[])append(DiskList, newDisk);
   return(true);
}

float maxDistance() {
   float maxd = Distance[0][0];
   for (int y=0; y<height; y++) {
      for (int x=0; x<width; x++) {
         maxd = max(Distance[y][x], maxd);
      }
   }
   return(maxd);
}

PVector getAnyPixelWithDistance(float d)
{
   int numPixels = 0;
   for (int y=0; y<height; y++) {
      for (int x=0; x<width; x++) {
         if (Distance[y][x] >= d) {
            numPixels++;
         }
      }
   }
   int whichPixel = int(random(0, numPixels));
   int pixelCount = 0;
   PVector result = new PVector();
   for (int y=0; y<height; y++) {
      for (int x=0; x<width; x++) {
         if (Distance[y][x] >= d) {
            result.x = x;
            result.y = y;
            if (pixelCount++ == whichPixel) {
               return(result);
            }
         }
```

```
        }
      }
    }
    // we should have returned by now, but safety first
    return(result);
}

void updateDistance(PVector center, float radius) {
    for (int y=0; y<height; y++) {
        for (int x=0; x<width; x++) {
            float d = dist(x, y, center.x, center.y);
            Distance[y][x] = min(Distance[y][x], d-radius);
        }
    }
}
```

(See output in Figure 18.63. Full program in patterns/sketches/circlefill05/circlefill05.pde)

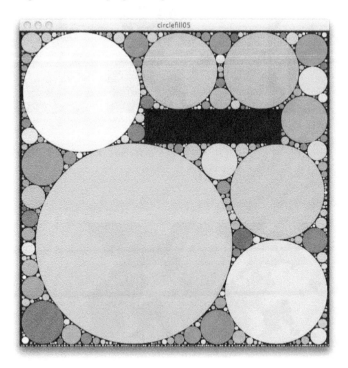

Figure 18.63. The circle-filling program. (patterns/sketches/circlefill05/circlefill05.pde)

I like the results, and best of all, they come out fast! It takes about five seconds to make this picture on my laptop.

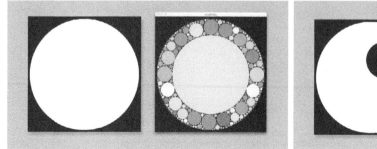

Figure 18.64. A mask and the result of filling it with circles.

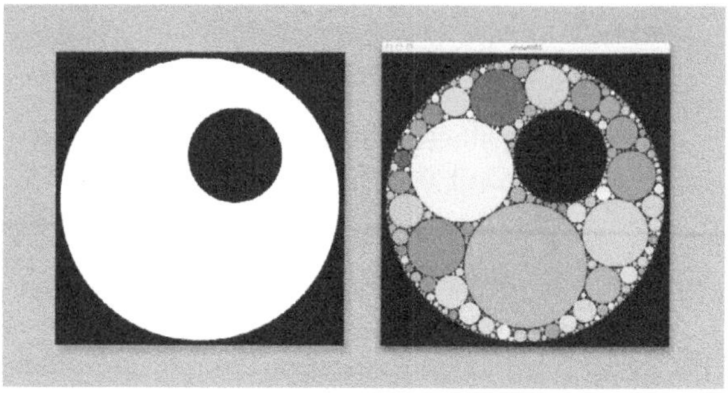

Figure 18.65. A mask and the result of filling it with circles.

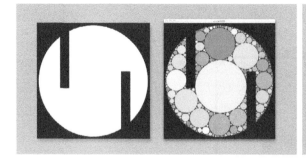
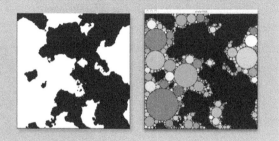

Figure 18.66. A mask and the result of filling it with circles.

Figure 18.67. A mask and the result of filling it with circles.

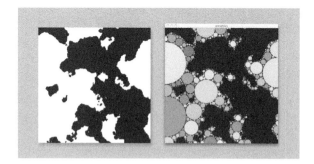

Figure 18.68. A mask and the result of filling it with circles.

In Figure 18.68, I removed the border around the mask that was present in the other figures, allowing the circles to extend out of the image (though their centers are always in the bounds of the mask).

In Figure 18.64 through Figure 18.68 I've shown a bunch of different masks that I ran through the above program. In each image but the last there's a border of black pixels around the outside of the mask. You can see that by removing that outer border in Figure 18.68, the circles are free to move offscreen (in fact, their centers fall on the edges). That's a cool effect, too.

Figure 18.69 shows a close-up of the picture generated without a border.

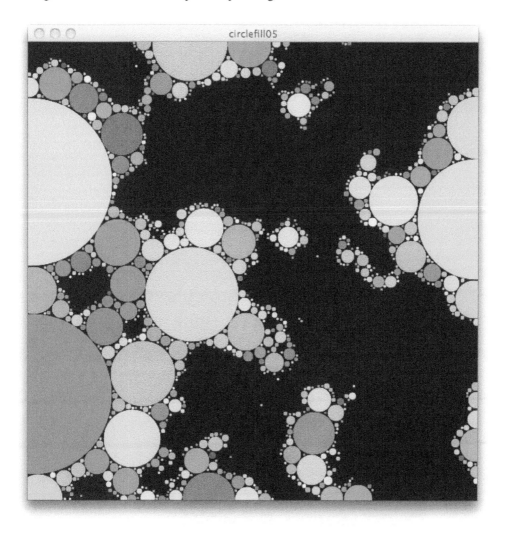

Figure 18.69. A close-up of a borderless fill.

Figure 18.70. A photograph of a kiwi sculpture in Queensland, NZ.

Figure 18.71. The mask of the kiwi.

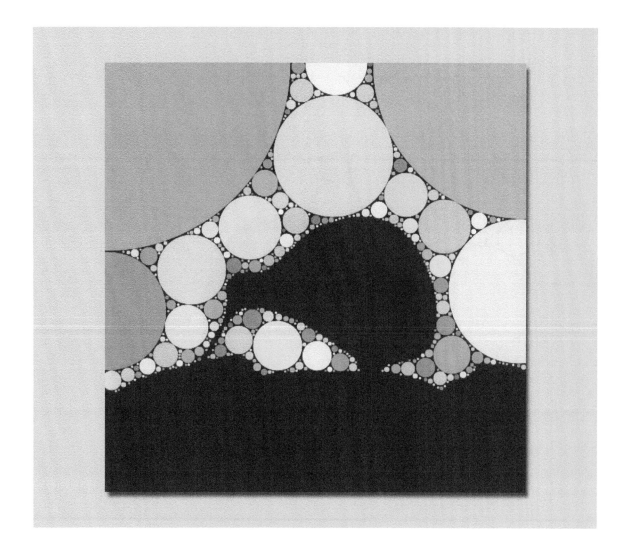

Figure 18.72. A circle fill of the borderless mask.

Let's see how this technique works on a real photograph. Figure 18.70 shows a picture I took of a kiwi sculpture in Queensland, NZ. I manually cut away the background, creating the mask of Figure 18.71.

Initially I didn't put a border around the mask. The resulting circle fill is in Figure 18.72.

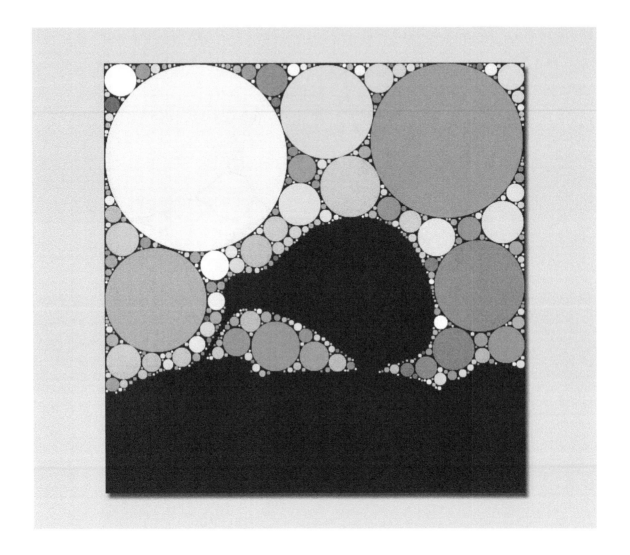

Figure 18.73. A circle fill of the bordered mask.

I then put a tiny black border around the mask and filled it again, resulting in Figure 18.73.

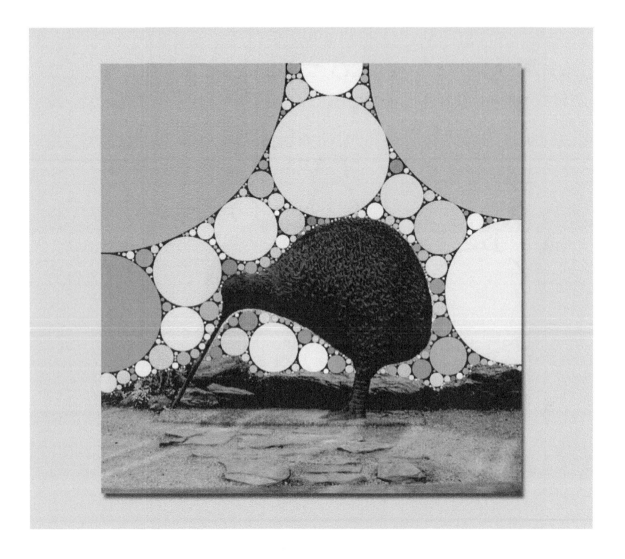

Figure 18.74. The kiwi in the borderless circle fill.

For fun, I then composited the kiwi sculpture back on top of the circle fills. Figure 18.74 shows the composite with the no-border fill.

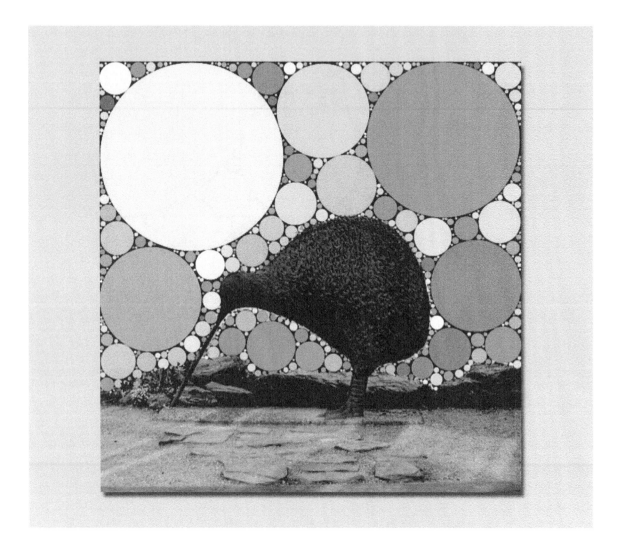

Figure **18.75.** The kiwi in the bordered circle fill.

Figure 18.75 shows the composite with the border fill.

Chapter 19
An Action Lamp

There's a really cool graphics primitive that we haven't seen yet. In the computer graphics field, it's known by the highly technical name of *blob*. A blob is what you might get if you squirted a big dollop of ketchup out of the bottle and let it hit the table. After it settled out, you'd have a kind of mound, high in the center and smoothly falling off to the sides. Anything with roughly that shape is known as a *blob*.

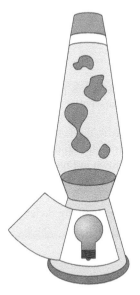

Figure 19.1. A schematic lava lamp.

Let's use some of our building blocks from Chapter 18 to make a Processing version of an *action lamp* (also called a *motion lamp*). The most popular version of this gadget was marketed under the brand name Lava Lamp. Rather than limit our discussion to a single brand, I'll use the generic term here. Figure 19.1 shows a schematic view of an action lamp.

Essentially, it's a glass tube that's filled almost to the top with oil. Inside the oil there's a glob of colored wax. Inside the base there's a lightbulb. That's pretty much the whole thing: it's a simple device. The magic lies in what happens while it's running.

When the lamp is cold, the wax usually collects at the bottom of the tube in a single thick layer. But when you turn on the lightbulb, the heat from the bulb warms the oil and the wax. Slowly, the wax starts to liquify and then as it gets warmer, it becomes an oozing goo. Now comes the magic, which is a result of very careful materials choices by the manufacturer. As the waxy goo warms up, it expands a little bit and becomes ever so slightly more buoyant than the surrounding oil. The result is that the warmer part of the wax starts to rise up. As the warm wax rises, it pulls away from the colder wax under it, stretching a long thin strand of wax behind it. Finally, the strand breaks and the warm blob of wax, roughly spherical now, rises to the top of the oil-filled tube.

The heat from the lightbulb falls off with distance, and it's not quite as warm at the top of the lamp as at the bottom. So after a moment, the wax cools down, and it sinks back to the base, where it remerges with the warmer wax. Once there, it starts to heat up again, and the cycle repeats.

Once the lamp gets going, it's mesmerizing: unpredictable globs of colored wax, some big and some small, rise up out of the base, break away, float to the top, and then float back down. The patterns are complicated and don't repeat. It's very pretty.

Let's make a simplified version of that. Rather than a 3D lamp, I'll make a 2D landscape in our familiar rectangular graphics window. At the bottom of the window will be a gently boiling glob of goo. Over time, circular pieces of the goo will break free and rise upward. In a real lamp, they'd hit the top, cool off, and float back down, but I think in our computer version I'll let them just float off the top of the window. Of course, if that doesn't look good, we can always change it.

This project could be overwhelming if we didn't cheat. Just imagine trying to keep track of the changing shape of a blob of wax as it warms up and rises out of a chunk of cooler wax. It's possible, but what a mess.

Instead, I'm going to think of my graphics window as a grid of *temperatures*. Each pixel represents a little rectangle with a specific temperature. At the bottom, near the lightbulb, the temperature will be warm. Inside that region, I'll introduce roughly circular regions that are hotter. They'll rise up out of the warmer stuff. On the screen, I'll color each pixel by temperature: cool pixels will be background colored, hot pixels will be wax colored.

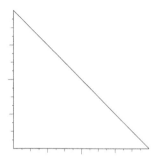

Figure 19.2. A profile for a cone-shaped blob.

So to approximate the hot rising globs of wax, I want to draw something roughly circular that's bright (hot) in the middle and dark (cool) at the edges. Figure 19.2 shows one way to do it: a cone.

In this figure I've shown a cross-section of the blob's shape. Imagine spinning this around the *y*-axis: you'll get an upside-down ice cream cone, as shown in Figure 19.3.

That's not exactly the kind of shape I'd get from dripping ketchup onto a table, but it's a start. Let's use it for now.

So let's get started with a little experimenting. As usual, I'll begin with my skeleton. I'll add a Blob class to it, create one instance, and draw it. I'll call that blob0 because I know I'll have more blobs coming.

```
void setup() {
    size(600, 400);
    Blob blob0 = new Blob(300, 200, 100);
    blob0.render();
}

void draw() {
}
```

```
class Blob {
    float cx, cy;   // blob center
    float r;        // blob radius

    Blob(float acx, float acy, float ar) {
        cx = acx;
        cy = acy;
        r = ar;
    }

    void render() {
    }
}
```

(Full program in lamp/sketches/blob0/blob0.pde)

It doesn't actually draw anything yet, but it doesn't crash, so I'm encouraged.

Now how do we draw this thing? I can't just use a circle; remember that the idea is to show the temperature in the image, and that varies smoothly from the blob's center to the outside.

I think I'll build up my picture pixel by pixel using a PImage (as we discussed in Chapter 16). I'll make it as large as the graphics window. Then I can draw the temperature of each pixel right into the image. I'll say that the blob has a height of 1 at the center, so my temperature range goes from 0 (cold) to 1 (hot). I'll use a color range to display that, running from black to yellow.

So I'll declare a global image variable at the start of the program:

```
PImage Img;
```

I'll create and initialize the image inside of setup(). I'll just put a black background color into every pixel:

```
Img = createImage(width, height, RGB);

color bgcolor = color(0, 0, 0);
for (int y=0; y<height; y++) {
    for (int x=0; x<width; x++) {
        Img.set(x, y, bgcolor);
    }
}
```

I could have saved both typing and running time if I'd used background() here instead of calling set() for every pixel:

```
Img.background(0);
```

But by using the two nested loops I'm free to make changes to the background if I want to. For example, I could introduce some minor variations in temperature over the image. Since I think I might want to do that later, I'll anticipate that by writing it this way now.

Now I have to write some code inside of `render()` in the `Blob` class to draw the thing.

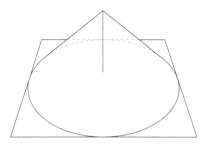

Figure 19.3. A cone-shaped blob.

My basic strategy begins with imagining a square that hugs the circular base of the blob, as in Figure 19.3.

For each point in the square, I'll first test to see whether it's in the circle defined by the blob's `radius`. If so, then I'll find the height of the blob at that pixel. This is easy because I know the blob has height 1 at its center and 0 at `radius`, and it goes down in between the two in a straight line. So `map()` will turn the distance range `(0, radius)` to the height range `(1, 0)`:

```
void render() {
    for (float y=cy-r; y<cy+r; y++) {
        for (float x=cx-r; x<cx+r; x++) {
            float d = dist(x, y, cx, cy);
            if (d > radius) continue;
            float h = map(d, 0, r, 1, 0);
            Img.set(int(x), int(y), color(255*h, 255*h, 0));
        }
    }
}
```

Note that I had to turn `x` and `y` into `int` types before I handed them to `set()` because that function expects `int` arguments. Finally, I'll remember to precede my call to `render()` with `loadPixels()`, and follow it with `updatePixels()` and then actually display the result.

Here's the program so far:

```
PImage Img;

void setup() {
    size(600, 400);

    Img = createImage(width, height, RGB);

    color bgcolor = color(0, 0, 0);
    for (int y=0; y<height; y++) {
```

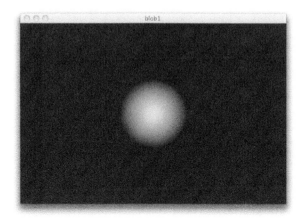

Figure 19.4. Our first blob. (lamp/sketches/blob1/blob1.pde)

```
      for (int x=0; x<width; x++) {
      Img.set(x, y, bgcolor);
      }
   }

   Blob blob0 = new Blob(300, 200, 100);

   Img.loadPixels();
   blob0.render();
   Img.updatePixels();
   image(Img, 0, 0);
}

void draw() {
}

class Blob {
   float cx, cy;  // blob center
   float r;       // blob radius

   Blob(float acx, float acy, float ar) {
      cx = acx;
      cy = acy;
      r = ar;
   }

   void render() {
      for (float y=cy-r; y<cy+r; y++) {
```

```
        for (float x=cx-r; x<cx+r; x++) {
            float d = dist(x, y, cx, cy);
            if (d > r) continue;
            float h = map(d, 0, r, 1, 0);
            Img.set(int(x), int(y), color(255*h, 255*h, 0));
        }
    }
}
}
```

(See output in Figure 19.4. Full program in lamp/sketches/blob1/blob1.pde)

So far, so good. Now let's add a second blob, right after the first:

```
Blob blob1 = new Blob(400, 230, 75);
```

We shouldn't forget to render it, again, right after the first one:

```
blob1.render();
```

(See output in Figure 19.5. Full program in lamp/sketches/blob2/blob2.pde)

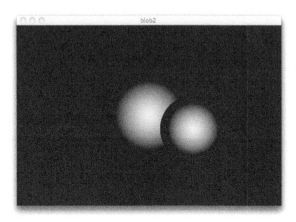

Figure 19.5. Two blobs. (lamp/sketches/blob2/blob2.pde)

Oops. That's not right. The temperatures should add up, not replace one another. So instead of just putting the color of the blob into each pixel, I'll first read back the existing color and add the blob's new color to it:

```
int ix = int(x);
int iy = int(y);
color oldColor = Img.get(ix, iy);
float newRed = (255*h) + red(oldColor)
```

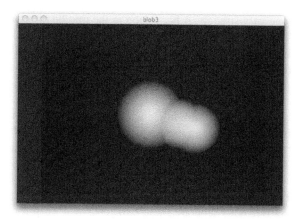

Figure 19.6. Two blobs with added colors. (lamp/sketches/blob3/blob3.pde)

```
float newGrn = (255*h) + green(oldColor)
float newBlu = blue(oldColor)
Img.set(int(x), int(y), color(newRed, newGrn, newBlu));
```

(See output in Figure 19.6. Full program in lamp/sketches/blob3/blob3.pde)

Well, that's kind of better, but there's a strange hump in the middle. If you think about it, that actually makes sense: where these two blobs overlap, their upside-down cones add up, so we get a kind of bulge in between them.

Maybe we can reduce the effect if I change the background color to gray:

```
color bgcolor = color(128, 128, 128);
```

(See output in Figure 19.7. Full program in lamp/sketches/blob4/blob4.pde)

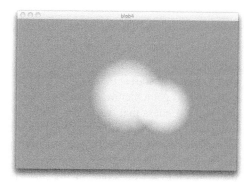

Figure 19.7. Two blobs with a gray background. (lamp/sketches/blob4/blob4.pde)

Something's gone very strange. A big region in the middle of my blobs has turned into a flat yellow field.

The problem is called *clipping*. Remember that the maximum value we can store into any of the three color channels (red, green, and blue) is 255. When I put 128 into all of them as the background color, then adding anything above 128 causes the value to get to 255 and *clip* there, meaning everything above 255 is lost.

If this is happening with two blobs, imagine what's going to happen with five or ten!

The problem is that I'm trying to use my image variable Img for two jobs at once: storing the temperature at each pixel and showing a picture representation of those temperatures. These two roles are in conflict because the temperature value should be able to be anything reasonable (heck, maybe even negative, if we want to drop ice into the lamp), while colors can only be a number from 0 to 255.

The easiest way out is to separate these two jobs. I'll keep Img for the image display, but I'll make a new 2D array of floats to hold the temperature. So when I call render() for a blob, it doesn't draw into the picture, but rather, stores values into this array of temperatures. Once the temperatures are all written, I'll run through that grid and find a good corresponding color value for the image. Then I'll display that. This will be straightforward because I'll make the temperature grid exactly the same size as the graphics window, so each float in the temperature grid has exactly one corresponding pixel in the image (and thus the window), and vice versa.

To get started, I'll declare the new 2D array of floats as a global variable:

```
float [][] Temperature;
```

I'll write a function to initialize this array by setting every element to 0:

```
void zeroTemperature() {
   for (int y=0; y<height; y++) {
      for (int x=0; x<width; x++) {
         Temperature[y][x] = 0;
      }
   }
}
```

Now I need a function to build the pixels in Img from the values in Temperature. I know that the temperature values will start at 0, but they could go as high as they want; way beyond 1, for instance. Just to get a picture up for right now, I'll look at my most recent figure of two blobs, and I'll guess that the values there range from 0 to 1.5. So I'll map the numerical range (0, 1.5) to the color range (black, yellow). It might still clip, or I might never make it to full-on bright yellow, but it'll be good enough to make sure everything is working so far.

For simplicity I'll use set() to set the color of the pixel for now, although I'll probably want to swap it out before I'm done and use the faster mechanism offered by the pixels array.

```
void buildImage() {
    for (int y=0; y<height; y++) {
        for (int x=0; x<width; x++) {
            float t = map(Temperature[y][x], 0, 1.5, 0, 255);
            Img.set(x, y, color(t, t, 0));
        }
    }
}
```

Now setup() changes a little bit. I no longer have to initialize the image to the background color, and I don't have to wrap the calls to render() in the pixel load and update functions. I'll call zeroTemperature() before I render the blobs and then I'll call buildImage() to create the image from the Temperature array.

Here's the new program:

```
PImage Img;
float [][] Temperature;

void setup() {
    size(600, 400);
    Img = createImage(width, height, RGB);
    Temperature = new float[height][width];

    Blob blob0 = new Blob(300, 200, 100);
    Blob blob1 = new Blob(400, 230, 75);

    zeroTemperature();
    blob0.render();
    blob1.render();

    Img.loadPixels();
    buildImage();
    Img.updatePixels();
    image(Img, 0, 0);
}

void draw() {
}

void zeroTemperature() {
    for (int y=0; y<height; y++) {
        for (int x=0; x<width; x++) {
            Temperature[y][x] = 0;
        }
    }
}
```

```
void buildImage() {
    for (int y=0; y<height; y++) {
        for (int x=0; x<width; x++) {
            float t = map(Temperature[y][x], 0, 1.5, 0, 255);
            Img.set(x, y, color(t, t, 0));
        }
    }
}

class Blob {
    float cx, cy; // blob center
    float r;      // blob radius

    Blob(float acx, float acy, float ar) {
        cx = acx;
        cy = acy;
        r = ar;
    }

    void render() {
        for (float y=cy-r; y<cy+r; y++) {
            for (float x=cx-r; x<cx+r; x++) {
                float d = dist(x, y, cx, cy);
                if (d > r) continue;
                float h = map(d, 0, r, 1, 0);
                Temperature[int(y)][int(x)] += h;
            }
        }
    }
}
```

(See output in Figure 19.8. Full program in lamp/sketches/blob5/blob5.pde)

I'm not winning any awards yet, but this is looking more like I think it should.

Now that we have a handy 2D array of temperatures to work with, I can do something cool: I'm going to draw an *isocurve*. This is a term used by mapmakers for a curve of constant elevation. The name comes from combining the prefix *iso* (which means "same") with *curve*. So an isocurve is a "same curve," which in this case is a curve where every pixel under the curve has the same temperature. Sometimes an isocurve is called an *isoline*, even when it's not a straight line.

When you look at a topographic map of a region with hills, you'll probably see a series of concentric wobbly curves with numbers near them. The numbers indicate the elevation. Let's say that they're marked in ten-meter increments. So on a hillside you might see a line marked *200*, and a little bit downhill would be *190* and uphill would be *210*. In theory, If you were stood on top of the *200* line, and you walked exactly where the line was drawn, you'd never go up or down. You can also see isocurves in

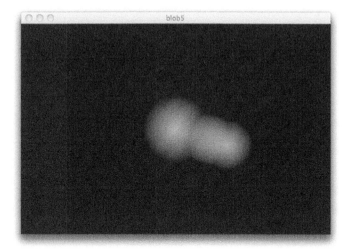

Figure 19.8. The new blobs from temperature. (lamp/sketches/blob5/blob5.pde)

the weather map in your local newspaper, where they're used to show lines of constant pressure, temperature, and humidity.

In this picture, I'm going to draw an isocurve where the temperature is exactly 0.4 (I picked that number out of thin air as something a little less than halfway between cool and hot). All I have to do is check the temperature value when I generate the image pixels. If the temperature is 0.4, I'll mark the pixel in an obvious way by painting it bright red. It's a tiny change to `buildImage()`:

```
if (Temperature[y][x] == 0.4) {
    Img.set(x, y, color(255, 0, 0));
} else {
    float t = map(Temperature[y][x], 0, 1.5, 0, 255);
    Img.set(x, y, color(t, t, 0));
}
```

(See output in Figure 19.9. Full program in lamp/sketches/blob6/blob6.pde)

That's not exactly a success. I don't see any red in there at all.

The problem is that none of my temperature values happen to have a value of precisely 0.4. What I really need is a range of values. I guess that would make this more of an *isoband* than an isocurve. Let's try a range of 0.05 on either side of our center temperature:

```
float midT = 0.4;
float rangeT = 0.05;
if ((Temperature[y][x] > midT-rangeT) &&
```

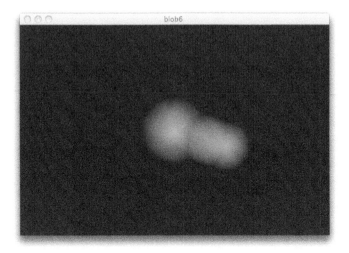

Figure 19.9. Where's my isocurve? (lamp/sketches/blob6/blob6.pde)

```
    (Temperature[y][x] < midT+rangeT)) {
}
```

Just what I wanted.

This works, but we can write a nicer version using the abs() function. We find the difference between the value in the Temperature grid and the center of the band and test whether that's less than the range of the band:

```
if (abs(Temperature[y][x] - midT) < rangeT) {
}
```

(See output in Figure 19.10. Full program in lamp/sketches/blob7/blob7.pde)

Much nicer. That's the band where the temperature is in the range $(0.35, 0.45)$.

Just for fun, and to get a better sense of how this is all coming together, let's add another blob:

```
Blob blob2 = new Blob(145, 270, 210);
```

And I'll add blob2.render(); to the end of the list, of course.
(Full program in lamp/sketches/blob8/blob8.pde)

Uh-oh. If I run this I get an error:

```
ArrayIndexOutOfBoundsException: -1
```

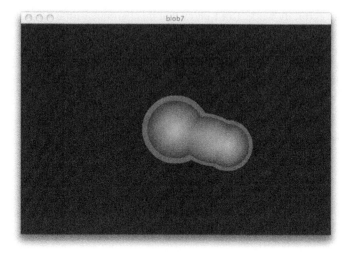

Figure 19.10. My first isoband. (lamp/sketches/blob7/blob7.pde)

The line near the end of the program, where I assign to Temperature, is high-lighted in yellow. So something's wrong with my indexing into the array.

And sure enough, this new blob has a big radius, and I'm trying to access the value of Temperature when x is less than 0. I haven't been checking my index bounds. That was lazy of me. I was writing this code quick and dirty just to see how it was working out, and I cut a corner. Now it's time to put that corner back and make sure we only write to actual entries in the array.

If all we want to do is avoid the error, we could put a big test right in front of the assignment statement. I'll create a couple of little temporary variables ix and iy to hold the integer values of x and y to simplify the test:

```
void render() {
    for (float y=cy-r; y<cy+r; y++) {
        for (float x=cx-r; x<cx+r; x++) {
            float d = dist(x, y, cx, cy);
            if (d > r) continue;
            float h = map(d, 0, r, 1, 0);
            int ix = int(x);
            int iy = int(y);
            if ((ix >= 0) && (ix < width) && (iy >= 0) && (iy < height)) {
                Temperature[iy][ix] += h;
            }
        }
    }
}
```

This would certainly work. But I know that this particular little bit of code is going to execute for every single pixel, so if I can speed it up, it'll probably pay off later, maybe by letting me use more blobs in my piece before the animation slows down.

Looking at this `render()` routine more closely, I can see that if I'm not going to write this value, there's no need to do all those other calculations involving `dist()` and `map()`, so I can move the test up:

```
void render() {
   for (float y=cy-r; y<cy+r; y++) {
      for (float x=cx-r; x<cx+r; x++) {
         int ix = int(x);
         int iy = int(y);
         if ((ix >= 0) && (ix < width) && (iy >= 0) && (iy < height)) {
            float d = dist(x, y, cx, cy);
            if (d > r) continue;
            float h = map(d, 0, r, 1, 0);
            Temperature[iy][ix] += h;
         }
      }
   }
}
```

Even better! But as long as we're shaving off speed, let's really go for it. Suppose a blob is near the left side of the screen. There's no reason to be looking at any pixels with an *x* value less than 0 since we're going to skip them. And the same logic holds for the other sides.

So we can reduce the size of the box we're scanning up front by chopping away the parts that are offscreen. Then we don't have to test the pixels one by one, since we know we won't be trying to get any pixels beyond the array limits. Let's do that:

```
void render() {
   int lox = max(0, int(cx-r));
   int hix = min(width, int(cx+r));
   int loy = max(0, int(cy-r));
   int hiy = min(height, int(cy+r));
   for (int y=loy; y<hiy; y++) {
      for (int x=lox; x<hix; x++) {
         float d = dist(x, y, cx, cy);
         if (d > r) continue;
         float h = map(d, 0, r, 1, 0);
         Temperature[y][x] += h;
      }
   }
}
```

(See output in Figure 19.11. Full program in lamp/sketches/blob9/blob9.pde)

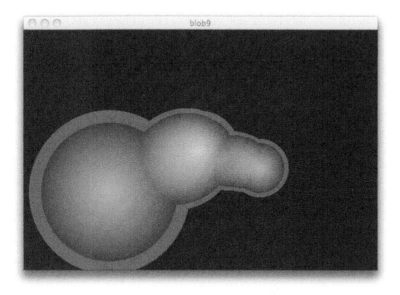

Figure 19.11. Blobs with bounds checking. (lamp/sketches/blob9/blob9.pde)

Not only are we bounds checking, but we're doing it very efficiently. Before we start the loops, we build the limits on x and y so that they only generate indices that are actually in the array.

And we've created a new picture!

Unfortunately, now that we've managed to draw this picture, I don't like it. It just doesn't do it for me. Remember that I started out with the idea of a goopy, gloppy action lamp. These red isobands have crisp, sharp corners where they meet up. They do have their own aesthetic appeal, and in another context I might be thrilled by this picture, but right now this just doesn't have the right feeling at all. Those sharp corners just don't say "oozing goo" to me.

The band also gets thicker around big blobs and thinner around smaller ones. That's also not really what I want, but it's a much smaller problem to my eye than those crisp corners.

19.1   Bell Curves

One solution to the problem of sharp corners comes from re-thinking the shapes of our blobs. Remember that these blobs are upside-down ice cream cone shapes. Imagine moving two of these things towards one another. Where they start to overlap, there's going to be an inevitable sharp edge because when the cones reach zero (at their radius) they don't kind of smoothly flatten out, but instead they plunge right down to zero and then come to a sudden, dead stop. Graphically, the problem comes from the right edge of Figure 19.2 (repeated here as Figure 19.12), where the line of the cone bangs into the horizontal *x*-axis and stops. That corner is causing the corners in my isobands.

Figure 19.12.   A cone-shaped blob.

What I really want is a blob shape something closer to the ketchup blob we talked about at the start of the chapter. This shape falls off gradually.

Compare Figure 19.13 to Figure 19.12. If we revolve Figure 19.13 around the *y*-axis, we'll get something a lot smoother than the ice cream cone. It will be flat at the top, not pointed. And it will fall off smoothly at the outer edge, not abruptly.

Figure 19.13. A blobbier blob.

Figure 19.13 is the famous *bell curve* that people refer to when they talk about grades, statistics, and public health, among other topics. Mathematicians call it a *Gaussian curve* (pronounced gows'-ee-in, and named for the mathematician Johann Gauss).

The Gaussian blob has the same general shape as the cosine curve, which I discussed in Chapter 18. The Gaussian isn't quite as common as the cosine, but it's a terrific shape that belongs in your toolbox, so let's use the Gaussian for this project.

Gaussian blobs will join up much more nicely than the linear, ice-cream-cone blobs. To see why, consider Figure 19.14. Here I've shown two linear blobs (in red and blue) and their sum (in black). You can see that the sum, like the cones, has some sharp corners. If we add up three blobs, as Figure 19.15, we just get more sharp corners.

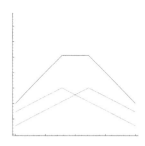

Figure 19.14.   Two linear blobs (in red and blue) and their sum (in black).

As I've briefly mentioned in earlier chapters, it turns out that the human visual system has evolved to be very, very good at detecting these kinds of sharp changes in the intensity of light. When our eyes and brains see this kind of abrupt change in brightness, it gets amplified in order to really grab our attention. Some people think that this helped us evade predators when they were hiding in the bushes and rustled the leaves or otherwise betrayed their presence through this kind of visual edge. Psychologists call these perceived edges *Mach bands* (named after the physicist Ernst Mach). You can see Mach bands in some of the figures at the start of this chapter. For example, look at in Figure 19.6 where the ice-cream-cone blobs join up with one another. There's no sharp edge there, but our eye detects the abrupt change in brightness and amplifies it.

Smooth blobs that gradually tail off to zero join up in a much smoother, nicer way that avoids Mach bands. Figure 19.16 shows a couple of smooth blobs and their sum. You can see how nicely they all join up. I've added a third blob in Figure 19.17, and we

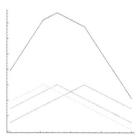

Figure 19.15. Three linear blobs and their sum.

can see that the blobs just keep adding together smoothly. Note that the left-most two blobs in the figure overlap closely enough that they add up into what looks like one big blob. If we moved them apart horizontally, the big blob in the sum would also separate into two smaller humps, like the one on the right. These kinds of blobs, based on the bell curve, are going to look much better in our action lamp animation!

There are lots of variations on the basic bell curve that you can use for specialized purposes, but the basic one I've used here does a great job in many situations, and it'll be a fine blob shape for this project. To make the bell curve, you call the building-block function `exp()`. You give it a number that's related to your distance from the center of the blob, and it gives you back a height for the blob.

I find the bell curve so incredibly useful in so many projects that I wish it had been built into Processing. As it is, Processing makes it easy to write your own bell curve function. Without going into the mathematics, you can write the value v for the bell curve at a point x almost this easily:

```
v = exp(-4*x*x);
```

Let's write a little program to see the results of this expression for inputs from 0 to 1:

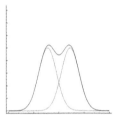

Figure 19.16. Two bell curve blobs (in red and blue) and their sum (in black).

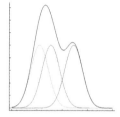

Figure 19.17. Three bell curve blobs and their sum.

```
void setup() {
    for (int i=0; i<11; i++) {
        float x = i/10.0;
        float v = exp(-4*x*x);
        println("x="+x+"   v="+v);
    }
}
```

(Full program in lamp/sketches/bellCount/bellCount.pde)

Here are the results:

```
x=0.0   v=1.0
x=0.1   v=0.96078944
x=0.2   v=0.85214376
x=0.3   v=0.6976763
x=0.4   v=0.5272924
x=0.5   v=0.36787945
x=0.6   v=0.23692775
x=0.7   v=0.14085843
x=0.8   v=0.07730473
x=0.9   v=0.039163902
x=1.0   v=0.01831564
```

So you give it a number x from 0 to 1, and you get back a number v from 1 to something that is *nearly* 0, but not quite. The reversal of the direction (inputs from 0 to 1 turn into outputs from 1 to almost 0) is easy to handle, but the fact that the output doesn't quite reach 0 is an important problem.

To see why this is an issue, let's use this bell curve expression to smoothly move a circle from one position (at frame 0) to another position (at frame 75).

As I mentioned in the discussion of the cosine curve, objects in the real world don't instantly go from standing still to moving at a high rate of speed, and they don't stop instantly, either. If you saw an object do that in your animation, it would look unnatural. Unless that's the effect you're going for, you need to find a way to get objects to accelerate when they start to move and decelerate as they prepare to stop. Like cosine, the bell curve is a fine tool for this job.

To get started, I'll just move the circle from the start to the finish linearly, setting the position simply by how far along we are in time. This is the bad-looking motion I just said we should try to avoid, so we'll soon change this code to make the motion look better.

```
void setup() {
    size(600, 400);
    background(128, 128, 128);
    noFill();
    stroke(255, 0, 0);
```

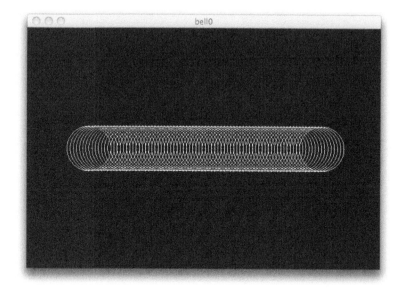

Figure 19.18. Moving a circle linearly. (lamp/sketches/bell0/bell0.pde)

```
}

void draw() {
    if (frameCount > 75) return;
    float centerx = map(frameCount, 0, 75, 100, 500);
    ellipse(centerx, 200, 75, 75);
}
```

(See output in Figure 19.18. Full program in lamp/sketches/bell0/bell0.pde)

Here I used map() to move the center of the circle, so as frameCount goes from 0 to 75, centerx goes from 100 to 500. Now let's dress this up a little bit, because that will make it easier to change later and see what's happening. First, I'll explicitly create a floating-point variable percent that will be 0 at the starting frame and 1 at the ending frame. I'll set this to another variable that I'll just call t. It's kind of superfluous right now, but we'll use it in the next version.

I'll use v to control the center x position with a call to lerp(). For fun, I'll adjust the center vertical y position, too. I'll use sin() to make a little vertical bump. I can see from Figure 18.20 that the first half of the sine curve starts at 0, rises to 1, and comes back down to 0. Since the full curve takes 360 degrees, this single bump runs the range from 0 to 180 degrees. So I'll just give it the number 180 (converted to radians, of course), scaled by our v variable (remember, that's just percent right now).

Finally, I'll change the color so it starts with red and ends at white.

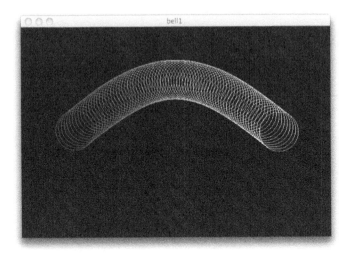

Figure 19.19. Moving a circle with some extra features. (lamp/sketches/bell1/bell1.pde)

```
void draw() {
   if (frameCount > 75) return;
   float percent = map(frameCount, 0, 75, 0, 1);
   float v = percent;
   float centerx = lerp(100, 500, v);
   float centery = lerp(200, 100, sin(v * radians(180)));
   stroke(255, 255*v, 255*v);
   ellipse(centerx, centery, 75, 75);
}
```

(See output in Figure 19.19. Full program in lamp/sketches/bell1/bell1.pde)

Great.

But also, awful. The circle suddenly leaps into motion at full speed, and at the end, it freezes in a sudden stop. This is not how physical objects behave, and it looks weird to human observers because we've spent our whole life watching objects get up to speed and then slow down.

So let's take the step we've been waiting for! I'll set the value of v using the bell curve formula. Since the value of percent is already in the range 0 to 1, I can just plug it into the bell curve expression I gave above and use the resulting value of v for the position and color of the circle:

```
float v = exp(-4*percent*percent);
```

(See output in Figure 19.20. Full program in lamp/sketches/bell2/bell2.pde)

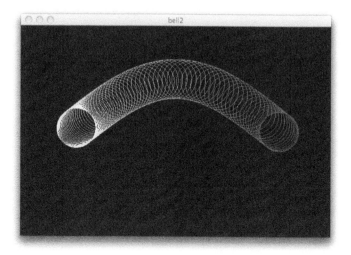

Figure 19.20. Moving with spacing control from the bell curve. (lamp/sketches/bell2/bell2.pde)

Two interesting things have happened. The first is that, as we expected, the ball is moving more slowly at the start and finish than before, so it's also moving a little more quickly in the middle to compensate. That's going to look great as animation: the ball will accelerate from its starting position and then decelerate into the ending position. This is one reason the bell curve is so useful.

The second interesting thing is that the ball has reversed direction!

That's because when we give the bell curve a value of 0, it gives us back 1, and when we give it 1, we get back (nearly) 0. To make the discussion that's coming up a little easier, I'll compute v as before, but I'll also make a variable w=1-v, and then use w from then on. Now we can keep talking about v, but the results look like the previous ones.

```
void draw() {
    if (frameCount > 75) return;
    float percent = map(frameCount, 0, 75, 0, 1);
    float v = exp(-4*percent*percent);
    float w = 1-v;
    float centerx = lerp(100, 500, w);
    float centery = lerp(200, 100, sin(w * radians(180)));
    stroke(255, 255*w, 255*w);
    ellipse(centerx, centery, 75, 75);
}
```

(See output in Figure 19.21. Full program in lamp/sketches/bell3/bell3.pde)

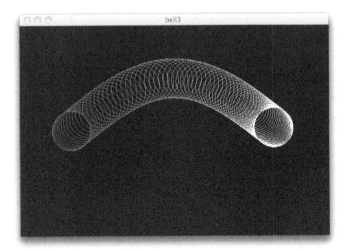

Figure 19.21. Reversing direction. (lamp/sketches/bell3/bell3.pde)

My real interest here is in what's happening at the very end. When `percent` is 0, v is 1. Perfect. Our starting position is our starting position. But when `percent` is 1, then v is nearly, but not quite, 0. That means that the circle isn't really coming to its resting place.

To see this, I'm going to get rid of the test at the top of `draw()`. Instead of returning when `frameCount` is past 75, I'll just manually set v to 0 and let things run normally. This will simulate a situation where we use this transition as an animation: the ball would be sitting at the start position, then we'd trigger the animation, and then the ball would rest at the end position.

```
if (frameCount > 75) v = 0;
```

(See output in Figure 19.22. Full program in lamp/sketches/bell4/bell4.pde)

In Figure 19.22 you can see that during the animation, the circle does not smoothly decelerate into the final position, which is shown by the circle at the far right that's some distance from the cluster of compressed circles just to its left. The circle comes close to the ending position, but not close enough. To make this very clear, I'll add a line at the end of `setup()` to draw a line along the bottom of the ball:

```
line(0, 237, 600, 237);
```

(See output in Figure 19.23. Full program in lamp/sketches/bell5/bell5.pde)

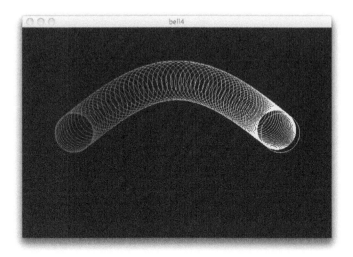

Figure 19.22. Drawing the final frame. (lamp/sketches/bell4/bell4.pde)

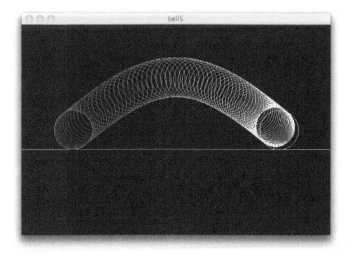

Figure 19.23. Including the baseline. (lamp/sketches/bell5/bell5.pde)

If we cleared the background before each frame and watched this as an animation, the ball would gently accelerate, come over the top, decelerate on its way down, and then *jump* to its ending position. That would look awful.

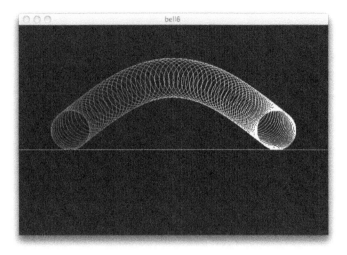

Figure 19.24. Using map() to get the ball to the ending location.
(lamp/sketches/bell6/bell6.pde)

The problem is, as I've said, that the little expression we wrote doesn't come to 0 when the input is 1. So let's fix that. The most straightforward way would be to use map().

What's the input range? We know that when percent=0, v = 1. And when percent = 1, v = exp(-4*1*1), which is just exp(-4), whatever number that happens to be. We want the output to be from 1 to 0. So we can use map() to fix this range just after the calculation of v:

```
v = map(v, 1, exp(-4), 0, 1);
```

(See output in Figure 19.24. Full program in lamp/sketches/bell6/bell6.pde)

So that's the trick.

I went through all of these steps because if you're not familiar with what's inside Processing's building blocks (like exp()), it can be a challenge to figure out how to handle them so that they produce the results you want. But if you're willing to ignore the internals and just work with the results, things can be very easy. Just take the range of values that the bell curve gives us and use map() to send them to the range $(0, 1)$. We don't have to even care what's happening inside of exp() at all.

A good route to working with these building blocks is to start with a recipe (like our exp(-4*x*x)). You can get this from a friend or colleague (or the web), or find it yourself by experimenting. Once you have a starting point, you can adjust the results by manipulating the input values, the output results, or both. If you're not mathematically inclined, I think you'll find your time is much better spent shaping the outputs (like we did with map()) than messing around with the input arguments.

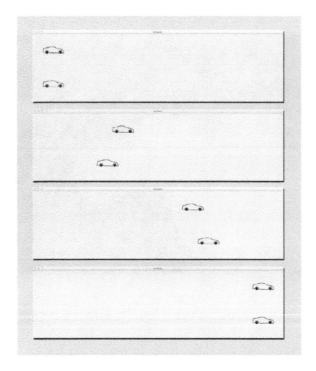

Figure 19.25. The upper car in each panel moves at a constant speed, while the lower one accelerates and decelerates. Reading from the top, these snapshots are at times 0, 1/3, 2/3, and 1.

Let's compare a car that starts and stops instantly with one that undergoes acceleration and deceleration, as in Figure 19.25. You can find the source of this sketch in the folder `carEasel`. The car in the top panel is moving at a constant speed, while the one below accelerates and decelerates. You can see it gets off to a slower start but then passes ahead of the other car so it has time to slow down.

This kind of smooth picking up and losing of speed is often called *ease in* and *ease out*. In the code for the car figure, I replaced our blob formula with yet a different type of curve, but the result is the same: a smooth start and a smooth ending.

19.2 A Blobbier Lamp

So now we have a little two-step process to compute a bell curve. Given a value of x, we can find the height v from

```
v = exp(-4*x*x);
v = map(v, 1, exp(-4), 0, 1);
```

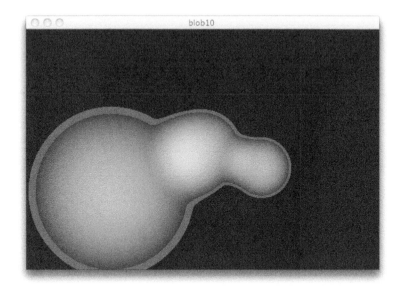

Figure 19.26. Blobs using the new blob function. (lamp/sketches/blob10/blob10.pde)

Let's put this into our blob-drawing program. It's a simple change. In `render()`, instead of computing h as before, we'll use this two-step expression instead:

```
void render() {
    int lox = max(0, int(cx-r));
    int hix = min(width, int(cx+r));
    int loy = max(0, int(cy-r));
    int hiy = min(height, int(cy+r));
    for (int y=loy; y<hiy; y++) {
        for (int x=lox; x<hix; x++) {
            float d = dist(x, y, cx, cy);
            if (d > r) continue;
            float h = map(d, 0, r, 1, 0);
            float v = exp(-4*h*h);
            v = map(v, 1, exp(-4), 0, 1);
            Temperature[y][x] += v;
        }
    }
}
```

(See output in Figure 19.26. Full program in lamp/sketches/blob10/blob10.pde)

Now there's the kind of blobby feeling I was hoping for. The sharp corners are gone and are now replaced by smooth curves. The band still varies in thickness a little, but I can live with that.

19.3   Optimization

Before pushing on with the action-lamp project, let's take a moment and think about what we've constructed. This code runs and produces good results, and that's 90 percent of the game.

Earlier I showed how to trim the `render()` routine so that it would run as fast as possible. That's why we're calculating variables like `lox` and `hix`, so we don't have to test each pixel. That's great.

But that inner loop, now six lines long, still gets repeated for every single pixel in every single blob. This is where our program is going to spend the great majority of its time. I don't know how many blobs I'll want on the screen in the final project, but I bet I'll want a lot of them. As I add in more blobs, the program's going to take longer and longer to draw them all, until my smooth fast motion becomes smooth slow motion and then jerky slow motion and then very slow, choppy, barely moving, not-really motion. To keep the speed up, and thus give myself the chance to have lots of blobs, I have to make sure each one draws as quickly as possible.

This takes us into *optimization*, that is, making things efficient. This is usually the very last step you do in any program. Once the whole program is working right and every option is in place and you're absolutely done making changes, then you go back and tweak the code until it's running fast. There are three good reasons for leaving this to the end.

First, not every piece of code you write while working on a project will survive to the end. We've seen that plenty of times already in this book, where we've taken out code and replaced it with something new. It's a waste of time to improve something that you might eventually remove.

Second, there's no need to spend your time optimizing something that doesn't need it. Maybe some piece of code that you thought was going to eat up all your time turns out to be a lot faster than you expected. Your time would be better spent speeding up something else. You only know where your final program is spending its time when you're actually dealing with the final program.

Third, optimization often makes your code ugly. A lot of the tricks you'll cook up to make your program faster will be strange and super specialized to the idiosyncrasies of that particular job. The more a piece of code gets optimized, usually the harder it is to figure out later. And, of course, if you can't figure it out, debugging any problems that might have crept in is going to be a nightmare. Also, when you do find a bug, optimized code can be hard to change because it's become so specialized to do exactly what it does; if what it is doing isn't quite right, unraveling that tangle and setting it straight can be a lot of work.

So typically we wait until the very end to optimize. And then we only target the places that really need it. And then we only optimize as much as needed to get the performance we want.

Of course, I'm going to ignore all those principles and optimize `render()` right now! That's because we've just spent some time with `render()` and it's fresh in our minds. So I'll do a little optimizing on it now, so you can see the general process. Then you'll have the tools you need if you want to dig into other pieces of this program, or other programs, later on.

A word of warning: optimization is a rabbit hole that you can easily disappear into. Some people spend far more time optimizing than they do writing the original program. They have massive tables of statistics in their head, and they're able to tell you exactly how long it takes a particular model of computer to execute one operation versus another. And they can putter around and tune their code all day. And the next day. And the next.

They do get improvements, but usually, you quickly hit a point of diminishing returns. So the general rule in optimizing is that you keep at it until you think more effort just isn't worthwhile.

There are two general ways to optimize: *strategy* and *tactics*. There's no hard-and-fast rule that separates these approaches. Rather, it's more of a mind-set. In a strategic optimization, you ask yourself whether there's a different, faster way to get the same results. In a tactical optimization, you focus on one little thing and make adjustments to just that so it runs as fast as possible.

We saw one kind of tactical optimization earlier, when I tweaked the loops that draw the blobs so that they only computed the blob values for pixels that could be affected.

Let's try both kinds of optimization. First I'll make a low-level, tactical improvement and then I'll look at making a larger, strategic change.

Let's return to the blob-drawing code, and look at the first two lines of that loop:

```
float d = dist(x, y, cx, cy);
if (d > r) continue;
```

You may remember from high school that the distance between two points is found by a rule named for Pythagoras. If we computed it ourselves, rather than calling `dist()`, it might look like this:

```
float dx = x-cx;
float dy = y-cy;
float d = sqrt((dx*dx)+(dy*dy));
if (d > r) continue;
```

In words, we find the distance between the *x* values and the *y* values. Then we square those (that is, multiply each one by itself), add them together, and take the square root.

I bet the square root operation (that is, the call to `sqrt()`) is a time eater. Figuring out a square root is a pretty complicated job. I know that there are some very efficient techniques out there for that operation, and I hope that Processing is using them, but even so, it's not free. Can we get rid of it?

We can't get rid of it entirely, but we can avoid it sometimes. Let's write the last example with one more intermediate step. First I'll calculate d1, the sum of the squared distances, and then I'll calculate d2, the square root of d1:

```
float dx = x-cx;
float dy = y-cy;
float d1 = (dx*dx)+(dy*dy);
float d2 = sqrt(d1);
if (d2 > r) continue;
```

The trick to optimizing this lies in the last couple of lines. In the test, we compare d2 to r. What if we square both sides of this test? We might write

```
if (d2*d2 > r*r) continue;
```

That would surely have the same result as the test that's in there now. After all, if d2 is larger than r, then d2*d2 will be larger than r*r, and similarly, if d2 is less than r, then d2*d2 will be less than r*r. But d2*d2 is, of course, just d1. So we can run the test *before* we calculate the square root! We do need to remember to test against r*r, of course.

```
float dx = x-cx;
float dy = y-cy;
float d1 = (dx*dx)+(dy*dy);
if (d1 > r*r) continue;
float d2 = sqrt(d1);
```

So now we only calculate the square root for pixels that are actually inside the circle. We can either calculate r*r right there in the test, as I did here, or we can save it beforehand (along with r itself) for just this purpose (and save ourselves one multiply per pixel—remember I said optimizing could be a rabbit's hole of endless tiny adjustments!).

OK, how much of a savings is this, really? The acid test is to try it out. Here's a little program I wrote that tries out both ways. It runs the same loop over and over 10,000 times, so I should get a nice average, even if the computer occasionally does other things (like check my email or update the clock). I'll call the system routine millis() at the start and end of each loop; this tells me how many milliseconds (thousandths of a second) have elapsed since the time the program started. The difference between the time at the start and end of the loop is the time taken by the loop.

I arbitrarily picked a circle with a radius of 100, since I think that's likely to be an average size for my blob. I also declared all the variables up top, so they don't have to get created in the loop. I added a single trivial statement (adding one to a variable I never use) just so I have something in the loop.

So this program does essentially what render() does: it scans a square and does something for each pixel inside. It just tests two ways: once using dist and the other using our manual version of that routine, where we split apart the calculations before and after the square root:

```
void setup() {
  int numsteps = 10000;
```

```
int i, x, y;
float dx, dy, dd, d;
int t1, t2;
float g=0;

int radius = 100;
int radius2 = radius * radius;
int lox = 100;
int loy = 100;
int hix = lox + (2*radius);
int hiy = loy + (2*radius);
int cx = lox + radius;
int cy = loy + radius;

t1 = millis();
for (i=0; i<numsteps; i++) {
  for (y=loy; y<hiy; y++) {
    for (x=lox; x<hix; x++) {
      dd = dist(x, y, cx, cy);
      if (dd > radius) continue;
      g++;
    }
  }
}
t2 = millis();
int delta1 = t2-t1;

t1 = millis();
for (i=0; i<numsteps; i++) {
  for (y=loy; y<hiy; y++) {
    for (x=lox; x<hix; x++) {
      dx = x-cx;
      dy = y-cy;
      dd = sq(dx)+sq(dy);
      if (dd > radius2) continue;
      d = sqrt(dd);
      g++;
    }
  }
}
t2 = millis();
int delta2 = t2-t1;

println("delta1="+delta1+"  delta2="+delta2);
}
```

(Full program in lamp/sketches/timing1/timing1.pde)

	dist (delta 1)	2-step (delta 2)
Desktop	9169	5044
Laptop	15632	9065

Figure 19.27. Timing results in milliseconds.

I ran this five times on my big desktop Mac and five times on my little laptop Mac and averaged the results. Happily, all the runs were within about a single percent of each other. Figure 19.27 shows the results.

Wow. On the big machine, using `dist()` took a bit over nine seconds, but using our two-step process took just about five seconds. That's huge! Even on my laptop, it still shaved off a third of the running time.

The nicest thing about this optimization is that there's no wasted effort. That is, we don't throw away any of our work: we compute the distances and the sums of their squares, and if we pass the test, we use those results to find the square root (and the distance).

Whether or not this savings will result in a visibly faster program is something I can't predict yet. As I said before, typically we optimize as a final step and only when we need to. So I'm getting ahead of myself here by doing it now. This effort will certainly speed up the program, but I can't say whether it's going to be enough to make a visible difference or not.

Nevertheless, let's push on and optimize some more, if we can. This time I'll try for something strategic.

Let's look at three lines near the end of `render()`:

```
float h = map(d, 0, r, 1, 0);
float v = exp(-4*h*h);
v = map(v, 1, exp(-4), 0, 1);
```

This all makes sense. But is there a way to speed things up?

There's a tactical speedup that hits my eye right away: in the third line, we're using `exp(-4)`. Whatever that number is, it's not changing, so there's no need to compute it every single time. A quick one-line program (nothing but `println(exp(-4));`) tells me it has the value 0.01831564. That's a lot of digits, but it's easy enough to copy and paste them in:

```
float h = map(d, 0, r, 1, 0);
float v = exp(-4*h*h);
v = map(v, 1, 0.01831564, 0, 1);
```

A little icky. As I said, optimizing can make your code harder to read, and harder to understand later. If you came to this program with fresh eyes, you would probably have no idea where that strange number came from. Future generations will sing the praises of the kind programmer who explained this with a comment, even if it's very short:

index	x	value
0	0.0	1.0
1	0.1	0.96078944
2	0.2	0.85214376
3	0.3	0.6976763
4	0.4	0.5272924
5	0.5	0.36787945
6	0.6	0.23692775
7	0.7	0.14085843
8	0.8	0.07730473
9	0.9	0.039163902
10	1.0	0.01831564

Figure 19.28. The exp() function in a table.

```
v = map(v, 1, 0.01831564, 0, 1);  // map (1,exp(-4)) to (0,1)
```

Storing this as a global would be even better because then we could refer to it by name, which would make things clearer. If we put this line at the top of the file

```
float MinBlobVal = 0.01831564;
```

then we could write the map() statement as

```
v = map(v, 1, MinBlobVal, 0, 1);
```

But how about that remaining call to exp()? Like sqrt(), I know it's not the fastest thing on the block. But unlike sqrt(), I don't have a handy little formula that I can use to pick it apart; besides, I'm not testing it against anything, so there would be no advantage to computing it in stages. I really do need to get the values this thing is computing for me, even though it takes a while.

One trick is to buy time with memory. I'll make an array of values that come out of exp() and then I'll use values from that precomputed array instead of using the function call (in this context, we often call the array a *lookup table*, or simply a *table*). This trick often works, but you have to be careful with it. Essentially what you're doing is throwing away some accuracy in favor of speed. By using a few precomputed values, you can get numbers that are close to the actual numbers, but they'll be wrong.

How wrong they are usually depends on how many entries you put in the table and how you use the table. To get us started, Figure 19.28 shows the exp() function with eleven entries.

There are a few ways to use a precomputed table. The simplest way is called *nearest neighbor*. That says you use whatever value that's in the table that's closest to the value you want.

For example, let's put the data from Figure 19.28 into an array:

```
float [] ExpTable = { 1.0,         0.96078944, 0.85214376,
                      0.6976763,  0.5272924,  0.36787945,  0.23692775,
                      0.14085843, 0.07730473, 0.039163902, 0.01831564 };
```

This array has 11 entries (with indices 0 to 10), which represent the value of exp() from 0 to 1 in equal steps of 0.1. Suppose we want the value of exp(x) at x = 0.73. That's somewhere between entry number 7 and entry number 8. It's a little bit closer to entry number 7, so the nearest-neighbor approach would just use table entry 7. To find the index 7 from the input 7.3, we can use the built-in function round(), which gives us the nearest integer for a given value. I'll multiply the input by ten; then round(7.3) will be 7:

```
x = 0.73;
float tableValue = ExpTable[round(10*x)];
```

Note that this example only works when we have exactly 11 entries for values from 0 to 1. If we plot the results of this process for all the values from 0 to 1, we get Figure 19.29.

That's kind of chunky. We can make it better in two ways. One way, of course, is just to use a much bigger table. Figure 19.30 shows an example with a table of 100 points.

That's a lot better. We'll probably want to build that table with a loop at the top of the program rather than put in all those numbers by hand.

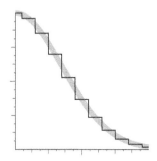

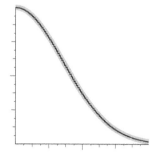

Figure 19.29. The bell curve approximated with 11 points using nearest-neighbor. The smooth curve is shown behind in light gray.

Figure 19.30. The bell curve approximated with 100 points using nearest neighbor. The smooth curve is shown behind in light gray.

There's another approach that takes a little more time but gives better results. It goes by a variety of names, but perhaps the clearest is simply *table interpolation*. The idea is to find the two table values that surround the value we want and then interpolate (or blend) between them. We can pull this off by using floor() (which gives us the nearest integer below its input), ceil() (which gives us the next integer above the input), and then lerp() to blend the values together.

```
x = 0.73;
int highIndex = ceil(x);
int lowIndex = floor(x);
float fraction = ((10*x)-lowIndex)/10.0;
float tableValue = lerp(ExpTable[lowIndex], ExpTable[highIndex],
                        fraction);
```

Again, this code only works in this exact example, where we have 11 values from 0 to 1. The expression for fraction is designed to turn 0.73 into 0.3. That is, it's 0.3 of the way from 0.7 to 0.8.

Figure 19.31 shows the result of this approach with 11 points, and Figure 19.32 shows the result with 100 points.

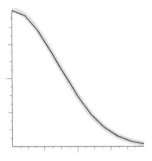
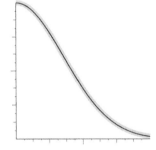

Figure 19.31. The bell curve approximated with 11 points using table interpolation. The smooth curve is shown behind in light gray.

Figure 19.32. The bell curve approximated with 100 points using table interpolation. The smooth curve is shown behind in light gray.

This table-interpolation technique gives you a lot more bang for the buck, but it's a little slower because you have to grab a second table entry and then blend it with the first. You have to figure for yourself which is the best way to go. But if you compare the 11-point, nearest-neighbor graph and the 11-point, table-interpolation graph, you can see that in this example (with a nice, smooth curve) the table-interpolation approach looks really good, even with just under a dozen points in the table.

So let's give this a try with real code and see what we save. Here's a little program to try out all three approaches: explicit computation, nearest neighbor, and table interpolation. One of the nicest things about the table approach is that we can do both the exp() and map() calculations just once per entry and save the combined result in the table.

```
void setup() {
  int numsteps = 100000000;
  int t1, t2;
  float x, v, fraction;
  int i, index0, index1;
```

```
float [] ExpTable;
ExpTable = new float[200];
for (i=0; i<ExpTable.length; i++) {
  x = i/(ExpTable.length-1.0);
  v = exp(-4*x*x);
  ExpTable[i] = map(v, 1, 0.01831564, 1, 0);
}

t1 = millis();
for (i=0; i<numsteps; i++) {
  x = i/(numsteps-1.0);
  v = exp(-4*x*x);
  v = map(v, 1, 0.01831564, 1, 0);
}
t2 = millis();
int delta1 = t2-t1;

t1 = millis();
for (i=0; i<numsteps; i++) {
  x = i/(numsteps-1.0);
  float xIndex = x * (ExpTable.length-1);
  index0 = floor(xIndex);
  v = ExpTable[index0];
}
t2 = millis();
int delta2 = t2-t1;

t1 = millis();
for (i=0; i<numsteps; i++) {
  x = i/(numsteps-1.0);
  float xIndex = x * (ExpTable.length-1);
  index0 = floor(xIndex);
  index1 = ceil(xIndex);
  fraction = xIndex - index0;
  v = lerp(ExpTable[index0], ExpTable[index1], fraction);
}
t2 = millis();
int delta3 = t2-t1;

  println("delta1="+delta1+"  delta2="+delta2+"  delta3="+delta3);
}
```

(Full program in lamp/sketches/timing2/timing2.pde)

I ran this program just like the last one, five times on each computer, and averaged together the results. The runs were very similar each time. The data are in Figure 19.33.

	calculation	nearest neighbor	table interpolation
Desktop	11240	6673	11588
Laptop	15458	9102	15228

Figure 19.33. Timing results in milliseconds.

The left-most column is our baseline, telling us what it costs to explicitly compute the blob using exp() followed by map(). The middle column is the nearest-neighbor approach, and it's about 60 percent of the left-most column. That's great! It's not quite doubling the speed, but it's getting there. The right-most column is a big surprise to me. On both computers, table interpolation was just about as slow as the explicit calculation. I guess exp() is a whole lot faster than I thought it would be. The cost of getting a second entry from the table and then calling lerp() to blend them together eats up all the savings we got from not calling exp() in the first place.

Normally a table lookup for a slow math function is a surefire win. And in this case it was, for the nearest-neighbor approach. But while exp() is slow, it turns out not to be *that* slow. If we were doing a bigger calculation, though, the tables would start to look better and better.

The data I've gathered tell me to stick with the explicit calculation for now. It's simple and clear and doesn't take all that long to run. Later, when I'm finishing the project, I might find that I need to squeeze out some more time from this routine to make my animation run a little more smoothly. Then I can come back and put in a table. I'll have to remember to use the nearest-neighbor approach, though, which means I'll have to use a pretty big table so that I don't see any visual artifacts deriving from the chunky stairsteps in Figure 19.29. It's no good going faster if the results look bad!

19.4   Building the Lamp

Now that we're back from our travels into the land of optimization, we can implement our discoveries. First, I'll apply our splitting up of the square root into the heart of render() and replace the call to exp(-4) with the global variable:

```
float d2 = sq(x-cx)+sq(y-cy);
if (d2 > r*r) continue;
float d = sqrt(d2);
float h = map(d, 0, r, 1, 0);
float v = exp(-4*h*h);
v = map(v, 1, MinBlobVal, 0, 1);
Temperature[y][x] += v;
```

(See output in Figure 19.34. Full program in lamp/sketches/blob11/blob11.pde)

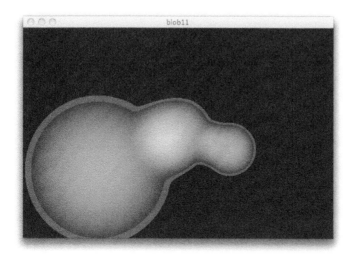

Figure 19.34. A more efficient square root. (lamp/sketches/blob11/blob11.pde)

I'll need to remember to define that variable up top, of course:

```
float MinBlobVal = 0.01831564;
```

Second, I'll keep the idea of a nearest-neighbor table lookup in the back of my head to replace that pair of calls to `exp()` and `map()`, but I won't bother with it now.

Now that all the pieces are in place and the blob-drawing code is nicely optimized, let's build the lamp! There are two things to do: build the blobs that represent the cold wax at the bottom, and build the blobs that rise up. Let's tackle them one at a time.

I want the lower blobs to completely cover the bottom of the window, and I want them to gently move around, as though they were warming up and oozing. The center blob in my pictures so far has had a radius of 100, and that looks pretty good to me.

So to get started, I'll make a row of blobs along the bottom of the window, each with radius 100. The left-most blob will sit right on the left edge, the right-most blob on the right edge, and the others will be equally spaced between them.

I'll create a global array called `Wax` to hold the blobs, and I'll write a routine to initialize them. Then I'll call that routine in `setup()`, which will also run through the array and tell each one to render itself.

As always, I'll start by making these structural changes in a way that shouldn't change the picture at all. I'll declare the array:

```
Blob [] Wax;
```

I need to initialize the blobs themselves:

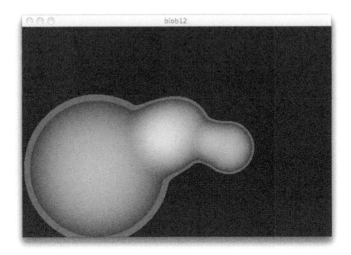

Figure 19.35. Using a blob array. (lamp/sketches/blob12/blob12.pde)

```
void makeWax() {
    Wax = new Blob[3];
    Wax[0] = new Blob(300, 200, 100);
    Wax[1] = new Blob(400, 230, 75);
    Wax[2] = new Blob(145, 270, 210);
}
```

In setup(), I'll call the routine to build the array. I'll set the temperature of every pixel to 0, and then I'll run through the array to tell each blob to draw itself:

```
makeWax();

zeroTemperature();
for (int i=0; i<ColdWax.length; i++) {
    Wax[i].render();
}
```

(See output in Figure 19.35. Full program in lamp/sketches/blob12/blob12.pde)

Ah, no change. Just the way it should be.

Now let's fix up makeWax() to create the line of blobs along the bottom. I'll make them really boring at first, all with radius 100, all spaced 100 units apart:

```
void makeWax() {
    int numColdBlobs = 1+int(width/100);
    Wax = new Blob[numColdBlobs];
    int xcenter = 0;
```

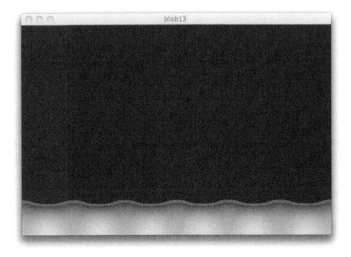

Figure 19.36. Creating the ground blobs. (lamp/sketches/blob13/blob13.pde)

```
    for (int i=0; i<numColdBlobs; i++) {
        Wax[i] = new Blob(i*100, height, 100);
    }
}
```

(See output in Figure 19.36. Full program in lamp/sketches/blob13/blob13.pde)

That looks utterly boring. Great! Now that we have them where we want them, we can move them around.

Animation, finally!

The first step, of course, is to move all the rendering stuff out of setup() and into draw():

```
void draw() {
    zeroTemperature();
    for (int i=0; i<Wax.length; i++) {
        Wax[i].move();
        Wax[i].render();
    }

    Img.loadPixels();
    buildImage();
    Img.updatePixels();
    image(Img, 0, 0);
}
```

You'll notice I added a procedure call that tells each blob to move itself. I'll have to write that, of course.

How should we make the blobs move around? I'll use a couple of Processing's building blocks. I mentioned in Chapter 18 that we can use sine and cosine (`sin()` and `cos()`) to create smooth, repeating patterns. So let's give them a whirl.

I'll save the original x center of each blob, and when I call `move()`, I'll add to that. The idea is that over time, the blob will move to the left, slow down and stop, then move to the right, slow down and stop, move back to the left, and so on. To get that to happen, I'll call `cos()` with an ever-increasing angle (I could have used `sin()` for this just as well). As time goes on and the angle goes up and up and up, the output of `cos()` will just keep going from 1 (pushing the blob to the right) smoothly down to -1 (pushing the blob to the left) and then back to 1, over and over. The speed with which the blob moves depends on how much the angle changes with time; big changes in the angle mean fast motion. The amount by which the blob moves left and right will be controlled by a scaling factor. If I use 1, then the blob will move just one pixel left and right, which will be just barely noticeable. So I'll try something larger.

While this is happening in x, I'm going to do the very same thing in y. I'll use a different angle that's incrementing by a different amount each time. And I'll scale the result by a different amount.

That means that the motions in x and y will be unrelated; we sometimes say they're *uncorrelated*, which just means that they don't have any relationship to one another. The left–right motion and the up–down motion are entirely independent, so the blob will have a more organic, randomly-varying feeling in its motion.

Let's write the code. I'll need six variables. For the left-right motion I'll need an angle, an increment to that angle, and a scaling factor (which I'll think of as the radius of the blob's motion). I'll need those three variables for the x motion, and another three for the y. I'll also want to save the original or starting x and y values of the blob so I'll know what I'm adding to.

I don't know what the numbers are going to be yet, but I can write down how they work:

```
void move() {
    cx = xorig + (xrad * cos(xangle));
    cy = yorig + (yrad * cos(yangle));
    xangle += xinc;
    yangle += yinc;
}
```

I need to declare these variables, of course, up in the variables associated with each blob:

```
float cx, cy;    // blob center
float r;         // blob radius
float xangle, xinc, xrad;  // for wobbling blobs left-right
```

```
float yangle, yinc, yrad;   // for wobbling blobs up-down
float xorig, yorig;         // starting x and y
```

So what values should these have? Well, now we're designing motion. As always, that's a matter of taste and your computer's speed. Your computer might be faster than mine, so when I get a gently rolling quiet motion, you might see a roiling, boiling madness. If your computer's a lot slower than mine, then my gentle motion might be imperceptible to you. If we really wanted to cement this down so the speed was consistent across computers, we could use some combination of `frameRate`, `frameCount`, and `millis()` as a kind of master clock. This is certainly possible, but it would make things more complex. So I'll proceed in a way that makes results that look good to me on my computer, and you can adjust the numbers as needed for your own system.

To keep things compartmentalized, I wrote a little routine to handle the wobbling. The constructor calls that routine with the values for the increments and radius, and it cooks up a starting angle itself. Finding good numbers was an interactive process; I pulled some values out of my hat and then adjusted them until the motion looked good on my computer. Then I kept changing them to find the range in which they looked nice, and that became the limits to the random-number generator. Here are the values that looked good to me, producing a softly bubbling gloopy goo:

```
Blob(float acx, float acy, float ar) {
   cx = acx;
   cy = acy;
   r = ar;
   startWobbles(radians(20)*random(-1, 1), r*random(0.1, 0.3),
                radians(20)*random(-1, 1), r*random(0.1, 0.3));
}

void startWobbles(float axinc, float axrad, float ayinc, float ayrad) {
   xangle = random(0, radians(360));
   yangle = random(0, radians(360));
   xinc = axinc;
   yinc = ayinc;
   xrad = axrad;
   yrad = ayrad;
   xorig = cx;
   yorig = cy;
}
```

(See output in Figure 19.37. Full program in lamp/sketches/blob14/blob14.pde)

If you run this (and get the numbers tuned up right), you may want to take a moment to just watch it. I've sat here for about a minute just now, enjoying the oozing, wobbling goop. I really like how this looks and feels.

Now let's add the rising blobs. To accomplish this, we could either take some of the existing blobs and let them "break free" of the mass at the bottom, or we could create new blobs and let them rise up and out of the goop. I'll go with the second approach.

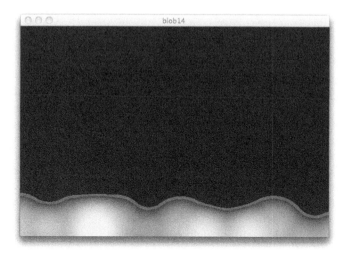

Figure 19.37. Bubbling ground blobs (frame from animation).
(lamp/sketches/blob14/blob14.pde)

So we'll make new blobs that are roughly the same as the blobs we've just made, but they have a few differences. First, they get born "underground," or below the window. That way they won't cause a sudden change in the appearance of the bubbling goo when they appear. Instead, they will gradually rise up and push their way through. So the second change is that instead of roiling around near the ground, they rise up, maybe moving a little to the left or right as they go.

19.5   Subclasses

So now we have an interesting dilemma. We have our own object called a `Blob`, and it's got a bunch of variables and a bunch of methods, or actions. Now we want to make another thing that is very much like this `Blob`, but a little different. Because it moves differently, the function that controls its motion will have to change a little, and we'll probably want to use a few new variables to control that new motion.

What to do? There are two clear choices given what we've seen so far.

First, we can create a whole new object. This will be just like the last `Blob`, but we'll add some new variables and code to make it rise upward. The routine to move the blob over time will have to be a little different, too, since it needs to detect when the blob has risen off the top of the window. So we'd copy the code for the existing `Blob` object and change it a little to make a new object.

I really don't like the idea of making a near carbon copy of the existing `Blob`, and you can guess why: we'd have to repeat a lot of stuff. In fact, we'd end up repeating almost everything in `Blob`, changing just a few little bits to get it to move differently. Then if we want to change how our blobs behave, we'd always have to remember to change both versions. And if we later want more types of blobs, the number of pieces of identical code we would have to make identical changes to would just keep increasing.

The second choice is to turn the existing `Blob` into a single beast with two heads. In addition to all the variables we just added to make the blobs move around, we could include the new variables to make them rise up. Then we could put in another variable, maybe a `boolean`, to tell us if this is a ground blob or a rising blob. Then we'd have `move()` test that variable and call one of two routines to move the blob appropriately. In essence, each blob would be a mashed-together object that could be used in either way.

I don't like that approach very much, either. It makes things complicated and ugly. I like how these ground blobs move and behave. That's how these blobs *should* move and behave. Blobs that move in some other way should be some other kind of blob. Almost the same, of course, but with a few differences.

Happily, there's a really great third choice available to us that does the job perfectly.

When we declare a new kind of object (that is, we define a class), we can tell Processing that this object is a *subclass* of some other class. What that means is that the new object *inherits* everything the other class has: all the variables, all the procedures, everything. The new subclass can then add its own stuff. That "other" class we're inheriting from is sometimes called the *parent class*, or the *super class* (sometimes this is written as just one word: *superclass*).

A subclass inherits everything from its superclass, but it has the option of substituting its own functions for those that the parent already has. If the subclass doesn't replace something from its parent, then Processing will use the parent's information. The idea is that the subclass starts out life by deferring to the parent on everything. Then one by one you can change the parent's routines, or even add entirely new routines.

This situation is something like global and local variables. Suppose you have a global variable that's defined at the top of your program. Every routine in your program "inherits" that variable: it can read it and write it. But suppose that some routine in your program declares a variable of the same name. Then inside that routine, it's the local copy that you're referring to. You can read and write it, as usual, but it doesn't touch the global version. The local definition supersedes the global one. This is normally a pretty bad idea from the point of view of writing clean and maintainable code, but it's not illegal. Let's write a little test program to demonstrate the idea:

```
int Avar = 5;

void setup() {
  test1();
  test2();
  test1();
}
```

```
void test1() {
  println("test 1: Avar=" + Avar);
}

void test2() {
  int Avar = 8;   // bad (but legal): this "hides" the global Avar
  println("test 2: Avar=" + Avar);
}
```

(Full program in lamp/sketches/localVars/localVars.pde)

Here's the output:

```
test 1: Avar=5
test 2: Avar=8
test 1: Avar=5
```

What's happening here? First, I declare the global variable Avar as an int with the value 5. The function test1() prints out the value of Avar. What happens when that println() statement is executed? Processing looks inside of test1() for a variable called Avar. It doesn't find one. So it looks outside the routine and finds the global. That gets printed. We sometimes say that Processing looks "up" rather than outward when it looks for objects and functions of a given name.

Now in test2() I've declared my own variable Avar (violating the convention that only globals begin with a capital letter). Now when println() is called in that procedure, Processing looks inside of test2() for a variable called Avar. It finds it and uses that for printing.

Just to confirm that the global hasn't changed, I've called test1() again, and we can see that the global still has the value 5. So the local version inside of test2() obscured the global copy as far as code inside of test2() was concerned, but it didn't touch, delete, replace, or in any way affect the global version. The local variable simply took over the name for the duration of the routine.

That's what happens in subclasses. A subclass inherits all of the procedures and variables from its parents automatically, without doing a thing (just as a routine "inherits" all of the global variables). But if it wants to, the subclass can give its own definitions of procedures, and as far as the subclass is concerned, those are the methods that get used.

A subclass can also replace its parent's variables simply by re-declaring them, but I strongly recommend against it. This is one of those situations where it's easy to make a single little slip while programming that can take many frustrating hours to track down. The problem is that when you're reading your code and you see the variable name, you can easily misinterpret which object it belongs to. You can always find out what procedures are getting called (with a print statement, if nothing else), but checking whether you're modifying a local or global variable is much harder and an invitation to confusion and head-scratching. And if you forget that you've redefined the variable, it can take forever to rediscover that fact. Be nice to yourself and use new variables with new names in your subclass rather than redefining variables from your parent. Although it is permissible for a subclass to redefine its parent's variables, I consider that such a dangerous practice that I never do it.

Let's see how a subclass is created by using every kid's favorite food: a goldfish cracker. I'll create an object called Goldfish. It contains a couple of arrays that define its shape and a color variable. The constructor takes only one piece of information: the color of the fish. When you want to draw a fish, you call its render() method with the location and size that you want the fish to have (I won't use the built-in transforms here because they also scale up the line weight, so I'll do my own translating and scaling in the render() procedure).

Most of the code is stuff we've seen before. The only unusual thing might be in the render() routine. The arrays fx and fy hold the coordinates for the upper outline of the fish. The fish is centered at (0,0), so the upper half has negative y values. To draw the fish, I start by calling beginShape() and then I run through the points that make the upper half of the fish. To draw the lower half, I just run through the points again in the opposite order, multiplying the y values by -1. Then I call endShape() to draw the fish. I use scl to control the size (or scale) of the drawing and cx and cy to position it.

```
Goldfish Fish;

void setup() {
   size(600, 400);
   background(83, 181, 169);

   Fish = new Goldfish(color(255, 184, 51));
   Fish.render(100, 100, .5);
}

class Goldfish {
   // Goldfish outline
   float [] fx = { 150, 130, 110,  90,   70,  50,
                     0, -40, -50, -80, -100, -80};
   float [] fy = {   0, -20, -30, -40,  -50, -50,
                   -30, -10, -10, -40,  -30,   0};

   // the color of this fish
   color fishColor;

   // Goldfish constructor
   Goldfish(color afishColor) {
      fishColor = afishColor;
   }
```

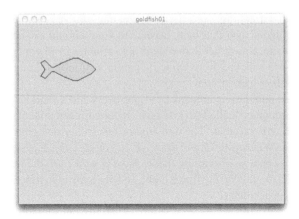

Figure 19.38. A delicious goldfish. (lamp/sketches/goldfish01/goldfish01.pde)

```
// draw a Goldfish using this fish's color
void render(float cx, float cy, float scl) {
    fill(fishColor);
    beginShape();
    for (int i=0; i<fx.length; i++) vertex(cx+(scl*fx[i]),
            cy+(scl*fy[i]));
    for (int i=fx.length-1; i>=0; i--) vertex(cx+(scl*fx[i]),
            cy+(scl*-fy[i]));
    endShape();
    }
}
```

(See output in Figure 19.38. Full program in lamp/sketches/goldfish01/goldfish01.pde)

I'd like to give this fish an action so that I can later show how a subclass of the fish deals with that action. So let's teach it to draw a little periscope, to help it see where it's going. I'll create two new arrays with the points for the periscope:

```
//periscope outline
float [] px = {  90,    90,    95,   100,   130,   130,   150,
                150,   130,   130,   120,   115,   110,   110 };
float [] py = { -40,  -110,  -117,  -120,  -120,  -125,  -125,
                -95,   -95,  -100,  -100,   -97,   -90,   -30};
```

I'll write a routine called drawPeriscope() that will just draw it.

```
// draw a periscope using this fish's color
void drawPeriscope(float cx, float cy, float scl) {
```

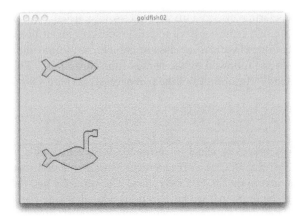

Figure 19.39. A delicious goldfish and its periscopic friend.
(lamp/sketches/goldfish02/goldfish02.pde)

```
    fill(fishColor);
    beginShape();
    for (int i=0; i<px.length; i++) vertex(cx+(scl*px[i]), cy+(scl*py[i]));
    endShape();
}
```

Finally, in `setup()` I'll draw a second fish and a periscope on top of it:

```
Fish.render(100, 300, .5);
Fish.drawPeriscope(100, 300, .5);
```

(See output in Figure 19.39. Full program in lamp/sketches/goldfish02/goldfish02.pde)

Figure 19.39 shows the result. The periscope is just drawn right over the fish. But because I don't close the periscope (that is, there's no line at its base), the bottom blends right into the body of the fish. That was a happy accident!

Now let's get into a subclass. I'm going to create a new kind of fish called a `Spotfish`. This is like a goldfish in every way except one: it has (you guessed it) a spot.

A `Spotfish` inherits everything from `Goldfish`: the body color, the variables holding the fish outline, the `render()` procedure, the variables holding the periscope outline, and the `drawPeriscope()` procedure.

But a `Spotfish` has three differences. First, the `Spotfish` has an extra variable (to hold the color of the spot). Second, its constructor is different because it takes a second argument (the color of the spot). Third, the `Spotfish` has its own version of `render()`, in order to draw the fish with the spot.

So let's see how to create all this stuff.

We begin by declaring `Spotfish` as a `class`, as usual. But because we want it to inherit from `Goldfish`, we have to tell Processing about that relationship. To express the idea that one class is a subclass of another, we follow the class name with the keyword `extends` followed by the name of the super class. The thinking is that this new class "extends" the abilities of the parent class. So here's how we start out:

```
class Spotfish extends Goldfish {
}
```

We use the curly braces as usual to surround all the stuff that's part of this class. Because of the `extends Goldfish` statement, you can imagine that the curly braces also include all the text in the `Goldfish` class. The variables and the routines are all right there, ready to be used. All we have to do is add what's new and overwrite what we want to change.

From now on, we basically have a normal class. We don't have to think about the parent class at all unless we want to. All of its capabilities are inherited and just sitting there, ready and waiting.

The first thing we want to add is a new variable to hold the color of the spot:

```
class Spotfish extends Goldfish {
    color spotColor;   // the color of the spot
}
```

Now how do we save that new color with the fish? We write a new constructor. Just like any other constructor, this has the name of the class, followed by any arguments, followed by the code to build the object.

But there's a special requirement for subclass constructors. Every constructor in a subclass has to call the constructor for its superclass. That's the rule. In this case, a `Spotfish` constructor must call the `Goldfish` constructor.

The best way to do this is to explicitly call the parent's constructor yourself. I strongly recommend this. If you don't, then Processing will look through the parent's code for a constructor that takes no arguments, and it will call that. This behavior can surprise you. First, you may not intend for the "no-arguments" constructor to be the one that gets run. Second, there may be no such constructor! In that case, you'll get a cryptic error message from Processing. In this example, if you tried to create a `Spotfish` without explicitly calling a constructor, you'd get this message:

```
Implicit super constructor localvars.Goldfish() is undefined.
Must explicitly invoke another constructor
```

To avoid this error message, and to be sure your parent object gets built the way you want, I urge you to manually call the parent's constructor yourself, as the first step in your object's constructor.

The notation is a little unusual. Anytime you want to talk about your parent (or super) class, you use the keyword `super`. So even though `Spotfish` knows that its

super class is named `Goldfish`, it never refers to it that way; it's always `super`. So
to create an object of the parent class, you just call `super()`:

```
super(afishColor);
```

When Processing sees this, it realizes you're calling the constructor for your superclass. The argument is `afishcolor`, which is of type `color`, so it looks inside of
`Goldfish` to find a constructor that takes a `color`. It runs that constructor, creates
the object, and associates the result with this `Spotfish`. Now the `Spotfish` object
can get at the `Goldfish` object at any time using `super`.

Curiously, even though our `Spotfish` can reach "up" into its parent object using
`super`, the parent cannot reach "down" into the `Spotfish`. In fact, the parent doesn't
even know that the subclass object exists! As far as the parent is concerned, it is an
object with methods and variables and that's all there is. The child is aware of its
relationship to its parent, but not vice versa.

Notice that we don't assign the result of the superclass constructor to anything.
Processing handles that automatically. It's not quite accurate, but you can think of
Processing as taking the result of the constructor and assigning it to the variable `super`.
Now you can access the contents of the constructed parent object using that variable (of
course, it's a keyword and not a variable; I'm just illustrating a conceptual similarity).

If your parent has a procedure that you haven't redefined, you can simply call it by
name. After all, the subclass inherited that procedure. If your parent has a procedure
that you've redefined in your subclass, then just calling that procedure will result in
your new version getting run. But what if you have redefined the procedure, but you
want to call the parent's version? You can do it with dot notation: prefix the call to the
parent's version with the keyword `super` followed by a period. That tells Processing
to use the superclass's version of the procedure, not your own. If you haven't redefined
a procedure from your superclass, you can still precede it with `super` and a dot, but
it's not necessary. Calling your parent's constructor doesn't follow this rule because it's
a special case.

Returning to constructors, we now know that the `Spotfish` constructor needs to
call the `Goldfish` constructor. The `Goldfish` constructor needs a fish color, and the
`Spotfish` itself needs a spot color, so the `Spotfish` constructor takes both colors.
It hands one color up the line to its parent to create the fish color, and it keeps one for
itself to make the spot color.

Here's the `Spotfish` constructor:

```
Spotfish(color afishColor, color aspotColor) {
    // call the superclass (Goldfish) constructor to save the fish color
    super(afishcolor);
    // now save my spot color
    spotColor = aspotColor;
}
```

So when you create a `Spotfish`, the first thing it does is call the `Goldfish` constructor with the necessary arguments. That initializes the values declared in the superclass. With that obligation out of the way, the `Spotfish` is free to do whatever it needs to. In this case, it just stores the spot color.

Now that we've constructed our `Spotfish` and saved its spot color, all we have left is to draw it. I'll write a new version of `render()`. The first thing that `render()` does is call the superclass's version of `render()`. In other words, the first thing a `Spotfish` does when it draws itself is to draw a `Goldfish`. Then it adds in the spot.

```
void render(float cx, float cy, float scl) {
    // ask the Goldfish to draw itself first
    super.render(cx, cy, scl);
    // and now draw our own spot
    fill(spotColor);
    ellipse(cx+(scl*75), cy+(scl* 10), 20, 20);
}
```

Note that I called `super.render()` here and not simply `render()`. That's because I wanted the parent's version of the program. Of course, we're already in the subclass's `render()` method, so if I called `render()` here, this routine would call itself in an infinite loop, causing the program to freeze and eventually crash when it ran out of memory.

This version of `render()` works because when we constructed the parent object of type `Goldfish`, we gave it its color. Again, as far as that parent object is concerned, it's just a normal `Goldfish` with its own color, variables, and routines. So when we ask it to draw itself, it just uses its color and shape data and the rest and proceeds. It doesn't know that a subclass object was the source of the request; as I said, it doesn't even know the subclass object is out there. It's just a `Goldfish`, and it's been asked to draw itself, and so it does. Lovely.

That wraps it up! Here's the whole `Spotfish` class in one place:

```
class Spotfish extends Goldfish {

    // the color of the spot
    color spotColor;

    // the Spotfish constructor
    Spotfish(color afishColor, color aspotColor) {
        // call the Goldfish constructor to save this color
        super(afishColor);
        // now save the color for the spot
        spotColor = aspotColor;
    }

    void render(float cx, float cy, float scl) {
```

Figure 19.40. Adding in a `Spotfish`. (lamp/sketches/goldfish03/goldfish03.pde)

```
    // ask the Goldfish to draw itself first
    super.render(cx, cy, scl);
    // and now draw our own spot
    fill(spotColor);
  ellipse(cx+(scl*75), cy+(scl* 10), 20, 20);
  }
}
```

All that's left is to use this. I'll declare a global variable to hold a `Spotfish`:

```
Spotfish Spot;
```

I'll make a new `Spotfish` by calling the constructor:

```
Spot = new Spotfish(color(219, 101, 73), color(173, 171, 26));
```

Finally, I'll draw a `Spotfish` by calling its `render()` procedure:

```
Spot.render(275, 100, .5);
```

(See output in Figure 19.40. Full program in lamp/sketches/goldfish03/goldfish03.pde)

Take a look at the code for `Spotfish` and you'll see the power of subclassing. It can do everything a `Goldfish` can do, and then some (like adding an extra spot!). To see that it really does inherit everything from `Goldfish`, let's draw another `Spotfish`, but now we'll add a periscope:

Figure 19.41. A Spotfish can draw a periscope, too.
(lamp/sketches/goldfish04/goldfish04.pde)

```
Spot.render(275, 300, .5);
Spot.drawPeriscope(275, 300, .5);
```

(See output in Figure 19.41. Full program in lamp/sketches/goldfish04/goldfish04.pde)

Just to drive the point home, notice that the Spotfish class doesn't say anything about periscopes! That came in from the parent class, for free, without any work at all.

So a subclass inherits everything a parent class has. It can add new procedures and new variables (like our variable spotColor), and it can overwrite the parent's procedures (like our new version of render()). The parent's versions are always around, though, if you use super (and period) first. So our new render() is the one that gets called for a Spotfish, but it can always reach up to the parent and call the parent's version of render() via super.render() (and, of course, we do exactly that).

Let's extend Goldfish again, but in a different direction. Instead of adding a spot, I'll change the shape of the fish. I think I'll create a two-finned Sharkfish, which is just like a Goldfish in every way, except that it has a different outline shape.

We begin as before, by creating a new class that uses extends Goldfish so that inherits from that object:

```
class Sharkfish extends Goldfish {
}
```

The thing that makes a Sharkfish special is its shape. In particular, it sports uniquely symmetrical, dual-use, supercharged atomic hyperfins. I just created them after several long seconds of research and development. To define them, I'll write two outline `sfx` and `sfy` arrays that have a fin in them:

```
// Sharkfish outline
float [] sfx = { 150, 130, 110,  90,  70,  50,   40,  20,  -10,
                   5,  10,   0, -40, -50, -80, -100, -80};
float [] sfy = {   0, -20, -30, -40, -50, -50,  -70, -80, -85,
                 -70, -50, -30, -10, -10, -40,  -30,   0};
```

Now I need a constructor. As usual, the very first thing I'll do is call the superclass's constructor. A `Sharkfish` doesn't have any additional constructor parameters, so this one line is all that's needed:

```
Sharkfish(color afishColor) {
   // call the Goldfish constructor to save this color
   super(afishColor);
}
```

Finally, I need to replace `render()`. I could write a new version of `render()` like we did last time, but let's try a different approach.

Suppose I don't write a `render()` function at all, and from my main program, I tell `Sharkfish` to render itself. Processing looks in `Sharkfish` and doesn't find a routine called `render()`. So it then goes up to the parent. It finds one there and calls it.

Which means that in effect, the `Goldfish` object is being told to render itself. Remember that the `Goldfish` doesn't know anything about the `Sharkfish`, or even that it exists at all. The `Goldfish` is in its own little world, and when it's told to render itself, it does.

So I need to tell the `Goldfish`, in some way, that when it's time to render itself, it should use a different set of points.

One way to do this, from the `Sharkfish` point of view, would be to overwrite the points in the `Goldfish`. We could reach up into the parent object and change the values in the parent's arrays to match those in its own. It would have to make the parent arrays longer, because there are more points in the `Sharkfish`. Then when the `Goldfish` goes to draw itself, it would use its points in the `fx` and `fy` arrays it holds, but they would be modified from their original values. This would work, but what a mess! And it's a terrible idea anyway, because it ruins the whole idea of what classes and subclasses are about. If a subclass reaches up into its superclass and modifies the superclass's variables, the distinction between "class" and "subclass" gets completely muddied up. A subclass ought never directly modify it's parent's variables in this way.

A cleaner approach is to make a little change to the `render()` procedure in `Goldfish`. I'll have it call another function and pass to that function the arrays that define the points. Then the `Sharkfish` can call that second function with its own arrays instead. The improvement here is that the `Sharkfish` is not modifying anything inside its parent but is merely calling one of its parent's routines with a particular set of arguments.

So let's change the `Goldfish` procedure `render()` to call a new routine called `drawOutline()`, that takes two arrays and draws the fish:

```
// draw a Goldfish using this fish's color
void render(float cx, float cy, float scl) {
  drawOutline(cx, cy, scl, fx, fy);
}

void drawOutline(float cx, float cy, float scl, float [] x,
                 float [] y) {
  fill(fishColor);
  beginShape();
  for (int i=0; i<x.length; i++) vertex(cx+(scl*x[i]),
        cy+(scl*y[i]));
  for (int i=x.length-1; i>=0; i--) vertex(cx+(scl*x[i]),
        cy+(scl*-fy[i]));
  endShape();
}
```

Note that this change, entirely within `Goldfish`, has no effect on our old friend `Spotfish`. Even though its parent has changed, `Spotfish` doesn't need to change at all.

Now my `render()` routine in `Sharkfish()` can call `drawOutline()` (which it inherits) using its own arrays:

```
void render(float cx, float cy, float scl) {
  drawOutline(cx, cy, scl, sfx, sfy);
}
```

Now I'll add a declaration for a `Sharkfish`:

```
Sharkfish Shark;
```

I'll create a `Sharkfish`:

```
Shark = new Sharkfish(color(158, 61, 88));
```

I'll tell it to draw itself:

```
Shark.render(450, 100, .5);
```

(See output in Figure 19.42. Full program in lamp/sketches/goldfish05/goldfish05.pde)

That does the trick! The sharkfish is out there looking lean and mean.

Figure 19.42. A Sharkfish. (lamp/sketches/goldfish05/goldfish05.pde)

The routine render() in Sharkfish looks almost like the line in Goldfish, but it has an entirely different effect. That's because when it gets executed, sfx and sfy refer to the arrays in Sharkfish, so that's what gets drawn.

Of course, a Sharkfish can use a periscope to see where it's going, too. Here's the complete listing, including a periscope-wielding Sharkfish (as though it didn't have enough advantages already):

```
Goldfish Fish;
Spotfish Spot;
Sharkfish Shark;

void setup() {
   size(600, 400);
   background(83, 181, 169);

   // create fish
   Fish = new Goldfish(color(255, 184, 51));
   Spot = new Spotfish(color(219, 101, 73), color(173, 171, 26));
   Shark = new Sharkfish(color(158, 61, 88));

   // show each fish, with and without a periscope
   Fish.render(100, 100, .5);
   Fish.render(100, 300, .5);
   Fish.drawPeriscope(100, 300, .5);

   Spot.render(275, 100, .5);
```

```
   Spot.render(275, 300, .5);
   Spot.drawPeriscope(275, 300, .5);

   Shark.render(450, 100, .5);
   Shark.render(450, 300, .5);
   Shark.drawPeriscope(450, 300, .5);
}

class Goldfish {
   // Goldfish outline
   float [] fx = { 150, 130, 110,  90,   70,  50,
                     0, -40, -50, -80, -100, -80};
   float [] fy = {   0, -20, -30, -40,  -50, -50,
                   -30, -10, -10, -40,  -30,   0};

   //periscope outline
   float [] px = {  90,  90,  95, 100, 130, 130, 150,
                   150, 130, 130, 120, 115, 110, 110 };
   float [] py = { -40, -110, -117, -120, -120, -125, -125,
                   -95,  -95, -100, -100,  -97,  -90,  -30};

   // the color of this fish
   color fishColor;

   // Goldfish constructor
   Goldfish(color afishColor) {
      fishColor = afishColor;
   }

   // draw a Goldfish using this fish's color
   void render(float cx, float cy, float scl) {
      drawOutline(cx, cy, scl, fx, fy);
   }

   void drawOutline(float cx, float cy, float scl, float [] x, float [] y) {
      fill(fishColor);
      beginShape();
      for (int i=0; i<x.length; i++) vertex(cx+(scl*x[i]),
            cy+(scl*y[i]));
      for (int i=x.length-1; i>=0; i--) vertex(cx+(scl*x[i]),
            cy+(scl*-y[i]));
      endShape();
   }

   // draw a periscope using this fish's color
   void drawPeriscope(float cx, float cy, float scl) {
```

```
        fill(fishColor);
        beginShape();
        for (int i=0; i<px.length; i++) vertex(cx+(scl*px[i]), cy+(scl*py[i]));
        endShape();
    }
}

class Spotfish extends Goldfish {

    // the color of the spot
    color spotColor;

    // the Spotfish constructor
    Spotfish(color afishColor, color aspotColor) {
        // call the Goldfish constructor to save this color
        super(afishColor);
        // now save the color for the spot
        spotColor = aspotColor;
    }

    void render(float cx, float cy, float scl) {
        // ask the Goldfish to draw itself first
        super.render(cx, cy, scl);
        // and now draw our own spot
        fill(spotColor);
        ellipse(cx+(scl*75), cy+(scl* 10), 20, 20);
    }
}
class Sharkfish extends Goldfish {
    // Sharkfish outline
    float [] sfx = { 150, 130, 110,  90,  70,  50,   40,  20,  -10,
                       5,  10,   0, -40, -50, -80, -100, -80};
    float [] sfy = {   0, -20, -30, -40, -50, -50,  -70, -80, -85,
                     -70, -50, -30, -10, -10, -40,  -30,   0};

    // the Sharkfish constructor
    Sharkfish(color afishColor) {
        // call the Goldfish constructor to save this color
        super(afishColor);
    }

    void render(float cx, float cy, float scl) {
        drawOutline(cx, cy, scl, sfx, sfy);
    }
}
```

(See output in Figure 19.43. Full program in lamp/sketches/goldfish06/goldfish06.pde)

Figure 19.43. A Sharkfish with a periscope. (lamp/sketches/goldfish06/goldfish06.pde)

Look how small the definition for Sharkfish is. There's just a few lines for the definition of the shape, and then two one-line functions: the constructor and render(). We've got everything that's in a Goldfish, with some extra features, at almost no cost.

The beauty of the subclass idea is that you can create a wide variety of similar objects without repeating yourself. You create a class that contains the essence that all the others share. Then each new object is just a subclass of the parent, replacing only what's different.

You can carry the subclassing chain as deep as you like by making a subclass of your subclass, and a subclass of that, and so on. So a Spotfish could have a couple of subclasses of its own, say one with a motorized propeller and another with a scuba mask. And the scuba fish could have subclasses as well, if you wanted them.

19.6 Ascending Blobs

It won't come as a surprise that I now have a great answer for our earlier problems. How can we have two different, but nearly similar, types of blobs in our lamp? Of course, we'll use subclasses. I'll rewrite my blob object as a single generic kind of blob. Then I'll have two subclasses, one for the blobs on the ground and another for the blobs that rise up through the goo.

So, let's get the ball rolling. I'll take the code for our `Blob` object and chop it up into two pieces. One piece I'll continue to call `Blob`, and that object will be the generic one:

```
class Blob {
   float cx, cy;    // blob center
   float r;         // blob radius
   float xangle, xinc, xrad;  // for wobbling blobs left-right
   float yangle, yinc, yrad;  // for wobbling blobs up-down
   float xorig, yorig;        // starting x and y

   Blob(float acx, float acy, float ar) {
      cx = acx;
      cy = acy;
      r = ar;
      startWobbles(radians(20)*random(-1, 1), r*random(0.1, 0.3),
                   radians(20)*random(-1, 1), r*random(0.1, 0.3));
   }

   void startWobbles(float axinc, float axrad, float ayinc, float ayrad) {
      xangle = random(0, radians(360));
      yangle = random(0, radians(360));
      xinc = axinc;
      yinc = ayinc;
      xrad = axrad;
      yrad = ayrad;
      xorig = cx;
      yorig = cy;
   }

   void move() {
      cx = xorig + (xrad * cos(xangle));
      cy = yorig + (yrad * cos(yangle));
      xangle += xinc;
      yangle += yinc;
   }

   void render() {
      int lox = max(0, int(cx-r));
      int hix = min(width, int(cx+r));
      int loy = max(0, int(cy-r));
      int hiy = min(height, int(cy+r));
      for (int y=loy; y<hiy; y++) {
         for (int x=lox; x<hix; x++) {
            float d2 = sq(x-cx)+sq(y-cy);
            if (d2 > r*r) continue;
            float d = sqrt(d2);
```

```
                    float h = map(d, 0, r, 1, 0);
                    float v = exp(-4*h*h);
                    v = map(v, 1, MinBlobVal, 0, 1);
                    Temperature[y][x] += v;
              }
          }
      }
}
```

So a generic `Blob` is just a thing with a center and a radius and some values to control its wobbling. It knows how to construct itself, how to add the wobble values, how to draw itself, and that's all.

Now let's make the blobs that bubble along the bottom. I'll call each of these a `WarmBlob`. It inherits (or extends) the basic `Blob` object. This subclass is pretty darned small; all it has is a custom constructor.

```
class WarmBlob extends Blob {

    WarmBlob(float acx, float acy, float ar) {
      super(acx, acy, ar);
      startWobbles(radians(3)*random(-1, 1), ar*random(0.1, 0.2),
                   radians(3)*random(-1, 1), ar*random(0.1, 0.2));
    }
}
```

Remembering our rules for subclass constructors, the first thing I do is call the superclass's constructor, using just `super()`. Then I change the blob's wobble values by calling `startWobbles()`. That routine belongs to the superclass, so I could have written `super.startWobbles()`, and that would have worked perfectly well. But since `WarmBlob` hasn't defined its own version of `startWobbles()`, there's no ambiguity. When we call `startWobbles()`, Processing first looks to see if `WarmBlob` has its own version; since it doesn't, Processing goes up to the parent and looks for a version there and finds it. Perfect.

To wire in my new subclass, I'll make the necessary name changes up at the top of the program. I'll declare my blobs:

```
WarmBlob [] WarmWax;
```

Of course, I need to create my new objects in `makeWax()`:

```
void makeWax() {
    int numWarmBlobs = 1+int(width/100);
    WarmWax = new WarmBlob[numWarmBlobs];
    int xcenter = 0;
    for (int i=0; i<numWarmBlobs; i++) {
       WarmWax[i] = new WarmBlob(i*100, height, 100);
    }
}
```

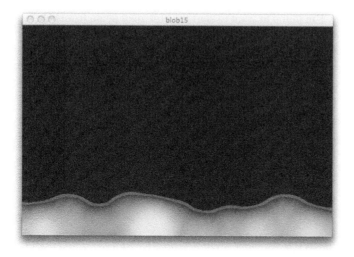

Figure 19.44. Globby subclass Blobs (frame from animation).
(lamp/sketches/blob15/blob15.pde)

I'll need to make sure I refer to these with the proper new name inside draw():

```
for (int i=0; i<WarmWax.length; i++) {
   WarmWax[i].move();
   WarmWax[i].render();
}
```

(See output in Figure 19.44. Full program in lamp/sketches/blob15/blob15.pde)

We've made an important change to the structure of the program, but the results look just the same as before. The new class is basically a normal Blob, with just a few different parameters controlling its motion.

Now comes the payoff, because it's duck soup to write a new, rising blob object. I'll call this a HotBlob.

Let's start with the new move() function since everything kind of flows from that. This new blob will ooze around a little like the others, of course, since it's in the same hot oil, but I think it's random motion should be a little more constrained. And of course, it has to move upward on every frame, which the warm blobs aren't doing. While I'm at it, I'll give the blob some horizontal drift too; just a tiny bit of leftward or rightward motion, because I think that will make them a little more interesting to watch.

So I'll start out by calling the parent's move(), which will take care of the wobble, and then I'll add in some upward motion. In this case, I do have to use the whole form of the call, super.move(), because I want to call the Blob version of move(), not this new one that we're already inside of!

I also know I'm going to want to start the blob over again from below once it passes off the top of the window. I could just throw away this blob object and create a new one (letting the garbage collector come along later and mop things up), but I'm trying to stay efficient here. Reusing an object is faster than allocating a new one. So when the blob goes offscreen, I'll call `restart()` (which doesn't exist yet) to move it to a new location and get it rising again:

```
void move() {
   super.move();
   cx += vx;
   cy += vy;
   if (cy+r < 0) {
      restart();
   }
}
```

I've got a couple of new "velocity" variables `vx` and `vy`, so let's declare them:

```
float vx, vy;    // blob velocity per frame
```

Let's now implement `restart()`. This routine is responsible for setting up the blob either for the first time, after it's just been made, or at some point in the future after it's risen off the top of the screen. In that case, we'll recycle the blob ourselves by loading it up with new starting values. The routine will pick a random radius for the blob and a random horizontal location for it to rise from. I'll start it just below the bottom of the window.

But what about the other values? Looking at `move()`, the blob has two basic controls on its motion. First, there's `vx` and `vy`, which tell it how much to move horizontally and vertically per frame. I'll give it a very tiny amount of horizontal drift (the value in `vx`), and I'll pick some value for `vy` based on the radius `r` so that small blobs rise more quickly than big ones. The second thing is the wobbling motion applied by the superclass. How should a rising blob wobble as it moves? I fooled around with these numbers a little and found that these looked good on my computer:

```
void restart() {
   r = random(40, 100);
   cx = random(width);
   cy = height+r;
   vx = 0.0;
   vy = map(r, 40, 100, -4, -2) * random(0.8, 1.2);
   startWobbles(radians(2)*random(-1, 1), r*random(0.3, 0.6),
                radians(2)*random(-1, 1),   random(0.3, 0.6));
}
```

Note that I'm freely using the variables `r`, `cx`, and `cy` that were defined by the parent. Since they were defined by the parent, the subclass inherits them automatically, so they're just sitting there, ready to be used.

Notice that I left off the `r*` in the last argument to `startWobbles()`. I want the wobbling in *y* to be subtle, and not scaled up by the radius of the blob itself.

Finally, we need to call the constructor. It doesn't need any arguments because `restart()` puts the blob in the right position and assigns it all the values it needs. But we do have to call the superclass's constructor, as always, even if we have nothing to tell it. I'll hand it all 0's since I'm going to directly set `cx`, `cy`, and `r` inside of `restart()`:

```
HotBlob() {
    // We must call the Blob constructor, but I'll over-write the values
    super(0, 0, 0);
    restart();
}
```

Now I just need the same little bits of glue as before. I'll declare a global array of hot blobs:

```
HotBlob [] HotWax;
```

I'll add their creation into `makeWax()` (I'll go for ten blobs right now):

```
int numHotBlobs = 10;
HotWax = new HotBlob[numHotBlobs];
for (int i=0; i<numHotBlobs; i++) {
    HotWax[i] = new HotBlob();
}
```

Finally, I'll make sure to update and render them inside of `draw()`:

```
for (int i=0; i<HotWax.length; i++) {
  HotWax[i].move();
  HotWax[i].render();
}
```

Here's the complete listing:

```
PImage Img;
float [][] Temperature;
float MinBlobVal = 0.01831564;
WarmBlob [] WarmWax;
HotBlob [] HotWax;

void setup() {
    size(600, 400);
    Img = createImage(width, height, RGB);
    Temperature = new float[height][width];
```

```
   makeWax();
}

void draw() {
   zeroTemperature();
   for (int i=0; i<WarmWax.length; i++) {
     WarmWax[i].move();
     WarmWax[i].render();
   }
   for (int i=0; i<HotWax.length; i++) {
     HotWax[i].move();
     HotWax[i].render();
   }

   Img.loadPixels();
   buildImage();
   Img.updatePixels();
   image(Img, 0, 0);
}

void makeWax() {
   int numWarmBlobs = 1+int(width/100);
   WarmWax = new WarmBlob[numWarmBlobs];
   int xcenter = 0;
   for (int i=0; i<numWarmBlobs; i++) {
      WarmWax[i] = new WarmBlob(i*100, height, 100);
   }
   int numHotBlobs = 10;
   HotWax = new HotBlob[numHotBlobs];
   for (int i=0; i<numHotBlobs; i++) {
      HotWax[i] = new HotBlob();
   }
}

void zeroTemperature() {
   for (int y=0; y<height; y++) {
      for (int x=0; x<width; x++) {
         Temperature[y][x] = 0;
      }
   }
}

void buildImage() {
   for (int y=0; y<height; y++) {
      for (int x=0; x<width; x++) {
         float midT = 0.4;
```

```
            float rangeT = 0.05;
            if (abs(Temperature[y][x] - midT) < rangeT) {
               Img.set(x, y, color(255, 0, 0));
            } else {
               float t = map(Temperature[y][x], 0, 1.5, 0, 255);
               Img.set(x, y, color(t, t, 0));
            }
         }
      }
}

class Blob {
   float cx, cy;    // blob center
   float r;         // blob radius
   float xangle, xinc, xrad;  // for wobbling blobs left-right
   float yangle, yinc, yrad;  // for wobbling blobs up-down
   float xorig, yorig;        // starting x and y

   Blob(float acx, float acy, float ar) {
      cx = acx;
      cy = acy;
      r = ar;
      startWobbles(radians(20)*random(-1, 1), r*random(0.1, 0.3),
                   radians(20)*random(-1, 1), r*random(0.1, 0.3));
   }

   void startWobbles(float axinc, float axrad, float ayinc, float ayrad) {
      xangle = random(0, radians(360));
      yangle = random(0, radians(360));
      xinc = axinc;
      yinc = ayinc;
      xrad = axrad;
      yrad = ayrad;
      xorig = cx;
      yorig = cy;
   }

   void move() {
      cx = xorig + (xrad * cos(xangle));
      cy = yorig + (yrad * cos(yangle));
      xangle += xinc;
      yangle += yinc;
   }

   void render() {
      int lox = max(0, int(cx-r));
```

```
        int hix = min(width, int(cx+r));
        int loy = max(0, int(cy-r));
        int hiy = min(height, int(cy+r));
        for (int y=loy; y<hiy; y++) {
            for (int x=lox; x<hix; x++) {
                float d2 = sq(x-cx)+sq(y-cy);
                if (d2 > r*r) continue;
                float d = sqrt(d2);
                float h = map(d, 0, r, 1, 0);
                float v = exp(-4*h*h);
                v = map(v, 1, MinBlobVal, 0, 1);
                Temperature[y][x] += v;
            }
        }
    }
}

class WarmBlob extends Blob {

    WarmBlob(float acx, float acy, float ar) {
        super(acx, acy, ar);
        startWobbles(radians(3)*random(-1, 1), ar*random(0.1, 0.2),
                     radians(3)*random(-1, 1), ar*random(0.1, 0.2));
    }
}

class HotBlob extends Blob {
    float vx, vy;    // speed per frame

    HotBlob() {
        // We must call the Blob constructor
        super(0, 0, 0);
        restart();
    }

    void restart() {
        r = random(40, 100);
        cx = random(width);
        cy = height+r;
        vx = random(-.1, .1);
        vy = map(r, 40, 100, -4, -2) * random(0.8, 1.2);
        startWobbles(radians(2)*random(-1, 1), r*random(0.3, 0.6),
                     radians(2)*random(-1, 1),   random(0.3, 0.6));
    }

    void move() {
```

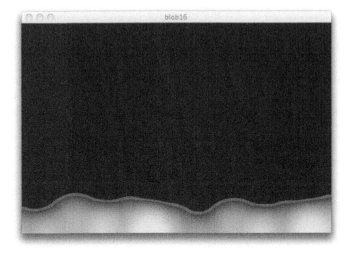

Figure 19.45. Where are the hot blobs? (frame from animation)
(lamp/sketches/blob16/blob16.pde)

```
    super.move();
    cx += vx;
    cy += vy;
    if (cy+r < 0) {
        restart();
    }
  }
}
```

(See output in Figure 19.45. Full program in lamp/sketches/blob16/blob16.pde)

And ... nothing. Nada. Well, not nothing at all, since we still have the animation we had before, but after all that work, I don't see a single change.

What could be going wrong? All the Blob stuff is clearly working correctly, so it must be our new subclass. The constructor is okay, and restart() is indeed putting the blob in the right place. Could there be a problem with move()? How could there be? It's a pretty simple routine.

Well, it does call the superclass's move(). Let's look at that again:

```
void move() {
    cx = xorig + (xrad * cos(xangle));
    cy = yorig + (yrad * cos(yangle));
    xangle += xinc;
    yangle += yinc;
}
```

The superclass's move() sets the values for cx and cy, which are the center of the blob. So in my new move(), I can't just add vy to cy, because that value gets moved back to a spot close to the beginning every time. In other words, each hot blob is moving just like a warm one, except that it's offscreen.

Here's an easy way out: the superclass's move() routine wobbles the location of the blob around the point (xorig, yorig). It thinks that's the unmoving starting (or original) location of the blob, but let's trick it. We'll change those values for each frame, moving the blob upward (and maybe left/right a little). Then the superclass's wobbling will take place around this moving origin.

Wait a second. Isn't this an example of "reaching up" and changing the parent's variables, the very thing I advised against doing in the last section? Nope. We're not changing the parent's variables, we're changing our own. When a HotBlob gets made, it inherits all the variables declared by its parent. But those variables, once inherited, belong to the child. So here, I'm playing a little fast and loose with the meaning of HotBlob's variables, but they all belong to the HotBlob. In other words, we're not changing super.xorig, which belongs to the parent Blob and shouldn't be monkeyed with, but instead, we're simply changing xorig, which belongs to HotBlob itself and is fair game for anything we want to do with it, just like any other object variable.

We have to be careful when we change these variables, though, and update the values of (xorig, yorig) *before* we call the superclass's move() routine. Note that the test at the end of the new move() still works, because cy does contain the current *y* location of the blob:

```
void move() {
    xorig += vx;
    yorig += vy;
    super.move();
    if (cy+r < 0) {
        restart();
    }
}
```

(See output in Figure 19.46. Full program in lamp/sketches/blob17/blob17.pde)

That little adjustment made everything just right again.

This is very close to satisfying, but I don't like the way it starts out, when all the blobs rise up at once. I'd like to stagger their first appearance a little bit.

I'll add a boolean to restart() to tell us if this is the first time through or not. If it is, I'll push each blob downward by a random amount, up to a whole screen height. That way, it'll take a moment longer for the pushed-down blobs to rise up.

```
void restart(boolean firstTime) {
    r = random(40, 100);
    cx = random(width);
```

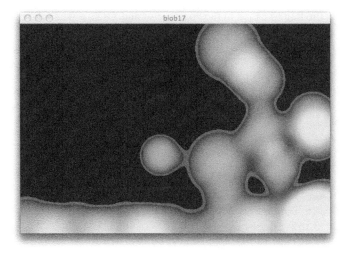

Figure 19.46. Hot blobs on the rise! (frame from animation).
(lamp/sketches/blob17/blob17.pde)

```
    cy = height+r;
    if (firstTime) cy += random(height);
}
```

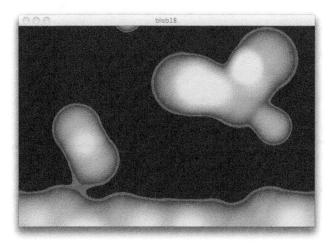

Figure 19.47. Hot and warm blobs with a staggered start (frame from animation).
(lamps/sketches/blob18/blob18.pde)

I'll then set the flag to `true` in the constructor and `false` when the blob is remade after passing off the top of the screen.

(See output in Figure 19.47. Full program in lamp/sketches/blob18/blob18.pde)

Oh, that's much better. Now this looks good from the very beginning.

All this time I've been drawing the temperature image, and that's been nice (and even kind of attractive), but let's leave it off. I'll draw just the isoband, and everything else will be black:

```
void buildImage() {
    for (int y=0; y<height; y++) {
        for (int x=0; x<width; x++) {
            float midT = 0.4;
            float rangeT = 0.05;
            if (abs(Temperature[y][x] - midT) < rangeT) {
                Img.set(x, y, color(255, 0, 0));
            } else {
                Img.set(x, y, color(0, 0, 0));
            }
        }
    }
}
```

(See output in Figure 19.48. Full program in lamp/sketches/blob19/blob19.pde)

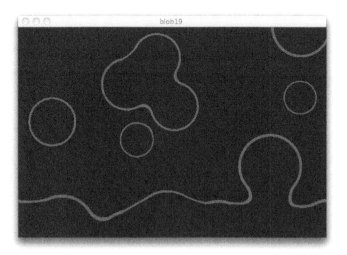

Figure 19.48. Just the isoband (frame from animation). (lamp/sketches/blob19/blob19.pde)

That's kind of appealing; I like the band.

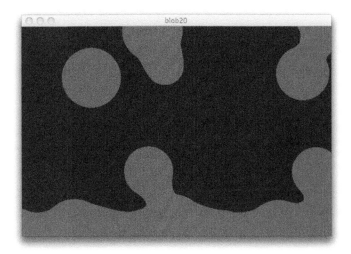

Figure 19.49. Solid blobs (frame from animation). (lamp/sketches/blob20/blob20.pde)

But what if we forgot about the band and just filled in everything that's above the threshold temperature?

```
if (Temperature[y][x] > midT) {
    Img.set(x, y, color(255, 0, 0));
} else {
    Img.set(x, y, color(0, 0, 0));
}
```

(See output in Figure 19.49. Full program in lamp/sketches/blob20/blob20.pde)

I think I like that. And it's moving pretty nicely on my computer. The colors need to be changed, of course. And I just noticed that buildImage() can be sped up a bit since I'm still using set() to draw the pixels. I know that set() is an expensive routine because it's running a bounds check on every pixel before it writes it. Of course, I know that all these pixels are valid, so I can do away with that and write to the pixels array directly. And it's a super-easy change because the call to buildImage() is already wrapped up between a loadPixels() and updatePixels() pair! So let's rewrite drawImage() to be better, stronger, and faster:

```
void buildImage() {
    color cool = color(18, 69, 94);
    color hot = color(207, 152, 14);
    float midT = 0.4;
    for (int y=0; y<height; y++) {
        for (int x=0; x<width; x++) {
```

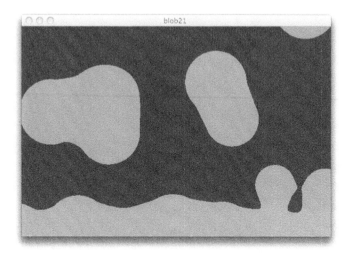

Figure 19.50. An improved `buildImage()` (frame from animation).
(lamp/sketches/blob21/blob21.pde)

```
        if (Temperature[y][x] > midT) Img.pixels[(y*width)+x] = hot;
                              else Img.pixels[(y*width)+x] = cool;
    }
  }
}
```

(See output in Figure 19.50. Full program in lamp/sketches/blob21/blob21.pde)

Oh yeah, there's the stuff. Figures 19.51 and 19.52 show another couple of frames from this animation.

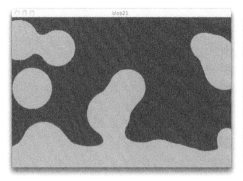

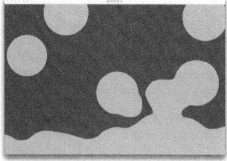

Figure 19.51. Another frame of rising blobs.   Figure 19.52. More blobs rising from the goo.

That's moving nice and fast on my computer now. I have all the blobs I want, and it's running nice and smooth.

I could watch this thing for hours.

19.7   Personalizing Your Lamp

If you're feeling adventurous, or if your computer's not as fast as mine, try putting the table lookup into the blob-drawing code so that you don't have to call `exp()` for every pixel in every blob and see if that gets you a perceptible increase in speed.

There are all kinds of fun experiments you can run with this program. For example, try creating cold blobs as well as hot ones. Instead of adding into the `Temperature` array, they subtract from it. How does that look? Should your cold blobs rise up from the bottom, like the hot ones, or should they fall down from the top? You could change the way the hot blobs work entirely, so that when they hit the top of the window, they cool off (perhaps becoming negative) and then sink until they fall below the bottom and then start up again, like a real action lamp.

I used round, symmetrical blobs. What about other shapes? How would this look if you used four-sided pyramids? Should they spin as they rise up? How about star-shaped blobs? You could easily scale the values used in the `render()` function to create elliptical blobs. They could even morph from one shape to another as they rose.

You might try letting regions of the oil influence the behavior of nearby blobs. If there are a lot of hot blobs in one location, for example, the oil could be very hot and the blobs could rise through it more quickly. Colder areas could slow blobs down.

You could add other objects into the lamp along with the blobs. They might just add visual effect, or they might influence the blob's motion. You might have something that pushes blobs away or pulls them towards it.

You might even want to extend the blobs themselves so that they can split into pieces or join up. A very big blob might rise slowly and hit an obstacle, which causes it to split into two (or more) smaller bits. Or multiple blobs that find themselves in nearly the same place might fuse together. Or they could fuse together loosely, as though joined by a spring, so the two blobs kind of vibrate towards and away from one another as they move together.

I made all my blobs the same color, but what if you had two or more different colors of blobs in the same project? Would they coexist but ignore each other? Would they glob together and mix colors? Would they break apart and retain the mixed color, or go back to the colors they had? Might some colors attract each other and others repel one another?

Once you start experimenting with this kind of thing, you can spend a lot of very happy hours playing around with ideas.

Chapter 20
Typography

We haven't done much with text so far. Sure, we've printed text messages out to the console to diagnose problems, but our drawings and animations haven't had any text in them. Let's do something about that now.

20.1 Strings

Typography is fundamentally about characters, and most of the time, characters are grouped into words. What's the best way to group characters? An array seems like a good starting point. We could make a word just by declaring an array of char variables and filling it up with individual characters.

A char is a data type that holds a single typographic character. You identify a character as a char by putting it between single quotes: ′a′, ′Q′, ′3′, and ′&′ are all of type char. If you want a single quote for your character, you precede it with the backslash (\); that's a special symbol that Processing interprets as a sign that the next character should be interpreted not as a letter, but as a code. For example, if you want a newline character, you'd use ′\n′, because n is the code for newline (there's no way to know this other than to be told or to look it up). If you want a tab, use the special code t, as in ′\t′. The code for single quote is, happily, just a single quote. So if you want a single-quote character, you'd write ′\′′ for it. I know that looks messy, but here's another one that's also messy: the code for a backslash is also a backslash, so to identify a backslash character, you'd write ′\\′ in your code. If you work with the English character set, those four codes will likely be all you'll ever need to know. If you need accented characters, you can find a full list of the codes to generate them in the online Processing documentation.

You can create an array of char types and use it the normal way:

```
char [] myText = { 'B', 'i', 'g', ' ', 'd', 'o', 'g' };
println(myText[2]);
```

Of course, this will print the letter g.

There's a lot to be said in favor of handling your text this way. Probably the nicest thing is that it gives you access to all of the array-manipulating routines saw in Chapter 13.

But this array of char variables has a whole lot of drawbacks, too. You're not really dealing with your characters as words; they're just individual characters one after the other. Initialization is cumbersome. Some of the array routines, like reverse(), are not frequently needed for strings. And some other routines we might find useful, like searching for a word in a piece of text, aren't available at all.

Processing offers a much better alternative: the String class. Like our array above, it's made up of individual characters. But a String is not an array, and the array functions we saw in Chapter 11 won't work on String types (you'll just get an error if you try).

Instead, there's a whole new bunch of specialized methods meant just for Strings.

Like any other object's methods, we call these functions by naming the string we want to modify, then a period, and then the name of the function, followed by any arguments. In most String methods, the String itself (the object to the left of the period) is modified by its method. You can store the result in another variable, if you like, but remember that unlike arrays, the original String object is usually changed.

To initialize a String, you just provide it your text within double quotes:

```
String myString = "Big dog";
```

So, in general, if we call a method doSomething() on a string, we write it this way:

```
myString.doSomething();
```

The result would be that myString gets changed. If you wanted to have both the old version of myString and the new one, make a copy of the old one first (we'll see how to do that). Then you'll have both the original and changed versions.

Let's look at the methods that are available specifically for doing cool things with variables of String type. Each of the little fragments below is just meant to illustrate the use of a method. But you can turn most of them into running programs by putting them into a setup() routine; just put a void setup() { at the top and a closing curly brace at the end. For these little things there's no need for a draw() routine (but it doesn't hurt, if you choose to include one anyway).

20.1.1   nf(), nfc(), nfp(), nfs()

The function nf() will turn a number into a String, so that you can then work with the digits as characters (the strange name is an abbreviation of *number formatter*). There are two overloaded versions.

The first is for integers. Because it's often convenient to have numbers line up nicely, this form of `nf ()` takes a second argument that tells it how many digits wide the result should be, and it puts 0's in front of your number until it's that wide:

```
int myNumber = 32;
String myString;

myString = nf(myNumber, 2);        // convert with 2 digits
println("myString with 2 digits = "+myString);

myString = nf(myNumber, 5);        // convert with 5 digits
println("myString with 5 digits = "+myString);
```

This prints out

```
myString with 2 digits = 32
myString with 5 digits = 00032
```

What happens if you ask for too few digits? Let's try it.

```
String myString = nf(8123, 2);        // convert with 2 digits
println("myString with 2 digits = "+myString);
```

Happily, Processing does the right thing.

```
myString with 2 digits = 8123
```

So your second input to `nf ()` can be thought of as your telling Processing that you want *at least* that many digits in your output. If necessary, you'll get more.

Let's try that with negative numbers, too.

```
int daysInYear = 365;
int negDays = -365;
String s1 = nf(daysInYear, 1);
String s2 = nf(negDays, 1);
println("s1 = "+s1+"  s2 = "+s2);
```

So in both cases, we're asking for only one digit, but that's too small to contain the input number. The output from this program shows that Processing will make the output at least as large as it needs to be:

```
s1 = 365   s2 = -365
```

The floating-point version of `nf ()` takes two arguments after the input number: the number of digits that you want appearing in your string to the left of the decimal point, and the number of digits in your string to the right of the decimal point. The result is padded with 0's left and right to meet your specifications:

```
float myNumber = 32.78;
String myString;

myString = nf(myNumber, 2, 1);
println("myString with 2,1 digits = "+myString);

myString = nf(myNumber, 5, 3);
println("myString with 5,3 digits = "+myString);
```

This prints out

```
myString with 2,1 digits = 32.8
myString with 5,3 digits = 00032.780
```

Notice in the first line of output that nf() rounded the fraction .78 to .8 because it had only a single digit in which to place the value.

The function nfc() only converts integers, but it does not pad the result with 0's. Instead, it inserts any needed commas to group digits in clusters of three, as is conventional in countries like the United States (thus the name includes a *c* for *comma*). Its arguments are not the same as nf(). You give it just an int or a float followed by the number of digits to the right of the decimal.

The function nfp() is another variant, which will explicitly include a plus sign (+) or a minus sign (-) in front of positive and negative numbers (think of the *p* as *plus*).

The function nfs() is kind of a combination of nf() and nfp(); it will pad your numbers with 0's, and also include the explicit plus or minus sign at the start (think of the *s* as *sign*).

20.1.2 join()

You can manually paste together two String objects with the plus sign (+):

```
String a = "apple";
String b = "baker";
String result = a+b;
println("result="+result);
```

This prints out

```
result=applebaker
```

Suppose I had a whole bunch of words that I wanted to put together, but I wanted spaces between them. I could do it by hand:

```
String a = "apple";
String b = "baker";
String c = "pie";
String d = "maker";
String result = a+" "+b+" "+c+" "+d;
println("result="+result);
```

This prints out

```
result=apple baker pie maker
```

That worked fine, but if I had a big list of words to assemble, typing in all the blanks by hand would become tiring very quickly. I could simplify things by putting the words into an array of `Strings`:

```
String [] poem = new String[4];
poem[0] = "apple";
poem[1] = "baker";
poem[2] = "pie";
poem[3] = "maker";
String result = "";   // This String starts out empty
for (int i=0; i<poem.length; i++) {
   result = result+' '+poem[i];
}
println("result="+result);
```

Better yet, I could initialize the array when I declare it:

```
String [] poem = { "apple", "baker", "pie", "maker" };
String result = "";
for (int i=0; i<poem.length; i++) {
   result = result+' '+poem[i];
}
println("result="+result);
```

Happily, there's a built-in command that runs this loop for us. It's called `join()`, and it takes two inputs. The first is an array of `String` objects. The second input is a `String` that will be inserted between each pair of `Strings` in the first argument. I can replace the *for loop* above with this line:

```
String result = join(poem, " ");
```

If you run this, the results are identical to what we saw before. Because `join()` takes a `String` in the second argument, we can put anything in there:

```
String result = join(poem, " <*ZING*> ");
```

This produces this result:

```
result=apple <*ZING*> baker <*ZING*> pie <*ZING*> maker
```

I think we can all agree this greatly improves the poem.

20.1.3   split()

The mirror-image routine to `join()` is `split()`. This takes a `String` and a single `char`. It chops up your `String` into words, using that `char` to determine where each word starts and ends, and returns to you an array of `Strings`.

Here's `split()` in action:

```
String recipe = "raspberries,chocolate,a roaring fire,and you";
String [] words = split(recipe, ',');
for (int i=0; i<words.length; i++) {
    println("words["+i+"] = "+words[i]);
}
```

This produces the output

```
words[0] = raspberries
words[1] = chocolate
words[2] = a roaring fire
words[3] = and you
```

You can split on any character you like. Probably the most common is the space, ' '. You can use `split()` with a space to break up a line of text into individual words. We did something like that in Chapter 17, where we used `split()` with a tab to break up our input lines, which were pairs of numbers separated by tabs.

If you want to split on multiple characters, you can use `splitTokens()`. As an example, I'll split the above example on both commas *and* spaces:

```
String recipe = "raspberries,chocolate,a roaring fire,and you";
String [] words = splitTokens(recipe, ", ");
for (int i=0; i<words.length; i++) {
    println("words["+i+"] = "+words[i]);
}
```

Notice that I changed the second argument from the single character ',' to the two-character `String` ", ". The single quotes (which identify the type `char`) had to change to double quotes (which identify the type `String`). The output of this program is

```
words[0] = raspberries
words[1] = chocolate
words[2] = a
words[3] = roaring
words[4] = fire
words[5] = and
words[6] = you
```

20.1.4 trim()

The trim() function is a great little utility that simply removes any white space (spaces, newlines, and tabs) from the start and end of your String:

```
String story = "\n\n        She threw back her head and laughed!    \n";
println("<"+story+">");
println("<"+trim(story)+">");
```

You'll notice that I've added angle brackets around each printed piece so we can clearly see where they begin and end. Here's the output of this program:

```
<

She threw back her head and laughed!
>
<She threw back her head and laughed!>
```

Yup, trim() works as advertised.

20.1.5 match() and matchAll()

Suppose that you have a String variable and you want to search within it for other strings. This would be useful if, for example, you wanted to do your own search-and-replace operation.

Processing offers you a powerful, high-octane searching function called match(). This routine takes the string you want to search and a *regular expression*, which is a structured way of writing a pattern that can match anything from a particular string to any string that has various pieces of the right form. For example, you might search for "all words that start with *a*, somewhere later have two *l*'s in a row, and end with *s*." You can write that in a regular expression, and you'd get back words like "alligators," "appellations," and "anthills" (if they were in your original string, of course).

Regular expressions are anything but simple. Entire books exist dedicated to this single topic! So I'm definitely not going to get into it here, particularly since this isn't something we often use when creating images and animations (for instance, I don't use regular expressions anywhere in this book). If you find that you really need to search for general patterns of strings inside of other strings, you'll find lots of terrific tutorials and documentation online; just search on *regular expression*. Since most languages use regular expressions in much the same way, if you understand how they're used in some other language, you're probably just a short hop from using them in Processing.

But it doesn't stop there. If you want do this kind of general pattern-based searching not on a single string but instead on a whole array of strings at once, then there's an even more super-hyper-atomic-powered upgrade called matchAll() that fills the bill. Check the online documentation if you find yourself doing a whole lot of searching for strings inside of other strings.

20.2 Showing Strings

Unlike the other graphics we've seen, drawing text in Processing requires you to do a little work up front. It's not much, but the steps you need to take will make a lot more sense once you have a general picture of what's going on behind the scenes, so let's discuss that a little bit now.

A *font*, or *typeface*, is a file on your hard drive that tells the computer how to draw every letter, number, and symbol that a designer has created for a specific style of text. Your computer probably came with a few dozen typeface files already installed as part of the operating system. You can also download free fonts from the web; there are thousands and thousands of them available, in endless variations and styles, designed by enthusiastic amateurs who share their work freely. And you can buy many thousands more professionally designed typefaces.

Once you have a font file on your disk, you have to tell the computer to *install* it. That means the computer reads the file and puts it into active memory. Installing a font is necessary if you want to use it. Before you've installed it, a font is just another file on your hard drive. Installing it makes it *active* and available. Your operating system comes with a bunch of preinstalled fonts so that you can do basic work like word processing and web surfing. If you want to use any of the tens of thousands of additional fonts out there, you'll need to install them first.

Each font that's installed takes up some memory and requires some time to read when your computer starts up, so most people who deal with huge numbers of typefaces manage their fonts by installing them when necessary for a given project and then un-installing them. If you have just a few dozen (or even a few hundred) typefaces, you probably don't have to worry about managing them.

Unlike most programs, Processing doesn't use these installed fonts directly. Instead, Processing first transforms each font you want to use into its own private format before it can use it. In practice, that means you have to explicitly tell Processing to do that.

Here is the general plan for using a given font in your project. First, make sure the font is installed. Next, go to Processing's *Tools* menu and select *Create Font*. From that window, select the font you want to use. Type in the size that you want to use it at and give it a name. Processing then goes off and draws every character in that font, saving the resulting image (and some other information) in a file. Processing looks for a folder called *data* in the same folder as your sketch. If there is no such folder, Processing makes one. Then it saves the font file in that folder.

Now whenever you ask Processing to draw a letter, such as a capital *A*, it finds the data folder, looks inside for the font image, reads that image, locates the piece of the picture that holds the capital *A*, and copies those pixels to the screen. That's why you have to tell Processing what size you want it to use for the font: it creates that image using characters of the size you specify.

You can later tell Processing to actually draw the characters onscreen at any size. Suppose that you originally saved your font at 24 points. If you then draw it smaller, say at 13 points, Processing will do its best to shrink down each letter-sized image, but that uses a different process than the high-quality process used when the font is built using Create Font. The result is that the text won't look as nice as if you'd saved it at 13 points in the first place.

You can also draw your characters larger than the size you saved them at, but if you have experience with enlarging digital pictures, you know how that's going to turn out if you enlarge by too much: the characters are going to look chunky and blocky. Often, scaling will work out nicely enough that you can get away with it for sizes that are close to the one you originally chose, but for the best results, you'll want to create your typeface image at the size you're going to display. If you're going to want to use the same typeface at multiple sizes, there's no reason not to save it multiple times; just be sure that your file names clearly identify the size (e.g., `Courier-14`) so that you can specify the proper one later.

You can't look at Processing's prerendered font file directly because it's not a standard image file like a .jpg or .tiff. It's in a strange custom format that you'll probably never deal with directly.

Why does Processing do all of this craziness? Remember that a font isn't available to most programs unless it's installed. Suppose you write a program in Processing and you've spent a long time choosing just the right typeface and making it look exactly the way you want it. Then you send your program to a friend, or you run it on someone else's computer. If they don't have that font installed, Processing won't be able to show the text in the font you worked so hard on. Like word processors and web browsers in this situation, it will try to find another font to substitute for your original. That might look okay, but it might look horrible.

Rather than force everyone who runs your program to obtain and install every typeface you use (which might involve purchasing them, if some or all are commercial fonts), Processing uses its own typeface images. As long as you have the typeface picture, you don't need to have the font installed; you don't even need to have the font at all. By predrawing fonts in this way, Processing is able to essentially keep a local copy of the typeface associated with your sketch but without running into issues of font purchasing, ownership, or installation.

The prerendered font images can be a hassle to create and manage, but they were designed to eliminate the even bigger hassle of dealing with fonts on every system that will run your program, whether it's a web browser, museum kiosk, or smartphone.

As I mentioned, these font files go into a folder called data located in the same directory as your sketch. If you're working on a temporary project with no name, Processing takes care of managing things for you. If you have named a folder for your sketch, then of course they go in there. This means that if you created a project and used the Create Font tool to build a certain font (say, 14-point Courier) and then you start a new project that will also use that typeface, you'll need to build that font again so that a new copy will exist in your new project (you could just copy the file over if you prefer).

By the way, there is a way to create a font from within a running program (rather than using the Create Font tool), but that's a tricky thing to do. See the documentation on `createFont()` if you need to do this.

That's the end of the background. To recap, you install fonts on your computer. You use Create Font to take an installed font and create a Processing-friendly "font picture" file of that font at a given size, and that file goes into a folder called data in your sketch's directory (you can recognize that file because it will have the name you gave it with an extension of `.vlw`). Then you can use it in Processing.

By the way, you can then uninstall the font at that point if you want because Processing will use its own version from then on.

So let's put something up on the screen already! We have to first create an object that will tell Processing which Processing-ready typeface file we want to use. That object has type `PFont`:

```
PFont MyFont;
```

To actually fill that object up with a font, call `loadFont()` with the name of the font file as you saved it. Processing's font files end with `.vlw`, so include that in the name. Here's an example of loading up a file I called `Courier-48.vlw` when I created it with Create Font. As you can tell from the name, this is the Courier font at 48 points:

```
MyFont = loadFont("Courier-48.vlw");
```

We can, as always, roll the declaration and assignment together into one statement:

```
PFont MyFont = loadFont("Courier-48.vlw");
```

Some of your sketches might have a whole lot of fonts defined at once for use in different places or times. When you want to draw some text, you have to tell Processing which of these fonts it should use. You do this by calling `textFont()` with the `PFont` object you want to use:

```
textFont(MyFont);
```

This is one place where you can change the size of your font, if you want. The call above will cause the characters in the object `MyFont` to be drawn onscreen at the same size that was used to save them. But if you give `textFont()` a second argument, the characters will be zoomed up or down before drawing so that they come out at the desired size. To get 36-point characters, I'd say

```
textFont(MyFont, 36);
```

Now to display text, just call `text()` with three arguments: the string to be drawn and the *x*- and *y*-coordinates of the lower-left corner of the first letter.

```
text("Blueberry Pie!", 50, 100);
```

The text is drawn using the current fill color. Let's package this all up into a program. I'll use a friendly typeface called Puschkin, which I saved at 48 points.

Figure 20.1. Displaying type. (type/sketches/type01/type01.pde)

```
void setup() {
   size(600, 400);
   background(92, 39, 44);
   fill(232, 200, 72);
   PFont myFont = loadFont("Puschkin-48.vlw");
   textFont(myFont);
   text("Blueberry Pie!", 50, 100);
}
```

(See output in Figure 20.1. Full program in type/sketches/type01/type01.pde)

If this doesn't work for you, you're probably getting an error, with the `loadFont()` call highlighted, and an error message like

```
Could not load font Puschkin-48.vlw.  Make sure that the font has
been copied to the data folder of your sketch.
```

That's a pretty darned good error message! If the Puschkin font isn't installed on your computer, but you once used Create Font in the past to make a 48-point image of it, then you can find that old file and copy it in. But if it's currently installed, it's probably easier and faster just to use Create Font and make a new version, which automatically is saved in the right place.

Of course, if you don't have the font file on your drive, or you don't have it installed, you can just copy the `.vlw` file I saved with this sketch.

I'd like to dress this up a bit. I know—I'll put a blue box under the phrase "Blueberry Pie!" because that's the kind of avant-garde thinking that builds reputations. I know that the lower-left corner of the first letter B is at $(50, 100)$, because that's where we put it with `text()`. But how wide and how tall should the background box be?

The width of a string of a text can be found from the function `textWidth()`. It basically pretends to draw the string you give it, using all the current settings, and tells you how wide the result will be. Let's use this to determine the width of the box. I'll draw the box so that there's a 25-pixel border around the phrase. We don't yet know the height of the box, so I'll make a guess; we'll fix that in a moment.

To keep things clear, I'll move the word we're going to print into a `String` variable so I can hand it to `textWidth()` first and then `text()` later. I'll also stash the lower-left corner of the box in some new variables.

```
void setup() {
   size(600, 400);
   background(92, 39, 44);
   float xText = 100;
   float yText = 200;
   float border = 25;

   PFont myFont = loadFont("Puschkin-48.vlw");
   textFont(myFont);

   String message = "Blueberry Pie!";
   float textWid = textWidth(message); //find the message width

   fill(60, 55, 196);    // blue color
   rect(xText-border, yText-100, textWid+2*border, 200);
   fill(232, 200, 72);     // draw type in yellow
   text(message, xText, yText);
   noLoop();
}
```

(See output in Figure 20.2. Full program in type/sketches/type02/type02.pde)

Figure 20.2. Putting a box around the type. (type/sketches/type02/type02.pde)

Figure 20.3. Type descriptors.

To find the width of the text we called `textWidth()`, so to find the height we use `textHeight()`, right? Strangely, there is no `textHeight()`. Weird. It just isn't there.

Happily, we can get this information, but it takes two function calls. By analogy, suppose you want to learn someone's height, but they will only tell us the distances from their toes to their belt and from their belt to the top of their head. We can just add up the two numbers to get their height.

Consider the word *frog*. Most of the letters sit on top of the same horizontal line; only the lower loop of the g drops below it. Similarly, most of the letters are only as high as another horizontal line; only the vertical part of the f rises above it. The height of the two letters in the middle, from their shared *baseline* to the shared line across their tops, is called by typographers the letter's *x-height*. The part of the f that rises up above the *x*-height is called the f's *ascender*, and the part of the g that drops below the baseline is called the *descender*. Naturally enough, the heights of the ascender and descender are called the *ascender height* and *descender height*. The distance from the baseline to the top of a capital letter is called the *cap height*. Figure 20.3 shows these measurements.

Processing lets us get the distance from the baseline to the top of the ascender with the call `textAscent()`. It tells us the distance from the baseline to the bottom of the descender with `textDescent()`. Figure 20.4 shows what these functions measure. Adding those together gives us the distance from the bottom of the g to the top of the f. Weirdly, not only is there no way to get the cap height, there's also no way to simply get the very useful x-height. You can't find out how tall the letter *e* is, for example.

For now, we can add together the two calls we've just seen to find the total text height from the bottom of the descender to the top of the ascender:

```
float textUpper = textAscent();
float textLower = textDescent();
float textHeight = textLower + textUpper;
```

Figure 20.4. Processing's type-measuring functions.

Of course, if we're drawing a string that doesn't have an ascender or descender, this measurement will be taller than the type itself.

We'll see in Chapter 22 that we can draw text to an *off screen* image rather than to the screen. I'll show how we can use that feature to write our own routine that can make a good guess of a font's *x*-height. Figure 22.13 shows the result.

Back to the main discussion, now that we know the height of the font from baseline to ascender, we can use that information to draw our background rectangle. To find the upper edge, we start at the bottom of the first letter, stored in `yText`, and move up by (that is, subtract) `textUpper` and then move up again by `border`. The height of the rectangle is the height of the text plus two borders:

```
float rectTop = yText - textUpper - border;
float rectHgt = textHeight + 2*border;
rect(xText-border, rectTop, textWid+2*border, recthgt);
```

We can even center everything. Here's the whole program:

```
void setup() {
   size(600, 400);
   background(92, 39, 44);
   float xText = 100;
   float yText = 200;
   float border = 25;

   PFont myFont = loadFont("Puschkin-48.vlw");
   textFont(myFont);        // make myFont the active font

   String message = "Blueberry Pie!";
   float textWid = textWidth(message);
   float textUpper = textAscent();
   float textLower = textDescent();
   float textHeight = textLower + textUpper;

   xText = (width/2.0) - (textWid/2.0);
   yText = (height/2.0) + (textHeight/2.0);

   noStroke();
   fill(60, 55, 196);       // the blue box
   float rectTop = yText - textUpper - border;
   float rectHgt = textHeight + 2*border;
   rect(xText-border, rectTop, textWid+2*border, rectHgt);
   fill(232, 200, 72);      // draw in yellow
   text(message, xText, yText);
   noLoop();
}
```

(See output in Figure 20.5. Full program in type/sketches/type03/type03.pde)

Figure 20.5. A nicely arranged box. (type/sketches/type03/type03.pde)

That's a long way to go for just one little message, but now that we're familiar with the tools, we can do something more interesting.

Let's strip this back down to just one simple message that I'll place on the screen by hand. I'll make it longer than before, though:

```
void setup() {
    size(600, 400);
    background(92, 39, 44);
    fill(232, 200, 72);       // draw in yellow
    PFont myFont = loadFont("Puschkin-48.vlw");
    textFont(myFont);         // make myFont the active font
    String message = "Blueberry Pie is a delicious summertime treat!";
    text(message, 50, 100);
}
```

(See output in Figure 20.6. Full program in type/sketches/type04/type04.pde)

That's not very good; the text runs right off the right edge of the screen. I can imagine a routine that would try to break up this text into shorter lines. It would use split() to break up the message into words and then it would use textWidth() to measure the width of each word. It would also measure the width of one space (that is, textWidth(" ")). Then the routine would display the words, starting at the left edge and showing one word after another, moving right by each word's width plus a space, until the next word would fall off the right edge. Then it would do what a text editor does: move down by the height of the text plus a little more for space, go to the far left, and start again.

Figure 20.6. The type is wider than the window. (type/sketches/type04/type04.pde)

If you're feeling in the mood, I encourage you to write that program! It's not too tricky, and it will give you a chance to apply some of the things we've been talking about.

If you're not in the mood, that's okay too, because Processing has a built-in function for doing just that. And it's just our old friend `text()`! We know that the first argument

Figure 20.7. Fitting type to a box. (type/sketches/type05/type05.pde)

Figure 20.8. Increasing the space between lines. (type/sketches/type06/type06.pde)

to text() is the string to draw and then come the *x*- and *y*-coordinates of the lower-left corner of the first letter. But if you give it two more values, they specify the width and height of a box in which the text should be displayed. If a word would fall off the right side of the box, it picks up again on a new line. Any text that falls off the bottom simply doesn't get displayed. Here's an example:

```
text(message, 50, 100, 500, 200);
```

(See output in Figure 20.7. Full program in type/sketches/type05/type05.pde)

You can increase or decrease the amount of space between each line by calling textLeading(). Larger values of *leading* will create more empty space between lines (leading is a typographer's term for how closely you set together successive lines of text):

```
textLeading(70);
text(message, 50, 100, 500, 300);
```

(See output in Figure 20.8. Full program in type/sketches/type06/type06.pde)

Note that I had to make the box a little deeper in order to include the spaced-apart lines.

We can also run the leading the other way and tighten the lines up:

```
textLeading(40);
```

(See output in Figure 20.9. Full program in type/sketches/type07/type07.pde)

You can change whether the text is left justified, right justified, or centered by calling textAlign() with the arguments LEFT, RIGHT, or CENTER.

Figure 20.9. Decreasing the space between lines. (type/sketches/type07/text07.pde)

Figure 20.10. Centering text. (type/sketches/text08/text08.pde)

```
textAlign(CENTER);
text(message, 50, 100, 500, 200);
```

(See output in Figure 20.10. Full program in type/sketches/test08/test08.pde)

Of course, you can use both of these calls:

```
textLeading(40);
textAlign(CENTER);
text(message, 50, 100, 500, 200);
```

(See output in Figure 20.11. Full program in type/sketches/type09/type09.pde)

Figure 20.11. Text with tighter leading. (type/sketches/type09/type09.pde)

Now that we can display text, let's do something more interesting. How about a fortune cookie program? Every time the frame updates, it displays a couple of new fortune cookies.

We could of course type in a few dozen cookies, but let's do it *Mad Libs* style. I'll write down two generic fortunes that have blanks and then we'll fill in the blanks with random entries chosen from a list. Here are my two generic fortunes, where I've marked the slots to be filled in with angle brackets:

1. <Number> <Animal>s are out to get <Person>.

2. <When>'s lucky sandwich is <Food> on <Bread>.

First off, I need some entries to go into the blanks. I just cooked up some random words and phrases to go into each of these slots.

```
String [] Number = split("Three,Seventeen,Some,A few,Lots of,Most,No", ',');
String [] Animal = split("lion,giraffe,elephantalope,worm", ',');
String [] Person = split("you,your neighbor,Uncle Bob,Crazy Harry", ',');
String [] When = split("Today,This week,Yesterday,March,2003", ',');
String [] Food = split("macaroni,roasted apple,peanut brittle,frog", ',');
String [] Bread = split("rye,wheat,multi-grain,pita,a hot-dog bun", ',');
```

You can see that I'm making life easy on myself by doing a few things at once. On each line I'm listing all the words for one category in a single string separated by commas, then I'm using `split()` to chop that up into an array of `Strings`, and then I'm assigning that resulting array into a newly declared array of `Strings`.

Next I need to define the little strings that will serve as the glue between these values; these are the fixed bits that will be the same in every fortune. I'll name them by fortune number and then where they are in the list:

```
String F1_1 = "1. ";
String F1_2 = " ";
String F1_3 = "s are out to get ";
String F1_4 = ".";
String F2_1 = "2. ";
String F2_2 = "'s lucky sandwich is ";
String F2_3 = " on ";
String F2_4 = ".";
```

Notice that I built spaces into some of these little glue strings. That way, I didn't have to put spaces into the big lists above, and I won't have to add them in manually later. I couldn't just use `join()` with spaces because some of the glue words don't begin with a space (for example, because I want to refer to animals in the plural, `F1_3` begins with s, not a blank).

Next, I'll declare and initialize the font, create the display window, and make a call to `frameRate()` to get updates every three seconds (by asking for 1/3 of a frame per second).

```
PFont FortuneFont;

void setup() {
   size(600, 400);
   smooth();
   FortuneFont = loadFont("AmericanTypewriter-48.vlw");
   textAlign(LEFT);
   textFont(FortuneFont, 36);
   frameRate(1/3.0);
}

void draw() {
   background(240);
}
```

(Full program in type/sketches/fortune01/fortune01.pde)

So far, so good. Let's dig into draw(). We want to clear the background first, of course. Then we'll pick a color for fortune number 1. For the fortune itself, I'll make up a single long string by sticking together each of the strings. The glue strings I'll just use by name. For each of the template words, I'll do something like this:

```
Animal[int(random(0, Animal.length))]
```

This call to random() gives me a number from 0 to the number of entries in the Animal array. Remember that a call of the form random(a, b) gives back numbers from a up to (but not including) b. That *not including* is essential for us. Suppose that the array Animal has five entries. We know that they're numbered 0 to 4. So asking for Animal[5] would cause the program to crash. If we ask for random(0, 5), we'll get back numbers from 0 to 4.9999..., but never quite reaching 5. When we pass those numbers to int(), it throws away everything to the right of the decimal point, leaving us with numbers from 0 to 4.

By pasting together the fixed glue words with these randomly chosen words, we get a fortune:

```
String message1 = F1_1 + Number[int(random(0, Number.length))] +
                  F1_2 + Animal[int(random(0, Animal.length))] +
                  F1_3 + Person[int(random(0, Person.length))] +
                  F1_4;
```

Then we can display this fortune, constrained to a box:

```
text(message1, 50, 50, 500, 150);
```

We can do the very same for fortune number 2. Here's the complete listing for the program, including the completed draw():

```
// Fortune cookie program
// version 1.0 - AG 24 April 2009
// 1. <Number> <Animal>s are out to get <Person>.
// 2. <When>'s lucky sandwich is <Food> on <Bread>.

String [] Number = split("Three,Seventeen,Some,A few,Lots of,Most,No", ',');
String [] Animal = split("lion,giraffe,elephantalope,worm", ',');
String [] Person = split("you,your neighbor,Uncle Bob,Crazy Harry", ',');
String [] When = split("Today,This week,Yesterday,March,2003", ',');
String [] Food = split("macaroni,roasted apple,peanut brittle,frog", ',');
String [] Bread = split("rye,wheat,multi-grain,pita,a hot-dog bun", ',');

String F1_1 = "1. ";
String F1_2 = " ";
String F1_3 = "s are out to get ";
String F1_4 = ".";
String F2_1 = "2. ";
String F2_2 = "'s lucky sandwich is ";
String F2_3 = " on ";
String F2_4 = ".";

void setup() {
   size(600, 400);
   smooth();
   PFont fortuneFont = loadFont("AmericanTypewriter-48.vlw");
   textAlign(LEFT);
   textFont(fortuneFont, 36);
   frameRate(1/3.0);
}

void draw() {
   background(240);

   fill(84, 65, 19);  // brown
   String message1 = F1_1 + Number[int(random(0, Number.length))] +
                     F1_2 + Animal[int(random(0, Animal.length))] +
                     F1_3 + Person[int(random(0, Person.length))] + F1_4;
   text(message1, 50, 50, 500, 175);

   fill(39, 68, 92);  // dark blue
   String message2 = F2_1 + When[int(random(0, When.length))] +
                     F2_2 + Food[int(random(0, Food.length))] +
                     F2_3 + Bread[int(random(0, Bread.length))] + F2_4;
   text(message2, 50, 200, 500, 175);
}
```

(See output in Figure 20.12. Full program in type/sketches/fortune02/fortune02.pde)

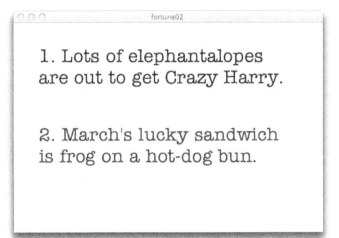

Figure 20.12. The fortune cookie program. (type/sketches/fortune02/fortune02.pde)

Another couple of fortunes are in Figure 20.13 and Figure 20.14.

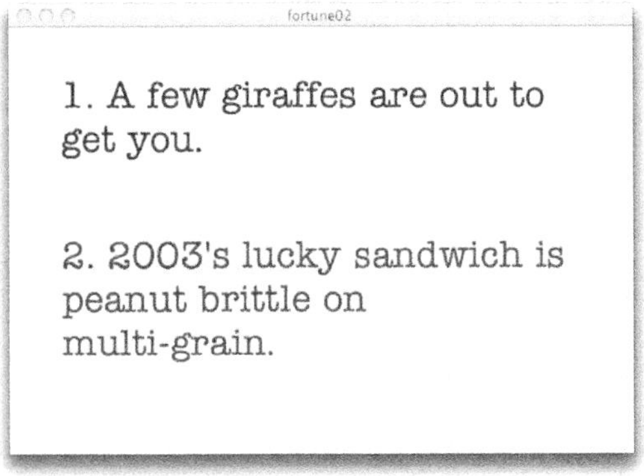

Figure 20.13. Another fortune. 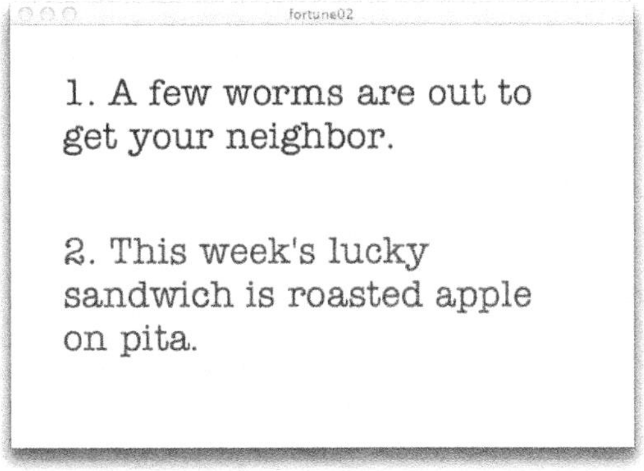   **Figure 20.14.** Another fortune.

20.2.1 Transforming Type

Text is a graphic object like any other, and if you apply transformations to your scene, the text will transform as well.

Let's make a simple text animation. For this little program, I'll set the text mode to CENTER and then translate and scale around the point where I want the bottom-center of the text to appear.

To control the scaling, I've made a little number pattern. By feeding a scaled version of frameCount to sin(), I get a smoothly changing value from −1 to 1 (I picked a scaling factor of 0.07 by trial and error—bigger values cause faster bouncing). I want the scale factor to be in the range 0.5 to 1, so I use map() to convert the number from (−1, 1) to (0.5, 1), and then I hand it to scale() to control the size of the text.

```
void setup() {
    size(600, 400);
    smooth();
    PFont fortuneFont = loadFont("MarkerFelt-Wide-48.vlw");
    textAlign(LEFT);
    textFont(fortuneFont, 36);
    fill(194, 122, 12);
}

void draw() {
    background(11, 55, 69);
    float sinVal = sin(frameCount * .07);
    float scaleMul = map(sinVal, -1, 1, .5, 1);
    translate(100, 200);
    scale(scaleMul);
    text("Delicious apricots!", 0, 0);
}
```

(See output in Figure 20.15. Full program in type/sketches/bouncer1/bouncer1.pde)

Figure 20.15. Bouncing type (frame from animation). (type/sketches/bouncer1/bouncer1.pde)

Notice that the scaling motion is pleasing at the extremes; there's no sharp change in size at either end. That's thanks to the `sin()` function, which produces this kind of smoothly changing pattern.

I mentioned earlier that you can choose at what size the font should appear on the screen when you set the active font with `textFont()`. You can also change the size on the fly with `textSize()`. This is great when you're developing your program. You can save the font at any convenient size with the Create Font tool, and then adjust it with `textSize()` as you work. When you're done, if you end up with just a few different sizes for each font, you can consider explicitly creating a file for each with the Create Font tool, which will give you the cleanest, sharpest-looking results for all your text. Of course, if you're changing the size of the text over a range, as in the scaling example above, you'll probably want to use just one font and stick with it. As a rule of thumb, build the font at the largest size you think it'll appear on the screen. Making the font smaller over the course of the program will, in general, look better than making it bigger.

Lots of projects use type like just another graphic element. Using the default renderer and rendering modes, most of the time type looks just fine. But some projects require beautiful, crisp type of the highest quality. If you need that kind of control, then you'll want to know about `textMode()`.

It takes three arguments: MODEL (the default), SCREEN, or SHAPE. The default is MODEL.

In the examples we've seen so far, I haven't called `textMode()`, so the default mode (MODEL) has been active, and it's worked well. We can put type anywhere we want, and we can rotate and scale it, too. It's simple and works fine.

Alternatively, you can switch to SCREEN mode. Things get a little messier here. With the optional P2D and P3D renderers, type drawn with this option will be drawn much faster and will usually look much better than with the default renderer. On the other hand, if you're using the default JAVA2D renderer or the optional OPENGL renderer, your renderings in SCREEN mode will be slower, but they will still look better. In SCREEN mode, the characters are copied directly out of the prerendered type image file and onto the window, so you can't change their size (any calls to `textSize()` just get ignored).

The SHAPE mode is more complicated still and works only with the PDF and OPENGL renderers. It's for special cases when you want to save your drawing commands directly into files.

I recommend sticking with the default unless you really need to switch. If you need the increased precision and beauty of SCREEN mode, make sure you're using a renderer that takes advantage of it and also supports all the other stuff your project requires. Also read the latest online documentation for `textMode()` and the renderer you're using because with each new release of Processing, the details can change, and the perfect choice for one version of the system might be less than perfect for another.

Let's do another project with animated type. This time I'll spin the type around, as if it was on a carousel.

Figure 20.16. A short message. (type/sketches/spintext01/spintext01.pde)

As usual, we'll start with a skeleton. Here I'll set up my colors and make my font.

```
void setup()
{
   size(600, 400);
   PFont MyFont = loadFont("ArnoPro-Bold-48.vlw");
   textFont(MyFont);
}

void draw() {
   fill(199, 172, 115);
   background(89, 9, 21);
   String message = "Pomegranate and lime juice ";
   text(message, 10, 200);
}
```

(See output in Figure 20.16. Full program in type/sketches/spintext01/spintext01.pde)

I'm using a font called ArnoPro-Bold which I've saved at 48 points.

Now let's grab these characters one by one so we can place them. I'll make a loop to access each character. Just to be sure it's working, I'll display each one along a diagonal, since I can cook up those coordinates pretty easily.

```
void draw() {
   fill(199, 172, 115);
   background(89, 9, 21);
   String message = "Pomegranate and lime juice";
```

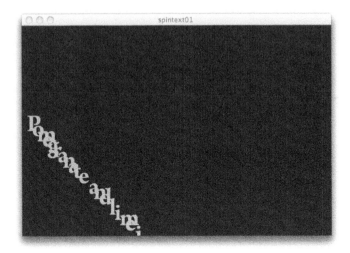

Figure 20.17. Placing characters one at a time. (type/sketches/spintext02/spintext02.pde)

```
for (int i=0; i<message.length(); i++) {
    char thisChar = message.charAt(i);
    text(thisChar, 10+(10*i), 200+(10*i));
  }
}
```

(See output in Figure 20.17. Full program in type/sketches/spintext02/spintext02.pde)

Pretty nice. Ugly, but working. A word on efficiency: you'll notice that in the loop, my test uses `i<message.length()`. Processing has to run that test once each time through the loop, meaning that if there are 26 characters (as there are here), then `message.length()` will get called 26 times. Each call takes some time. Now in this little program that's completely under the radar, but in an animation where there's lots of other things going on, we could save a tiny bit of time by calling `message.length()` just once and storing the result in a variable. In general, this is a good idea because you want your tests to be tight and fast (if that function was a slowpoke, even in a little program like this you might see a slowdown).

So let's make our program shipshape. I'll find the message length just once, save it, and write the test to use that saved value:

```
int numChars = message.length();
for (int i=0; i<numChars; i++) {
```

(Full program in type/sketches/spintext03/spintext03.pde)

Now let's put these on a circle. I'll compute an angle from 0 to 360 degrees based on how far `i` has made it through the loop and then I'll apply the recipe from Chapter 18

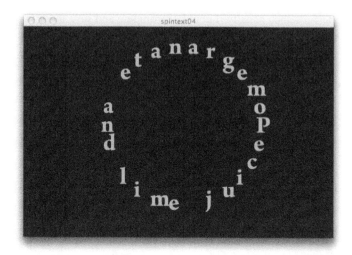

Figure 20.18. Type in a circle. (type/sketches/spintext04/spintext04.pde)

for computing the points around a circle using calls to `sin()` and `cos()`. After taking the sine and cosine of that angle, I'll add it to the center of the screen and place the character. I'll create a variable called `radius` to set the size of the circle. I'll call my angle `theta` (for the Greek letter θ), which is often used in geometry to indicate an angle.

```
void draw() {
    fill(199, 172, 115);
    background(89, 9, 21);
    String message = "Pomegranate and lime juice";
    float radius = 150;
    int numChars = message.length();
    for (int i=0; i<numChars; i++) {
        char thisChar = message.charAt(i);
        float theta = map(i, 0, numChars, radians(0), radians(360));
        float xpos = 300 + (radius * cos(theta));
        float ypos = 200 - (radius * sin(theta));
        text(thisChar, xpos, ypos);
    }
}
```

(See output in Figure 20.18. Full program in type/sketches/spintext04/spintext04.pde)

Uh-oh. Now that the letters are in a loop, I need to add a space to the end of the word "juice." No problem.

You'll see I'm calling `radians(0)` and `radians(360)` for every letter. These values never change, so there's no reason for me to call `radians()` every time and pay that little performance penalty. I could precompute and save these two values, and then use the saved variables, like I did for the message length. For now, I'll leave these in.

Let's get this moving. All I need to do is change the angle `theta` on every frame. I can just add (or subtract) a number based on `frameCount`. After a little trial and error, I found that subtracting 0.01 on each frame caused the letters to spin at a pleasing rate on my computer:

```
float theta = map(i, 0, numChars, radians(0), radians(360));
theta -= frameCount * .01;
```

(See output in Figure 20.19. Full program in type/sketches/spintext05/spintext05.pde)

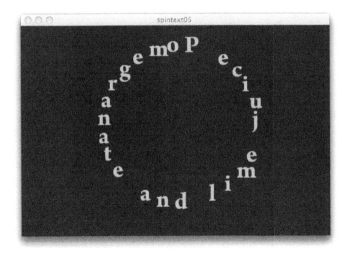

Figure 20.19. Type spinning in a circle (frame from animation).
(type/sketches/spintext05/spintext05.pde)

They look like they're spinning in a circle, not like they're going around some surface in 3D. I'll try making the circle a little shorter than it is wide by scaling the *y* value by something less than one.

```
float ypos = 200 - (radius * 0.6 * sin(theta));
```

While I'm at it, I'll also increase the size of `radius` to fill more of the window. Here's the complete program:

```
void setup()
{
  size(600, 400);
```

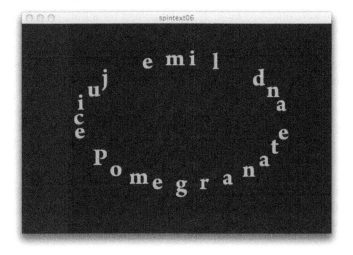

Figure 20.20. Type spinning in a squished circle (frame from animation). (type/sketches/spintext06/spintext06.pde)

```
  PFont MyFont = loadFont("ArnoPro-Bold-48.vlw");
  textFont(MyFont);
}

void draw() {
   fill(199, 172, 115);
   background(89, 9, 21);
   String message = "Pomegranate and lime juice ";
   float radius = 200;
   int numChars = message.length();
   for (int i=0; i<numChars; i++) {
      char thisChar = message.charAt(i);
      float theta = map(i, 0, numChars, radians(0), radians(360));
      theta -= frameCount * .01;
      float xpos = 300 + (radius * cos(theta));
      float ypos = 200 - (radius * 0.6 * sin(theta));
      text(thisChar, xpos, ypos);
   }
}
```

(See output in Figure 20.20. Full program in type/sketches/spintext06/spintext06.pde)

Because the path is compressed a little bit vertically, this looks to me like type that's going around a carousel. The illusion might be enhanced if there was something like a pole in the middle of the ring so that the "near" letters were in front of the pole, but the "far" letters were obscured by it. If you're itching for a little project, enhance this version to have one or more objects like that. (Hint: The easiest way to pull this off is to draw everything in the order that you want it to appear in, back to front. That means you'd draw the far-away letters, then the pole or other objects that are in front of them, then the nearer letters.)

The 3D feeling could be further enhanced by simulating perspective. If the letters scaled in size so that those near the bottom of the graphics window were larger than those near the top, the larger letters would probably appear to be nearer, and smaller letters would probably appear to be farther away, particularly if they smoothly changed in size as they rotated around the ring (and, seemingly, moved towards and away from us).

Another way to fake depth is to pretend that there's some fog in the scene. As letters get farther away they could take on a color that approaches the background color (reducing contrast).

Chapter 21
3D

Processing isn't just for 2D graphics. As I've mentioned earlier, it supports 3D graphics as well. I love 3D, and it's a lot of fun to develop 3D projects, but it's a huge subject of its own. I could write whole books about nothing but 3D. In fact, I have!

But deep and complex 3D tools aren't part of Processing's bag of tricks. In line with its basic principles to keep things lightweight and easy to use, Processing's 3D functions are nowhere near as extreme or powerful as those you'd find in full-featured 3D programs. If you really want to get into sophisticated or realistic 3D images and movies, you'll probably want to invest your time and energy in one of the large 3D systems designed for just that purpose. But if you just want to mess around with 3D, or you want to do the same sorts of visual sketches in 3D that Processing supports in 2D, then you can have a lot of fun with Processing's 3D features.

The heart of the idea is, of course, that there are now three dimensions (called x, y, and z) rather than only two. But this small change can have big effects.

To get into 3D, I'll start with a boilerplate (or skeleton), like the one we used for 2D. The boilerplate I'm going to use sets up the world as in Figure 21.1. Like 2D, the origin is in the upper-left corner. The positive x-axis runs to the right, and the positive y-axis runs down. But there's also a z-axis, and its positive direction comes towards us out of the screen.

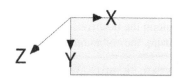

Figure 21.1. The default 3D view.

It might seem a little strange, but the positive z direction indeed comes *towards* you. Points that are placed in the plane of the page (or screen) have a z value of 0. As we push points away from us, they have larger and larger negative values. To bring them closer, we give them larger positive z values.

One way to keep this straight in your head is to remember something called the *left-hand rule* . Processing's 3D system is often called a left-handed coordinate system. Take your left hand and hold it out in front of you, your fingers out straight and pointing down, your thumb pointing to the right, your palm facing you, as in Figure 21.2. Your thumb points in the direction of the positive x-axis, your fingers in positive y, and if you

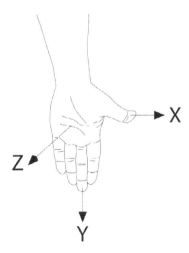

Figure 21.2. The left-hand rule. Your left thumb points towards positive *x*, your fingers towards positive *y*, and your palm towards positive *z*.

push with your palm (holding your hand in this strange way, pushing means bringing it towards you), you're moving in positive *z*.

The left-hand rule tells us not only how to move things by knowing which way is positive but, as we'll soon see, also how to rotate things by knowing which direction around each axis corresponds to a positive angle.

I'm going to jump ahead for a moment and create some 3D objects in order to show you how Processing uses these ideas. I'll create an image that has four boxes. A gray box will sit at the origin, which is now the 3D point $(0,0,0)$. I'll put a red box some distance along the positive *x*-axis, a green box along the positive *y*-axis, and a blue box along the positive *z*-axis. So the colored boxes will be arranged on the *x*, *y*, and *z* axes, using the colors red, green, and blue.

```
void setup() {
  size(600, 600, P3D);
  translate(300, 300, 0);
  background(191, 223, 227);
  fill(128, 128, 128); makeBox(0, 0, 0);      // gray box at origin
  fill(209,  98, 133); makeBox(150, 0, 0);    // red box on +X axis
  fill(153, 229, 149); makeBox(0, 150, 0);    // green box on +Y axis
  fill( 45, 111, 173); makeBox(0, 0, 150);    // blue box on +Z axis
}

void makeBox(float tx, float ty, float tz) {
  pushMatrix();
  translate(tx, ty, tz);
```

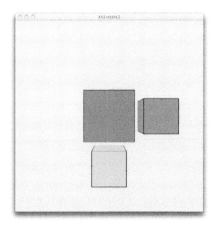

Figure 21.3. The colored boxes in the default view. (3d/sketches/XYZrotate0/XYZrotate0.pde)

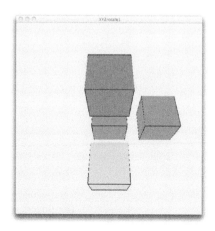

Figure 21.4. Rotating the boxes +30 degrees around the x-axis.
(3d/sketches/XYZrotate1/XYZrotate1.pde)

```
  box(100);
  popMatrix();
}
```

(See output in Figure 21.3. Full program in 3D/sketches/XYZrotate0/XYZrotate0.pde)

In the default view of this scene, we can see the blue box in the middle of the screen. That's because we're located, by default, at a point along the positive z-axis, and we're looking down that axis towards the origin. Since the blue box is also on the positive z-axis, it's right in front of us. We don't see the gray box at the origin because the blue box hides it. To the right, you can see the red box on the positive x-axis, and below is the green box on the positive y-axis. Thanks to perspective, those boxes are a little bit smaller than the z box, and we can see a little of their sides.

Now let's rotate the whole scene around the positive x-axis. I'll rotate it by 30 degrees. All I have to do is add a call to rotateX() near the top:

```
rotateX(radians(30));
```

(See output in Figure 21.4. Full program in 3D/sketches/XYZrotate1/XYZrotate1.pde)

To understand this result, use the left-hand rule. Hold out your left hand with your thumb pointing to the right (like the positive x-axis), and curl your fingers. Figure 21.5 shows the idea.

In Figure 21.4, our little collection of boxes was rotated 30 degrees around your thumb, in the direction from your knuckles to your fingertips.

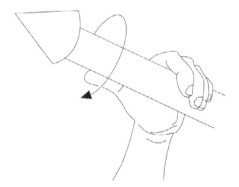

Figure 21.5. The fingers of your left hand curl in the direction of positive rotation when your thumb points along the positive direction of the axis.

If we rotate by -30 degrees, everything spins the other way.

```
rotateX(radians(-30));
```

(See output in Figure 21.6. Full program in 3D/sketches/XYZrotate2/XYZrotate2.pde)

We can also rotate around the other axes. Let's first rotate by positive 30 degrees around the y-axis. Just point your left thumb along the positive y-axis, and your fingers curl in the direction of positive rotation.

```
rotateY(radians(30));
```

(See output in Figure 21.7. Full program in 3D/sketches/XYZrotate3/XYZrotate3.pde)

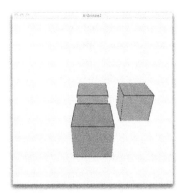

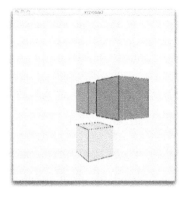

Figure 21.6. Rotating the boxes −30 degrees around the x-axis.
(3d/sketches/XYZrotate2/XYZrotate2.pde)

Figure 21.7. Rotating the boxes +30 degrees around the y-axis.
(3d/sketches/XYZrotate3/XYZrotate3.pde)

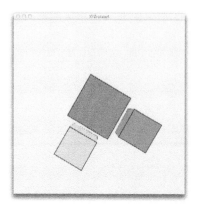

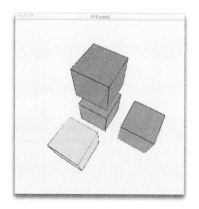

Figure 21.8. Rotating the boxes +30 degrees around the *z*-axis. (3d/sketches/XYZrotate4/XYZrotate4.pde)

Figure 21.9. Rotating the boxes +30 degrees around the *x*-axis, then +30 degrees around *z*. (3d/sketches/XYZrotate5/XYZrotate5.pde)

Now let's rotate by a positive 30 degrees around the *z*-axis.

```
rotateZ(radians(30));
```

(See output in Figure 21.8. Full program in 3D/sketches/XYZrotate4/XYZrotate4.pde)

We can of course accumulate lots of transformations if we want. But just as in 2D, in general, *the same operations in different orders give different results.* Let's see this with two different rotations. First, I'll rotate +30 degrees around *x*, and then +30 degrees around *z*:

```
rotateX(radians(30));
rotateZ(radians(30));
```

(See output in Figure 21.9. Full program in 3D/sketches/XYZrotate5/XYZrotate5.pde)

Now let's simply switch the order and rotate around *z* and then *x*.

```
rotateZ(radians(30));
rotateX(radians(30));
```

(See output in Figure 21.10. Full program in 3D/sketches/XYZrotate6/XYZrotate6.pde)

Different! Although there are occasional exceptions to the rule, in general the order of your transformations matters. Always think through what you're trying to achieve, so you do things in the right sequence. If you think you might not be transforming in the order you mean to, your best bet is always to think it through carefully. You can, of course, just try different sequences and see if one of them does the job, but the number

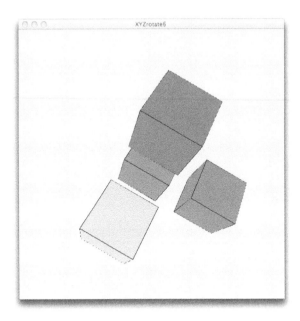

Figure 21.10. Rotating the boxes $+30$ degrees around the z-axis, then $+30$ degrees around x. (3D/sketches/XYZrotate6/XYZrotate6.pde)

of possibilities goes up very fast (if you have three transformations, there are only six possible orders, but if you have six transforms there are 720 possibilities!).

Now that we know how the coordinate system is set up, we can look into putting objects into our scene. In 2D we had all kinds of primitive shapes available: rectangles and ellipses, lines and points, and so on. In 3D it's much simpler. There's only one basic shape: the *polygon* . You can think of a polygon as a little flat piece of cardboard bounded by straight edges. All the triangles and rectangles and quads we've been drawing so far are polygons, though they've all been lying flat in the graphics window. Now we can reach in and peel them off.

21.1   3D Objects

Here's our first program to draw a single 3D polygon on the screen. I'll use some boilerplate code to set up the 3D world inside of `draw()` and then I'll draw a single polygon:

```
import processing.opengl.*;

void setup() {
  size(600, 600, OPENGL);
```

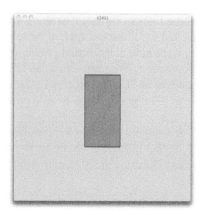

Figure 21.11. Our first 3D polygon. (3D/sketches/p3d01/p3d01.pde)

```
}

void draw() {
  background(225, 192, 145);
  lights();
  camera();
  translate(width/2, height/2);
  scale(width/2, height/2);
  drawPicture();
}

void drawPicture() {
  fill(241, 100, 95);
  drawPolygon();
}

void drawPolygon() {
  beginShape();
  vertex(-.2, -.4, 0);
  vertex( .2, -.4, 0);
  vertex( .2,  .4, 0);
  vertex(-.2,  .4, 0);
  endShape(CLOSE);
}
```

(See output in Figure 21.11. Full program in 3D/sketches/p3d01/p3d01.pde)

Wow. I bet you're impressed. This looks *very* three-dimensional.

Ignore for a moment all the lines in draw() except for the last one. Those other lines are just the boilerplate, and we'll discuss each of those new function calls below. The stuff I want to focus on right now is the actual drawing code, which I've put into its own routine in drawPolygon(). We start with a call to fill(), which specifies the color of the polygon, just like in 2D. The other style functions (like stroke weight and stroke color) also apply to 3D objects. Then I call drawPolygon() to actually draw something.

In drawPolygon() I'm using old friends: beginShape() and endShape(). In between these, I'm using another old friend, vertex(), though you'll see that I'm now calling it with three values. These are the 3D locations of the points of the polygon, named in the order x, y, and z.

So right now we have a rectangle that runs from $(-0.2, 0.2)$ in x, $(-0.4, 0.4)$ in y, and sits at a constant z value of 0.

Let's move things around with the transformation functions.

In 2D, the routine translate() took two values: how far to move in x and y. To move in 3D, just give translate() a third argument, describing how you want to move in z.

Similarly, in 2D, the routine scale() could take two arguments: how much to scale the coordinate system (and thus all further objects) in x and y. In 3D, you can give it a third value to describe how things get stretched in z. But as in 2D, you can give scale() just a single argument, and it will apply to all three axes.

Finally, in 2D, the rotate() command spun things around. In 3D, we have three similar commands: rotateX(), rotateY(), and rotateZ(). These, quite naturally, spin things around each of the three axes. But which way do they go?

As we saw earlier, the left-hand rule gives the answer. With your left hand in front of you, curl your fingers around as though you were holding a carrot. Now hold your thumb straight out, as though you were hitchhiking. Figure 21.5 shows the idea in case it's been a while since you've thumbed a ride while holding a carrot. Holding your hand this way, the direction from your knuckles to your fingertips is the direction of positive rotation.

Now that we know how to create shapes and how to move them, let's get this party started! I'll add one line to our program. Just before we draw the polygon, I'll rotate it around the x-axis. I'll use an angle that's a scaled value of frameCount, so it will grow slowly over time, and the polygon will just spin around and around:

```
rotateX(frameCount * .02);
```

(See output in Figure 21.12. Full program in 3D/sketches/p3d02/p3d02.pde)

It's hard to tell from a still image, of course, but this thing's going around and around. To make that a little more obvious, let's draw another polygon above it. I'll just use translate() to move the coordinate system a little bit farther from us in z (that is, I'll move by a negative amount), so the two polygons are parallel to each other, like two pieces of bread in an air sandwich.

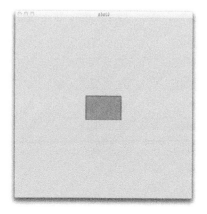

Figure 21.12. A spinning 3D polygon (frame from animation).
(3D/sketches/p3d02/p3d02.pde)

```
translate(0, 0, -.1);
fill(128, 173, 135);
drawPolygon();
```
(See output in Figure 21.13. Full program in 3D/sketches/p3d03/p3d03.pde)

Figure 21.13.   A   pair   of   spinning   3D   polygons   (frame   from   animation).
(3D/sketches/p3d03/p3d03.pde)

To make this a little more interesting, I'll also spin them around the *y*-axis, at a slightly slower speed:

```
rotateY(frameCount * .013);
```

(See output in Figure 21.14. Full program in 3D/sketches/p3d04/p3d04.pde)

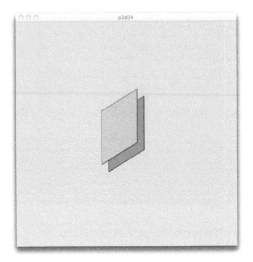

Figure 21.14.   A pair of even-more spinning 3D polygons (frame from animation).
(3D/sketches/p3d04/p3d04.pde)

That's much better. But to really see this in action, let's make a loop out of this. I'll
build a big stack of these polygons and spin them all.

```
color color0 = color(241, 100, 95);
color color1 = color(128, 173, 135);
int numSteps = 30;
for (int i=0; i<numSteps; i++) {
    float a = map(i, 0, numSteps-1, 0, 1);
    fill(lerpColor(color0, color1, a));
    translate(0, 0, -1.0/numSteps);
    drawPolygon();
}
```

(See output in Figure 21.15. Full program in 3D/sketches/p3d05/p3d05.pde)

Remember from Chapter 4 that lerpColor() lets us compute a color "between"
two other colors.

Polygons like these are the heart and soul of 3D in Processing. The system does
offer you two shortcuts for making more complicated objects: a box and a sphere. But
they're both made out of polygons!

The command box() takes either one or three arguments. With three arguments,
you're defining the lengths of the sides of the box in x, y, and z. If you give it just one
argument, all three lengths are the same (giving you a cube). The box is centered at the
origin. This procedure is just a convenience; you can always build your own boxes out
of six rectangles.

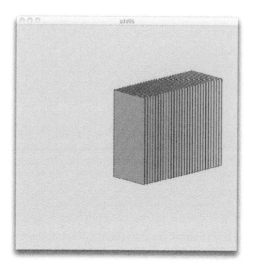

Figure 21.15. A stack of spinning 3D polygons (frame from animation).
(3D/sketches/p3d05/p3d05.pde)

Here's a version of our last program, using just a single box rather than a stack of polygons. This box is centered at the origin (like all boxes) and runs from -0.2 to 0.2 in x, -0.4 to 0.4 in y, and -0.5 to 0.5 in z.

```
void drawPicture() {
  fill(128, 173, 135);
  rotateX(frameCount * .02);
  rotateY(frameCount * .013);
  box(.4, .8, 1);
}
```

(See output in Figure 21.16. Full program in 3D/sketches/box3d01/box3d01.pde)

The command sphere() draws a ball out of triangles. It takes just one argument: the radius of the sphere. Like the box, the sphere is also centered at the origin. Unlike the box, a sphere should be smooth and round, so no number of flat triangles is ever going to combine to make a perfect sphere. But more triangles will usually look better, and you can tell Processing how many triangles to use in each sphere you create.

How many triangles should you use to make a sphere? There's no fixed answer. The more triangles you use, the smoother the sphere will look. But those triangles can add up fast, and each one requires some memory to store and some time to draw. If you get too many polygons on the screen, your program can start slowing down. This is why video game artists spend a lot of time figuring out how to make their characters look good with the fewest number of polygons.

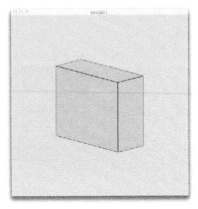

Figure 21.16. A spinning box (frame from animation). (3D/sketches/box3d01/box3d01.pde)

The rule of thumb is that you want to use as few polygons as possible to make any shape. In the case of a sphere, consider how big it is on your screen and how round it has to look. If you're using a ton of little spheres to look like pebbles or raindrops, you might be able to get away with very crude spheres made up of only a couple of dozen triangles each. That way you can have lots of them on the screen at once, and your program will still run smoothly. But suppose you're creating a close-up view of a pool table with a bunch of pool balls on it. Then the spheres will be relatively large on the screen, and you'll want them to look very smooth, so you'll use more triangles. There's no formula that can tell you what will look good in your project for your sense of aesthetics: you have to take a guess and then hand-tune the results.

Processing's default is to use 1,800 triangles for a sphere. That's a fine place to start. To use a different number of triangles, call sphereDetail() before you make the sphere. To see what this routine does, consider how Processing builds a sphere. It starts at the north pole and draws a ring of triangles. Then it moves down and builds another ring just under that. Then another ring, and another, and so on, until it draws a ring of triangles around the equator. Then it continues on until it reaches the south pole.

You can tell Processing how many steps to take around each ring (this is called the *latitude resolution*) and how many steps to take along the way from the north pole to the south (this is called the *longitude resolution*).

You can call sphereDetail() with two arguments, one each for the longitude and latitude resolutions. By default, these are each 30. If you give it just one value, it assumes that's the longitude resolution, and it leaves the latitude resolution alone. The minimum for each resolution is three. Once you set these resolutions with a call to sphereDetail(), they stay in force for all future spheres until you change them again.

To illustrate this, let's draw a grid of spheres. I'll change the latitude resolution with the horizontal position and the longitude resolution with the vertical position. I'll also change the code in draw() a little bit; I'll discuss these changes in a moment.

```
void setup() {
  size(600, 600, P3D);
}

void draw() {
  background(225, 192, 145);
  directionalLight(255, 255, 255, -1, 0,  -1);
  fill(128, 183, 135);
  perspective(radians(20), 1, -10, 10);
  drawPicture();
  noLoop();
}
```

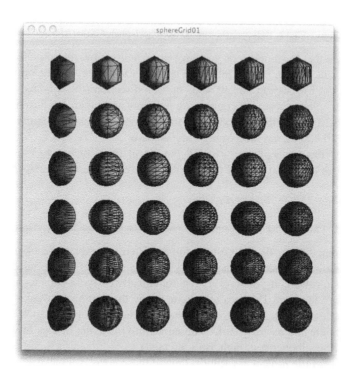

Figure 21.17. Changing sphereDetail(). (3D/sketches/sphereGrid01/sphereGrid01.pde)

```
void drawPicture() {
  int ysteps = 6;
  int xsteps = 6;
  for (int y=0; y<ysteps; y++) {
    for (int x=0; x<xsteps; x++) {
      float xalpha = x/(xsteps-1.0);
      float yalpha = y/(ysteps-1.0);
      float xpos = lerp(230, 370, xalpha);
      float ypos = lerp(230, 370, yalpha);
      int latitudeRes = int(lerp(3, 30, xalpha));
      int longitudeRes = int(lerp(3, 30, yalpha));
      sphereDetail(latitudeRes, longitudeRes);
      pushMatrix();
      translate(xpos, ypos, 0);
      sphere(10);
      popMatrix();
    }
  }
}
```

(See output in Figure 21.17. Full program in 3D/sketches/sphereGrid01/sphereGrid01.pde)

You can see that the more steps you have in each direction, the smoother the sphere appears. The sphere in the upper left has 3 steps in each direction (the minimum), and the sphere in the lower right has 30 steps in each direction (the default). If you need even smoother spheres, you can crank those numbers up higher. Each step generates a rectangle, and each rectangle is made up of two triangles. So at the defaults of 30-by-30 steps, we get $30 * 30 * 2 = 1,800$ triangles per sphere.

Let's draw the same picture, but I'll put a call to noStroke() at the top of drawPicture() so that we don't get the distracting black lines around each triangle:

```
noStroke();
```

(See output in Figure 21.18. Full program in 3D/sketches/sphereGrid02/sphereGrid02.pde)

There's something really interesting going on here: the spheres look a lot rounder than you might have expected. They look kind of smooth. That's because Processing (and your 3D hardware, if you have it) is automatically carrying out a technique called *smooth shading* for you. This is a technique where the computer tweaks the color of every triangle in a way designed to make the collection of polygons look smooth. It's entirely automatic and usually works well enough to make the insides of your spheres look smooth (the silhouette, though, isn't affected).

Let's make a little project to explore some of these ideas. I'll make a bunch of little rectangles that spin in place around a central sphere, making a nice pattern to watch. Since they form a ring, I think of these polygons as forming a kind of necklace made out of polygonal "beads."

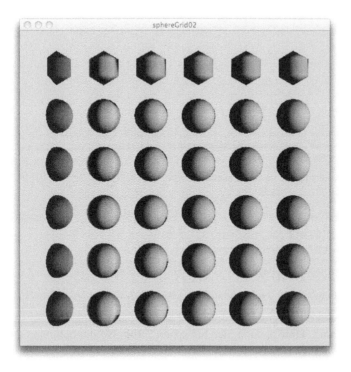

Figure 21.18. Changing sphereDetail() without strokes.
(3D/sketches/sphereGrid02/sphereGrid02.pde)

I'll start with a standard 3D skeleton, but I'll add a couple of lines to the end of draw(). The first will translate my origin to the center of the window (I'll include a z value, because we're in 3D, but I'll move 0 units in z). The second line will scale the coordinate system so that it runs from $(-1, 1)$ both horizontally and vertically. I'll do this by scaling by half the window's width in x, and half the window's height in y. Since we're in 3D, I'll also scale in z, but since I don't quite know what that will mean yet for my picture I'll put the z scaling factor at 1, which effectively does nothing to z. I'll use the OpenGL renderer for this project.

```
import processing.opengl.*;

void setup() {
  size(600, 400, OPENGL);
}

void draw() {
  background(180, 219, 180);
  lights();
```

Figure 21.19. Starting the necklace sketch (I hope!). (3D/sketches/necklace01/necklace01.pde)

```
camera();
translate(width/2, height/2, 0.0);
scale(width/2, height/2, 1.0);
}
```

(See output in Figure 21.19. Full program in 3D/sketches/necklace01/necklace01.pde)

Well, we got a background color up! Let's put something in there so we can see what's happening. How about a nice big sphere? I'll give it a color and a low amount of detail.

```
fill(50, 106, 102);
sphere(0.5);
```

(See output in Figure 21.20. Full program in 3D/sketches/necklace02/necklace02.pde)

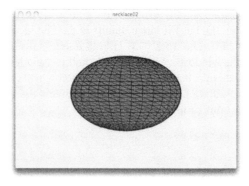

Figure 21.20. Adding a sphere. (3D/sketches/necklace02/necklace02.pde)

That's not right: the ball is stretched out horizontally. The problem is that my window is wider than it is tall. So my scaling is not uniform. That's easy to see because

I'm giving three different numbers to `scale()`. If I want my sphere to look round, then I can't stretch space by different amounts in different directions. Since I know that my window is shorter than it is wide, I'll change `scale()` so that it stretches in *x* and *z* by the same amount as in *y*. I can just repeat the expression `height/2` three times, but remember that if you give `scale()` just one value, it applies it to all dimensions. That approach is shorter, easier to read, and leaves less room for bugs. Let's make that change:

```
scale(height/2);
```

(See output in Figure 21.21. Full program in 3D/sketches/necklace03/necklace03.pde)

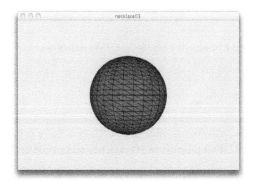

Figure 21.21. Making the sphere a sphere. (3D/sketches/necklace03/necklace03.pde)

Whew! I feel a lot better about that sphere now.

To get started, I'll make just one rectangle, representing one bead on my necklace. I'll set it up so that it is in the plane of the screen (that is, *z* = 0), and it's taller than it is wide. I'll put it into its own little routine so that I can make lots of these beads later:

```
void drawBead() {
    beginShape();
    vertex(-.1, -.2, 0);
    vertex( .1, -.2, 0);
    vertex( .1,  .2, 0);
    vertex(-.1,  .2, 0);
    endShape(CLOSE);
}
```

Now let's actually create this polygonal bead. I'll move out to the right side of the sphere (using `translate()`) and then call this function. While I'm at it, I'll give it a different color, too.

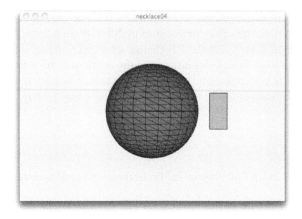

Figure 21.22. Adding a bead to the necklace. (3D/sketches/necklace04/necklace04.pde)

```
fill(226, 125, 156);
translate(0.75, 0, 0);
drawBead();
```

(See output in Figure 21.22. Full program in 3D/sketches/necklace04/necklace04.pde)

Now let's make a whole string of beads. All we need to do is pivot around the *y*-axis at the origin (located at the center of the screen) before we move outwards. So I'll put this into a loop. Using map(), I'll get us to rotate a full circle (that is, 360 degrees) around the *y*-axis over the course of the loop.

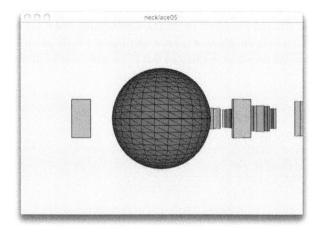

Figure 21.23. Where's the necklace? (3D/sketches/necklace05/necklace05.pde)

```
int numBeads = 25;
for (int i=0; i<numBeads; i++) {
   float a = map(i, 0, numBeads-1, 0, 1);
   rotateY(radians(a * 360));
   translate(0.85, 0, 0);
   drawBead();
}
```

(See output in Figure 21.23. Full program in 3D/sketches/necklace05/necklace05.pde)

Simply horrible. What went wrong? Each time through the loop, I rotate and then translate, and then the next time I rotate and translate again, and then again, and so on. The transformations just keep stacking up, and there's the problem. I want to position each bead anew, not cumulatively. I need to wrap my transforms in a pushMatrix() and popMatrix() pair so that I've essentially isolated each transformation.

Happily, pushMatrix() and popMatrix() work in 3D exactly as they do in 2D. There's a stack of matrices, and you can push new ones on the top of the stack and then pop them off later. In fact, Processing uses the same stack for both 2D and 3D transformations. I don't recommend you mix and match, though, as it can become confusing when you try to figure out what's happening to your coordinate system. Generally speaking, you'll save yourself a lot of grief by sticking to 2D transformations when you're working in 2D and sticking to 3D transformations when you're working in 3D.

You might be tempted to save a line and call resetMatrix() at the top of the loop, but then we'd lose our calls to translate() and scale() above as well. What we want is to save the state of the transform when we start the loop and put it back the way we found it when we're done. And that's just what the push and pop functions are for.

```
for (int i=0; i<numBeads; i++) {
   float a = map(i, 0, numBeads-1, 0, 1);
    pushMatrix();
        rotateY(radians(a * 360));
        translate(0.85, 0, 0);
        drawBead();
    popMatrix();
}
```

(See output in Figure 21.24. Full program in 3D/sketches/necklace06/necklace06.pde)

That's starting to look like my necklace.

I'd like to see this a little bit from above. There are lots of ways to do this. Later on, we'll see a function called camera() that lets us move our viewpoint around without affecting the model. But for now, I'll just move the whole space in which the model resides (remember that the transformation commands in 2D affect the flat coordinate system in which objects get drawn; the same thing is true in 3D, except now the 3D

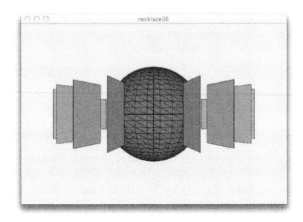

Figure 21.24. The start of the necklace. (3D/sketches/necklace06/necklace06.pde)

coordinate system represents a volume of space). I think I'll rotate it in x so that the nearest part tips down. The left-hand rule tells me that positive rotation in x would push the far part down and the near part up, so I'll rotate by a negative angle. Thirty degrees sounds about right, so I'll try that. Since the necklace (and sphere) seem pretty much in the right place, I'll add the rotation after the scaling operation:

```
translate(width/2, height/2, 0.0);
scale(height/2);
rotateX(radians(-30));
```

(See output in Figure 21.25. Full program in 3D/sketches/necklace07/necklace07.pde)

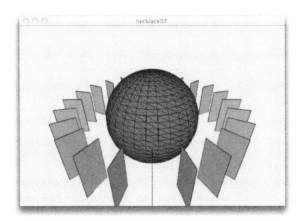

Figure 21.25. Looking for a better view. (3D/sketches/necklace07/necklace07.pde)

That's not really what I wanted; the necklace has moved downward and is even falling off the bottom of the screen.

The problem is that I've already moved my whole model (with the translation). I think what I want is to rotate first, so that the translation then takes it downward and closer to me. So I'll move the rotation to the start of the list.

```
rotateX(radians(-30));
translate(width/2, height/2, 0.0);
scale(height/2);
```

(See output in Figure 21.26. Full program in 3D/sketches/necklace08/necklace08.pde)

Figure 21.26. Finding a better view. (3D/sketches/necklace08/necklace08.pde)

There we go! The rectangles look a little too close to the sphere, so I'll move them out a little more by translating farther:

```
translate(1.1, 0, 0);
```

(See output in Figure 21.27. Full program in 3D/sketches/necklace09/necklace09.pde)

Not a giant leap for mankind, I grant you, but it looks a little better to me. Now let's get this necklace moving!

We can do pretty much anything that we'd like in order to animate these rectangular beads. Let's get them to spin in place, rotating around the string that would be joining them if this was a real necklace. Since each rectangle thinks it lies in the z plane, we only need to rotate it around the z-axis (and the z-axis is in the right place when we come to draw the rectangle, thanks to the transformation commands). I'll rotate all the beads by the same amount. The angle will start at zero and go up a little bit on every frame, because I'll just use a scaled version of frameCount for the angle.

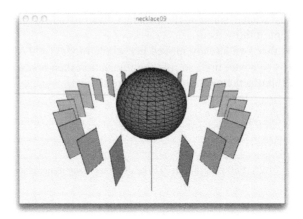

Figure 21.27. Making the necklace bigger. (3D/sketches/necklace09/necklace09.pde)

```
rotateZ(.02 * frameCount);
drawBead();
```

(See output in Figure 21.28. Full program in 3D/sketches/necklace10/necklace10.pde)

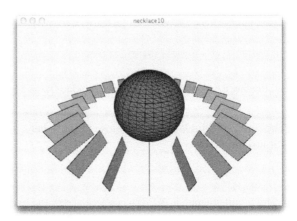

Figure 21.28. Animating the necklace (frame from animation).
(3D/sketches/necklace10/necklace10.pde)

I like the way this looks! Let's try putting in lots more beads. How about 250 of them?

```
int numBeads = 250;
```

(See output in Figure 21.29. Full program in 3D/sketches/necklace11/necklace11.pde)

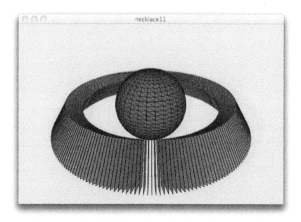

Figure 21.29. Animating a denser necklace (frame from animation). (3D/sketches/necklace11/necklace11.pde)

At this point, you can start creating lots of really cool variations on the necklace. Here's just a couple of ideas. How about if we add one full rotation to the beads as they go around, so that they look like the whole thing has been twisted once? We only need to add an angle from 0 to 360 degrees as we work our way around:

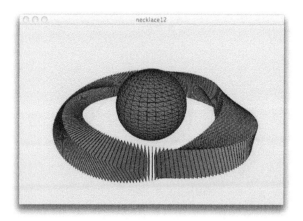

Figure 21.30. Animating a twisted necklace (frame from animation). (3D/sketches/necklace12/necklace12.pde)

```
rotateZ(radians(a*360) + (.02 * frameCount));
```

(See output in Figure 21.30. Full program in 3D/sketches/necklace12/necklace12.pde)

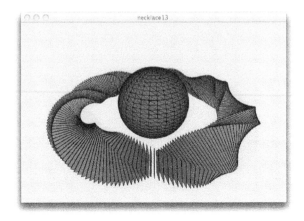

Figure 21.31. Animating a very twisted necklace (frame from animation).
(3D/sketches/necklace13/necklace13.pde)

I like that! What if instead of one full turn, we used more? Let's try three turns:

```
rotateZ(radians(a*3*360) + (.02 * frameCount));
```

(See output in Figure 21.31. Full program in 3D/sketches/necklace13/necklace13.pde)

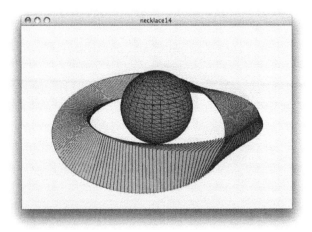

Figure 21.32. Adding *y* rotation (frame from animation).
(3D/sketches/necklace14/necklace14.pde)

Let's go back to one rotation but add another around the *y*-axis. Again, we'll just let it grow over time, but a little faster than the other rotation:

```
        rotateY(.03 * frameCount);
```

(See output in Figure 21.32. Full program in 3D/sketches/necklace14/necklace14.pde)

For fun, let's add some texture to this. Recall from Chapter 16 that we can add a PImage to any graphics element, including these rectangular shapes. Here, that will cause the image to be drawn in each rectangular bead. I'll pull back on the number of beads to just 25 so we can see the texture:

```
int numBeads = 25;
```

Then I'll declare and read in the texture file up top:

```
PImage Hike;

void setup() {
    size(600, 400, OPENGL);
    Hike = loadImage("myPhoto.jpg");
}
```

Finally, I'll just add texture coordinates to each call to vertex():

Figure 21.33. Putting texture on the necklace (frame from animation). (3D/sketches/necklace15/necklace15.pde)

```
void drawBead() {
    beginShape();
    texture(Hike);
    vertex(-.1, -.2, 0,   0,   0);
    vertex( .1, -.2, 0, 600,   0);
    vertex( .1,  .2, 0, 600, 450);
    vertex(-.1,  .2, 0,   0, 450);
    endShape(CLOSE);
}
```

(See output in Figure 21.33. Full program in 3D/sketches/necklace15/necklace15.pde)

You can play with this code for a long time, adding transformations here and there of different kinds. You can work in any way that pleases you. If you like to plan, you can sit down with pencil and paper and design a particular kind of motion and then work out how to achieve it. You could imagine a kind of motion in your head and then fool around with the code by the seat of your pants to find out how to make it. Or you can just mess with the program, sticking in transformations completely intuitively, making up angles and axes and seeing what they do. You can build an infinite variety of simple and complex motions this way.

21.2   Making Shapes in 3D

In Chapter 6 we made polygons from points with beginShape() and endShape(). As we saw above, we can use those functions to create 3D objects as well, just by including a third value (the *z* value) to each vertex() in the shape.

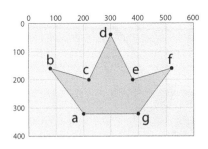

Figure 21.34. Our three-pointed leaf.

When working in 3D, you'll often produce huge numbers of duplicated vertices. For example, imagine making a simplified bird's wing. You might have a long string of side-by-side rectangles that gradually move up and down over time. Each vertex in that shape is repeated twice: once for the polygon on its left and again for the polygon on its right. To eliminate this duplication, you can create your polygons in one of two special forms: a *fan* or *strip*.

These are both options in beginShape(). Let's illustrate these with the same leaf shape we used in Chapter 6. I've repeated Figure 6.31 here as Figure 21.34.

We've seen the results of calling beginShape() with no arguments, or the optional arguments POINTS and LINES. Here are the remaining choices:

TRIANGLES. Each set of three points is taken to be a single triangle. This is convenient for making a whole bunch of independent triangles without having to call

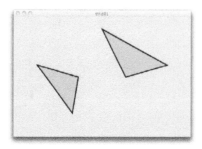

Figure 21.35. Using `beginShape(TRIANGLES)`. (3D/sketches/strip01/strip01.pde)

`beginShape()` and `endShape()` over and over for each one.

`beginShape(TRIANGLES);`

(See output in Figure 21.35. Full program in 3D/sketches/strip01/strip01.pde)

TRIANGLE_STRIP. In this mode, the points are assumed to form a long strip of triangles. The first three points form the first triangle. Then each new point builds a new triangle by adding one point to the two most recent ones. In our example, the first triangle would be formed by the points `(a,b,c)`. Then the next triangle is `(b,c,d)`, then `(c,d,e)`, `(d,e,f)`, and finally `(e,f,g)`.

`beginShape(TRIANGLE_STRIP);`

(See output in Figure 21.36. Full program in 3D/sketches/strip02/strip02.pde)

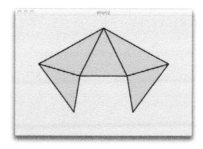

Figure 21.36. Using `beginShape(TRIANGLE_STRIP)`. (3D/sketches/strip02/strip02.pde)

This creates a strange result when I give it the leaf points as I've defined them here. That's because I didn't arrange these points so that this kind of interpretation made sense. To fix things up, I could put in another point (let's call it h) at the base of the leaf. Then I could draw most of the leaf as one strip. I'd have to add the top triangle manually.

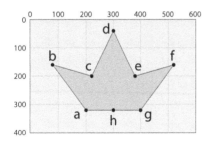

Figure 21.37. Another point at the leaf base.

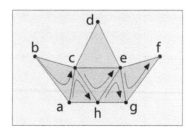

Figure 21.38. Creating a triangle strip. Each arrow starts at the first point of its triangle and continues on to points 2 and 3.

Figure 21.37 shows the location of h, which I'll include in all the rest of the examples of the beginShape() options.

Here's the definition of h, which is just halfway between a and g:

```
float hx = 300;   float hy = 320;
```

To use TRIANGLE_STRIP effectively, first I'll draw the left-most triangle. Because the next triangle builds off the last two points of the previous one, it's important to name the points in the right order. Figure 21.38 shows the order in which I'll create the triangles

I'll build the first triangle in the order (b,a,c). Then I'll give the point h, which defines the triangle (a,c,h). Then the next point, e, makes the triangle (c,h,e), and so on.

```
void drawLeaf() {
   beginShape(TRIANGLE_STRIP);
   vertex(bx, by);
   vertex(ax, ay);
   vertex(cx, cy);
   vertex(hx, hy);
   vertex(ex, ey);
   vertex(gx, gy);
   vertex(fx, fy);
   endShape(CLOSE);
}
```

(See output in Figure 21.39. Full program in 3D/sketches/strip03/strip03.pde)

Note that alternating triangles go clockwise and counterclockwise. As I mentioned, I'll have to draw the upper triangle (c,d,e) separately, since it's not part of this strip.

TRIANGLE_FAN. This is another way to efficiently create triangles. It's a variation on TRIANGLE_STRIP. The first point is special and is shared by all following triangles.

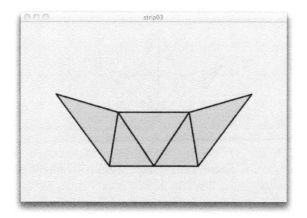

Figure 21.39. Building a triangle strip for the base. (3D/sketches/strip03/strip03.pde)

It's considered the "center" of a "fan" of triangles, like the fabric segments of an opened umbrella. Point 1 is joined with points 2 and 3 to make the first triangle (1, 2, 3). Now point 2 is forgotten, and the next point is used to build on the last edge, creating triangle (1, 3, 4). Then we forget about point 3 and build (1, 4, 5), and so on. To show this figure, I've return my points to their original order, a through g, with h at the end.

```
beginShape(TRIANGLE_FAN);
```

(See output in Figure 21.40. Full program in 3D/sketches/strip04/strip04.pde)

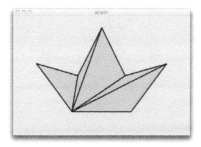

Figure 21.40. Using `beginShape(TRIANGLE_FAN)`. (3D/sketches/strip04/strip04.pde)

This works just fine, but I'd like my triangles to be more uniformly shaped. The figure is symmetrical, after all, so it would be nice if the underlying structure was as well. That's easy to achieve by just using point h as the center of our fan, rather than point a. I'll just add a line at the start of the calls to `vertex()` so we begin with point h:

Figure 21.41. A better fan. (3D/sketches/strip04b/strip04b.pde)

```
vertex(hx, hy);
```

(See output in Figure 21.41. Full program in 3D/sketches/strip04b/strip04b.pde)

Now that's what triangle fans are for!

QUADS. This is just like the TRIANGLES mode, but it builds four-sided figures rather than three-sided ones. So the first four points make up a single quad, then the next four points, and so on.

```
beginShape(QUADS);
```

(See output in Figure 21.42. Full program in 3D/sketches/strip05/strip05.pde)

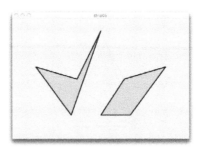

Figure 21.42. Using beginShape(QUADS). (3D/sketches/strip05/strip05.pde)

QUAD_STRIP. This is like the triangle strip, but for quads. It's a bit different than the triangle strip, though, because in this mode each pair of points goes in the same direction. That is, the first four points don't go around the quad (like they would if we called quad()), but rather, they form two parallel edges that go in the same direction (this would make a bowtie if we named them in this order to quad()).

Figure 21.43 shows a stab at using QUAD_STRIP. The first quad is made up of the edge (a,b) and then the edge (h,c) (again, note that these are opposite sides that go in the same direction). My next quad builds on the last pair (h,c) and adds the pair (e,d). You might see that I'm about to run into trouble: the next quad wants to build off of (e,d), but that edge isn't shared with the next quad. Just for grins, let's go ahead and put those points in there anyway, so the last two points to the strip will be (g,f). This will create a weird quad.

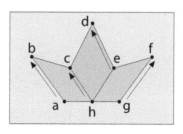

Figure 21.43. Creating a quad strip.

Let's try this out:

```
void drawLeaf() {
   beginShape(QUAD_STRIP);
   vertex(ax, ay);
   vertex(bx, by);
   vertex(hx, hy);
   vertex(cx, cy);
   vertex(ex, ey);
   vertex(dx, dy);
   vertex(gx, gy);
   vertex(fx, fy);
   endShape(CLOSE);
}
```

(See output in Figure 21.44. Full program in 3D/sketches/strip06/strip06.pde)

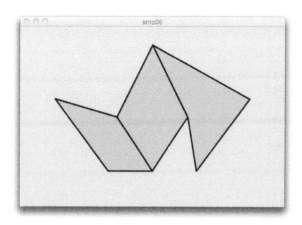

Figure 21.44. A bad result from beginShape(QUAD_STRIP).
(3D/sketches/strip06/strip06.pde)

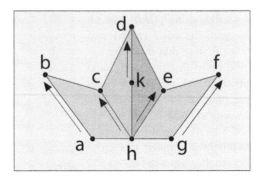

Figure 21.45. Repairing a quad strip. (3D/sketches/strippoints05/strippoints05.pde)

Yeah, that's wrong. The problem isn't with QUAD_STRIP but just that this isn't the sort of shape for which it's a natural fit. But with a little effort, we can still draw the leaf.

I'll add a new point, k, midway between d and h:

```
float kx = 300;  float ky = 180;
```

(See output in Figure 21.45. Full program in 3D/sketches/strippoints05/strippoints05.pde)

Now I have four quads: the ones on the left and right and the two in the middle. Admittedly, the quads in the middle sure look like triangles. But they have four sides and the pieces all go together the right way.

So the first quad joins pairs (a,b) and (h,c) as before. The next quad builds off that last pair and adds (k,d). The next quad builds off of that to add the pair (h,e). And finally, we build on that by adding edge (g,f).

```
void drawLeaf() {
   beginShape(QUAD_STRIP);
   vertex(ax, ay);
   vertex(bx, by);
   vertex(hx, hy);
   vertex(cx, cy);
   vertex(kx, ky);
   vertex(dx, dy);
   vertex(hx, hy);
   vertex(ex, ey);
   vertex(gx, gy);
   vertex(fx, fy);
   endShape(CLOSE);
}
```

(See output in Figure 21.46. Full program in 3D/sketches/strip07/strip07.pde)

Figure 21.46. Improving beginShape(QUAD_STRIP). (3D/sketches/strip07/strip07.pde)

That did the trick. Admittedly, it's not the most elegant way to handle this particular shape, but it does show that you can draw quads that look like triangles if you need to.

The different modes offered by beginShape() are there primarily for efficiency's sake. You could produce any of these results with the default mode (that is, no argument to the routine, so the points are just joined up in the order you name them). But if your shape's points take a lot of effort to compute, or there are huge numbers of them that you have to deal with, then one of these modes can make your program a little easier to write and maintain.

It's not uncommon to have situations where a fan or strip is just the right way to describe a big collection of polygons, except for one or two places where the geometry doesn't perfectly match up. That's when it pays off to add (or remove) an extra point or two here or there so you can use the efficient fan and strip forms.

In these examples, I listed all the vertices by hand in a big list. In practice, your vertices will usually be collected together in an array, and you'd just run through the array, handing off each point to vertex() to build up your object.

Now that we know how to make polygons, boxes, and spheres, let's talk about the pieces of the 3D boilerplate that I haven't addressed yet.

21.3   Controlling 3D

Before we get into the way these 3D functions work, I have an important word of warning.

You may recall that in Chapter 6 I discussed the different renderers (the underlying code that actually draws your pictures, which you choose with an optional third parameter to size()). In that section, I said that each renderer is a little different from the others. You'll find that this is very much the case in 3D.

The P3D renderer is optimized for software rendering, while the OPENGL renderer is optimized for using any 3D hardware that's installed on your computer. The intent is that the P3D renderer, though slower, should produce the very same picture on every computer because it does everything in software. The OPENGL version should run much faster, but due to differences in hardware and operating systems, might not generate the same results from one system to another.

This means that if you switch from one renderer to another, even on your own computer, your images may change. In practice, I find that the different renderers almost always produce different images. Sometimes the differences are minor, but often they change the picture significantly.

To make things more complicated, each of these two renderers has its own set of bugs and idiosyncrasies, and these change with each new release.

I've found that a good approach to getting started on a new project is to locate a piece of code that runs on your system and does something close to what you want to do and then build on that. Often I find that starting code in my own previous projects, but sometimes I find something on the Processing site or the Internet that comes closer, and I'll use that. With this approach, at least you'll know that you're starting with a solid base: your renderer is running, its settings are okay, and so on. If things start to go screwy later on, you can isolate just the latest step and see what's going wrong with that. If the problem is in your code, you can fix it. If the renderer itself is acting badly (by misunderstanding, or even ignoring, one of your instructions), then you can try to find a way around the problem. You can almost always find a way to do what you want in the face of a bug because there's usually more than one way to achieve any result. If you get really stuck, the online forums are always a good place to look for help.

To see an example of the differences between renderers, let's take the program I wrote earlier to draw the grid of spheres and replace the P3D renderer with the OPENGL renderer. It just takes two changes: use the import statement to import the library and then specify OPENGL rather than P3D in the call to size().

```
import processing.opengl.*;
void setup() {
  size(600, 600, OPENGL);
}
```

(See output in Figure 21.47.
Full program in 3d/sketches/sphereGrid02OPENGL/sphereGrid02OPENGL.pde)

In this case, Figure 21.47 isn't a total disaster, but it's certainly different from Figure 21.18. In other circumstances, the differences could be more dramatic or confusing. The different renderers have their own idiosyncrasies, and if you don't read up on the bugs, you can drive yourself crazy trying to figure out what's wrong with your code (I speak from experience here). If you're embarking on a 3D project, definitely go to the website and read up on the current bugs and limitations of the renderers and choose the one that is able to best accomplish what you're after.

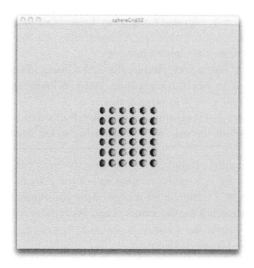

Figure 21.47. The sphere grid in OpenGL.

In the following discussion, I'm going to pretend that we're a little bit in the future, when all the bugs have been worked out, and all renderers are 100 percent perfect and implement every function call. Much of the time, you can get away with this fantasy. But if your programs start to act wonky, try to quickly decide whether it's your fault or the renderer's before you go crazy trying to debug your bug-free program!

Before we dig in, here's another essential point to remember: each time we enter `draw()`, we have to remind Processing about *everything* in our 3D world. That's because as soon as we exit `draw()`, Processing forgets all of our transformations and other 3D instructions (like the ones we'll cover below that control the lights and camera). We have to completely rebuild our 3D scenes from scratch each time we enter `draw()`. The only exceptions are the commands we inherited from 2D, like `stroke()` and `fill()`, which retain their settings.

It's best to set up all the 3D information before we start to draw anything, of course.

There are two principal things we need to do in `draw()` to get things ready for drawing (in addition to clearing the screen to a background color): we need to set up the camera, and we need to set up the lights. Let's look at these one at a time.

21.4 3D Camera

As we've seen, in a 3D scene there's a convenient default that puts the origin in the upper-left corner, with x going right, y down, and z coming towards us. We're positioned somewhere on the positive z-axis, looking straight down that axis towards the origin.

What if we want to move around? One way to go is to move the world by calling transformations like `translate()`. Alternatively, you can leave the coordinate system where it is and move the *camera* instead.

Think of the camera like a real, simple physical camera in the world. It has a location, it has a direction in which it's pointing, and you know which way is up. The camera in Processing has the very same qualities.

To define the camera in Processing, call the function `camera()`. With no arguments, it creates the default scenario we've been using so far, and that's the most common usage.

But you can hand it a list of nine values to customize your camera (yes, nine!). The first three numbers are the x, y, and z coordinates of the camera's location. The next three numbers give the x-, y-, and z-coordinates of the point that the camera is looking at. The last three numbers tell the direction of up. With these values, you can put the camera anywhere you want in the scene, you can point it at anything, and you can rotate it around the axis formed by those two points.

It's often a lot easier, and more natural, to move the camera than to move the scene. For example, suppose you've created a 3D model of a building and you'd like to move around it both inside and outside so you can get a feeling for the space. Rather than leave the camera fixed and move the building around you in space, it's a lot more sensible to leave the building where it is, unchanged in every frame, but simply move the camera around from one place to another, looking around at interesting things.

Most of the time, `camera()` can do everything you want. For those times when you need more precise control, here's a brief description of the advanced options that are available to you.

Typically, a computer-graphics camera will create pictures with some kind of *perspective*. This is the familiar effect whereby objects that are farther away seem smaller than those nearby, and parallel lines (like train tracks) converge in the distance. The standard camera that's created when you call `camera()` has a 60-degree viewing angle, which usually looks pretty good. If you want to crank that up (for example, to simulate a fish-eye lens) or crank it down (for example, to simulate a long zoom lens), you can do that manually. You can use either `perspective()` or `frustum()` to set the perspective (a *frustum* is a four-sided pyramid with the top bit sliced off; sometimes that's an easier way to define how you want your perspective to be set up).

If you want to turn off perspective altogether, that's called an *orthographic* view. Architects use orthographic views in blueprints so that they can accurately measure the size of objects (otherwise, they'd have to constantly correct for the size distortion introduced by perspective). To create an orthographic camera, call `ortho()`.

The commands `perspective()`, `frustum()`, and `ortho()` all take options that are more detailed than it's worth getting into here. If you need this sort of precise control, check out the documentation on these functions.

It's often easier to tweak the camera from its default settings rather than setting it up from scratch. Call `beginCamera()` to start defining the camera and then call `camera()` with no arguments to load up the defaults. Now, in this special mode, you can issue the standard transformation commands (translations, rotations, and scales), and they will apply to the camera. Call `endCamera()` when you're done. These commands will throw away any existing transformations you've already done, so if you're going to transform your scene, place your camera before you apply any transformations to your world. For that reason, it's best to put the camera calls very near the start of `draw()`.

Because Processing forgets everything about 3D when it exits `draw()`, if you want to use a customized camera you'll have to declare it again every time `draw()` gets called.

Debugging cameras can be kind of tricky. If you're mathematically inclined, you can get Processing to reveal some of the internal guts of the camera by printing information to the console. You can print out the current camera with `printCamera()`, and you can print the perspective matrix using `printProjection()`. These two routines are meant for people who are comfortable with the mathematics that makes the cameras work; if that's not you, I suggest you ignore them.

To figure out where the camera is located, my favorite technique is to use a simple scene like the one at the start of this chapter. I put a gray box at the origin and three other boxes colored red, green, and blue along the positive x, y, and z axes, in that order. Then I can easily make sense of where I am, where I'm looking, and which way is up. Of course, if nothing is visible at all, I might have to add some more objects or move the boxes farther out, but much of the time, that little scene can help me get sufficiently oriented that I can get right to work on putting my camera where I want it to be.

When you're getting started, I recommend the colored-box setup until you feel comfortable with how Processing handles 3D. Just grab the source code for one of the opening sketches in this chapter and use it as your starting point, adding your graphics to everything that's already there. That way you'll get my boilerplate with a camera and some lights, and a few handy pieces of geometry to give you both the current orientation and a sense of scale.

21.5 3D Lights

So now we've got a world with objects in it and a camera to view them. In 2D, I gave objects a fill color, and that was it. They simply got drawn with that color.

But remember how the spheres in Figure 21.18 looked smoothly shaded? They're not simply drawn with a flat color. Instead, they look like they've been lit with a *light source*. And that's just what's happening.

Take a second and think about why it is that we can see anything in the real world. The only reason we can see anything at all is because light is leaving the surface of that object and ultimately going into our eyes, where it hits our retina. Then a chain of information goes up the optic nerve to the brain, and we can see!

There are two ways light can leave an object's surface: it can be *emitted* or *propagated*. Emitters generate light all on their own. Emitters include electric lightbulbs, the sun, and bioluminescent fish. If we took one of these into a dark closet, they would still be visible because of the light that they generate themselves.

But most objects *reflect* light. Think of a paper coffee cup, for instance. If you took that cup into a dark closet and closed the door, you wouldn't see a thing. But take it back outside, and there it is again. The light from the sun strikes the coffee cup, some of that light is reflected, and eventually that reflected light hits your eye. So we see that coffee-cup shaped blob of color in our visual field, and from experience and intuition, we associate that with a coffee cup. Without some kind of externally generated light falling on (and getting reflected by) the coffee cup, we wouldn't be able to see it at all.

Some objects also *transmit* light. That term refers to the light that passes through a transparent, or partially transparent, object. So light that passes through a stained-glass window, a clear plastic bottle, or a windowpane has been transmitted by the material.

Taken together, we refer to reflected and transmitted light as propagated light. This is to remind us that the light started somewhere else (that is, from an emitter), and this object simply propagated it, or passed it on. Of course, the light can change in intensity or color or both as it's reflected or transmitted, but nonemitters only absorb and pass on light, they don't create their own.

Processing doesn't have any explicit tools for describing transmitted light in 3D; it focuses just on how objects reflect light. If you want transparent objects in Processing, you're out of luck (assigning transparency to a fill color creates transparent objects in 2D, but unfortunately, that doesn't also work in 3D). So from here on, I'll only talk about emitted light and reflected light.

As we'll see, Processing doesn't let you build objects that emit light. Light is only emitted by special, built-in objects called *light sources*, which we'll discuss in a moment. So when setting up a 3D scene, our job is to place the camera, place the light sources, and then create our objects that will reflect the light, and thus give rise to the scene we see.

Returning to our idea of the coffee cup outdoors, I said that we could only see it because light from an emitter struck the surface, got reflected, and ultimately reached our eye. In 2D, we didn't have to worry about this process. In essence, everything was an emitter and created its own light. If we filled an ellipse with a color, in effect, the ellipse was a light source glowing with that color. But in 3D, where we want to *shade* objects, we have to take two steps. The first is to paint the object with a color, and the second is to shine a light source onto it.

You can get Processing to give you a default batch of light sources by calling `lights()`. This routine takes no arguments: it simply says, "Create the default lights." There are two default lights: a kind of all-around glow and a specific light that's pointing straight down the middle of the screen. Think of it like the light on a miner's helmet sitting on your head.

If you want to create your own lights, you have a bunch of options. Generally each kind of light has a *color*. Many lights have a *direction* that describes which way they're pointed. To specify a direction, you give a point in space (that is, three numbers, for *x*, *y*, and *z*). Imagine an arrow that starts at (0,0,0) (the origin) and goes to that point. That arrow is the direction of the light. Keep in mind that this is the direction in which the light is moving. So, for example, if you give a direction of $(-1,0,0)$, then the light is moving to the left, which means if it hits a sphere, it will illuminate the right side of the ball.

Also keep in mind that you never see light sources directly. They don't have any shape, and they never get drawn. If you want to see your lights (for example, if you want your scene to include a glowing lightbulb where your light source is located), then you have to make that shape yourself and place it in the proper spot. In other words, you have to fake it. In Processing, lights are conceptual objects, and they don't have any shape or visual appearance.

Processing isn't meant for really subtle lighting situations, like late-afternoon sun streaming through a broken window shade, creating a shaft of soft light in a dust-filled room. For that, you'll want to use a full-blown 3D package. But for simpler scenes where you're primarily interested in showing your objects, Processing's lights do a fine job.

To create your own set of lights, you'll probably want to begin with a call to noLights(). This turns off all the lights. Then you can start adding in your own.

The simplest light is probably the *directional light*. This is essentially a light that's so far away that all the light from it is coming into your scene in the same direction. The sun is a great example of a directional light. To create a directional light, you call directionalLight() with the color of the light and the direction of the arriving light.

A *point light* is like a tiny lightbulb or a candle. It has a location and a color, and light flows from it in all directions. You create one with a call to pointLight().

Somewhere between these two types of lights is a *spotlight*. This is meant to model something like a theatrical spotlight, or even a flood-type lightbulb in your house. The idea is that the light streams away from the spotlight in a cone. If the cone is narrow, this is something like a flashlight or searchlight. If the cone is wide, you've got something like a flood light mounted above a painting in a museum. Like a point light, a spotlight has a color and a location. Like a directional light, it sends off its light in a specific direction. To create a spotlight, you call spotLight() with a color, position, and direction. The function takes two additional arguments. The first is the angle, which tells Processing how much the light spreads out. A flashlight would probably have a small angle, while a light meant to illuminate the side of a building would probably have a wide angle. The last value controls what happens inside the cone defined by this angle. A value of 0 means that the light is smoothly distributed in the cone, while a large value (like 20) concentrates most of the light in the middle of the cone, so that it falls off sharply.

Let's build a grid of spheres and light them with each of these lights. I'll start with a directional light.

```
void setup() {
  size(600, 600, P3D);
}
```

```
void draw() {
  background(144, 196, 224);
  lightSpecular(255, 255, 255);
  directionalLight(255, 255, 255, -1, 0,  -1);
  perspective(radians(20), 1, -10, 10);
  drawPicture();
  noLoop();
}
void drawPicture() {
  noStroke();
  color fillLeft = color(0, 0, 0);
  color fillRight = color(255, 0, 0);
  color specTop = color(0, 0, 0);
  color specBottom = color(0, 255, 0);
  int ysteps = 6;
  int xsteps = 6;
  for (int y=0; y<ysteps; y++) {
    for (int x=0; x<xsteps; x++) {
      float xalpha = x/(xsteps-1.0);
      float yalpha = y/(ysteps-1.0);
      float xpos = lerp(230, 370, xalpha);
      float ypos = lerp(230, 370, yalpha);
      pushMatrix();
      translate(xpos, ypos, 0);
      sphere(10);
      popMatrix();
    }
  }
}
```

(See output in Figure 21.48. Full program in 3D/sketches/directionalLight/directionalLight.pde)

In Figure 21.48, I've put the light source off to the right of the grid. Except for minor changes due to the effect of perspective, you can see that all of the spheres are lit the same way.

Let's change one line. I'll replace the directional light with a point light, located a bit above and to the right of the center of the image:

```
pointLight(255, 255, 255, 330, 270, 0);
```

(See output in Figure 21.49. Full program in 3D/sketches/pointLight/pointLight.pde)

You can see that the location of the point light is easily revealed by the illumination it throws off. Finally, let's replace the point light with a spotlight.

```
spotLight(255, 255, 255, 330, 270, 10, -1, -.25,  -1,
  radians(180), 0.5);
```

(See output in Figure 21.50. Full program in 3D/sketches/spotLight/spotLight.pde)

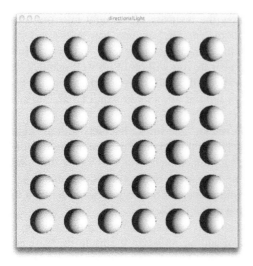

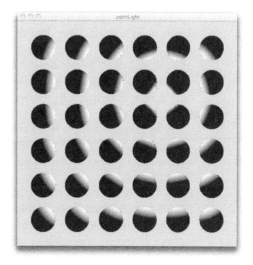

Figure 21.48. Illumination from
a directional light off to the right.
(3D/sketches/directionalLight/directionalLight.pde)

Figure 21.49. Illumination from a
point light located near the upper right.
(3D/sketches/pointLight/pointLight.pde)

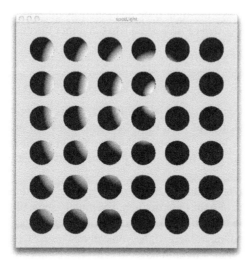

Figure 21.50. Illumination from a spotlight located near the upper right.
(3D/sketches/spotLight/spotLight.pde)

The spotlight is located in the same place as the point light from before, but it's
pointing to the left, a little bit up, and into the screen. I've made the cone very broad so
that it throws light in a half-circle in front of itself.

You can see in all of these examples how the intensity of the light falls off with distance. Processing handles this for you by default, but you can adjust it with `lightFalloff()`. Imagine that you shine a flashlight in a long, dark room full of watermelons. The watermelons that are near to you will be lit up well enough for you to see them clearly, but those farther away will be dimmer, and the watermelons even farther than that will receive almost no light at all, so you won't be able to see them.

Now suppose that the room is filled with smoke. The smoke interacts with the light from your flashlight, absorbing some of it and reflecting some of it. That means that the watermelons you were able to see very well a moment ago would now look dim, and those that used to be dim will be receiving no light at all, and you won't be able to see them. In other words, one thing the smoke did was cause the brightness of the light to fall off with distance faster than in the room without smoke.

The default value of `lightFalloff()` is 1, corresponding to a room without smoke. If you increase that number, it's like adding smoke to the room in the sense that the light dissipates more rapidly. You can also do something unnatural and set the value to a number less than 1. If the value is between 0 and 1, the light will fall off very slowly; when you reach 0, the intensity of the light won't change at all. If you give `lightFalloff()` a negative number, the light will actually get brighter with distance!

For example, I'll make the light drop away half as quickly as in Figure 21.50 by setting the first value in `lightFalloff()` to 0.5 rather than the default of 1:

```
lightFalloff(.5, 0, 0);
```

(See output in Figure 21.51. Full program in 3D/sketches/falloff/falloff.pde)

An oddball light source is called *ambient light*. This is a pretend light source that is meant to capture the idea of light that is coming from "all around." For example, suppose that you're outside on a sunny day with a friend. Your friend's back is to the sun, but you can still see your friend's face just fine. How is that possible, if the sun is at their back?

What's going on is the light from the sun is hitting the dirt, the trees, the grass, even you, and bouncing back into the environment. Eventually some of that light strikes your friend's face, and some of that is reflected into your eyes. Thus, you see your friend. To create this all-around, or ambient, light, you call `ambientLight()` with the color you'd like this "free-floating" light to have.

Another odd function controls the "specular" quality of reflected light. I'll talk about that in the next section, when we discuss material properties.

Remember, like everything else that's 3D, you need to explicitly recreate your lights at the start of every frame, so you'll want to put their definitions near the start of `draw()`.

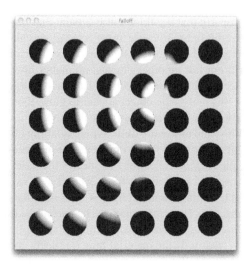

Figure 21.51. Changing how fast the light fades with distance by adjusting `lightFalloff()`. (3D/sketches/falloff/falloff.pde)

21.6 Materials

In 2D, every object had either a single fill color or a texture image, and that was that. In 3D, objects can reflect light in a variety of ways. Generally, the way an object reflects light is referred to as *shading*.

When the way an object reflects light is controlled by a little nugget of programming, we refer to that piece of software as a *shader*. We say that objects have shaders applied to them in order to control their appearance.

Some shaders are inspired by what happens in the real world, and some of them are not. These unreal types of effects are the result of how the mathematics of the shading process is done. Processing lets you get right into the midst of the process so that you can fiddle with some of the steps. This fiddling can lead to decidedly unreal types of results. You can create some really interesting visual effects by experimenting with shaders.

Processing's general approach to creating shaders for your objects is to let you cover every object in your scene with one or more special paints. These paints control not just the color of the object but the texture of its surface. So some paints are red or blue, others are rough or smooth.

We call each of these "paints" a *material property* . To apply these properties, we take an approach like that in 2D, where we defined a fill color and then all objects after that took on that color. In 3D, we define all the material properties for an object and then all objects that come after that (until we change those properties) will have those properties.

The first material property that we'll look at is a paint that glows all by itself. That is, it causes the object to emit light. To cause an object to glow, call emissive() with the color that the object should emit. Note that this doesn't turn it into a light source, so this emitted light will not fall on other objects, no matter how near or far they are. It merely makes an object visible even if no light from actual light sources are falling upon it. In other words, this makes the object appear to glow, though no other object in the scene can receive any of the light it seems to be emitting.

Some objects are shiny, and others are dull. Typically, shiny objects are smooth, and dull ones are rough. The quality of a rough object is that incoming light is reflected in all directions. This is called *diffuse* reflection. To specify the base, or rough, color of an object, you can simply use fill(), just as for a 2D object.

You can also control how much ambient light is reflected (that is, light that was created by ambientLight()). This really ought to be part of the diffuse reflection handled by fill(), but Processing lets you give it a different color if you want. If you give a color to ambient(), that tells the material how it reflects ambient light. So to set the color of the ambient light falling on your scene, you use ambientLight(), but to control how much of that light is reflected by a particular object, use ambient(). Normally you'll either skip calling ambient(), or you'll call it with the same value you use for the object's fill(), but you can give it a different value if you want to for special effects. The reason why the effect is special is because objects in the real world don't know where the light that's hitting them is coming from. My coffee cup doesn't know that some light is coming directly from an overhead lightbulb and other light is being reflected off the table. As far as the cup is concerned, light hits it, interacts with the material, and then gets reflected. But in the computer, an object knows which light is coming directly from a light source (and thus gets reflected with the color from fill()) and which light is coming from the ambient light (and thus gets reflected with the color from ambient()).

If an object's surface is shiny, then reflected light can take a form we call a *highlight*. A highlight is caused when the light that strikes a surface bounces off it in a predictable direction, like a ping pong ball bouncing off of a table. This is called a *specular* reflection.

Typically, the color of a highlight (that is, light that has been reflected specularly) is not the same as the base (or diffuse) color of the object. Think of a shiny, black 8-ball that's lit by a yellow light. The highlight is yellow, even though the base color of the ball is black. One frequent cause of this is that the light that bounces off to create the highlight is actually bouncing off an outer, transparent layer (like the transparent, hard plastic on the outside of the 8-ball).

You can specify the color of a highlight by giving a color to the function specular().

But how shiny is shiny? Some objects, like a perfectly smooth 8-ball, have a very tightly focused shiny highlight. Some objects, like a smooth tabletop, also have a highlight but it's spread out. Typically, the smoother the surface that the light is bouncing off of, the smaller the highlight. You can specify how smooth a surface is with the function shininess(), which takes a single number. When the value of that number is 1, the material is rough. As the value increases, the material gets smoother and the highlight gets sharper: a value of 5 is a pretty smooth surface and a value of 10 is very smooth.

When you create a light, in addition to all the parameters we've covered (like its color, position, direction, and so on), you can tell the light what color its specular reflections should be. In the real world, this makes no sense at all: the color of the light is the color of the light. Whether it's bouncing off of a rough piece of cardboard or a smooth sheet of metal, the light emits the same color. But in Processing, you can totally cheat the real world and tell the light source that when an object reflects the light specularly (that is, when the light bounces off like a highlight), then it should have a specific highlight color. You assign that color to the light source using the function lightSpecular(). As I said, this doesn't have any kind of physical analogue, but it can be used to create unusual effects.

Let's see how the diffuse and specular values interact. In this grid, I'll increase the diffuse color (which I'll make pure red) from left to right, and I'll increase the specular color (pure green) from top to bottom. The diffuse and specular lights that are hitting the spheres are both white.

```
void setup() {
  size(600, 600, P3D);
}

void draw() {
  background(225, 192, 145);
  lightSpecular(255, 255, 255);
  directionalLight(255, 255, 255, -1, 0,  -1);
  perspective(radians(20), 1, -10, 10);
  drawPicture();
  noLoop();
}

void drawPicture() {
  noStroke();
  color fillLeft = color(0, 0, 0);
  color fillRight = color(255, 0, 0);
  color specTop = color(0, 0, 0);
  color specBottom = color(0, 255, 0);
  int ysteps = 6;
  int xsteps = 6;
  for (int y=0; y<ysteps; y++) {
    for (int x=0; x<xsteps; x++) {
      float xalpha = x/(xsteps-1.0);
      float yalpha = y/(ysteps-1.0);

      color fillColor = lerpColor(fillLeft, fillRight, xalpha);
```

```
        color specColor = lerpColor(specTop, specBottom, yalpha);
        fill(fillColor);
        specular(specColor);
        shininess(8);

        float xpos = lerp(230, 370, xalpha);
        float ypos = lerp(230, 370, yalpha);
        pushMatrix();
        translate(xpos, ypos, 0);
        sphere(10);
        popMatrix();
      }
    }
}
```

(See output in Figure 21.52. Full program in 3D/sketches/difspecGrid/difspecGrid.pde)

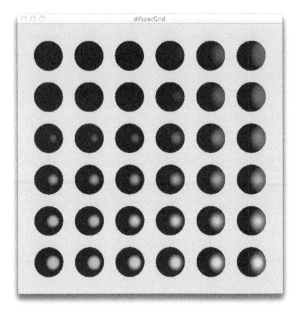

Figure 21.52. The diffuse color (red) increases from left to right; the specular color (green) increases from top to bottom. (3D/sketches/difspecGrid/difspecGrid.pde)

The sphere in the upper left is black because it's been told to reflect no light in a diffuse way and no light in a specular way. Physically, a sphere that didn't reflect any incoming light would be absorbing it all, making it a little warmer.

As we move to the right along the top row, the spheres reflect more and more light diffusely. So these spheres have a rough surface, and as we work our way to the right, they absorb less light and reflect more.

As we move down along the left column, the spheres reflect more and more light in a specular way. Think of each sphere getting a hard, smooth shell wrapped around it. The light bounces off of that shell, creating a highlight.

In the middle of the grid we have combinations of these two types of reflection. In the bottom right, the sphere is reflecting in both ways. In the bottom-right corner, light from the green specular reflection is mixing with the red diffuse reflection, creating yellow.

21.7 Other 3D Tools

Processing offers a few other commands that may be useful for you when working with 3D. Most of them are only useful in specific, unusual situations, but it's worth knowing that they exist.

Part of the process of figuring how how much light is hitting a surface involves finding out what direction the surface is pointing in. Think of a flat sheet of paper that's facing a light head-on. That paper will be hit with much more light than if we turn it so that it's increasingly edge-on to the light. That's why the spheres we've been drawing look round: the amount of light reflected by the triangles that are facing the light source is much more than those that are edge-on, and the ones in between are reflecting intermediate amounts of light.

The direction in which an object is facing can be found mathematically, resulting in something called the *surface normal* or just *normal*. If you're mathematically inclined, you can compute your own surface normals for your shapes and manually set them with the routine `normal()`.

Suppose in the process of building your scene you've called and accumulated a whole bunch of transformations. You've done some rotations, translations, and maybe even scales to get things placed right where you want them. Now suppose that you're about to create another shape, and you wonder to yourself where it's going to end up. That is, you're about to name a point (with x-, y-, and z-coordinates), and you know that it's going to get transformed to some other position, but you want to know what that other position is going to be. So you want an answer to this question: what will the current transformations do to a specific point?

You can find out with three routines. If you want to know the final x-coordinate of your point, hand the x, y, and z values of the input point to `modelX()`. It will return a single `float` that gives you the final x coordinate of your input point, after all the transforms have been applied. If you want the y or z coordinates, naturally you can call `modelY()` and `modelZ()`, respectively. Although each of these routines gives you back only a single coordinate, they all require all three coordinates of the input point as arguments in order to do their work.

That's great if you want to know where the point will land in 3D space, but sometimes you want to know where it will fall on the screen. After all, the camera is going to take that 3D point and turn it into a 2D (x, y) pair for display. Interestingly, a result of this process is that the final point will also have a z value. Often this is ignored, and we just draw the color of the point at the x and y values, but if you want to use the final z value, you can. If you converted the z value to a color, for instance, you could create an image where the color of each pixel showed you how far away the object at that pixel is from the viewer.

To find the screen x-coordinate of a point use the function screenX(), which takes three floats (the input point) and returns one float (the x-coordinate on the screen). For the other two values, you call screenY() and screenZ().

21.8 Greebles

Science fiction spaceships were once imagined to be smooth and clean. The spaceships built on Earth were long, pointed tubes with fins, while ETs arrived in flying saucers that were something like a sphere sitting in the middle of a thick, rounded disk. But then everything changed: the giant Empire ships of *Star Wars* were covered in tiny little bits of detail. Boxes and tubes and cylinders and all kinds of little shapes covered the surface of the ships, and smooth, streamlined spaceships were quickly out of fashion.

Over the years, the little pieces of bric-a-brac that cover spaceships and other surfaces have been described by a number of names, but the one that I like the most is *greebles*.

There's nothing formal about a greeble. It's just some little bit of stuff you put onto an otherwise smooth surface to break it up and give it that science fiction spaceship look.

There are lots of ways to create greebles. Let's take a look at one approach by building a piece of a spaceship exterior that's covered in greeble *tiles*. I'll make a little square shape with some objects on it (our prototype tile), and then I'll repeat that single tile over and over, plunking it down like a rubber stamp, to create our surface detail.

The first step in this process will be to make a little tile. To make things even easier, let's make a couple of helper functions. The first will just draw a sphere at a given point. We'll save the matrix, translate to that point, draw the sphere, and then restore the matrix:

```
void drawSphere(float cx, float cy, float cz, float r)
{
    pushMatrix();
    translate(cx, cy, cz);
    sphere(r);
    popMatrix();
}
```

Let's also write a little routine for a box. Since I'm going to draw all of my objects on a surface, I'd like to specify my box by placing its center in the middle of its bottom face. But in Processing, boxes are built symmetrically around the origin. So like the sphere, I'll translate first to put the box in the desired position, but I'll also translate up by half the desired height of the box. This will move the center up so that it's floating in space above the surface. When we draw the box, the lower face will just touch the ground.

```
void drawBox(float cx, float cy, float cz, float dx, float dy, float dz)
{
    pushMatrix();
    translate(cx, cy+(dy/2.0), cz);
    box(dx, dy, dz);
    popMatrix();
}
```

Now I'll use these to make a little greeble. Since I expect to eventually have a few of them, I'll call this one number 00 (so the next one will be 01, then 02, and so on). Like Processing, I'll use a left-handed coordinate system for the greeble. So the tile is spanned by x and z, and y goes upwards, telling us the altitude of an object above the tile's surface. In my design, I'll say that the tile extends one unit in both x and z (so both run from 0 to 1), and I'll scale it as needed when I draw it. I'll just make a little collection of boxes along with one sphere. I doodled this on a piece of graph paper, and when it looked pretty good to me, I just read off the coordinate values for x and z and typed them in. I just estimated the y values as I typed in the others, since I knew roughly how high I wanted each box to appear.

The first object in the greeble will be a big thin box that forms the base of the tile. All the other shapes sit on top of that base.

```
void drawGreeble00() {
    drawBox(.5, -.1, .5, 1, .1, 1);
    drawSphere(.4, 0, .35, .2);
    drawBox(.3, 0, .05, .2, .1, .1);
    drawBox(.25, 0, .75, .2, .05, .15);
    drawBox(.75, 0, .25, .1, .1, .1);
    drawBox(.75, 0, .4, .1, .1, .1);
    drawBox(.75, 0, .55, .1, .1, .1);
    drawBox(.9, 0, .8, .2, .15, .25);
    drawBox(.55, 0, .8, .08, .2, .22);
}
```

Now let's put a simple 3D wrapper around this. I'll use the OPENGL renderer this time, so I'll remember to import that at the top. My setup() routine will simply make the graphics window.

In draw() I'll set the background, move the origin to the center, scale things so the tile isn't too monstrously large, and then I'll draw it. I'll also tilt everything down a little so I can see the top of the tile by rotating a few degrees around *x*.

```
import processing.opengl.*;

int Window = 600;

void setup(){
   size(Window, Window, OPENGL);
}

void draw() {
   background(25, 42, 51);
   translate(Window/2.0, Window/2.0, -400.0);
   scale(Window, -Window, Window);
   lights();

   noStroke();
   fill(255);
   rotateX(radians(35));
   float gScale = 0.5;
   scale(gScale);

   drawGreeble00();
}

void drawGreeble00() {
   drawBox(.5, -.1, .5, 1, .1, 1);
   drawSphere(.4, 0, .35, .2);
   drawBox(.3, 0, .05, .2, .1, .1);
   drawBox(.25, 0, .75, .2, .05, .15);
   drawBox(.75, 0, .25, .1, .1, .1);
   drawBox(.75, 0, .4, .1, .1, .1);
   drawBox(.75, 0, .55, .1, .1, .1);
   drawBox(.9, 0, .8, .2, .15, .25);
   drawBox(.55, 0, .8, .08, .2, .22);
}

void drawSphere(float cx, float cy, float cz, float r)
{
   pushMatrix();
   translate(cx, cy, cz);
   sphere(r);
   popMatrix();
}
```

Figure 21.53. Our first greeble. (3D/sketches/greeble01/greeble01.pde)

```
void drawBox(float cx, float cy, float cz, float dx, float dy, float dz)
{
    pushMatrix();
    translate(cx, cy+(dy/2.0), cz);
    box(dx, dy, dz);
    popMatrix();
}
```

(See output in Figure 21.53. Full program in 3D/sketches/greeble01/greeble01.pde)

Not a bad start, but if you look closely, you can see some little stairsteps on the edges of the boxes. I'll include a call to smooth() into setup() to help clean that up.

Now I'll put these tiles together into a big grid to simulate the outside of my ship. I'll make a couple of global variables to declare the size of this grid:

```
int GridX = 13;
int GridY = 10;
```

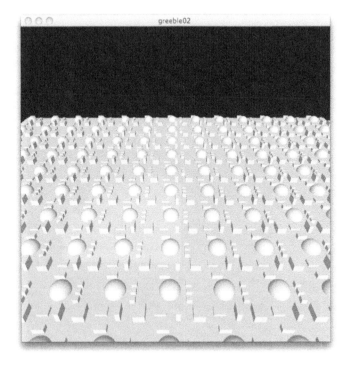

Figure 21.54. A great greeble grid. (3D/sketches/greeble02/greeble02.pde)

I'll back the scale off a little bit so I can fit more greebles onto the screen, and I'll replace our single call to drawGreeble00() with a loop that will push the matrix, translate us to a point in the grid, draw the greeble, and then pop the matrix:

```
for (int iz=0; iz<GridZ; iz++) {
    for (int ix=0; ix<GridX; ix++) {
        pushMatrix();
        translate(ix-(GridX/2.0), 0, iz-(GridZ/2.0));
        drawGreeble00();
        popMatrix();
    }
}
```

(See output in Figure 21.54. Full program in 3D/sketches/greeble02/greeble02.pde)

It's a start, but that grid is so flat it doesn't look good to me at all. I think I'll give it just a little bit of a curve, like we're looking down the middle of a rounded tunnel. I'll just add a little bit of rotation around z so that the tiles on the left will rotate so their left side's a little higher, and those on the right will rotate so the right side's a little higher.

I'll translate to the tile's center (that is, $(0.5, 0, 0.5)$), do the rotation, and translate back. Note that we don't want to push and pop the matrix because we want this rotation to accumulate on top of the translation that puts the tile in position. I'll use the tile's x position in the grid to determine how much rotation to apply.

```
translate(.5, 0, .5);
rotateZ(radians(5.0*(ix-(GridX/2.0))));
translate(-.5, 0, -.5);
```

(See output in Figure 21.55. Full program in 3D/sketches/greeble03/greeble03.pde)

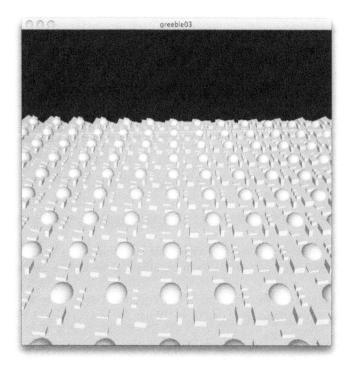

Figure 21.55. A great greeble grid in a faked, shallow tunnel. (3D/sketches/greeble03/greeble03.pde)

Oops! That's a little too much. Since I'm not actually moving the tiles upwards to make my tunnel but just rotating them to give that impression, I can't rotate them by too much, or it just looks wrong. So I'll try backing off that angle multiplier of 5 to just 3. I'll also give these just a little bit of color. Even in space, a little color is welcome.

The results are in Figure 21.56.

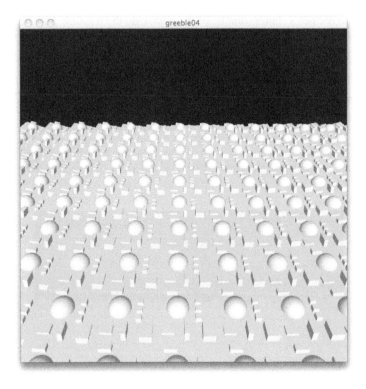

Figure 21.56. A little less rotation.

That's definitely better. Let's make this a little more interesting by rotating each tile. I'll spin each one around the *y*-axis by some multiple of 90 degrees, so they still make up a square grid.

Now that we're starting to create per-tile information, I think I'll create a Greeble class to package everything up in one place. When we make a Greeble, we give it the *x*- and *z*-coordinates of its location in the grid. The Greeble itself then saves its translation and rotation values. Then they're all right there and handy when it's time to render the tile.

This will also make it easy to spin around the *y*-axis. I'll pick a random angle when I make the tile, and then just before drawing the geometry, after rotating around *z*, I'll rotate around *y* as well.

I'll begin with a new global variable that will hold a 2D array of tiles:

```
Greeble Ggrid[][];
```

The Greeble class isn't much more than a repackaging of what we already have, plus a couple of extra little bits to handle *y* rotation. This is all stuff we've seen before, so I won't go into each line of code individually.

```
class Greeble {
   float tx, tz;
   float angleY;
   float angleZ;

   Greeble(int x, int z) {
     tx = x-(GridX/2.0);
     tz = z-(GridZ/2.0);
     int i4 = int(random(0, 1000))%4;
     angleY = radians(i4*90);
     angleZ = radians(3.0*(x-(GridX/2.0)));
   }

   void render() {
     pushMatrix();
         translate(tx, 0, tz);
         translate(.5, 0, .5);
         rotateZ(angleZ);
         rotateY(angleY);
         translate(-.5, 0, -.5);

         drawBox(.5, -.1, .5, 1, .1, 1);
         drawSphere(.4, 0, .35, .2);
         drawBox(.3, 0, .05, .2, .1, .1);
         drawBox(.25, 0, .75, .2, .05, .15);
         drawBox(.75, 0, .25, .1, .1, .1);
         drawBox(.75, 0, .4, .1, .1, .1);
         drawBox(.75, 0, .55, .1, .1, .1);
         drawBox(.9, 0, .8, .2, .15, .25);
         drawBox(.55, 0, .8, .08, .2, .22);
     popMatrix();
   }
}
```

Now setup() creates and initializes this grid, and draw() just tells every tile to render itself:

```
void setup(){
   size(Window, Window, OPENGL);
   smooth();
   Ggrid = new Greeble[GridZ][GridX];
   for (int z=0; z<GridZ; z++) {
     for (int x=0; x<GridX; x++) {
       Ggrid[z][x] = new Greeble(x, z);
     }
   }
}
```

```
void draw() {
   background(25, 42, 51);
   translate(Window/2.0, Window/2.0, -400.0);
   scale(Window, -Window, Window);
   lights();

   noStroke();
   fill(255, 255, 200);
   rotateX(radians(35));
   float gScale = 0.2;
   scale(gScale);

   for (int iz=0; iz<GridZ; iz++) {
      for (int ix=0; ix<GridX; ix++) {
         Ggrid[iz][ix].render();
      }
   }
}
```

(See output in Figure 21.57. Full program in 3D/sketches/greeble05/greeble05.pde)

Now we're cooking!

Enough of having just one tile. I drew a few more greeble tiles, and typed in the ones I liked best.

To specify which geometry goes with which tile, I'll assign a random greeble number to each tile when it gets made. Then when it's time to render, I'll use a switch statement to choose one of several different methods to draw the chosen tile.

While doodling out my new greebles, I decided it would be nice to have some cones and cylinders to play with. So I wrote another little shape-drawing routine to draw these. By giving it a radius at the top and bottom, I could make a cylinder (same radius at both ends), a cone (set one radius to 0), or a flared shape by using different radii. In the case where the top doesn't come to a point, I decided to provide an option to draw a cap on the top to cover it up.

A cylinder is a perfect use of the QUAD_STRIP shape type: I just tell it how many quads to put around the outside and make them (in the argument list, I call this number res, standing for *resolution*). The cap is a perfect place to use TRIANGLE_FAN, since I can put the center of the fan in the center of the lid and just draw triangles out to the tops of the surrounding quads.

```
void drawCone(float cx, float cy, float cz, float rLo, float rHi,
              float yTop, int res, boolean cap)
{
   pushMatrix();
   translate(cx, cy, cz);
```

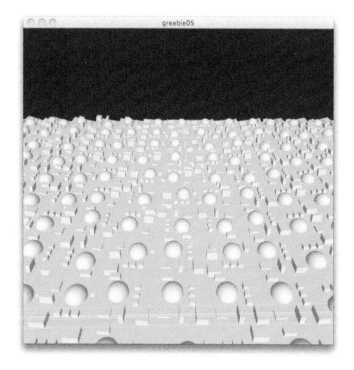

Figure 21.57. Greebles with random *y* rotation. (3D/sketches/greeble05/greeble05.pde)

```
beginShape(QUAD_STRIP);
for (int i=0; i<=res; i++) {
    float theta = radians(map(i, 0, res, 0, 360));
    vertex(rLo*cos(theta),  0.0, rLo*sin(theta));
    vertex(rHi*cos(theta), yTop, rHi*sin(theta));
}
endShape();
if (cap) {
    beginShape(TRIANGLE_FAN);
    vertex(0, yTop, 0);
    for (int i=0; i<=res; i++) {
        float theta = radians(map(i, 0, res, 0, 360));
        vertex(rHi*cos(theta), yTop, rHi*sin(theta));
    }
    endShape();
}
popMatrix();
}
```

The additional greebles aren't very interesting code; they're just lists of boxes, spheres, and cones placed in each tile where I doodled them. I just put the graph paper next to me and typed in where I drew the shapes, one after the other. As before, I read the *x* and *z* values right off the page, and I chose *y* values by picturing the greeble in my imagination and estimating the heights that I "saw" there.

Here's the whole new class in one place:

```
class Greeble {
    float tx, tz;
    float angleY;
    float angleZ;
    int tileType;

    Greeble(int x, int z) {
        tx = x-(GridX/2.0);
        tz = z-(GridZ/2.0);
        int i4 = int(random(0, 1000))%4;
        angleY = radians(i4*90);
        angleZ = radians(3.0*(x-(GridX/2.0)));
        tileType = int(random(0, 1000))%4;
    }

    void render() {
        pushMatrix();
            translate(tx, 0, tz);
            translate(.5, 0, .5);
            rotateZ(angleZ);
            rotateY(angleY);
            translate(-.5, 0, -.5);

            switch (tileType) {
                case 0: drawGreeble00(); break;
                case 1: drawGreeble01(); break;
                case 2: drawGreeble02(); break;
                case 3: drawGreeble03(); break;
                default: drawGreeble03(); break;
            }
        popMatrix();
    }

    void drawGreeble00() {
        drawBox(.5, -.1, .5, 1, .1, 1);
        drawSphere(.4, 0, .35, .2);
        drawBox(.3, 0, .05, .2, .1, .1);
        drawBox(.25, 0, .75, .2, .05, .15);
        drawBox(.75, 0, .25, .1, .1, .1);
```

```
        drawBox(.75, 0,  .4,  .1,  .1,  .1);
        drawBox(.75, 0,  .55, .1,  .1,  .1);
        drawBox(.9,  0,  .8,  .2,  .15, .25);
        drawBox(.55, 0,  .8,  .08, .2,  .22);
    }

    void drawGreeble01() {
        drawBox(.5, -.1, .5, 1, .1, 1);
        drawCone(.625, 0, .32, .23, .14, .35, 20, true);
        drawBox(.85, 0, .3, .3, .1, .2);
        drawBox(.25, 0, .2, .15, .2, .4);
        drawBox(.25, 0, .7, .3, .15, .2);
        drawBox(.325, 0, .9, .15, .15, .1);
        drawBox(.725, 0, .8, .025, .1, .22);
        drawBox(.775, 0, .8, .025, .1, .22);
        drawBox(.825, 0, .8, .025, .1, .22);
    }

    void drawGreeble02() {
        drawBox(.5, -.1, .5, 1, .1, 1);
        drawCone(.12, 0, .37, .11, 0, .25, 10, false);
        drawCone(.2, 0, .6, .11, 0, .25, 10, false);
        drawCone(.4, 0, .71, .11, 0, .25, 10, false);
        drawCone(.62, 0, .65, .11, 0, .25, 10, false);
        drawSphere(.45, 0, .35, .2);
        drawBox(.4, 0, .3, .1, .05, .4);
        drawBox(.55, 0, .15, .3, .05, .1);
        drawBox(.85, 0, .35, .1, .25, .2);
        drawBox(.35, 0, .925, .5, .1, .15);
        drawBox(.8, 0, .825, .2, .075, .05);
        drawBox(.925, 0, .925, .05, .075, .15);
    }

    void drawGreeble03() {
        drawBox(.5, -.1, .5, 1, .1, 1);
        drawBox(.425, 0, .6, .4, .1, .4);
        drawBox(.425, 0, .6, .3, .2, .3);
        drawBox(.425, 0, .6, .2, .3, .2);
        drawBox(.425, 0, .6, .1, .4, .1);
        drawBox(.35, 0, .9, .1, .05, .2);
        drawCone(.175, 0, .9, .05, 0, .15, 15, false);
        drawCone(.475, 0, .9, .05, 0, .15, 15, false);
        drawBox(.8, 0, .625, .2, .03, .03);
        drawBox(.8, 0, .675, .2, .03, .03);
        drawBox(.8, 0, .725, .2, .03, .03);
        drawBox(.8, 0, .775, .2, .03, .03);
```

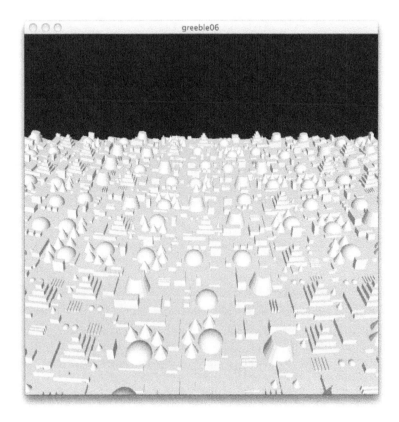

Figure 21.58. Four greebles are better than one. (3D/sketches/greeble06/greeble06.pde)

```
        drawBox(.8, 0, .825, .2, .03, .03);
        drawSphere(.8, 0, .275, .05);
        drawSphere(.8, 0, .425, .05);
        drawBox(.9, 0, .075, .1, .1, .15);
        drawBox(.3, 0, .2, .4, .1, .2);
        drawBox(.075, 0, .175, .05, .05, .05);
        drawBox(.025, 0, .35, .05, .1, .5);
    }
}
```

(See output in Figure 21.58. Full program in 3D/sketches/greeble06/greeble06.pde)

Great! The geometry is more interesting, but the image is still very plain.

For fun, I'll give each tile a random color and use fill() to set that as the drawing color when I draw each tile.

Figure 21.59. Colored greebles with moving lights (frame from animation).
(3D/sketches/greeble07/greeble07.pde)

Let's make this scene a little more interesting by replacing the default lights. In place of the call to lights(), I'll put in a couple of lights of my own, with slightly different colors. And I'll move them around a little bit from frame to frame using noise(); the shapes become more interesting as they react to the changing lights.

```
float lightDirX = lerp(-1, 1, noise((frameCount+151)*.02));
float lightDirY = lerp(-1, 1, noise((frameCount+307)*.02));
directionalLight(128, 128, 100, lightDirX, lightDirY, -.2);

float lightDirX2 = lerp(-1, 1, noise((frameCount+500)*.02));
float lightDirY2 = lerp(-1, 1, noise((frameCount+800)*.02));
directionalLight(64, 128, 128, lightDirX2, lightDirY2, -.2);
```

(See output in Figure 21.59. Full program in 3D/sketches/greeble07/greeble07.pde)

That's nice; I think the animated lights make the shapes read more clearly.

You can make this project more interesting by creating more greebles of your own, perhaps including even more primitive shapes. One easy addition would be to add another argument to `drawCone()` that would let you move the height of the center point. Then you could draw, for example, a cylinder with a pointed cap.

Right now it's obvious that the greebles are placed on a grid of square tiles. You can experiment with other ways of laying out your pieces so that the underlying grid is harder to see, or even completely hidden.

For a bigger challenge, you could change the approach entirely so that there is no underlying grid. Your program would take in a piece of geometry (like a segment of a spaceship's outer hull or some other flat surface) and would return a new version full of greebles, ready to be drawn.

Chapter 22
Useful Odds and Ends

There are some bits and pieces that I've left out of earlier chapters. My goal has been to remain focused on the material at hand, so I skipped some topics that weren't essential to the discussion. They're not unimportant, but they just didn't fit the flow of the discussion.

There are also a few really handy and common programming techniques that I want to share with you but that didn't fit into the flow of the previous examples.

Let's fill in some of those omissions.

Before we dig in, note that many of the built-in function calls we've seen in previous chapters, as well as those we have yet to cover, have multiple, overloaded versions. I'm sticking here to the ones that I think are the most important. If you're getting strange behavior from a function, make sure you're passing it the right arguments for the version you intend to invoke. If you do find yourself wondering if you're getting the right version, check the documentation. There you can find lists of all the variants for each function, including the obscure and rarely used versions that I haven't discussed.

22.1 Push and Pop Styles

You can push and pop the drawing style (which describes things like the fill color, stroke color, stroke width, etc.) just as you would transformation matrices. Use `pushStyle()` and `popStyle()`:

```
pushStyle();
popStyle();
```

They're maintained on a stack, just like transformations. So when you push, a copy of the current style goes onto the top of the stack. If you make changes to the current style, the stack is unaffected because it's holding a copy of how the style was defined when you pushed. When you pop, the most recently pushed style is removed from the stack, and it becomes the current style, overwriting all the settings that were in effect.

For a complete list of what makes up a style, see the documentation for `pushStyle()`.

22.2 Libraries

Lots of people have shared their Processing source code on the web. Some people have taken their work a step further, and they've packaged up their programs in the form of *libraries*. You can find dozens of free, powerful libraries on the Processing website. They're designed to extend Processing's reach, so that it can be used to control musical equipment, video gear, custom hardware, and more.

Libraries are easy to download and install; the instructions are on the main Libraries page. You probably won't need any of these for a while, but it's worth checking the list from time to time to see what's new. Sometimes just reading the description of what a library can do can give you some great ideas for doing stuff with it.

There are two types of libraries.

The first are the "official" Processing libraries. These are considered part of Processing. We've already used this kind of library when we wrote code that used the OpenGL renderer.

The other kind of library is user contributed. These libraries are created, debugged, and then freely shared by civic-minded people who want you to be able to build on their work. This is a wonderful thing! But like volunteer work in any field, it comes with no guarantees. The biggest problem is that user-contributed libraries can fall behind and "break" when they're not updated to keep track of new releases of Processing. This doesn't happen often since new releases tend to only fix bugs and extend the language, but it's a possibility. If you use a user-contributed library for something that will run unattended for a long time (like an information kiosk or museum exhibit), you might want to be careful about applying updates to Processing so you don't accidentally break your program. You could test out the updates on another computer first before installing them on the public version. Of course, for smaller personal projects, this is much less of a concern.

To bring a library into your sketch, you use the `import` keyword, just as we imported the `opengl` library when we used the OpenGL renderer. For one of the built-in libraries, you can save a bit of effort and simply go to the *Sketch* menu in your Processing window and choose *Import Library*.

Every library is different and reflects the personality and style of the person (or people) who wrote it. To learn how to use any library, consult the latest documentation for it on the Processing website.

22.2.1 System Libraries

As of Processing 1.1, there are nine system libraries.

You might be wondering why these system libraries exist at all. If they're part of the Processing system, why not just make them part of the language?

The answer is as much social as technical. The idea is that Processing is meant to offer language tools that will be useful to a broad cross-section of people. Everyone needs an *if statement*, and a `PGraphics` object is useful in all kinds of projects. Because of their general-purpose utility, those ideas are part of the core definition of the Processing language.

By contrast, libraries typically focus on more specific topics with more specialized audiences. By keeping the tools in the library out of the main language, you don't have to read up on and learn them if you don't need them, but they're never far away if your work calls for them. In many ways, they're like the books in your local public library versus the books in your home. They're available to you, but you check them out only when you need them.

The libraries themselves are open-source, meaning you can see (and modify) the code that goes into them. They're automatically downloaded along with Processing, so you've already got them all on your hard drive, ready to be imported and used.

Here's an overview of the nine system libraries as of this writing.

Video. (Read, display, and create video.) This library gives you access to QuickTime, which is a free download available for both Macs and PCs. With this library, you can read QuickTime videos, display them, and create your own. You can also read from a video camera and treat it as input for your sketch.

For example, with this library you can write a program that uses a webcam to watch you and displays that image on the screen. As you wave your hands around, you might create "trails" on the screen that change color over time. Or the program puts a hat on your head. Or it reads a video that you downloaded from the web and crops it to display just the upper-right corner, or it takes a color video and turns it into an old-fashioned newsreel by converting it to a range of sepia tones and showing it at a low, jerky frame rate.

Network. (Communications between computers.) If you want your sketch to communicate with a sketch running on another computer, this gives you the tools. So you can have two computers on opposite sides of the world talking to one another.

You might use this library to create a system for collaborative music making. One person creates the rhythm track, another the bass, another the lead melody, and so on. Each person is running their own program, but they're also communicating in real time with the others.

Or you could write a game where multiple players are on different computers but all participating in the same event.

Serial. (Communications with external devices.) Many peripheral devices, from musical keyboards to mice, communicate with the computer using a technique known as *serial communication*. Your mouse is probably a USB mouse, meaning that it talks to the computer by plugging into a USB slot on the side of the machine. That means you're already using a serial device: USB stands for "Universal Serial Bus."

Lots of different devices, including those you can build yourself, can "talk" USB in order to communicate with a computer. If a device has been set up with the right hardware and software, you can just plug it into the computer, and it's ready to communicate.

You might use this library to create a computer-controlled Christmas light show for your house, where your program is in charge of turning on and off different strings of lights at different moments, perhaps while synchronized to music. Or you might steer a little toy radio-controlled (RC) helicopter around the room. Or you could control an audio music synthesizer, telling it what notes to play with which "voices," or sounds.

PDF Export. (Write PDF files.) PDF is a common and useful format for saving resolution-independent images. I talked about using PDF files earlier, particularly in Chapter 17, where I imported and used this library to save our results in PDF format.

OpenGL. (Use the OpenGL renderer.) We've already seen this library many times since we had to import it every time we used that renderer. There's not much to the library beyond giving you the opportunity to specify OPENGL in your call to size().

Minim. (Audio input and output.) With this library, you can read, write, and work with audio files. You can "listen in" on the microphone attached to your computer (if there is one) and play sounds through the speakers. You can read the contents of audio files and manipulate them.

You can use this library to write a program that lets you mash up some of your favorite songs from your music library. Or you can play them back with effects like reverb and echo, giving them the sound of playing in a big empty room. You might create a project that listens to the computer's microphone and enhances that incoming audio with music that's tuned to the sounds and rhythms that are coming in. You can analyze the audio and clean it up by removing clicks and pops or dirty it up by adding lots of random little noises.

DXF Export. (Write to DXF files.) Just as PDF, jpg, and mp3 are common file formats for 2D vector art, 2D raster art, and music, the DXF format is common for 3D objects. Using this library lets you save your 3D creations to a DXF file, where they can be read in by almost any 3D program.

For example, suppose you wanted to create a 3D scene of a spiral staircase. You might have a great 3D modeling and rendering program around, but its tools are just not right for this job; it would be awkward and take forever: you'd have to spend hours drawing each step and then moving and rotating it into exactly the right position. But this kind of repetitive, transformation-heavy task is just right for a program, where you can use all the tools of Processing to write a little loop that creates as many steps as you need. Better yet, you can put that code in a routine with arguments, so you can easily make spiral staircases of any height, any radius, any number of steps, any number of turns, etc. So you write that program and export your final model into DXF. Then you read the DXF file into your 3D program and proceed as usual, as though you'd made the shape right in that program. If you later want another staircase, or you want to modify this one a little, you can just crank up Processing to create another model.

Unfortunately, this is a one-way process. You can export your 3D models to DXF format, but you can't read DXF models back into Processing. It's possible, of course, and you could write your own Processing code to read DXF files into Processing, but it would be a real challenge.

Arduino. (Work with an *Arduino*.) The Arduino is a little one-board computer that was designed to allow rapid, creative exploration of projects that involve computers. It's easy to connect devices of all kinds to the Arduino, so it can read and write and talk to everything from a sound synthesizer to a professional lighting rig, or even control the steering of your home-built UFO or blimp. There's a thriving community of people building all kinds of devices with the Arduino, and they freely share their hardware, software, and expertise with one another on the web and in hands-on workshops.

In terms of their philosophies, the Arduino is kind of the hardware version of Processing: small, friendly, and approachable.

Of course, it *is* hardware, so you have to put in some considerable effort to master the basics, but once you're over the hump, the Arduino is a great way to mess around with controlling external devices. Since it's a real thing, it isn't free, but there are a wide range of options available to you for buying or building an Arduino board. You can buy a complete, finished system ready to plug in the minute you receive it, or you can build one yourself from one of many different kinds of kits, or you can even download the entire design and list of parts for free on the web and do it all yourself.

You can run the Arduino while it's connected to your computer. But you can also download your Processing program into the Arduino and then disconnect it. Now you have a little stand-alone computer that runs your code and controls whatever you might plug into the Arduino board. People put Arduinos in their backpacks, on their bicycles, and in endless other public and private places, running code to control a never-ending sequence of creative and unusual devices.

Netscape.JavaScript. (Communicate from JavaScript to Java.) This one's a little weird. As we've seen, Processing normally gets compiled into Java. But applets on the web run in a different language called JavaScript (although the two names are very similar, and the languages have some overlap, they're actually entirely different languages).

This library lets JavaScript applets call Java methods, and vice versa. It's like a bridge between the two languages. This is a large and complex library for very specialized needs, and I recommend you only approach it if you're already well versed in both of its underlying languages.

22.2.2   User-Contributed Libraries

As of Processing 1.1, there are 105 (yes, 105!) user-contributed libraries. Holy smokes! Each one of these represents significant time, energy, and effort by one or more people to create something useful. And then each person put in even more time, energy, and effort to make sure their work was as free of bugs as they could make it, then each author worked even more to package it up and make it available to the rest of the world. Most people also add documentation and notes to help you learn their library and use it well. And it's all free, all the result of volunteer effort. I find that really inspiring.

The Processing website organizes these 105 libraries into 12 categories: Sound, Import/Export, Tools, Hardware, Animation, Typography/Geometry, Computer Vision/ Video, 3D, Simulation/Mathematics, Graphic Interface, Compilations, and Data Protocols.

As you might imagine, the level of complexity and sophistication in these libraries varies all over the map. Some libraries are small, carefully focused little packages intended to do one specific thing very well. Others are large, wide-ranging collections of algorithms and techniques that essentially provide you with a whole tool kit for exploring many different kinds of projects. Some libraries are straightforward little routines, and others embody very sophisticated algorithms taken from the latest research literature. But they all have the same goal: to give you new tools to use in your own projects.

I won't summarize all the libraries here; it would take many, many pages, and some libraries update frequently, making anything I said here become out of date almost as soon as I wrote it. Instead, I suggest you head over to the Processing website and scan through the list yourself. Each library has a little blurb that summarizes what it does. If you click on the library's name, you'll be taken to a webpage that describes it in more detail and offers you a download link.

Many libraries are designed to help Processing talk to other hardware and software. So if you have a favorite program or device that you'd like to hook up to Processing, before you dig into figuring out how to communicate with it using one of Processing's general-purpose system libraries, look through the user libraries. Someone may have already done the work for you.

Even if you can't find a library that does what you want, they can still be an enormous asset. Often you can find a library that does something close to what you're after. Since the libraries are open-source, downloading them means you get the Processing code that went into them. You can then take that code and use it as a starting point, pulling out what you don't need, adding in new stuff, and gradually transforming it into the library you need. This can give you a huge head start over beginning from scratch.

Libraries are also a great way to see how other people have approached large Processing projects. You can see how they broke down the problem, how many files they used and what went into which one, where they used global variables and where they used classes, and so on. Everyone has their own style, so no two libraries are likely to reflect the very same approach. By browsing all of this rich, working code, you can expand your own style, picking and choosing those techniques that appeal to you the most.

I find that reading through library source code for something I'm interested in is frequently a great learning experience. You can often discover a new trick or a new way to use an old idea, and that becomes another arrow in your quiver for your own projects.

The level of documentation that comes with the user-contributed libraries varies all over the map, of course. Some people write tons of documentation and comment their code extensively. Others give you just a few words of advice and leave it to you to figure things out.

I find that the best way to learn a new library is to write a series of little stand-alone sketches. I don't try to integrate it right away into some large, ongoing project. Rather, I'll build up a little toy project that starts out as small as possible: maybe just a `setup()` routine that calls one library function. Then I'll add another call, and another, until it starts to do something useful or interesting. In this little sandbox, I can play around with the library and try all kinds of experiments without worrying about the rest of my project. When I feel like I know how to do what I'm after, then I can either copy the code from my little toy or write new code for my project that uses the library based on what I've learned.

The value of this approach is that if things don't work right, you can usually figure out whether it's your code that's misbehaving, the library itself, or (most usually) the way you're using the library. If you try to learn the library in the midst of your own code, distinguishing these three categories of problems can be much more difficult.

New libraries pop up from time to time as people create and contribute them, so it's worth going back to the library page and checking it out for new entries every now and then.

22.3 Time and Date

A bunch of functions built into Processing will provide you with the current time and date. They all ask the operating system for that information, so they're only as accurate as your computer's reckoning. You can get the time with `hour()`, `minute()`, and `second()` and the date with `day()`, `month()`, and `year()`. The function `millis()` will tell you how many milliseconds (that is, 1/1000 of a second) have elapsed since your program started running.

Related to timing is the command delay(). You give it an argument in milliseconds, and your program will pause for that long.

22.4 Saving Your Images

As we saw in Chapter 17, you can save the image in your graphics window at any time with save(), which takes a filename as an argument and saves the current image as a file with that name. If you want to capture a series of images, then include a call to saveFrame() at the end of draw(). It will save the current image in a numbered file (starting with 0) and then each subsequent image produced by draw() will be saved with a number one greater than the one before. Be careful with saveFrame() because it will happily save images for you on every frame until your program stops, your disk fills up, or the universe collapses due to a black hole run amok, whichever comes first.

22.5 Window Wraparound

Sometimes it's useful to "wrap" the graphics window. To illustrate this idea, take a look at the animation we made at the end of Chapter 11 (a frame is in Figure 11.25). This looks to me like a type of meandering shape sometimes called a "drunkard's walk." Let's create a bunch of balls doing this at once. I'll take a few steps to modify the program and then we'll return to the question of wrapping the screen.

To make things easier, I'll put the balls into a class of their own. Below is the final program; this is just the program from Chapter 11, reorganized so that it's in an OOP structure. I'll call my objects Flies since they remind me of aimlessly wandering flies.

```
Ball [] Flies;

void setup() {
   size(600, 400);
   Flies = new Ball[3];
   Flies[0] = new Ball(300, 200,  2,  3, 30, 138,  59,  59, 255);
   Flies[1] = new Ball(400, 100, -2, -1, 50, 151, 166,  95, 255);
   Flies[2] = new Ball(100, 200,  3, -3, 20,  78, 120, 145, 255);
}

void draw() {
   background(128, 103, 103);
   for (int i=0; i<Flies.length; i++) {
      Flies[i].render();
      Flies[i].move();
   }
}
```

```
class Ball {
   float cx, cy;
   float vx, vy;
   float radius;
   float cr, cg, cb, ca;

   Ball( float acx, float acy, float avx, float avy,
   float aradius, float ar, float ag, float ab, float aa) {
      cx = acx;  cy = acy;
      vx = avx;  vy = avy;
      radius = aradius;
      cr = ar; cg = ag; cb = ab; ca = aa;
   }

   void render() {
      fill(cr, cg, cb, ca);
      ellipse(cx, cy, 2*radius, 2*radius);
   }

   void move() {
      float noiseScale = 0.02;
      radius += lerp(-1, 1, noise(frameCount*noiseScale));
      radius = constrain(radius, 10, 100);
      vx += lerp(-0.25, 0.25, noise(noiseScale*cx, noiseScale*cy));
      vy += lerp(-0.25, 0.25, noise(noiseScale*cy, noiseScale*cx));
      cx += vx;
      cy += vy;
      if ((cx-radius < 0) || (cx+radius >= width)) {
```

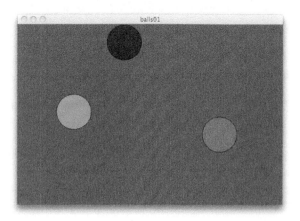

Figure 22.1. Multiple flies (frame from animation). (oddsends/sketches/balls01/balls01.pde).

```
        vx = -vx;
        cx += 2*vx;
    }
    if ((cy-radius < 0) || (cy+radius >= height)) {
        vy = -vy;
        cy += 2*vy;
    }
  }
}
```

(See output in Figure 22.1. Full program in oddsends/sketches/balls01/balls01.pde)

If you watch this animation, you'll see that all the balls are changing size in unison. Of course, that's because they're all using frameCount to get their noise value. Let's change that to something else that's convenient, say, simply cx.

```
radius += lerp(-1, 1, noise(cx*noiseScale));
```

(See output in Figure 22.2. Full program in oddsends/sketches/balls02/balls02.pde)

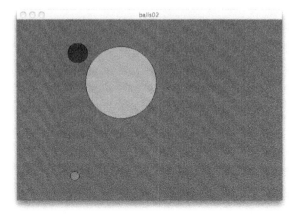

Figure 22.2. Improved flies (frame from animation). (oddsends/sketches/balls02/balls02.pde)

Ah, much better. I'm not crazy about manually entering in all that information for each ball, so I'll add a blank constructor that will fill everything in randomly. This has another advantage, in that I don't have to manually update the length of the array each time I add or remove one ball. I'll just create a single variable called numFlies, and everything flows from there. By rolling up my colors using the random-number generator, I risk getting some garish results; I can always replace this with a list of harmonious colors if I prefer, as we did for the leaves in Chapter 15.

```
void setup() {
  size(600, 400);
```

```
    int numFlies = 4;
    Flies = new Ball[numFlies];
    for (int i=0; i<numFlies; i++) {
        Flies[i] = new Ball();
    }
}

Ball() {
    cx = random(50, width-50);
    cy = random(50, height-50);
    vx = random(-3, 3);
    vx = random(-3, 3);
    radius = random(10, 30);
    cr = random(100, 255);
    cg = random(100, 255);
    cb = random(100, 255);
    ca = random(100, 255);
}
```

(See output in Figure 22.3. Full program in oddsends/sketches/balls03/balls03.pde)

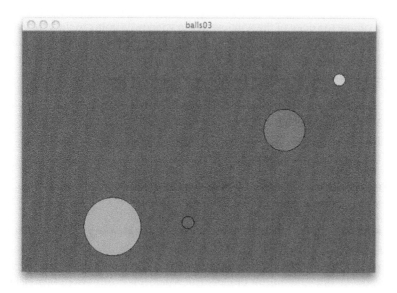

Figure 22.3. A few more balls, randomly constructed (frame from animation). (oddsends/sketches/balls03/balls03.pde)

I could get rid of the more complicated constructor and save a few lines, but since I might want it later, and it's not hurting anything, I'll leave it in for now.

Figure 22.4. A wraparound screen. The spaceship has just flown off the top left of the screen and has reappeared at the bottom left. You can still see the lower left fin of the ship at the top of the screen.

Now we can address the point of this section. What if the balls didn't bounce off the edges of the window? What if they just rolled right around from one side to the next? Lots of video games do this by providing a *wraparound* effect for the graphics window. In the classic *Asteroids* arcade game, if you fly your spaceship off the top of the screen, it reappears on the bottom. If you fly off the left side, you come back in from the right. Figure 22.4 shows how this looks in an *Asteroids*-type game as the ship leaves the top of the screen.

We can do the same thing, but we have to work a little to make the effect look convincing. Let's follow the motion of a circle with radius 100 as it moves up. When the center of the circle is at $y = 200$, say, the whole circle is in the window. When the center is at $y = 100$, the top edge is just touching the top side of the window. If the circle moves one more unit up, putting the center at $y = 99$, then a tiny, one-pixel tall sliver falls off the top edge of the window. If the window is going to look like it's wrapping around, then that little sliver has to show up on the bottom side of the window. Now the circle keeps moving up, and when the center is at $y = 50$, a big wedge has fallen off the top edge, and needs to appear on the bottom. Finally, the circle's center reaches $y = 0$, and half the circle appears at the bottom. As the circle keeps moving, say to $y = -25$, we see less and less of it on the top and more and more of it on the bottom. Figure 22.5 shows this in action.

The same kind of thing happens when the circle moves across any of the window's sides. How can we draw circles to make it look like the window is wrapped around?

The trick is to draw a second circle on the other side of the screen. So when the circle is partly falling off the top edge of the window, we'll draw another, identical circle at the bottom edge of the window. Let's call that second circle a *mirror* circle, not because it's a reflection, but because it moves the way the original circle moves.

Where do we draw the mirror circle? The window is `height` pixels tall. If we draw the mirror circle `height` pixels below the original, all will be well. Think of it this way: suppose every circle has four others attached to it

Figure 22.5. Window wraparound: the ball moves up as we read left to right. Any piece of the ball that disappears off the top edge needs to be drawn at the bottom.

by rods, making a giant plus sign with a circle in the middle and circles on the ends. The left and right rods have length `width`, and the upper and lower rods have length `height`. When the original circle starts to move past the top side of the window, the

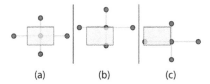

(a)　　　　　　(b)　　　　　　(c)

Figure 22.6. Wrapping the disk around the screen using a "plus sign" made of other balls. As the center ball crosses an edge, another ball appears at the opposite edge. (a) The center disk is fully onscreen, so none of the other disks are visible. (b) The center disk straddles the upper edge, so the lower disk is partly visible. (c) The center disk straddles the right edge, so the left disk is partly visible.

circle at the end of the lower rod starts to appear. Figure 22.6 shows the idea. We'll need to change `move()` so that we don't bounce any more, and we'll need to change `render()` to draw the mirror circles. Let's take these one at a time.

In `move()`, I'll take out the bouncing code. When a ball moves off the left side (that is, the center is less than zero), I'll add the window's width to it. In essence, the ball is jumping to the position that was occupied by its mirror, and its old position becomes a mirror of the new one. The ball and mirror change places. Because `render()` will always draw all the necessary mirrors, we won't see any visual effects of this swap. I'll need to check all four sides. The last eight lines of `move()` get replaced by this:

```
if (cx >= width) cx -= width;
if (cx < 0) cx += width;
if (cy >= height) cy = height;
if (cy < 0) cy += height;
```

Now we'll draw the mirror balls. We could, of course, just draw all four mirror balls every time. Usually they'll be offscreen and so Processing will just skip the rendering step. But this is wasteful and could use up valuable time we might prefer to be using to make our game better. So instead, I'll just draw the mirror balls when needed. When a ball is crossing a wall, I'll draw the mirror ball on the opposite wall:

```
void render() {
    fill(cr, cg, cb, ca);
    ellipse(cx, cy, 2*radius, 2*radius);
    if (cx < radius) ellipse(cx+width, cy, 2*radius, 2*radius);
    if (width-cx < radius) ellipse(cx-width, cy, 2*radius, 2*radius);
    if (cy < radius) ellipse(cx, cy+height, 2*radius, 2*radius);
    if (height-cy < radius) ellipse(cx, cy-height, 2*radius, 2*radius);
}
```

(See output in Figure 22.7. Full program in oddsends/sketches/balls04/balls04.pde)

Because each side of the window is handled independently, this nicely handles situations where the ball is crossing over two walls at once, like when it drifts into a corner.

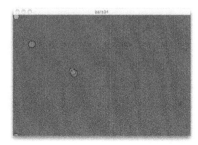

Figure 22.7. Balls in a wraparound window (frame from animation).
(oddsends/sketches/balls04/balls04.pde)

22.6 Debugging

Sometimes error messages can be confusing. Suppose you have a line like this:

```
for (int y=0; y<100; y+) {
```

When you try to run this program, you'll find that the line gets highlighted, and in the message area, you'll get the error message

```
unexpected token: )
```

Well, that's confusing.

First of all, what's a token?

Second of all, what's wrong with that parenthesis?

In general, when you get an error message that isn't entirely obvious, try to get a general idea of the problem if you can and then use your own eyes to figure out what it's complaining about. Here it's saying that the right parenthesis is unexpected. We know that the *for loop* has to have those parentheses, so it seems entirely expected to me.

So I look at the line more closely. Aha, instead of writing y++, I wrote y+. Processing saw this and figured there was more to come; maybe it was going to be y+3 or y++. Instead, it got y+). Of course, I wanted y++ and fixing that solves the problem.

When error messages don't seem to make any sense, just accept that something is off and don't worry too much about what the message is telling you. Something's wrong, and Processing's helped as much as it knows how. To continue, you'll need to locate and solve the problem yourself. There are two types of tools that will quickly become your best friends in this process.

The first tools are the print() and println() statements. You've seen me use them. They can take a mix of strings and numerical values, pasted together with + signs. They give you a great way to find out what's happening in your code by printing out the results of your work. The difference is that println() puts a newline at the end of the line. If you want to include a newline of your own, use the sequence "\n".

```
print("y = " + y + "  and z = " + z + "\n");
```

Your other friend is the comment. This is particularly useful when you're having trouble figuring out just where the error is located. It's unfortunate, but sometimes the line that Processing identifies as the error line isn't really where the problem lies. What's happening is that something goes a little bit wrong in your program, but Processing doesn't really get confused until later on. It announces the error where it got confused, but that line looks (and is) entirely correct and innocent.

Here's an example of an error message that takes some decoding:

```
void setup() {
}

int countApples(float a) {
    float f = a;
    return(f);
}
```

If you run this, the `return` statement is flagged in yellow, and Processing says

```
Cannot convert from float to int.
```

How can the *return statement* be doing anything wrong? It must be that something's wrong with f, but f is just a `float` that gets assigned from another `float`. What's left? The type of the function! The function `countApples()` is declared to return an `int`, but the statement returns a `float`. Processing caught the error, but it didn't explicitly tell you that the reason was that you were returning a `float` when you said you'd return an `int`. It's your job to work out that this was the problem, given only the flagged yellow line and the error message.

Here's another weird error:

```
void setup() {
    int wid = 300;
    if (wid < 1) {
        float g = random(200, wid-200));
    }
}
```

If you run this, the line starting `float g` is highlighted, and you get the error message

```
unexpected token: float
```

If you look at this for a while, you'll see that the problem is that there is an extra closing parenthesis at the end of that line. To explain why that error caused this error message, we'd have to make a temporary digression and spend a few weeks or months talking about compiler theory, preferably with a good textbook or two to help. Short of that, we have to use our wits.

Ultimately, if the error isn't obvious, we have to just poke and prod in the suspected area of the code, commenting things out until we isolate the problem. If we comment out a line and the bug goes away, we can then drill into every character on that line and force ourselves to spot the mistake.

Here's a run-time bug. This produces no error message during the compilation step, so it turns into an executable Java program without any problem. But it really messes up the project when it runs (hence the name):

```
float v = sqrt(x*x)+(y*y);
```

In this code I'm trying to find the distance from the point $(0,0)$ to the point (x,y) (if I'd used norm(), then I'd have avoided this error, but let's assume I want to do it manually for some reason). You could run a program with this statement in it for a long time, with things never seeming to be quite right, and never really know what was going wrong.

The problem here is that this is a perfectly legal statement in Processing. There's no way Processing can possibly know that I didn't intend to write exactly this. If you remember the Pythagorean Theorem from high school, you've probably guessed that what I meant was to find the square root of the sum of these two subexpressions. I need another set of parentheses:

```
float v = sqrt((x*x)+(y*y));
```

This is often the nature of a run-time bug. You make a typo that compiles and runs cleanly but produces the wrong result. It's often very satisfying to catch these errors, but it can be frustrating to figure them out. If you really start pulling out your hair, take a break and relax, clear your mind, and come back later when you can see things with fresh eyes and a positive attitude.

Let's return to compile-time errors. When you just can't find the code that's responsible for Processing's error statement, try to isolate the problem by commenting out huge chunks of lines until the error goes away. For this job, the multiline comment pair /* and */ will be the most convenient. For example, consider one of our earlier examples, but with some surrounding context:

```
a = 47;
for (int y=0; y<100; y+) {
    drawLine(y);
}
b = 33;
```

When Processing complains about the unexpected token, you might not spot the problem right away. If you think that this line might be perfectly fine, and so the error is of the runaway kind (that is, something went wrong much earlier), try commenting

out the part it's complaining about. In this case, commenting out just the line with the
`for` statement would cause its own errors, so you'll want to comment out the whole *for
loop*:

```
a = 47;
/*
for (int y=0; y<100; y+) {
    drawLine(y);
}
*/
b = 33;
```

Processing will display the commented-out lines in light gray text, confirming that
they'll be ignored. Now try running the program again.

If you were getting a runaway error due to something happening earlier in the program, you'll get a new, unlikely looking error at the line where you're assigning 33 to
b, or shortly after. That'll be more evidence that something is wrong up above. You can
then continue the process, working your way up the program and commenting things
out until the error goes away. When you finally get the program to compile properly,
you'll know your most recent change was the one that removed the source of the problem. Then you'll know you're in the right spot (or close to it), and you can focus your
search.

It's very satisfying to go through this process, fix an error, and then uncomment out
huge blocks of code that then run perfectly!

Remember that you can't put one multiline comment inside of another. When Processing sees `*/`, that tells it, "Comments are over, back to program text." So keep an
eye on your comments. Processing will help by color-coding your comments (on my
system, comments are gray). If you see code that should be commented, but it's not in
the commenting color, you'll know you've slipped somewhere.

But let's step back and suppose that commenting out the *for loop* removed the error
(as it would, in this case). That tells us that the error really is coming from something
to do with this loop.

The next step then is to restore the loop but leave out the code inside it:

```
a = 47;
for (int y=0; y<100; y+) {
/*
    drawLine(y);
*/
}
b = 33;
```

Ah, the error is back. So something is wrong with the lines we just put back in. One
of them is just a closing curly brace. The other is the *for loop* itself. So now we can
pick through both lines, one letter at a time, until we spot that missing + sign.

This general strategy is time consuming, but it's a great way to isolate problems. You can comment out the entire contents of great hulking blocks of code and then un-comment them one chunk at a time, step by step, to locate precisely where the problem is.

Human beings being what we are, sometimes I can stare at a line of code like this for five minutes and not see the problem. I know I meant to type y++, and somehow I just always see y++ every time I look at it. Typos persist.

When I'm really up against the wall, sometimes I'll delete and retype the offending line. In this case, that would almost certainly fix the problem, since I'm unlikely to make that same dumb typo twice. I usually delete the line before I retype it so that I don't accidentally just mimic my mistake.

If that doesn't work, I'll often grab the whole block that's causing me trouble, copy it, paste it somewhere else (in another window or another file), and save it. Then I'll delete it from my source code and write it again. Unless the code is really simple (like it was in this example), I'll probably implement the steps in at least a slightly different way, and that can be enough to steer a new course that avoids whatever sharp rocks I was running into before.

Another trick for isolating run-time errors is to completely replace procedures that you think might be causing trouble. For example, suppose you had a procedure like this:

```
float makeCoffeeshop(int numberChairs, int numberTables)
{
    // huge complicated stuff here
    return(finalResult);
}
```

Say that your code compiles, but something is going wrong somewhere along the line. If you're having trouble figuring out where the problem is coming from, you can try removing procedures one by one. Rather than actually remove them, I just *rename and replace*. That is, I rename the existing procedure with a similar name and replace it with something else that's as simple as possible. In this case, I might replace the code above with this:

```
float makeCoffeeshop(int numberChairs, int numberTables) {
    return(1.0);
}

// this was the original makeCoffeeshop
float old_makeCoffeeshop(int numberChairs, int numberTables)
{
    // huge complicated stuff here
    return(finalResult);
}
```

Now my code can call this routine as usual, but if there's something wrong inside the original version, I've just placed a short circuit around it. If my program works now, that's a strong suggestion that something's wrong with my original version of the function. If the problem persists, I'll try this little replacement strategy again and again. Ultimately, I'll end up with a program that does almost nothing, but it will do it correctly! Then I'll try adding the functions back in, simply by switching the names of the little replacement functions and the originals. When I'm all done and things are working, I try to remember to delete the little substitution functions so I won't later confuse them for real code.

Sometimes debugging can drive you up a wall. Whatever is wrong is just not revealing itself to your eyes. It's probably right there in front of you, but you simply can't see it. Talking to a friend or getting help from someone else is always a good ultimate backup when you're really stuck. Sometimes fresh eyes can see something that you've looked right at and missed 20 times in a row.

22.7 Types and Type Conversion

In Chapter 3 I talked about some of Processing's built-in data types and how to convert between them. We've seen some of the other types in later chapters.

Figure 22.8 lists all the *primitive types* in one place.

It's often useful to be able to convert from one type to another (see Figure 22.9). You've seen me use `int()` to convert a `float` to an `int` type (though of course we lose anything to the right of the decimal point when we do that).

We've seen some advanced constructions like arrays and objects. What types are those?

type	values
boolean	true or false
byte	127 to -128
char	a single character (16 bits, in Unicode format)
color	32 bits, 8 bits per channel
double	64-bit float
float	32 bits, -3.40282347E+38 to 3.40282347E+38
int	32 bits , -2,147,483,648 to 2,147,483,647
long	64 bits, -9,223,372,036,854,775,808 to 9,223,372,036,854,775,807

Figure 22.8. Primitive types in Processing and their ranges.

function	from	to
binary()	byte, char, int, color	a String of 0 and 1 chars
boolean()	primitive, String, array	true unless the input is 0
byte()	primitive	a number from -128 to 127
char()	primitive	a number
float()	primitive, String, array	a float
hex()	byte, char, int, color, String	a String of characters in hex notation
int()	primitive, string, array	an int
str()	primitive, array	a String or String array
unbinary()	String	an int from a String of 0's and 1's
unhex()	String	a hex-format int from a String

Figure 22.9. Type conversions in Processing.

It turns out that arrays are actually of type Array, and a general "object" is of type Object. You'll normally never need to directly refer to these types, but you'll see them occasionally.

22.7.1 Working with Bits

Warning! This next section covers very low-level detailed stuff. You will probably never need to use this information. I'm including it here because you may see it in other people's code, and I don't want you to be mystified. But I'm going to go through it pretty quickly and not in a lot of depth. If you get the general gist of this section, you'll be more than fine.

Every once in a while it's useful to dig down deep into the guts of a number and get at the 1's and 0's that the computer is using. Usually you'll do this because you want to talk to some external piece of hardware (like a sound synthesizer or lighting controller) or you know something about your numbers that lets you do something sneaky that saves some time.

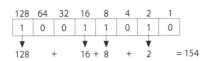

Figure 22.10. The number 154 in binary.

To illustrate these ideas, consider the number 154. Inside the computer, this is represented by the sequence 10011010.

To decode this *binary representation* of a *decimal number*, you add up the values of the slots that have a 1 in them. The value of each slot starts with 1 at the far right and doubles with each step you take to the left. So the values of the slots, read right to left, go 1, 2, 4, 8, 16, 32, and so on.

To work out the decimal (or everyday) value of the binary number 10011010, we begin with a total of 0. Now we'll work our way from the far right to the far left, adding in the value for any slot that has a 1 in it, as shown in Figure 22.10.

As we can see in the figure, the right-most slot holds a 0, so we skip it. The next slot to the left holds a 1. That slot has value 2, so we add 2 into our running sum. The next slot is 0, and the next one is a 1. That slot is worth 8, so we add that to our sum: $8 + 2 = 10$. The next slot is also a 1, and that slot is worth 16, so we add that into the sum: $10 + 16 = 26$. The next two slots are 0 and then finally the left-most slot, worth 128, has a 1, so we add that in: $26 + 128 = 154$. Ta-da!

For humans, 154 is the most convenient way to write this number. Inside the computer, 10011010 is more convenient. But they're the same thing.

If you push (or *shift*) this sequence one step to the right, the right-most 0 drops off and you have 1001101, which works out to 77. We just divided by two! Similarly, if we shift it one step to the left, we get 100110100, which is 308. We just multiplied by two! Shifting right and left to divide and multiply by two works perfectly for positive integers, but *only* for positive integers. Other numbers are stored in other formats where the 0's and 1's have different interpretations. If you shift the bits of, say, a floating-point number, you'll just get back nonsense.

This bit-shifting business is just one of an endless number of little tricks that people have developed to squeeze every drop of speed out of their programs. I don't suggest getting too much into this yourself, but you might see other people doing it in their code, so you should be aware of the concept. These kinds of tricks used to be much more important, but modern software has become sophisticated enough that the computer will automatically apply them for you whenever it can.

To manipulate these binary representations, Processing gives you *bit operators*, so named because they operate on the 0's and 1's (that is, the bits) in the number.

To push (or shift) a binary number to the right, you use the *right shift* operator, written >>. On the left you put the number to shift, and on the right, the number of steps to shift it. So we might write the above example this way:

```
int value = 154;
int halfValue = value >> 1;   // superfast divide-by-2
```

To shift a binary number to the left, you use the *left shift* operator, written <<.

You can also apply *logical operations* to binary numbers. Two of the most common are called *and* and *or*. Recall that the test operators && and || work on `boolean` types, which can be `true` or `false`.

The bit operators do the very same things as their `boolean`-based cousins, but they use the bit 1 to mean `true` and the bit 0 to mean `false`.

The *bitwise and* operator is written & (just a single &). So if both of its arguments are 1, it returns a 1 as well, otherwise it returns 0.

The *bitwise or* operator is written | (just a single vertical |). So if either (or both) of its arguments are 1, it returns a 1 as well, otherwise it returns 0.

These operators can work on entire numbers in bit format at once.

To avoid confusion with the logical testing operators && and ||, the bitwise-and and bitwise-or operators are usually pronouced out loud as "bitwise and" and "bitwise or."

I'll show them in action in the next program fragment, but I recommend you just kind of glance at this for now. If you need to get into bit operations, you can come back to this section and carefully go through the details.

```
void setup() {
  int a = 218;
  int b = 185;
  int a_or_b = a|b;
  int a_and_b = a&b;
  int a_shift_r = a>>1;
  int a_shift_l = a<<1;

  println("a="+a+"            in binary="+binary(a));
  println("b="+b+"            in binary="+binary(b));
  println("a_or_b="+a_or_b+"     in binary="+binary(a_or_b));
  println("a_and_b="+a_and_b+"     in binary="+binary(a_and_b));
  println("a_shift_r="+a_shift_r+"  in binary="+binary(a_shift_r));
  println("a_shift_l="+a_shift_l+"  in binary="+binary(a_shift_l));
}
```

(Full program in oddsends/sketches/bitOps/bitOps.pde)

This gives the following result:

```
a=218            in binary=11011010
b=185            in binary=10111001
a_or_b=251       in binary=11111011
a_and_b=152      in binary=10011000
a_shift_r=109    in binary=1101101
a_shift_l=436    in binary=110110100
```

This is really specialized stuff. When you see someone doing bit operations, you'll know they're digging deep into the guts of their computer for some very careful, low-level work.

22.8   Offscreen Drawing

When you draw graphics, normally they all go straight to the screen. But you can create an *offscreen image* if you want. It's called *offscreen* because you can use it just like a graphics window, but it doesn't appear on the screen anywhere. In fact, it's nothing more than a simulated screen in the computer's memory.

An offscreen window might be useful as a place to store graphics that take a while to draw but that you'll want to use over and over. Processing itself does this for fonts, as I discussed in Chapter 20, where a font is rendered into an offscreen image and then the letters are just copied back onto the screen.

If you want to do this yourself, you create a new object of type PGraphics with the call createGraphics(), which takes the desired width and height of your offscreen window, along with the renderer you want to use when drawing into it. To start drawing into your new offscreen window, you must first tell Processing to direct its attention to that window with a call to beginDraw(). Then you issue your drawing commands (prefixing each one with the PGraphics object you created) and then end with endDraw(). Don't forget to include the calls to beginDraw() and endDraw() or you may end up not drawing anything into your offscreen window. Note that beginDraw() and endDraw() are methods of the offscreen object. So if your PGraphics object is called offscreen, to start drawing into it, you'd call offscreen.beginDraw(), and to end your drawing you'd call offscreen.endDraw().

In Chapter 20 I said that we could write our own routine to make a good guess about a font's x-height (that's the height of a lower-case letter with no ascender or descender, like the letter x). Now that we know how to create (and draw into) an offscreen window, we can bring that idea to life.

The heart of the approach is to render the type into an offscreen window and measure the height of a lower-case x over there. Let's build this up in pieces. I'll start with a skeleton that makes a typical onscreen graphics window and then draws some text into it:

```
void setup() {
    size(600, 400);
    PFont myFont = loadFont("ChaparralPro-Bold-96.vlw");
    textFont(myFont);

    background(240, 215, 175);
    String message = "raspberry!";

    fill(145, 44, 66);
    text(message, 50, 200);
}
```

(See output in Figure 22.11. Full program in oddsends/sketches/xheight01/xheight01.pde)

No surprises there.

Now my goal will be to find the x-height. How will I know I've done it? I'll dress up this display with three stripes: one from the baseline down to the bottom of the descender, one from the baseline up to the x-height, and another from the top of the x-height to the top of the ascender. I'll offset the three stripes so I can be sure they're not overlapping each other incorrectly. When the stripes look right, I'll know I've found these heights correctly.

Figure 22.11. Drawing some text. (oddsends/sketches/xheight01/xheight01.pde)

I'll stash the width of the text in a variable for convenience. I'll also call a function to compute the *x*-height. Of course, we haven't written that yet, so I'll just take a random guess and have it return 25 for now. I positioned the three stripes by hand so that they would form a little three-step pyramid.

```
void setup() {
   size(600, 400);
   PFont myFont = loadFont("ChaparralPro-Bold-96.vlw");
   textFont(myFont);

   background(240, 215, 175);
   String message = "raspberry!";
   float messageWidth = textWidth(message);
   int xheight = getXHeight();

   // top stripe
   fill(189, 176, 130);
   rect(75, 200-textAscent(), messageWidth, textAscent()-xheight);

   // center stripe
   fill(126, 189, 152);
   rect(45, 200, messageWidth+60, -xheight);

   // bottom stripe
   fill(145, 185, 189);
   rect(15, 200, messageWidth+120, textDescent());


   fill(145, 44, 66);
   text(message, 75, 200);
}
```

```
int getXHeight() {
  return(25);
}
```

(See output in Figure 22.12. Full program in oddsends/sketches/xheight02/xheight02.pde)

Figure 22.12. Drawings stripes to show the text heights.
(oddsends/sketches/xheight02/xheight02.pde)

The stripes are fitting around the text just right, and only the *x*-height is wrong. Now we can flesh out the function `getXHeight()`. When that's properly working, the central bar (in light green) should be just as tall as the lower-case letters.

So let's take a stab at `getXHeight()`:

```
int getXHeight() {
   PGraphics pg = createGraphics(10, 10, JAVA2D);
   pg.beginDraw();
   // do something
   pg.endDraw();

   int xheight = 25;
   return(xheight);
}
```

(Full program in oddsends/sketches/xheight03/xheight03.pde)

The main program uses the default renderer (that is, I didn't pick a different one with `size()`). But when you create an offscreen window with `createGraphics()`, it doesn't automatically use the default and requires you to tell it which renderer you want to use. So I've given it the same renderer as the one used by the main program, and since I haven't changed that, it's the default renderer `JAVA2D`.

I know that different renderers display fonts differently, so if I change the renderer I use in `size()`, I will definitely want to change the one in `getXHeight()` as well.

In this little start to the routine, I've done the essential things: I created the off-screen graphics window (which I've called pg), and I've called `pg.beginDraw()` and `pg.endDraw()` so that I can actually do things with it. So let's start doing things!

How big should the offscreen window be? I'm using (10, 10) right now, but that's just a placeholder. It should definitely be as wide and tall as the letter x we're going to put in there. Assuming that we've already loaded up the right font and set it to the active font using `textFont()`, we can just call `textWidth()` on the letter x. I don't know how tall to make the graphics window (finding out the height of the letter x is the whole point of this routine!), but I do know how to get the distance from the baseline to the ascender: `textAscent()`. Except for really bizarre fonts, a lower-case x shouldn't be any taller than a letter with an ascender, like the letter h. So that'll be my height.

In other words, the offscreen window will be as wide as a letter x and as tall as a letter h:

```
int hwid = int(textWidth("x"));
int hhgt = int(textAscent());
PGraphics pg = createGraphics(hwid, hhgt, JAVA2D);
```

Now I'm going to draw the letter x into the window, and...oh, wait. I have to set up the offscreen graphics window pg with all the font information I was using before. Remember, this is a brand-new world of graphics. It doesn't automatically inherit *any* information about the graphics state in the onscreen window. So I have to tell it what font I'm using. Which this routine doesn't know.

So I'll make the font a parameter to the routine.

```
int getXHeight(PFont myFont) {
```

Now let's put the x in there. I'll start by setting the background to 0 and the fill color to white. Then I'll tell the graphics window to use this font and then I'll draw a lower-case x starting in the lower-left corner:

```
pg.background(0);
pg.fill(255);
pg.textFont(myFont);
pg.text("x", 0, hhgt);
```

(Full program in oddsends/sketches/xheight03/xheight03.pde)

Note that I'm placing the x at (0, hhgt). That tells Processing to put the lower-left corner of the letter in the lower-left corner of the window.

I can't see the offscreen window. I could of course copy its pixels into the onscreen window, but short of that, it's just another piece of computer memory with stuff in it. Working with offscreen windows is a little bit like flying an airplane through the clouds when you have no visibility. You trust your instruments, but it's up to you to make sure that you're giving the instructions you intend to get the results you want; there's no onscreen feedback to help you know you're getting it right.

So if this code works properly (and I think it should), we now have a little graphics window that has a white *x* sitting on a black background. All we have to do is find out how tall the *x* is.

We know it starts at the bottom of the window, because we put it there, so we only really need to find its top. Suppose we start looking at the pixels of the window, starting at the top and working our way down. As soon as we find a pixel that isn't black, that's the topmost pixel of the letter, so the letter's height is the distance from this first nonblack pixel to the bottom of the window.

So let's do that. I'll write a little loop that runs down from the top of the window and looks across the pixels of each row, looking for the first nonblack pixel. I'm not testing for pure white because Processing might use intermediate shades of gray to help the letters look nicer on the screen. But anything that isn't the black background must be part of the *x*, and that's all I'm after.

So I'll just scan the graphics window, top–down left–right, until I find something. For simplicity, I'll just test the red value of the color. Since I've drawn a white *x* on a black background, all three color components will be the same at every pixel. Then I'll return the distance from that line to the bottom of the window; that's the height of the letter *x*.

Figure 22.13. The *x*-height! (oddsends/sketches/xheight04/xheight04.pde)

```
int ytop = 0;
// scan down from top
for (ytop=0; ytop<hhgt; ytop++) {
  for (int x=0; x<width; x++) {
    color c = pg.get(x, ytop);
    if (red(c) != 0) {
```

```
        int xheight = 1 + hhgt - ytop;
        return(xheight);
      }
    }
  }
  return(hhgt);
```

(See output in Figure 22.13. Full program in oddsends/sketches/xheight04/xheight04.pde)

That does it!

If I find a pixel that isn't white, I return the height to the bottom. If I don't, I assume something went wrong and I return the entire height of the window (that is, the value from textAscent()).

Figure 22.14. Three more fonts with their *x*-heights.

You can see the results for three other fonts that I have on my computer in Figure 22.14. The topmost example shows an interesting situation: in this font, the letter *p* has a little extra bit that sticks up above the other lower-case letters. So the *x*-height isn't perfectly consistent across all the letters in a typeface, and if the letter *x* happens to be one of the weird ones, the estimate returned by this routine will be wrong by the amount that the *x* is unlike the rest of the typeface. But in general, I think *x* is a reasonable guess (the height is called the *x*-height, after all), and the algorithm seems to do a pretty good job most of the time.

Offscreen graphics can be a huge efficiency boost for all kinds of programs. Anytime you have some graphics that get redrawn in the same way (or nearly the same way) on every frame, you might want to think about drawing them in an offscreen window. Then you can just throw your image up on the screen quickly rather than computing it anew.

This is a classic trade-off in programming: you're spending some memory to buy some time. Specifically, you're using the computer's memory to save the graphics, which enables you to save the time it would otherwise cost to redraw them every frame.

One popular use of offscreen windows (also called *offscreen buffers*) is to save a complicated background image. If you have a game or an art piece that uses the same background for every frame, why draw it over and over? Just draw it once and save it.

Another use for offscreen buffers is for little animated objects that move around. You might be writing a game where a hundred little creatures are running up and down hills, building bridges, digging tunnels, and doing other actions of your bidding. You could read in a single big image from the disk that holds a grid of drawings: one each for every pose your characters can take. Then to create each frame, you just find the necessary pose and copy it to the screen in the proper position for every character.

Of course, your program can also create these little drawings at run time if you prefer and your graphics are simple enough. That might be a better way to go if your characters are little robots, and you want them to look different each time someone plays your game. Your program might have a few routines for drawing different robots, but it uses random numbers to choose whether each one has wheels or treads, whether or not it has an antenna on the top, whether it's made out of red metal or blue plastic, and so on.

How do you copy an offscreen buffer to the screen? You wouldn't guess from its definition, but our friend image() from Chapter 16 does the job. Instead of giving it a variable of type PImage for its first argument, you give it a PGraphics object. Happily, image() will treat that as a PImage, and it will copy its contents to the screen. As usual, you must also give image() an upper-left x and y to tell it where to place the pixels. And again as usual, you can give it two additional arguments to define the width and height of the rectangle into which the pixels should be drawn.

If you would like to explicitly create a PImage object from a PGraphics object, you can use get(). For example, if you have a PGraphics object named pg, you could write

```
PImage newImage = pg.get(0, 0, pg.width, pg.height);
```

To show the power of offscreen buffers, let's make a very simple simulation of a radar screen. I'll take my inspiration from every low-budget TV show and movie that shows such a screen. The most important thing is that it's all green. For whatever reason, TV radar screens are traditionally green. So ours will be, too.

The radar screen is a grid with a bunch of circles on top of it. A narrow, bright green segment sweeps around the circle, leaving a glowing trail behind. When the segment passes over an object, a little circle appears under the segment. It, too, fades out with time.

Of course, we could easily decorate our radar with a million other details, but this is enough to get us started and demonstrate how to use an offscreen buffer.

To get started, I'm going to draw the background image in an offscreen buffer that I'll name Background. Note that this doesn't interfere with Processing's own function background(), both because it's a variable (rather than a function) and because it starts with a a capital letter, and Processing considers capital and lower-case letters to be entirely different.

I'll set the offscreen window's background to a dark green color. Then using a bright green, I'll draw a rectangular grid of thin lines.

On top of that, I'll draw some concentric circles that are somewhat thicker and more obvious. Cutting across the circles will be some radial lines that don't quite meet in the center. And around the outside, a whole bunch of little hash marks.

Since I don't really know exactly how I want this to look, I'll cook up a bunch of variables to control it. That way I can make more circles (or fewer of them), more lines (or fewer of them), space everything farther apart or closer together, and so on. After all, I'm not working from any kind of real radar screen here, but I'm just trying to draw something that feels to me like the simple radar screens I've seen in the movies. Here's my code to draw the background, with the variables set to the values that I finally tweaked them to.

The result of this code is shown in Figure 22.15.

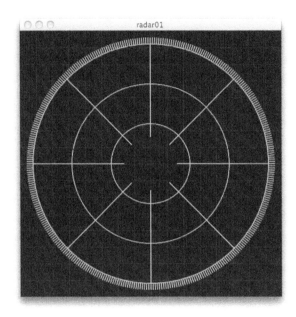

Figure 22.15. The radar background. (oddsends/sketches/radar01/radar01.pde)

```
PGraphics Background;

int Window = 480;        // size of the graphics window
float Cx = Window/2.0;   // center x
float Cy = Window/2.0;   // center y

int NumRings = 3;        // number of circles around the center
float RingLo = 0.3;      // percentage of window for first radius
float RingHi = 0.9;      // percentage of window for last radius

int NumLines = 8;        // how many radial lines
float RadialLineLo = 0.2;  // percentage of window where they start
float RadialLineHi = 0.9;  // percentage of window where they end

int NumHashMarks = 360;  // number of little hash marks around outside
```

```
float HashLineLo = 0.9;     // percentage of window where they start
float HashLineHi = 0.95;    // percentage of window where they end

color BrightGreen = color(140, 215, 85);  // bright-green color

void setup() {
   size(Window, Window, P2D);
   smooth();
   makeBackground();           // create the background
}

void draw() {
   image(Background, 0, 0);    // draw the background
}

void makeBackground() {
   Background = createGraphics(Window, Window, P2D);
   Background.beginDraw();
   Background.smooth();
   Background.background(24, 44, 18);    //dark green background

   // draw background grid
   Background.stroke(42, 94, 30);
   Background.strokeWeight(1);
   float lineGap = (Window/16.0);
   Background.noFill();
   for (int i=1; i<16; i++) {
      Background.line(0, i*lineGap, Window, i*lineGap);
      Background.line(i*lineGap, 0, i*lineGap, Window);
   }

   // draw inner graphics
   Background.stroke(red(BrightGreen), green(BrightGreen), blue(BrightGreen));
   Background.strokeWeight(2);

   // inner rings
   float diameter;
   for (int ring=0; ring<NumRings; ring++) {
      diameter = Window * lerp(RingLo, RingHi, ring*1.0/(NumRings-1));
      Background.ellipse(Cx, Cy, diameter, diameter);
   }

   // radial lines
   for (int lineCount=0; lineCount<NumLines; lineCount++) {
      float theta = radians(360.0 * lineCount/NumLines);
      float r0 = RadialLineLo * (Window/2.0);
```

```
        float r1 = RadialLineHi * (Window/2.0);
        Background.line(Cx+(r0*cos(theta)), Cy+(r0*sin(theta)),
                       Cx+(r1*cos(theta)), Cy+(r1*sin(theta)));
    }

    // outer hash marks
    for (int lineCount=0; lineCount<NumHashMarks; lineCount++) {
        float theta = radians(360.0 * lineCount/NumHashMarks);
        float r0 = HashLineLo * (Window/2.0);
        float r1 = HashLineHi * (Window/2.0);
        Background.line(Cx+(r0*cos(theta)), Cy+(r0*sin(theta)),
                       Cx+(r1*cos(theta)), Cy+(r1*sin(theta)));
    }

    Background.endDraw();
}
```

(See output in Figure 22.15. Full program in oddsends/sketches/radar01/radar01.pde)

Notice that draw() has a very easy life. All it does is use image() to splat the precomputed background image onto the graphics window. The background is already the correct size, so this step happens in no time at all.

There's not much to makeBackground(), which merely draws a bunch of lines and circles. But there are a few things to keep in mind when drawing into the off-screen window. First, every graphics command has to be preceded by Background. (that is, the name of the PGraphics object Background followed by a period), so that Processing knows we're trying to draw into that offscreen buffer and not the on-screen graphics window. Second, we can't forget to call beginDraw() at the start and endDraw() at the end!

Okay, let's get this radar moving. The most obvious thing that's missing is the sweeping bright beam and the trail it leaves behind. How can we draw that?

If we were using a graphic-arts program we might have a gradient tool that would let us draw a smoothly changing field from bright, opaque green to transparent nothingness. Alas, there's no such tool in Processing.

I can think of a way to create this image, but it'll run at a snail's pace. I can scan the window, and for every pixel, test where it is in relation to the beam. If it's in the beam, it's bright green. If it's in the big circle of the radar screen, but behind the beam, it's increasingly transparent as it's farther and farther from the beam itself. After a certain angle, it'll be fully transparent.

This calculation will crawl because I'll have to do a bunch of math at every pixel. If only there was a way to use an offscreen buffer for this, then I could just draw it once, slowly, and reuse it. But the beam isn't fixed in place like the background because it rotates.

Wait a second. The beam picture never changes. It's got a bright wedge and a fading trail. The only change that happens is that it rotates around the center. If I drew this into a buffer, then I could use Processing's transformation commands to simply rotate the coordinate system for each frame before I call image() to draw the picture.

So let's do that! I'll make another offscreen buffer called Pulse and draw that at the start of the program, just like the background. It'll take a little while, but it will only happen once.

To make the Pulse, I'll create the offscreen window and set it up as usual. I'll clear the background to completely transparent black (the black color is arbitrary because all that matters here is that the pixels are completely transparent; because of that transparency, the color itself could be black or purple or eggshell and it wouldn't matter). Then I'll scan every pixel, and when I find a pixel that's part of the image, I'll set it to green and some opacity.

The first step in this pixel-by-pixel scan will be to find the distance of the pixel from the center of the window (which is the center of the radar screen). That's easy to do with mag(). If the pixel's outside of the big circle, then I use continue to stop all further work on this pixel and move on to the next (I'm only building up this picture once, but there's no reason to waste time if I don't have to).

If the pixel is in the circle, I use the built-in atan2() function to find its angle. I discussed this function back in Chapter 18. The idea is that you give it the y and x-coordinates of your point (in that order), and it tells you the angle of that point. In Processing, the angle is figured clockwise starting at three o'clock.

I use a few angles to determine the look of the pulse. First is PulseBeamWidth. That's the angle of the very bright part of the beam itself and is pretty narrow. Those pixels are almost entirely opaque (but not completely).

Behind that is PulseTrailWidth, and that's the angle of the big trail behind the beam. Pixels that are right up against the beam are very opaque, and at an angle of PulseTrailWidth from the beam they're fully transparent. Any pixels at an angle greater than that have no effect on the image.

Here's the code to draw the offscreen Pulse buffer:

```
void makePulse() {
   Pulse = createGraphics(Window, Window, P2D);
   Pulse.beginDraw();
   Pulse.smooth();
   Pulse.background(0, 0);

   for (int y=0; y<Window; y++) {
      for (int x=0; x<Window; x++) {
         float r = mag(x-Cx, y-Cy);
         if (r > RingHi*Window/2.0) continue;
         float theta = 360-degrees(atan2(y-Cy, x-Cx)+PI);
         if (theta < PulseBeamWidth) {

            Pulse.set(x, y, color(red(BrightGreen),
               green(BrightGreen), blue(BrightGreen), 224));
```

```
        } else if (theta < PulseBeamWidth + PulseTrailWidth) {
          float amp = map(theta-PulseBeamWidth, 0,
            PulseTrailWidth, 1, 0);
          if ((amp>0) && (amp<1)) {
            Pulse.set(x, y, color(red(BrightGreen),
            green(BrightGreen),blue(BrightGreen), 192*amp));
          }
        }
      }
    }
  }
  Pulse.endDraw();
}
```

Now that we have the picture, we need to draw it. I'll write a function that takes an angle in degrees and draws the beam at that angle.

```
void drawPulse(float angle) {  // angle in degrees
  pushMatrix();
  translate(Window/2.0, Window/2.0);
  rotate(radians(angle+180));
  translate(-Window/2.0, -Window/2.0);
  image(Pulse, 0, 0);
  popMatrix();
}
```

All we need to do now is some housekeeping. First, of course, we have to declare the global Pulse itself:

```
PGraphics Pulse;
```

Next, I'll declare the globals and give them some values:

```
float PulseBeamWidth = 5;    // bright wedge width in degrees
float PulseTrailWidth = 110; // dimming trail width in degrees
```

And then I'll adjust setup() and draw() to make the Pulse and render it:

```
void setup() {
  size(Window, Window, P2D);
  smooth();
  makeBackground();          // create the background
  makePulse();               // create the glowing beam and trail
}

void draw() {
  float angle = frameCount % 360;
```

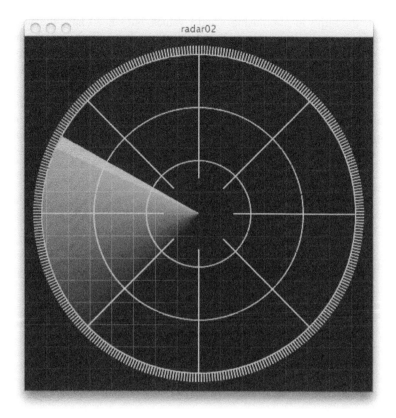

Figure 22.16. The radar screen with a moving beam (frame from animation).
(oddsends/sketches/radar02/radar02.pde)

```
    image(Background, 0, 0);      // draw the background
    drawPulse(angle);             // draw the pulse
}
```

(See output in Figure 22.16. Full program in oddsends/sketches/radar02/radar02.pde)

When we put that all together, we get Figure 22.16.

The only thing missing now are the little blips that the radar picks up as it rotates. For simplicity, I'll assume that the blips aren't moving. I think the easiest way to keep track of all the blips is to make a little class. Then each blip can be responsible for itself and can take care of figuring out when it needs to be drawn, how it should look, and so on.

What defines a blip? I think there are three things at a minimum: its distance from the center of the radar screen, its angle around the screen, and its size. We could of course write the blip's location using *x* and *y* values, but since I have the angle of the pulse already, it seems easiest to use this description. Representing the location of a point using its radius and angle, rather than its *x*- and *y*-coordinates, is called representing that point in *polar coordinates*. The more traditional *x* and *y* format is called *Cartesian coordinates*, named for the philosopher René Descartes.

I'll call this class `Blip`. So when we make a `Blip` object, it will randomly give itself an angle, radius, and size. I'll compute the size as a random value between a small fraction of the window's size and something a little more than twice that; I tuned these numbers up a bit until they looked good to me. Here's the `Blip` class so far:

```
class Blip {
    float angle;
    float radius;
    float size;

    Blip() {
        float smallSize = Window/80.0;
        float bigSize = 2.25*smallSize;
        angle = random(0, 360);
        radius = random(RingLo*Window/2.0,
                    (RingHi*Window/2.0)-bigSize);
        size = random(smallSize, bigSize);
    }
}
```

That makes a `Blip`, but how do we draw them? As usual, I'll make a `render()` routine. This one will take the current angle of the rotating pulse as input.

I want the blips to fade out like the rotating beam, but I want them to glow long enough that they're still fading out after the beam has completely passed them by. There's no physical reason for this, it's just what feels right to me for this imaginary radar screen. So I'll find the difference in the angle between where the beam is now and where the `Blip` object itself is located and compare that to a scaled-up version of `PulseTrailWidth`. That will tell me how far the object is from the bright wedge of the rotating pulse. The farther we are, the dimmer (or more transparent) the blip appears, until it's finally invisible.

By the way, after computing the angle difference, I check to make sure it's positive, and if it isn't, I add 360. That's to cover situations where the `Blip` object is at, say, 355 degrees, and the beam is at 5 degrees. In this case the beam just passed the object (it's only 10 degrees past it), but $5 - 355 = -350$. If I add 360 to that, I get 10 degrees, which is what I want.

I compute a variable called `glowLength` to tell me how far I am within the fading beam, and use that to calculate the opacity. Then I draw the `Blip` object as a circle with a little disk inside of it.

Here's the render() routine:

```
void render(float pulseAngle) {
    float glowLength = PulseTrailWidth*1.5;
    float angleDiff = pulseAngle - angle;
    if (angleDiff < 0) angleDiff += 360;
    float opacity = lerp(255, 0, angleDiff/glowLength);
    if ((opacity < 0) || (opacity > 255)) return;
    noFill();
    strokeWeight(2);
    stroke(red(BrightGreen), green(BrightGreen), blue(BrightGreen), opacity);
    ellipse(Cx+radius*cos(radians(angle)), Cy+radius*sin(radians(angle)),
            2*size, 2*size);
    noStroke();
    fill(red(BrightGreen), green(BrightGreen), blue(BrightGreen), opacity);
    ellipse(Cx+radius*cos(radians(angle)), Cy+radius*sin(radians(angle)),
            1.5*size, 1.5*size);
}
```

As before, we need a little housekeeping. At the top of the program, I'll declare a global for the total number of Blip objects and an array to hold them. I'll add a line in setup() to call a function called makeBlips() and then I'll use that procedure to create the array and fill it in with objects. Finally, I'll run through the list of Blip objects in draw(). Here's the complete program:

```
PGraphics Background;
PGraphics Pulse;
Blip BlipList[];
int NumBlips = 25;

int Window = 480;        // size of the graphics window
float Cx = Window/2.0;   // center x
float Cy = Window/2.0;   // center y

int NumRings = 3;        // number of circles around the center
float RingLo = 0.3;      // percentage of window for first radius
float RingHi = 0.9;      // percentage of window for last radius

int NumLines = 8;            // how many radial lines
float RadialLineLo = 0.2;    // percentage of window where they start
float RadialLineHi = 0.9;    // percentage of window where they end

int NumHashMarks = 360;   // number of little hash marks around outside
float HashLineLo = 0.9;   // percentage of window where they start
float HashLineHi = 0.95;  // percentage of window where they end

float PulseBeamWidth = 5;     // bright wedge width in degrees
float PulseTrailWidth = 110;  // the dimming trail width in degrees
```

```
color BrightGreen = color(140, 215, 85);   // bright-green color

class Blip {
   float angle;
   float radius;
   float size;

   Blip() {
      float smallSize = Window/80.0;
      float bigSize = 2.25*smallSize;
      angle = random(0, 360);
      radius = random(RingLo*Window/2.0, (RingHi*Window/2.0)-bigSize);
      size = random(smallSize, bigSize);
   }

   void render(float pulseAngle) {
      float glowLength = PulseTrailWidth*1.5;
      float angleDiff = pulseAngle - angle;
      if (angleDiff < 0) angleDiff += 360;
      float opacity = lerp(255, 0, angleDiff/glowLength);
      if ((opacity < 0) || (opacity > 255)) return;
      noFill();
      strokeWeight(2);
      stroke(red(BrightGreen), green(BrightGreen), blue(BrightGreen), opacity);
      ellipse(Cx+radius*cos(radians(angle)), Cy+radius*sin(radians(angle)),
                 2*size, 2*size);
      noStroke();
      fill(red(BrightGreen), green(BrightGreen), blue(BrightGreen), opacity);
      ellipse(Cx+radius*cos(radians(angle)), Cy+radius*sin(radians(angle)),
                 1.5*size, 1.5*size);
   }
}

void setup() {
   size(Window, Window, P2D);
   smooth();
   makeBlips();
   makeBackground();            // create the background
   makePulse();                 // create the glowing beam and trail
}

void draw() {
   float angle = frameCount % 360;
   image(Background, 0, 0);   // draw the background
   drawPulse(angle);          // draw the pulse
   for (int b=0; b<NumBlips; b++) {
```

```
      BlipList[b].render(angle);
   }
}

void makeBlips() {
   BlipList = new Blip[NumBlips];
   for (int b=0; b<NumBlips; b++) {
      BlipList[b] = new Blip();
   }
}

void makeBackground() {
   Background = createGraphics(Window, Window, P2D);
   Background.beginDraw();
   Background.smooth();
   Background.background(24, 44, 18);    //dark green background

   // draw background grid
   Background.stroke(42, 94, 30);
   Background.strokeWeight(1);
   float lineGap = (Window/16.0);
   Background.noFill();
   for (int i=1; i<16; i++) {
      Background.line(0, i*lineGap, Window, i*lineGap);
      Background.line(i*lineGap, 0, i*lineGap, Window);
   }

   // draw inner graphics
   Background.stroke(red(BrightGreen), green(BrightGreen), blue(BrightGreen));
   Background.strokeWeight(2);

   // inner rings
   float diameter;
   for (int ring=0; ring<NumRings; ring++) {
      diameter = Window * lerp(RingLo, RingHi, ring*1.0/(NumRings-1));
      Background.ellipse(Cx, Cy, diameter, diameter);
   }

   // radial lines
   for (int lineCount=0; lineCount<NumLines; lineCount++) {
      float theta = radians(360.0 * lineCount/NumLines);
      float r0 = RadialLineLo * (Window/2.0);
      float r1 = RadialLineHi * (Window/2.0);
      Background.line(Cx+(r0*cos(theta)), Cy+(r0*sin(theta)),
                      Cx+(r1*cos(theta)), Cy+(r1*sin(theta)));
   }
```

```
    // outer hash marks
    for (int lineCount=0; lineCount<NumHashMarks; lineCount++) {
        float theta = radians(360.0 * lineCount/NumHashMarks);
        float r0 = HashLineLo * (Window/2.0);
        float r1 = HashLineHi * (Window/2.0);
        Background.line(Cx+(r0*cos(theta)), Cy+(r0*sin(theta)),
                       Cx+(r1*cos(theta)), Cy+(r1*sin(theta)));
    }

    Background.endDraw();
}

void makePulse() {
    Pulse = createGraphics(Window, Window, P2D);
    Pulse.beginDraw();
    Pulse.smooth();
    Pulse.background(0, 0);

    for (int y=0; y<Window; y++) {
        for (int x=0; x<Window; x++) {
            float r = mag(x-Cx, y-Cy);
            if (r > RingHi*Window/2.0) continue;
            float theta = 360-degrees(atan2(y-Cy, x-Cx)+PI);
            if (theta < PulseBeamWidth) {
                Pulse.set(x, y, color(red(BrightGreen), green(BrightGreen),
                          blue(BrightGreen), 224));
            } else if (theta < PulseBeamWidth + PulseTrailWidth) {
                float amp = map(theta-PulseBeamWidth, 0, PulseTrailWidth, 1, 0);
                if ((amp>0) && (amp<1)) {
                    Pulse.set(x, y, color(red(BrightGreen), green(BrightGreen),
                              blue(BrightGreen), 192*amp));
                }
            }
        }
    }
    Pulse.endDraw();
}

void drawPulse(float angle) {  // angle in degrees
    pushMatrix();
    translate(Window/2.0, Window/2.0);
    rotate(radians(angle+180));
    translate(-Window/2.0, -Window/2.0);
    image(Pulse, 0, 0);
    popMatrix();
}
```

(See output in Figure 22.17. Full program in oddsends/sketches/radar03/radar03.pde)

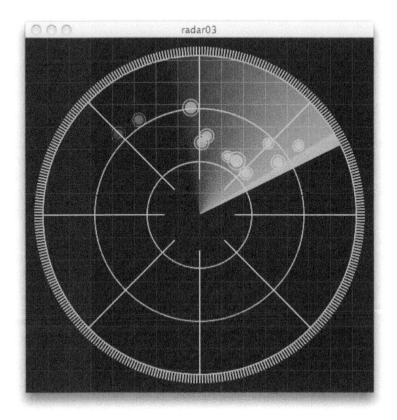

Figure 22.17. The complete radar screen with blips (frame from animation).
(oddsends/sketches/radar03/radar03.pde)

Our very own fake radar!

There's definitely a lot of code there, but none of it is terribly tricky (with the exception of the `atan2()` stuff if you haven't seen it before).

The interesting thing to note here is the structure of the program. In `setup()`, we call three routines: two to make offscreen images and one to build the array of blips.

And `draw()` is simple, simple, simple. That makes it fast, which is what we want for `draw()`. It computes the angle of the beam, draws the `Background` image in one step, draws the `Pulse` image using just a few steps, and then draws each `Blip`. The blips take almost all of the time, and if things were too slow, we could speed up their `render()` routine or even simplify their images.

On my machine, the radar beam spins smoothly, and the blips appear and fade out smoothly. It looks great. There's just no way we'd get good speed from this if we drew every frame from scratch, including all that background stuff and a pixel-by-pixel scan of the whole window. By precomputing all those expensive images, our program pauses for a brief moment when it first starts up but then runs smoothly forever more.

22.9   Reading and Writing Modes

Part of how Processing manages graphics for you is by maintaining a collection of settings collectively called the graphics state. Every PGraphics object (for example, the screen or an offscreen graphics object you've created) has an associated graphics state, independent of any other PGraphics objects that might exist in your program. When you issue any kind of command that affects how future graphics get drawn (for example, fill() or noStroke()), an associated variable in the graphics state for that PGraphics object records that information.

Because each PGraphics object has its own state, you can have multiple offscreen images that behave differently. For example, one might draw shapes with a three-point red outline and no fill color, and another might draw them with no outline but a fill of 25 percent transparent yellow.

Processing gives you a variety of dedicated routines for setting values in the graphics state (e.g., strokeWeight() and fill()), but there are no corresponding routines that will give you back the value that's currently being used.

But you can read these values back if you're willing to dig a little. Deep in Processing's online documentation (as of this writing, at http://dev.processing.org/reference/core/javadoc/processing/core/PGraphics.html), you'll find a list of all the fields in the graphics state. If you have a PGraphics object named, say, pg, then you can read back the current stroke weight for that object from the floating-point variable pg.strokeWeight.

You can also read back the mode settings that you change with calls such as rectMode() and ellipseMode(). There are seven of these mode variables. Each one is an integer that's named for the Processing function you call to set them: colorMode, ellipseMode, imageMode, rectMode, shapeMode, textMode, and textureMode.

In Chapter 6 I mentioned that there was a way to read back these mode settings for the onscreen window. What makes this possible is that the on-screen graphics are described by a PGraphics object just like any other. The trick is knowing that Processing lets you get at that object. It's a global variable with the simple, one-letter name g.

So if you want to know the current value of the rectangle-drawing mode for the graphics window, you could just read g.rectMode. Each time you call the function rectMode(), you're setting this variable.

Using rectMode() to set the variable and g.rectMode to read it lets you save the current mode, set it to something new for a while, and then put it back where it was.

But you can already do that with pushStyle() and popStyle(), which exist to do precisely that job.

What would be really useful is if you could read these mode variables and tell from them which mode you're in (for example, whether rectMode is set to CORNER or CENTER). Unfortunately, the mode variable is an integer, and these names are system-defined values, so it's up to us to figure out which mode name corresponds to each possible value of the variable.

For example, on my system with Processing 1.1, if I call rectMode(CORNER) and then read back the value of g.rectMode, it has the value 0. The mode CORNERS sets it to value 1, RADIUS to 2, and CENTER to 3. But those values aren't guaranteed to stay the same in the future. It's unlikely, but without a promise of consistency, it's possible that in the next release of Processing these correspondences could move around, so when you call rectMode(CORNER), the variable rectMode might get set to something other than 0.

This means that while you can read back each of the graphics modes, you can't tell for sure what they mean to Processing (you could write a little routine to try all the possibilities, read them all back, and save the results, but what a hassle!).

It's nice to know that we can read back the mode settings while your program is running. But that doesn't help at all when you're trying to figure out what mode is in effect when you're reading your source code. This kind of issue makes debugging much harder than it needs to be. So I still recommend leaving all modes at their defaults as much as possible.

22.10   Blurring

Blurring is a great general technique to know. You can use blurred images in tons of applications, from creating drop shadows to showing out-of-focus pictures.

There are lots of ways to blur an image, ranging from very simple to very complex. If you're working with high-quality photographs you'll want to use one of the complex, mathematically sophisticated methods offered by professional photo editing software. But for the types of projects we typically do with Processing, and certainly those in this book, we only need something that can run reasonably quickly and looks good.

The first criterion is the hardest one. High-quality blurring involves a lot of math and a lot of calculations. The results are lovely, but slow. So I usually use a quick-and-dirty approach. Even so, there's no getting around the fact that blurring is a slow operation. The amount of time it takes depends on the size of your image and how blurry you want to make it. The easiest way to make your blurs run faster is to blur a smaller picture. So it's not unusual to find that projects that do a lot of blurring either need to run on a very fast computer or use a smaller window size in order to create smooth animations.

The blur I'll discuss here is called a *box blur*. The idea is simple: for each pixel in the image, find the average color of all the pixels in a box around it and replace the pixel with that average color.

There's one little subtlety we have to keep in mind when implementing this, though: each pixel has to work with the colors in the original image. So we can't find an average value for a pixel, overwrite it with the new color, and then use that as part of the calculation for its neighbor. Instead, we have to keep around two images. One holds the original image, and the other one collects the blurred pixel colors.

The simplest box blur, which I'll use here, is illustrated in Figure 22.18.

When each pixel has had its average computed, we have built a second image that contains the blurred picture. Then we typically copy that blurred version back into the original, overwriting it, and return.

Every time you enter a blur routine, you typically have to pay a setup cost in the time it takes to create the second image that will hold the blurred version, and then you pay again when you copy all the pixels out of the blurred version back into the original. If you want to blur a picture a few times, you'd have to repeat this each time. To cut down on lost time, many blur routines let you specify how many times you want to repeat the blur. Then the routine blurs the picture repeatedly, saving you some time. Each time through the loop is typically called a *pass*, so one input to a blur routine is the number of passes you want to make. Three passes is just like calling the blur routine three times, but it's a little faster.

The size of the box (called its radius, even though it's not circular) determines how fuzzy the image becomes: the bigger the radius, the more fuzzy the result. Unfortunately, the bigger the radius, the slower the routine.

Here's a straightforward implementation of a blur routine. It takes as input a PImage, the number of passes, and a radius. For clarity, at the end of each pass, I copy the blurDst array (which receives the blurred pixels) back into the blurSrc array (which holds the

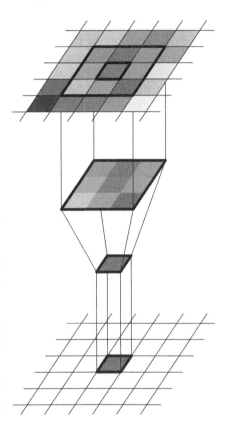

Figure 22.18. A box blur in action. For each pixel, we select a box around it (in this case, three-by-three pixels), average the colors in that box, and store that averaged color in the corresponding pixel in a second image.

original). You could certainly speed this up by eliminating that step. Then the second pass (if there was one) would use blurDst as the source and blurSrc as the destination, and each following pass would continue to flip the meanings of the two arrays back and forth.

Figure 22.19. A sharp image, scaled to fit the 600-by-400 window.

To illustrate blurring, I'll start with my New Zealand photo, shown in Figure 22.19.

```
void setup() {
   size(600, 400);
   background(110, 120, 126);
   PImage pic = loadImage("myPhoto-600-400.jpg");
   blurImage(pic,  1, 5);
   image(pic, 0, 0);
}

void blurImage(PImage img, int numPasses, int blurRadius) {
   color [][] blurSrc = new color[img.height][img.width];
   color [][] blurDst = new color[img.height][img.width];

   // copy the input layer's pixels into the source
   img.loadPixels();
   for (int y=0; y<img.height; y++) {
      for (int x=0; x<img.width; x++) {
         blurSrc[y][x] = img.pixels[(y*img.width)+x];
      }
   }

   // blur the image in blurSrc and save that in blurDst
   for (int pass=0; pass<numPasses; pass++) {
      for (int y=0; y<height; y++) {
         for (int x=0; x<width; x++) {
            int count = 0;
            float rSum = 0;
```

```
            float gSum = 0;
            float bSum = 0;
            float aSum = 0;
            int ixlo = max(0, x-blurRadius);
            int ixhi = min(width, x+blurRadius);
            int iylo = max(0, y-blurRadius);
            int iyhi = min(height, y+blurRadius);
            for (int iy=iylo; iy<iyhi; iy++) {
                for (int ix=ixlo; ix<ixhi; ix++) {
                    count++;
                    color srcColor = blurSrc[iy][ix];
                    rSum += red(srcColor);
                    gSum += green(srcColor);
                    bSum += blue(srcColor);
                    aSum += alpha(srcColor);
                }
            }
            if (count == 0) count = 1;
            blurDst[y][x] = color(rSum/count, gSum/count,
                                  bSum/count, aSum/count);
        }
    }

    // copy dst into src
    for (int y=0; y<height; y++) {
        for (int x=0; x<width; x++) {
            blurSrc[y][x] = blurDst[y][x];
        }
    }
}

// copy src back to the layer
img.loadPixels();
for (int y=0; y<img.height; y++) {
    for (int x=0; x<img.width; x++) {
        img.pixels[(y*img.width)+x] = blurSrc[y][x];;
    }
}
img.updatePixels();
}
```

(See output in Figure 22.20. Full program in oddsends/sketches/blur01/blur01.pde)

Figure 22.20 shows the result of a single pass of blurring using a radius of five pixels. That image is a little bit softer than the original.

Figure 22.20. Blurring with one pass with a radius of 5 pixels.
(oddsends/sketches/blur01/blur01.pde)

Sometimes you can get the look you want by applying a small-radius blur several times (that is, with several passes). Other times you'll need to use a large radius, but you might be able to use only one or two passes.

Compare Figure 22.21 (one pass with a radius of 25 pixels) with Figure 22.22 (five passes with a radius of 5). Though blurring five times with a box of radius 5 is not nearly as fuzzy as blurring once with a box of radius 25, it's about 21 times faster!

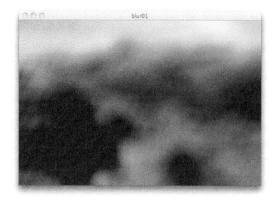

Figure 22.21. Blurring with one pass with a radius of 25 pixels.

Figure 22.22. Blurring with fives passes with a radius of 5 pixels.

If you look at these pictures closely, you may notice some subtle vertical and horizontal edges. These are artifacts of using such a simple blurring technique. If we used more sophisticated math, we could get rid of those little effects, but it would take even longer to run. I find that this box blur is usually good enough for the sorts of things I do with Processing. If you need a fancier approach, search for *blur algorithm* or *Gaussian blurring* on the web.

You have to experiment a bit with this sort of technique and find the choice of number of passes and blur radius that gives you the fastest route to the kind of look you're after. I usually start with one pass and a blur radius around 5 and then change the radius. I'll tinker with the number of passes, too, and see if they help; sometimes a few passes with a small radius looks better and runs faster than does one pass with a large radius.

The only way to find out how big a radius to use and how many passes to make is to make a guess and see how it looks. Then you can increase or decrease each value, run it again, change it again, run it again, and so on, until it looks right.

If all else fails and you still can't get your blur to run fast enough, you can reduce the size of your graphics window and cut down the number of pixels that have to be blurred on each pass. If you halve the window in each dimension, the blur will take about one-quarter the time.

22.11   Web Applets

You can easily embed your Processing programs into a webpage so people can enjoy them online. When embedded into a webpage, your program is often called an *applet*.

Generally speaking, your web applet can do anything that your program can do on your own computer. The big exception is that your applet cannot access files outside of its own directory. This is for security reasons; nobody would want to run an applet if it could read the password file or other confidential information on the computer. You can read files in your program's own directory and in subdirectories (for example, the data subdirectory where font files reside), but you can't reach beyond that directory and out into the computer's file system for files in other folders.

As you know, when you press the *Run* button your Processing code is translated to Java. When you export your code as an applet, the same thing happens, and it's the Java version that actually gets saved and shared.

Your program can test to see whether it's in a browser or not by checking the system `boolean` variable `online`:

```
if (online) {
  status("I know I'm in a browser!");
}
```

Here I've called the function status(), which writes a line of text to your browser's status area (usually a little region in the lower-left corner of your browser's window).

You can do a few things related to other webpages. Your applet can replace itself with another webpage. This might be useful if your Processing applet is a control page for a larger site; when someone presses the mouse over one of your animated buttons, that's your cue to load another page. To load a new page, call link() with the full name of the page you want to go to. If, instead of replacing the page, you'd rather open up a new browser window with the desired page loaded into it, give link() a second parameter of _new:

```
void mousePressed() {
  if (button1()) link("http://www.link1.com");
         else link("http://www.link2.com", _new);
}
```

You can read some values that are stored in other webpages with the param() command; this is very specialized stuff and somewhat tricky so I won't go into it here.

Suppose that your program uses a bunch of images. It would be natural to read them all in during setup() by calling loadImage() for each one and saving the results. Now the images are ready and available for your program. Unfortunately, loadImage() can take some time to run, and it can take even more time when the images are obtained over the web. So someone would start your program and then there would be a pause as it read in its images, pulling each one over the web from some other computer. We all know that people get bored waiting for a page to load and will often click away if something doesn't happen soon after they open a page. Processing offers you a tool so you can run right away and let the images catch up with you.

If you have a lot of images to load into your applet, you can use requestImage() rather than loadImage(). This tells Processing to get the images, and save them in your applet. You can then use them just as if you'd called loadImage(), but unlike that function (which loads the image immediately), this process happens in the *background*. This means your code doesn't stop and wait until the images are loaded; it can continue to run as the images are arriving. Of course, your program shouldn't use any of the images that haven't yet loaded; if it does try to use one, it'll pause until that image is read into memory. To track the progress of each image, check its width parameter. As long as that's 0, your image is still loading. If it goes to -1, then there was an error. Otherwise, it will eventually take on a positive number, and your image is ready for you to use.

When your applet is ready to share with the world, all you have to do is choose *File* from the main menu, and then *Export*. You'll get a new subdirectory in your sketch directory that contains all the files for your applet. The webpage itself is called index.html, which is a common name for a generic HTML file. You'll probably want to change that to something more meaningful for your website.

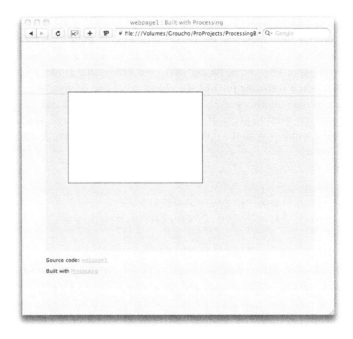

Figure 22.23. A typical webpage created with the Export command.

Let's build a short program and export it; the result is in Figure 22.23.

```
void setup() {
  size(600, 400);
  rect(50, 50, 300, 200);
}
```

The index.html page automatically includes a nice link to your source code so other people can see what you've done and a link to Processing itself if people want to download it. Your visitors will need to have the Java plug-in installed in their browser to see your running program, but if they don't, they will get a message telling them so and offering a link to the site where they can download and install it (for free, of course).

If you want, you can include some descriptive text along with your applet. Normally any comments in your code are ignored. But you can provide a special kind of comment, called an *export comment*. It starts with /** (that is, one more star than the standard multiline comment) and ends with */ (like the standard multiline comment). Everything on the line after the /** and until the line with */ will be printed out in small type just under your applet's window.

In this example, I'll add some text to explain the deeper meaning behind this deceptively simple example.

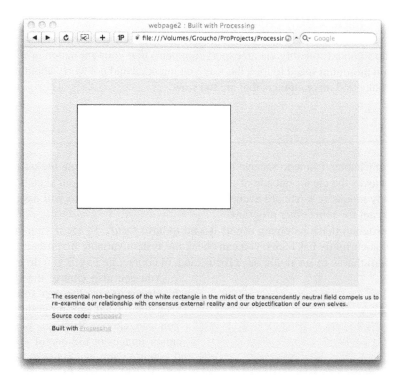

Figure 22.24. Adding an export comment. (oddsends/sketches/webpage2/webpage2.pde)

```
/**
The essential non-beingness of the white
rectangle in the midst of the transcendently
neutral field compels us to re-examine our
relationship with consensus external reality
and our objectification of our own selves.
*/
void setup() {
  size(600, 400);
  rect(50, 50, 300, 200);
}
```

(See output in Figure 22.24. Full program in oddsends/sketches/webpage2/webpage2.pde)

When you export an applet for the web, remember that you have no idea what kind of computer it's going to run on. It could be an insanely fast gaming rig or a glacially slow ancient clunker. If your frame rate is important, remember to request the speed you'd like to achieve with frameRate() and then check the variable frameRate to see what you're actually getting. If things are much too slow, you might want to consider simplifying your graphics or taking other actions. On the other hand, you can just include a note (probably via an export comment) that your animation needs to run at a certain minimum speed to look the way you intended and not worry about trying to make it look good on computers that are too slow.

22.12 User Events

We saw in Chapter 7 how to receive mouse and keyboard events from the user. But if the user moves the cursor outside of the Processing window, then your sketch will not receive any mouse or keyboard events because the operating system will assume that they're meant for some other program.

The program that's receiving events is said to have *focus*. To see if your sketch is the one that currently has focus, you can check the system variable focused. This is a boolean that is true if you have focus (and, of course, false if you do not).

Figure 22.25. The six predefined cursors for the Mac OS X operating system. From left to right: ARROW, CROSS, HAND, MOVE, TEXT, and WAIT.

You can also control the shape of the cursor to give the user some feedback about what your program's doing. You can choose from six predefined cursor images or use one of your own. If you use your own, it has to be a little PImage of size 32 by 32. To change the cursor image, call cursor(). You can name one of the six predefined shapes, or give it your own image (along with the *x* and *y* offsets that tell it which pixel in the image should be placed directly under the cursor itself).

The six choices predefined for you are ARROW, CROSS, HAND, MOVE, TEXT, and WAIT. The images of these cursors varies a little from one operating system to another. One set is illustrated in Figure 22.25.

To make the cursor image disappear entirely for a while, call noCursor(). You can bring it back by calling cursor() again. If you give it no arguments, cursor() will bring back the cursor with the last image it was loaded with.

22.13 Gotchas

Throughout the book, I've mentioned a few things that seemed unusual to me about Processing or worthy of special note. Of course, this is a very subjective thing to do: an idea that feels strange to me might be perfectly natural to you, and vice versa.

But there are a few things that I find myself stumbling over time and again. I get an error, I check the documentation, and I think to myself, "Oh no, *that* again!"

To save you the head slapping, I'll list here the top "gotchas" that I think are worth keeping in mind. We've seen each of these before; I'm just collecting them together here.

Integer division. Any division that involves only integers will cause the fractional part to be thrown away: 5/2 evaluates to 2. If you want the fractional part, remember to make at least one of the arguments a floating-point value, either by using a float type variable or explicitly including a decimal point or the letter f after the value: 5.0/2, 5./2, and 5f/2 all evaluate to 2.5. If your expression has all integer variables, multiply something by 1.0 (or 1. or 1f).

Modes. Processing loves to give you different modes, which cause the same function calls with the same arguments to behave differently. These mode-changing functions include rectMode(), ellipseMode(), shapeMode(), imageMode(), and textureMode(). Primarily because it can be very hard to tell what mode you're in when you're reading code, I consider these modes dangerous and potentially very confusing, and I recommend avoiding them. Almost always, you can change your code a very little bit and be able to use the default modes. The only modes that are hard to avoid are colorMode() and textMode(). If you *must* change a mode, I recommend that you set it back to the default as soon as possible.

Arguments to lerp(). There are three closely related functions: map(), norm(), and lerp(). Each one takes a control variable and some other values and produces a value that blends the others based on the value of the control. In map() and norm(), the control value comes first. In lerp(), the control value comes at the end. This inconsistency is a real shame, and it trips me up all the time.

```
map(alpha, low0, high0, low1, high1);
norm(alpha, low, high);
lerp(low, high, alpha);
```

The routine lerpColor() also puts the control at the end of the list.

No textHeight(). You can find out all kinds of information about a font, but you can't get the *x*-height. You can call textWidth(), but there's no textHeight(). I presented a work-around earlier in this chapter.

No ush() before close(). When you close a file (by sending a close() method to a PrintWriter), Processing doesn't automatically flush the buffer. That means you'll lose anything you've told the PrintWriter to put into the file but that it hasn't yet happened to write. You need to always call flush() before you call close(), or you risk losing your work. Forgetting this can drive you crazy.

System globals. You can change many of Processing's system wide globals. For example, you can write your own value into `frameCount` or `height`. I can't see any good reason for changing the value of one of these system globals; you can always accomplish the same ends with far less drastic intervention. And if you do change one of these values by accident, it can be incredibly hard to debug because everyone expects system variables to be dependable and reliably hold the correct values.

curveVertex() and bezierVertex(). When you make a Catmull-Rom curve using `beginShape()` and `endShape()`, you provide the points of the curve one at a time using the function `curveVertex()`. This takes two arguments: the point's x and y values. When you make a Bézier curve with the very same functions, you call `bezierVertex()`, but this routine takes six arguments, naming the next three points in the curve all at once. This difference is weird, and I always have to remind myself which format to use for each kind of curve.

Renderers differ. Processing offers you a choice of several different renderers. In a perfect world, they would all produce identical results. In the real world, they can vary by a lot. If you change renderers while working on a project, make sure to check that everything is working properly before moving on.

Classes without new. Although you use `new()` to create new instances of your objects, and new instances of lots of Processing's objects, there are a few oddball objects that don't get created with `new()` but have their own custom procedures. These include `PImage`, `PGraphics`, and `PShape`.

Hiding de nitions. If you have a global variable in your program, and inside a procedure you declare a variable of the same name, the version inside the procedure "hides" the global, which is then unaffected. For me, this is almost always a bug, and I usually introduce it when I'm editing my code.

For example, suppose I have a function like this:

```
void countApples() {    // version 1
   int AppleCount = 0;
   // count the apples and save in AppleCount
}
```

Suppose I later decide that `AppleCount` should be a global variable. So I declare it as a global near the top of the program, but I forget to remove the declaration in the procedure:

```
int AppleCount = 0;

// other code here

void countApples() {    // still version 1
```

```
    int AppleCount = 0;  // oops!
    // count the apples and save in AppleCount
}
```

In this case, anything that happens to AppleCount inside of countApples() has no effect on the global. This is almost never what I want since it defeats the whole reason I made that variable a global.

The problem is that pesky int that declares AppleCount again. If we get rid of it, then the local version no longer hides the global:

```
int AppleCount = 0;

// other code here

void countApples() {    // version 2
    AppleCount = 0;  // use AppleCount but don't re-declare it
    // count the apples and save in AppleCount
}
```

This problem is just as common, and even harder to catch, when it happens inside a class.

Pretend the examples above were part of a class. Then AppleCount (which we'd probably write with a lower-case a) would be an instance variable, but inside the first version of the method countApples, it gets ignored. Accidentally hiding a variable like this is much too easy, and I find it's hard to spot when I use everyday words like weight or count for variable names.

I wish the language didn't let you do this; I'd be delighted if the compiler flagged it as an error anytime a variable definition would hide a previous definition. But it doesn't mind a bit, and you can do it freely. My advice is to make life easy on yourself and never deliberately redeclare a variable so that it hides another definition.

This advice holds only for redefining class variables. Redefining the procedures (or methods) of a class is not only common but it's what inheritance in object-oriented programming is all about. The difference is that you can easily determine which version of a procedure is being called, while it can be very challenging to figure out the same thing for a variable.

Anytime you're tempted to redefine a global or class variable, create a new variable instead.

22.14 Going Beyond

We've come to the end of our voyage.

In the next chapters, I'll offer you a bunch of projects and help you write them if you like, but this chapter wraps up our discussion of the ideas and techniques behind creating images and animations with Processing. I've had a blast; I hope you have, too.

So what's left?

As I said before, we haven't seen everything there is to Processing, and we sure haven't seen everything that it can do. People are inventing new applications every day! If you want to know more, what's the best way to learn new elements of Processing to add to your tool kit?

Usually, it's from other people.

If you have friends who are also into Processing, share your experiences with them, and they'll tell you of theirs, and every now and then, one of them will mention something that will grab your attention and you'll ask, "What? How did you do that?" If your experience is like mine, they'll look at you like you're from Mars. "Why, I used the `zapbampow()` function. Don't you know about it?" And then, of course, it's time to discreetly change the subject ("Hey, do you think there's life on Venus?"). Or, I suppose, you could instead ask them what they're talking about, and in the process, learn about that function or technique. The same thing happens on the online discussion boards. You can learn a huge amount by reading other people's questions and the answers they get, and you can even contribute and give back by chiming in and helping other people who are having problems that you can solve.

In a similar vein, you can also learn from other people's code. Like many people who pursue something for pleasure, programmers who use Processing to make art and other personal-expression pieces often share not just their results but also their creative process. That means that there are tons of Processing programs out there, just waiting to be run and then picked apart. Some artists have pages full of one project, after another, after another. Each one can be run in your browser, and each one has a link to the source code. If you find the work of someone you admire, your understanding and skill can take a huge jump forward by studying their techniques and results.

There's no faster way to learn something new than to do it. So the next few chapters offer you a bunch of projects for you to dig into and implement. The more code you write, the faster you'll get, the better you'll get, and the more fun you'll have at every step along the way. So come on in—the water's great!

Chapter 23
Projects

Most of the projects in the preceding chapters were designed to highlight or illustrate one or more particular techniques. Now we have enough skills and knowledge to take on a few projects that have nothing in common except that they're fun and see what happens when we're free to approach them any way we want.

This chapter is something of a bridge. In previous chapters, we mostly built up programs together, step by step, often starting with a skeleton and adding one layer at a time. That's the way just about everybody programs, but as you've probably noticed, it takes up a lot of book pages! In the next chapter, I'm going to suggest a couple of large projects and encourage you to just dig in yourself and tackle them.

Here I'm going to take the middle road. I'll first describe an idea for a project that I think will be fun and interesting to write. Once you've read the description, I encourage you to put down the book and write your own implementation. The first few times will probably be challenging as you figure out how to begin and how to get building, but once you get the rhythm, you'll be producing great code in no time!

If a particular project doesn't grab you, or you're having trouble with it, keep reading. I'll describe my code in general terms. I'll get into the detailed nitty-gritty when there's something tricky or unusual going on, but most of the time, I'll stick to a big-picture view of the general approach. You'll probably be able to imagine what the code looks like.

But in case something doesn't quite come into focus, I'll also give you the code for my solution. I'm certainly not saying that this is the only solution, or even the smallest or fastest one! As before, I'm trying to keep my code clear, even if that makes it a little slower or a little longer. Of course, if you want to try your hand at optimizing, you can always dig into my solution (or your own) and make it faster or smaller.

In these examples, I'll include a comment here and there, but as before I'll mostly let the code speak for itself. This is almost entirely to save space and help you take in more of the code at a glance. In real programs, I encourage you to be liberal and generous in your commenting. It helps other people, and it helps you later on when you come back to your own program to change it or use it as a starting point for something new.

If you write your own programs for these little projects, you'll probably end up with very different solutions from mine, and they might even look entirely different as well. That's great! There's no right or wrong here, just some ideas for programs and presentations of how I solved them. You'll make your own choices when you write your own versions, reflecting your own aesthetics and preferences, with the result that you'll have created your own work that has something of yourself in it. That's success.

These projects aren't in any particular order, so you can take them in whatever sequence appeals to you.

23.1 Stacked Contours

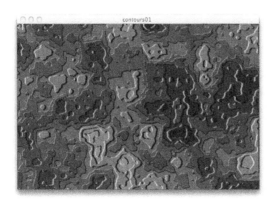

Figure 23.1. The shifting grounds of Tremorous.

In Chapter 16 we chopped up a field of noise into a stack of contours and then animated where the contours began and ended, making them appear to grow. That was just a fun project, but here on the planet of Tremorous it's a daily affair. The land is made up of sheets that are constantly moving over and under one another, like a vibrating layer cake. The layers are thick and clearly make up a moving, quivering stack.

Create an animation that shows other people what it's like here on Tremorous.

If you're feeling ready to program, go ahead and write this up! I know that this description is incredibly vague and undefined; that's how projects begin. It's only by rolling up your sleeves and digging in that you confront each question, each detail, and each missing piece of information, and figure out for yourself how to fill it in.

If you'd like to see a picture from my solution, Figure 23.1 shows a frame from my sketch.

23.1.1 My Approach

The basic question here is how to get the individual slices up on the screen quickly on each frame. I decided to draw them one by one into offscreen buffers, one per slice. Then for each frame all I'll have to do is find each slice's origin and draw it there. So my setup() routine builds the images that hold the slices, and my draw() routine simply copies them to the screen.

To create the slices, I first fill up a 2D array with noise values; this way I don't have to calculate them again for each slice. Then I create a single offscreen buffer that I'll use over and over again. I also create two colors, one each for the lowest and highest layers.

Then I run through a loop, stepping through it once for each layer. First, I initialize the buffer to transparent black. Then I find the minimum and maximum noise values that define this layer; any pixel with a noise value between these limits is part of this layer. Finally, I blend the high and low colors to find the color for this layer.

Then I run through every pixel in the image and test to see if its noise values are within the limits for this layer. If they are, then I set this pixel to that layer's color. When I'm done, I save the resulting offscreen buffer into a PImage using get(). I also set a variable that controls where the image is located on the screen.

That's it for the preparation. When that routine is done, I have a global array of PImage objects, each one transparent except for the pixels that are in its layer.

The draw() routine sets the background to black and then simply runs through the layers and draws them all. The one little interesting bit is how the layers move around. I don't want to simply use random(), since that would make them jump erratically. So instead of keeping each layer's x and y values and moving them, I save a PVector that has x and y values that I give to noise(). On each frame, I update those values, so I have a little point that's moving slowly through a noise field. I use the value of the noise under that point to position the layer.

The last trick is to make the layers look like they're embossed. That's actually easier than it sounds! If the layers were all drawn with their origins at (0,0), then every pixel in the screen would be covered (since every pixel belongs to one layer). Suppose that we've drawn the first layer, and now we're drawing the second one, and this is located a few pixels above and to the left of the first. That will leave a little gap between the layers where the background pokes through; remember, the background is black. When I draw each layer, I don't just draw it on top of the image that's been built up so far, but instead I use blend() with the ADD mode. That means each pixel gets added to the one underneath.

For most pixels, this just means that they get drawn with the color in their image, since they're getting added to the black background. But when a pixel overlaps a previous layer, the values add up and become bright, approaching white.

The result is that depending on how they move, many layers will have a black "shadow" along one part of their boundary, and a lighter "highlight" along another. This gives them a look of being embossed, as though light was striking the brighter side and casting a shadow on the other side.

Even better, because the layers are moving around at random, these bright and dark zones move around as well. So some layers appear to be "above" their neighbors at one time and then they seem to sink "below" them a little later, alternating back and forth over time.

Of course, this whole 3D embossed appearance is a total fake. It's just that we're so used to seeing this sort of thing in the real world that when these shapes have these

kinds of opposite dark and light boundaries, we automatically interpret them as a stack
of 3D shapes.

That's it for my solution; the code appears below. It runs pretty fast on my computer,
but the results aren't quite as I'd like because the layers don't move around smoothly,
but instead shift in little jumps. That's because the blend() routine won't let us pass
a floating-point value for the *x* and *y* origin of an image when we draw it. So when
the images move, they do so in steps of one or more whole pixels. Pixels are small,
but not *that* small, and I can see the little jumps very easily. This might be a desirable
effect sometimes, but I'd like to be able to turn it off and get smooth motion as well.
Unfortunately, unless we're willing to do a ton of programming and write our own
version of blend() that lets us position images at floating-point coordinates, we have
to live with this little jumpy motion.

```
int NumSlices = 12;
PImage Slices[];
PVector SliceOrigins[];

void setup() {
    size(600, 400, P2D);
    Slices = new PImage[NumSlices];
    SliceOrigins = new PVector[NumSlices];
    buildSlices();
}

void draw() {
    background(0, 0, 0);
    for (int slice=NumSlices-1; slice>=0; slice--) {
        SliceOrigins[slice].x += .02;
        SliceOrigins[slice].y += .02;
        int offx = int(lerp(-5, 5, noise(SliceOrigins[slice].x)));
        int offy = int(lerp(-5, 5, noise(SliceOrigins[slice].y)));
        blend(Slices[slice], 0, 0, width, height, offx, offy, width,
                height, ADD);
    }
}

void buildSlices() {
    float [][] noiseField = new float[height][width];
    color sliceColor;
    color orangeColor = color(255, 127, 0, 255); // opaque orange
    color blueColor = color(40, 41, 128, 255);   // opaque blue
    color blackColor = color(0, 0, 0, 0);        // transparent black

    for (int y=0; y<height; y++) {
        for (int x=0; x<width; x++) {
            noiseField[y][x] = noise(x*0.015, y*0.015);
```

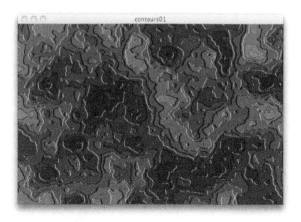

Figure 23.2. Moving contour layers (frame from animation).
(projects/sketches/contours01/contours01.pde)

```
      }
   }

   PGraphics layer = createGraphics(width, height, P2D);
   for (int slice=0; slice<NumSlices; slice++) {
      layer.beginDraw();
      layer.background(blackColor);
      float lerpVal = slice*1.0/(NumSlices-1);
      sliceColor = lerpColor(orangeColor, blueColor, lerpVal);
      float minVal = slice * 1.0 / NumSlices;
      float maxVal = (slice+1) * 1.0 / NumSlices;
      for (int y=0; y<height; y++) {
         for (int x=0; x<width; x++) {
            float noiseVal = noiseField[y][x];
            if ((noiseVal >= minVal) && (noiseVal <= maxVal)) {
               layer.set(x, y, sliceColor);
            }
         }
      }
      layer.endDraw();
      Slices[slice] = layer.get(0, 0, width, height);
      SliceOrigins[slice] = new PVector(random(slice*100),
         random((slice+1)*100));
   }
}
```

(See output in Figure 23.2. Full program in projects/sketches/contours01/contours01.pde)

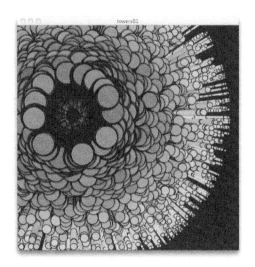

Figure 23.3. A field of cylindrical towers.

Figure 23.4. Another view of the cylindrical towers.

23.2 Crystal Towers

I'm relaxing in my protective underwater bubble here on the Ocean Planet of Hydraulicus IX. Things here are much calmer than on Tremorous.

Deep under the surface, I'm dreaming about the underwater crystals I found growing around a vent in the sea floor. A steady stream of nutritious chemicals are flowing up from this little hole in the floor, and the crystals use those chemicals to grow. They can't get too close to the rising stream, though, because it's incredibly hot. The crystals far from the vent are thin and blue, but as they get closer, they absorb more of the delicious chemicals and they grow thicker and turn a bright, healthy orange. The bigger crystals think nothing of growing right up through the smaller ones.

Now one day we journey down to the sea floor and take a picture of this strange crystal garden. How would it look?

A couple of images that show my answer to that question are shown in Figure 23.3 and Figure 23.4.

23.2.1 My Approach

This project is interesting because it's full of little tweaks designed to make the picture interesting. I started with something very simple that drew big orange disks near the middle of the screen and smaller blue ones at the edges and then added more stuff to it, one bit at a time, to make it look better. I threw away most of what I tried, but a bunch of little things survived.

So this sketch is really just a collection of many little ideas layered on top of one another. None of them are terribly deep or general purpose. They just grew out of my looking at the picture so far and asking myself what it was missing and then cooking up something to supply that missing element. Then I'd change it, and change it again, and that would cause me to change some of the other things. Putting together this program was organic, like the original idea itself!

So in this description I'll just document the many little things that made it into my final program. There's no good way to give you a really well-structured description, starting with an overview and then increasing detail, since everything got jumbled together as the program took shape. I've left it that way because this is often the way these things develop: the program starts with a base and grows and changes as you work on it.

This program is basically a one-shot, special-purpose bit of code. Of course, you can change anything here—delete some of the effects and add others—to make something that satisfies your taste.

The basic structure of the program is that `setup()` creates the graphics window and then draws some fixed number of crystals, which I've called towers. It creates just a single image, so there isn't even a `draw()` routine implemented.

I draw the towers one after the other, starting with the outermost ones and working my way inward. That way the nearer ones naturally overwrite the ones farther away, creating a nice kind of 3D effect. That 3D effect is completely fake, however, since everything here is entirely 2D. I kind of like that and went to some effort to really emphasize it.

The `setup()` routine does the usual stuff of making the graphics window and drawing the background and then it calls a little procedure to draw the towers. That procedure simply goes through a loop, once for every tower. It creates the parameters that describe the tower and then calls a routine to draw it. A tower is described by the center of the collection (that is, the location of the central vent around which the towers all grow) and a distance from that vent. Everything else is handled by the tower-making routine.

The tower maker essentially draws a whole bunch of filled-in circles, or disks. I start by using the vent location and distance that are handed to the routine: I imagine a line that has one end at the the start of the vent and a length given by the distance argument. The line is oriented in a random direction. The second endpoint of that line is the starting location of the tower. I pick a radius for the disk at that point. Then I make the line longer, and that gives me the ending location. I pick a new radius for the disk at that point by scaling up the first radius. By making the disks bigger as they grow, it simulates perspective (where an object appears smaller as it moves away from us). Disks near the center get scaled up more than those farther away because that looked good to me.

To draw the tower, I just draw a series of disks, beginning at the starting point and growing the radius along the way until I reach the ending point. This gives the illusion of a cylinder in perspective. When there are lots of cylinders all presenting the same perspective, the illusion is strengthened.

I pick a color based on the starting distance. If we're near the base of the vent, it's orange, and with increasing distance, the color becomes increasingly blue. I add a little random variation to the colors to keep things interesting visually.

By drawing the cylinders from the smallest ones (located farthest from the vent) to the largest ones (located near the vent), the near ones naturally obscure the far ones, and it seems even more like a 3D object.

I put three little tricks into the tower program to strengthen the 3D illusion.

The first trick isn't much of a trick at all. I just draw the black outline of the last disk in each stack. This makes it look like the circular top of a cylinder.

Secondly, because there's no 3D shading on the cylinder, I wanted some way to suggest that it's round. So every now and then, I draw a stroke around the disk (in the code, I do that for about one disk in ten). You can see those little lines on the sides of the cylinders in the figure; mostly they show up in the outermost blue towers. I think they give just the right amount of effect to suggest the round cross-section of a cylinder.

The last trick is that before I draw each disk, I first draw a very faint, nearly transparent black disk that's a little bit bigger. On their own, these faint black disks are almost invisible, and most of them get completely covered up by the disk itself (and the disks yet to come). But not all of the black disks get covered up, and those little bits that survive can accumulate until they're visible. This creates a little black halo around each tower, which acts like a drop shadow. It really helps to set off each tower from the ones around it.

This also has a happy side effect: it causes the inside of the central tunnel to get darker. The "farthest" part of the tunnel isn't as dark because there aren't as many disks there to add up, but I think that gives the whole thing a kind of nice inner glow. This was an accident of the drop-shadow idea, but I think it really helps the image by giving it some much-needed contrast.

Along the way I decided that I wanted the towers to bunch up more towards the middle, giving the impression of a steep mound of crystals. So up in the routine that calls the tower generator, I pass the distance through the first 90 degrees of a cosine curve. If you look at the figures, you'll see that the towers are denser at the center and outer edge and sparser in the middle, following the shape of the cosine curve.

I experimented with different sizes of the central gap, from closing it up all the way to opening it way out. I played with the numbers a bit, and these were the settings I liked the most. I put all five of the key numbers (the starting radius of the innermost and outermost towers, the center of the vent, and the number of towers to draw) at the top as global variables so I could easily adjust them.

The program demands a little patience while it builds the image. When I run it, it takes a few seconds for the picture to appear on my computer. I'm sure there are lots of places where the code could be optimized to make it run faster if you want it to.

```
int NumTowers = 1500;    // the total number of towers to draw
float MinStartD = 0.05;  // distance to the base of the
                         // innermost tower
```

```
float MaxStartD = 0.2;    // distance to the base of the outermost tower

float Xoffset = .5;       // X location (as a percent of the window) of the vent
float Yoffset = .5;       // Y location (as a percent of the window) of the vent

void setup() {
   size(600, 600);
   smooth();
   noStroke();
   background(0);
   drawTowers();
}

void drawTowers() {

   PVector origin = new PVector(Xoffset*width, Yoffset*height);
   for (int i=0; i<NumTowers; i++) {
      float alfa = i*1.0/(NumTowers-1);
      alfa = 1-cos(radians(90*alfa));
      float startDistancePercent = lerp(MaxStartD, MinStartD, alfa);
      drawTower(startDistancePercent, origin);
   }
}

void drawTower(float startDistancePercent, PVector origin) {
   PVector start;
   PVector end;
   float farRadius, nearRadius;
   color clr;

   float windowRadius = dist(0, 0, width, width)/2;
   float distToStart = startDistancePercent * windowRadius;
   float distToEnd = 5*distToStart;

   PVector direction = new PVector(random(-1, 1), random(-1, 1));
   direction.normalize();
   start = new PVector(origin.x + distToStart * direction.x, origin.y
                       + distToStart * direction.y);
   end   = new PVector(origin.x + distToEnd   * direction.x, origin.y
                       + distToEnd   * direction.y);

   float normDist = norm(startDistancePercent, MinStartD, MaxStartD);
   farRadius = width/100.0;
   nearRadius = lerp(farRadius*10, farRadius, normDist);
```

Figure 23.5. The world of cylindrical towers. (projects/sketches/towers01/towers01.pde)

```
color base0 = color(226, 105, 8);
color base1 = color(27, 205, 226);
float dr = 25;
base0 = color(red(base0)+(dr*random(-1, 1)), green(base0)
               +(dr*random(-1, 1)), blue(base0)+(dr*random(-1,1)));
base1 = color(red(base1)+(dr*random(-1, 1)), green(base1)
               +(dr*random(-1, 1)), blue(base1)+(dr*random(-1,1)));
clr = lerpColor(base0, base1, normDist);

int numSteps = width/4;
for (int step=0; step<numSteps; step++) {
    float alfa = step*1.0/(numSteps-1);
    boolean drawStroke = (random(0, 1000) > 900) ;
    if (step == numSteps-1) drawStroke = true;

    float rHere = lerp(farRadius, nearRadius, alfa);
    float xHere = lerp(start.x, end.x, alfa);
    float yHere = lerp(start.y, end.y, alfa);

    float bigr = rHere * 1.2;
    fill(0, 0, 0, 16);
```

```
    noStroke();
    ellipse(xHere, yHere, bigr, bigr);

    fill(clr);
    if (drawStroke) stroke(0); else noStroke();
    ellipse(xHere, yHere, rHere, rHere);
  }
}
```

(See output in Figure 23.5. Full program in projects/sketches/towers01/towers01.pde)

23.3 Skyline

Those guys on the Ocean Planet of Hydraulicus IX have it easy, looking out on a beautiful blue ocean every day. Here on the Urban Planet of Hirise, people have taken city living to an extreme. It's all rectangular glass-and-steel buildings everywhere you look. Particularly here on the harbor, where the city comes right up to the water.

Let's show the folks back on Earth what's happening up here. Make some images of the city at night, seen from a boat in the calm harbor.

You can see a screenshot from my program in Figure 23.6.

Figure 23.6. An urban skyline.

23.3.1 My Approach

To prepare for this project, I carried out an extended process of research and education, involving searching online for skyline pictures and looking at them for a minute or two. I gathered a few principles from these that I thought would guide my own skyline.

Generally, the sky looks best just after sunset, when there's still a glow radiating from where the sun went down. It's nice to see a few stars. They're mostly near the top of the sky (where it's darkest), and they're less intense near where the sun set (where they're a bit dimmed out).

The buildings near the water tend to be low, maybe because the ground is less stable there. Taller buildings are behind them. It seems that, roughly speaking, the buildings get taller with distance. Each building is filled with a grid of windows, some of which are glowing with light. It seems that in each building, the number of lit-up windows is about the same over the face of the building.

In front of the buildings the water reflects their light. At the waterline, there are sometimes some bright lights, maybe from streetlights on poles along the waterfront, and these are reflected in the water as well.

I organized the program in three distinct layers: the sky and water, the buildings, and the harbor lights. The biggest cheat is that the water doesn't reflect the buildings but uses noise to give the impression of reflected light. I do reflect the little harbor lights, though, which I think helps unify the midground buildings and foreground water.

My `setup()` routine creates the graphics window and determines two values that control the overall composition: the vertical location of the waterline and the maximum height of the buildings. These are saved in global variables named `Waterline` and `MaxHeight`. Then I call a routine named `drawSkyline()` to actually make the picture. There's no `draw()` routine for this project.

The `drawSkyline()` procedure has a pretty simple life. It draws the background and then it draws several layers worth of buildings (from back to front) and then it draws the harbor lights. Let's take these in turn.

The `drawBackground()` routine randomly places the setting sun somewhere near the right side of the image, close to the waterline. I find the distance of this point from the upper-left corner of the graphics window. I define two sky colors, one light blue and one dark blue. The idea is that pixels near the sun's center will be light, and they will smoothly get darker with distance, finally reaching the darker color in the upper-left corner.

To create the sky, I just run through every pixel above the waterline. I find its distance from the sun and divide it by the distance from the sun to the upper-left corner, giving me a value from 0 to 1 telling me how to blend the light and dark colors.

I wanted some stars in the sky. As I mentioned above, the stars vary across the image in two ways. First, they're more frequent near the top of the image than down near the waterline. To account for that, I compute a value `ya` (a super-shorthand for "y alpha") that tells me each pixel's vertical distance from the top of the screen to the waterline; it's 1 at the top of the screen and 0 at the waterline itself. I found that it looked nice to have about 1 pixel in 1,000 turn into a star, so I make a `threshold` value by multiplying 0.001 by `ya`. Now I can generate a random number from 0 to 1, and if it's less than the `threshold`, I know that this pixel should be a star.

But I also want the stars to be dimmer closer to the sun (since they should be a little washed out). So I use the distance I computed earlier that tells me how far this pixel is from the sun, and I scale the star's color by this distance (all of my stars are white). I found that the stars weren't quite fading in fast enough when I did this, so I first take the square root of the distance before using it to scale the star's color.

To draw the water, I again go through each pixel one at a time. I again find the vertical distance from the waterline and save this as `ya` (but now that distance is how far below the line we are, not above). Looking at the photographs, I saw that there was usually a very thin, dark region just under the waterline. So I make another value `ya2` that runs from 0 at the waterline to 1 just three pixels below it. I compute some 2D noise that's stretched out horizontally to simulate shallow waves. Then I scale that noise by first squaring it (so the brighter regions are smaller and more compact) and then multiplying it by the two scaling factors `ya` and `ya2`. This gives me the little dark band at the top and makes the noise less bright as we move down the image. I then use the scaled noise value to blend between the dark blue water color and the yellow average window color.

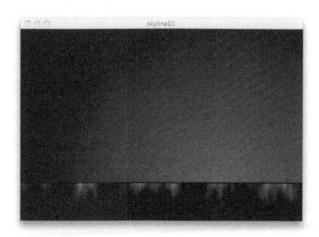

Figure 23.7. The sky, water, and fake reflections.

This gives me little vertical streaks of yellow that dim out with distance from the waterline. The streaks aren't really reflections of the buildings, since there aren't any buildings yet! But this usually gives me the kind of fuzzy reflection that I associate with this kind of image.

Figure 23.7 shows the background. Notice that the stars are slightly more frequent near the top, and they fade out in color near where the sun set. There's a small dark band just under the waterline and then there's carefully shaped yellow noise that I hope will ultimately look like reflections of the buildings yet to come.

Next up, it's time to draw the buildings. I do this in a series of layers, back to front. So `drawSkyline()` runs through a loop, calling `drawLayer()` for each layer of buildings. I found that between six and ten layers looked right to me most of the time, so I find a random value in that range and make that many layers.

To draw a layer, I first determine the average height and width of the buildings in that layer. The layers in back create buildings that are tall and narrow, while those in front are short and wide. I also make a random value called `layerDensity()`, which tells me how many of the buildings I compute I should actually draw.

Then I start at the left side of the picture and generate buildings left to right. Each building is found by taking the average height and width for that layer and randomizing it a bit. Then I check a random number, and if it's less than the building density, I call `drawBuilding()`. I move to the right by the building's width (whether I actually drew it or not) and repeat the process.

The `drawBuilding()` routine has two jobs: draw the building itself and draw the windows inside of it. The building part is easy: I just find a random gray value and draw a rectangle of that value.

I decided that all the windows in a given building should have the same color, so I take the average yellowish window color and randomize it a little. Then I get some more random numbers to tell me how many rows and columns to use when I draw the grid of windows. I find the size of each window from that, and I also generate a random number called `windowDensity`. I use this as I used the density value for buildings: before drawing each window, I test a random number against this value, and I only draw the window if that random value is smaller than the density.

Drawing the windows involves just a couple of nested loops that run through the rows and columns, drawing a rectangle of the window's color for each window that passes the threshold test.

Now I have a sky with stars, reflective water, and buildings. But the picture didn't seem to hold together for me; the illusion that I wanted from the fake reflections wasn't strong enough. I considered changing the program so that the reflections would actually be based on the buildings I drew, but that would have been a lot of work. Instead, I decided to lock the cityscape and the water together visually with another element: lights.

I draw just a few lights along the waterline. They vary in color, and they have a little vertical variation, too. Each light is drawn as two circles, one half-transparent and then a smaller, opaque one on top of it. This makes the light look a little fuzzy and more realistic.

Then I draw a vertical reflection of that light on top of the water that's already there. I start at the light itself and work my way down the image in a little column of pixels just under the light. I find the noise at each pixel using the same noise coordinates that I used for the building reflections so that the two sets of reflections will be consistent (remember that if you call `noise()` multiple times with the same inputs, you'll get back the same value every time). I fade out the light reflection faster than I faded the building reflections, because the light is lower to the water. I then blend in the light reflection to that pixel.

When I look at the pictures, I get the impression that the lights are part of the ground above the water and that they're reflected in the water. This little connection between the land and water ties them together for me and makes it easier for me to accept that the big, yellow, fuzzy shapes in the water are reflections of the buildings, even though there's no connection between them at all.

```
int NumLayers;
int Waterline;
float MaxHeight;
color WindowColor = color(220, 220, 20);

void setup() {
   size(600, 400);
   smooth();
   noStroke();
   Waterline = int(height * 0.8);
   MaxHeight = random(.2*height, .6*height);
   NumLayers = int(random(6, 10));
   drawSkyline();
}

void drawSkyline() {
   drawBackground();
   for (int layer=0; layer<NumLayers; layer++) {
      drawLayer(layer);
   }
   drawLights();
}

void drawLayer(int layer) {
   float a = norm(layer, 0, NumLayers-1);
   float avgWidth = lerp(width/50.0, width/20.0, a);
   float avgHeight = lerp(MaxHeight, height/20.0, a);
   float layerDensity = lerp(.1, 1, a);
   float left = -avgWidth;

   while (left < width) {
      float buildingWidth = vary(avgWidth, .1);
      float buildingHeight = vary(avgHeight, .2);
      boolean drawMe = random(0, 1) < layerDensity;
      if (drawMe) {
         drawBuilding(left, Waterline, buildingWidth, buildingHeight);
      }
      left += buildingWidth;
   }
}

void drawBuilding(float bLeft, float bBottom, float bWid, float bHgt) {
   float buildingGrayColor = random(30, 90);
   fill(buildingGrayColor);
```

```
    rect(bLeft, bBottom, bWid, -bHgt);

    color windowColor = color(vary(red(WindowColor), .1),
                              vary(green(WindowColor), .1),
                              vary(blue(WindowColor), .1));
    fill(windowColor);

    // figure out how many windows to draw, then draw each one
    int numAcross = int(random(10.0, 20.0));
    int numHigh = int(random(10.0, 20));
    float wWid = bWid / (numAcross*2.0);
    float wHgt = bHgt / (numHigh*2.0);

    float windowDensity = random(0.1, 0.7);
    for (int wx=0; wx<numAcross; wx++) {
        for (int wy=0; wy<numHigh; wy++) {
            float wLeft = (1.0/(numAcross*2.0)) + (wx*2*wWid);
            float wBottom = (1.0/(numHigh*2.0)) + (wy*2*wHgt);
            if (random(0, 1) < windowDensity) {
                rect(bLeft+wLeft, bBottom-wBottom, wWid, -wHgt);
            }
        }
    }
}

void drawBackground() {
    // draw the sky: a radial blend from (cx, cy)
    float cx = width * random(.6, .8);
    float cy = vary(Waterline, .1);
    float distToUL = dist(cx, cy, 0, 0);
    color lighter = color(5, 60, 130);
    color darker = color(0, 15, 45);

    for (int y=0; y<height; y++) {
        for (int x=0; x<width; x++) {
            float a = dist(x, y, cx, cy)/distToUL;
            a = constrain(a, 0, 1);
            color clr = lerpColor(lighter, darker, a);
            float ya = 1 - norm(y, 0, Waterline);
            float threshold = .001 * ya;
            if (random(0, 1) < threshold) {
                a = sqrt(a);
                clr = lerpColor(clr, color(255), a);
            }
            set(x, y, clr);
        }
```

```
    }

    // draw the (fake) building reflections
    color waterColor = color(10,10,30);
    for (int y=Waterline; y<height; y++) {
        for (int x=0; x<width; x++) {
            // ya is distance from Waterline
            float ya = 1-norm(y, Waterline, height-1);
            // ya2 creates a short fade right at the Waterline
            float ya2 = constrain((y-Waterline)/3.0, 0, 1);
            float wnoise = noise(x*.04, y*.01);
            wnoise = ya2 * ya * sq(wnoise);
            color clr = lerpColor(waterColor, WindowColor, wnoise);
            set(x, y, clr);
        }
    }
}

void drawLights() {
    int numLights = 20;
    noStroke();
    int lradius = 8;
    for (int l=0; l<numLights; l++) {
        int lx = int(random(0, width));
        int ly = int(Waterline-lradius+vary(lradius, .1));
        color lightColor = color(
                random(210, 255),  random(210, 255),  random(210, 255));

        // draw the light as two circles to fake a glow
        fill(red(lightColor), green(lightColor), blue(lightColor), 128);
        ellipse(lx, ly, lradius, lradius);
        fill(red(lightColor), green(lightColor), blue(lightColor), 255);
        ellipse(lx, ly, lradius/2, lradius/2);

        // draw fake reflections and add to water color
        for (int y=Waterline; y<height; y++) {
            for (int x=lx-2; x<lx+2; x++) {
                float ya = 1-norm(y, Waterline, height-1);
                float wnoise = noise(x*.04, y*.01);
                wnoise = sq(ya) * sq(wnoise);  // fade out noise
                color oldclr = get(x, y);
                color clr = lerpColor(oldclr, lightColor, wnoise);
                set(x, y, clr);
            }
        }
    }
}
```

Figure 23.8. A city skyline.
(projects/sketches/skyline01/skyline01.pde)

Figure 23.9. Another skyline.
(projects/sketches/skyline01b/skyline01b.pde)

```
}

float vary(float value, float percent) {
  float range = value * percent;
  value += random(-range, range);
  return(value);
}
```

(See output in Figure 23.8. Full program in projects/sketches/skyline01/skyline01.pde)

Figure 23.9 shows another city here on Hirise.

23.4   Neon Sign

One of the coolest things about visiting other planets is that they offer us whole new kinds of nightlife. If someone were to open an extraterrestrial nightclub, they might put up an animated neon sign in front to welcome all passing rocket ships.

Design a neon sign that uses four or five steps of animation and get it to step through them nicely. Then find a way to draw the sign so it looks like it really is made of neon lights.

You can see a screenshot of one frame of my version of this after a few seconds of execution in Figure 23.10.

23.4.1 My Approach

I doodled up a little rocket ship out of Bézier curves (plus a circular porthole so people can see where they're going). I then drew it in five positions, starting at a big blue planet and landing on a smaller green one. It accelerates in the second frame by burning fuel (causing lines to come out the back), and it decelerates in the fourth frame the same way. Of course, by then it's reversed direction and is flying backwards.

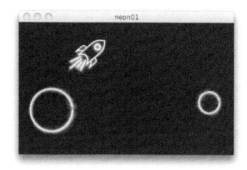

Figure 23.10. A frame from my spaceship neon sign.

The only trick now is to figure out how to draw neon. I tried a few experiments and came up with this approach. It's flexible and works pretty well even when you have a few tubes of different colors near one another. Its major drawback though is speed: I need to blur the whole graphics window twice for every frame, and that takes time. So I kept the screen size a little smaller than usual for this project so that it will run nicely even on a slow computer.

The trick to drawing neon is to observe that it's made up of three components. First, there's the background glow. That's a faint, fuzzy halo around the neon tube itself. It has the same color as the tube, but it's darker and much less intense.

Then there's the tube itself. Neon signs typically use very bright and saturated colors. The tube is so bright that it has a little faint halo around it as well.

And finally, to make this look really nice, I add a core layer, which is just a white stripe up the middle of the tube. This makes it look partly reflective (as though the white was a reflection of light from somewhere else), and it also matches what we see when a neon sign is really cranked up.

Most of my code is taken up with creating these three layers and managing all the x and y values for the frames. After all, this is essentially a five-frame, hand-animated movie!

Each time I enter `draw()`, I render every graphics element (a curve, line, or ellipse) three times. First, I draw a very thick line of the neon's color into the glow image. Second, I draw a medium-weight line of that color into the tube image. And finally, I draw a thin white line into the core image.

When they've all been drawn, I display the layers. First, there's a rusty metal background. On top of that comes the glow, but before I add the glow to the background, I blur it up a bit so that the glow fades out nicely. I also make it darker and transparent.

On top of that I draw the tube image, but again, I blur and darken it a little first (I blur and darken it by less than the glow layer).

Finally, I draw the core layer right on top, and that's that.

To blur the layers, I use the box-blurring technique we saw in Chapter 22.

```
color EarthColor = color(0, 200, 200, 200);
color MoonColor = color(0, 200, 0, 200);
color ShipColor = color(200, 0, 0, 200);
color PortholeColor = color(0, 200, 200, 200);
color Blast1Color = color(200, 200, 0, 200);
color Blast2Color = color(200, 128, 0, 200);
color NeonColor;

PGraphics GlowLayer;
PGraphics TubeLayer;
PGraphics CoreLayer;

PGraphics Layer;   // the current drawing layer
int PassNumber;    // three passes per graphic: glow, tube, core

PImage Background;

// These arrays are used to blur an image.  I'm making them
// globals so I don't have to reallocate them for every blur.
color [][] BlurSrc;
color [][] BlurDst;

void setup() {
   size(415, 250, JAVA2D);
   GlowLayer = createGraphics(width, height, JAVA2D);
   TubeLayer = createGraphics(width, height, JAVA2D);
   CoreLayer = createGraphics(width, height, JAVA2D);
   Background = loadImage("rust.jpg");

   BlurSrc = new color[height][width];
   BlurDst = new color[height][width];
}

void draw() {
   initLayers();
   int frameNumber = (millis() / 1000) % 5;
                     // display each image for 1 second

   for (PassNumber=0; PassNumber<3; PassNumber++) {
      switch (PassNumber) {
         case 0: Layer = GlowLayer;  Layer.strokeWeight(24);  break;
         case 1: Layer = TubeLayer;  Layer.strokeWeight( 7);  break;
         case 2: Layer = CoreLayer;  Layer.strokeWeight( 2);  break;
         default: break;
      }
```

```
        drawPlanets();
        drawFrame(frameNumber);
    }
    showLayers();
}

// all layers start out black and transparent
void initLayers() {
    GlowLayer.beginDraw();
    GlowLayer.noFill();
    GlowLayer.smooth();
    GlowLayer.background(0, 0, 0, 0);
    GlowLayer.endDraw();

    TubeLayer.beginDraw();
    TubeLayer.noFill();
    TubeLayer.smooth();
    TubeLayer.background(0, 0, 0, 0);
    TubeLayer.endDraw();

    CoreLayer.beginDraw();
    CoreLayer.noFill();
    CoreLayer.smooth();
    CoreLayer.background(0, 0, 0, 0);
    CoreLayer.endDraw();
}

void showLayers() {
    image(Background, 0, 0);

    blurLayer(GlowLayer, 1, 5, 0.5, 0.5);
    blend(GlowLayer, 0, 0, width, height, 0, 0, width, height, ADD);

    blurLayer(TubeLayer, 1, 3, 1.0, 0.75);
    blend(TubeLayer, 0, 0, width, height, 0, 0, width, height, ADD);

    blend(CoreLayer, 0, 0, width, height, 0, 0, width, height, ADD);
}

void drawPlanets() {
    setNeonColor(EarthColor);
    drawNeonEllipse(62, 165, 80, 80);  // earth
    setNeonColor(MoonColor);
    drawNeonEllipse(365, 150, 40, 40);  // moon
}
```

```
void drawFrame(int frameNumber) {
   boolean blast1 = false;
   boolean blast2 = false;
   float angle = 0;
   float tx = 0;
   float ty = 0;
   switch (frameNumber) {
      case 0: tx =  82; ty = 175; break;
      case 1: tx =  92; ty = 120; angle =  50; blast1 = true; break;
      case 2: tx = 140; ty =  72; angle =  80; break;
      case 3: tx = 362; ty =  92; angle = -50; blast2 = true; break;
      case 4: tx = 385; ty = 180; break;
      default: break;
   }
   drawShip(tx, ty, angle, blast1, blast2);
}

// draw ship with origin between the bottom fin tips
// it has height 65 and width 40
void drawShip(float tx, float ty, float angle, boolean blast1, boolean blast2) {
   Layer.pushMatrix();
   Layer.translate(tx, ty);
   Layer.rotate(radians(angle));
   Layer.translate(-40, -110);

   setNeonColor(ShipColor);
   mirrorY(20,   0, 12,   7,  8,  11,  8,  25); // body upper
   mirrorY( 8,  25,  8,  36,  8,  50,  8,  55); // body lower
   mirrorY( 8,  55, 10,  49, 15,  45, 20,  45); // body base
   mirrorY( 8,  35,  4,  35,  0,  35,  0,  42); // fin upper
   mirrorY( 0,  42,  0,  50,  0,  50,  0,  55); // fin lower
   mirrorY( 0,  55,  2,  48,  5,  45,  8,  45); // fin inside

   setNeonColor(PortholeColor);
   drawNeonEllipse(20, 18, 10, 10);

   if (blast1) {
      setNeonColor(Blast1Color);
      drawNeonLine(13, 55,  8,  75);
                  drawNeonLine(18, 57, 17,  83);
                  drawNeonLine(22, 60, 25,  72);
                  drawNeonLine(25, 52, 32,  70);
              }
              if (blast2) {
                  setNeonColor(Blast2Color);
                  drawNeonLine(13, 53,  8, 70);
                  drawNeonLine(18, 48, 14, 80);
```

```
      drawNeonLine(22, 55, 22, 74);
      drawNeonLine(25, 52, 30, 68);
   }
   Layer.popMatrix();
}

void mirrorY(float x0, float y0, float x1, float y1,
             float x2, float y2, float x3, float y3) {
   drawNeonBezier(x0, y0, x1, y1, x2, y2, x3, y3);
   drawNeonBezier(40-x0, y0, 40-x1, y1, 40-x2, y2, 40-x3, y3);
}

void setNeonColor(color clr) {
   NeonColor = clr;
   if (PassNumber == 2) NeonColor = color(255, 255, 255, 255);
   Layer.stroke(NeonColor);
}

void drawNeonBezier(float x0, float y0, float x1, float y1,
                    float x2, float y2, float x3, float y3) {
   Layer.bezier(x0, y0, x1, y1, x2, y2, x3, y3);
}


void drawNeonEllipse(float x, float y, float r0, float r1) {
   Layer.arc(x, y, r0, r1, radians(0), radians(350));
                              // leave a little gap like real neon signs
}

void drawNeonLine(float x0, float y0, float x1, float y1) {
   Layer.line(x0, y0, x1, y1);
}

// Blur the layer using a box average of the given radius.  Run the
// blur once for each pass.  When done, scale the output colors by
// the value in clrScale, and opacities by alphaScale
//
void blurLayer(PGraphics layer, int numPasses, int blurRadius, float clrScale,
               float alphaScale) {
   layer.loadPixels();
   for (int y=0; y<height; y++) {
      for (int x=0; x<width; x++) {
         BlurSrc[y][x] = layer.pixels[(y*width)+x];
      }
   }
```

```
// blur the image in BlurSrc and save that in BlurDst
for (int pass=0; pass<numPasses; pass++) {
   for (int y=0; y<height; y++) {
      for (int x=0; x<width; x++) {
         int count = 0;
         float rSum = 0;
         float gSum = 0;
         float bSum = 0;
         float aSum = 0;
         int ixlo = max(0, x-blurRadius);
         int ixhi = min(width, x+blurRadius);
         int iylo = max(0, y-blurRadius);
         int iyhi = min(height, y+blurRadius);
         for (int iy=iylo; iy<iyhi; iy++) {
            for (int ix=ixlo; ix<ixhi; ix++) {
               count++;
               color srcColor = BlurSrc[iy][ix];
               rSum += red(srcColor);
               gSum += green(srcColor);
               bSum += blue(srcColor);
               aSum += alpha(srcColor);
            }
         }
         if (count == 0) count = 1;
         BlurDst[y][x] = color(rSum/count, gSum/count,
                               bSum/count, aSum/count);
      }
   }

   // copy dst into src
   for (int y=0; y<height; y++) {
      for (int x=0; x<width; x++) {
         BlurSrc[y][x] = BlurDst[y][x];
      }
   }
}

// copy src back to the layer, with scaling on colors
// and alpha
layer.beginDraw();
layer.loadPixels();
for (int y=0; y<height; y++) {
   for (int x=0; x<width; x++) {
      color clr = BlurSrc[y][x];
```

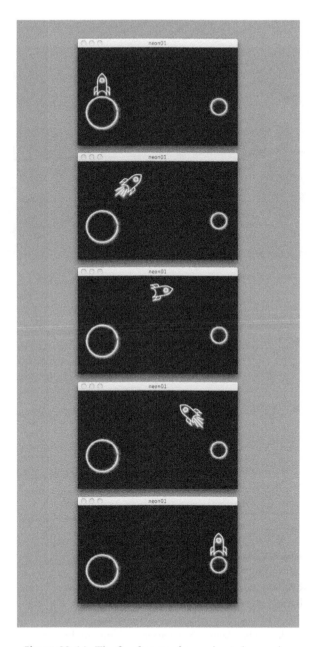

Figure 23.11. The five frames of my animated neon sign.

Figure 23.11 shows five frames from the running, animated sign.

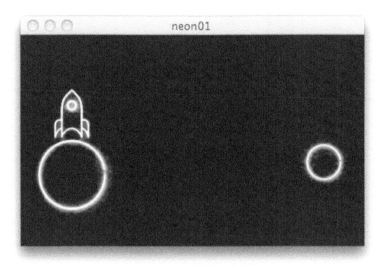

Figure 23.12. Frame 1 of an animated spaceship move. (projects/sketches/neon01/neon01.pde)

```
            layer.pixels[(y*width)+x] = color(red(clr)*clrScale,
                                          green(clr)*clrScale,
                                          blue(clr)*clrScale,
                                          alpha(clr)*alphaScale);
      }
    }
    layer.updatePixels();
    layer.endDraw();
}
```

(See output in Figure 23.12. Full program in projects/sketches/neon01/neon01.pde)

23.5   Streams

Oh, those lucky guys on The Urban Planet of Hirise. They get to see their beautiful cities every night, shining brightly in the clear, crisp air.

Here on the Rain Planet of New Seattle, it's the opposite story. It rains all day, every day. Clouds and water everywhere you look. Nobody here has had a dry martini in weeks.

The whole population has become an expert on rain and how it falls and the trails it leaves behind. We've even taken to mapping out the drainage basins, so we can tell you what happens to every drop of rain that strikes the ground.

Write a program that creates a ground terrain and then follows the path of the rain-drops from their moment of impact as they roll downhill.

You can see an image of my program after a few thousand raindrops have fallen in Figure 23.13.

23.5.1 My Approach

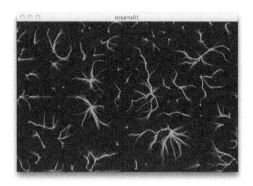

Figure 23.13. The streams created by a few thousand raindrops on a random terrain.

To create my world of running droplets, I start off with a 2D array of floating-point values that tell me the height of the surface. The array has the same dimensions as the graphics window, so every pixel has a height. I just call `noise()` for each pixel and save it in the array. Once that array has been created, `setup()` sets the background to black and it's done.

When `draw()` is called, it calls a procedure to follow the path of a single drop of water. Since one drop per frame builds up the picture very slowly, I run a little loop inside of `draw()` so that I follow many drops each frame.

To draw one drop, first I pick a random color so that the droplets stand out from one another a little bit. I set the stroke to that color, making it almost entirely transparent. That way I get a nice additive effect when many tiny strokes add up.

I then track the center of the drop. The starting point is a random point in the graphics window. Then I run a loop, moving the drop one step at a time. All I need to remember is that water flows downhill, so if I can find the steepest direction around this point, that's where the water will go. I search all the points in a circle around the center and locate the lowest one. Then I move one unit (that is, the size of one pixel) in the direction of that lowest point, and I draw a little line behind the drop to record its motion.

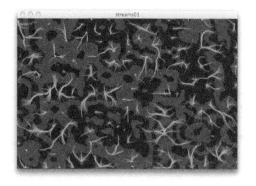

Figure 23.14. The streams with contours.

I follow the drop this way, drawing one tiny line behind it for every step, until one of three conditions holds true. First, I stop if the drop stops moving (that happens when it settles in some low bowl in the terrain and there's nowhere left to flow down to). Second, I stop if I've followed it for too many steps (this is just defensive programming so I won't end up following one drop forever if, for example, it gets caught in a little loop bouncing back and forth between two locations). Finally, I stop following it if it goes offscreen.

In the following code, I left in a function that draws the underlying topographical map (that is, the height field). If you comment out the call to drawTopoMap() in setup() you can see how it looks; Figure 23.14 shows an example. I just used a couple of dark blue colors for contrast with the yellowish raindrops.

It's fun to watch as the water flows from one level to the next, always seeking the fastest route downhill.

Because the drops take a while to follow and each drop's path is so transparent, it can take a long time to build up a nice image. On my computer it typically takes a couple of minutes to make a picture that I like. If this is too slow for you, an easy way to speed things up is to make each stroke more opaque, say by increasing the opacity value of 32 to 64 or more. You can also take larger steps; after normalizing the vector that describes how the drop moves, you can scale it up by two or three or more, so the drop will move a greater distance each time. The larger this value, the less smooth the curves will look, but the faster they'll be drawn.

```
float TopoMap[][];

void setup() {
   size(600, 400);
   TopoMap = new float[height][width];
   initTopoMap();
   background(0);
   //drawTopoMap();
}

void draw() {
   int numDropsToFollow = 50;
   for (int i=0; i<numDropsToFollow; i++) {
      drawOneDrop();
   }
}

void initTopoMap() {
   for (int y=0; y<height; y++) {
      for (int x=0; x<width; x++) {
         TopoMap[y][x] = noise(x*.01, y*.01);
      }
   }
}

// draw the topo map in blue isobands
void drawTopoMap() {
   background(0);
```

```
   for (int y=0; y<height; y++) {
      for (int x=0; x<width; x++) {
         float v = TopoMap[y][x];
         int vphase = int(v/.1);
         if (vphase%2 == 0) set(x, y, color(0, 0, 192));
         else set(x, y, color(0, 0, 128));
      }
   }
}

void drawOneDrop() {
   // pick a color for this drop
   float rval = random(100, 255);
   float gval = random(100, 255);
   float bval = random(20, 150);
   stroke(rval, gval, bval, 32);
   noFill();

   // pick a random point on the window to start from
   PVector center = new PVector(random(0, width), random(0, height));

   // as long as we don't have a reason to stop, keep moving
   PVector motion = new PVector(0, 0);
   int stepCount = 0;
   boolean updateAgain = true;
   while (updateAgain) {
      int searchRadius = 7;

      float minx = center.x;
      float miny = center.y;
      float minv = 999;

      // find the smallest value in a circle around the current center
      int angleSteps = round(12 * searchRadius);
      for (int i=0; i<angleSteps; i++) {
         float theta = map(i, 0, angleSteps-1, 0, TWO_PI);
         int px = round(center.x + (searchRadius * cos(theta)));
         int py = round(center.y + (searchRadius * sin(theta)));
         if ((px<0) || (px >= width-1) || (py<0) || (py >= height-1)) continue;
         float v = TopoMap[py][px];
         if (v < minv) { minv = v;  minx = px;  miny = py; }
      }

      // move 1 unit in that direction and draw a short line behind us
      motion.x = minx-center.x;
      motion.y = miny-center.y;
```

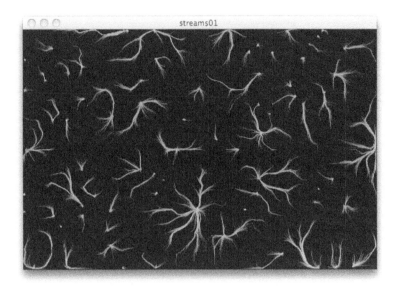

Figure 23.15. Streams created by drops of water running downhill.
(projects/sketches/streams01/streams01.pde)

```
motion.normalize();
line(center.x, center.y, center.x+motion.x, center.y+motion.y);
center.x += motion.x;
center.y += motion.y;

// stop if we're not moving, off screen, or have taken too many steps
if (mag(motion.x, motion.y) < 0.01) updateAgain = false;
if ((center.x < 0) || (center.x >= width) ||
    (center.y < 0) || (center.y >= height)) updateAgain = false;
if (++stepCount > width*2) updateAgain = false;
    }
}
```

(See output in Figure 23.15. Full program in projects/sketches/streams01/streams01.pde)

23.6   Puppet Show

I've got this great script for our puppet theater. One of the big love scenes involves a man telling his girlfriend about the ocean during a romantic, starry night under a full moon. I think the way to do this is to make a bunch of cut-out waves. We'll stack them one behind the other and move each one around, in front of a backdrop of a starry sky.

Please program this up in time for opening night! Figure 23.16 shows my version.

Figure 23.16. Layers of waves moving around as part of a puppet show (frame from animation).

23.6.1 My Approach

I love this type of art direction. It derives from live theater and, of course, puppet shows. I've seen a renaissance of this kind of moving cut-out art in popular media recently, from films and music videos to video games.

There are three main challenges here. The first is drawing the cut-out waves and making them look good. The second is deciding how to move them. The third is figuring out how to do all of this fast enough to support real-time animation (and leave enough time available for other objects to become part of the scene as well, like a boat or some jumping dolphins).

The third task is the easiest. When the program begins, I'll create each layer of wave in an offscreen buffer and then save it as a PImage. Then I can simply draw that wave layer to the screen, each wave in front of the other.

Oh, wait. That's not quite enough. If you do that, the waves don't look like they're separated in space. We need something that sets them apart. In a real scene, we'd see shadows cast by each wave on the waves behind. These little shadows that are associated with a layer in an image are often called *drop shadows*.

(a)

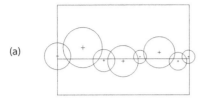

(b)

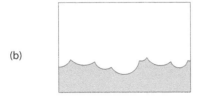

Figure 23.17. Making waves. (a) Creating circles above and below a baseline. (b) The resulting mask after subtracting those circles.

How can we create these drop shadows? The answer's easy: we'll draw them in offscreen buffers and save them as layers! Then each time we want to draw a wave, we draw its shadow first and then the wave itself on top. I have a hunch that it might look nice to move each shadow around a little bit from frame to frame relative to the wave that is "casting" it, so I'll keep the shadows and the waves in separate images.

So how do we make a wave? I drew a couple of potential stylized waves on a piece of paper, and I realized that I was drawing a series of circular arcs that would dip down and rise and then dip down again. The arcs were from circles of different radii and vertical position. Figure 23.17 shows the idea.

That seemed like a perfect recipe! So that will be my algorithm for making waves. I'll start by making a *mask*. This will be a PGraphics object that will tell me the shape of my wave. It will be opaque near the bottom, where the wave is visible, and transparent everywhere above.

To start with, the whole mask will be opaque. Then I'll imagine a horizontal line along which the circles will start out, and I'll make everything above that line transparent. Then I'll move across the line, from left to right, making overlapping circles. I'll place each one on the horizontal line, but with some vertical variation, and I'll make sure that they overlap, which will create the pointy cusps that, to me, say "wave." I'll draw each circle as a transparent shape so it has the effect of cutting away the mask inside the circle. When I've reached the right edge, the only nontransparent pixels left will be the ones below the circles I've removed. And that's the kind of stylized wave shape I was after!

Now that I have the mask, I can create the image of the wave and its shadow. I start with the shadow.

The idea behind making a nice shadow is simple, but the code takes a bunch of lines. I'll create a 2D array of float values that's the same size as the mask (so it's also the same size as the graphics window). Into each element of that array, I'll put a 1 if the corresponding mask entry is fully opaque, a 0 if it's fully transparent, and a value between those for intermediate levels of transparency (these will be created by Processing on the edges of the circles when it draws them into the mask).

But I want the shadows to look a little fuzzy, so I'll blur them first, using the same approach as I used to blur the glows in the neon-sign project and as described in Chapter 22.

At the end of the blurring step, I turn the array of float values into colors and use set() to write them into the PGraphics object that holds the blurred shadow. The object is black everywhere, but the opacity value follows the blurred shadow. So above the wave edge the shadow is transparent, below the edge it's opaque, and along the edge it has a broad, fuzzed-out transition that makes the shadow.

Now it's time to create the image. I took it easy and just used our old friend noise() to create a pattern of watery blue and frothy white. Again I used set() to write this color into each pixel of a PGraphics object. But I also remembered to set the opacity of each pixel using the mask. That way, the pixels in the waves are opaque colors, and those above are transparent.

I do this a bunch of times to create multiple pairs of wave and shadow layers.

Finally, I need to find some technique to get them to move around. I thought a nice approach would be to model this as though it was an actual, physical mechanism. If I was building something like this, I might attach each wave to a little circular crank mounted on a wheel. As I turned the crank, the wave would follow the motion of the wheel, going around and around. I thought it would be even more fun to simulate a little perspective, so the "closer" waves would move faster than those farther away, and move in circles with a larger radius as well.

The motion of the waves is all handled by draw(). First, I draw the background, which is just a picture I made by combining a couple of images I found at one of the free online stock photo sites. Then I draw each layer, from the farthest to the nearest. I use the layer number to determine the size and speed of my imaginary circular crank. Once I have the position, I draw the fuzzy, blurred-out shadow and then the wave. Then I move on to the next layer and draw its shadow and wave, and so on, all the way to the front.

```
int NumLayers = 4;
PGraphics LayerImage[];
PGraphics LayerShadow[];
float MotionRadius = 10;

// starry sky: http://www.sxc.hu/photo/1005288
// moon: http://www.sxc.hu/photo/1115121
PImage Background;

void setup() {
   size(600, 400, JAVA2D);
   LayerImage = new PGraphics[NumLayers];
   LayerShadow = new PGraphics[NumLayers];

   Background = loadImage("nightbg01.png");

   for (int layer=0; layer<NumLayers; layer++) {
      makeLayer(layer);
   }
}
```

```
void draw() {
    image(Background, 0, 0);
    for (int layer=0; layer<NumLayers; layer++) {
        int distanceFromBack = (NumLayers-1)-layer;
        float angleAtBack = 2.5 * frameCount;
        float theta = radians(angleAtBack) + (1.3 * layer);
        float radius = MotionRadius * pow(.8, distanceFromBack);
        float xoff = radius * cos(theta);
        float yoff = (layer * 20) + (radius * abs(sin(theta)));
        image(LayerShadow[layer], (-MotionRadius)+xoff, (-MotionRadius)+yoff);
        image(LayerImage[layer], (-MotionRadius)+xoff, (-MotionRadius)+yoff);
    }
}

void makeLayer(int layer) {
    int layerWidth = round(width + (2.5*MotionRadius));
    int layerHeight = round(height + (2.5*MotionRadius));

    PGraphics thisMask = createGraphics(layerWidth, layerHeight, JAVA2D);
    LayerShadow[layer] = createGraphics(layerWidth, layerHeight, JAVA2D);
    LayerImage[layer] = createGraphics(layerWidth, layerHeight, JAVA2D);

    // create the mask.  0=transparent, 255=opaque
    thisMask.beginDraw();
    thisMask.background(0, 255); // start completely opaque
    thisMask.smooth();
    thisMask.noStroke();
    thisMask.fill(255, 255);      // draw = erase opacity

    float circleYLine = layerHeight * 0.6;
    thisMask.rect(0, 0, layerWidth, circleYLine);

    float minRadius = layerHeight/10.0;
    float maxRadius = layerHeight/7.0;
    float radius = random(minRadius, maxRadius);
    float xCenter = -random(0, radius);
    while (xCenter-radius < layerWidth) {
        float yCenter = circleYLine + ((radius/4.0) *lerp(-1, 1, random(0,1)));
        thisMask.ellipse(xCenter, yCenter, radius*2, radius*2);
        xCenter += radius;
        radius = random(minRadius, maxRadius);
        xCenter += random(.25, .9)*radius;
    }
    thisMask.endDraw();
                    // create the shadow: black with alpha
                    // the float array is 1 for black (shadow), else 0
                    float blurSrc[][] = new float[layerHeight][layerWidth];
```

```
float blurDst[][] = new float[layerHeight][layerWidth];
for (int y=0; y<layerHeight; y++) {
   for (int x=0; x<layerWidth; x++) {
      color c = thisMask.get(x, y);
      blurSrc[y][x] = red(c)/255.0;
   }
}

int numPasses = 1;
int blurRadius = 8;
for (int pass=0; pass<numPasses; pass++) {

   for (int y=0; y<layerHeight; y++) {
      for (int x=0; x<layerWidth; x++) {
         int ixlo = max(0, x-blurRadius);
         int ixhi = min(layerWidth, x+blurRadius);
         int iylo = max(0, y-blurRadius);
         int iyhi = min(layerHeight, y+blurRadius);
         int numAdded = 0;
         float blurSum = 0;
         for (int iy=iylo; iy<iyhi; iy++) {
            for (int ix=ixlo; ix<ixhi; ix++) {
               blurSum += blurSrc[iy][ix];
               numAdded++;
            }
         }
         if (numAdded == 0) numAdded = 1;
         blurDst[y][x] = blurSum/numAdded;
      }
   }

   // copy dst back into src to prepare for next pass
   for (int y=0; y<layerHeight; y++) {
      for (int x=0; x<layerWidth; x++) {
         blurSrc[y][x] = blurDst[y][x];
      }
   }
}

LayerShadow[layer].beginDraw();
for (int y=0; y<layerHeight; y++) {
   for (int x=0; x<layerWidth; x++) {
      float blurVal = blurDst[y][x];
      LayerShadow[layer].set(x, y, color(0, 0, 0, 255*(1-blurVal)));
   }
}
```

```
LayerShadow[layer].endDraw();

// draw the image
color c0 = color(255, 255, 255);
color c1 = color(0, 0, 255);
LayerImage[layer].beginDraw();
for (int y=0; y<layerHeight; y++) {
    for (int x=0; x<layerWidth; x++) {
        float a = noise((x+(layerWidth*layer))*.02, (y+(layerHeight*layer))*.02);
        color maskColor = thisMask.get(x, y);
        float opacity = 255 - red(maskColor);
        color imgColor = lerpColor(c0, c1, a);
        imgColor = color(red(imgColor), green(imgColor), blue(imgColor), opacity);
        LayerImage[layer].set(x, y, imgColor);
    }
}
LayerImage[layer].endDraw();

}
```

(See output in Figure 23.18. Full program in projects/sketches/puppetshow01/puppetshow01.pde)

Figure 23.18. A puppet theater version of an ocean at night.
(projects/sketches/puppetshow01/puppetshow01.pde)

23.7 Spooky Plants

Those guys on the Urban Planet of Hirise and the Rain Planet of New Seattle have it easy. Here on the Scary Planet of Pitius, everything is out to eat us. The armor-covered flying Skeleton Birds drip acid from the skies, giant awful Blobbybeasts ooze into everything, and creepy long-spindled Razorweed grows in the few tiny holes that exist in the hard-packed ground.

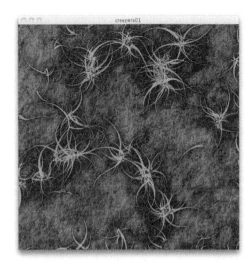

Figure 23.19. A picture of the creepers growing out of the tough ground.

You've never seen Razorweed? It's a green–blue kind of plant that grows from a central bulb, sending out long spindly blades that start out wide and taper to a point. A dangerous, malicious point.

Some of us have been trying to make it sound less scary by calling them creepers. As a public-spirited citizen, I'll call them that, but they'll always be Razorweed to me.

Figure 23.19 shows an image from one of my recent nature walks. You can see some of the creepers growing out of the tiny dark cracks in the rock-hard ground.

Let's make some pictures of this to send to the explorers on the other planets, so they'll know just how rough we have it here.

23.7.1 My Approach

I make my pictures of creepers by stacking up three images. First, there's the ground. This is a photograph that I found on a free online site, which I mix with some 2D noise to give it a crunchier feel. Then there are some black regions that represent cracks in the ground. On top of the stack are the creepers themselves, created by drawing a few thousand random, tapered blades. In between these is a shadow layer that's derived from the creeper picture, so that they appear to be growing a little bit above the surface.

This isn't an animation, so there's no `draw()` routine.

The process begins by building the ground. This actually creates two images: one to hold the picture of the ground itself and another to hold a mask. My use of the mask is a lot like in the last wave-making project.

I make the mask by initializing it to 255 and then calling `noise()` at every pixel. If the noise is above some threshold, the mask is set to 0. I found a pleasing value for the threshold using the same guess-and-refine technique I used in earlier projects.

Then I read in the background photograph of the ground from a file and run through every pixel of the background image. If the mask is 0, I set the color of the image to 0, otherwise it's a blend of the photograph and the black-and-white noise. This gives the photo a little bit of extra complexity and makes it a little different each time we run the program.

Next, I grow the creepers. I'll discuss that in detail in a moment, but it ends up in a single image that holds all the blades.

Finally, I create the shadows cast by the creepers. As in the waves example, I make a black-and-white version of the creepers image and then blur it a few times. I use the very same blurring technique that I used for the waves.

Once these things are done, I just draw the ground, the shadow, and the creepers, in that order.

So how do we draw the creepers? I draw a thousand or more of them, one by one, and accumulate them.

I decided to create a single object called a `Blade`. My original thought was that I might want the growing blades to know about one another, so they could cluster together and maybe even influence one another's growth. I ended up abandoning that idea, but it was still convenient to have the `Blade` object around. With it, I can just make a `Blade` and tell it to render itself, then make another and tell that one to render itself, and so on, as many times as I need.

The vein of a blade is made up of a single Bézier curve with a seed, a tip, and two control points. But because I want the blades to have thickness, I offset the two control points to create a pair of curves, one above the vein and one below. This is just like how I made my leaves in Chapter 15. When I first make a new blade, I give it a random color somewhere between green and blue that I picked.

Then the blade gets planted. That just means I find a pixel where the seed of the blade will be located. To find such a pixel, I look at random points on the image until I find one where the mask value tells me I'm on top of dirt (rather than the textured ground).

Then I build the blade by picking a random point some distance from the seed to act as the tip, followed by the two control points along the vein. I store the two control points that form the upper curve and the two that make the lower curve.

To render the blade, my first approach was just to draw the blade itself by setting the fill color to the blade's color and drawing the two Bézier curves. But the blades all seemed to sit right on top of each other; I wanted them to have a little bit of distinction.

I decided to reuse the shadow trick from the crystal-tower project above, but in a different way. There, I was able to draw a bigger circle under each disk. Here, there's no easy way to make the whole blade larger. So instead, I create a thick stroke in a nearly transparent black color, and I draw around the outside of the blade, which gives it a very light shadow. Then I draw the blade itself. I also draw a circle on the seed end so the sharp corners don't draw the eye.

The result is that the blades shadow one another slightly, giving them some depth and separation. And the clumps shadow the ground, so they seem to be growing above it.

```
PGraphics LayerGroundMask;
PGraphics LayerGroundPicture;
PGraphics LayerGrass;
PGraphics LayerGrassShadow;

class Blade {

   color clr;
   PVector seed, seedA, seedB;
   PVector c1, c1A, c1B;
   PVector c2, c2A, c2B;
   PVector tip;
   float r0, r1, r2;

   // Blade grows from seed to tip.  pA and pB are along the way.
   // c1 and c2 are perpendiculars at pA and pB.  A and B values
   // are points above and below seed, c1, and c2 for blade thickness.
   //
   //                                       c2A
   //                         c1A          *****(c2)**
   //                     **(c1)*****          c2B      **
   //                  **    c1B               |          **
   //       sA      **          |              |            **
   //      (seed)***------(pA)----------(pB)--------***(tip)
   //       sB
   //

   Blade() {
      color color0 = color(109, 204,  55, 192);  // greenish
      color color1 = color(  9, 178, 150, 192); // blueish
      clr = lerpColor(color0, color1, random(0, 1));
      seed = new PVector(0, 0);
      tip = new PVector(0, 0);
   }

   void plantSeed(PGraphics mask) {
      boolean foundSeed = false;
      while (!foundSeed) {
         seed.x = random(0, width);
         seed.y = random(0, height);
         int maskx = round(seed.x);
         int masky = round(seed.y);
         float rval = red(mask.get(maskx, masky));
         if (rval < 1) foundSeed = true;
      }
   }
}
```

```
void buildBlade(PGraphics layer) {
    float minLength = layer.width/20;
    float maxLength = layer.width/5;
    float bladeLength = lerp(minLength, maxLength, pow(random(0,1), 3));

    float bladeAngle = random(0, TWO_PI);
    tip = new PVector(seed.x + (bladeLength * cos(bladeAngle)),
                        seed.y + (bladeLength * sin(bladeAngle)));

    float aPercent = random(0.2, 0.4);
    float bPercent = random(0.6, 0.8);
    PVector pA = new PVector(lerp(seed.x, tip.x, aPercent),
                             lerp(seed.y, tip.y, aPercent));
    PVector pB = new PVector(lerp(seed.x, tip.x, bPercent),
                             lerp(seed.y, tip.y, bPercent));

    PVector tipMinusSeed = new PVector(tip.x-seed.x, tip.y-seed.y);
    PVector perp = new PVector(-tipMinusSeed.y, tipMinusSeed.x);
                                                // counter-clockwise
    perp.normalize();

    float c1sign = 1;
    if (random(1000) > 500) c1sign = -1;
    float c2sign = 1;
    if (random(1000) > 500) c2sign = -1;

    c1 = new PVector(pA.x + (c1sign*((aPercent*bladeLength)*perp.x)),
                    pA.y + (c1sign*((aPercent*bladeLength)*perp.y)));
    c2 = new PVector(pB.x - (c2sign*(((1-bPercent)*bladeLength)*perp.x)),
                      pB.y - (c2sign*(((1-bPercent)*bladeLength)*perp.y)));


    r0 = bladeLength * random(.01, .04);
    r1 = r0 * random(.5, .75);
    r2 = r1 * random(.5, .75);

    PVector c1MinusSeed = new PVector(c1.x-seed.x, c1.y-seed.y);
    PVector c1MSperp = new PVector(-c1MinusSeed.y, c1MinusSeed.x);
    c1MSperp.normalize();
    seedA = new PVector(seed.x+(r0*c1MSperp.x), seed.y+(r0*c1MSperp.y));
    seedB = new PVector(seed.x-(r0*c1MSperp.x), seed.y-(r0*c1MSperp.y));
    c1A = new PVector(c1.x+(r1*c1MSperp.x), c1.y+(r1*c1MSperp.y));
    c1B = new PVector(c1.x-(r1*c1MSperp.x), c1.y-(r1*c1MSperp.y));

    PVector tipMinusC2 = new PVector(tip.x-c2.x, tip.y-c2.y);
    PVector tMC2perp = new PVector(-tipMinusC2.y, tipMinusC2.x);
    tMC2perp.normalize();
```

```
            c2A = new PVector(c2.x+(r2*tMC2perp.x), c2.y+(r2*tMC2perp.y));
            c2B = new PVector(c2.x-(r2*tMC2perp.x), c2.y-(r2*tMC2perp.y));
        }

        void renderVein(PGraphics layer) {
            layer.beginDraw();
            layer.noFill();
            layer.stroke(clr);
            layer.bezier(seed.x, seed.y, c1.x, c1.y, c2.x, c2.y, tip.x, tip.y);
            layer.endDraw();
        }

        void renderBlade(PGraphics layer) {
            layer.smooth();
            layer.beginDraw();

            layer.noFill();
            layer.stroke(0, 16);
            layer.strokeWeight(5);
            drawCurves(layer);

            layer.noStroke();
            layer.fill(clr);
            drawCurves(layer);
            layer.ellipse(seed.x, seed.y, r0, r0);

            layer.endDraw();
        }

        void drawCurves(PGraphics layer) {
            layer.beginShape();
            layer.vertex(seedA.x, seedA.y);
            layer.bezierVertex(c1A.x, c1A.y, c2A.x, c2A.y, tip.x, tip.y);
            layer.bezierVertex(c2B.x, c2B.y, c1B.x, c1B.y, seedB.x, seedB.y);
            layer.endShape(CLOSE);
        }
    }
}
void setup() {
    size(600, 600, JAVA2D);
    smooth();
    background(69, 51, 40);

    LayerGroundMask    = createGraphics(width, height, JAVA2D);
    LayerGroundPicture = createGraphics(width, height, JAVA2D);
    LayerGrass         = createGraphics(width, height, JAVA2D);
    LayerGrassShadow   = createGraphics(width, height, JAVA2D);
```

```
    buildGround();
    growGrass();
    makeGrassShadow();

    image(LayerGroundPicture, 0, 0);
    image(LayerGrassShadow, 0, 0);
    image(LayerGrass, 0, 0);
}

void buildGround() {
    LayerGroundMask.beginDraw();
    LayerGroundMask.background(255);
    for (int y=0; y<LayerGroundMask.height; y++) {
        for (int x=0; x<LayerGroundMask.width; x++) {
            if (noise(x*.02, y*.02) > 0.7) LayerGroundMask.set(x, y, color(0));
        }
    }
    LayerGroundMask.endDraw();

    color c0 = color(65, 65, 65);
    color c1 = color(128, 128, 128);

    PImage concreteImage = loadImage("ground600.png");

    LayerGroundPicture.beginDraw();
    for (int y=0; y<LayerGroundPicture.height; y++) {
        for (int x=0; x<LayerGroundPicture.height; x++) {
            float opacity = (red(LayerGroundMask.get(x,y)) == 0) ? 0 : 255;
            float a = noise(x*.02, y*.02);
            color clr = color(
                lerp(red(c0), red(c1), a),
                lerp(green(c0), green(c1), a),
                lerp(blue(c0), blue(c1), a),
                opacity);

            color concreteColor = concreteImage.get(x,y);
            float ablend = 0.20;
            color cnew = color(red(concreteColor), green(concreteColor),
                               blue(concreteColor), opacity);
            color blendColor = lerpColor(clr, cnew, ablend);

            LayerGroundPicture.set(x, y, blendColor);
        }
    }
    LayerGroundPicture.endDraw();
}

                void growGrass() {
```

```
   LayerGrass.background(0, 0);
   for (int g=0; g<1000; g++) {
      Blade blade = new Blade();
      blade.plantSeed(LayerGroundMask);
      blade.buildBlade(LayerGrass);
      blade.renderBlade(LayerGrass);
   }
}

void makeGrassShadow() {
   float blurLayerSrc[][] = new float[height][width];
   float blurLayerDst[][] = new float[height][width];
   for (int y=0; y<height; y++) {
      for (int x=0; x<width; x++) {
         blurLayerSrc[y][x] = 0;
         color clr = LayerGrass.get(x,y);
         if (alpha(clr) > 0) blurLayerSrc[y][x] = 1;
      }
   }

   int numPasses = 3;
   int blurRadius = 8;
   for (int pass=0; pass<numPasses; pass++) {
      // blur src into dst
      for (int y=0; y<height; y++) {
         for (int x=0; x<width; x++) {
            int numAdded = 0;
            float blurSum = 0;
            int ixlo = max(0, x-blurRadius);
            int ixhi = min(width, x+blurRadius);
            int iylo = max(0, y-blurRadius);
            int iyhi = min(height, y+blurRadius);
            for (int iy=iylo; iy<iyhi; iy++) {
               for (int ix=ixlo; ix<ixhi; ix++) {
                  numAdded++;
                  blurSum += blurLayerSrc[iy][ix];
               }
            }
            if (numAdded == 0) numAdded = 1;
            blurLayerDst[y][x] = blurSum/numAdded;
         }
      }

      // copy dst into src
      for (int y=0; y<height; y++) {
         for (int x=0; x<width; x++) {
```

```
            blurLayerSrc[y][x] = blurLayerDst[y][x];
        }
    }
}

// copy src into the layer
LayerGrassShadow.beginDraw();
for (int y=0; y<height; y++) {
    for (int x=0; x<width; x++) {
        float opacity = 96 * blurLayerSrc[y][x];
        LayerGrassShadow.set(x, y, color(0, 0, 0, opacity));
    }
}
LayerGrassShadow.endDraw();
}
```

(See output in Figure 23.20. Full program in projects/sketches/creepers01/creepers01.pde)

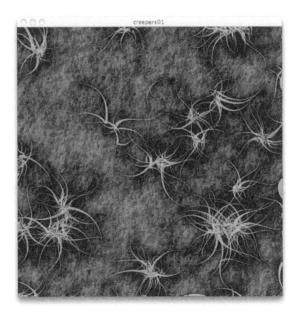

Figure 23.20. More growing creepers. (projects/sketches/creepers01/creepers01.pde)

Chapter 24
Big Projects

Now comes the time for you to grab the reins and take control of this dragon for yourself! In the last chapter we took on a series of small to medium sized projects. Now we'll tackle two big projects (not huge, but still big). These are intended to make you stretch. They will probably be a challenge, but I hope they will be fun challenges.

Let's talk about some of the different ways to tackle a large project.

24.1   Tackling a Project

After this introductory section, I'll describe the first project to you in a couple of sentences. I strongly encourage you to stop reading right then and there! Start working on the program.

For most people, that does not mean firing up Processing! For most of us, it means getting away from the computer.

You might want to put on some music and relax on the couch with some scratch paper. You might want to take a long walk. Or have a brainstorming session with a friend and fill up a few napkins with wild drawings.

Then once you have a plan in mind and a way to approach the problem, you can launch Processing and try writing some little programs to experiment with your ideas, seeing which ones work the way you'd hoped.

As the project grows, you'll probably hit a wall somewhere: you'll realize you need to do something that you don't know how to do. You'll be adrift.

And that is the moment you'll cross the threshold from journeyman programmer to an artist using Processing as a creative medium.

When you're out there in the dark, try to figure out a way—any way—to do anything even close to the thing you want. Nobody's watching. Make objects, make variables, cook up bizarre routines. Mess around. Go forwards, go backwards. Play.

Even the most crazy approach can teach you a lot if you really try to understand it, and it will help you appreciate the issue facing you in a deeper and more informed way.

You can't break anything, and you simply cannot do anything wrong. If something gets too complicated, try to simplify it, but don't give up as long as you're learning.

If one of the built-in functions doesn't seem to be working the way you think it should, reread this book or the online documentation and correct any misconceptions. And you can always search the Processing website (and the web at large) for a program that someone else has written that does something close enough to your task that it helps illuminate the way.

When you're ready to put the first few pieces together into a program, start with a skeleton and get it to draw something really simple, like a single box. Then get it to draw something a little closer to what you're thinking of. Then get it a little closer. And so on, one step at a time. Add new layers of operations and images, build new scaffolding, take it down when you no longer need it.

Go ahead: you can't hurt the computer, you can't hurt yourself, and everything you do will ultimately be good for you. So strap on your wings and give it a go.

If you're having trouble getting airborne, or your flights aren't lasting very long, you can come back here. The section after I describe the project will outline the architecture of my solution. I've already finished both of these projects, and I've found nice ways to organize them that pleased me and produced attractive results. So after you've played with each project for a while, if you're having trouble finding an organization that you like, you can see how I broke things down.

Again, at that point I encourage you to stop reading and get back to programming! I want to help you, but I want to give you only the least amount of help I can at each step.

If you're still having some flight troubles, I'll provide two more levels of discussion. The next section will give a detailed description of each file and object. Again, stop reading after that and go program!

Finally, I'll give you the code I wrote. And at the end, I'll give you my whole program in one place.

Then we'll do it again, with a whole new project. This one will encourage you to take on a whole new range of creative design decisions and stretch your skills in new directions.

24.2   Organizing a Project

Although you can always write any Processing program in one giant source file, it's often more convenient to break up a big project into a few different files. That can help you focus your attention just on one particular aspect of the problem. When you have several big classes in your project, it's often helpful to put each one in its own file. Processing makes this kind of organization easy to create and manage.

To make a new source file, go to the tab bar on the Processing window and click on the right-pointing arrow at the far right end, as shown in Figure 24.1.

Choose *New Tab* and give the new file a name. It will open a new tab next to the existing one, as shown in Figure 24.2.

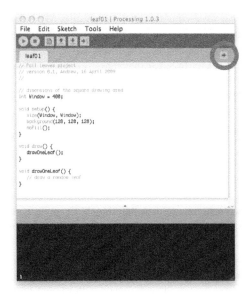

Figure 24.1. Click on the right arrow in the tab bar to create a file.

Figure 24.2. After giving the file a name, a new tab appears.

Now enter your code in the new tab. When you save your sketch, Processing puts all the source files together into the same folder. Processing knows that all the files in a folder belong together. When you open any of the files in this folder, Processing will open and display the other tabs for you automatically. This is true for all the files in a folder; they're all considered part of the same sketch, and saving any one of them will save them all.

Breaking things up into these separate files is really just a convenience for you, to help you keep any given bit of the program from getting too large. When it compiles your program, Processing treats all of the files as though they were just one big file. You do have to keep blocks together, though. That is, you can't split a single routine across multiple files or break up a class. Generally speaking, any opening curly brace has to have a matching closing curly brace in the same file.

If you're writing a program in the object-oriented style, you'll typically put each class into its own file. Then you can create and manipulate objects of that class in other files and not have to even see the code that implements the class itself. Until you need to change or fix the class, that code can just sit there in its own tab, quietly ignored. When you do need to change the object, just click on the tab and make your changes.

Always remember to save your work! As I've mentioned earlier, Processing does not automatically save your changes when you run a new sketch. If something goes wrong and you have to quit Processing (or it crashes, or the computer crashes), you'll probably lose any work you haven't saved. So save your sketches frequently. My habit is to save them every time I run them. If Processing gave me an option to have it do that for me automatically, I'd turn it on immediately. Until then, I do it manually.

Once you start any large project, you'll quickly discover that there are a seemingly endless number of big and little choices to be made. Some choices are analytic: how can I do this next step in a logical and elegant way? And some are artistic: what colors should this thing have? And some, perhaps the most challenging and the most fun, are both: how should this thing move, what should it look like, and what programming will bring that about?

Your answer to every one of these questions will be personal, and the result of all your decisions will be a solution that is yours and yours alone. Your programs might end up something like mine, or they might be a million miles away. Your pictures and animations might look like mine, or viewers might never guess that they both came from the same original inspiration. And that's fine. We're not building an air-traffic-control system here, we're expressing ourselves.

I encourage you to make lots of little experiments. Just pop open a new sketch, create `setup()` and `draw()` routines, and try things out. Draw things, change them, make them move. Figure out little solutions in isolation so you're not burdened with making them fit the rest of your program. When you finally know where you're going, you can go back to the big system and add them in. There's no bad experimenting. You can't break Processing, and you can't break the computer. Programming like this is about as responsibility-free as finger painting with water-soluble paints in the garage. When you're just goofing around and trying things out, messy is fine. Messy is good! You can clean up later.

So let's dig in!

24.3   Project 1: Sandstorm

An endless stream of little particles are falling down the screen. As they fall, they get caught up in moving, rotating fields, which spin them around before they break free and finally disappear off the bottom of the screen.

That's it. Put down the book and dig in. Have fun!

24.3.1   Level 2: My Architecture

Here's the overall structure of my solution to this project.

In this discussion, I'll use typography to distinguish between class definitions and objects of that class. We'll see that I have a class called `Grain`. An instance of that class will be simply a Grain, written without the typewriter font. Similarly, there's a class called `Wind`, and an instance of that class is a Wind. The capital letters are to help us distinguish actual objects in the program from the nouns they're roughly based on.

I decided I'd build my program around two custom classes. The first class is `Grain`, which corresponds to a single falling particle, like a grain of sand. The second class describes a wind field, and is fittingly called `Wind`.

There are two arrays: one of `Grain` objects, and one of `Wind` objects. Each Grain gets initialized at the start, and then on each frame I update its position and draw it. I also update each Wind object.

The general scheme is that I run `setup()` and `draw()` as usual. When `draw()` runs, it first moves each Grain into its new position by telling each one to update itself. Each Grain adds together the forces that are acting on it. It starts with gravity pulling it downward, and then adds in the amount and direction of force that each `Wind` object is exerting on it. It also adds in a little push in the direction it was moved during the last update, to simulate inertia. After adding all these forces together, the grain moves accordingly. Once all the grains have moved into position, I tell each one to draw itself.

When that's done, `draw()` calls each of the `Wind` objects and tells them to update themselves, which they do by moving a little bit from frame to frame. Then `draw()` exits until the system calls it again.

I broke this down into four files.

24.3.2   Sandstorm.pde Overview

The main file for my system is called *Sandstorm.pde*. This contains the globals for the arrays holding Grains and Winds, and code for `setup()` and `draw()`. In `setup()` I create the window and initialize the arrays. In `draw()` I update the Grains and draw them, and then update the Winds. There's also an implementation of `keyPressed()` so I can press a key to freeze to screen if I see something I really like and want to take a snapshot of it.

24.3.3   Grain.pde Overview

This file defines the `Grain` class. Each Grain is described by a handful of parameters:

```
PVector center;
float radius;
float cr, cg, cb;
PVector oldVelocity;
PVector oldCenter;
```

The Grain is located at `center`. When it gets drawn, it has a size given by `radius` and color given by `cr`, `cg`, and `cb`. The position it had in the last frame is stored in `oldCenter`, and the amount by which it moved in the last frame is stored in `oldVelocity`.

The `Grain` constructor calls another routine that actually fills in the `Grain` variables with random numbers. There's a `render()` routine to draw the Grain.

The move() routine figures out the direction and speed of the wind (if any) at the Grain's center. It combines that with the effects of gravity and the Grain's motion on the last frame to figure out its new position.

What should be done if a Grain falls off the bottom of the screen? I could manage my own pool of preallocated Grains and add this to the pool, since it's available for reuse. Or I could abandon the pointer and let the garbage collector scoop it up eventually. But I know that each time a Grain disappears, I'll simply want to start it again at the top of the screen. So the easiest solution is also the one that runs the fastest: I'll just recycle the object myself. I'll fill it up with new values like a brand-new Grain, and it will just naturally drop down into the screen again.

24.3.4 Wind.pde Overview

This file defines the Wind class. Each Wind object is described by four parameters:

```
PVector center;
PVector velocity;
float radius;
float strength;
```

Each wind gust has a center, a radius, and a strength. The wind has a maximum effect of strength units at the center, and that effect falls off linearly to 0 at the distance of radius. The value of strength describes the maximum power of the wind source. Figure 24.3 shows the idea.

The center moves each time the Wind is updated; the movement in screen coordinates is described by the value of velocity.

The constructor builds a new, random Wind object somewhere on the screen. The update() routine moves the Wind object around on the screen. When it hits one of the walls, it bounces off, just like the bouncing balls in earlier chapters.

An action called windAt() takes a 2D point in screen coordinates as input and returns a 2D point that describes the direction and strength of the Wind at that point.

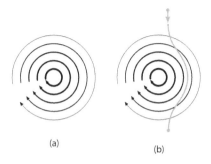

(a)   (b)

Figure 24.3. The wind source. (a) The wind blows in a circle. It's strongest in the center and falls off to 0. (b) The path of a falling object influenced by the wind.

24.3.5 End of Level 2

That's it for the overview. There's a main file and a couple of classes.

If this approach appeals to you, put down the book and give it a shot. See if you can breathe fire into this recipe and make it come alive.

If this particular organization doesn't do it for you, think about what's going on and come up with your own approach. Then implement it and make it run!

24.3.6 Level 3: Detailed Breakdown

In this section I'll describe my program in words. I'll try to be complete enough that you'll be able to write a program based just on this text. But of course, there are tons of details that defy a nice verbal description, so you'll still have some thinking to do in order to convert these descriptions to code.

After this description, the next section gives you my final code.

24.3.7 Sandstorm.pde Details

The `setup()` function first creates the graphics window. Then I define the number of `Grain` objects, create their global array, and run through the array calling the `Grain` constructor for each element. I then repeat the process for the `Wind` objects by stating how many there should be, creating an array, and then running through that array and creating a new `Wind` object for each element.

In `draw()`, I don't clear the screen (because I want the paths of the Grains to accumulate over time). I run through all the Grains, updating and drawing each one. Then I run through all the Winds and update them as well.

I found that I wanted to sometimes freeze the program so I could take a screenshot of a particularly nice pattern. I decided I'd use the keyboard to help me do this. If I press any key while the program is running, it will freeze and stop updating. If I press any key while it's frozen, it will resume running.

I implemented `keyPressed()` so that I would know when a key is pressed. I defined a global `boolean` variable that was `true` when the program was updating the screen and `false` when it was frozen. When `keyPressed()` gets called, it checks this `boolean`. If the program is updating the screen, I call `noLoop()` to stop the updates and set the `boolean` to `false`. If the program is *not* updating the screen, I call `loop()` to get it running again and set the `boolean` to `true`.

24.3.8 Grain.pde Details

The `Grain` object describes a single grain of sand, which is the only thing the program draws. Each Grain has a location, a color, and a size. It also has a couple of variables to remember the location and velocity it had the last time it was updated.

A Grain has only a few methods. There's a constructor, of course. This calls another function that actually creates random initial values for the Grain. There's a method that moves the Grain into position for each new frame and a method to draw the Grain. Let's look at these in turn.

The constructor is just one line long: it calls another routine called `fillGrain()` that fills the Grain with random starting values. By putting all the initialization in its own routine, I can easily recycle my Grain objects when they go offscreen. I merely need to call `fillGrain()` directly, and I have an essentially new Grain object.

The `fillGrain()` routine sets the Grain's center to a random point with an x value in the range `(0, width)` (so it's at a random point horizontally across the graphics window) and a y value in the range `(-height, 0)`. If they all started at a y value of 0, they would be located right at the top of the screen, and when the program started, they would all fall together in one giant clump. I wanted them to be spaced out vertically. So I imagine an entire graphics window sitting above the one that's actually drawn, and I start them somewhere in that window. While a little inefficient (the Grains spend some time offscreen, where we can't see them), this makes sure that the Grains are well-distributed vertically and don't clump up. I give the Grain a `radius` in the range (0.25, 2.0).

Each Grain remembers its position and value from the previous frame. But when I build a new Grain, there is no previous value to remember. So I set `oldCenter` to the same value as the `center` (so it has a reasonable, if kind of useless, value).

I give `oldVelocity` a y value between $(0.4, 1.8)$ in y, to give it a good push downward so it seems to be responding to gravity, and I give it an x value between $(-0.02, 0.02)$ so it picks up a little bit of horizontal drift.

Finally, I wanted the Grains to run through a few different colors across the screen. I created an array with five different HSB values that I picked by hand. The idea is that the five colors correspond to the left side of the window, three equally-spaced locations across it, and the right side. Grains in between these locations get color values in between these set colors. Once I build that color, I add some randomness to it because I think it adds visual interest. Since I'm adding a random value to the color, I don't bother spending a lot of work smoothly blending the colors I've provided but just use a quick linear blend from one to the next.

The `render()` routine draws a short line from the Grain's center position in the last frame to its center position in the new frame. I set the color of the line to the Grain's color and the stroke's weight to the Grain's radius. (I originally drew the Grains as circles, but I didn't like the gaps that appeared in their trails.)

The `move()` routine first saves the current center location (that is, the one that was used in the last frame) into `oldCenter`, so I'll have that around the next time `draw()` gets called. Then I figure out how the Grain should move. Since the Grain will move in both x and y, I create a `PVector` to hold the changes in position that I'll add to the Grain on this update.

That point gets initialized by setting x to 0 and y to a random number between 1.5 and 2. This simulates gravity pulling the grain downward, with a little bit of randomness for visual interest, so they don't all fall at exactly the same speed. I could make up some plausible physical reason why the grains fall at different speeds, I guess, but I'm not trying to do real physics here. If it looks better to have some get pulled downward a little faster than others, that's all that matters.

Then I run through a loop of the `Wind` objects (using the global array created in `SandStorm.pde`). I ask each Wind for it's value at the Grain's center. Each Wind gives me back a `PVector` telling me the *x* and *y* components of the wind there. I just add them all in to the point I created above, so now the Grain is feeling not just gravity but the sum of all the Wind objects.

Now I do a trick that I found by messing around. I want the grains to have a little bit of inertia as they move, as though they had some mass and couldn't change direction instantly. So I find out how much the Grain moved on the last update (saved in `oldVelocity`) and add a little bit of that into the new velocity.

To do this, I take the old velocity and scale it by 0.3 before adding it in. I found that number by trial and error. If it's too small, the Grains get thrown around by the combined effects of the Wind objects too easily. If the value is too big, the Grains resist the Wind and I don't get pretty patterns. To my eye, on my computer, 0.3 seemed just right.

With the combination of gravity, wind, and inertia I have the value of the velocity for this update. I then add that to the Grain's center position.

Finally, I test to see if the Grain has fallen off the bottom of the screen. If it hasn't, I'm done. But if it has, then I'll recycle the object. As I mentioned earlier, my technique for managing memory with these objects is to simply recycle them myself. I call `fillGrain()` to load the Grain up with new values, as though it was a fresh new object built by the constructor.

24.3.9 Wind.pde Details

The `Wind` object has only three methods: a constructor, a function to find the strength of the wind at a given point, and a function to move the wind around from frame to frame.

The constructor for `Wind` fills it up with random values. The `center` gets put somewhere in the graphics window, but within a 50-pixel border all around so that it's initially not too close to one of the edges.

I give the Wind a `radius` from $(40, 220)$ and a `strength` between $(-5, 5)$. Negative values of `strength` will push the Grains around clockwise, and positive values will push them counter clockwise

I also give the Wind object itself a `velocity` where both *x* and *y* are in the range $(-1, 1)$. This isn't the velocity of the wind that the object creates in order to push around the Grains, but rather, it's the velocity of the moving center of the Wind itself. In other words, it describes how the center of the Wind object is moving on the screen. I decided to treat the Wind objects like the bouncing balls we saw in earlier chapters. So each one moves in a straight line until it hits an edge and then it bounces off and continues in the new direction. This led to interesting patterns as the particles were pushed around by these spinning fields that were themselves moving around.

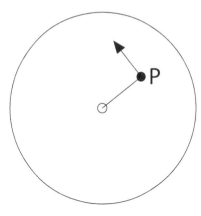

Figure 24.4. Figuring out the wind speed. Draw a line from the Wind's center to the point *P* and find the perpendicular to that line. That's the direction in which the point *P* is pushed, shown here with an arrow.

The windAt() procedure takes a PVector as input (let's call that *P*) and returns a PVector that describes the wind generated by this Wind object at point *P*. First, I find the distance between *P* and the Wind object's center. If that distance is greater than the Wind's radius, I return a wind strength of $(0, 0)$ because that Wind isn't contributing to point *P* at all. Otherwise, I use map() to scale that distance to the range (strength, 0) to find out how strong the wind is at point *P*. Next, I have to find the direction of that Wind at point *P*.

As I thought about it, I realized that *P* is going to be pushed around a circle that's centered at the Wind's origin and passes through point *P*. So if I draw a line from the origin of the circle out to point *P*, and I find the line perpendicular to that one, that gives me the direction in which point *P* is going to be pushed. Figure 24.4 shows the idea.

I can find the perpendicular using the technique from Figure 12.27 for finding the perpendicular line for any other line. So first I find the line from the center of the Wind object to point *P*. If that line has values (dx, dy) then using that technique, the wind direction is (-dy, dx). I scale that so it has length 1 and then I scale it again so it has a length equal to the strength of the wind at that point, as I computed just above. I return this scaled direction as the direction and strength of the Wind at that point.

The update() procedure is responsible for moving the Wind object itself around on the screen. It adds the current velocity of the Wind object to its center. It then checks to see if the Wind has bounced off any wall, and if so, it bounces it off the wall using the very same technique we used before for our bouncing balls.

24.3.10   Level 4: My Solution

24.3.11   SandStorm.pde

```
// Sandstorm project
// version 1.0 - AG 30 April 2009
//

boolean LoopingEnabled;  // true if draw() is being called

Grain [] Sparks;       // the grains that fall down the screen
Wind [] Gusts;         // the winds that push them around
```

```
// Create the graphics window.  Then create the global
// arrays of Sparks and Gusts and initialize them with
// objects.  Turn on the flag that indicates we're looping.
//
void setup() {
   size(600, 400);
   int numSparks = 5000;
   Sparks = new Grain[numSparks];
   for (int i=0; i<numSparks; i++) {
      Sparks[i] = new Grain();
   }
   int numGusts = 8;
   Gusts = new Wind[numGusts];
   for (int i=0; i<numGusts; i++) {
      Gusts[i] = new Wind();
   }
   LoopingEnabled = true;
}


// Draw each Spark and update it.
// Then update all the Gusts.
void draw() {
   for (int i=0; i<Sparks.length; i++) {
      Sparks[i].render();
      Sparks[i].move();
   }
   for (int i=0; i<Gusts.length; i++) {
      Gusts[i].update();
   }
}

// If the user presses a key, stop looping if it's
// enabled, or start again if it's been stopped.
//
void keyPressed() {
   if (LoopingEnabled)  noLoop();
   else loop();
   LoopingEnabled = !LoopingEnabled;
}
```

24.3.12   Grain.pde

```
// Grain class
// version 1.0 - AG 30 April 2009
//

class Grain {
```

```
PVector center;        // center location
PVector velocity;      // movement per frame
float radius;          // size in pixels
float ch, cs, cb;      // color
PVector oldCenter;     // position as of previous frame

Grain() {
   fillGrain(true);
}

// Fill in the grain with random values.  Pick a point above the
// screen so that the grain will take a while to fall.  This is
// not very efficient!  Assign a color based on the grain's
// horizontal position.
//
void fillGrain(boolean firstFill) {
   center = new PVector(random(0, width), random(-height, 0));
   if (!firstFill) center.y = 0;
   oldCenter = new PVector(center.x, center.y);
   velocity = new PVector(random(-.02,.02), random(.4, 1.8));
   radius = random(0.25, 2.0);

   float colorSets [] = {   // five hand-picked HSB colors I like
       35, 238, 133,
       42, 231, 210,
       21, 232, 235,
       18, 204, 115,
        9, 248, 210, };

   int colorSteps = int(colorSets.length/3)-1;
   float setWidth = 1.0*width/colorSteps;
   int setNumber = int(center.x/setWidth);
   float a = (center.x - (setNumber * setWidth))/setWidth;
   ch = lerp(colorSets[(setNumber*3)], colorSets[(setNumber*3)+3], a);
   cs = lerp(colorSets[(setNumber*3)+1], colorSets[(setNumber*3)+4], a);
   cb = lerp(colorSets[(setNumber*3)+2], colorSets[(setNumber*3)+5], a);

   ch = (ch + (frameCount * .02)) % 255.0;
   cs = constrain(cs+random(-10, 10), 0, 255);
   cb = constrain(cb+random(-10, 10), 0, 255);
}

// draw this grain as a short stroke from the oldCenter to center
void render() {
   strokeWeight(radius);
   colorMode(HSB);
```

```
         stroke(ch, cs, cb);
         line(oldCenter.x, oldCenter.y, center.x, center.y);
      }

   // update the grain's position.  First, store where it is now into
   // oldCenter.  Take the velocity from the last update and scale it
   // to simulate drag due to the effects of atmosphere.  Add in
   // gravity.  Then add in the total contribution of all wind gusts.
   // move the grain to the new position.  If it's fallen off the bottom
   // of the screen, recycle it by loading it with new random values.
   void move() {
      // save the current center
      oldCenter.x = center.x;
      oldCenter.y = center.y;

      // reduce the old velocity to account for atmospheric drag
      velocity.mult(.3);

      // start the new effect (in totalWind) with some gravity
      PVector totalWind = new PVector(0, random(1.5, 2.0));

      // add in the effects of each wind gust
      for (int i=0; i<Gusts.length; i++) {
         PVector w = Gusts[i].windAt(center);
         totalWind.add(w);
      }

      // add the new effect (in totalWind) to the old velocity,
      // giving a new velocity.  Add that to the center.
      velocity.add(totalWind);
      center.add(velocity);


      // if the grain has fallen below the screen, recycle it.
      if (center.y > height) {
         fillGrain(false);
      }
   }
}
```

24.3.13 Wind.pde
```
// Wind class
// version 1.0 - AG 30 April 2009
//
class Wind {
   PVector center;     // center of the wind
```

```
PVector velocity;   // speed of the wind
PVector wind;       // direction of the wind
float radius;       // radius of wind effect
float strength;     // strength of the wind

// create a new object with random values
Wind() {
    center = new PVector(random(50, width-50), random(50, height-50));
    velocity= new PVector(random(-1, 1), random(-1, 1));
    wind= new PVector(random(-3, 3), random(-1, 1));
    radius = random(40, 220);
    strength = random(-5, 5);
}

// find the effect of this wind at this point
PVector windAt(PVector p) {
    PVector windHere = new PVector(0, 0);  // by default, there's no effect
    float pointToWind = dist(p.x, p.y, center.x, center.y);
    if (pointToWind < radius) {
        // we're inside radius.  Find the strength from the distance
        // of this point to the center.
        float wstrength = map(pointToWind, 0, radius, strength, 0);
        // compute the line perpendicular to the line from
        // the center to this point; that's where the wind is pointing.
        PVector dPoint = new PVector(p.x-center.x, p.y-center.y);
        PVector windDir = new PVector(dPoint.y, -dPoint.x);
        // scale the wind based on its strength at this point
        windDir.normalize();
        windDir.mult(wstrength);
        windHere.add(windDir);
    }
    return(windHere);
}

// move the wind around on the screen like a bouncing ball
void update() {
    center.add(velocity);
    if ((center.x < 0) || (center.x >= width)) {
        velocity.x = -velocity.x;
        center.x += 2*velocity.x;
    }
    if ((center.y < 0) || (center.y >= height)) {
        velocity.y = -velocity.y;
        center.y += 2*velocity.y;
    }
}
}
```

(Full program in bigprojects/sketches/SandStorm/SandStorm.pde)

Figures 24.5– 24.10 show some screenshots of the animation. Of course, for the real fun you should watch it run.

Figure 24.5. A screenshot from *SandStorm*.

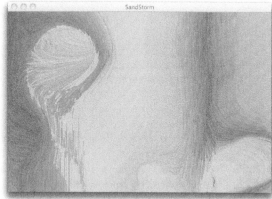

Figure 24.6. Another screenshot from *Sand-Storm*.

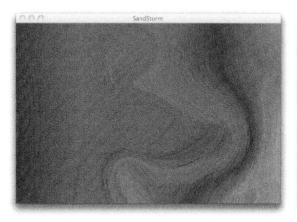

Figure 24.7. Another screenshot from *Sand-Storm*.

Figure 24.8. Another screenshot from *Sand-Storm*.

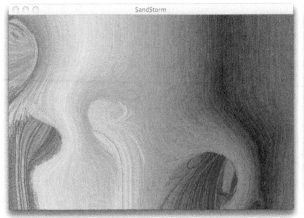

Figure 24.9. Another screenshot from *SandStorm*.   Figure 24.10. Another screenshot from *SandStorm*.

24.4   Project 2: Postcards from Another Planet

Lots of people like to visit the Ice Planet of Frozerra for a little while, but hardly anyone sticks around for very long. It's always overcast, and the sun is diffused by a hazy glow. The only saving grace are the tall, thin trees, which are topped by balls of fuzz like giant, colored dandelions.

Write a program that makes an endless variety of postcards from the planet of Frozerra.

24.4.1   Level 2: My Architecture

My program started out very simply and then it grew one little piece at a time. I added a piece, then another piece, then I changed something, took something out, and so on, building it up here and there as I explored what the feeling of the Frozerra world should be. I spent a lot of time playing with colors and shapes and compositions.

Finally it started to take form, and I had a general idea of how my cards would look and what pieces were involved in them.

My postcards are made up of three main visual elements. The background is a sun in a hazy sky. In front of that, there are layers of snowbanks and trees with puffballs on top. I wrapped up each of these elements in its own class and its own file.

In the descriptions to come, keep in mind that none of this existed when I started! I played around with this project for quite a while and let it grow organically. It was only once things started to settle down that I stepped back and took stock of what I was doing and decided on a way to organize it all.

The program itself is in five files: one each for the sun, the snow, and the trees, one for `setup()` and the routine that calls the three visual elements, and one little utility file that holds a couple of convenient procedures used by the others.

24.4.2   Landscape.pde Overview

The main file for my program is called *Landscape.pde*. It has a tiny `setup()` that calls `size()` and `smooth()` and then it draws the postcard by calling `drawPostcard()`.

This function takes up the rest of the file. It's responsible for creating the composition of the card. It first sets up the background by picking variables like the size and position of the sun and the brightness of the clouds in the sky. When these parameters have been chosen, I create a `Sky` object and tell it to draw itself. This creates a backdrop that covers the entire graphics window.

The objects in the card are drawn in a series of layers. Each layer contains several trees and then a snowbank that sits in front. To create the layers, `drawPostcard()` runs through a loop, once per layer. I draw the trees and snowbank in the farthest layer first, and then the next-closer elements on top of them, and then the next-closer elements, and so on. That way, nearer objects naturally cover up those farther away.

For each layer, I first select a big bunch of parameters, like the depth of the layer and its position on the screen.

Then I run through a loop to create `Tree` objects. Each `Tree` takes a big list of parameters that describes its geometry and color, so I build all of those first. To give the card a sense of perspective, the trees that are far away are smaller than those nearby. After each `Tree` has been made, I tell it to render itself to the screen.

Once the trees are made, I create a `Snow` object. This builds a snow-covered hill. Once it's made, I tell each `Snow` to render itself.

Two parameters that control this process are the number of layers and the number of trees per layer. Once all the layers have been drawn on top of the sky, the postcard is done, and the program is complete.

A key step in the routine is to pick all object sizes based on their depth, in order to create a sense of perspective. Distant snowbanks are flatter than those nearby, and distant trees are shorter, with smaller puffballs at the top.

There's no `draw()` routine in this project because there's no interactivity or updating (though it would be fun to let the recipient drag the sun around or plant new trees).

24.4.3   Sky.pde Overview

I came up with a sky that has four components: a sun, a hazy glow around the sun, a background sky, and clouds. The idea is that the sun is a bright circle in the sky. Around it, its light is diffused by the surrounding haze, creating a kind of fuzzy glow around the sun. As we get farther from the glow, we start to see the color of the surrounding sky and its clouds.

I draw the sky one pixel at a time. Each pixel is either part of the sun, part of the haze around the sun, or part of the sky. If it's in the sun, the pixel is just the sun's color. If it's in the haze, then the pixel is a smooth blend from the sun's color to the haze's color. Otherwise, the pixel is part of the sky. The base color of the sky blends from the haze color (at the edge of the haze) to a dark blue at the farthest corner of the window. I also add some stretched-out white clouds to the sky to give it a more textured feel. The clouds are invisible under the sun and haze but gradually fade in as we get farther away from the sun.

24.4.4   Snow.pde Overview

I want each snowbank to look like a smooth, snow-covered hillside. The top of a snow-bank is a bright color, since it's reflecting the hazy sunlight. The sides of the snowbank are darker, since they catch less sun, and the natural variation of the hillside introduces some large shadows. All of these features are influenced by how far away the snowbank is located.

To create a snowbank, I start with a vertical position on the screen that represents the "average" height of the hill the snow has accumulated on. To make the rolling hills, I build two Bézier curves whose control points can move a little above and below the snowbank's vertical position. The top few pixels of the snowbank are the bright reflection color and then there's a transition zone where that color blends into a color that combines the snow's base color and the shadows.

The colors are all adjusted based on how far away the snowbank is from us. To simulate atmospheric perspective, I gradually blend the colors towards the overall scene's haze color based on distance. An object far away will blend away completely into the haze, while one close up will retain most of its color and contrast.

24.4.5   Tree.pde Overview

Each tree is made up of a trunk and a puffball at the top.

To draw a tree, I first draw a Bézier curve for the trunk. At the top of the curve, I draw a puffball using a cloud of points. The points are densest near the center and sparser near the edge. Because I want the trees to appear to be receiving light from the sun, each puffball has two colors: a highlight color for dots that are receiving sunlight and a base color for the rest of the puff. These colors are blended over the puff to give it an illusion of three-dimensionality.

All the colors involved are also adjusted by depth to simulate the effect of atmosphere with distance.

24.4.6   Utilities.pde Overview

The utilities file contains two little routines that are used by several of the objects.

The first is a tiny procedure that "wiggles" a number by adding or subtracting a random amount. This function replaces just a single line of code, but I like packaging it up this way because it makes it more obvious that I'm starting with a value I like and then adding a little bit of randomness to it.

The other routine is responsible for simulating the change in color that we see as an object recedes from us on a hazy day. The routine takes an object color, the background haze color, and the distance of the object, and returns the color of the object as it might appear at that distance.

24.4.7   End of Level 2

That's the basic structure of my postcards: a sky, and then several layers of trees and snowbanks.

Go ahead and see where your imagination takes you with this rough outline. Try just getting something up on the screen and then ask yourself what you might do to make it a little bit better. Try that, and then take another little step, and another.

Or if while reading this you thought of a different approach, go for it! The planet Frozerra can look any way you want.

24.4.8   Level 3: Detailed Breakdown

In this breakdown, I'll describe the specifics of my code. This program isn't really the result of a single master plan but many little things all brought together. There are lots of places where I pick numbers, or shape numbers, or adjust the blending, that are simply the result of trying a whole bunch of variations until I found one that looked good to me. There's very little here that is based on any kind of physical reality; it's all about finding ways to draw an endless variety of pictures that share the kind of feeling I get when I think about this imaginary place.

I'll change the order a bit and present the main file, *Landscape.pde*, after the three classes. It will be easier to discuss how the overall postcard-making routine generates data for the visuals once we've seen what parameters they require.

24.4.9   Sky.pde Details

The sky is dependent on eight input parameters. The first four describe the sun. The sun is a circle, so it requires a center x and y, a color, and a radius.

The next two parameters describe the hazy circle around the sun. That's built from the color of the haze and its radius (that is, how much farther the circle of the haze extends beyond the sun).

Finally, there's the color of the sky and the intensity of the clouds in the sky.

I draw the sky by scanning the graphics window pixel by pixel. I decide what part of the sky it belongs to and then set its color.

The basic idea behind the structure of the sky is shown in Figure 24.11.

Before I start filling in pixels, I find the
distance from the center of the sun to the farthest corner of the window. In Figure 24.11,
that's along the line marked B. I call this
cdist (for "corner distance"). I'll describe
how this is used in a moment.

Each pixel falls into one of three categories: inside the sun, inside the haze, or in
the sky.

If a pixel is inside the innermost circle,
then it's part of the sun. It simply gets set to
the color of the sun.

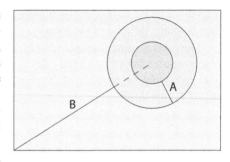

Figure 24.11. The geometry of the sky.

If a pixel is inside the hazy zone, shown in the figure as a tan-colored circle, then it
gets a color that blends the sun's color (at the inside of the zone) with the haze's color
(at the outside of the zone). In the figure, I've shown the size of this transition zone with
a line marked A.

I found that if I linearly blended the colors along the line A, I could just barely make
out an edge around the sun and another around the outside of the haze, where the color
transitions started and stopped. Because I wanted everything to look smooth, I use the
first half of a cosine curve to blend the colors, as discussed in the section on the cosine
in Chapter 18. That way the colors change smoothly as they move through the transition
zone. RGB blending looked fine for this job, and it also worked well throughout the rest
of the project. Since I don't change the color mode, all of my color blends take place in
the default RGB color space.

If a pixel is outside of the hazy zone, then it's part of the sky. The sky has two
components: the sky's color and the clouds. Let's see how the sky pixel gets built and
then discuss how it gets blended.

First I find the distance from the pixel to the nearest point of the hazy zone. This is
easy: just find the distance from the pixel to the center of the sun and then subtract the
sun's radius and the thickness of the hazy zone. What's left is the distance to the haze.

I then use map(), along with cdist (the value I mentioned above), to scale this
distance into a number from 0 to 1. If it's 0, then I'm right on the edge of the hazy zone.
If it's 1, then I'm at the farthest corner from the sun. And, of course, values in between
tell me, as a percentage, how far I am between those two extremes.

Now I find the clouds at that pixel. That's just a call to the 2D version of noise()
using the pixel's x and y values, only I scale the y value three times more than the x.
That means that the noise is stretched out horizontally, which gave me the feeling of
big, wide clouds in the sky. I tried just adding the clouds into the sky color, but then the
sky only got lighter, so I subtracted 0.5 from the cloud value so it runs from $(-0.5, 0.5)$.

I want the clouds to be hidden by the haze but show up more with distance from the
sun. I originally scaled them by the distance of each pixel from the haze, as computed
above, but the clouds came in too slowly. I tried shaping that distance and found that
the square root looked good to me. So I find the cloud color at a given pixel by calling

Figure 24.12. The postcard sky only.   Figure 24.13. Another sky image.

`lerp()` on a range from 0 to the cloud's noise color (as computed above), using the square root of the distance to control the blending.

The final cloud color is the result of this scaling, multiplied by the overall cloud brightness given as an input to the procedure.

To get the pixel's color, I start by simply blending from the haze color to the sky color based on the distance to the outer edge of the haze. That zone is labeled B in the figure. Then I add in the cloud's contribution (since the clouds are gray, I just add the same amount to all three color channels).

Note that the clouds blend in at a slightly different rate than the sky color (since they use the square root of the distance to the haze, not the distance itself, to control the blending). There's no principle behind that; it's just what looked good to me as I tried different experiments.

That gives me the pixel color. I set it into the pixel and move on to the next.

As you can see, this has been a process of combining lots of little steps, each one designed to create or enhance one or more subtle effects. The result of this process is shown in Figure 24.12 and Figure 24.13 (I just took the final listing of the project, commented out the snowbanks and plants, and ran it a couple of times).

24.4.10   Snow.pde Details

The general idea behind snowbanks is that they are positioned vertically on the screen. The top few pixels of the snowbank are bright because they're reflecting the sunlight that's striking the top of the snow. Then there's a transition zone, where the color darkens and shadows start to appear.

The colors of the snowbank are changed before they're drawn to accommodate *atmospheric perspective*. This is the phenomenon we've all seen in the real world on foggy days. An object that's right in front of us is easy to see, but as it gets farther away, it seems to blend into the fog, eventually disappearing completely. I have a routine in the *Utilities.pde* file that simulates this effect, so we'll cover the mechanics of it when we talk about that file. But to calculate this change in color, the routine needs to know the starting color, the depth of the object (that is, how far away from us it's located), and the color of the haze, or fog, in the air. So the snowbank procedure also needs to know the snowbank's distance and the color of the haze so it can pass this information to the color-shifting routine.

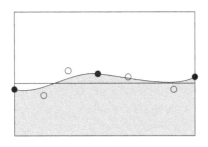

To create the basic shape of the snowbank, I build two side-by-side Bézier curves. I only need seven points because the center point is shared by both curves. I used two curves because only one didn't look bumpy enough, but three looked too bumpy. Given the normal variation in random points, two curves generally looked just right. The points at the far left and right of the window are stuck to those edges, but otherwise, all the points start on the vertical position of the top of the snowbank and are then free to move a little bit in x and y.

Figure 24.14. The snowbank is made from two Bézier curves.

So the snowbank's parameters are the snowbank's starting vertical position, it's top and body colors, the strength of the shadows, the height of the transition zone from the top color to the body color, the depth of the snowbank and the color of the background haze, and the maximum vertical height by which the Bézier curve points can move.

Figure 24.14 shows the starting vertical position of a snowbank and two curves that might be built from it.

Using the top color as a fill color, I draw a shape that matches the gray region shown in the figure. Because I've called smooth() at the start of the program, the top edge of the snowbank is nicely blended into whatever was on the screen before it.

Now I go through the snowbank, pixel by pixel, changing the colors to those of the darker snowbank and the shadows. So I work my way across the image, left to right, modifying one column of pixels at a time.

Figure 24.15 shows the general idea. First I call a little utility function to tell me the floating-point height of the curve for this column (that is, this value of x). Since I've made the Bézier curve using the setup of Figure 24.14, I know it will have only a single y value for each x, and it won't have crazy loops or other features that would confuse the process of finding y from x.

That routine works just the same way as the routine we saw in Chapter 12. Though that was written for Catmull-Rom curves, the strategy works perfectly well for Bézier curves.

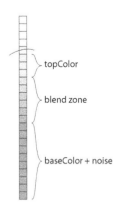

Figure 24.15. Changing the colors of a column of the snowbank.

Figure 24.16. A far-away snowbank.   Figure 24.17. A nearer snowbank.

There's one little extra step, though. Because I have two Bézier curves across the graphics window, I test the value of x against the x value of the right-most point in the first curve (which is also the left-most point of the second). Based on where the input x falls, I hand my y-finding routine either the first Bézier curve or the second. I want the top few pixels of the column to stay the bright color in which I drew them, so I add three to the value I get back from the routine. That gives me three bright pixels at the top, and now I enter the blending zone. I played around with changing the height of this bright zone based on depth, thinking that snowbanks farther away should have smaller bright zones than those nearby, but I found that this constant, relatively thin 3-pixel band across the top of each snowbank looked just right. Below that is the transition to the darker, shadowed snowbank face.

I want the snowbank to appear curved, so I find where I am in the zone as a value from 0 to 1 and then I run it through the first 90 degrees of the sine curve. That shapes the transition so that it starts slowly and then goes more quickly, as if it really was rounded.

The shadows come from a call to the 2D `noise()` function, though I make sure to use a different piece of the function from one layer to the next so the shadows won't appear to all belong to one big piece of noise. I scale the strength of the shadow by the input parameter that tells me how strong they should appear.

Then I just blend the top color with the combined color of the snowbank body and noise. I adjust the final color based on the snowbank's distance and fill in the pixel.

Then I move down to the next pixel in the column. When that column's complete, I move right and repeat the process.

The result of just drawing the farthest snowbank is shown in Figure 24.16, and a nearer snowbank is shown in Figure 24.17. Notice that as the snowbanks recede from us, the size of the hills decreases, the blend zone of reflected light off the top becomes smaller, and the overall colors lose intensity and contrast. Three snowbanks together are shown in Figure 24.18 (to make these pictures, I just took the final listing of the project and commented out the code to draw anything but the snowbanks).

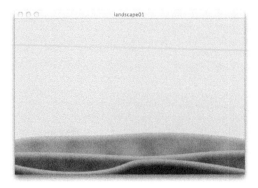

Figure 24.18. Three snowbanks.

24.4.11 Tree.pde Details

Each tree is a trunk with a puffball on top.

The trees may look pretty simple, but each one is defined by 13 parameters!

Let's run through the construction process, so the parameters will make sense.

We start by making the trunk, which is a Bézier curve that runs from the tree's base to the tree's top, which also serves as the center of the puffball.

To find the top of the tree, I first add the tree's height to the base. To make the trees look a little more organic, I let them lean left and right by adding some randomness to the horizontal location of the top point. After some experimenting, I found that moving the point left and right by up to ten percent of the tree's height looked pretty good.

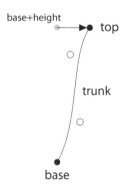

Figure 24.19. Building the tree trunk.

Figure 24.19 shows the process.

As with the snowbank, I create a couple of control points along the trunk and then wiggle them left and right (by up to 20 percent of the tree's height).

Now that I have four points, I'm ready to draw. I take the color of the trunk and pass it through my perspective routine, so it fades into the haze with distance. I set the line weight to the value handed to it as an input and draw the Bézier curve for the trunk. I experimented with tapered trunks that got thinner towards the top, but they required a lot more effort and I didn't like the results as much as I did this single, curvy line.

I draw the puffball using a circular cloud of dots. The dots are densest in the center and sparser towards the edge. I start by generating a random point location in the puffball. Then I get its color, which I wiggle around a little bit randomly for interest. I also fade out the transparency of the color at the outermost 20 percent of the puffball's radius. Then I adjust the color for atmospheric perspective and draw the dot.

To find the random point, I pick a random angle. I choose the radius by calling a function. That function creates a random number from 0 to 1. Then I pass that through the first 90 degrees of the sine curve so that it falls off a little more sharply near 1 and then I take the square root of that. This recipe was the result of some experimenting as I looked for something that created a distribution of points that felt right for this kind of object.

The colors of the puffballs took some work. There are two colors: the base color and the highlight color. The idea is that where the sun is striking the puffball, it'll have the highlight color, and the parts that aren't getting direct light will be the base color. That way, the puffs will appear to be illuminated by the sun.

As an added benefit, the color changes can make the puff look more 3D since they're simulating the shading that might appear on a real 3D object.

So for each dot in the puffball, I need to find a value that tells me how much to blend from the highlight color to the base color to create the illumination and 3D illusion.

Since I have a 3D background, my first idea was to treat the puffball and the sun like real 3D objects, and find out how much the sun was striking each point in the puffball. So I used equations that I know capture some of the real physics of how light interacts with the surface of an object such as a sphere. It worked beautifully, but I didn't like the results. Though they were mathematically right, they didn't *feel* right in this image. I wanted something softer and a little more dreamy than the physics were giving me. The upsides of a physical simulation are that it can capture some aspects of the real world, and you can get a lot of complex results relatively easily. The downsides are that if you don't like what you get, there's not much you can usually do about it. Of course, you can change the equations, but that often becomes a very tricky process, and I find it often takes me far away from the kind of visually based thinking that I've been focusing on so far.

So I started over and tried several different ideas for making the puffballs appear to be illuminated by the sun, yet have the kind of general feeling that fit the mood I was after. I finally found something I really liked.

The heart of the idea is shown in Figure 24.20. I start by drawing a line from the center of the puffball to the center of the sun, and I travel along that line to the edge of the puff. That gives me a point that I've labeled S in the figure (I call that point `spark` in the code, since I think of it as the center of a burst of light, like a spark from a fire).

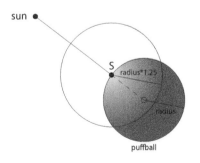

Figure 24.20. Illuminating a puffball.

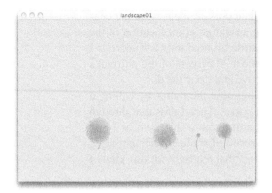

Figure 24.21. The farthest trees only.

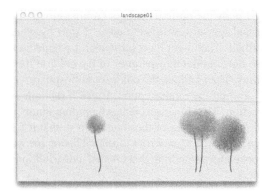

Figure 24.22. The middle trees only.

Point S is the point on the puffball that's closest to the sun, and so it's the brightest (or most illuminated) point on the puff.

Then I imagine a circle centered at point S with a radius given by 1.25 times the radius of the puffball itself (there's nothing special about the value 1.25; I tried a bunch of different values and that's the number that made the pictures I liked best).

The idea is that the puffball has the highlight color at S, and that color falls off to the base color with distance. At the edge of this circle of radius 1.25 times the puffball's radius, the color has become the base color.

So to find the color of any dot, I find its distance from point S. If I'm right at S itself, the distance is 0. If I'm on the edge of the circle, the distance is 1 (and points beyond the circle get set to 1 as well). Points inside the circle get a value from 0 to 1 based on their distance from the center.

Figure 24.23. The nearest trees only.

Figure 24.24. Three layers of trees.

To my surprise, a simple linear blend (rather than a cosine blend) looked just fine to me, so I left it like that.

As you probably guessed, I use this value to blend from the highlight color to the base color.

I like how this looks. It's not realistic, but neither is anything else in the picture, really. It just looks right, and for this project, that's what's important.

With that, I have the color of the dot. As I described above, I add some random noise to the color and then I tune its transparency if it's near the edge. Finally, I adjust the color based on the depth of the tree.

In addition to the color changing, the effect of perspective is strengthened by the trunks getting thinner with distance and the puffs getting smaller in size.

The input parameters to building a tree are the position of the sun, the color of the haze, the position of the base of the tree, its depth, and its height. There's the trunk's width and color. Finally, the puff is described by its highlight color, base color, radius, and density.

Figure 24.21 shows a faraway layer of trees (I manually placed the sun horizontally centered in the window and about a third of the way down for these images). Figure 24.22 shows a closer layer, and Figure 24.23 shows a set very near to us. Three layers of trees are shown together in Figure 24.24 (as before, I made these images by manually commenting out all the drawing routines but those for the trees).

24.4.12 Landscape.pde Details

The routine `drawPostcard()` is the brains of this outfit. It basically creates the composition, builds the objects that it needs, and then tells them to draw themselves.

So `drawPostcard()` is responsible for picking the colors, placing the sun and the snowbanks, determining the locations and sizes of the trees, and taking care of all the other little parameters that add up to create a nice picture, from the height of the snowbank's transition zone to the width of the tree trunks. Most of these details make only a small contribution to the overall image, but taken together, they help it look unified and as though all the pieces are part of the same scene.

If I didn't care about making the cards different from one run to another, I could just pick values for all these parameters, and the routine would be pretty short. But for me, a big part of the fun in a project like this is the surprise I get each time I run the program because I get a new, unpredictable image. So this routine is really about setting up the basic structure of a postcard and the type and range of variation that each element can assume.

The first step sets up the sky. I pick the colors for the sun, haze, and background; the intensity of the clouds; the location and radius of the sun; and the radius of the haze around it.

Then I pick the colors for the top and body of the snowbanks and the strength of the shadows on them.

Finally, I choose how many layers to draw (recall that each layer contains trees and a snowbank in front of them) and how many trees to draw per layer.

Then I'm ready to make the picture. I start by drawing the sky, which covers the entire window. Because I place the sun vertically anywhere in the window, sometimes it ends up partly or completely behind the snowbanks. I like those images, too, since they feel like they're made just before (or during) the early-morning sunrise.

Then I enter a loop that runs for each layer, first drawing the trees and then the snowbank. Remember, these are drawn back to front.

I set up the snowbank's parameters first. These all depend on the layer number. The first layer (layer 0) is the one that's farthest away, and each succeeding layer number is closer to us. I use the layer number to determine the snowbank's vertical position on the screen, as well as how much it can wiggle (far away snowbanks have less wiggle than do those nearby), the size of the transition zone from bright to dark (the closer the snowbank, the larger the zone), and the depth of the snowbank.

For the background haze color, I used the same color as the haze around the sun in the sky. I found that this gave me yet another little bit of connection between the different pieces of the image and helped pull them together visually to create a more unified picture.

Then I start a loop for the trees, running through it once for each tree. I find the base of the tree (using the height of the snowbank as a guide) and determine its height (again, trees closer to us are taller than those farther away). I use the same depth for the tree as I used for the snowbank (the trees should be slightly farther away, but since the depth is just used to adjust the colors, that difference wouldn't be noticeable). I then determine the size of the puff and the thickness of the trunk, both of which get larger as the tree gets closer to us.

Before I'm ready to draw the tree, I need to pick colors for the trunk, the puffball, and the highlight on the puffball. I choose starting colors for these, but then I modify them all with random numbers.

For this project, modifying the colors is much easier with HSB than with RGB. That's because I want the saturation and brightness of the colors to stay where I picked them; those are basic parts of the composition that I don't want to change. It's just the hue that I want to vary. So I change the color mode from the default RGB to HSB.

In this book I've talked about the dangers of switching modes, and I do it rarely. You'll see that I have big hard-to-miss comments in the code where I switch to HSB. I build the three colors and then I set the mode right back to RGB.

Except for the exciting diversion into HSB mode, the color picking doesn't involve too much. I pick a color somewhere from red to yellow for the puff and then push the hue around a little bit for the highlight. The saturation and value of the highlight are both larger than for the puff, so it will have that sense of illumination I want. Then I pick a blue-like hue for the trunk. I remembered to convert the HSB values to RGB using the constants 0.71 and 2.55 when creating the colors, as discussed in Chapter 5. Sometimes the hues of the base and the highlight aren't physical in any way (we might get a red highlight and a yellow puff), but the highlights will always be a little bit brighter.

Once the trees are drawn for a given layer, the snowbank is drawn in front of them. That ends the loop, and when all the loops are done, the postcard's ready for sharing.

24.4.13 Utilities.pde Details

The program uses a few utilities to do some repeated or easily isolated tasks.

There's basically a one-liner that I use to wiggle the value of a floating-point number. It takes a center value and a range. I find a number from (-range, range) add that to the center, and return the result. It's just a little convenience function so that I don't have to write all that random-number stuff every time I want to vary a single number by some amount.

The other utility function is more interesting since it figures out how to change the color of an object based on distance. The routine takes three inputs: the object color, the haze color, and the depth (or distance of the object from us). The idea is to simulate atmospheric perspective by blending the object's color into the haze color as it recedes from us.

I decided that a depth of 0 means the object is right in front of us and is unaffected, while a depth of 100 is where it gets lost in the haze. In between, of course, is where it fades away.

I could have changed the colors linearly and just blended based on the depth, but I remember seeing some physically based models of atmospheric perspective that use the exp() function. As with the lighting on the puffballs, there was no reason to rely on realism, but it seemed like a good place to start. So I map the depth range (0, 100) to the range (0, 1) and give that to exp(). I use the result as a parameter to lerpColor() to blend from the object color to the haze color. When the depth is 0, the object color is unchanged. As the object recedes, the color starts to change a little, and then it changes more and more quickly until, at a depth of 100, the color has shifted completely to the haze.

24.4.14 Level 4: My Solution

24.4.15 Landscape.pde

```
void setup() {
    size(600, 400);
    smooth();
    drawPostcard();
}

void drawPostcard() {
    // the sun and sky
    color sunColor = color(255, 255, 255);     // sun color
    color hazeColor = color(180, 180, 192);    // sun halo and sky
    color skyColor = color(30, 40, 70);        // dark part of the sky
```

```
   float sunX = random(width*.1, width*.9);    // sun x location
 float sunY = random(height*.1, height*.9); // sun y location
 float sunR = wiggle(25, 3);                     // sun radius
 float hazeR = wiggle(30, 5);                    // sun halo size
 float cloudIntensity = wiggle(40, 5);       // brightness of clouds

 // snowbank colors
 color snowTopColor = color(145, 150, 160, 255); // top of snowbank
 color snowBodyColor = color(50, 60, 70, 255);   // body of snowbank
 float shadowNoiseStrength = wiggle(20, 2);      // strength of snow shadows

 // Number of snowbanks, and number of trees per bank
 int treesPerLayer = 4;
 int numLayers=3;

 // create the sun and sky, then draw them
 Sky sky = new Sky(sunColor, sunX, sunY, sunR,
                   hazeColor, hazeR, skyColor, cloudIntensity);
 sky.render();

 // draw each layer: build the trees and render them, then the snowbank
 for (int layerNum=0; layerNum<numLayers; layerNum++) {

    float a = norm(layerNum, 0, numLayers-1);
    float layerHeight = lerp(300, 390, a); // vertical location
    float hillWiggle  = lerp( 10,  20, a); // wiggle vertical extent
    float glowHeight  = lerp( 15,  25, a); // height of glow transition zone
    float layerDepth  = lerp( 70,   0, a); // distance of layer from us

    // create the parameters for a tree and draw it
    for (int i=0; i<treesPerLayer; i++) {
       float treex = random(width*.1, width*.9);   // x base of tree
       float treey = layerHeight + (2*hillWiggle); // y base of tree
       float treeh = lerp(40, 180, a);             // height by layer
       treeh +=  wiggle(0, treeh/4.0);             // wiggle it a bit
       float treed = layerDepth;                   // depth
       float puffRadius = lerp(5, 40, a);          // puff size
       puffRadius = random(puffRadius, puffRadius+30);  // let puff grow a lot!
       float trunkWidth = lerp(1, 4, a);           // trunk thickness
       float puffDensity = 3.0;                    // higher numbers = more dots

       // pick basic puff color in red-to-yellow range
       float puffHue = random(0, 130.0);
       float puffSat = 25;
       float puffBrt = 50;
```

```
            // pick related but brighter highlight color
            float highHue = puffHue + wiggle(0, 50);
            while (highHue >= 360) highHue -= 360;  // make sure 0<= hue <=360
            while (highHue < 0) highHue += 360;
            float highSat = 36;
            float highBrt = 74;

            // make trunk color in blue-ish range
            float trunkHue = wiggle(225, 20);
            float trunkSat = 50;
            float trunkBrt = 46;

            colorMode(HSB); ////// ****** SWITCHING TO COLOR HSB MODE ******
                color puffColor      = color( puffHue*.71,  puffSat*2.55,
                                                    puffBrt*2.55);
                color highlightColor = color( highHue*.71,  highSat*2.55,
                                                    highBrt*2.55);
                color trunkColor      = color(trunkHue*.71, trunkSat*2.55,
                                                    trunkBrt*2.55);
            colorMode(RGB); ////// ****** RETURNING TO COLOR RGB MODE ******

            Tree tree = new Tree(sunX, sunY, hazeColor,
                    treex, treey, treed, treeh,
                    trunkWidth, trunkColor,
                    puffRadius, puffDensity, puffColor, highlightColor);
            tree.render();
        }

        // draw the snowbank
        Snow snow = new Snow(snowTopColor, snowBodyColor, shadowNoiseStrength,
                            glowHeight, hazeColor, layerHeight, hillWiggle,
                            layerDepth);
        snow.render();
    }
}
```

24.4.16 Sky.pde

```
class Sky {
    color sunColor;
    float sunX;
    float sunY;
    float sunR;
    color hazeColor;
    float hazeR;
    color skyColor;
    float cloudIntensity;
```

```
Sky(color asunColor,  float asunX,  float asunY, float asunR,
    color ahazeColor, float ahazeR,
    color askyColor,
    float acloudIntensity) {
  sunColor = asunColor;
  sunX =  asunX;
  sunY =  asunY;
  sunR =  asunR;
  hazeColor =  ahazeColor;
  hazeR = ahazeR;
  skyColor = askyColor;
  cloudIntensity = acloudIntensity;
}

void render() {

  // cdist is the distance from sun's center to the farthest screen corner
  float cdist = dist(sunX, sunY, 0, 0);
  cdist = max(cdist, dist(sunX, sunY, width, 0));
  cdist = max(cdist, dist(sunX, sunY, 0, height));
  cdist = max(cdist, dist(sunX, sunY, width, height));

  for (int y=0; y<height; y++) {
    for (int x=0; x<width; x++) {
      float r = dist(x, y, sunX, sunY);
      if (r < sunR) {
        set(x, y, sunColor);  // when in the sun, we're sun color
      } else if (r < sunR+hazeR) {
        float a = map(r, sunR, sunR+hazeR, 0, 180);  // distance into degrees
        float v = map(cos(radians(a)), -1, 1, 1, 0);// cosine over transition
        color hc = lerpColor(sunColor, hazeColor, v);// blend colors
        set(x, y, hc);
      } else {
        float dist = map(r, sunR+hazeR, cdist, 0, 1); // distance into (0,1)
        float cloudClr = noise(0.01*x, 0.03*y);       // cloud strength
        cloudClr -= 0.5;                              // center cloud color at 0
        float cloudStrength = sqrt(dist);             // cloud strength
        cloudClr = lerp(0, cloudClr, cloudStrength);  // scale cloud
        float cgray = cloudClr * cloudIntensity;      // cloud grayness
        color sc = lerpColor(hazeColor, skyColor, dist); // blend haze to sky
        sc = color(red(sc)+cgray, green(sc)+cgray, blue(sc)+cgray);
        set(x, y, sc);
      }
    }
  }
}
}
```

24.4.17 Snow.pde

```
class Snow {
    color topColor;
    color baseColor;
    float shadowNoiseStrength;
    float glowHeight;
    color hazeColor;
    float yValue;
    float hillSize;
    float depth;
    PVector[] pts;

    Snow(color atopColor, color abaseColor, float ashadowNoiseStrength,
            float aglowHeight, color ahazeColor, float ayValue,
            float ahillSize, float adepth) {
        topColor = atopColor;
        baseColor = abaseColor;
        shadowNoiseStrength = ashadowNoiseStrength;
        glowHeight = aglowHeight;
        hazeColor = ahazeColor;
        yValue = ayValue;
        hillSize = ahillSize;
        depth = adepth;
        pts = new PVector[7];
    }

    void render() {
        // create two Bezier curves across the screen to create a rolling snowbank
        for (int i=0; i<7; i++) {
            pts[i] = new PVector(0, 0);
            pts[i].x = map(i, 0, 6, 0, width);
            pts[i].y = yValue + wiggle(0, hillSize);
            if ((i>0) && (i<6)) pts[i].x += wiggle(0, width/15.0);
        }
        pts[4].x = pts[3].x + (pts[3].x - pts[2].x);//the curves join smoothly
        pts[4].y = pts[3].y + (pts[3].y - pts[2].y) //by setting pts(4-3) = pts(3-2)

        // create a big filled region the top color of this snowbank
        noStroke();
        color topColorInDistance = distanceContrast(topColor, hazeColor, depth);
        fill(topColorInDistance);
        beginShape();
        vertex(0, height);
        vertex(pts[0].x, pts[0].y);
        bezierVertex(pts[1].x, pts[1].y, pts[2].x, pts[2].y, pts[3].x, pts[3].y);
        bezierVertex(pts[4].x, pts[4].y, pts[5].x, pts[5].y, pts[6].x, pts[6].y);
```

```
   vertex(width, height);
   endShape(CLOSE);

   // For each column of pixels, leave a few topColor pixels at the top,
   // then blend downward over the distance glowHeight to a combination
   // of baseColor and shadow noise.

   loadPixels();
   for (int x=0; x<width; x++) {
      float gh = getHillHeightAtX(x)+3;  // get curve y, add 3 to skip smoothing
      for (int y=int(gh); y<height; y++) {
         float a = constrain((y-gh)/glowHeight, 0, 1); // amount in transition
         a = sin(radians(90.0 * a));                   // shape transition with sine

         float shadowNoise = noise((0.02*x)+width, (0.02*y)+height+yValue);
         shadowNoise = shadowNoiseStrength * map(shadowNoise, 0.0, 1.0, -1.0,
                                                 1.0);
         // blend top color to (bottom and shadow)
         float rval = lerp(red(topColor), red(baseColor)+shadowNoise, a);
         float gval = lerp(green(topColor), green(baseColor)+shadowNoise, a);
         float bval = lerp(blue(topColor), blue(baseColor)+shadowNoise, a);

         color clr = color(rval, gval, bval);
         clr = distanceContrast(clr, hazeColor, depth);
         pixels[(y*width)+x] = clr;
      }
   }
   updatePixels();
}

// Find the height of a snowbank at a given x.  First find which of the two
// Bezier curves we want, then use those points for the actual work.
// Test to see if we're left or right of the rightmost point of the left curve.
//
float getHillHeightAtX(float x) {
   PVector [] bpts = new PVector[4];
   int inputOffset = 0;
   if (x > pts[3].x) inputOffset = 3;
   for (int i=0; i<4; i++) {
      bpts[i] = new PVector(pts[i+inputOffset].x, pts[i+inputOffset].y);
   }
   return(getBezYforX(x, bpts));
}

// Assuming a Bezier curve that has just a single y value for each x, find the
// value of t that lands us at that x, and return the y value for that t.
// Simply put, return the y value for the given x.
//
```

```
float getBezYforX(float x, PVector [] bpts) {
    float tLo = 0.0;
    float tHi = 1.0;
    float threshold = 0.0001; //if we get back a t within 1/10,000, good enough
    int numIterations = 500;   //we'll only try this many times
    while (numIterations-- > 0) {
        float tMid = (tLo+tHi)/2.0;
        float bx = bezierPoint(bpts[0].x, bpts[1].x, bpts[2].x, bpts[3].x, tMid);
        if (abs(bx-x) < threshold) {
            float by = bezierPoint(bpts[0].y, bpts[1].y, bpts[2].y, bpts[3].y,
                                   tMid);
            return(by);
        }
        if (bx > x) tHi = tMid;
            else tLo = tMid;
    }
    return((tLo+tHi)/2.0);
}
}
```

24.4.18   Tree.pde

```
class Tree {

    float sunX;
    float sunY;
    color hazeColor;
    float baseX;
    float baseY;
    float depth;
    float treeHeight;
    float trunkWidth;
    color trunkColor;
    float puffRadius;
    float puffDensity;
    color puffColor;
    color highlightColor;

  Tree(float asunX, float asunY, color ahazeColor,
       float abaseX, float abaseY, float adepth, float atreeHeight,
       float atrunkWidth, color atrunkColor,
       float apuffRadius, float apuffDensity, color apuffColor,
                 color ahighlightColor) {
        sunX = asunX;
        sunY = asunY;
        hazeColor = ahazeColor;
        baseX = abaseX;
```

```
        baseY = abaseY;
        depth = adepth;
        treeHeight = atreeHeight;
        trunkWidth = atrunkWidth;
        trunkColor = atrunkColor;
        puffRadius = apuffRadius;
        puffDensity = apuffDensity;
        puffColor = apuffColor;
        highlightColor = ahighlightColor;
    }

    void render() {

        // find the top of the tree, allowing it to tilt a little
        float topX = baseX;
        float topY = baseY - treeHeight;
        baseX += wiggle(0, treeHeight/10.0);

        // make a Bezier curve for the trunk
        PVector p0 = new PVector(baseX, baseY);
        PVector p1 = new PVector(lerp(baseX, topX, 0.3), lerp(baseY, topY, 0.3));
        PVector p2 = new PVector(lerp(baseX, topX, 0.6), lerp(baseY, topY, 0.6));
        PVector p3 = new PVector(topX, topY);
        // wiggle the control points left and right so the trunk is curvy
        p1.x += 0.2 * treeHeight * wiggle(0, 1);
        p2.x += 0.2 * treeHeight * wiggle(0, 1);

        // draw the trunk with the given width, and color adjusted for distance
        trunkColor = distanceContrast(trunkColor, hazeColor, depth);
        noFill();       stroke(trunkColor);
        strokeWeight(trunkWidth);
        bezier(p0.x, p0.y, p1.x, p1.y, p2.x, p2.y, p3.x, p3.y);
        strokeWeight(1);

        // number of dots is puffball area (pi*radius*radius) times the density
        int numDots = int(puffRadius * puffRadius * PI * puffDensity);

        // find the point on the outer edge of the puff that's nearest the sun
        PVector spark = new PVector(sunX-topX, sunY-topY);
        spark.normalize();
        spark.mult(puffRadius);
        spark.add(new PVector(topX, topY));

        for (int p=0; p<numDots; p++) {

            // get a distance and angle for this dot, then find its (x,y)
            float thisR = getPuffR(puffRadius);
            float thisT = random(0.0, 360.0);
            float px = topX + (thisR * cos(thisT));
            float py = topY + (thisR * sin(thisT));
```

```
            // get distance to puff's spark (the source of highlight)
            float d2 = dist(px, py, spark.x, spark.y);
            // find highlight strength based on distance from spark
            float hlPower = constrain(map(d2, 0, puffRadius*1.25, 0, 1), 0, 1);

            // find the color, and add some noisy variation for effect
            float clrWiggle = 40.0;
            float rval = lerp(red(highlightColor), red(puffColor), hlPower)
                        + wiggle(0, clrWiggle);
            float gval = lerp(green(highlightColor), green(puffColor), hlPower)
                        + wiggle(0, clrWiggle);
            float bval = lerp(blue(highlightColor), blue(puffColor), hlPower)
                        + wiggle(0, clrWiggle);

            // puffball fades out in the outermost 20 percent
            float aval = 255;
            float dimRadius = puffRadius * .8;
            if (thisR > dimRadius) {
                aval = map(thisR, puffRadius*.8, puffRadius, 255, 0);
            }

            // build the color, adjust it for distance, and draw the dot
            color clr = color(rval, gval, bval, aval);
            clr = distanceContrast(clr, hazeColor, depth);
            stroke(clr);
            point(px, py);
        }
    }
}
// A little hack to make a puffball shape that I find pleasing.  Then
// frequency of dots is given by the square root of the first 90 degrees
// of the cosine curve.  There's no theory here; I just fooled around
// with different patterns and liked this one the best.
//
float getPuffR(float puffRadius) {
    float x = 0;
    float y = 0;
    float thresh = 0;
    while (true) {
        x = random(0, 1);
        y = random(0, 1);
        thresh = cos(radians(x*90));
        thresh = sqrt(thresh);
        if (y < thresh) return(x*puffRadius);
    }
}
}
```

Figures 24.25–24.27 show another couple of postcards from the frozen planet.

Figure 24.25. A postcard from Frozerra.

Figure 24.26. Another postcard from Frozerra.

Figure 24.27. A different postcard from Frozerra.

24.4.19   Utilities.pde

```
// A little convenience procedure to return a
// random number from (center-distance) to (center+distance)
//
float wiggle(float center, float distance) {
    float offset = random(-distance, distance);
    return(center+offset);
}

// Fake distance perspective.  The object color is lerped into the
// background color by an amount given by depth.  When depth=0,
// the object is touching our nose and the color is unaffected.
// When depth=100, the object blends completely into the background.
// In between the blend is exponential, meant to sort-of fake reality.
//
color distanceContrast(color objectColor, color bgColor, float depth) {
    float expAt1 = 2.71828;    // Euler's constant, exp(1)
    float a = map(exp(depth/100.0), 1, expAt1, 0, 1);
    a = constrain(a, 0, 1);
    color newclr = lerpColor(objectColor, bgColor, a);
    return(newclr);
}
```

Appendix A
Keywords

Here is a summary of each keyword (and symbol) defined in Processing. Note that many functions have multiple forms, depending on the number of arguments it receives and their types. Also, some words are used in multiple ways and their interpretation depends on context (for example, `height` is a global variable holding the height of the graphics window, but it is also a property of a `PImage` object). When a keyword can be used in multiple ways, for this quick summary, I picked what I thought was the most useful or common context.

I wrote these microsummaries to fit on one line. They're just to remind you of the meaning and purpose of each entry, but of course, these are not complete, in-depth descriptions. When you use any part of Processing for the very first time, it's a good idea to at least skim the documentation to make sure that you use it correctly and you know what alternatives are available.

Not every entry here is available on every system. In particular, the functions that control drawing styles vary from one renderer to another (recall that you choose your renderer with an optional third argument to `size()`). If a particular renderer doesn't support some option, it will just ignore those calls. If you're not getting the kinds of visual results you're expecting, it's worth reading the documentation for that function call to see if it's renderer-specific. Renderers, and their capabilities, sometimes change with new releases of Processing. It always pays to keep your copy up to date by occasionally visiting the Processing webpage at http://www.processing.org and seeing if there's a new version available for download.

Most of Processing's built-in objects and classes have a variety of special methods and fields built into them, such as the `String` methods discussed in Chapter 20. After the listings, I've included a summary of the methods and fields on a half-dozen of the most useful types.

The information here is presented in two forms: alphabetical and functional. The categories here are informal and are only meant to be suggestive; there's no hard-and-fast rules for categorizing language entries like this.

Each entry contains the keyword, its category, a short description, and the page number where it's first discussed.

Category	Refers to
2D curve	create a 2D curve
2D graphics	general 2D graphics work
2D shape	create 2D shapes
3D camera	define and control 3D camera
3D light	define 3D light sources
3D material	define materials for 3D shapes
3D shape	define 3D shapes
I/O	input and output
UI	user interface
array	array-related functions
assignment	assignment and related functions
color	color creation and manipulation
constant	fixed constants
file	reading and writing files
image	working with images
language	general Processing language
math	math operations
operator	things that change variables
random	random-number routines
string	specialized lists of characters
style	2D drawing style
test	testing conditions
time/date	checking time and date
transform	change the coordinate system
type	one of Processing's data types
type change	convert a variable of one type to another
typography	using fonts

A.1 Alphabetical Listing

Symbols

!	test	logical not	71
!=	test	test inequality	70
%	operator	modulo	96
&&	test	logical and: true if both terms are true	72
&	operator	bitwise and	791
()	language	multiple uses, typically to group expressions	46
*=	assignment	multiply and assign	57
*	operator	multiply	53
++	operator	increment (pre or post)	54
+=	assignment	add and assign	56
+	operator	addition	53
,	language	multiple uses, generally separates list elements	46
- -	operator	decrement (pre or post)	54
-=	assignment	subtract and assign	57

-	operator	minus sign	53
.	language	refer to an object's methods and variables	350
/* */	language	multiline comment (comments do not nest)	38
/** */	language	special comment used by the Export command	820
//	language	start of a comment that runs to end of line	29
/=	assignment	divide and assign	57
/	operator	divide	53
;	language	marks the end of a statement	35
<<	operator	left shift	791
<=	test	test less than or equal to	70
<	test	test less than	70
==	test	test equality	68
=	assignment	assignment	28
>=	test	test greater than or equal to	70
>>	operator	right shift	791
>	test	test greater than	66
?:	language	shortcut for an if/else test	74
|	operator	bitwise or	791
||	test	logical or: true if either or both terms are true	73
[ ]	language	array elements	234
{ }	language	multiple uses, generally forms a block of code	47

Capital Letters

Array	array	formal type for an array	790
ArrayList	array	advanced object for array manipulation	250
BufferedReader	file	object for reading files line by line	530
HALF_PI	constant	$\pi/2 \approx 1.57079\ldots$	110
HashMap	array	advanced object for associative arrays	251
Infinity	constant	special value for "infinite" numbers	530
Object	language	formal type for a generic object	790
PFont	typography	a font object	688
PGraphics	2D graphics	a 2D graphics object	793
PI	constant	$\pi \approx 3.14159\ldots$	110
PImage	image	an image object	462
PShape	2D shape	type of an SVG-format vector object	499
PVector	math	an object for a 2D or 3D point	397
PrintWriter	file	an object for writing text files	508
QUARTER_PI	constant	$\pi/4 \approx 0.78539\ldots$	110
String	string	special object for character strings	680
TWO_PI	constant	$2\pi \approx 6.28318\ldots$	110
XMLElement	file	advanced object for processing XML	535

A

abs()	math	absolute value of x	545
acos()	math	arc-cosine (inverse cosine)	546
alpha()	color	get the alpha value from a color	176
ambient()	3D material	set the ambient reflectance of a material	752
ambientLight()	3D light	create ambient light	750
append()	array	extend the array by 1 and insert the new element	244
applyMatrix()	transform	apply the given matrix to the current matrix	200
arc()	2D shape	draw a section of an ellipse (or circle)	109
arrayCopy()	array	copy some or all of one array into another array	245
asin()	math	arc-sine (inverse sine)	546
atan()	math	arc-tangent (inverse tangent)	547
atan2()	math	2-variable form of arc-tangent	547

B

background()	2D graphics	set the background of the graphics window	60
beginCamera()	3D camera	start customizing the camera model	744
beginDraw()	2D graphics	start drawing into offscreen image	793
beginRaw()	file	start capturing 3D data to a file	535
beginRecord()	file	open a file to record all drawing commands	532
beginShape()	2D shape	start defining a 2D shape	122
bezier()	2D curve	draw a Bézier curve	313
bezierDetail()	2D curve	set the drawing precision for a Bézier curve	336
bezierPoint()	2D curve	find a single point on a Bézier curve	336
bezierTangent()	2D curve	find the tangent to a Bézier curve	337
bezierVertex()	2D curve	provide the next 3 points in a Bézier curve	323
binary()	type change	a String of 0 and 1 chars	789
blend()	color	merge two images in a variety of ways	486
blendColor()	color	combine two colors in many different ways	488
blue()	color	get the RGB blue value from a color	92
boolean()	type change	true unless the input is 0, which is false	789
boolean	type	can take on values true and false	33
box()	3D shape	create a box (or cube)	718
break	language	exit the innermost loop	172
brightness()	color	get the HSB brightness value from a color	95
byte()	type change	a number from −128 to 127	789
byte	type	a number from −128 to 127	535

C

camera()	3D camera	describe the current camera	744
case	language	start a choice clause in a switch statement	75
catch	language	start a clause to handle errors	530
ceil()	math	smallest integer greater than or equal to x	547

char()	type change	a character corresponding to the given number	789
char	type	a single typographic character	679
class	language	start a class declaration	344
color()	color	specify a color in RGB or HSB	88
color	color	a color	88
colorMode()	color	specify if colors are given as RGB or HSB	94
concat()	array	combine two arrays one after the other	246
constrain()	math	restrict x to a range	548
continue	language	jump to the next iteration of the loop	173
copy()	2D graphics	copy PImage or window pixels to window	484
cos()	math	cosine (in radians)	548
createFont()	typography	advanced call to generate a font file	687
createGraphics()	2D graphics	create a new PGraphics	793
createImage()	image	create a new PImage	462
createInput()	I/O	advanced Java: open an input stream	535
createOutput()	I/O	advanced Java: open an output stream	535
createReader()	I/O	open a text file for line reading	530
createWriter()	file	create a file and a PrintWriter	509
cursor()	UI	set the cursor's bitmap image	822
curve()	2D curve	draw a Catmull-Rom curve	274
curveDetail()	2D curve	set the drawing precision for a curve	295
curvePoint()	2D curve	find a point on a Catmull-Rom curve	295
curveTangent()	2D curve	compute a tangent to a Catmull-Rom curve	297
curveTightness()	2D curve	specify how taut the curve should be	291
curveVertex()	2D curve	provide a point in a Catmull-Rom spline	288

D

day()	time/date	current day from 1 to 31	777
default	language	default clause in a switch	76
degrees()	math	convert radians to degrees	110
delay()	time/date	stops program for given milliseconds	778
directionalLight()	3D light	create a directional light source	747
dist()	math	distance between two 2D points	181
do	language	do loop	169
double	type	a double-precision float (use infrequently)	32
draw()	language	called once per frame	60

E

ellipse()	2D shape	draw an ellipse (or circle)	108
ellipseMode()	2D shape	set the style for interpreting ellipse() values	108
else	language	clause to execute when an "if" test fails	71
emissive()	3D material	set the emissive color of a material	752
endCamera()	3D camera	stop customizing the camera model	745
endDraw()	2D graphics	stop drawing into offscreen image	793
endRaw()	file	stop capturing 3D data to a file	535

endRecord()	file	stop recording drawing commands	532
endShape()	2D shape	end definition of a 2D shape	122
exit()	language	forces the program to end	50
exp()	math	raise e (Euler's constant) to the given power	549
expand()	array	increase the size of the array	244
extends	language	create a subclass	652

F

false	constant	value for a boolean data type	33
fill()	style	set the color for filling in shapes	117
filter()	2D graphics	apply a built-in filter to the graphics window	488
final	language	create a constant variable, procedure, or class	28
float()	type change	a float	33
float	type	a single-precision float	28
floor()	math	largest integer less than or equal to x	550
focused	UI	true if the sketch is receiving user events	822
for	language	for loop	169
frameCount	UI	the current frame number, starting at 0	80
frameRate()	UI	set the desired frame rate in frames per second	80
frameRate	UI	current estimated frames per second	80
frustum()	3D camera	define the viewing frustum for the camera	744

G

get()	2D graphics	retrieve the color of one or more pixels	466
green()	color	get the RGB green value from a color	92

H

height	2D graphics	the height of the graphics window	128
hex()	type change	a String of characters in hex notation	789
hint()	2D graphics	set miscellaneous renderer features	130
hour()	time/date	current hour from 0 to 23	777
hue()	color	get the HSB hue value from a color	95

I

if	language	start an if statement	66
image()	image	display a PImage on the graphics window	463
imageMode()	image	specify how to interpret values in image()	467
implements	language	declares an implementation of an interface	374
import	language	load a library	772
int()	type change	an int	33
int	type	an integer from $-2,147,483,648$ to $2,147,683,647$	28

J

| join() | string | combine a String array with a separator | 683 |

K

key	UI	value of most recently pressed or released key	151
keyCode	UI	detect modifier keys (e.g., Control and Alt)	152
keyPressed()	UI	called when a key is pressed	151
keyPressed	UI	true if a key is pressed	152
keyReleased()	UI	called when a key is released	152
keyTyped()	UI	called when non modifier key is pressed	152

L

lerp()	math	linearly blend two values	140
lerpColor()	color	linearly blend two colors	99
lightFalloff()	3D light	specify how lights get dimmer with distance	750
lightSpecular()	3D light	describe the specular highlight of a light	753
lights()	3D light	enable the use of lights	746
line()	2D shape	draw a line	114
link()	UI	points your web browser at a given URL	819
loadBytes()	file	reads a file or URL	535
loadFont()	typography	load a .vlw font file	688
loadImage()	image	create a PImage from a disk file	462
loadPixels	image	load the pixels array with current values	474
loadShape()	2D shape	read an SVG-format shape	499
loadStrings()	string	builds an array of Strings, one per file line	519
log()	math	natural logarithm of x	551
long	type	a super-large integer (use infrequently)	31
loop()	language	restarts automatic calling of draw()	80

M

mag()	math	distance of a 2D point from (0,0)	181
map()	math	transform a point from one range to another	136
match()	string	advanced: find regular expressions in a String	685
matchAll()	string	like match() but for arrays of Strings	685
max()	math	maximum of two numbers	551
millis()	time/date	total milliseconds since program started	777
min()	math	minimum of two numbers	552
minute()	time/date	current minutes from 0 to 59	777
modelX()	transform	x value of a point under the current matrix	755
modelY()	transform	y value of a point under the current matrix	755
modelZ()	transform	z value of a point under the current matrix	755
month()	time/date	current month from 1 to 12	777
mouseButton	UI	identifies which mouse button is down	150
mouseClicked()	UI	called when a mouse button is released	147
mouseDragged()	UI	called when mouse moves with a button down	146
mouseMoved()	UI	called when mouse moved and no buttons are down	146
mousePressed()	UI	called when a mouse button is pressed	148

mousePressed	UI	true if a mouse button is pressed	144
mouseReleased()	UI	called when a mouse button is released	148
mouseX	UI	horizontal position of the mouse	133
mouseY	UI	vertical position of the mouse	133

N

new	language	create a new object (typically array or class)	234
nf()	string	convert numbers to strings with padded 0's	680
nfc()	string	convert numbers to strings with commas	682
nfp()	string	like nf() but includes a + or − in front	682
nfs()	string	like nfp() but uses a blank instead of +	682
noCursor()	UI	hide the cursor from view	822
noFill()	2D shape	disable filling	120
noLights()	3D light	disable the use of lights	747
noLoop()	language	stops automatic calling of loop()	80
noSmooth()	style	turn off smoothing	123
noStroke()	style	set the color for drawing strokes	120
noTint()	image	stop applying tints	484
noise()	random	smooth, infinite noise field	254
noiseDetail()	random	set parameters controlling noise()	262
noiseSeed()	random	generate a particular pattern for noise()	262
norm()	math	find a value $(0, 1)$ for x in given range	142
normal()	3D shape	set the surface normal for a point	755
null	language	placeholder for empty data	346

O

online	UI	true if the program is running in a web browser	818
open()	file	open an application on your computer	535
ortho()	3D camera	set the camera to produce orthographic images	744

P

param()	UI	read a parameter from a web page	819
perspective()	3D camera	set the camera to produce perspective images	744
pixels	2D graphics	pixels in a PImage; must load and update	474
pmouseX	UI	value of mouseX in the most recent frame	149
pmouseY	UI	value of mouseY in the most recent frame	149
point()	2D shape	draw a single point	115
pointLight()	3D light	create a point light source	747
popMatrix()	transform	remove and use top matrix on the stack	196
popStyle()	transform	pop the style stack and set the current style	771
pow()	math	exponentiation	552
print()	language	print to the console	38
printCamera()	3D camera	print the current camera to the console	745

printMatrix()	transform	print the current matrix to the console	200
printProjection()	transform	print the current projection matrix	745
println()	language	print to the console and add a newline	38
private	language	make class elements unreadable to other classes	374
public	language	allow other classes to see class elements	374
pushMatrix()	transform	push current matrix onto the matrix stack	196
pushStyle()	style	push the current style onto the style stack	771

Q

quad()	2D shape	draw a four-sided figure	113

R

radians()	math	convert degrees to radians	110
random()	random	random numbers from a given range	225
randomSeed()	random	generate a particular pattern for random()	230
readLine()	file	read one line from a file	530
rect()	2D shape	draw a rectangle (or square)	104
rectMode()	2D shape	set the style for interpreting rect() values	105
red()	color	get the RGB red value from a color	92
redraw()	language	calls draw() once	80
requestImage()	file	load a PImage from disk in the background	819
resetMatrix()	transform	set the current matrix to the identity matrix	196
return	language	return a value; type must match function's type	48
reverse()	array	reverse the order of the elements in the array	247
rotate()	transform	rotate a 2D object clockwise	180
rotateX()	transform	rotate around the x-axis	716
rotateY()	transform	rotate around the y-axis	716
rotateZ()	transform	rotate around the z-axis	716
round()	math	nearest integer to x	553

S

saturation()	color	get the HSB saturation value from a color	95
save()	file	save the graphics window in a file	531
saveBytes()	file	write an array of bytes to a file	535
saveFrame()	file	save generated frame in files	531
saveStream()	file	advanced Java: save a stream to a file	535
saveStrings()	file	save an array of strings, one string per line	529
scale()	transform	scale an object (x and y scales can differ)	190
screen	UI	screen's dimensions	128
screenX()	transform	x value of a 3D point projected to the screen	756
screenY()	transform	y value of a 3D point projected to the screen	756
screenZ()	transform	z value of a 3D point projected to the screen	756
second()	time/date	current seconds from 0 to 59	777

`selectFolder()`	UI	dialog box for choosing a folder	529
`selectInput()`	UI	dialog box for choosing an input file	529
`selectOutput()`	UI	dialog box for choosing an output file	529
`set()`	2D graphics	set the color of a pixel	467
`setup()`	language	first procedure called when a program runs	59
`shape()`	2D shape	display a PShape object	499
`shapeMode()`	2D shape	set the style for interpreting `shape()` values	499
`shininess()`	3D material	set how shiny the material is	753
`shorten()`	array	discard the last element of the array	244
`sin()`	math	sine (in radians)	553
`size()`	2D graphics	create a graphics window; choose a renderer	59
`smooth()`	style	turn on smoothing	123
`sort()`	array	sort the elements of the array	247
`specular()`	3D material	set the specular color of a material	752
`sphere()`	3D shape	create a sphere (from triangles)	719
`sphereDetail()`	3D shape	number of triangles to make a sphere	720
`splice()`	array	insert an array into another array	246
`split()`	string	cut a `String` into an array using the divider	684
`splitTokens()`	string	like `split()` but can use multiple dividers	684
`spotLight()`	3D light	create a spotlight source	747
`sq()`	math	$x*x$	554
`sqrt()`	math	square root of x	554
`static`	language	create class variables and class methods	375
`status()`	language	display a message in the browser's status area	819
`str()`	type change	a `String` form of the type or array	789
`stroke()`	style	disable stroke drawing	119
`strokeCap()`	style	set the style for line endpoints	121
`strokeJoin()`	style	set the join style for lines	122
`strokeWeight()`	style	set the thickness of all strokes	121
`subset()`	array	extract a range of elements from an array	247
`super`	language	access the superclass of this class	652
`switch`	language	start a `switch` statement	75

T

`tan()`	math	tangent (in radians)	555
`text()`	typography	display the text in the current font	688
`textAlign()`	typography	set horizontal and vertical text positions	695
`textAscent()`	typography	distance from baseline to top of ascender	691
`textDescent()`	typography	distance from baseline to bottom of descender	691
`textFont()`	typography	specify the current font	688
`textLeading()`	typography	set vertical space between lines of text	695
`textMode()`	typography	sets how text is drawn to the screen	702
`textSize()`	typography	set the size of displayed text	702

textWidth()	typography	get the width of a string in the current font	689
texture()	image	assign a PImage to be used as a texture	495
textureMode()	image	set the coordinates for applying texture	498
this	language	points to the object that called a method	357
tint()	image	apply a colored tint to an image	483
translate()	transform	move an object	186
triangle()	2D shape	draw a triangle	113
trim()	string	removes white space from String ends	685
true	constant	value for a boolean data type	33
try	language	start a clause for catching errors	530

U

unbinary()	type change	an int from a String of 0's and 1's	789
unhex()	type change	an int from a String in hex format	789
updatePixels()	2D graphics	update a PImage with current pixels array	474

V

vertex()	2D graphics	define a single point in a shape	122
void	language	return type for functions with no return	51

W

while	language	while loop	164
width	2D graphics	the width of the graphics window	128

Y

year()	time/date	current year	777

A.2   Listing by Function

2D Curve

bezier()	2D curve	draw a Bézier curve	313
bezierDetail()	2D curve	set the drawing precision for a Bézier curve	336
bezierPoint()	2D curve	find a single point on a Bézier curve	336
bezierTangent()	2D curve	find the tangent to a Bézier curve	337
bezierVertex()	2D curve	provide the next points in a Bézier curve	323
curve()	2D curve	draw a Catmull-Rom curve	274
curveDetail()	2D curve	set the drawing precision for a curve	295
curvePoint()	2D curve	find a point on a Catmull-Rom curve	295
curveTangent()	2D curve	compute a tangent to a Catmull-Rom curve	297
curveTightness()	2D curve	specify how taut the curve should be	291
curveVertex()	2D curve	provide a point in a Catmull-Rom spline	288

2D Graphics

PGraphics	2D graphics	a 2D graphics object	793
background()	2D graphics	set the background of the graphics window	60
beginDraw()	2D graphics	start drawing into offscreen image	793
copy()	2D graphics	copy PImage or window pixels to window	484
createGraphics()	2D graphics	create a new PGraphics	793
endDraw()	2D graphics	stop drawing into offscreen image	793
filter()	2D graphics	apply a built-in filter to the graphics window	488
get()	2D graphics	retrieve the color of one or more pixels	466
height	2D graphics	the height of the graphics window	128
hint()	2D graphics	set miscellaneous renderer features	130
pixels	2D graphics	pixels in a PImage; must load & update	474
set()	2D graphics	set the color of a pixel	467
size()	2D graphics	create a graphics window; choose a renderer	59
updatePixels()	2D graphics	update a PImage with current pixels array	474
width	2D graphics	the width of the graphics window	128
vertex()	2D graphics	define a single point in the shape	122

2D Shape

PShape	2D shape	type of an SVG-format vector object	499
arc()	2D shape	draw a section of an ellipse (or circle)	109
beginShape()	2D shape	start defining a 2D shape	122
ellipse()	2D shape	draw an ellipse (or circle)	108
ellipseMode()	2D shape	set the style for interpreting ellipse() values	108
endShape()	2D shape	end definition of a 2D shape	122
line()	2D shape	draw a line	114
loadShape()	2D shape	read an SVG-format shape	499
noFill()	2D shape	disable filling	120
point()	2D shape	draw a single point	115
quad()	2D shape	draw a four-sided figure	113
rect()	2D shape	draw a rectangle (or square)	104
rectMode()	2D shape	set the style for interpreting rect() values	105
shape()	2D shape	display a PShape object	499
shapeMode()	2D shape	set the style for interpreting shape() values	499
triangle()	2D shape	draw a triangle	113

3D Camera

beginCamera()	3D camera	start customizing the camera model	744
camera()	3D camera	describe the current camera	744
endCamera()	3D camera	stop customizing the camera model	745
frustum()	3D camera	define the viewing frustum for the camera	744
ortho()	3D camera	set the camera to produce orthographic images	744
perspective()	3D camera	set the camera to produce perspective images	744
printCamera()	3D camera	print the current camera to the console	745

3D Light

ambientLight()	3D light	create ambient light	750
directionalLight()	3D light	create a directional light source	747

lightFalloff()	3D light	specify how lights get dimmer with distance	750
lightSpecular()	3D light	describe the specular highlight of a light	753
lights()	3D light	enable the use of lights	746
noLights()	3D light	disable the use of lights	747
pointLight()	3D light	create a point light source	747
spotLight()	3D light	create a spotlight source	747

3D Material

ambient()	3D material	set the ambient reflectance of a material	752
emissive()	3D material	set the emissive color of a material	752
shininess()	3D material	set how shiny the material is	753
specular()	3D material	set the specular color of a material	752

3D Shape

box()	3D shape	create a box (or cube)	718
normal()	3D shape	set the surface normal for a point	755
sphere()	3D shape	create a sphere (from triangles)	719
sphereDetail()	3D shape	number of triangles to make a sphere	720

I/O

createInput()	I/O	advanced Java: open an input stream	535
createOutput()	I/O	advanced Java: open an output stream	535
createReader()	I/O	open a text file for line reading	530

UI

cursor()	UI	set the cursor's bitmap image	822
focused	UI	true if the sketch is receiving user events	822
frameCount	UI	the current frame number, starting at 0	80
frameRate()	UI	set the desired frame rate in frames per second	80
frameRate	UI	current estimated frames per second	80
key	UI	value of most recently pressed or released key	151
keyCode	UI	detect modifier keys (e.g., Control and Alt)	152
keyPressed()	UI	called when a key is pressed	151
keyPressed	UI	true if a key is pressed	152
keyReleased()	UI	called when a key is released	152
keyTyped()	UI	called when non modifier key is pressed	152
link()	UI	points your web browser at a given URL	819
mouseButton	UI	identifies which mouse button is down	150
mouseClicked()	UI	called when a mouse button is released	147
mouseDragged()	UI	called when mouse moves with a button down	146
mouseMoved()	UI	called when mouse moved and no buttons are down	146
mousePressed()	UI	called when a mouse button is pressed	148
mousePressed	UI	true if a mouse button is pressed	144
mouseReleased()	UI	called when a mouse button is released	148
mouseX	UI	horizontal position of the mouse	133
mouseY	UI	vertical position of the mouse	133

noCursor()	UI	hide the cursor from view	822
online	UI	true if the program is running in a web browser	818
param()	UI	read a parameter from a web page	819
pmouseX	UI	value of mouseX in the most recent frame	149
pmouseY	UI	value of mouseY in the most recent frame	149
screen	UI	screen's dimensions	128
selectFolder()	UI	prompts you to choose a folder for input files	529
selectInput()	UI	prompts you to choose a file for input	529
selectOutput()	UI	open a dialog box to create a save file	529

array

Array	array	formal type for an array	790
ArrayList	array	advanced object for array manipulation	250
HashMap	array	advanced object for associative arrays	251
append()	array	extend the array by 1 and insert the new element	244
arrayCopy()	array	copy some or all of one array into another array	245
concat()	array	combine two arrays one after the other	246
expand()	array	increase the size of the array	244
reverse()	array	reverse the order of the elements in the array	247
shorten()	array	discard the last element of the array	244
sort()	array	sort the elements of the array	247
splice()	array	insert an array into another array	246
subset()	array	extract a range of elements from an array	247

assignment

/=	assignment	divide and assign	57
*=	assignment	multiply and assign	57
+=	assignment	add and assign	56
-=	assignment	subtract and assign	57
=	assignment	assignment	28

color

alpha()	color	get the alpha value from a color	176
blend()	color	merge two images in a variety of ways	486
blendColor()	color	combine two colors in many different ways	488
blue()	color	get the RGB blue value from a color	92
brightness()	color	get the HSB brightness value from a color	95
color()	color	specify a color in RGB or HSB	88
color	color	a color	88
colorMode()	color	specify if colors are given as RGB or HSB	94
green()	color	get the RGB green value from a color	92
hue()	color	get the HSB hue value from a color	95
lerpColor()	color	linearly blend two colors	99
red()	color	get the RGB red value from a color	92
saturation()	color	get the HSB saturation value from a color	95

constant

HALF_PI	constant	$\pi/2 \approx 1.57079\ldots$	110
Infinity	constant	special value for "infinite" numbers	530
PI	constant	$\pi \approx 3.14159\ldots$	110
QUARTER_PI	constant	$\pi/4 \approx 0.78539\ldots$	110
TWO_PI	constant	$2\pi \approx 6.28318\ldots$	110
false	constant	value for a boolean data type	33
true	constant	value for a boolean data type	33

file

BufferedReader	file	object for reading files line by line	530
PrintWriter	file	an object for writing text files	508
XMLElement	file	advanced object for processing XML	535
beginRaw()	file	start capturing 3D data to a file	535
beginRecord()	file	open a file to record all drawing commands	532
createWriter()	file	create a file and a PrintWriter	509
endRaw()	file	stop capturing 3D data to a file	535
endRecord()	file	stop recording drawing commands	532
loadBytes()	file	reads a file or URL	535
open()	file	open an application on your computer	535
readLine()	file	read one line from a file	530
requestImage()	file	load a PImage from disk in the background	819
save()	file	save the graphics window in a file	531
saveBytes()	file	write an array of bytes to a file	535
saveFrame()	file	save generated frame in files	531
saveStream()	file	advanced Java: save a stream to a file	535
saveStrings()	file	save an array of strings, one string per line	529

image

PImage	image	an image object	462
createImage()	image	create a new PImage	462
image()	image	display a PImage on the graphics window	463
imageMode()	image	specify how to interpret values in image()	467
loadImage()	image	create a PImage from a disk file	462
loadPixels	image	load the pixels array with current values	474
noTint()	image	stop applying tints	484
texture()	image	assign a PImage to be used as a texture	495
textureMode()	image	set the coordinates for applying texture	498
tint()	image	apply a colored tint to an image	483

language

noLoop()	language	stops automatic calling of loop()	80
()	language	multiple uses, typically to group expressions	46
,	language	multiple uses, generally separates list elements	46
.	language	refer to an object's methods and variables	350
/* */	language	multiline comment (comments do not nest)	38
/** */	language	special comment used by the Export command	820

`//`	language	start of a comment that runs to end of line	29
`;`	language	marks the end of a statement	35
`?:`	language	shortcut for an if/else test	74
`Object`	language	formal type for a generic object	790
`[ ]`	language	array elements	234
`break`	language	exit the innermost loop	172
`case`	language	start a choice clause in a `switch` statement	75
`catch`	language	start a clause to handle errors	530
`class`	language	start a class declaration	344
`continue`	language	jump to the next iteration of the loop	173
`default`	language	default clause in a switch	76
`do`	language	do loop	169
`draw()`	language	called once per frame	60
`else`	language	clause to execute when an "if" test fails	71
`exit()`	language	forces the program to end	50
`extends`	language	create a subclass	652
`final`	language	create a constant variable, procedure, or class	28
`for`	language	for loop	169
`if`	language	start an if statement	66
`implements`	language	declares an implementation of an interface	374
`import`	language	load a library	772
`loop()`	language	restarts automatic calling of `draw()`	80
`new`	language	create a new object (typically array or class)	234
`null`	language	placeholder for empty data	346
`print()`	language	print to the console	38
`println()`	language	print to the console and add a newline	38
`private`	language	make class elements unreadable to other classes	374
`public`	language	allow other classes to see class elements	374
`redraw()`	language	calls `draw()` once	80
`return`	language	return a value; type must match function's type	48
`setup()`	language	first thing that Processing runs	59
`static`	language	create class variables and class methods	375
`status()`	language	display a message in the browser's status area	819
`super`	language	access the superclass of this class	652
`switch`	language	start a `switch` statement	75
`this`	language	points to the object that called a method	357
`try`	language	start a clause for catching errors	530
`void`	language	return type for functions with no return	51
`while`	language	while loop	164
`{ }`	language	multiple uses, generally forms a block of code	47

math

`PVector`	math	an object for a 2D or 3D point	397
`abs()`	math	absolute value of x	545
`acos()`	math	arc-cosine (inverse cosine)	546
`asin()`	math	arc-sine (inverse sine)	546
`atan()`	math	arc-tangent (inverse tangent)	547
`atan2()`	math	2-variable form of arc-tangent	547
`ceil()`	math	smallest integer greater than or equal to x	547
`constrain()`	math	restrict x to a range	548

`cos()`	math	cosine (in radians)	548
`degrees()`	math	convert radians to degrees	110
`dist()`	math	distance between two 2D points	181
`exp()`	math	raise e (Euler's constant) to the given power	549
`floor()`	math	largest integer less than or equal to x	550
`lerp()`	math	linearly blend two value	140
`log()`	math	natural logarithm of x	551
`mag()`	math	distance of a 2D point from (0,0)	181
`map()`	math	transform a point from one range to another	136
`max()`	math	maximum of two numbers	551
`min()`	math	minimum of two numbers	552
`norm()`	math	find a value $(0,1)$ for x in given range	142
`pow()`	math	exponentiation	552
`radians()`	math	convert degrees to radians	110
`round()`	math	nearest integer to x	553
`sin()`	math	sine (in radians)	553
`sq()`	math	$x*x$	554
`sqrt()`	math	square root of x	554
`tan()`	math	tangent (in radians)	555

operator

`%`	operator	modulo	96
`*`	operator	multiply	53
`++`	operator	increment (pre or post)	54
`+`	operator	addition	53
`--`	operator	decrement (pre or post)	54
`-`	operator	minus sign	53
`/`	operator	divide	53
`<<`	operator	left shift	791
`>>`	operator	right shift	791
`&`	operator	bitwise and	791
`|`	operator	bitwise or	791

random

`noise()`	random	smooth, infinite noise field	254
`noiseDetail()`	random	set parameters controlling `noise()`	262
`noiseSeed()`	random	generate a particular pattern for `noise()`	262
`random()`	random	random numbers from a given range	225
`randomSeed()`	random	generate a particular pattern for `random()`	230

string

`String`	string	special object for character strings	680
`join()`	string	combine a `String` array with a separator	683
`loadStrings()`	string	builds an array of `Strings`, one per file line	519
`match()`	string	advanced: find regular expressions in a `String`	685
`matchAll()`	string	like `match()` but for arrays of `Strings`	685
`nf()`	string	convert numbers to strings with padded 0's	680
`nfc()`	string	convert numbers to strings with commas	682

nfp()	string	like nf() but includes a + or − in front	682
nfs()	string	like nfp() but uses a blank instead of +	682
split()	string	cut a String into an array using the divider	684
splitTokens()	string	like split() but can use multiple dividers	684
trim()	string	removes white space from String ends	685

style

fill()	style	set the color for filling in shapes	117
noSmooth()	style	turn off smoothing	123
noStroke()	style	set the color for drawing strokes	120
pushStyle()	style	push the current style onto the style stack	771
smooth()	style	turn on smoothing	123
stroke()	style	disable stroke drawing	119
strokeCap()	style	set the style for line endpoints	121
strokeJoin()	style	set the join style for lines	122
strokeWeight()	style	set the thickness of all strokes	121

test

&&	test	logical and: true if both terms are true	72
!	test	logical not	71
||	test	logical or: true if either or both terms are true	73
==	test	test equality	68
!=	test	test inequality	70
>=	test	test greater than or equal to	70
>	test	test greater than	66
<	test	test less than	70
<=	test	test less than or equal to	70

time/date

day()	time/date	current day from 1 to 31	777
delay()	time/date	stops program for given milliseconds	778
hour()	time/date	current hour from 0 to 23	777
millis()	time/date	total milliseconds since program started	777
minute()	time/date	current minutes from 0 to 59	777
month()	time/date	current month from 1 to 12	777
second()	time/date	current seconds from 0 to 59	777
year()	time/date	current year	777

transform

applyMatrix()	transform	apply the given matrix to the current matrix	200
modelX()	transform	x value of a point under the current matrix	755
modelY()	transform	y value of a point under the current matrix	755
modelZ()	transform	z value of a point under the current matrix	755
popMatrix()	transform	remove and use top matrix on the stack	196
popStyle()	transform	pop the style stack and set the current style	771
printMatrix()	transform	print the current matrix to the console	200
printProjection()	transform	print the current projection matrix	745

`pushMatrix()`	transform	push current matrix onto the matrix stack	196
`resetMatrix()`	transform	set the current matrix to the identity matrix	196
`rotate()`	transform	rotate a 2D object clockwise	180
`rotateX()`	transform	rotate around the x-axis	716
`rotateY()`	transform	rotate around the y-axis	716
`rotateZ()`	transform	rotate around the z-axis	716
`scale()`	transform	scale an object (x and y scales can differ)	190
`screenX()`	transform	x value of a 3D point projected to the screen	756
`screenY()`	transform	y value of a 3D point projected to the screen	756
`screenZ()`	transform	z value of a 3D point projected to the screen	756
`translate()`	transform	move an object	186

type

`boolean`	type	can take on values true and false	33
`byte`	type	a number from -128 to 127	535
`char`	type	a single typographic character	679
`double`	type	a double-precision float (use infrequently)	32
`float`	type	a single-precision float	28
`int`	type	an integer from $-2,147,483,648$ to $2,147,683,647$	28
`long`	type	a super-large integer (use infrequently)	31

type change

`binary()`	type change	a `String` of 0 and 1 chars	789
`boolean()`	type change	true unless the input is 0, which is false	789
`byte()`	type change	a number from -128 to 127	789
`char()`	type change	a character corresponding to the given number	789
`float()`	type change	a float	33
`hex()`	type change	a `String` of characters in hex notation	789
`int()`	type change	an int	33
`str()`	type change	a `String` form of the ptype or array	789
`unbinary()`	type change	an int from a `String` of 0's and 1's	789
`unhex()`	type change	an int from a `String` in hex format	789

typography

`PFont`	typography	a font object	688
`createFont()`	typography	advanced call to generate a font file	687
`loadFont()`	typography	load a .vlw font file	688
`text()`	typography	display the text in the current font	688
`textAlign()`	typography	set horizontal and vertical text positions	695
`textAscent()`	typography	distance from baseline to top of ascender	691
`textDescent()`	typography	distance from baseline to bottom of descender	691
`textFont()`	typography	specify the current font	688
`textLeading()`	typography	set vertical space between lines of text	695
`textMode()`	typography	sets how text is drawn to the screen	702
`textSize()`	typography	set the size of displayed text	702
`textWidth()`	typography	get the width of a string in the current font	689

A.3   Object Methods

Several of Processing's objects contain a number of additional methods and fields related to instances of the object. Here is a summary:

String. Contains a sequence of chars. It is conceptually like an array, but it does not respond to array function calls. Instead, it has its own methods.

> **charAt**(). return the character at this location
>
> **equals**(). test if two strings are the same
>
> **indexOf**(). the index of the first instance of this character
>
> **length**(). the length of the String
>
> **substring**(). a new String that is a piece of the input
>
> **toLowerCase**(). convert all characters to lower case
>
> **toUpperCase**(). convert all characters to upper case

PShape. Contains a vector shape in the SVG format, typically created by some other program and read from the disk.

> **width**. image width
>
> **height**. image height
>
> **isVisible**(). boolean describing if image is visible
>
> **setVisible**(). set visibility
>
> **disableStyle**(). use Processing's drawing styles
>
> **enableStyle**(). use the shape's built-in drawing styles
>
> **getChild**(). return a child of the PShape
>
> **translate**(). move the shape
>
> **rotate**(). rotate the shape in the graphics window
>
> **rotateX**(). rotate the shape around the x-axis
>
> **rotateY**(). rotate the shape around the y-axis
>
> **rotateZ**(). rotate the shape around the z-axis
>
> **scale**(). change the shape's size

PrintWriter. This object lets you write text to an output file.

> **print**(). print the contents to the stream
>
> **println**(). print the contents to the stream and add a newline
>
> **flush**(). make sure stream has been fully written
>
> **close**(). close the stream

PImage. An object for holding a photograph or other image from the disk. A PImage can be created from files in .gif, .jpg, .tga, or .png formats. Once an image is in memory, you can manipulate it.

> **width**. image's width
>
> **height**. image's height
>
> **pixels**. array of pixel colors (must load and update)

get(). retrieve the color of a pixel

set(). set the color of a pixel

copy(). copy the entire image

mask(). set part of the image to not display

blend(). copies a rectangle of pixels using different modes

filter(). convert image to grayscale

save(). save as .tif .jpg, .tga, or .png (note .tif, not .gif)

resize(). rebuild image at new width and height

loadPixels(). load the pixels array

updatePixels(). save the pixels array back to the `PImage`.

PFont. This object holds a single font descriptor.

list(). return an array of `Strings`, one for each font installed on the system

PVector. An object that can hold a 2D point (x,y) or a 3D point (x,y,z). In certain mathematical contexts, we can consider these numbers to describe a similar idea called a vector, hence the name. Put simply, to think of a point as a vector imagine an arrow that begins at the origin (either $(0,0)$ or $(0,0,0)$) and ends at the point. This arrow is a vector: it has a start point (the origin), an end point (the `PVector`'s values), and a direction (from the origin to the `PVector`). Vectors are useful in a variety of geometric calculations, some of which are made easier with the methods available to `PVector` objects. For more information on these types of operations, look up *linear algebra* on the web. This isn't necessary, though; you can get very far with just the basics.

x. The x component of the vector

y. The y component of the vector

z. The z component of the vector

set(). sets the vector's components

get(). returns the vector's components

mag(). returns the length of the vector

add(). adds two vectors

sub(). subtracts one vector from another

mult(). multiplies all components of a vector by a single value

div(). divides all components of a vector by a single value

dist(). returns the distance between two points

dot(). computes the dot product of two vectors

cross(). computes the cross-product of two vectors

normalize(). scales the vector to have length 1.0

limit(). scales a vector if it's longer than the given amount

angleBetween(). finds the angle between two vectors

array(). returns the vector's components in an array

Index

Printed and bound by CPI Group (UK) Ltd, Croydon, CR0 4YY

22/10/2024

01777633-0002